JAPAN ART REVOLUTION

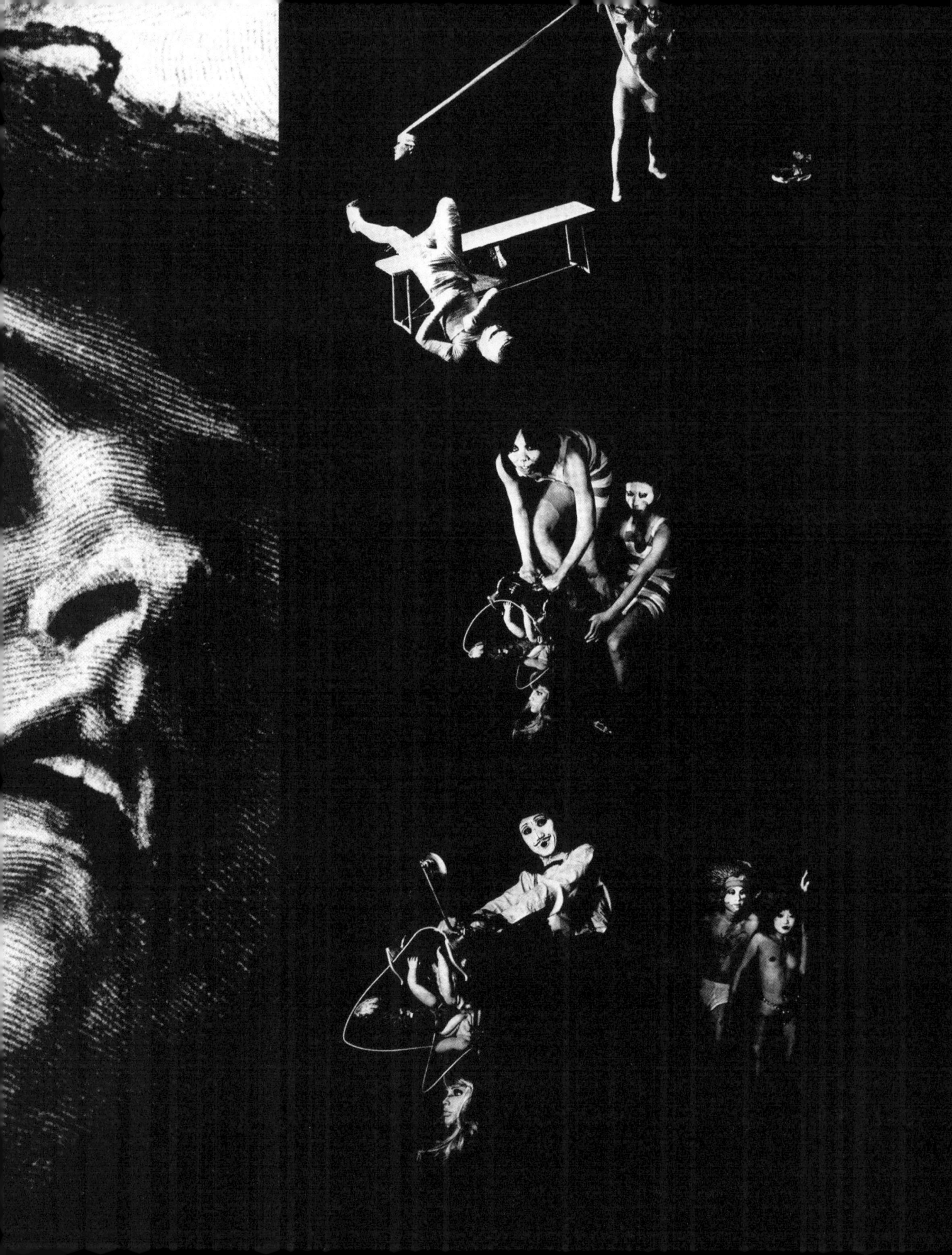

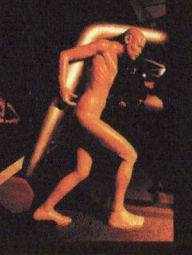
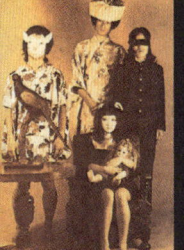
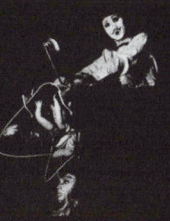
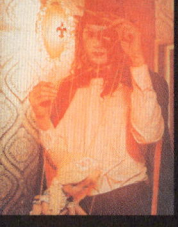
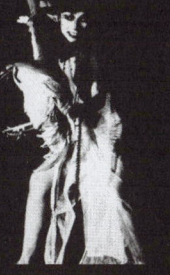
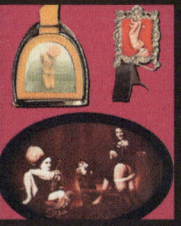
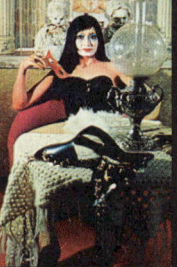

THE JAPANESE AVANT-GARDE

JAPAN ART REVOLUTION

FROM ANGURA TO PROVOKE

Amélie Ravalec

アメリー・ラヴァレック

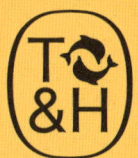

日本のアヴァンギャルド

アングラからプロヴォークまで

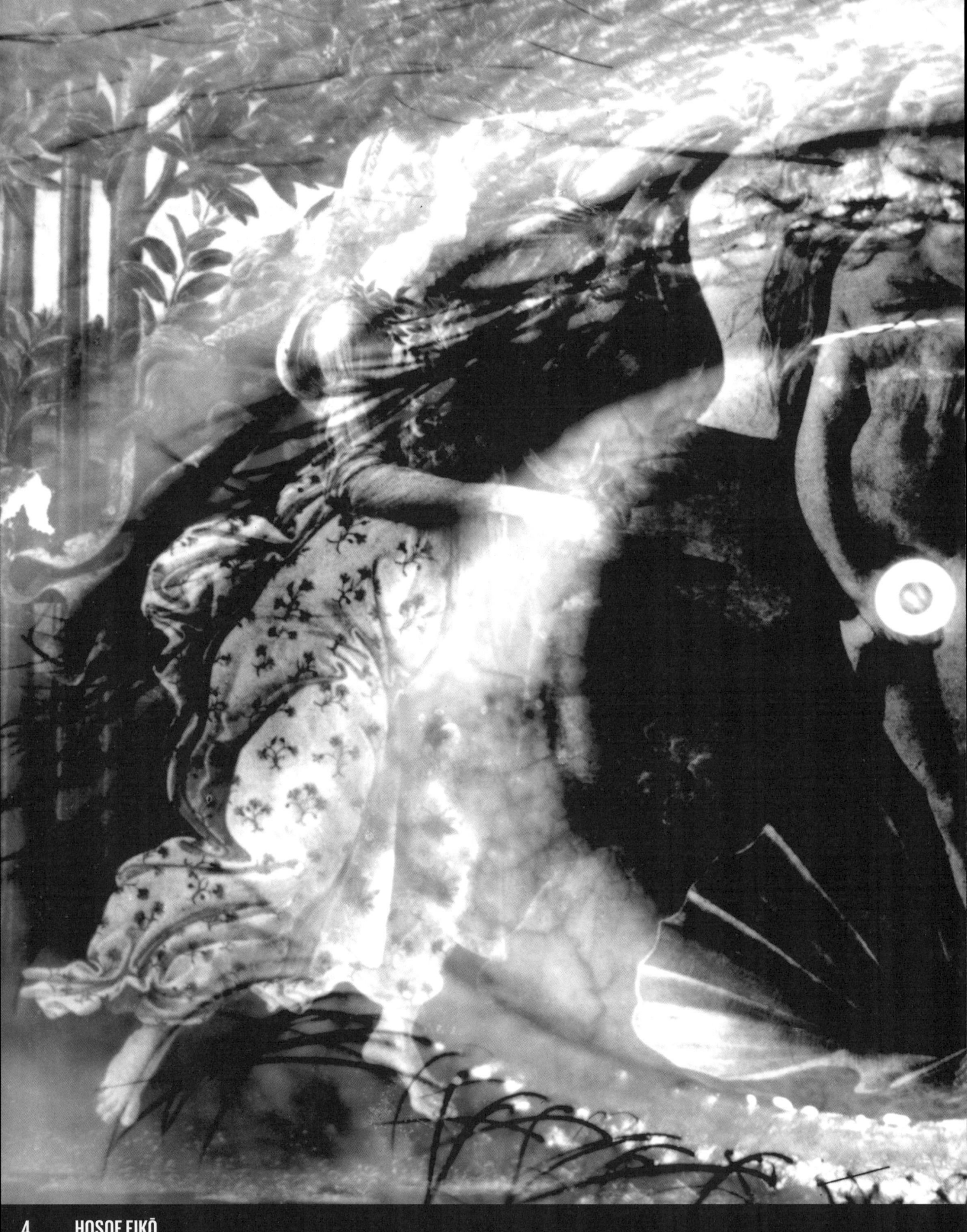

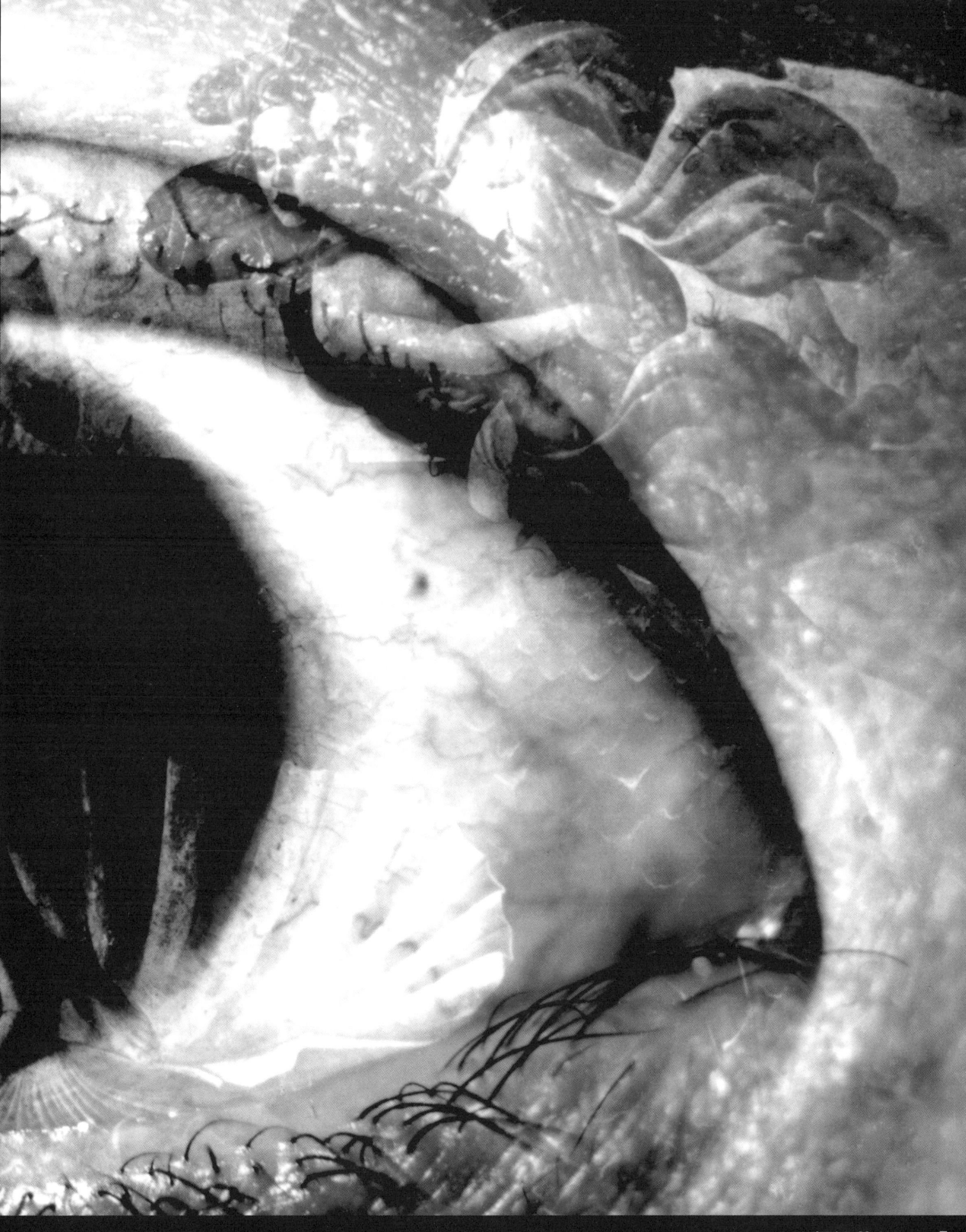

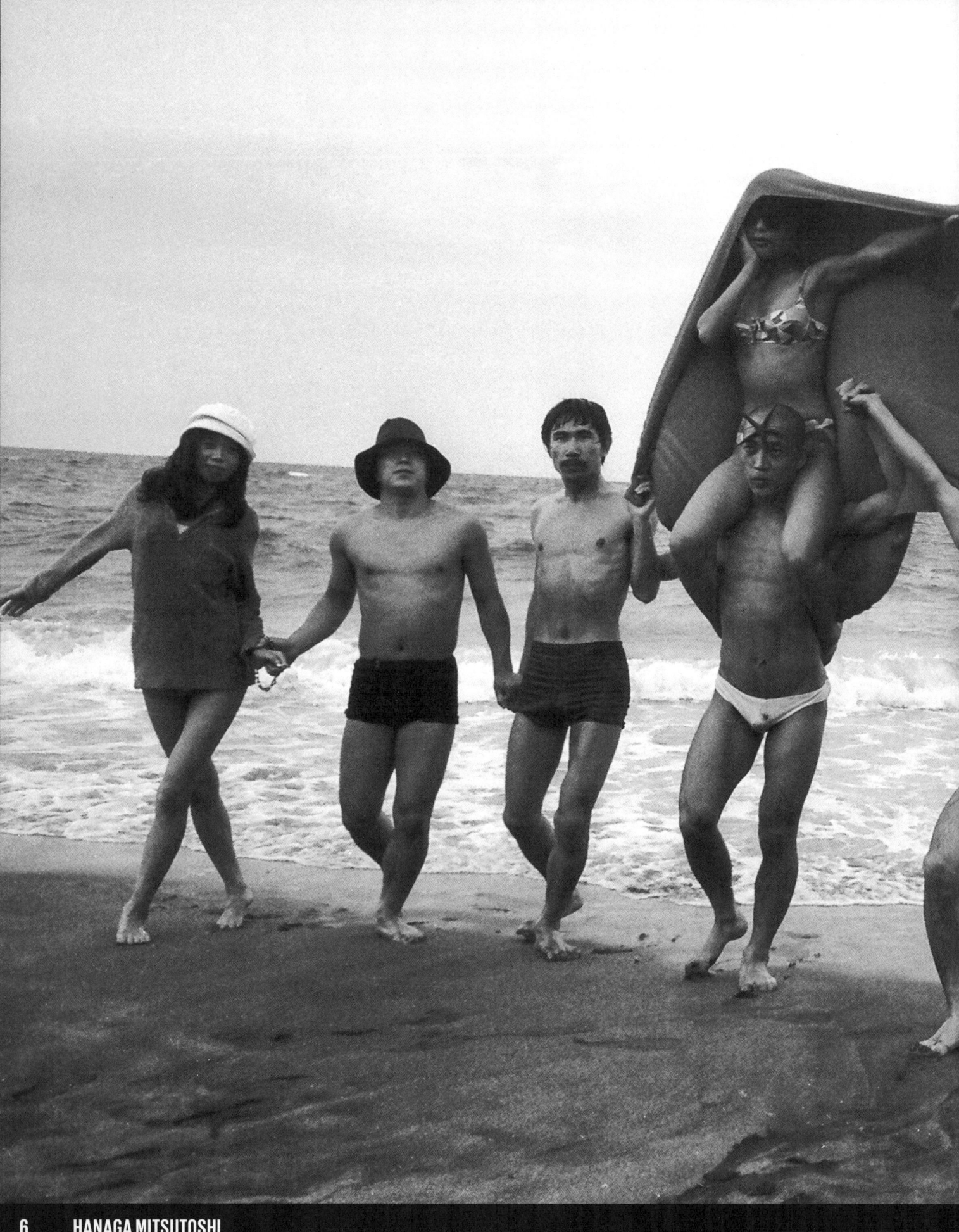

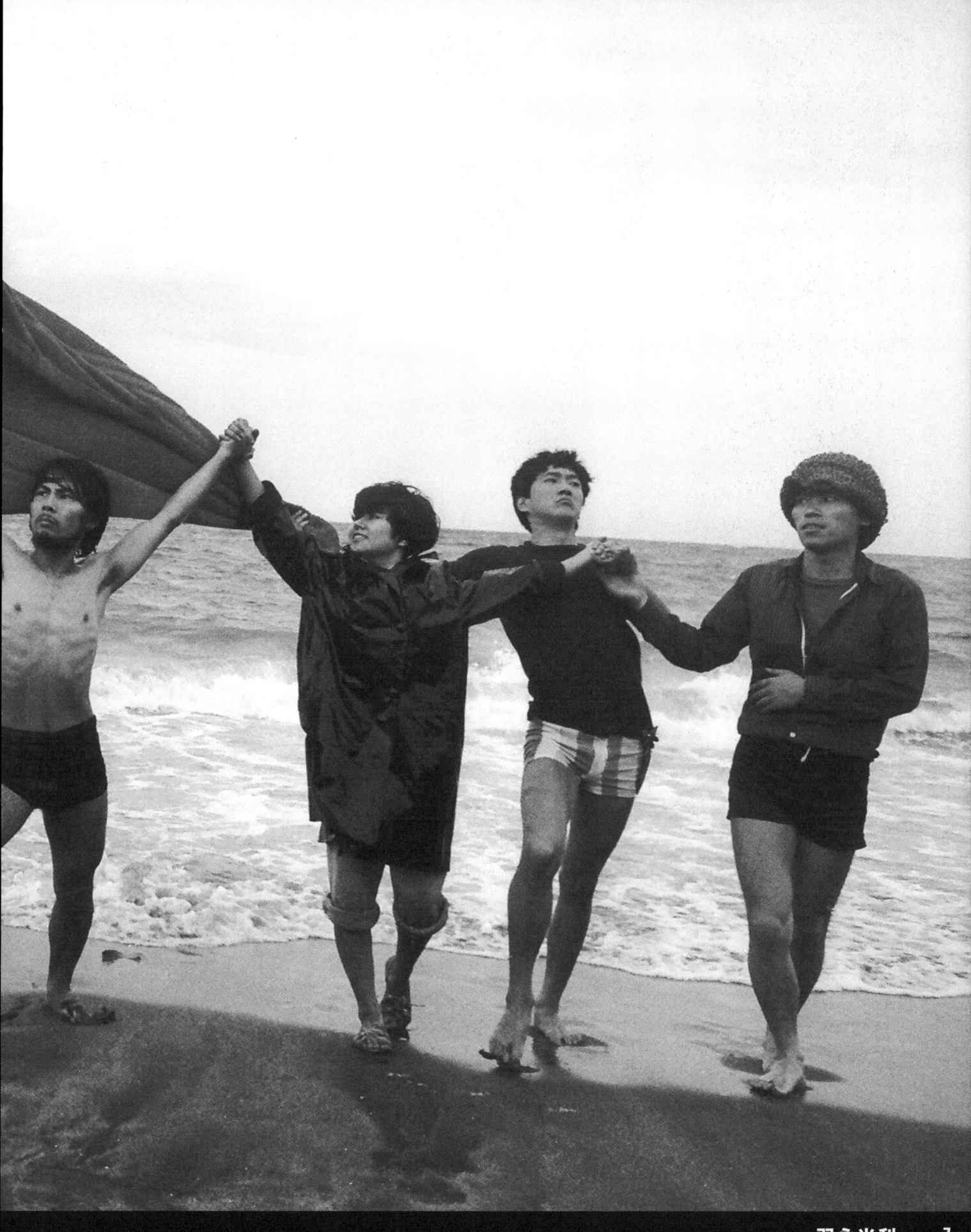
羽永光利

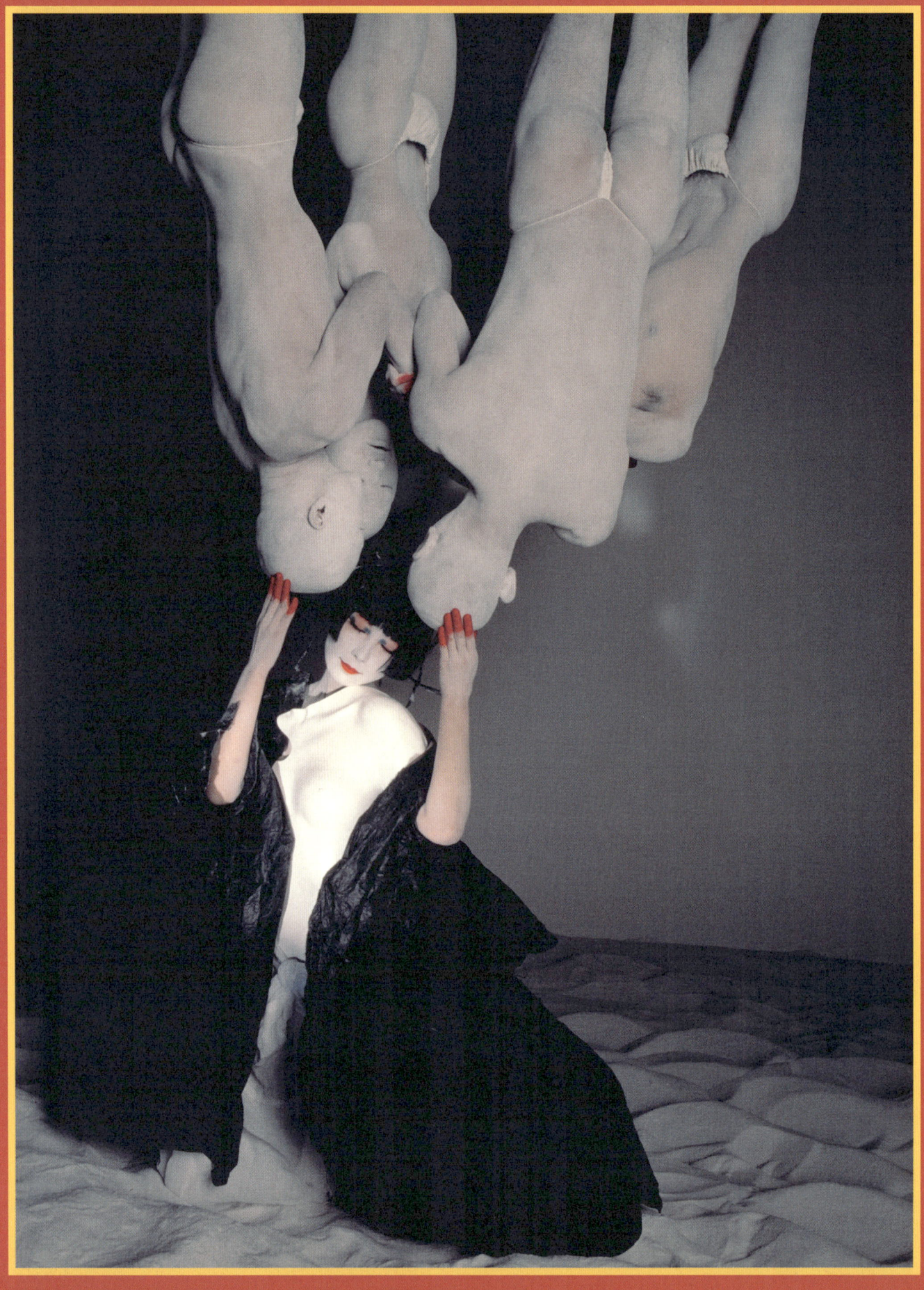

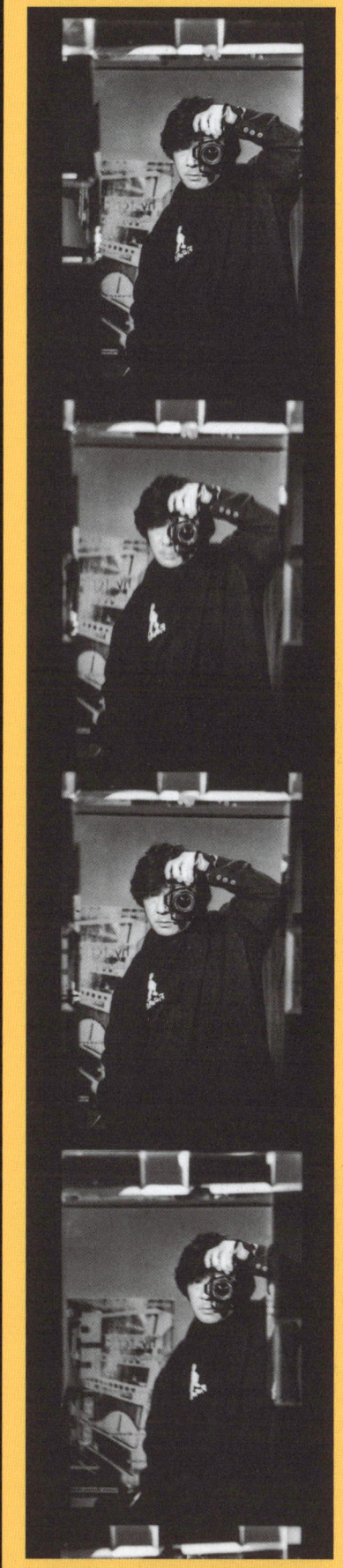

THE JAPANESE AVANT-GARDE	Yokoo Tadanori	10
PREFACE	Amélie Ravalec	14
INTRODUCTION	Alexandra Munroe	18
ANPO PROTESTS	1959/1960/1970	20
WATANABE HITOMI	1942–	30
TANAAMI KEIICHI	1936–2024	36
KAWADA KIKUJI	1933–	56
HOSOE EIKŌ	1933–2024	64
MISHIMA YUKIO	1925–1970	70
YOKOO TADANORI	1936–	86
BUTOH	1959	106
HIJIKATA TATSUMI	1928–1986	114
OHNO KAZUO	1906–2010	126
AWAZU KIYOSHI	1929–2009	136
TERAYAMA SHŪJI	1935–1983	148
ARAKI NOBUYOSHI	1940–	174
KINBAKU	1952	190
MORIYAMA DAIDO	1938–	200
PROVOKE	1968–69	220
NAKAHIRA TAKUMA	1938–2015	226
NEO-DADA ORGANIZERS	1960–62	234
HI-RED CENTER	1963–64	246
HANAGA MITSUTOSHI	1933–1999	256
ISHIUCHI MIYAKO	1947–	268
SAEKI TOSHIO	1945–2019	280
YOKOSUKA NORIAKI	1937–2003	304
ARTISTS AND CONTRIBUTORS		312
ACKNOWLEDGMENTS		314
CREDITS		315
INDEX		317

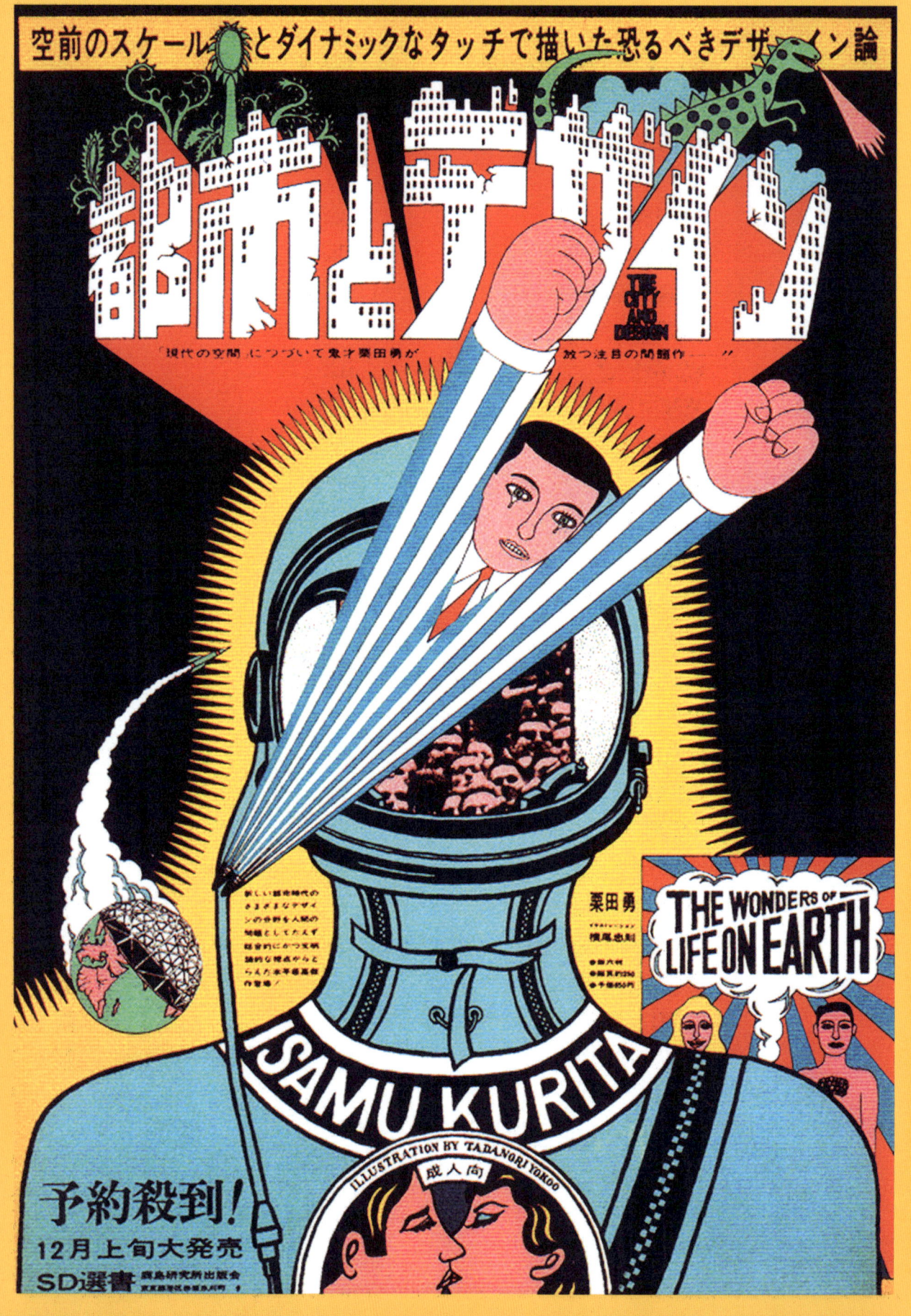

THE JAPANESE AVANT-GARDE
Yokoo Tadanori

From the 1960s to the 1970s, Japan experienced major changes in its underground movements. It's difficult to pinpoint exactly where it all started; across different fields, young people with similar mindsets and ideas emerged all at once. When you look back at it now, it might seem like there was an organized cultural movement. But that's not really how it was.

The number of people shaping that cultural movement was very small. Just a handful of individuals created the culture of that time, which I think is one of its defining characteristics. It was something incredibly concentrated, happening in very small spaces, over short periods of time. That's what makes it so interesting.

In theatre, for example, you had Terayama Shūji, Hijikata Tatsumi and Kara Jūrō leading the underground performance scene. These three were at the core of the movement. In film, there was Ōshima Nagisa. In avant-garde music, there were composers like Takemitsu Tōru and Ichiyanagi Toshi.

In photography, Hosoe Eikō was a central figure of that era. Moriyama Daido started out as Hosoe's assistant. Later, of course, Moriyama and Araki became hugely influential, and their work expanded internationally. At the same time, there were towering figures like Mishima Yukio and Kurosawa Akira. They didn't engage with the underground movement, but their presence was undeniable.

I was lucky enough to collaborate with almost all of these people. They didn't just think about things intellectually – they engaged through physical actions. Intellectual pursuits based only on knowledge and education lack real energy. These were all individuals who acted through their bodies.

I believe that engaging with art through physicality is crucial. Cerebral and academic approaches alone are not enough – true energy comes through the body. Now, people think too much, overanalyse everything; they process everything intellectually. It's a dull time compared to back then.

These artists got to know each other, and later, some of them collaborated. Each of them was an individual artist, but at the same time, they were inspiring one another. This underground cultural movement played a major role in shaping Japanese art as we know it today, bringing together so many forces. It was truly a wonderful time.

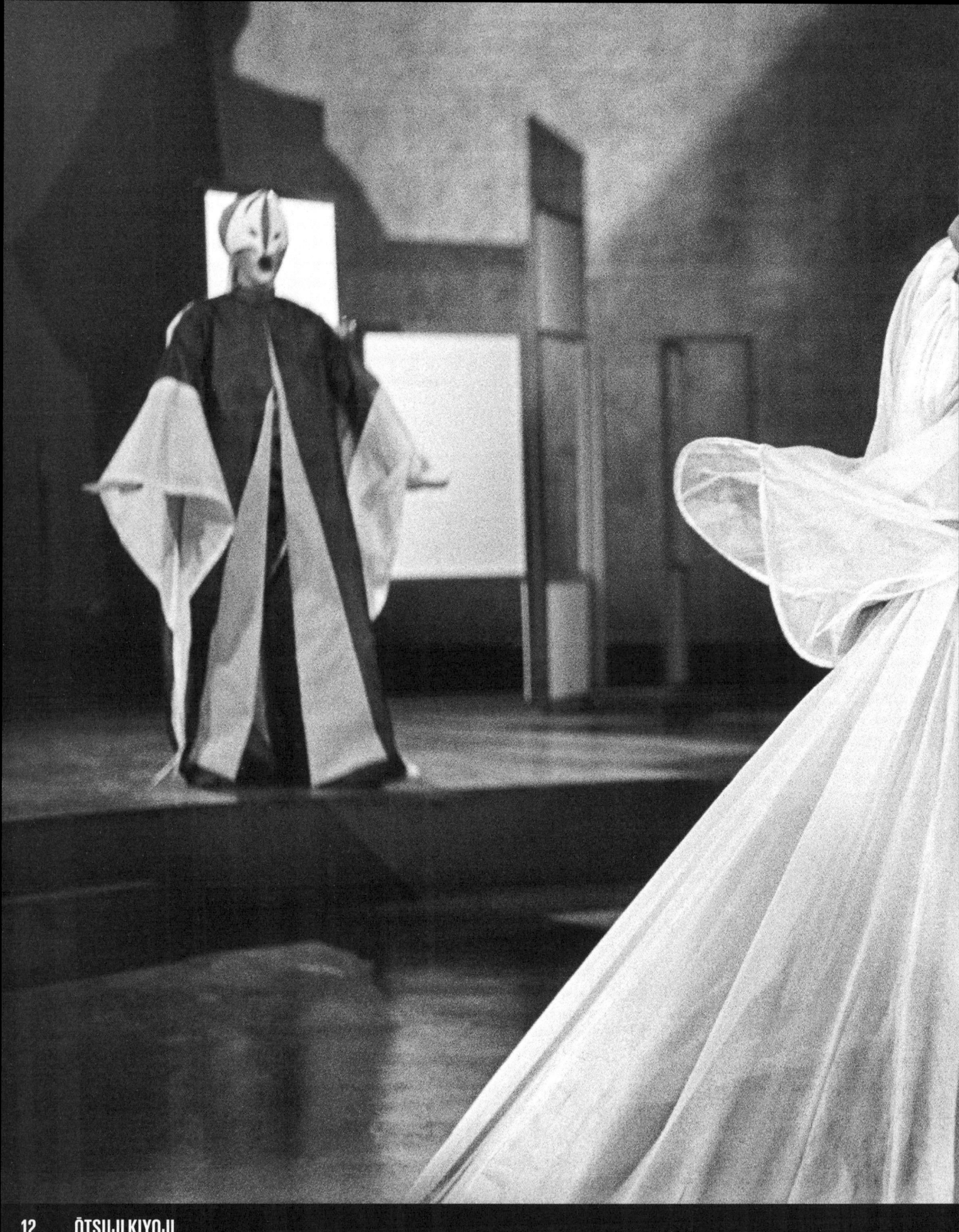

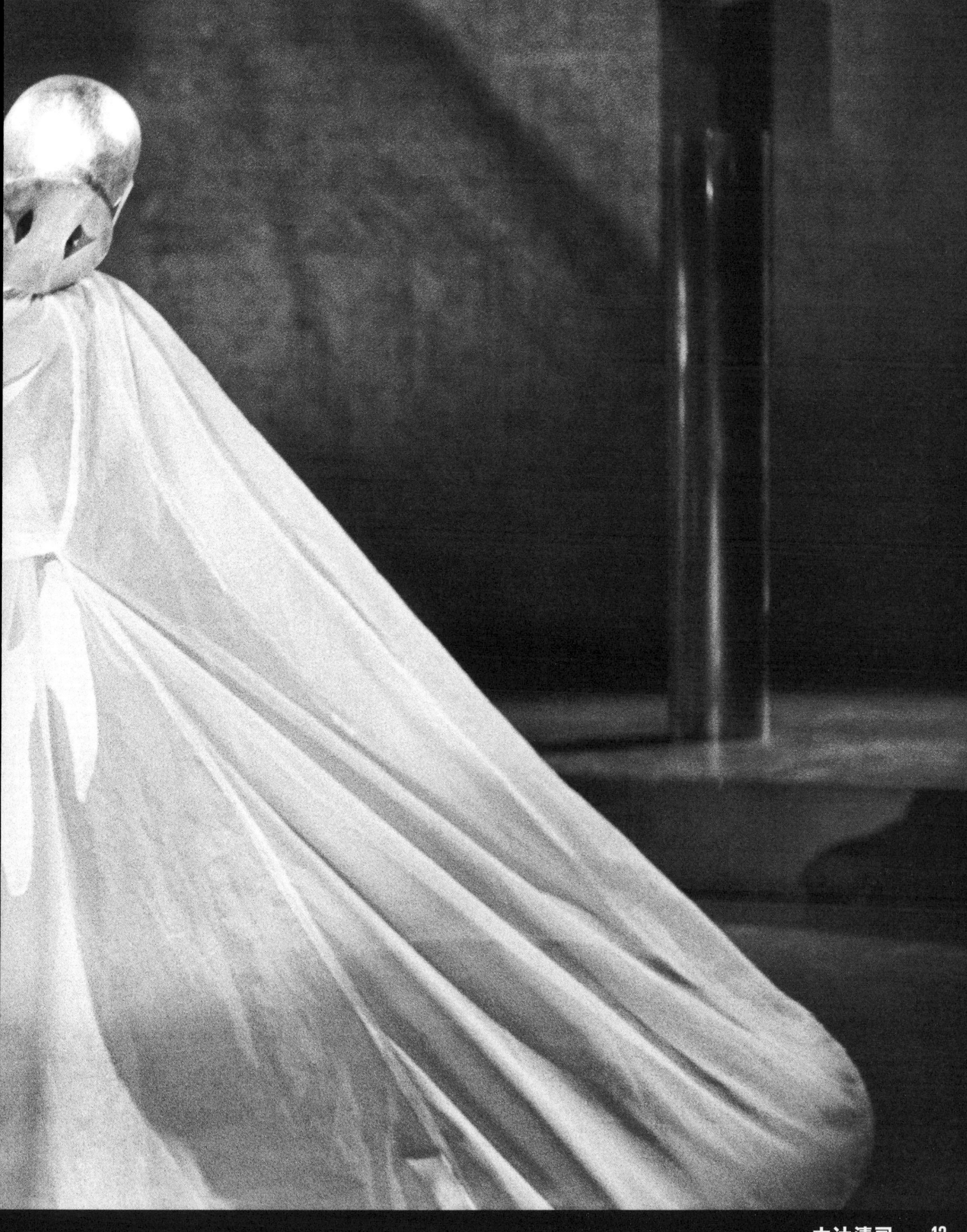

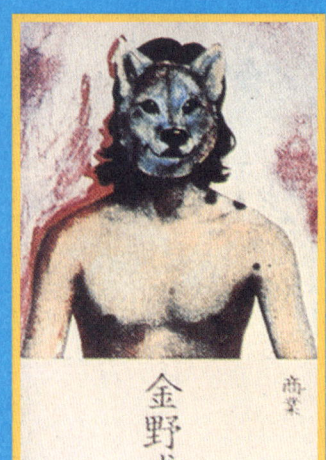

pp. 2-3: **Terayama Shūji**, Images from *Photothèque imaginaire de Shuji Terayama* (1975).

pp. 4-5: **Hosoe Eikō**, *Ordeal by Roses #19*, 1961, gelatin silver print.

pp. 6-7: **Hanaga Mitsutoshi**, *Fuwa Mansaku, Nakajima Natsu at Jōkyō Gekijō (Situation Theater)*, 1967, gelatin silver print.

p. 8: Photograph from **Yokosuka Noriaki**, *The Photon and Ogre*, 2006.

p.9: **Moriyama Daido**, *Self-Portrait*, 1997, gelatin silver print.

p. 10: **Yokoo Tadanori**, *The City and Design, The Wonders of Life on Earth, Isamu Kurita*, 1966, silkscreen.

pp. 12–13: **Ōtsuji Kiyoji**, *Pierrot Lunaire*, 1955, gelatin silver print.

Above, right and p. 17: **Terayama Shūji**, Images from *Photothèque imaginaire de Shuji Terayama* (1975).

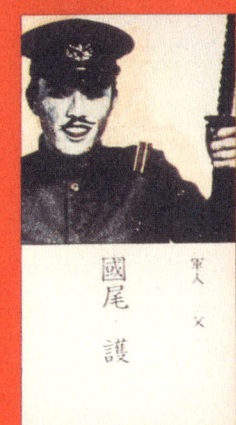
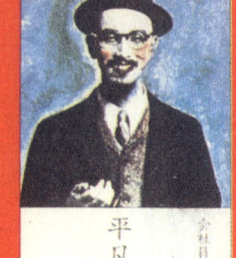
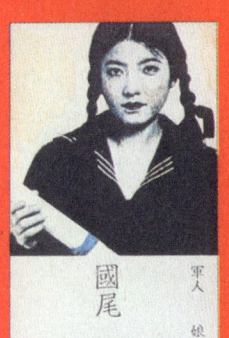
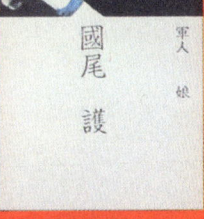
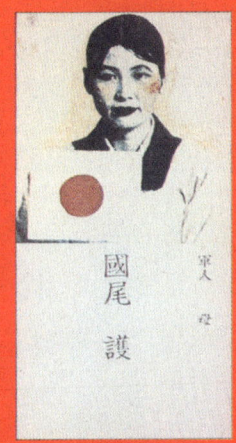
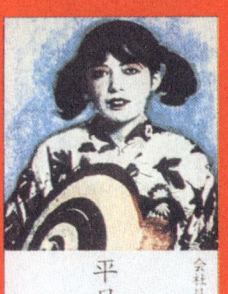
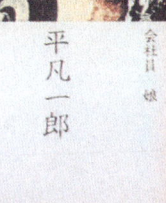
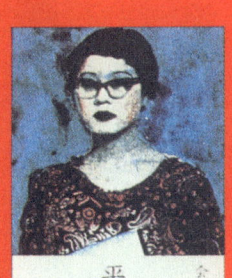
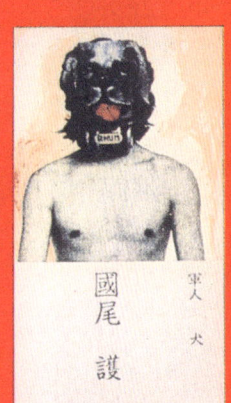
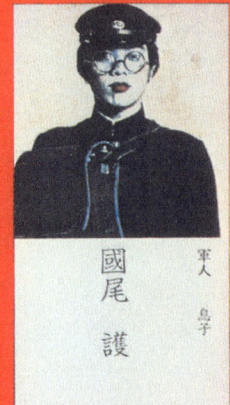
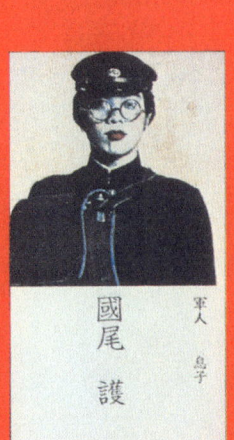
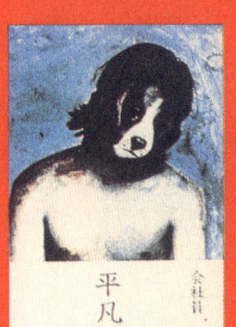
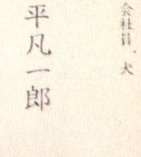
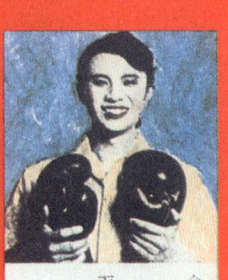

PREFACE
Amélie Ravalec

My first encounter with the world of Japanese avant-garde art was through Terayama Shūji's *Photothèque imaginaire de Shuji Terayama – Les gens de la famille Chien-Dieu* (1975). The book was a revelation: a kaleidoscope of vivid colours, simultaneously playful and provocative, imbued with an aura of dreamlike strangeness and disturbing beauty. It was a masterpiece that seemed to exist between reality and fantasy. This initial encounter sparked an obsession that led me to delve into the works of a plethora of avant-garde Japanese artists. Hosoe Eikō captivated me with his strikingly intense portraits of Mishima Yukio, while Yokoo Tadanori's psychedelic theatre posters demonstrated how you could push the boundaries of graphic design, elevating the medium into art itself.

These discoveries urged me to direct my documentary *Japanese Avant-Garde Pioneers* (2025), a labour of love over five years in the making. The film explores the chaos, beauty and defiance of the 1960s and 1970s in Japan while capturing the very essence of a cultural revolution that felt both urgent and inevitable. It's a story of outcasts and visionaries, many of whom are little known beyond the niche of Japanese art and photography collectors.

The art of this era was deeply political, shaped by the societal upheavals of the 1960s. Both my film and this book document the turbulence that followed: the impassioned student protests that swept across Japanese universities, the radical experimentation in photography that upended traditional aesthetics and the relentless subversion embodied by avant-garde performances. This was encapsulated in *Provoke*, a short-lived but highly influential photographic journal that became synonymous with a new photographic aesthetic. Emerging in the late 1960s, *Provoke* challenged conventional photographic traditions, combining raw, grainy and high-contrast images with philosophical texts and manifestos to redefine visual language. It was a time when underground theatre groups like Tenjō Sajiki and performance art collectives such as Neo-Dada Organizers and Hi-Red Center shattered conventions with radical performances that defied and challenged authority, societal norms and capitalism. Politics, art and body performances were interwoven, forming a potent rebellion that still provokes and inspires.

This generation of artists grew up in the shadow of the Second World War, and many of them experienced as children the bombings of Tokyo – life-altering events that would profoundly shape their artistic visions in the decades that followed. Themes of Eros and Thanatos – the interplay of desire and death – permeated many influential works, from Araki Nobuyoshi's provocative photography to Saeki Toshio's surreal illustrations, where eroticism and existential dread coalesced. The trauma of the atomic bomb found poignant expression in Kawada Kikuji's now classic photobook *The Map* (1965), which grappled with the aftermath of Hiroshima, and Hosoe Eikō's film *Navel and A-Bomb* (1960), a haunting reflection on the scars left by that devastation. Butoh, a new and harrowing form of dance, emerged as an exploration of humanity's darkness and light, drawing from the aftermath of the nuclear apocalypse. This visceral art form transformed human movement into a visual and emotional symphony, with performances that were simultaneously grotesque and transcendent, exploring themes of life, death and rebirth with an otherworldly intensity.

Japan Art Revolution spans a wide range of disciplines – art, photography, film, theatre, performances, butoh dance, illustration and graphic design – highlighting how avant-garde artists refused to be confined by a single medium. The post-war era in Japan became a paragon of creativity, a time when traditional art forms were cast aside in favour of radical experimentation. The era was defined by unprecedented collaborations: photographers working alongside butoh dancers; theatre directors and graphic designers conjuring new, electrifying worlds together. Their works often defied categorization, existing instead in a liminal space where disciplines merged to form a singular cultural phenomenon.

Building on the film's narrative, this book takes full advantage of the tactile and immersive nature of the printed medium. Breaking away from the traditional essay form prevalent in art publications, the text is structured like a fragmented documentary narration, weaving together a chorus of voices: artists, photographers, scholars, archivists, experts and writers, each bringing their unique perspective. Direct testimonies from artists who experienced this era at first hand are woven with archival texts, manifestos and the clarifying insights of contemporary art historians and experts. This approach creates a polyphonic narrative, an ever-shifting landscape of ideas that pays homage to the boundless energy of the avant-garde scene.

Japanese book design has profoundly influenced my work as a photographer and a book designer. I am a lifelong collector of art and photography books, and the design of *Japan Art Revolution* has been as important to me as the art within the pages. Encountering books designed by Japanese artists like Yokoo Tadanori and Awazu Kiyoshi was nothing short of a revelation. Their designs are a complete sensory overload: an explosion of colours, bold typography and dynamic graphical elements that leave no space untouched, yet somehow retain a unifying balance. Each page draws you irresistibly into a kaleidoscopic world where every detail matters. This sense of visual immersion, this vibrant and deliberate chaos, is what I've aspired to replicate in my own book.

Designing the book layout myself felt necessary, as it allowed me to fully express the rich and complex universe of the Japanese avant-garde in the exact way I had envisioned. As a filmmaker, I've always thought visually, and as a film editor, I thrive on bringing disparate elements together into a cohesive whole. My work as a colourist also played a significant role in shaping the book design. The transition from film to book was an incredibly exciting challenge. For several intense months, I found myself in a state of pure, frenzied inspiration, where the design seemed to flow effortlessly from concept to page, as if the book were designing itself. This is a work that I hope reflects the spirit and energy of the Japanese avant-garde.

Despite years of research and creative output on the subject, the world of Japanese avant-garde remains an endless source of fascination for me. Each new discovery feels like peeling back another layer of a complex universe that continues to influence fashion, music and culture today. I hope this book will inspire you to dive deeper and perhaps, like me, become lost in this extraordinary world of beauty, defiance and boundless creativity.

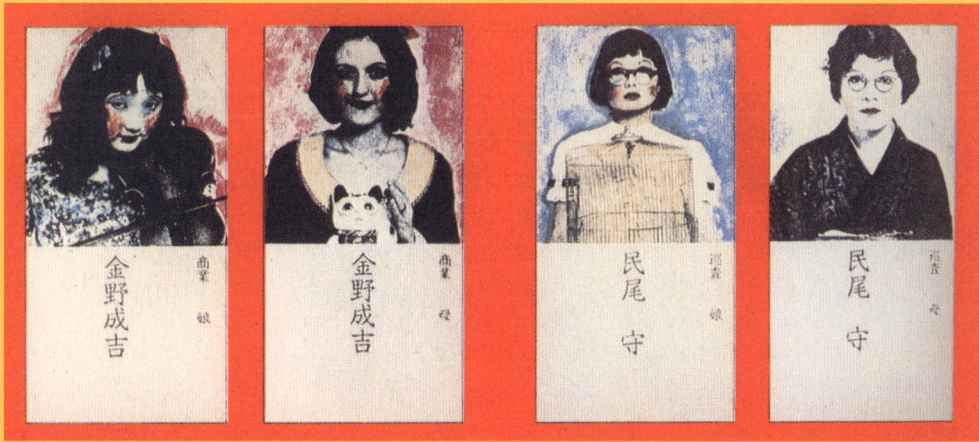

INTRODUCTION: AVANT-GARDE PIONEERS

Avant-garde art in Japan was translated very early on in the Taishō period (1912–26) as *zen'ei bijutsu*, meaning art that is advanced, or art that comes before.

'Avant-garde' originally referred to those in the military who were literally the front line, and that kind of militant aspect of change, of eradicating what came before in order to create a new world, was very much part of the spirit of the Japanese avant-garde as well.

Japan had always been a very hierarchical, conformist, classist society, and the artists of this period were thrilled to see themselves as outside that structure. They were there at a foundational moment intellectually, politically, philosophically and, of course, artistically.

The idea of the purpose of art, the audience of art, and the definition of the artist in society was changing. They wanted to be outside; they gained strength and identity and power in their being outside. They wanted to be mavericks. They wanted to be eccentrics.

Japanese artists in this avant-garde lineage have a way of reaching an edge of psychic truth, an edge of psychic being, that is almost unmatched. There is a fearlessness that is really very close to suicide, and very close also to spiritual transcendence.

There are few other artists that as a group deal so naturally with the unthinkable and the unfathomable. And it is in that unthinkable that the grotesque holds a very powerful place of honour. Japanese artists throughout time have been exemplary in articulating that for all mankind.

ALEXANDRA MUNROE

Moriyama Daido, *Self-Portrait*, 1997, gelatin silver print.

Opposite: **Hanaga Mitsutoshi**, *Akasegawa Genpei at his Residence in Tokyo*, 1967, gelatin silver print.

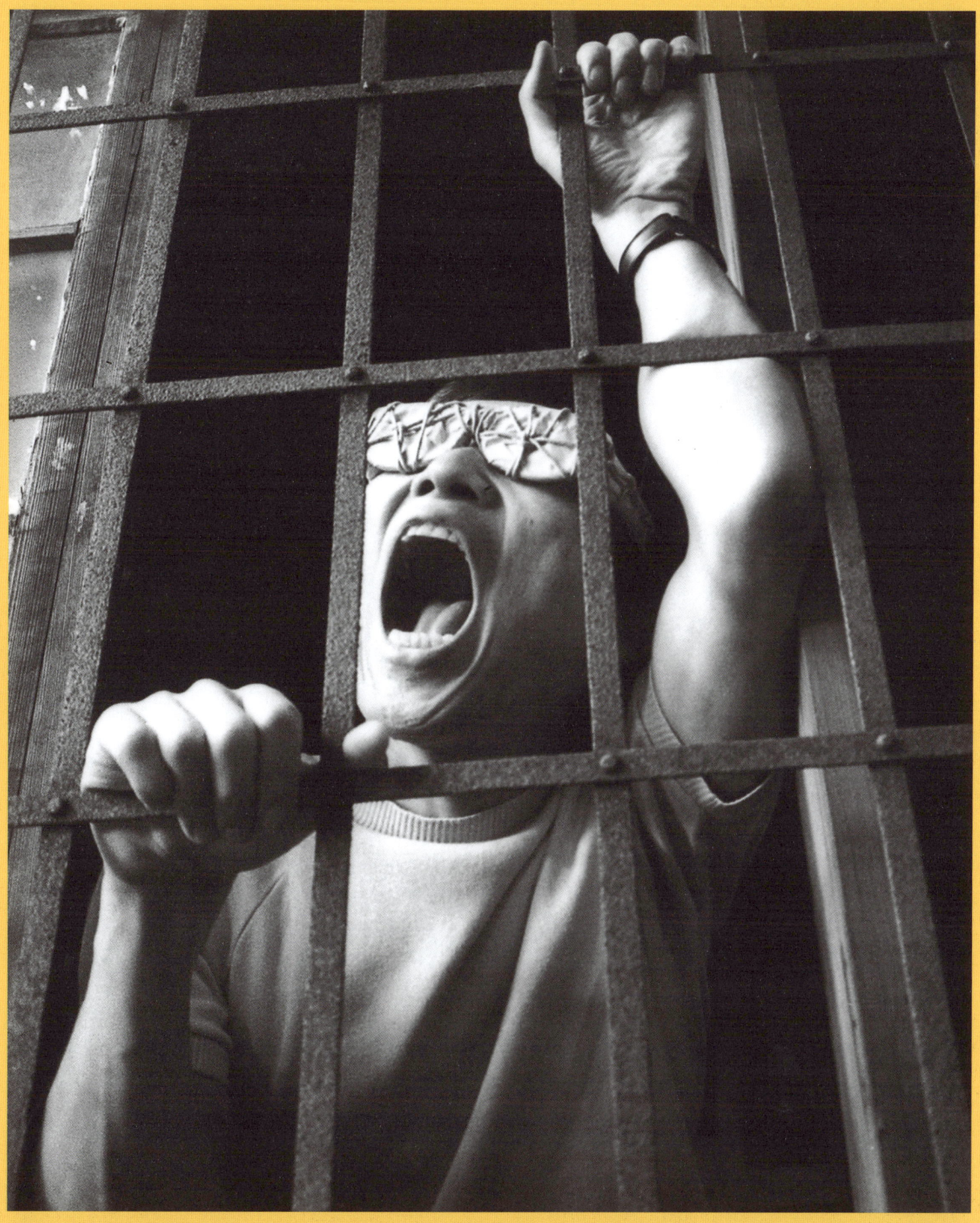

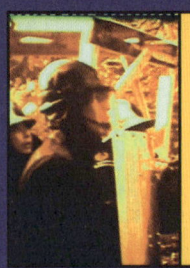

ANPO PROTESTS
1959/1960/1970

安保闘争

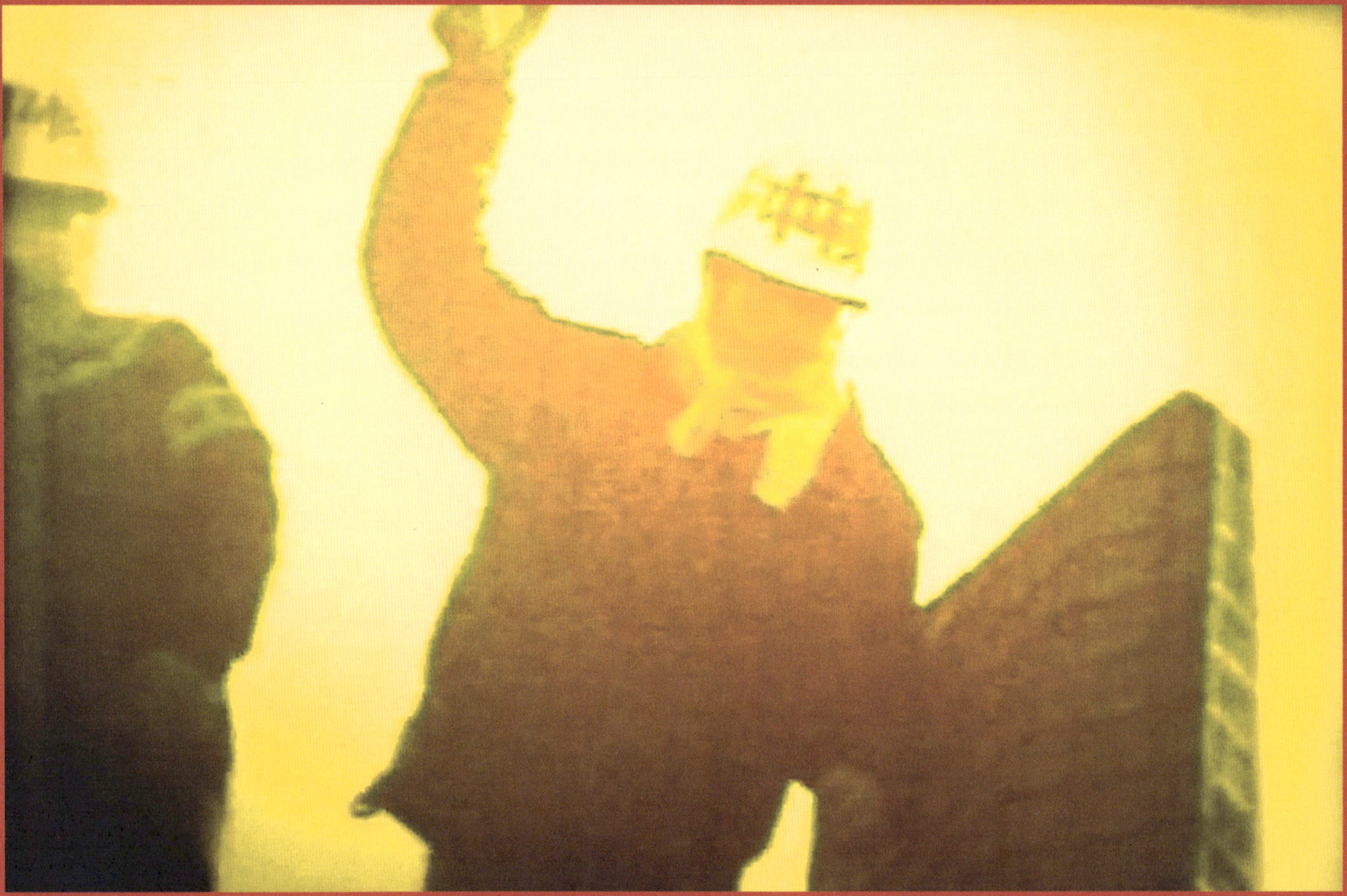

Above and opposite: Stills from **Michael Rogge**, *An American Views Japan in 1968* (1968).

pp. 24–25: Stills from **All University Joint Struggle Committee of Nihon University**, *A Record of the Struggle at Nihon University* (1968).

Japanese mass participation in popular unrest first came to a head in 1960, when hundreds of thousands of Tokyo residents took to the streets and more than 10 million Japanese citizens signed petitions in opposition to the renewal of the Treaty of Mutual Cooperation and Security between Japan and the United States, nicknamed 'Anpo'.

LUCY FLEMING-BROWN

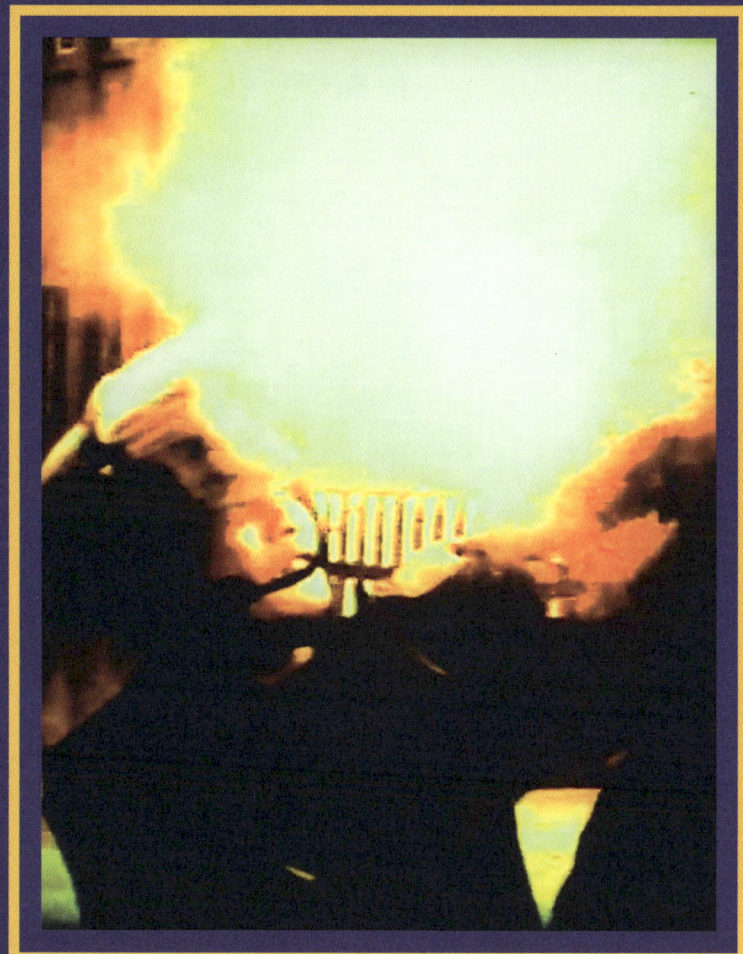
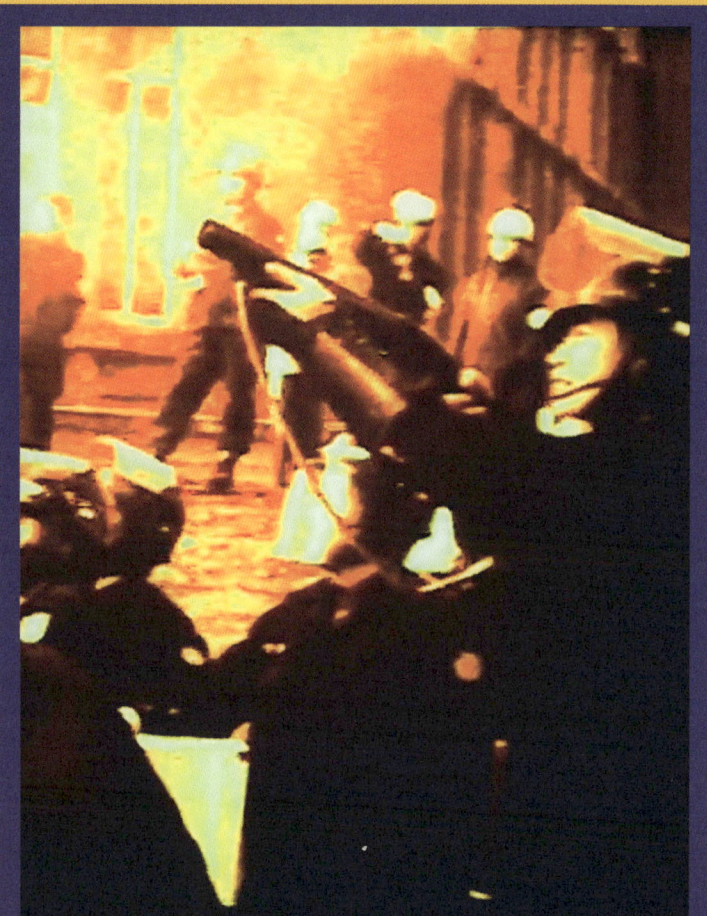

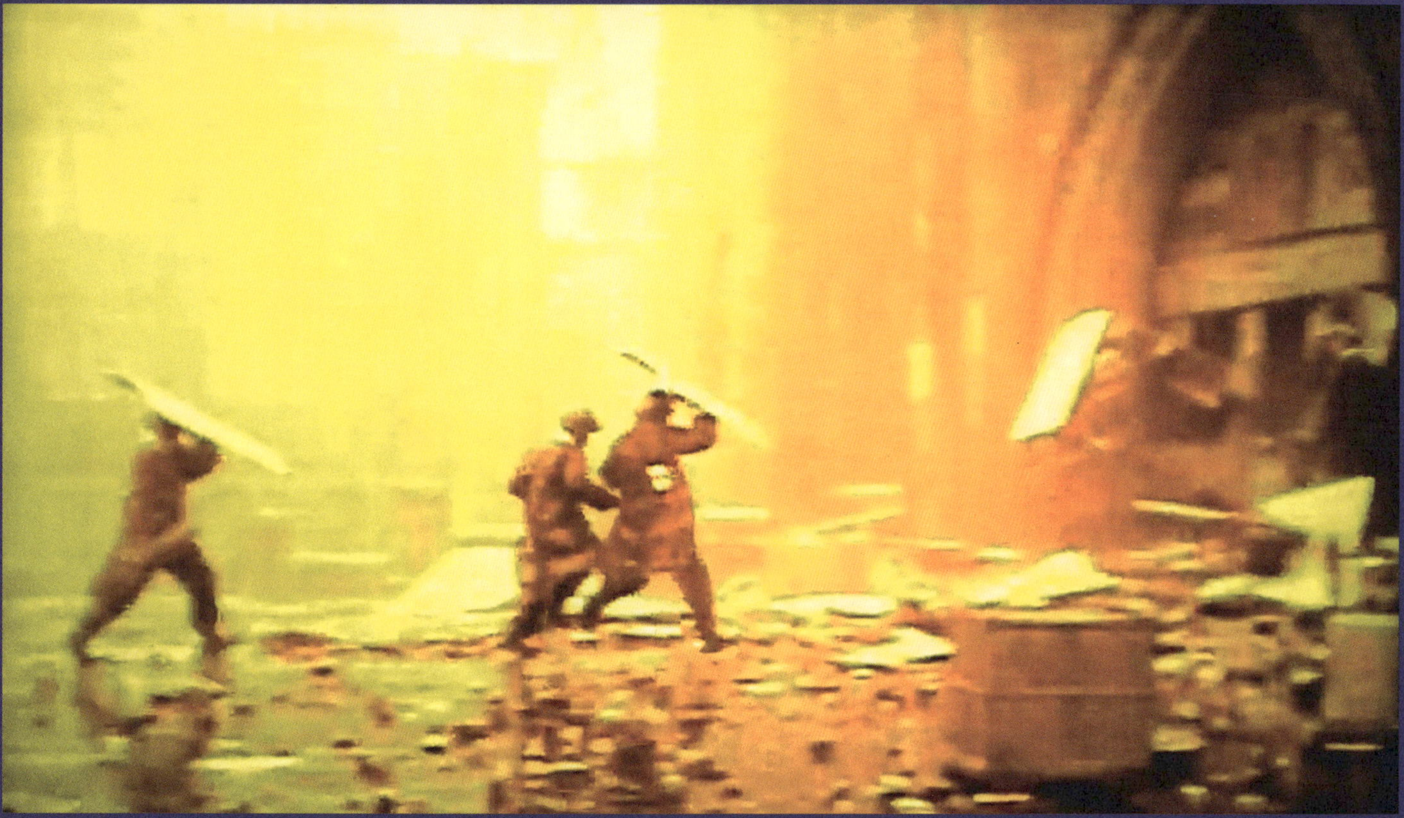

The treaty had come to represent the burden of American-Japanese tensions following the Occupation, and it came under fire from both left- and right-wing factions.

As Cold War pressure and American involvement in the Vietnam War continued to escalate throughout the 1960s, Japanese resentment towards the exploitation of their country in support of American militarism increased, and it was accompanied by unprecedented public participation in dissent. The ongoing occupation of Okinawa, the informal colonization of strategic towns as military bases, the forced construction of a new airport at Narita, necessitated by American air traffic, and more general pan-Asian solidarity against foreign intervention fuelled resistance throughout the 1960s.

The intensification of the Vietnam War during the second half of 1967 gave rise to a renewed wave of political activism, and the impact of this popular dissent was magnified for Tokyo's creative avant-garde. Their close-knit interlocking circles, based in Ginza by day and Shinjuku by night, rendered interaction with street politics inevitable. Some artists held overtly revolutionary sympathies, with contributors to the photography publication *Provoke* hosting student activists and actively engaging in radical debates and street riots.

Others, like Tōmatsu Shōmei, who navigated political themes in their work but who were not aligned with any single cause, found themselves caught up in the action and forced to pick a side as a result of the positions they held at Tokyo's politicized art schools.

Through the city's overlapping networks of professional associations, shared workspaces, educational outfits and committees responsible for exhibitions and publications, artists from across the political spectrum were thrown together in creative solidarity during the 1960s, resulting in diverse feats of cultural activism.

Photographs from **All University Joint Struggle Committee of Nihon University**, *Nihon University Protests* (1969).

Opposite: **Takuma Akio, Iida Takao et al.**, *NON*, vol. 2: *Okinawa wa niga-yo/Okinawa is a Bitter World* (1969), cover.

LUCY FLEMING-BROWN

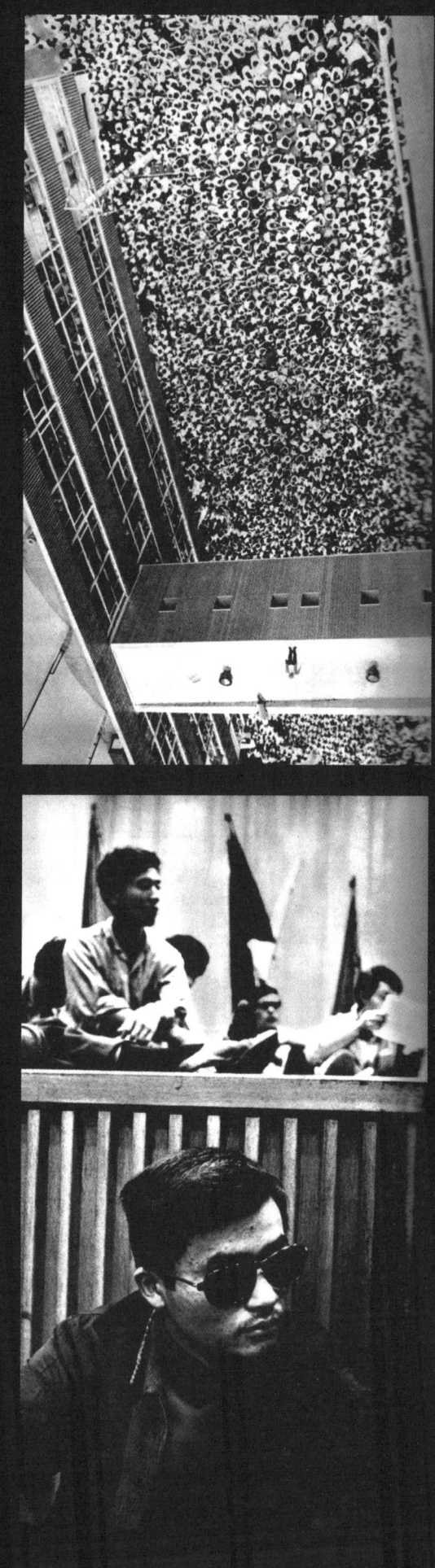

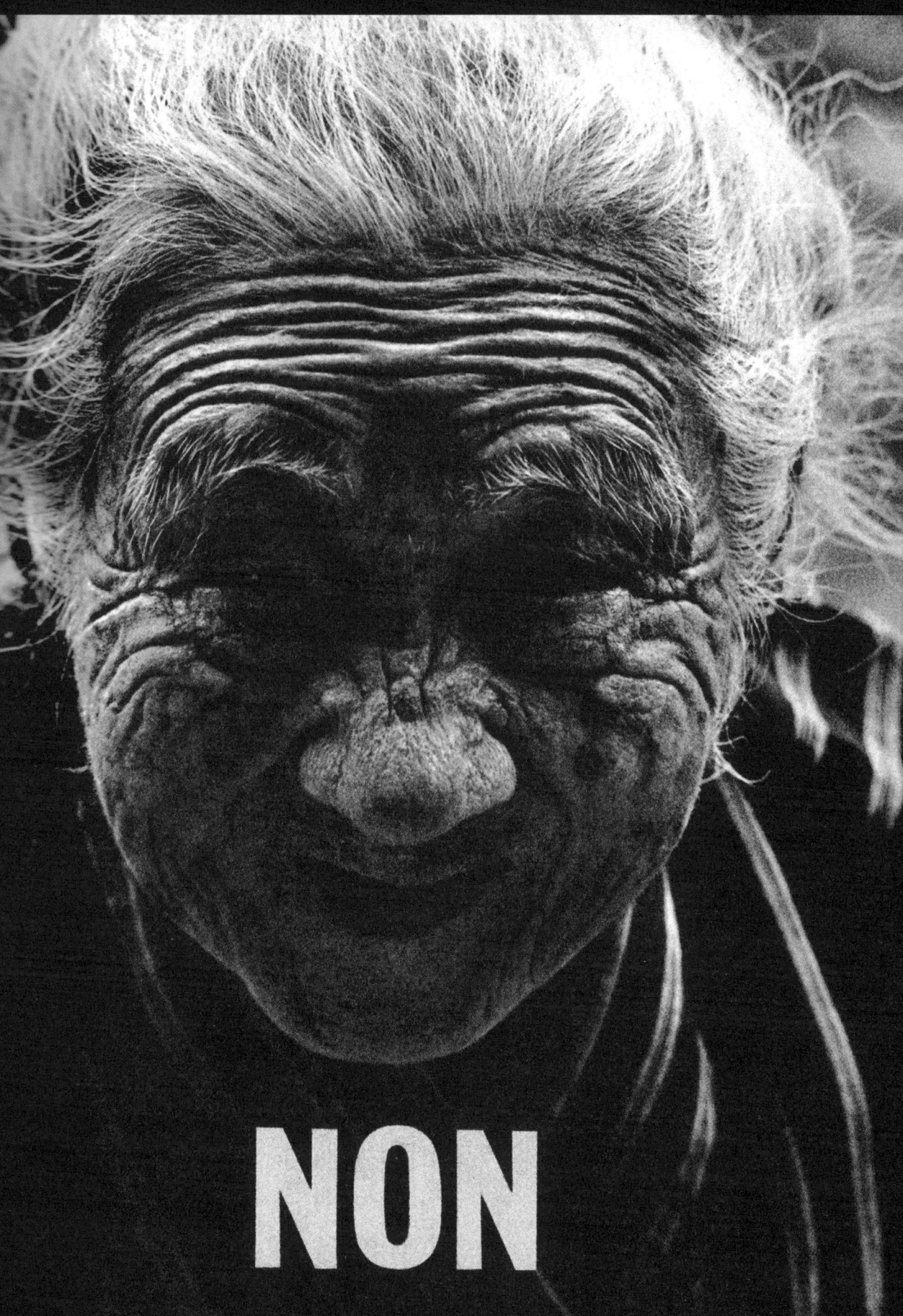

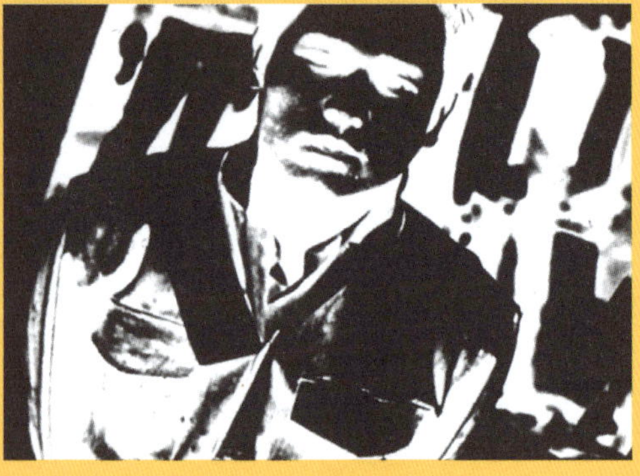

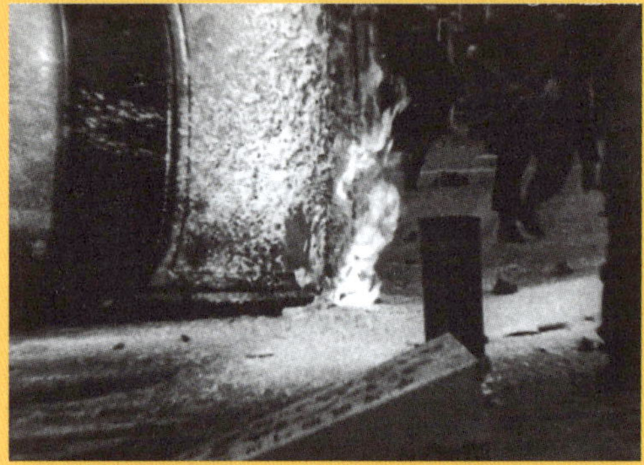

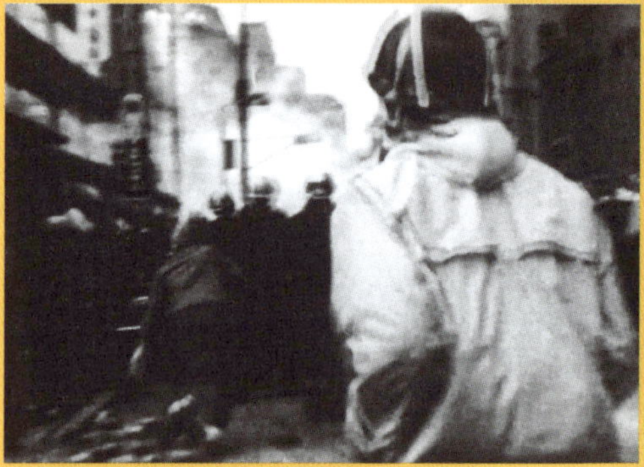

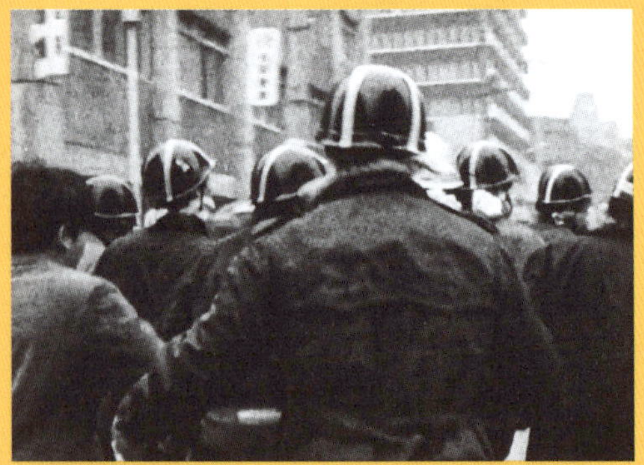

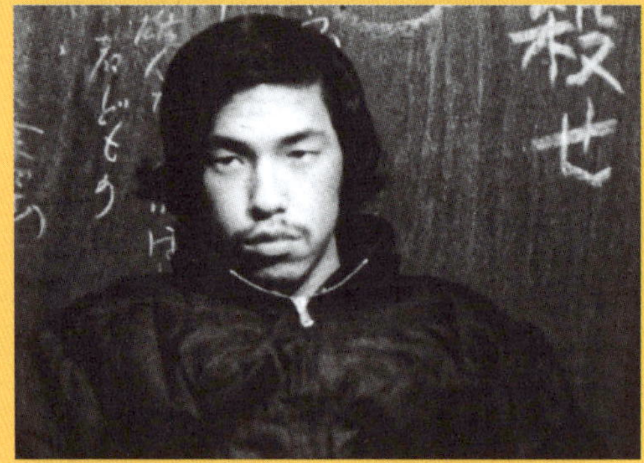

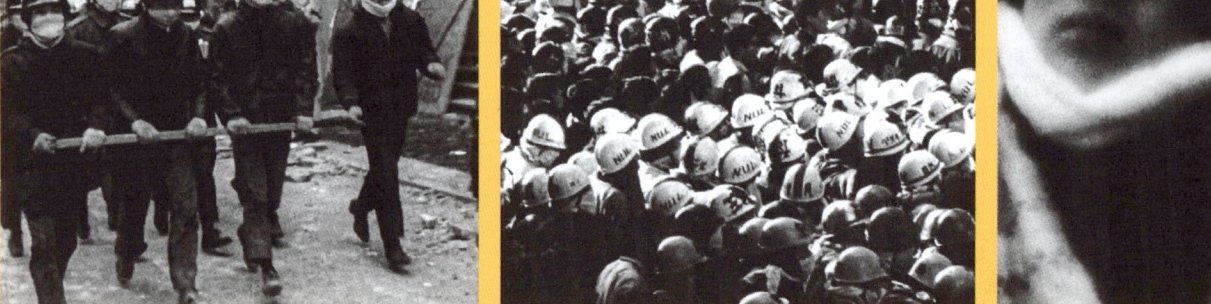
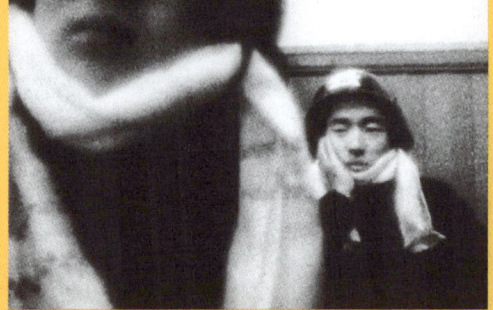

ANPO PROTESTS

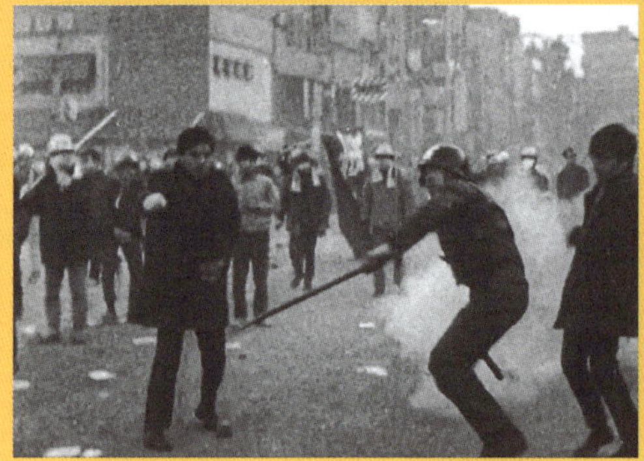

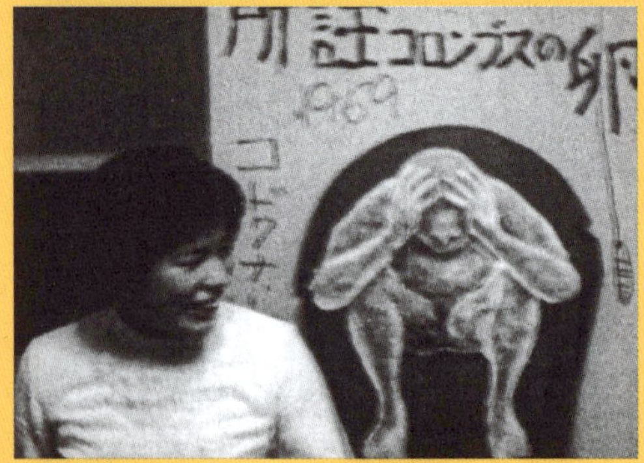

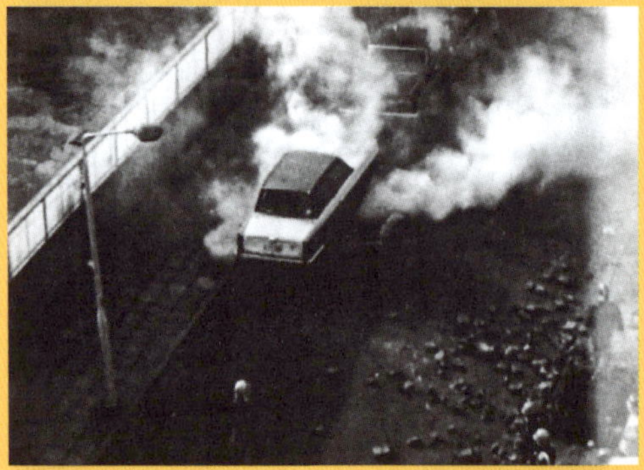

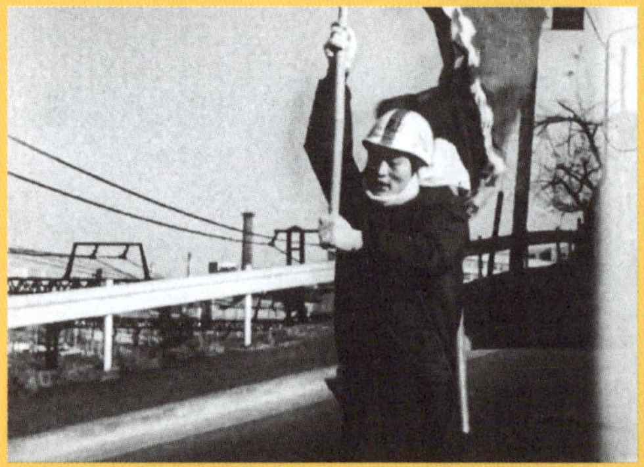

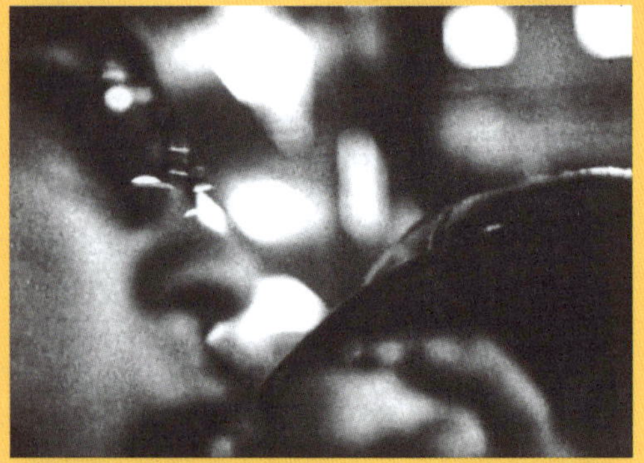

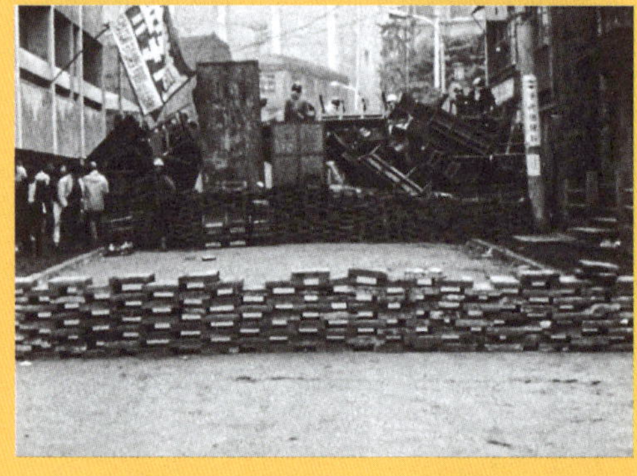

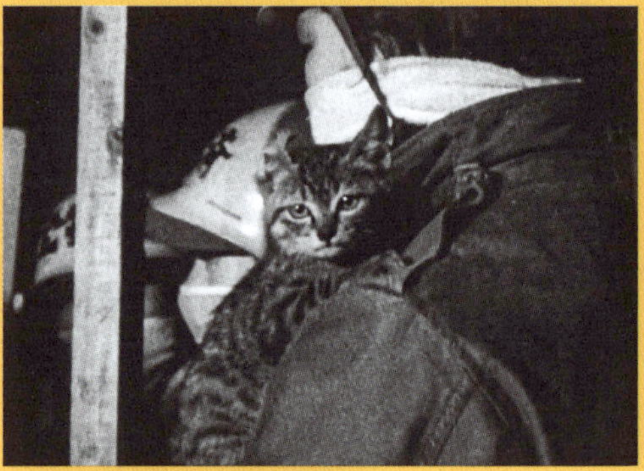

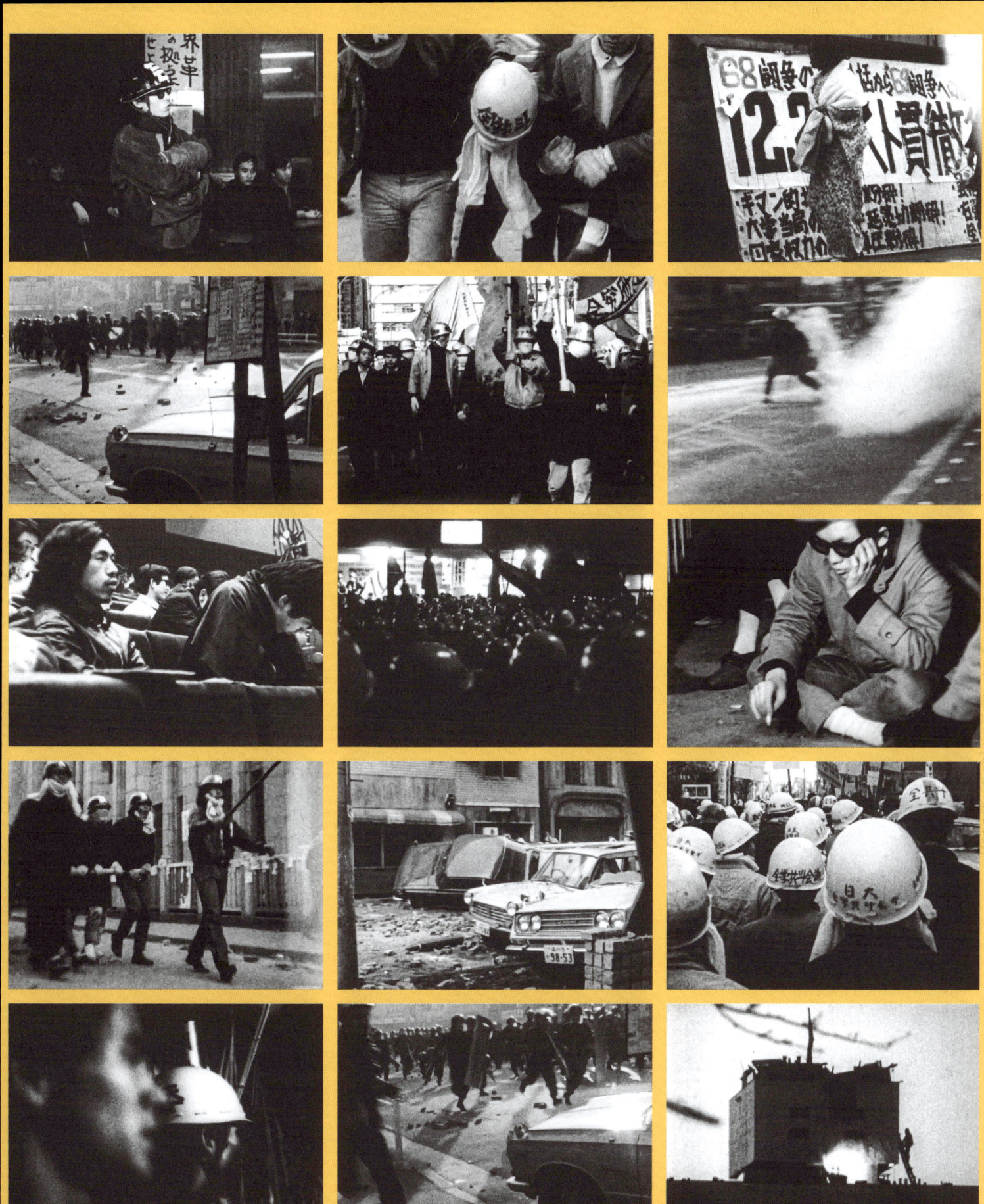

安保闘争

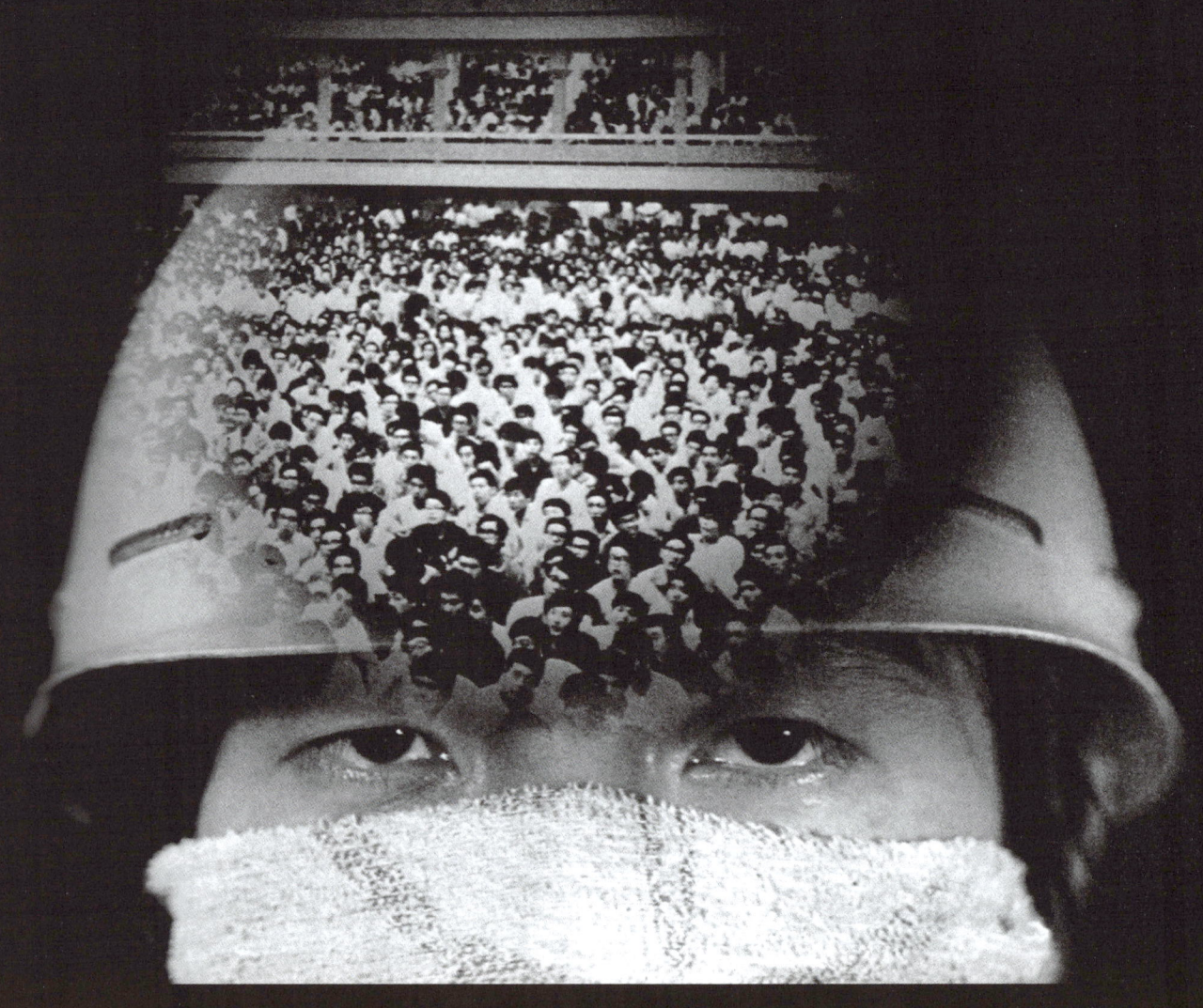

All University Joint Struggle Commitee of Nihon University, *Nihon University Protests* (1969), cover.

Overleaf: Stills from **Nihon University Zenkyōtō**, *A Record of the Struggle at Nihon University* (1968).

> THERE WERE BARRICADES AGAINST TOKYO UNIVERSITY. THERE WERE FIRES. THERE WERE FIREBOMBS. THERE WERE RIOTS. ALL OF THAT WAS ULTIMATELY DEFEATED.
>
> ALEXANDRA MUNROE

I became a student in the mid-1960s and in the '70s, US–Japan security treaty protests were going on when I had just joined university. This was a time when people could rethink society. There was the '60s treaty and the '70s treaty, so it was a political era, and there was the student movement. I was encountering this period of turbulence in real life and it was a great experience.

I decided to go into the barricades. I thought it would be interesting to enter it, so I decided to live there. It was almost fifty years ago, but we were more free back then. We could do such things normally. Students as well as citizens could quite clearly state what they wanted and revendicate it. So the whole atmosphere was different.

ISHIUCHI MIYAKO

They'd had a collapse of values, a collapse of the ideological regime that existed before. And they wanted to make something new. Vast numbers of people were coming into the big cities from the countryside. During the war, Japan was still largely a rural country. But in the '50s and '60s, it became a very urban country. A huge influx of people came from the countryside to the towns, mainly young people, and they created their own lifestyle, their own values.

PETER TASKER

1968 was a time of great global revolution. The revolution caused us to rethink different institutions, whether politics, economy or culture. All of these things were questioned, re-read and made into something new. This was the global movement of the '60s and '70s. They said 'no' to everything in the world and rejected it, thereby creating a new worldview.

KANEKO RYŪICHI

Societies experience social unrest through student protests, their desires, their demands, and at the same time cultural shifts emerge. Politics, society and culture are closely intertwined.

MORISHITA TAKASHI

The young people held an ideology of creating their own culture and society. From this moment, the cultural movements of the '60s and '70s were shaped. I graduated in 1969, during the second Anpo treaty. Without those movements, I wonder if Japan would have been as culturally interesting. It was an instance when you had to rethink society. Political movements are very important. The desire to create something new was very strong during the '60s and '70s. Since then, it has been about prioritizing the economy.

ENOMOTO RYOICHI

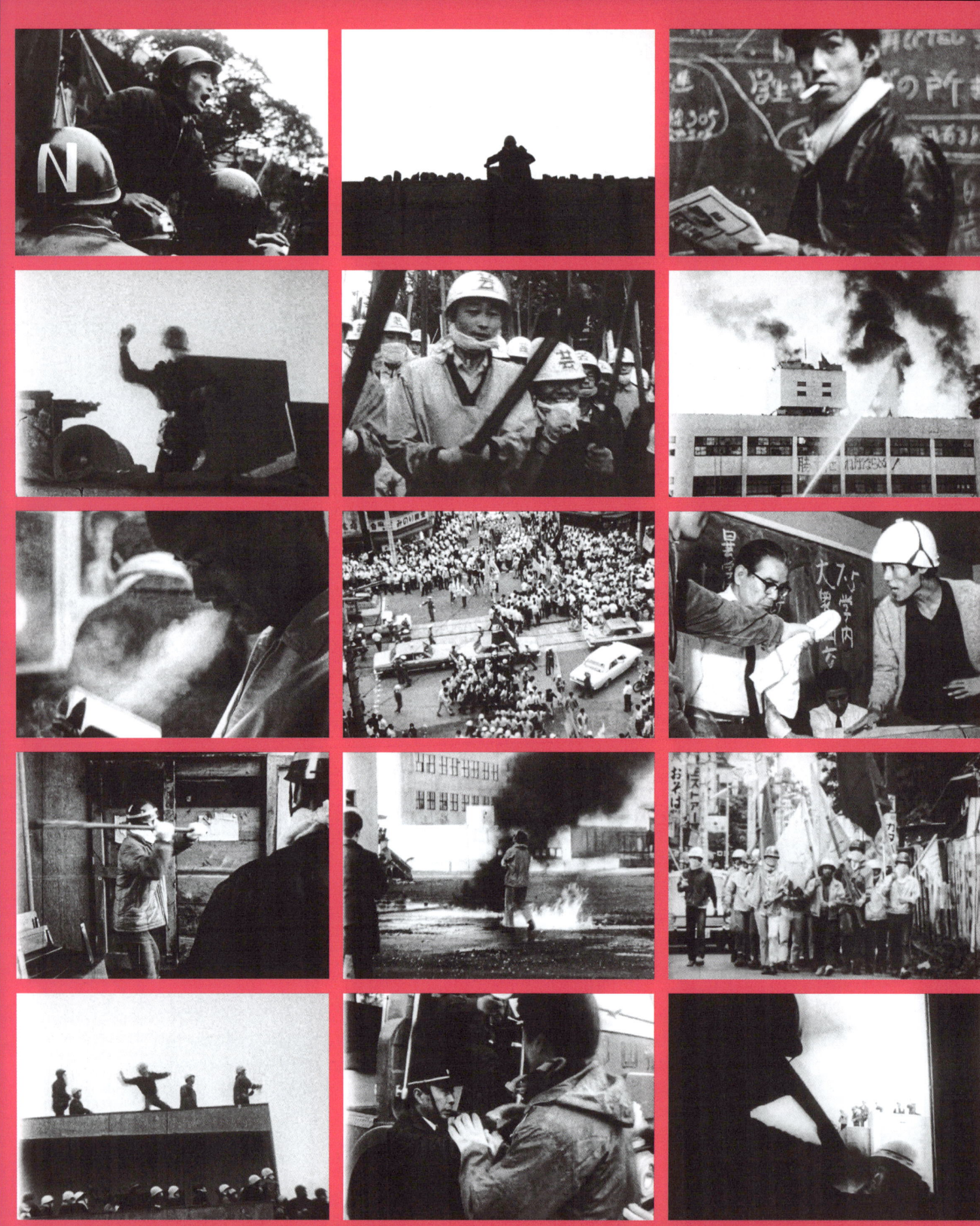

ANPO PROTESTS

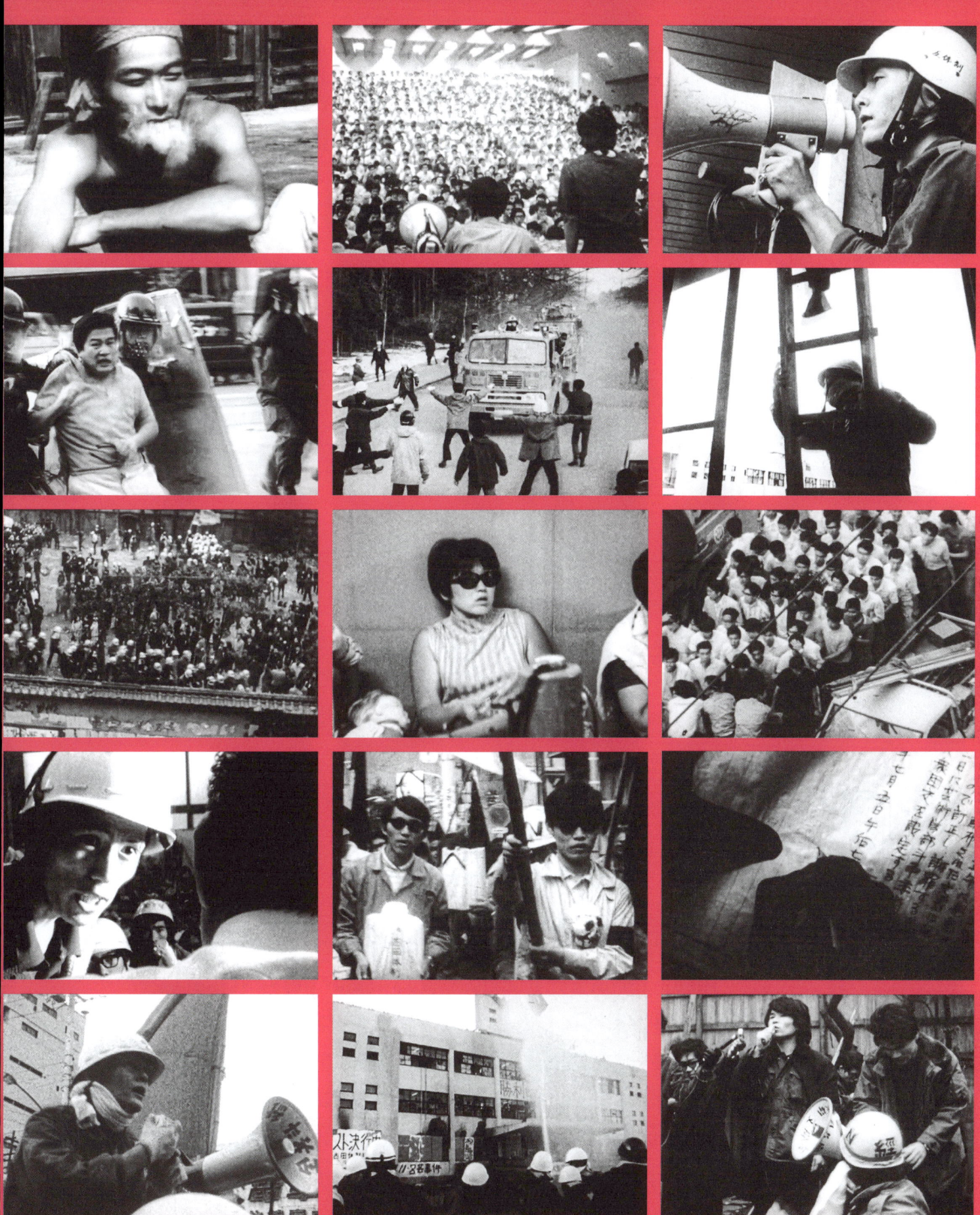

安保闘争

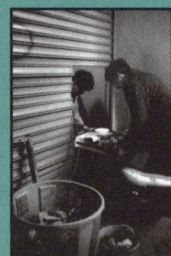

WATANABE HITOMI
1942–
渡辺眸

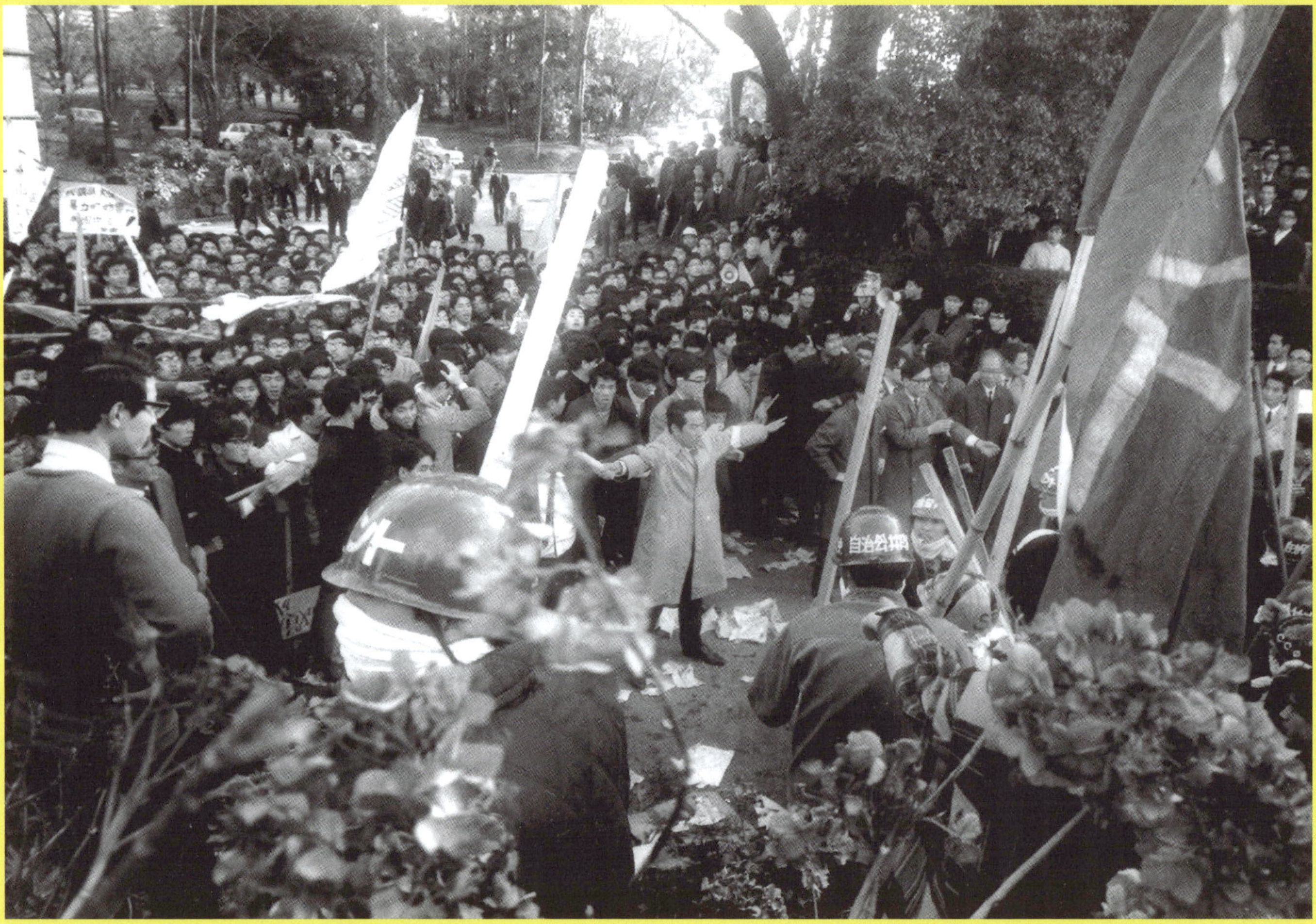

Above, opposite and overleaf: **Watanabe Hitomi**, *Untitled, 1968–1969*, from the series *Tōdai Zenkyōtō*, gelatin silver print.

p. 35: **Watanabe Hitomi**, *Untitled, 1968–1969*, from the series *Tōdai Zenkyōtō*, gelatin silver print.

'Nihon University (Nichidai) was one of the first places where protests really took off, especially because of its art department, which attracted many politically engaged students. At the time, everyone involved in the Zenkyōtō movement had their own role to play, and for some reason, my role became capturing its visual history.'

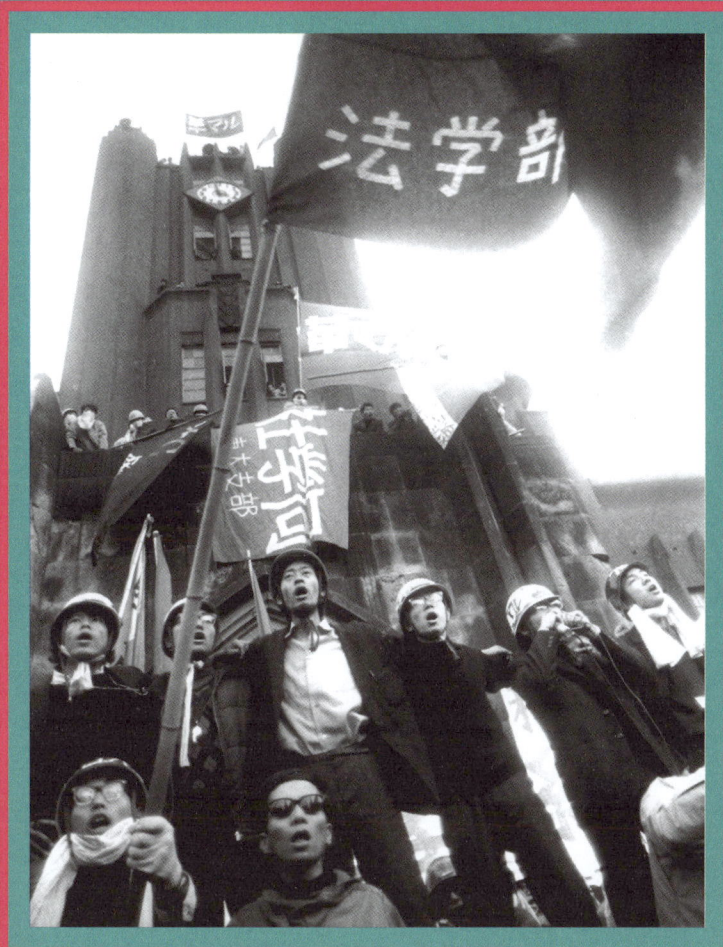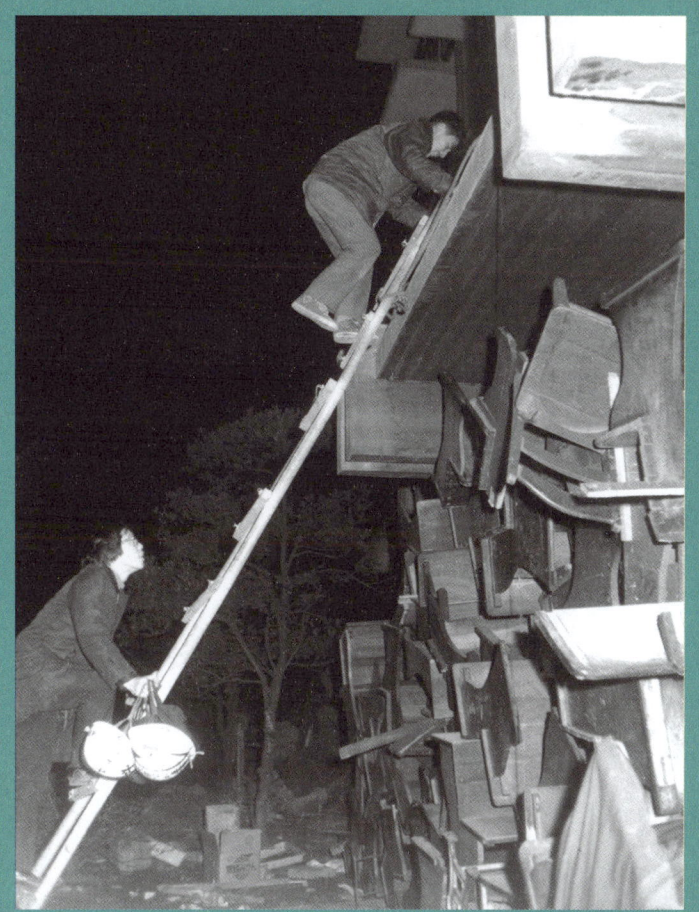

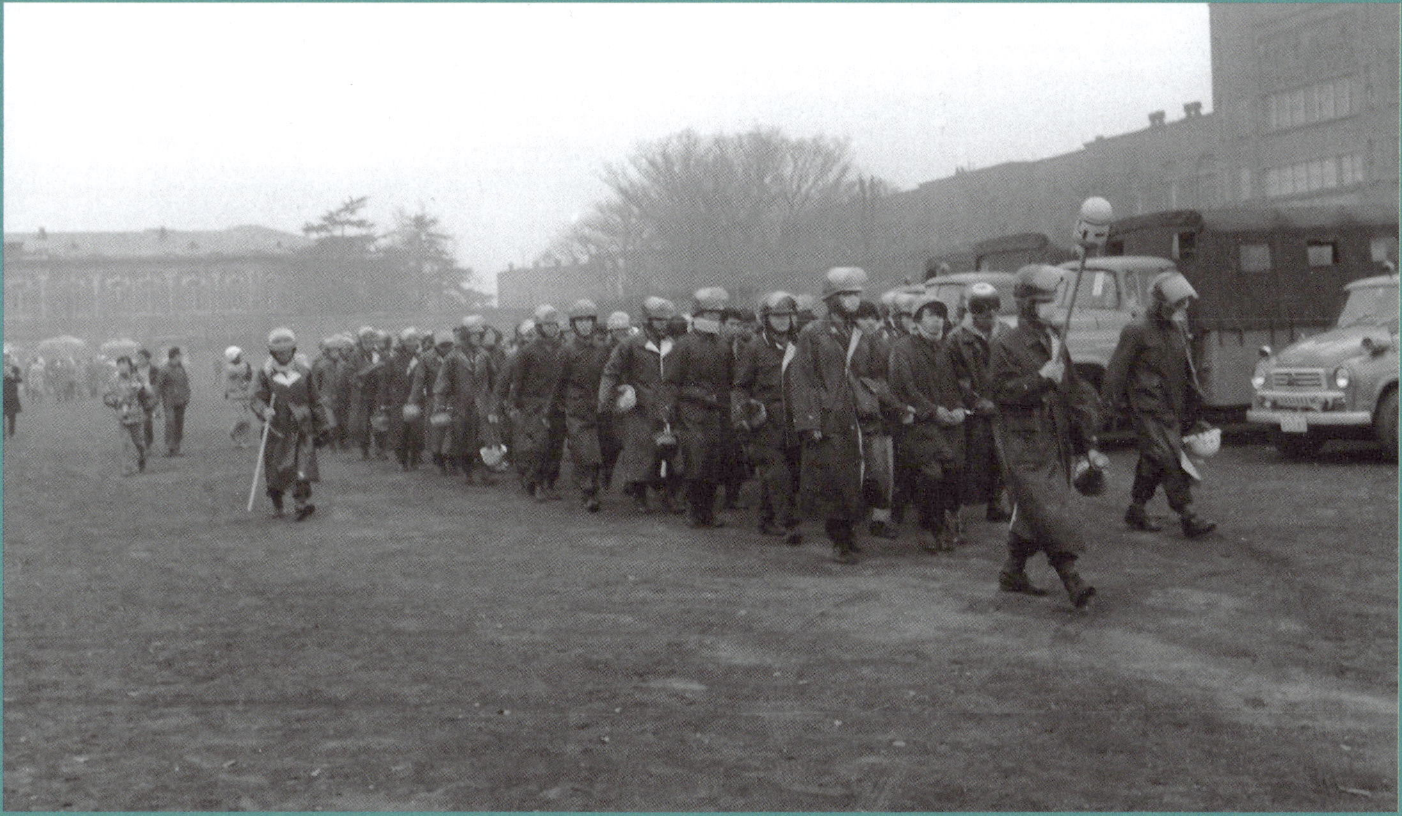

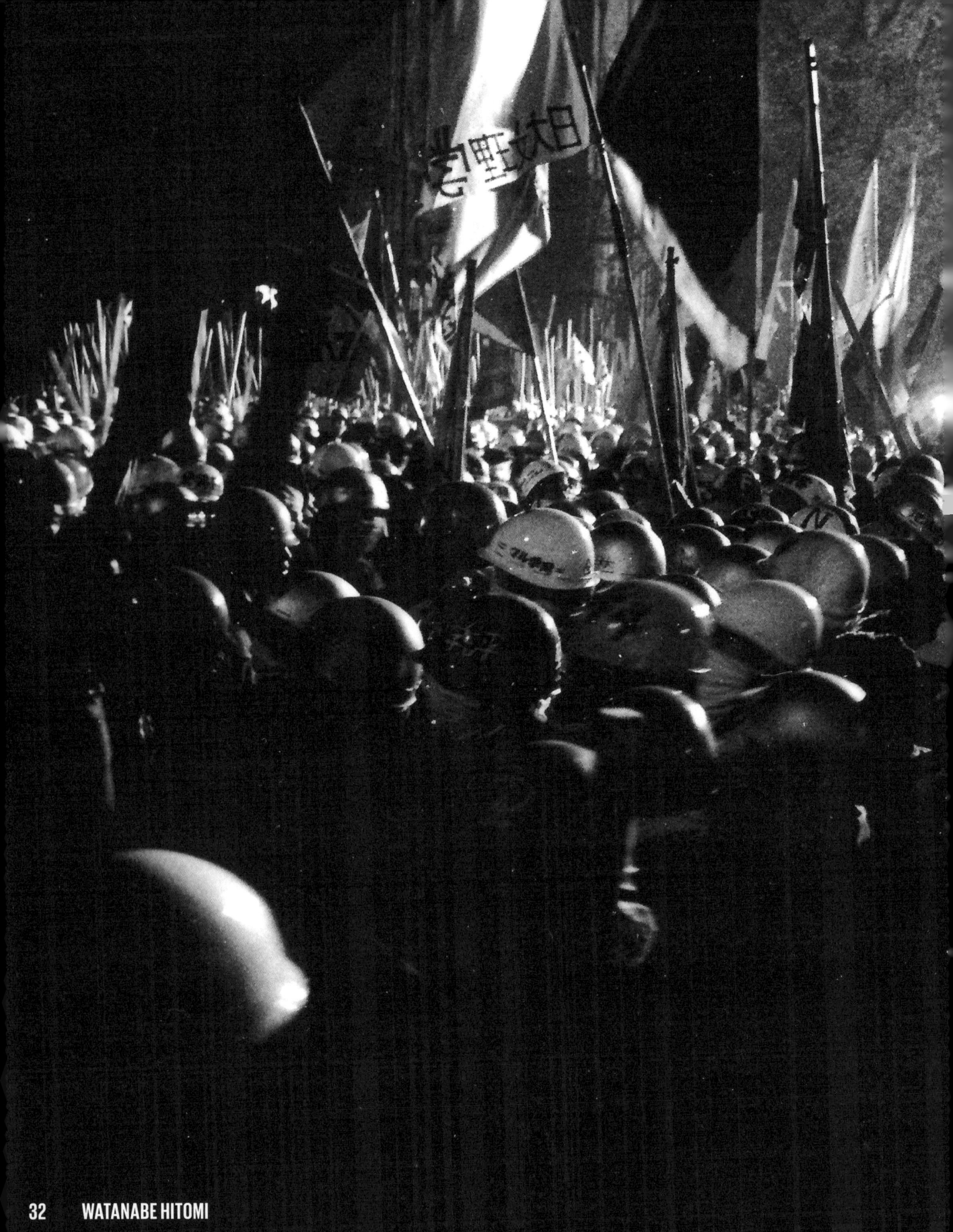

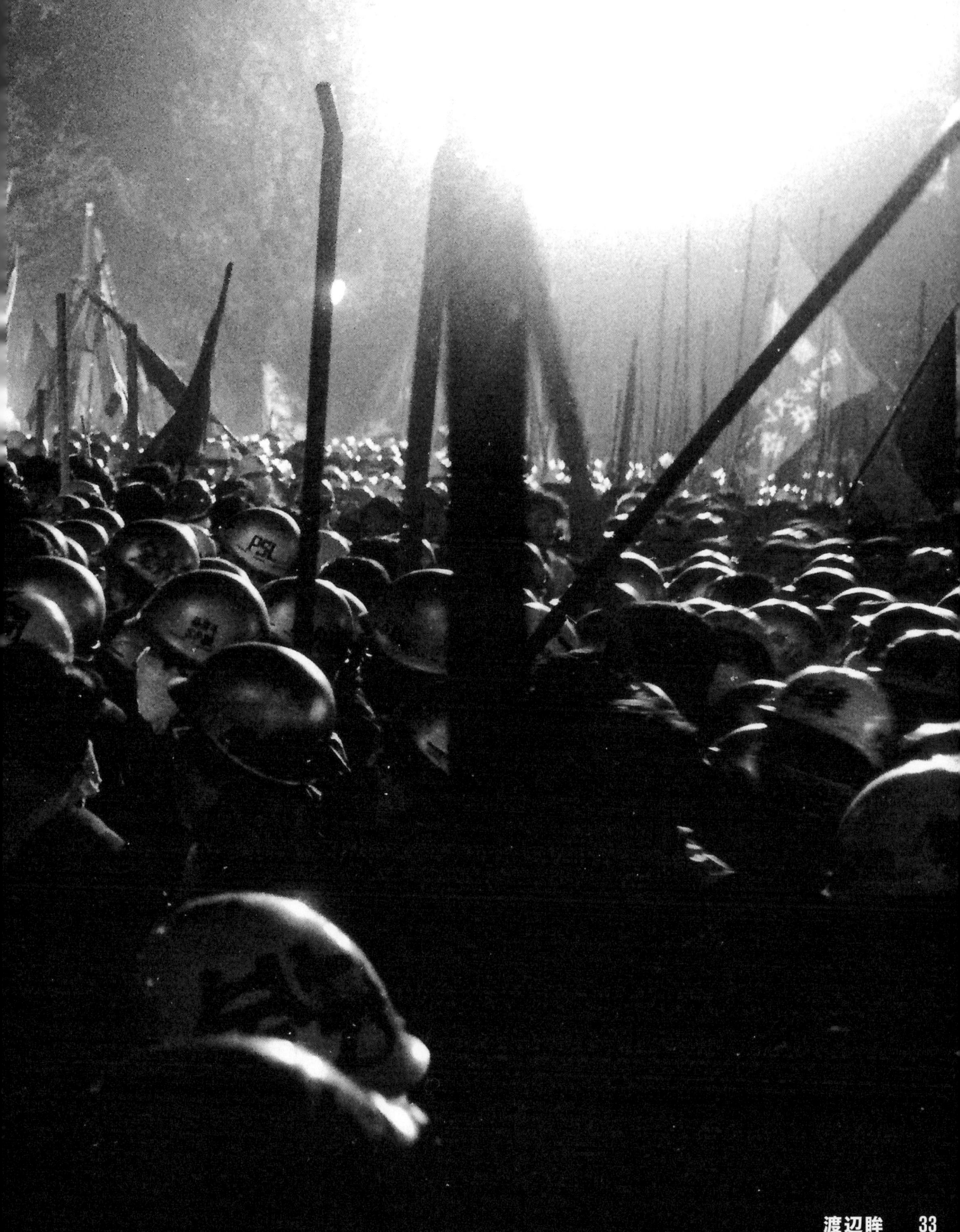

'It all began in 1968 at the University of Tokyo, with the Zenkyōtō, the student protest movement. There were places in Shinjuku where student activists from Nihon University (Nichidai) would gather – bars, meeting spots and underground venues. I had a friend who was involved with the Zengakuren (All-Japan Federation of Student Self-Government Associations) group, and I often met with him in Shinjuku, which is why I started taking photos there. Nihon University was one of the first places where protests really took off, especially because of its art department, which attracted many politically engaged students. At the time, everyone involved in the Zenkyōtō movement had their own role to play, and for some reason, my role became capturing the visual history of it. I became deeply immersed in it.

Back then, even before the main student movements, there was opposition from groups associated with the Communist Party. But the Zengakuren movement was different – it wasn't tied to any particular party, it emerged organically through the student protests, rather than from an established political movement. It was a response to the government's oppressive policies. The era was completely different from today – there was real opposition. Now, I don't think that kind of resistance exists anymore. I was taking photographs near the gates when students were being arrested en masse. Everyone knew that getting caught meant facing brutal consequences. I remember clearly capturing those moments – the tension, the fear.

We had a phrase we used as a warning: "18–19". It referred to the 18th and 19th of the month, when police crackdowns were expected. I managed to get inside Yasuda Auditorium before the final crackdown. Then word spread that the police were about to raid the building. Someone told me, "You need to get out now." If I was arrested, all my photos would become evidence. That was the biggest risk – not just being arrested, but losing the documentation of everything that had happened. On that day, I witnessed everything, from the barricades to the final moments before the police stormed in. The police were relentless – they were determined to capture anyone involved. I took precautions by hiding my film in a different location, so even if they came for me, they wouldn't find my negatives. In the end, they didn't search my place, but if they had, all of my photographs would have been confiscated.'

'PHOTOGRAPHY IS A WAY TO BRING BACK MEMORIES. WITHOUT PHOTOGRAPHS, SOME THINGS MIGHT COMPLETELY FADE. I'VE BEEN DOING THIS FOR A LONG TIME, AND WHEN I LOOK AT MY OLD PHOTOS, THEY HELP ME REMEMBER NOT JUST THE MOMENT ITSELF, BUT EVERYTHING SURROUNDING IT – WHAT HAPPENED BEFORE AND AFTER.

THERE WERE HARDLY ANY WOMEN IN THE FIELD OF PHOTOGRAPHY BACK THEN – MAYBE ONLY ONE OR TWO OTHERS. IN MOST OF MY JOBS, I WORKED WITH MEN. THAT WAS JUST THE WAY THINGS WERE. BECAUSE I WAS OFTEN THE ONLY WOMAN, I DID GET MEDIA ATTENTION, ESPECIALLY FROM TV AND MAGAZINES. IT WAS A COMPLETELY DIFFERENT TIME. NOW, ALMOST HALF OF THE STUDENTS IN PHOTOGRAPHY SCHOOLS ARE WOMEN. BUT BACK THEN, WOMEN PHOTOGRAPHERS WERE EXTREMELY RARE.'

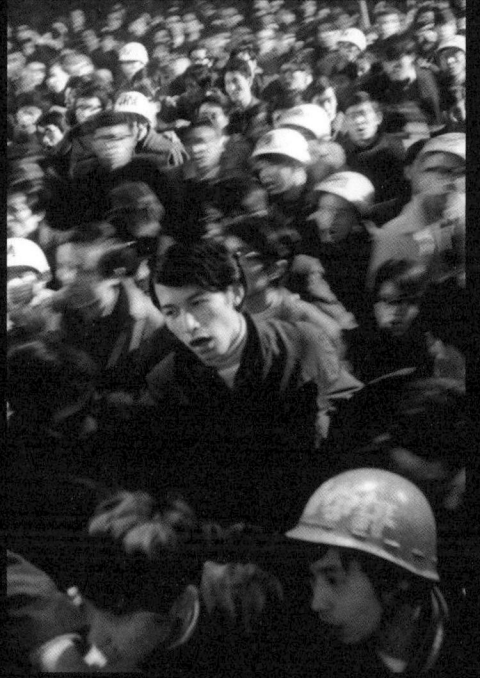
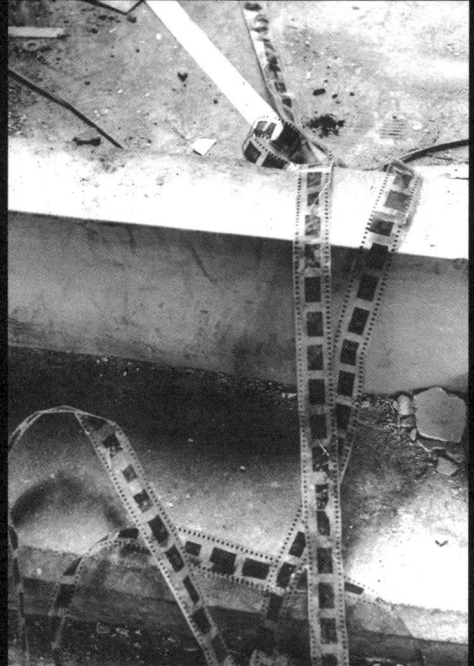
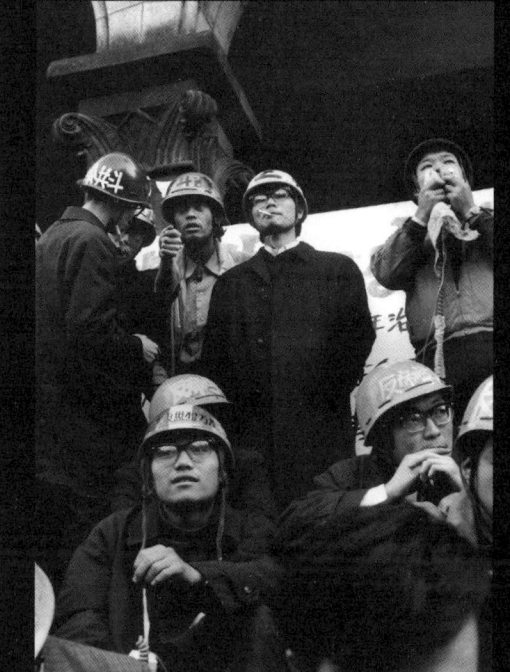
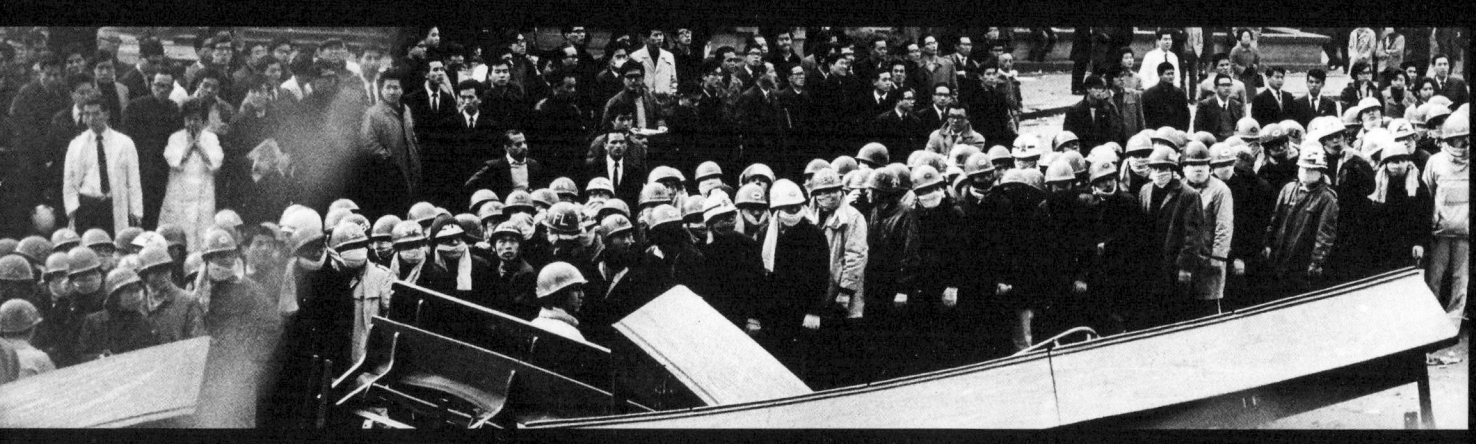
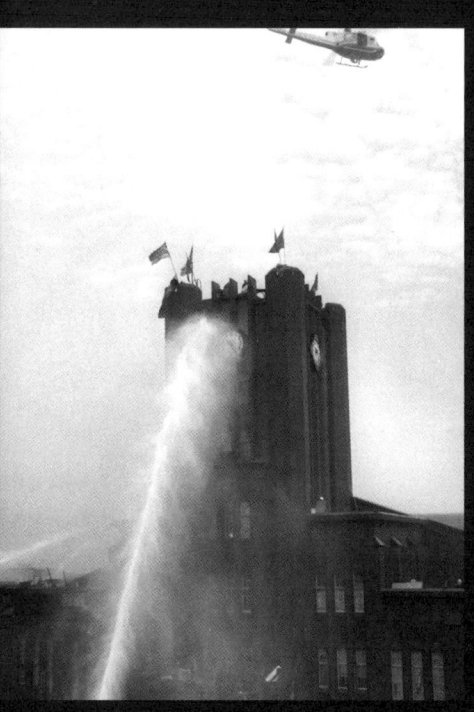
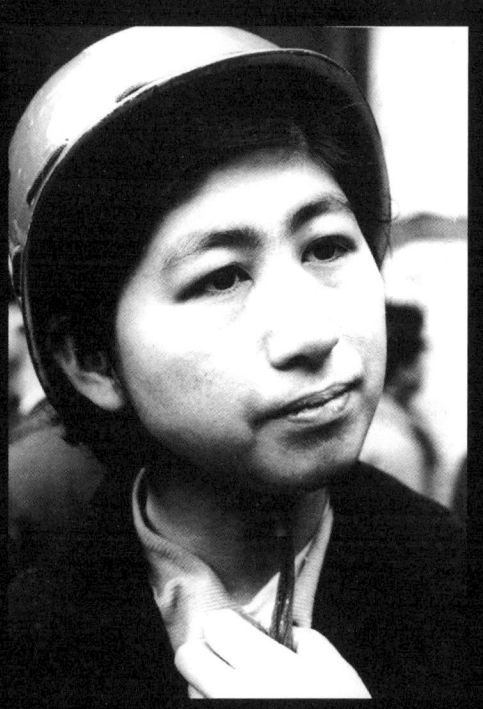
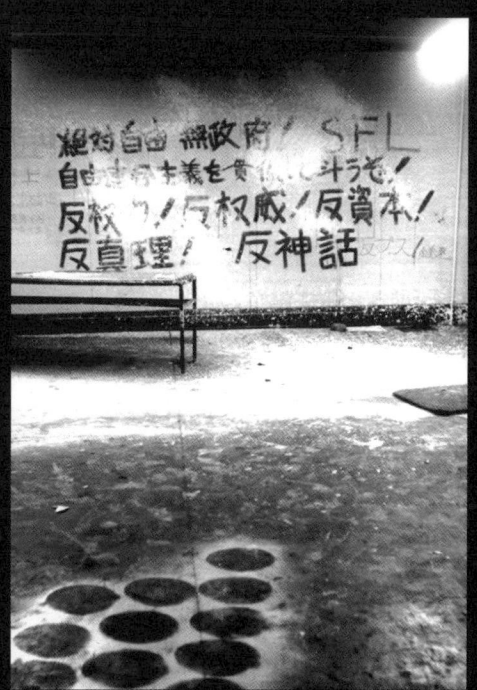

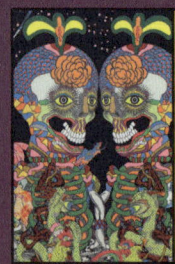

TANAAMI KEIICHI
1936–2024

田名網敬一

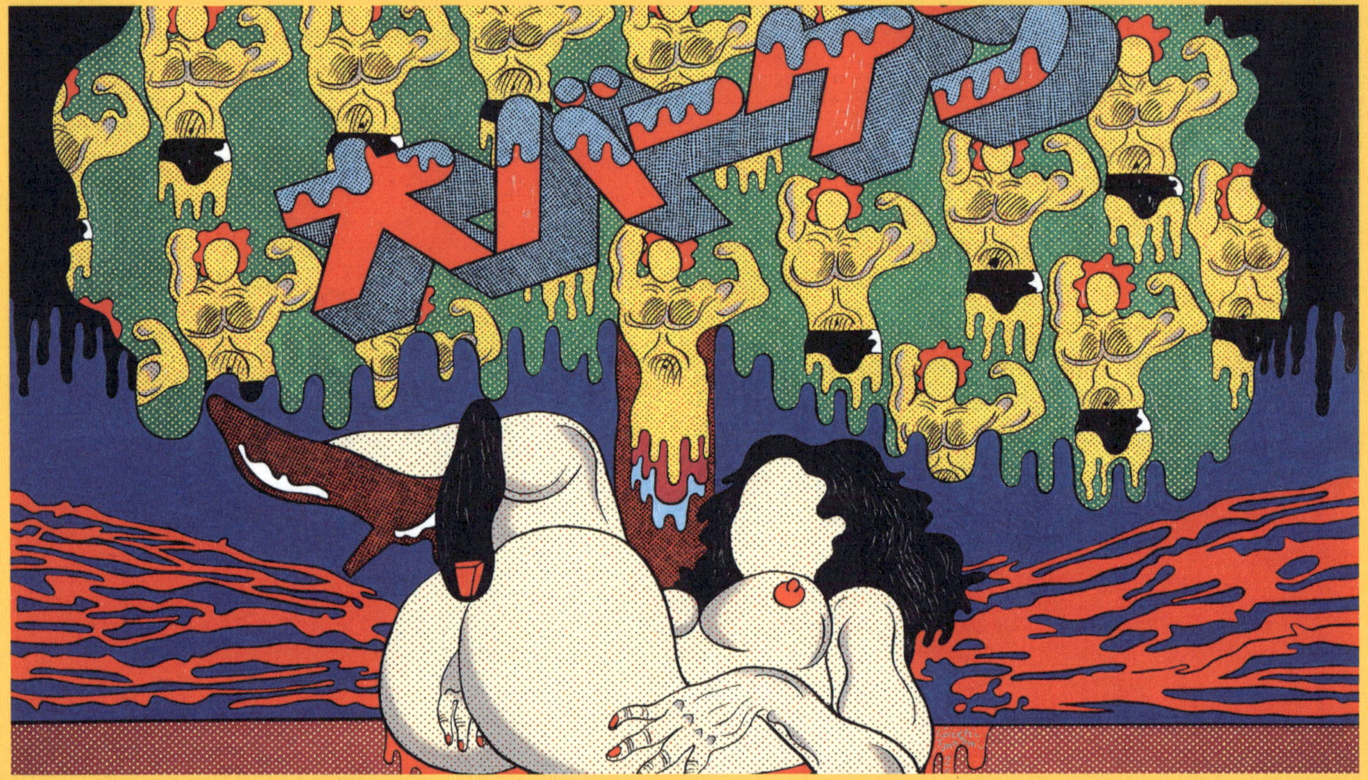

Tanaami Keiichi, *Big Bargain*, 2008, acrylic on canvas.

Opposite (above): **Tanaami Keiichi**, *Dream Diary 021*, 2012, coloured pencil and paper collage on paper.

Opposite (below): **Tanaami Keiichi**, *Dream Diary 013*, 2012, coloured pencil and paper collage on paper.

Tanaami Keiichi was exposed to Tokyo's Neo-Dada scene during the 1960s, and this encounter with artists like Shinohara Ushio set him on the course to become a leading figure in the city's underground art community. His early career, which coincided with the advent of psychedelic culture and Pop art in Japan, was focused on design and advertising projects, through which he refined his signature blend of kitsch and erotic humour rendered in a dramatically saturated palette. Tanaami began to experiment with video art during the second half of the 1960s, and he went on to develop his fine art practice through painting, sculpture and installation art in the decades that followed.

LUCY FLEMING-BROWN

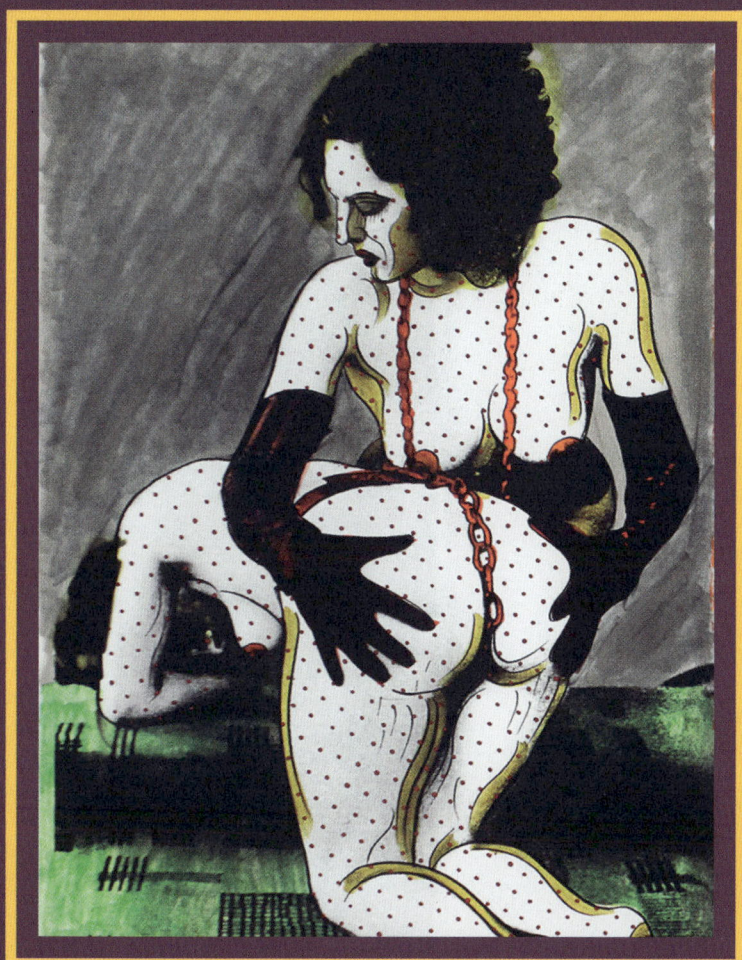
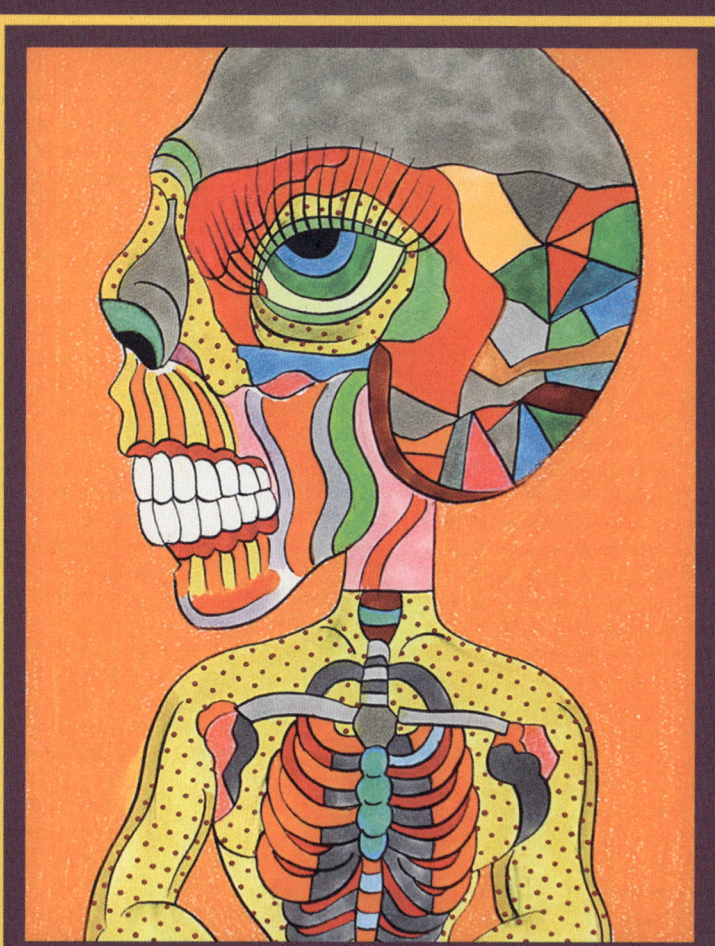

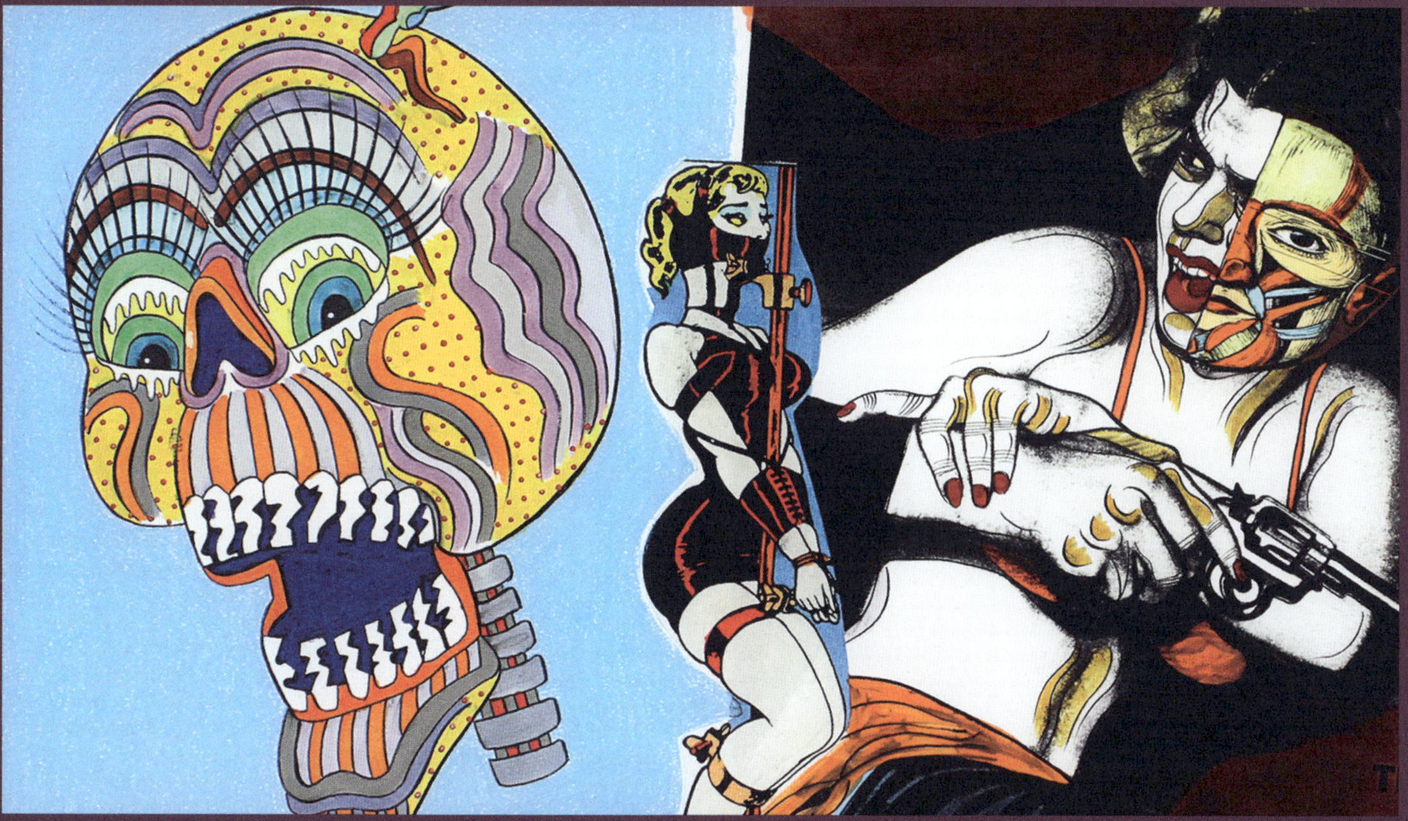

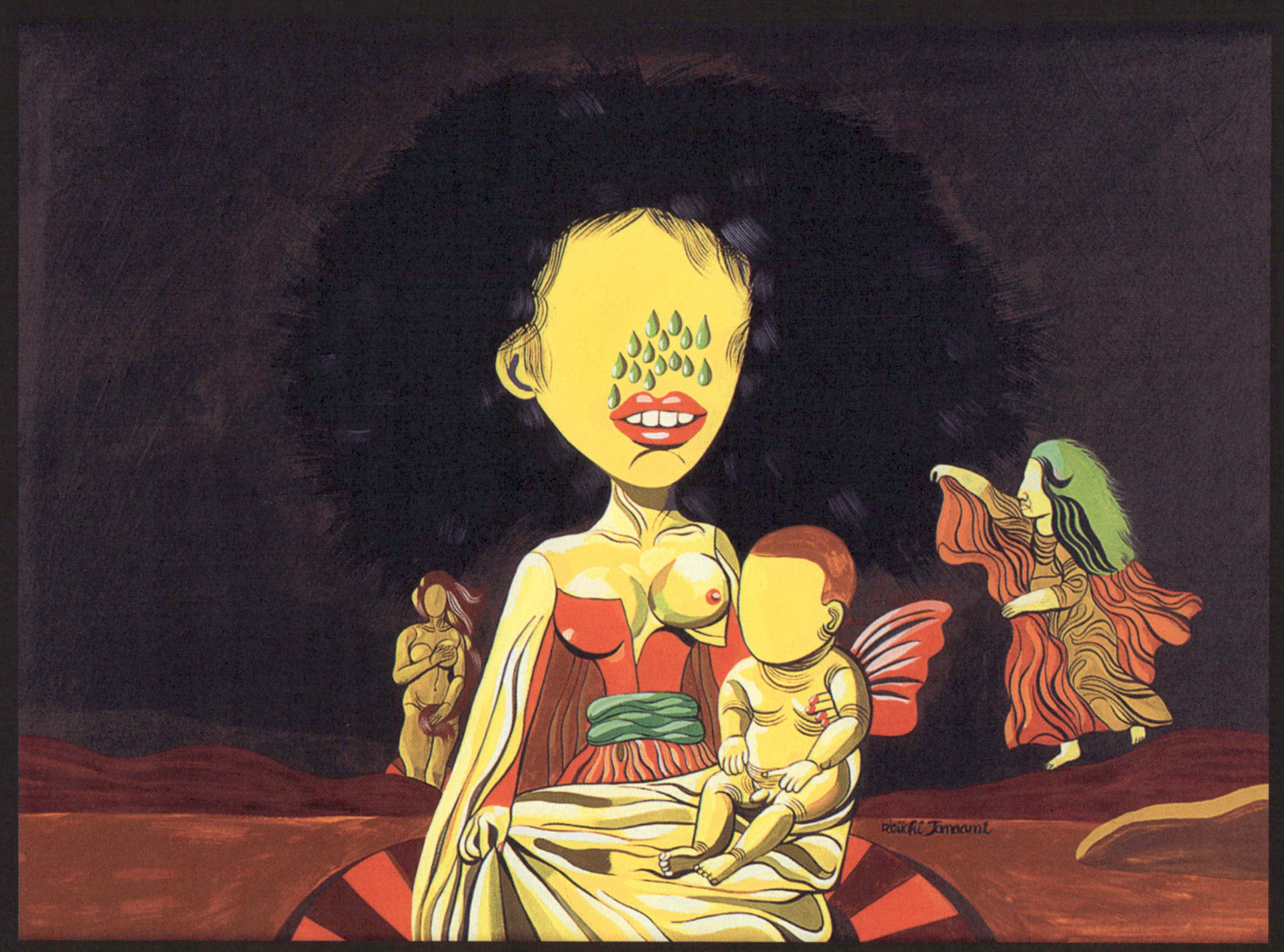

'I was only around four or five years old during the war period, so I was a small child, but when the Americans started to bomb Japan with B-29s, I could tell by looking at the adults that something very serious was happening. When night fell, the bombs would start falling, so I hid in the bunkers, and when the attack was over, I would come out in the afternoon with my mother and go home. On the way home you'd see countless dead bodies.

Tanaami Keiichi, *Mother and Child*, 1973, oil on illustration board.

Opposite: **Tanaami Keiichi**, *Ephemerality and Eternity*, 2019, ink, colour pencil, acrylic paint and mixed media on canvas.

Overleaf: **Tanaami Keiichi**, *No More War 4* (left) and *5* (right), 1968, silkscreen print on paper.

I was evacuated to Niigata with my mother and when I returned to Meguro, I stood at the station and looked down. It had completely burnt to the ground, so the red soil had surfaced. And because all the buildings were gone, the horizon was a straight line, and on top of that there was a cloudless blue sky. Back then, there was no smog, there were no cars, the sky was as blue as if it had been painted and the bottom was all red burnt soil. This contrast between red and blue, when I think about it, became my starting point for colour. Simply blue sky and red burnt ground. This was the most vivid of my colour experiences. My life since has been very long and I've experienced a lot, but nothing can top the experiences I had in the war. It's the hardest memory I have, both mentally and physically.'

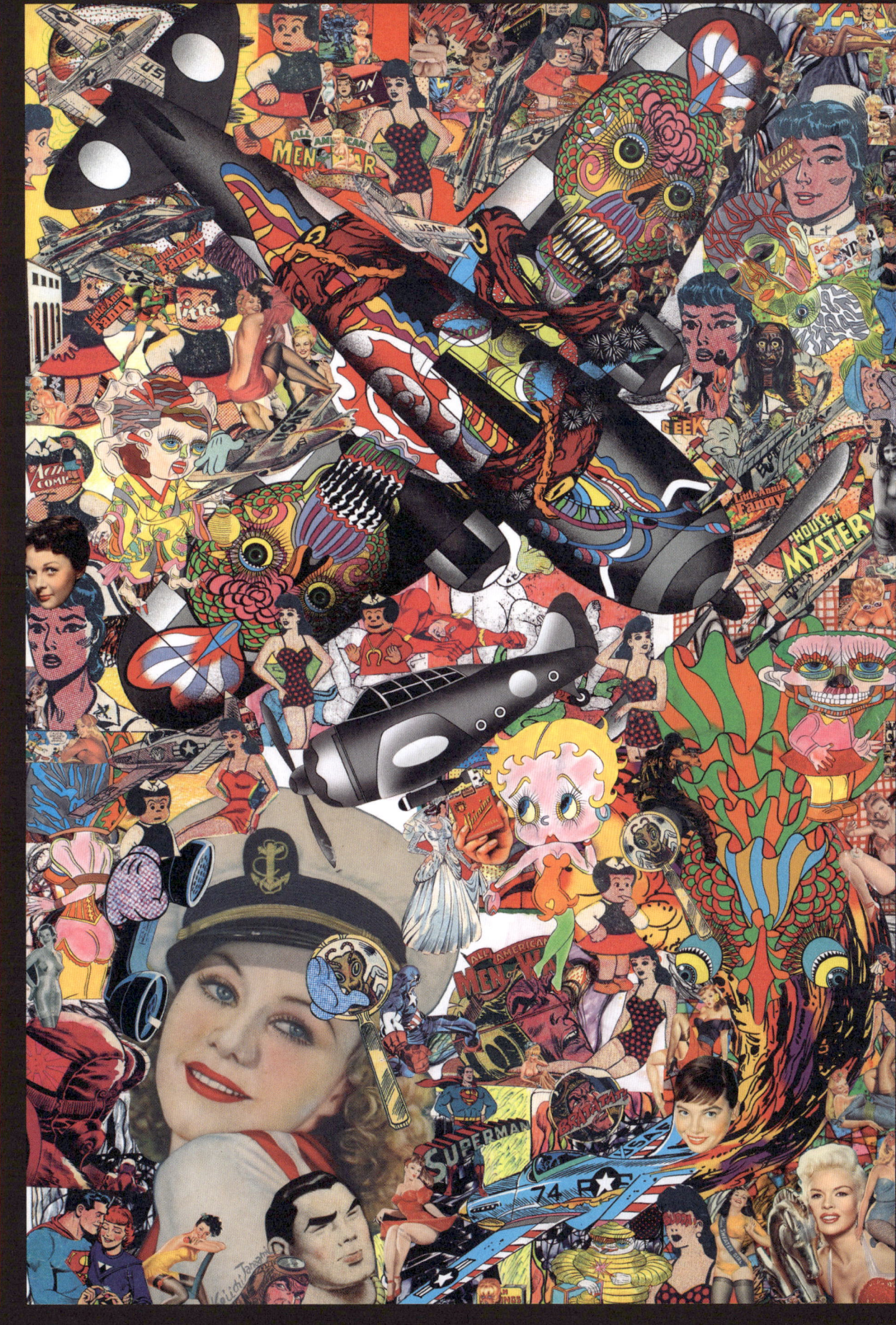

田名網敬一

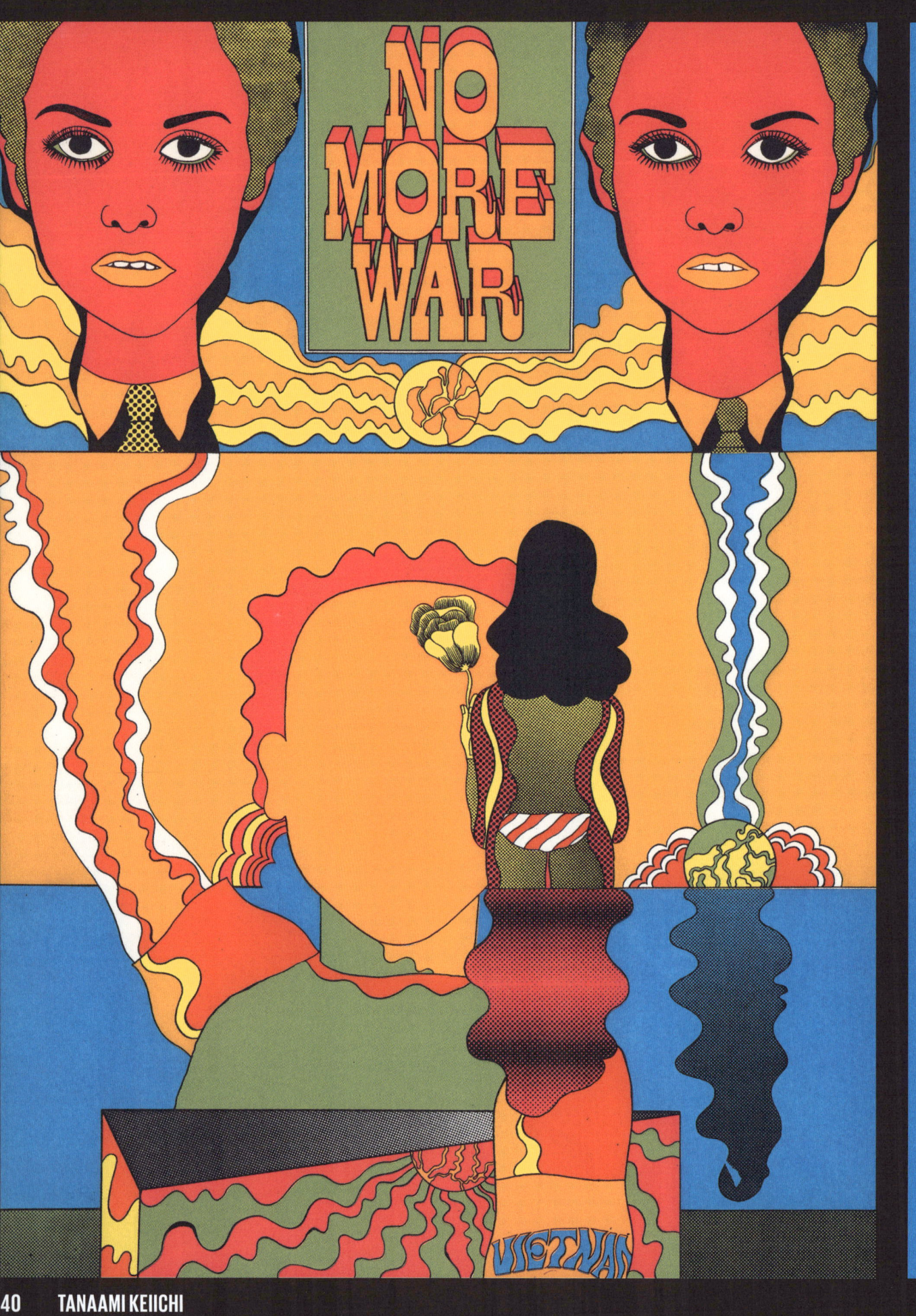

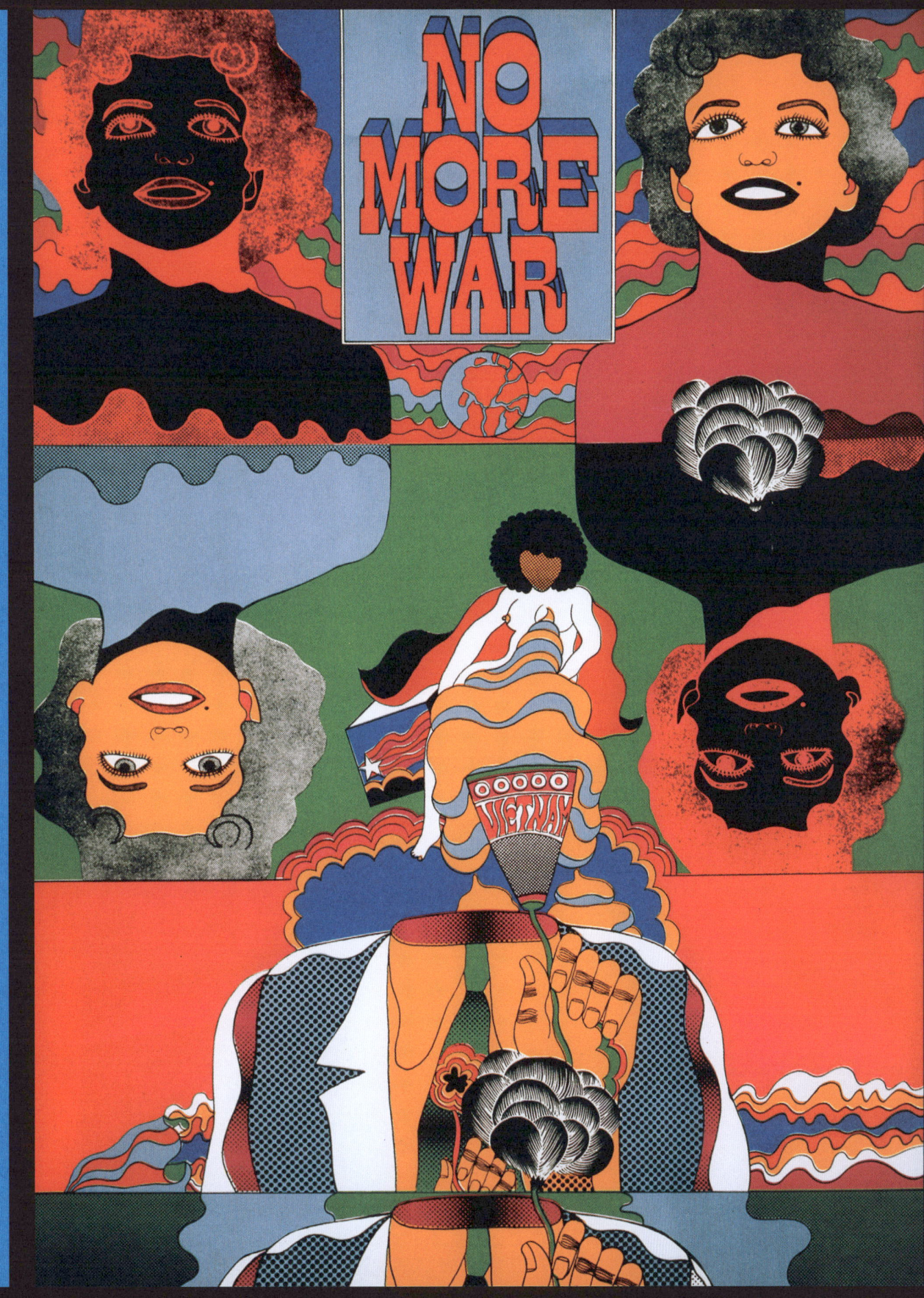

田名網敬一

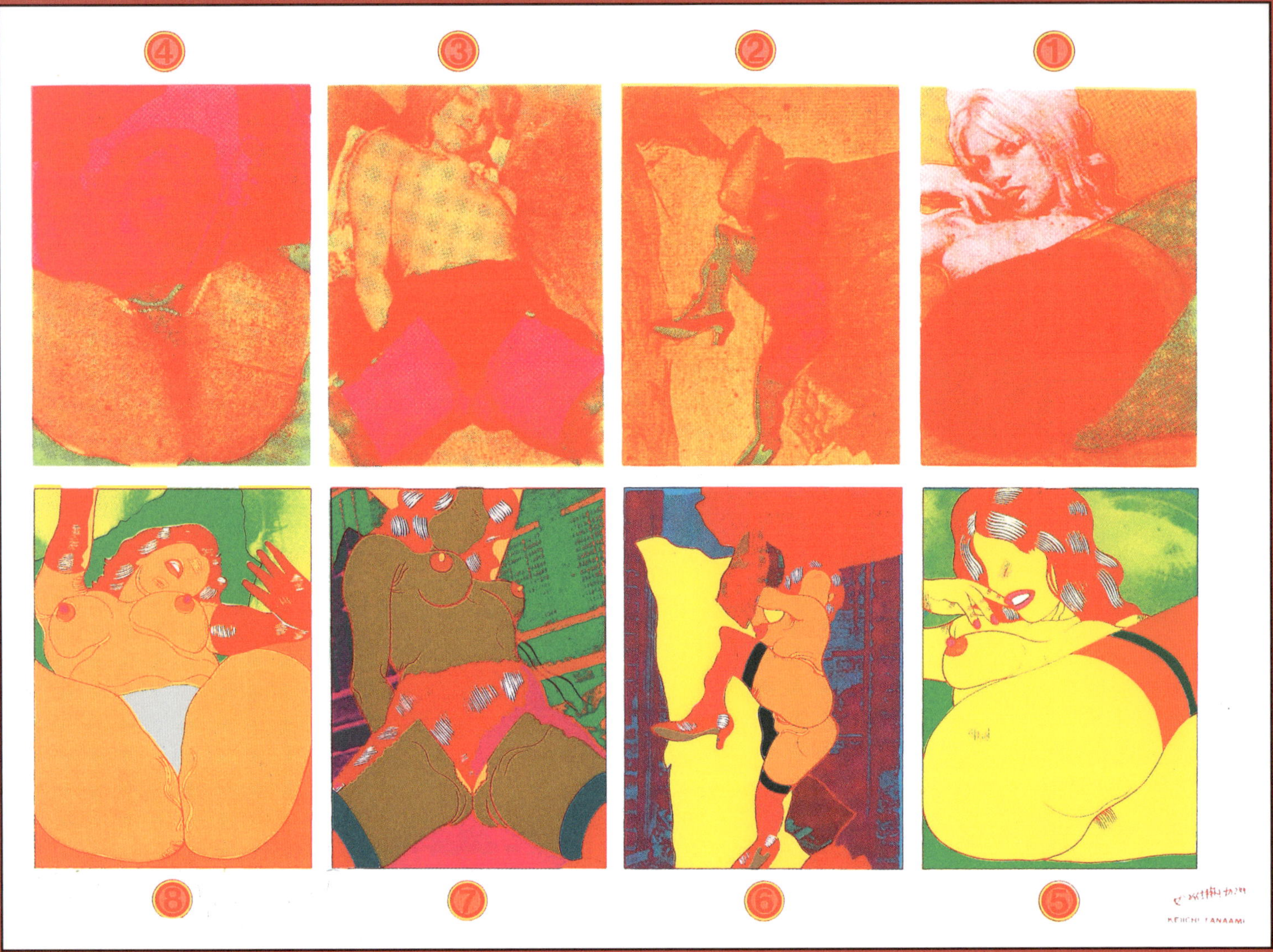

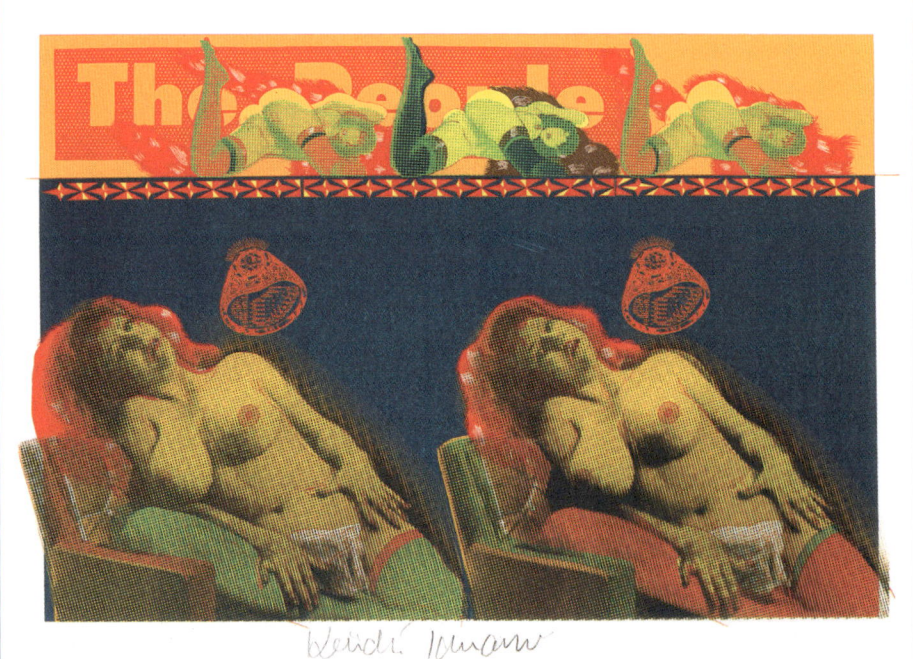

Above: **Tanaami Keiichi**, *Clock Work Marilyn_9*, 1972, silkscreen print on paper.

Right: **Tanaami Keiichi**, *A Pancake for Breakfast_6*, 1974, silkscreen print on paper.

Opposite: **Tanaami Keiichi**, *Clock Work Marilyn_3*, 1971, silkscreen print on paper.

Overleaf: **Tanaami Keiichi**, *Collage Book 4_23*, c. 1975, ink, marker and collage on paper.

'The 1960s was an era of the body. It was a period where many art forms were expressed using human bodies. Eroticism isn't just about naked bodies. Buildings, food and living spaces can also be erotic. I think eroticism can be found in so many places.

Things are attractive due to their eroticism. For instance, there are erotic sofas, and without Eros, the sofa might have lost its charm. So the '60s brought the body-flesh into focus, and in this sense it was a very iconic period.

Then in the '70s, beauty became more important. For instance, if you looked at fashion magazines, a boy's room would be completely white with nothing in it, a clean room.

So from the '60s, which was all about our physical bodies, we entered the '70s, where all the different, dirty and decorative elements were shaved off and we entered an extremely conceptual period. Painting, butoh, cinema … They all started to change.'

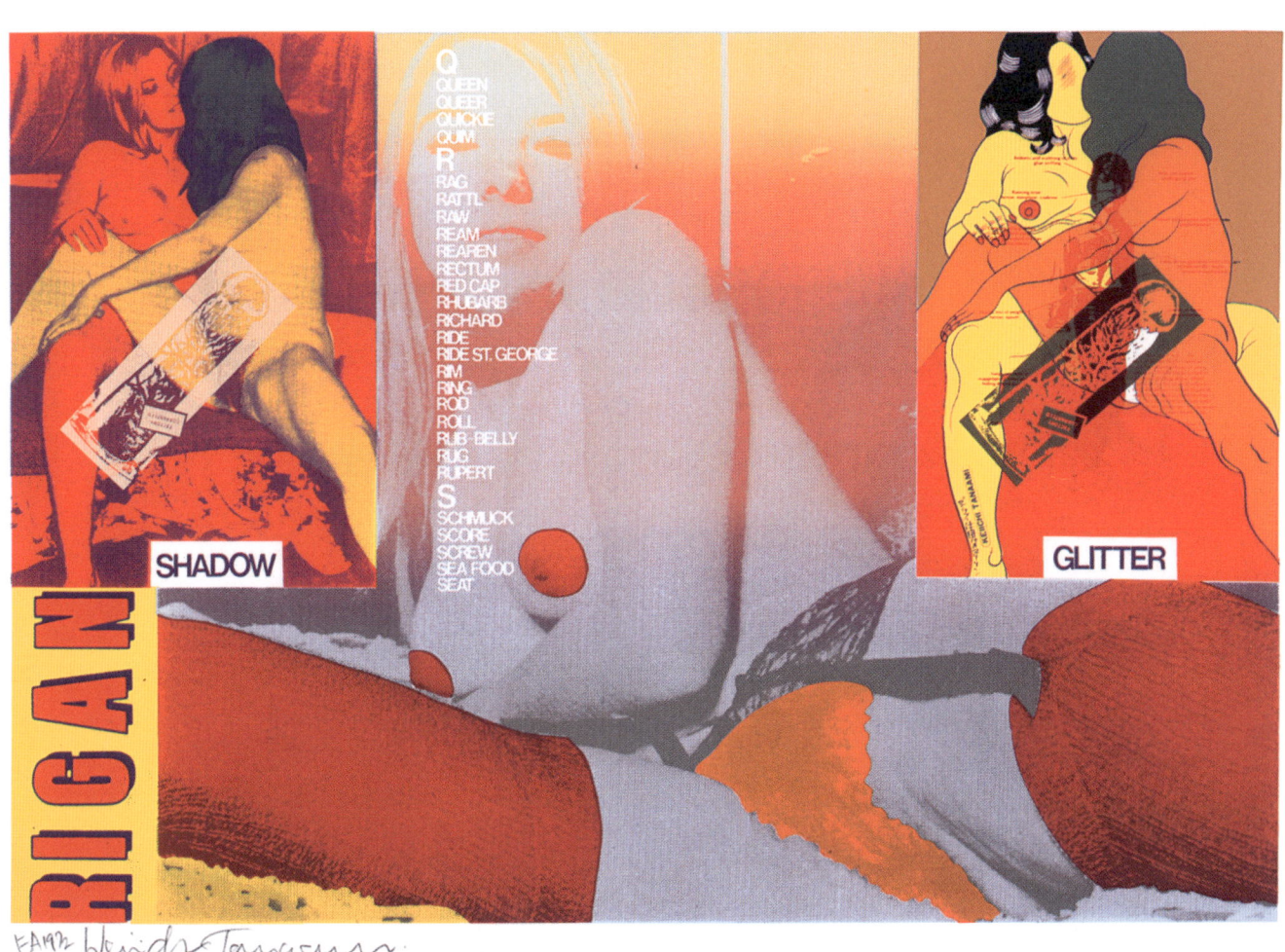

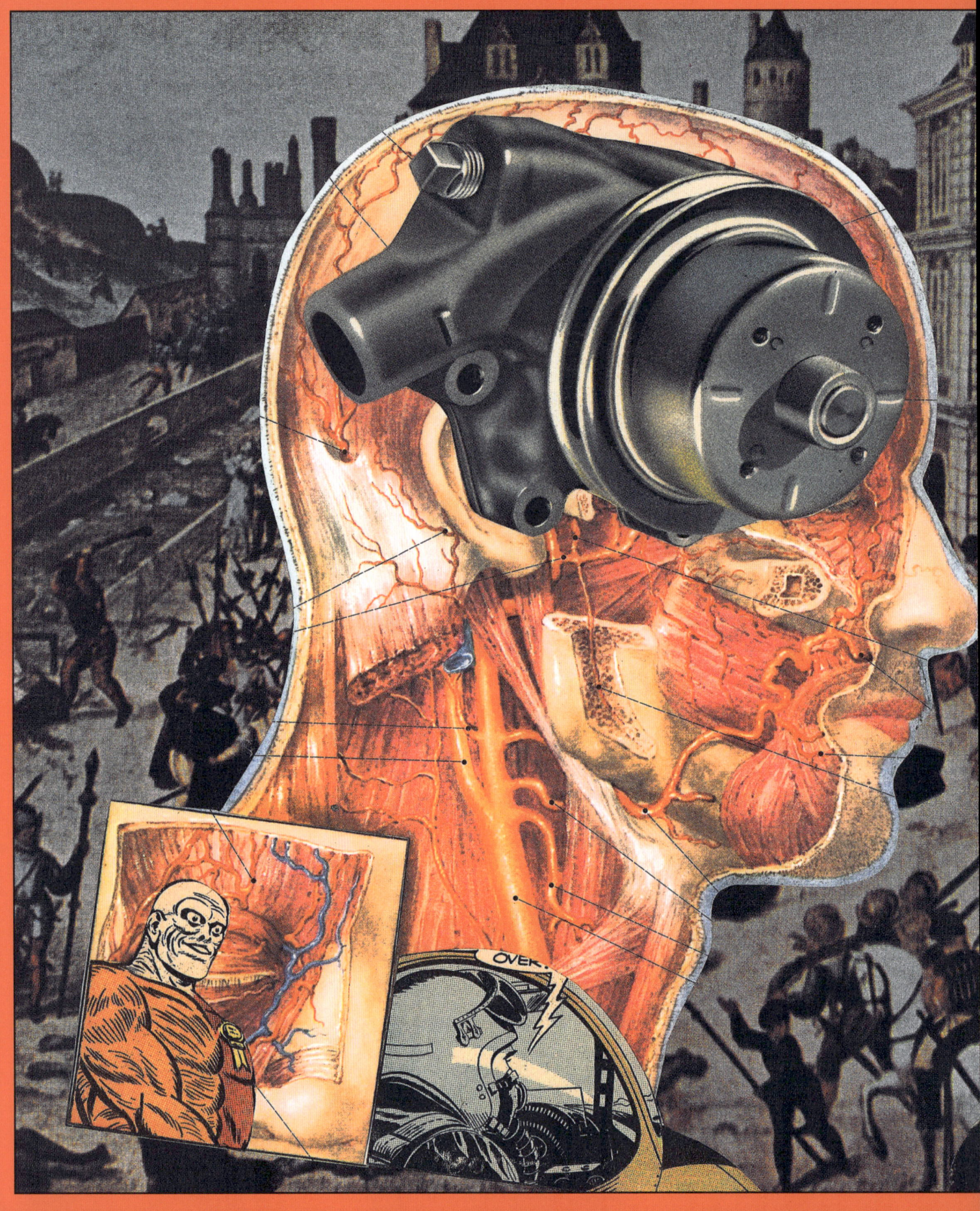

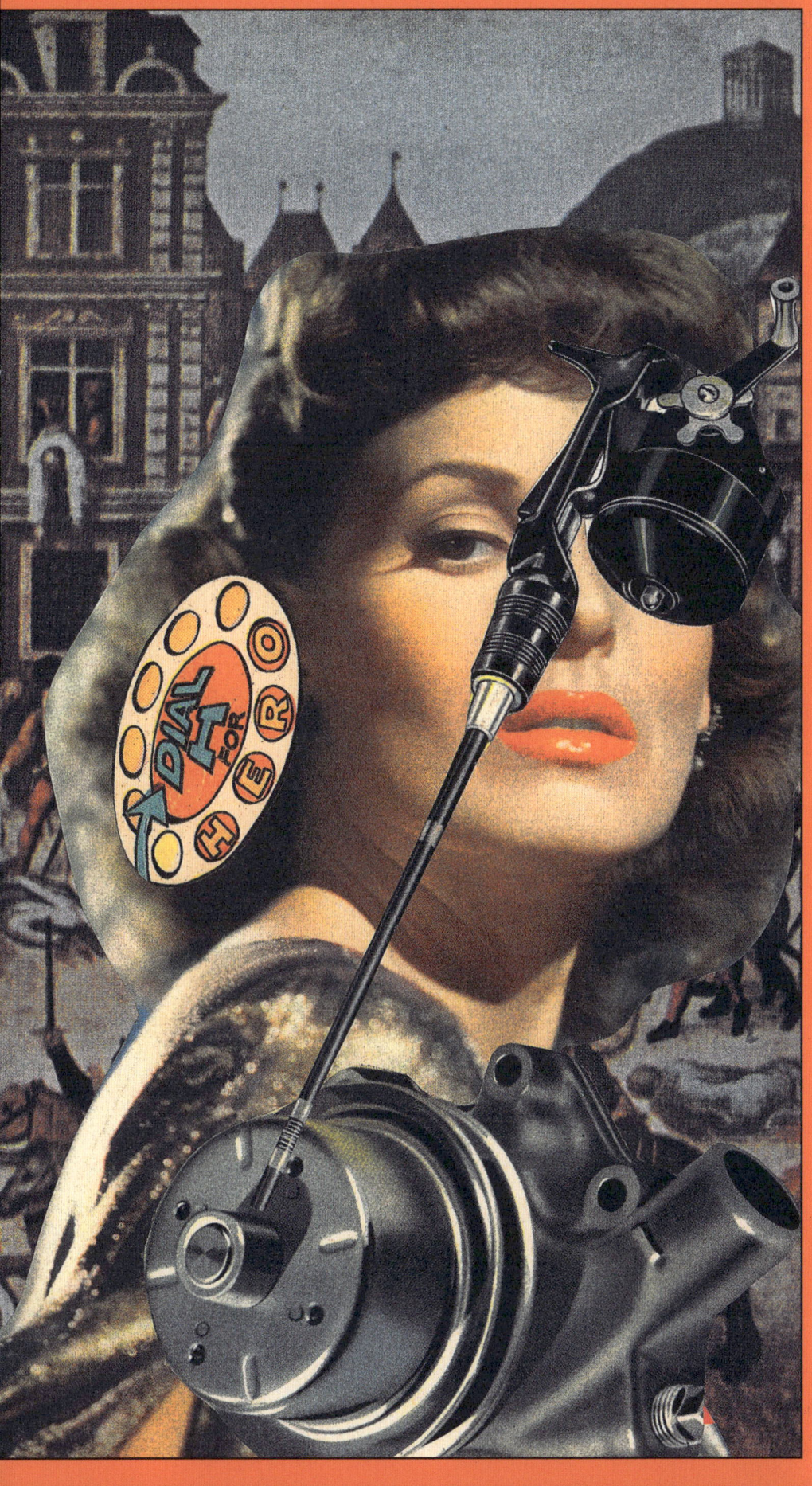

'FROM THE '60S, WHAT HAS REMAINED EXTREMELY VIVID IN MY MEMORY IS KENNEDY'S ASSASSINATION IN 1963.

THEN IN 1969, THERE WAS WOODSTOCK, AND THAT WOULD SIGNAL THE CURTAIN FALL OF THE '60S.

IN THAT TIME, THINGS YOU COULDN'T IMAGINE NOW HAPPENED, LIKE THE KILLING OF MARTIN LUTHER KING JR OR THE VIETNAM WAR, WOMEN'S LIBERATION AND THE EMERGENCE OF HIPPIES.

WITH AMERICA IN THE CENTRE, THERE WERE SO MANY MOVEMENTS THAT OCCURRED IN THIS PERIOD.'

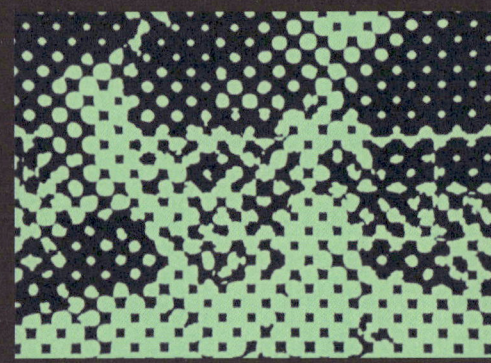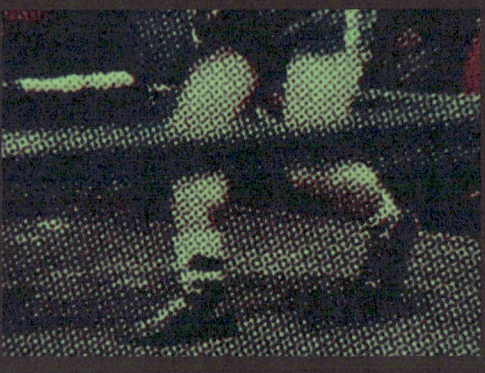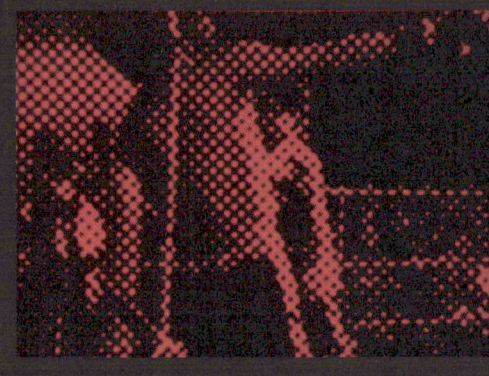

'In the 1970s, the boundary between image and reality became indistinguishable. Often what you thought was an image turned out to be real, or what you thought was real turned out to be imagined. For instance, with boxing champions like Muhammad Ali (or Cassius Clay), the match would crop up in the sports papers the next day.'

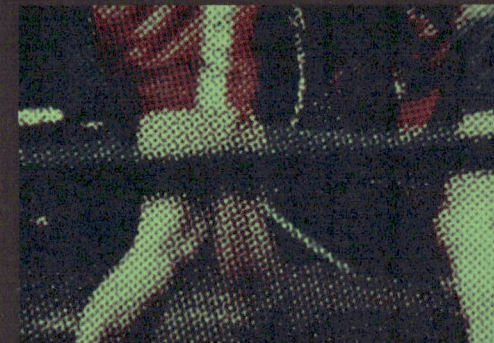
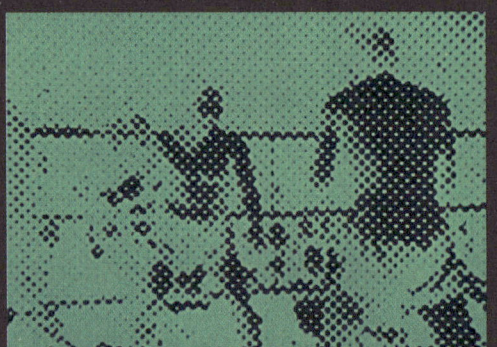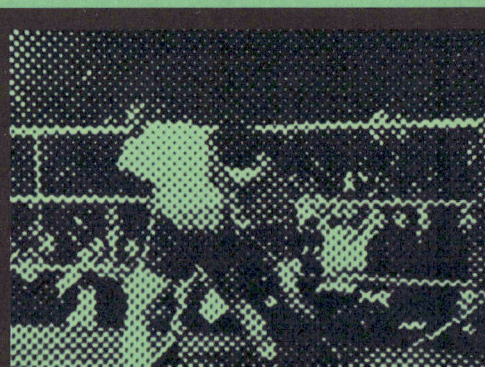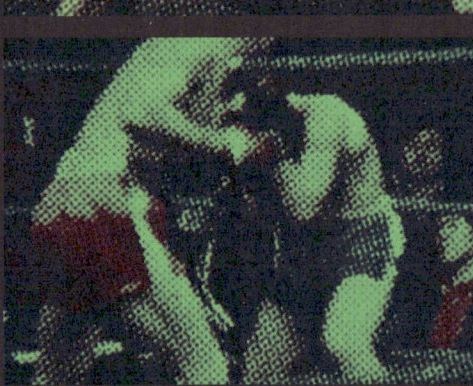

'Even though you'd seen the match, when you saw the picture of it the next day, the impact of the image that appeared in the paper surpassed that of the real life experience. Back then, film wasn't used much, so the newspaper photograph was critical. The reproduced photograph held a reality that surpassed the real experience.'

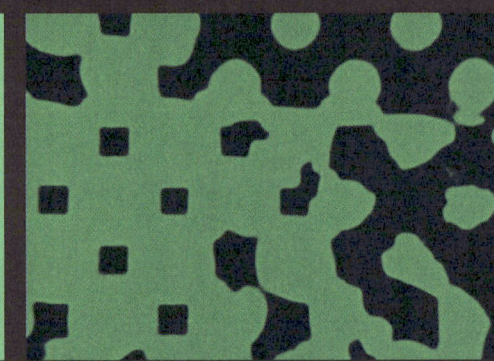
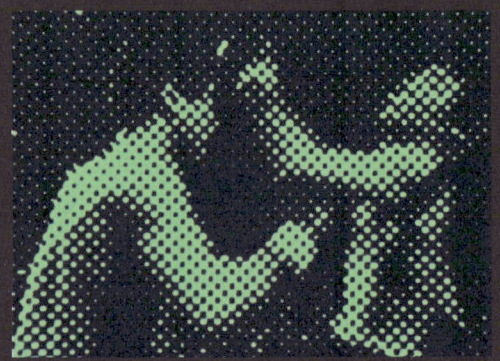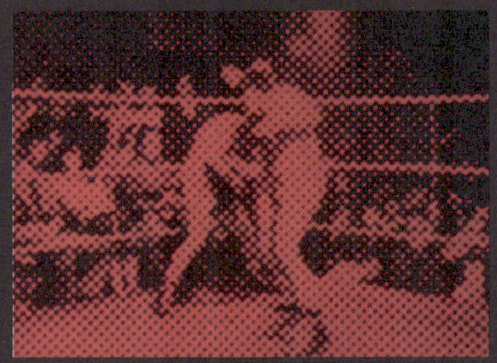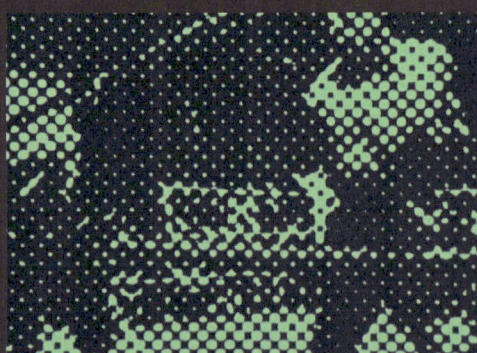

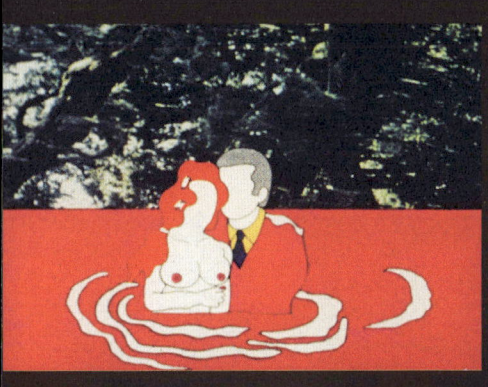 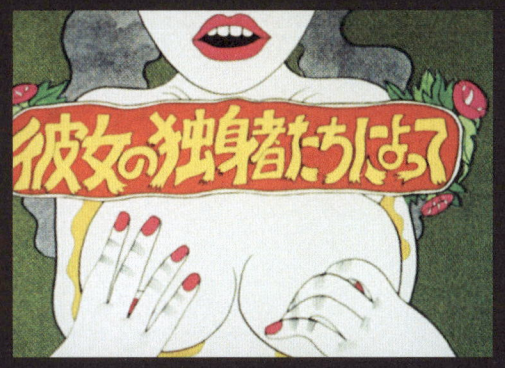 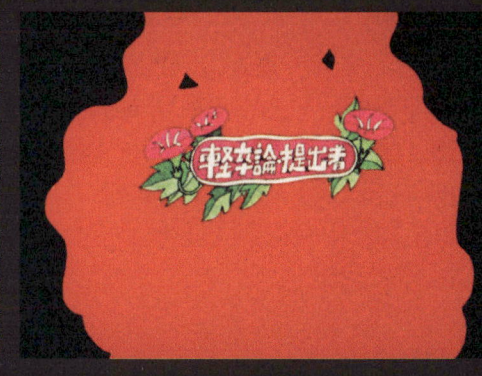
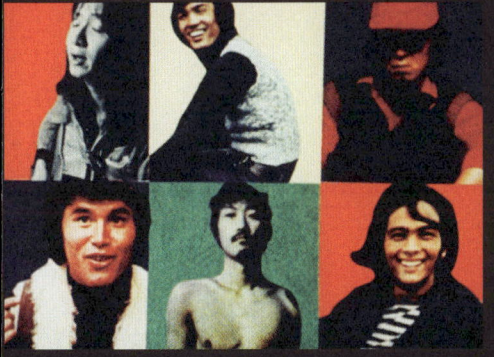 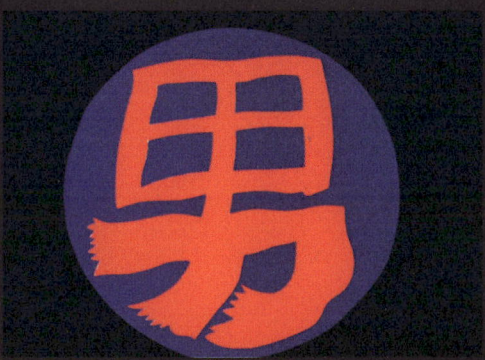 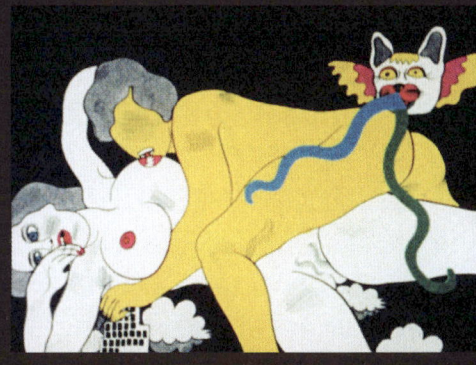
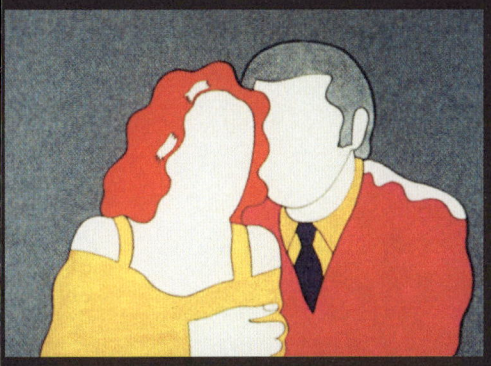

'I first went to New York in the 1960s. At that time, people like Jonas Mekas or Kenneth Anger, and of course Andy Warhol, made very experimental films and many small venues were showing them, they were quite popular in NYC. I thought, "This is what I want to do," so when I returned to Japan I started creating experimental films. I showed them at Parco in Shibuya, and also at Terayama Shūji's theatre.'

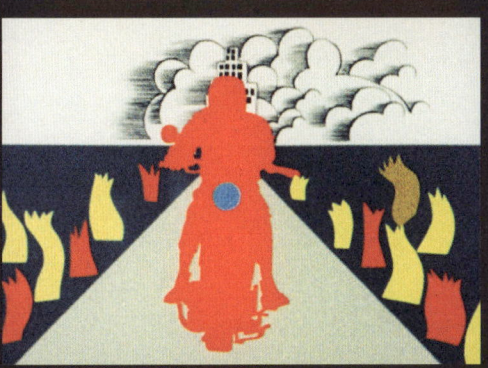 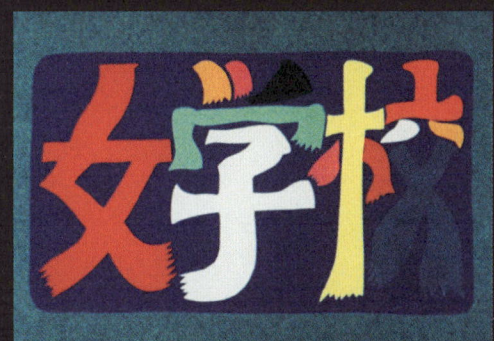 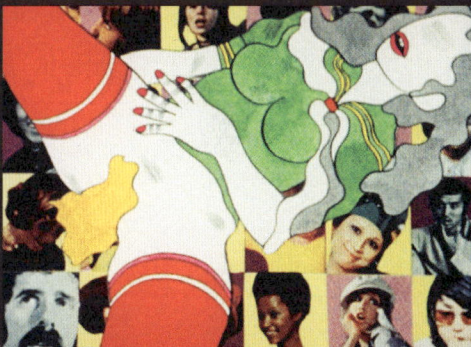
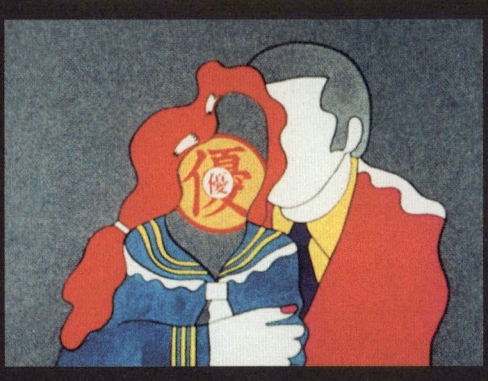

'I think of my own paintings as products of the editing process. You collect your elements and you position them and then give them colour and so on, it's nothing other than editing. I do have an overall image of what I want it to look like, but the finished painting never looks like that. In the process of drawing, there are twists and turns, and the resulting image is completely different to the one I had in mind.'

'PEOPLE DON'T REALLY CHANGE THAT MUCH. I LEAD THE SAME KIND OF LIFE AS I DID IN THE '60S, AND WHAT IS FUNDAMENTAL TO ME ARE THE THINGS I EXPERIENCED IN THE '60S.

THE METHODS AND CONTENTS OF EXPRESSION HAVE CHANGED BUT MY SENSIBILITIES HAVEN'T CHANGED. WHAT I EXPERIENCED WHEN I WAS VERY YOUNG IS STILL STRONGLY EMBEDDED IN MY MEMORY. TO THIS DAY, THOSE EXPERIENCES HAVE A LASTING EFFECT ON ELEMENTAL PARTS OF MYSELF.

I'VE LIVED TO THIS AGE, AND IF YOU ASK ME HOW MUCH I'VE GROWN UP AND BECOME AN ADULT, I HAVEN'T. I'M STILL AT THE SAME LEVEL AS I WAS WHEN I WAS IN HIGH SCHOOL. PEOPLE DON'T BECOME COMPLETE LIKE THAT, THAT'S WHY LIVING IS INTERESTING.'

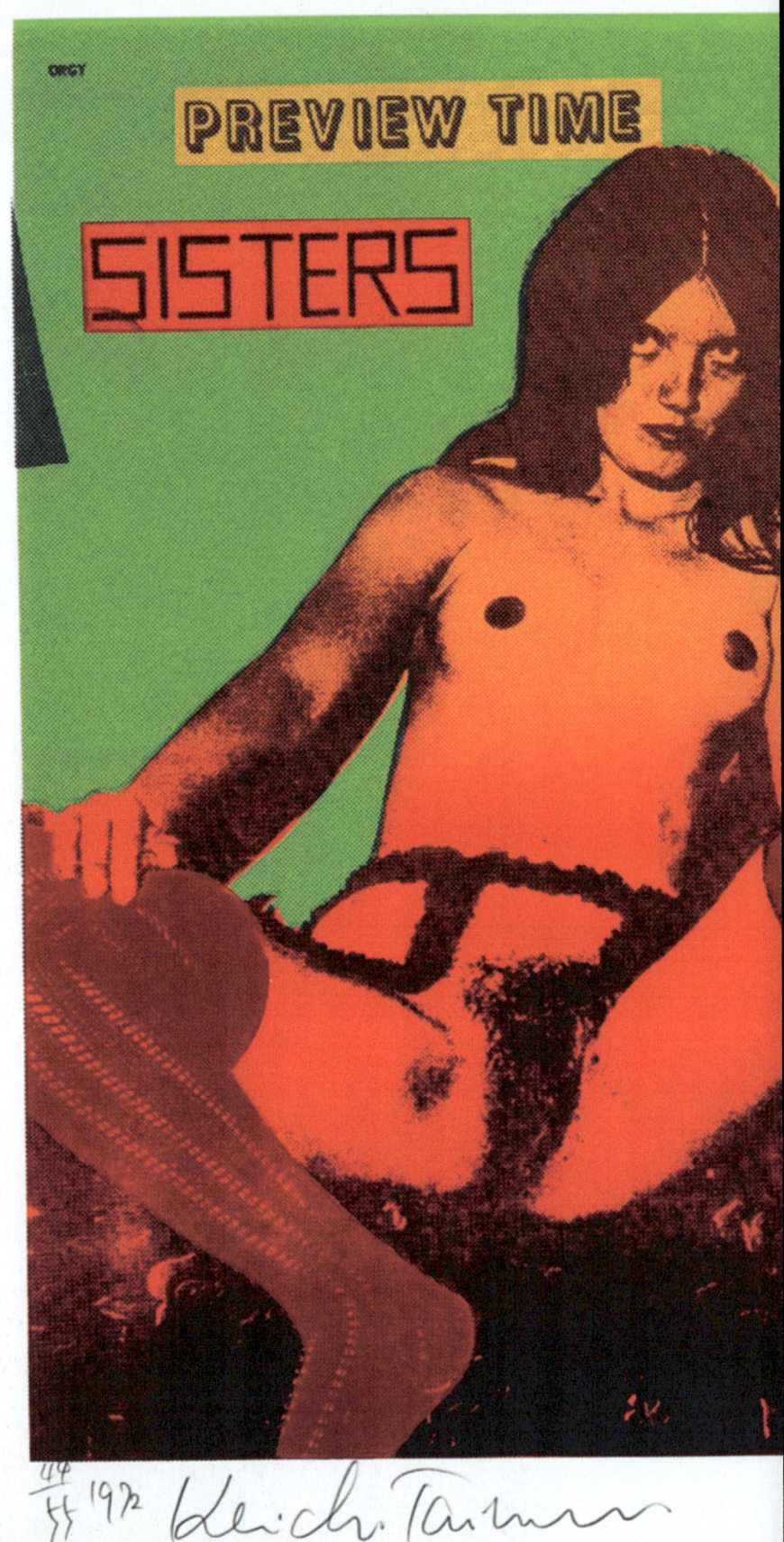

p. 46: Stills from **Tanaami Keiichi**, *Why* (1975), short film.

p. 47: Stills from **Tanaami Keiichi**, *Study of the Virgin in School Uniform . . .* (1972), short film.

Right: **Tanaami Keiichi**, *Clock Work Marilyn_8*, 1972, silkscreen print on paper.

Overleaf: **Tanaami Keiichi**, *Jakuchu: Birds and Flowers*, 2015, pigmented ink, acrylic silkscreen medium, crushed glass, glitter acrylic paint, acrylic paint on canvas.

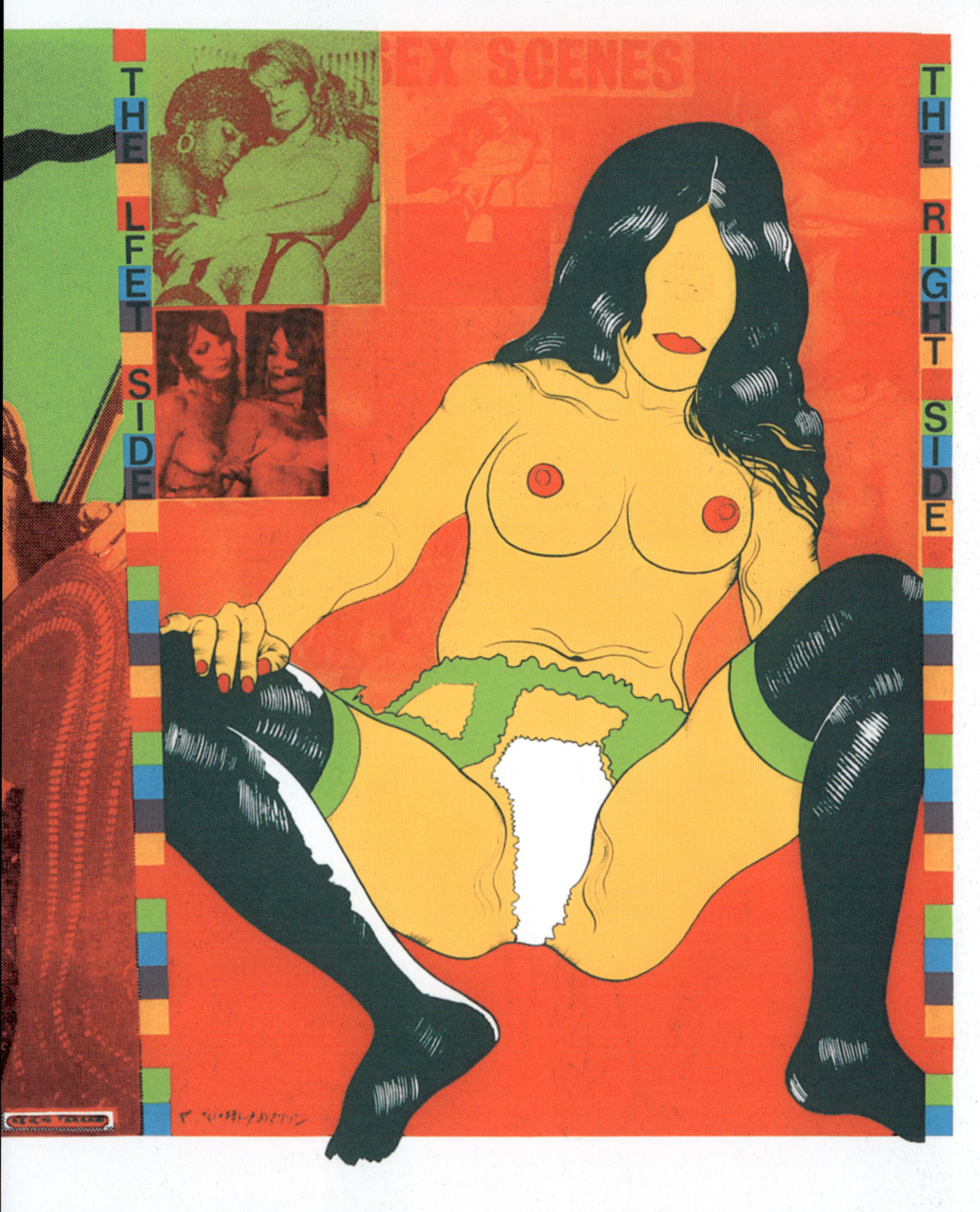

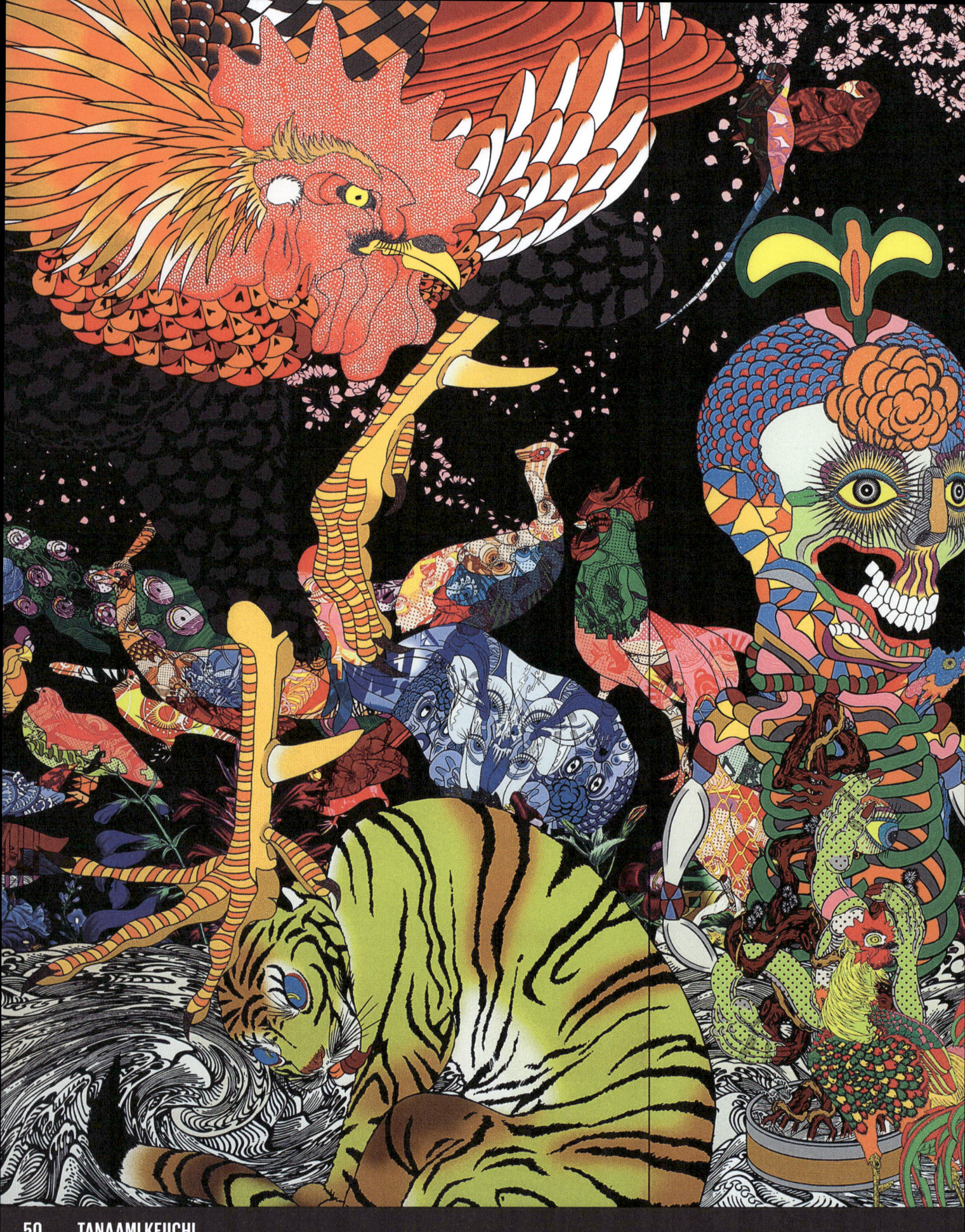

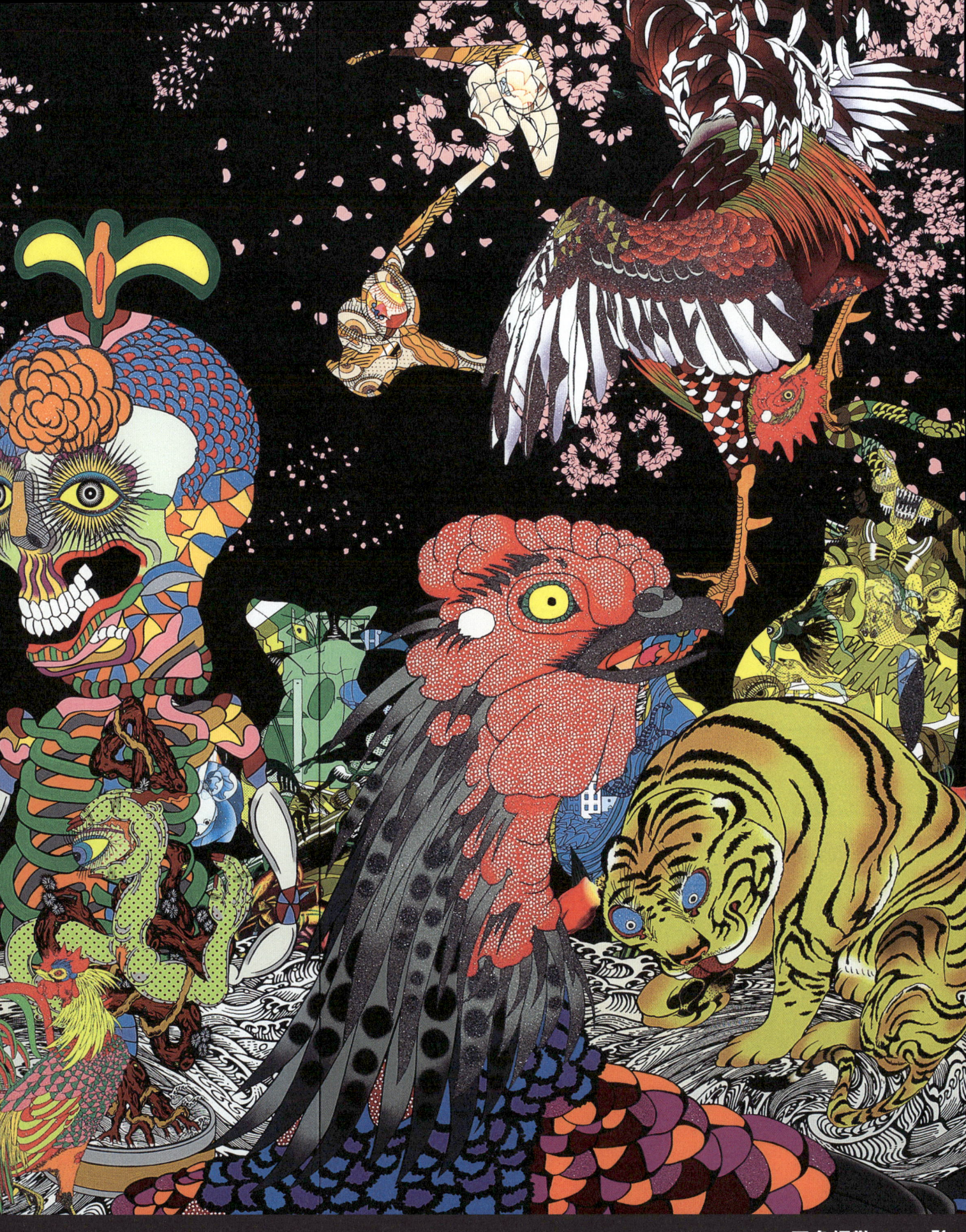

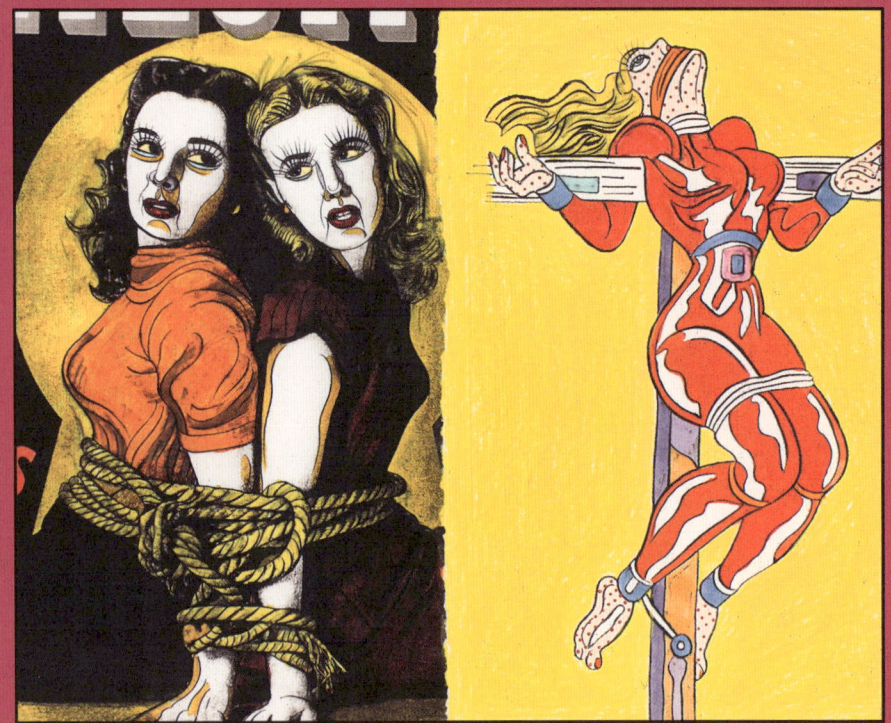

'When I was sick, death was always there inside of me, and considering my age, it is almost as if there is not a moment that I am not thinking about death. Not just about how you're going to die, but also when reflecting on what you've achieved in your life, as it also relates to death.

When you're young, you don't think about death much, but as you grow older, death becomes a closer reality. Even if I try not to think about it, when I'm painting, the topic of death just comes out on the canvas. This is the real meaning of us humans, so I think it is thought-provoking.

We humans want to live because of death, right? Because they are opposites.'

Tanaami Keiichi, *Dream Diary 039*, 2012, coloured pencil and paper collage on paper.

Opposite: Tanaami Keiichi, *Collage Book 7_50*, 1969, ink and magazine scrap collage on paper.

Overleaf: Tanaami Keiichi, *The Last Supper*, 2015, pigmented ink, acrylic silkscreen medium, crushed glass, glitter acrylic paint, acrylic paint on canvas.

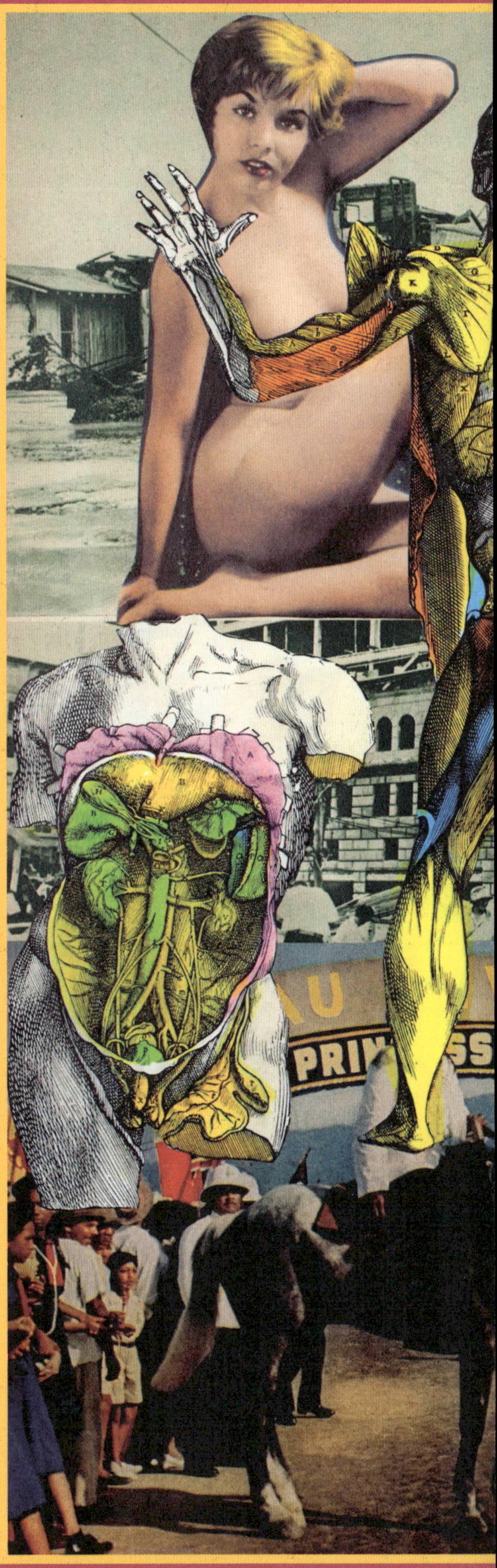

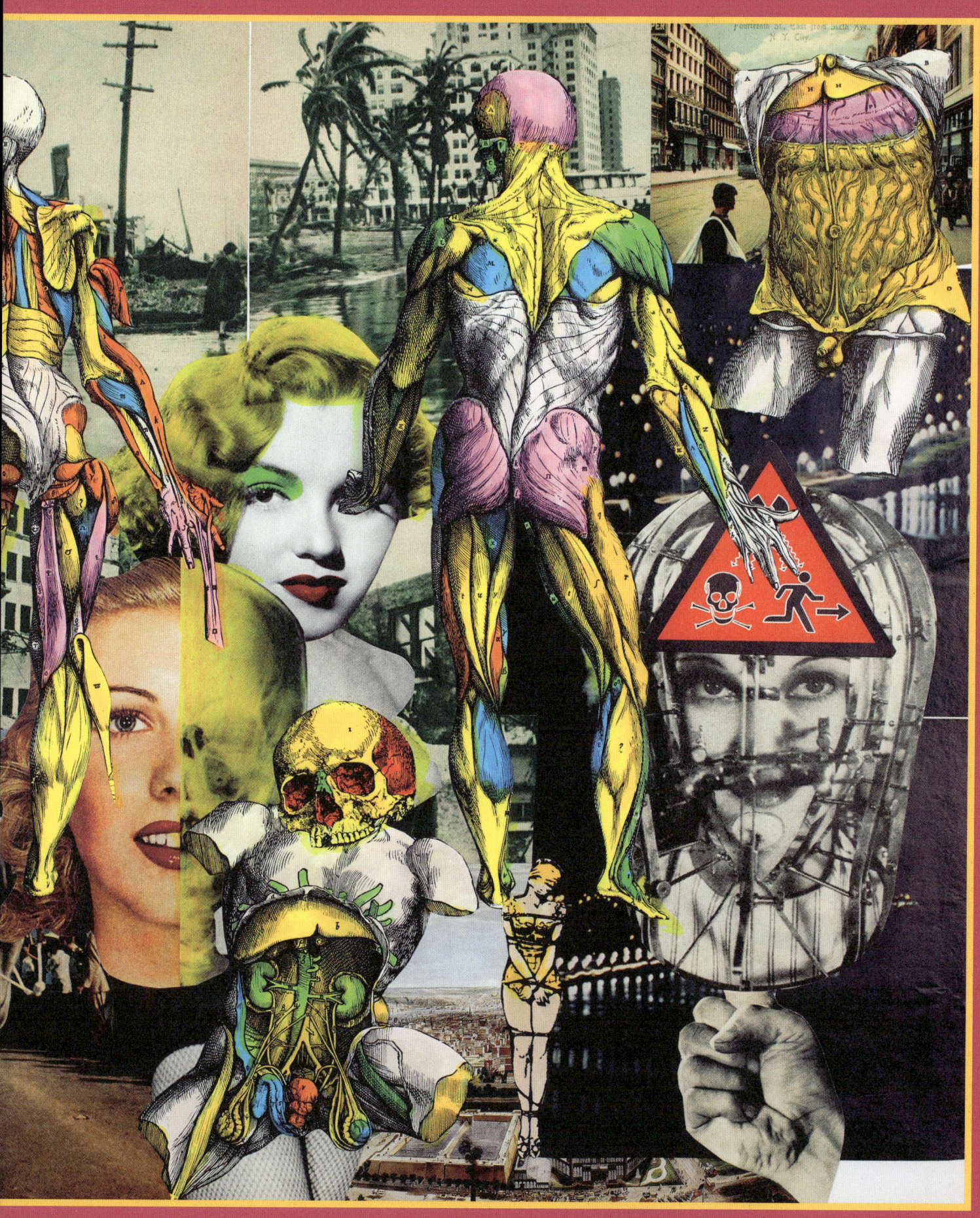

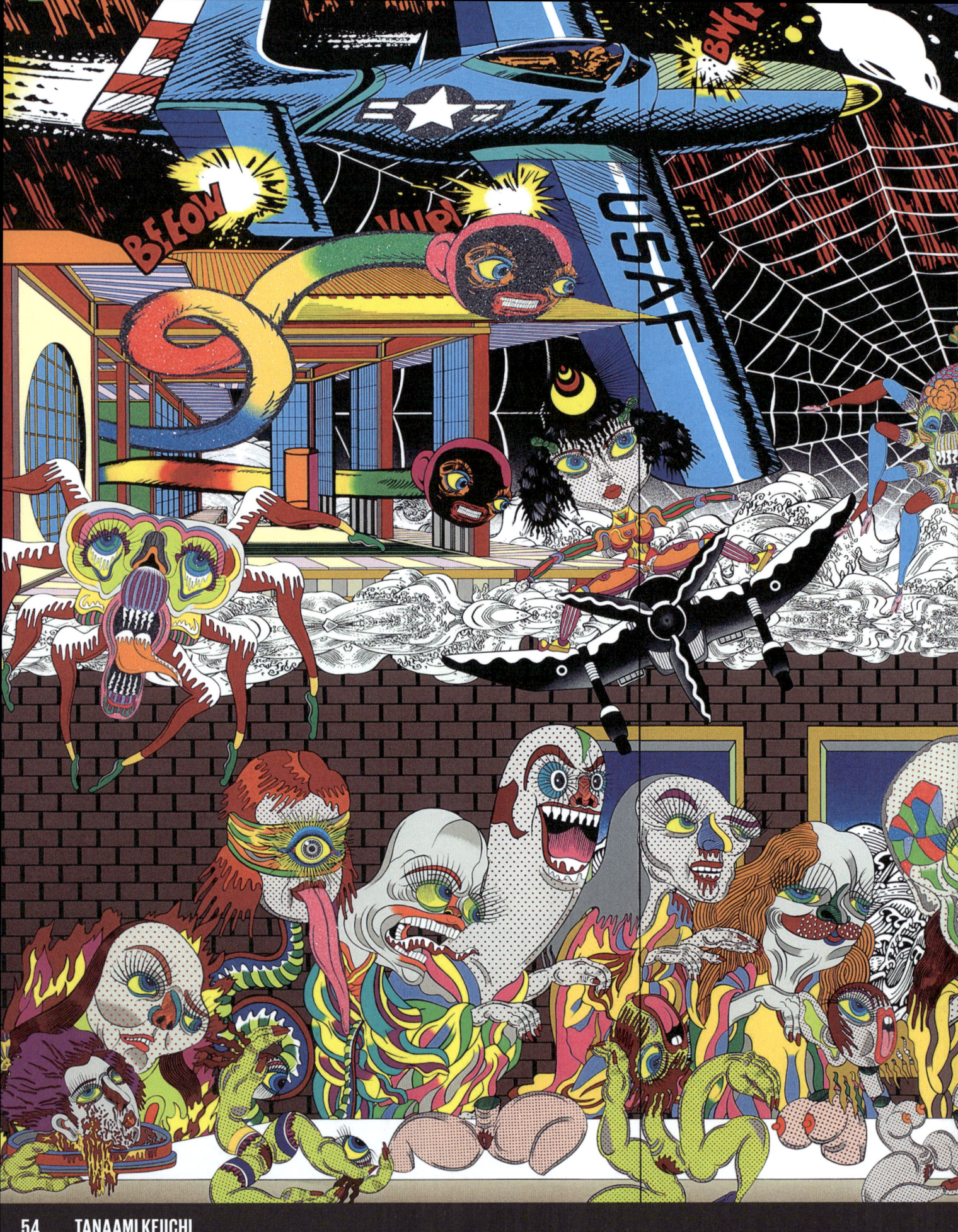

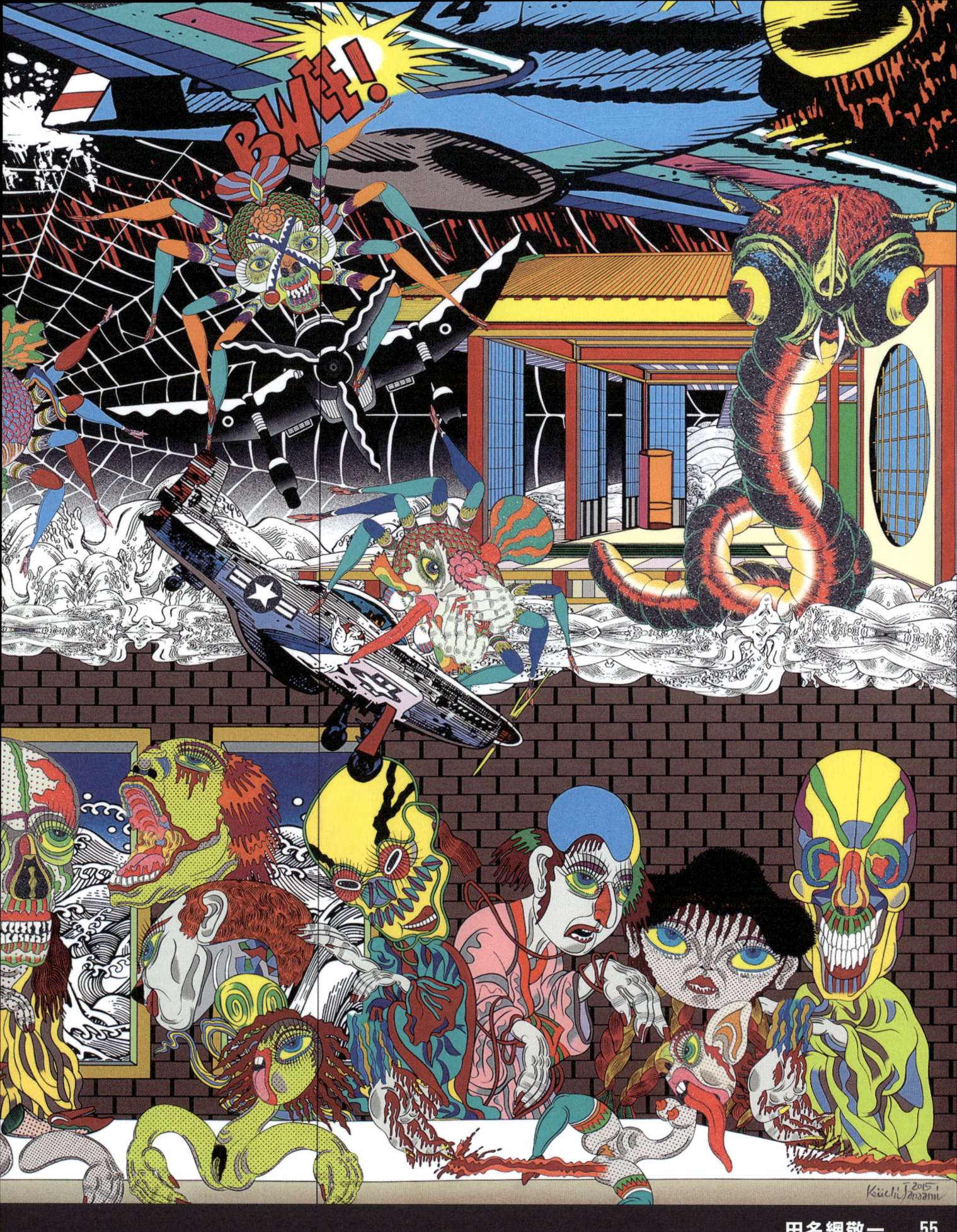

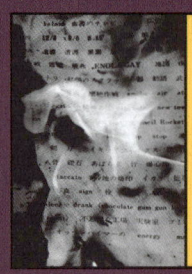

KAWADA KIKUJI
1933–

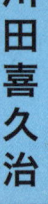

川田喜久治

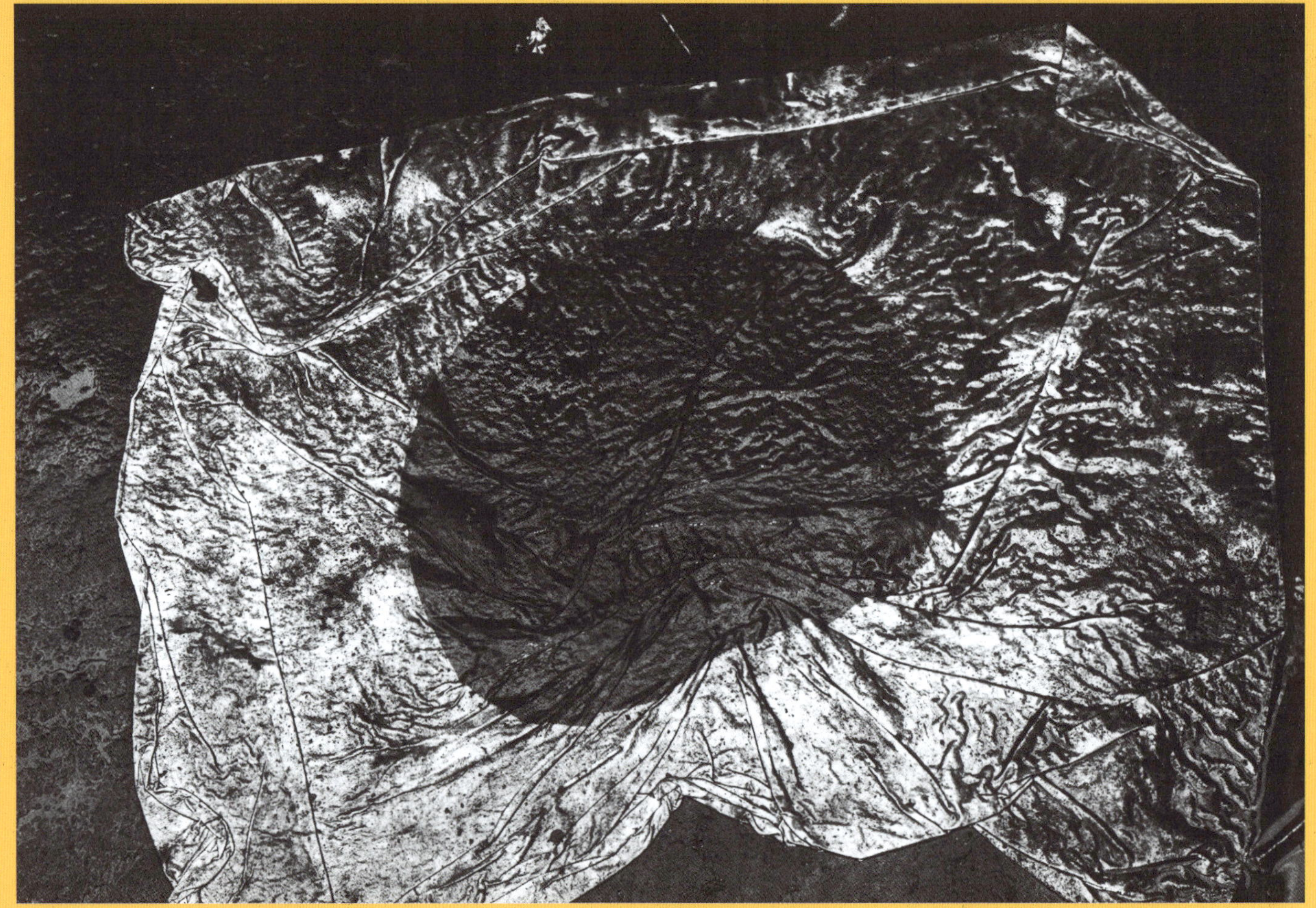

Kawada Kikuji, *The Japanese National Flag*, from the series *The Map* (*Chizu*), 1960–65, gelatin silver print.

Opposite: Photographs from **Kawada Kikuji**, *The Map* (*Chizu*) series, 1960–65, gelatin silver prints.

'As a child, I felt completely unsafe due to the Americans coming to Japan. We were told that the military tanks would come and run us all over. However, as it turned out, the merry American soldiers entered the town on their jeeps and gave us chocolate and chewing gum. I was very curious to see how it tasted, so I would tell the GIs, "Gimme chewing gum."'

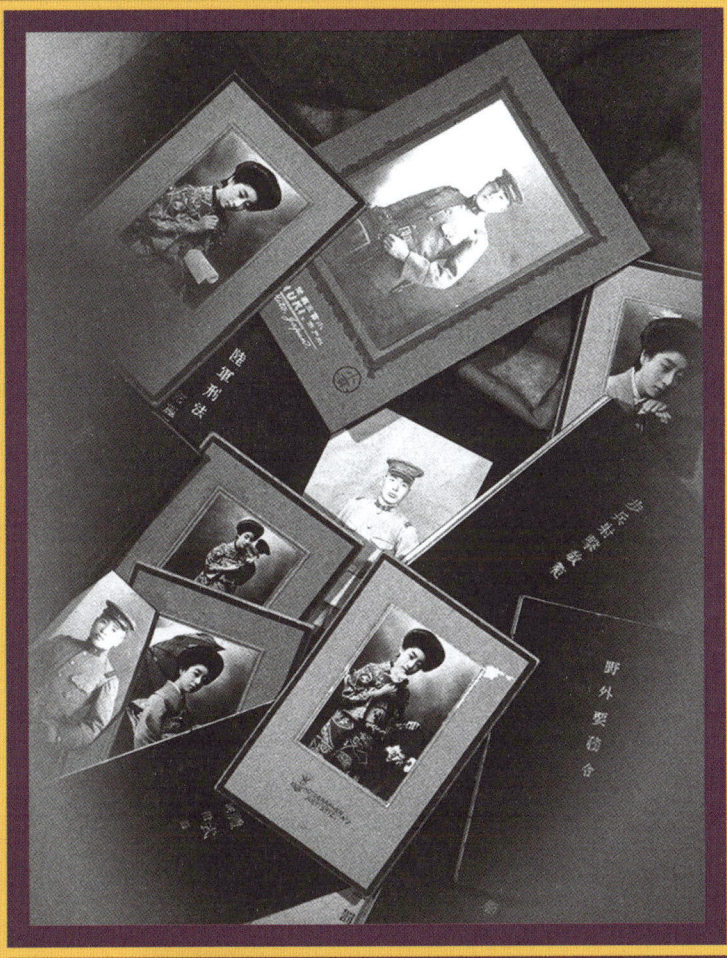
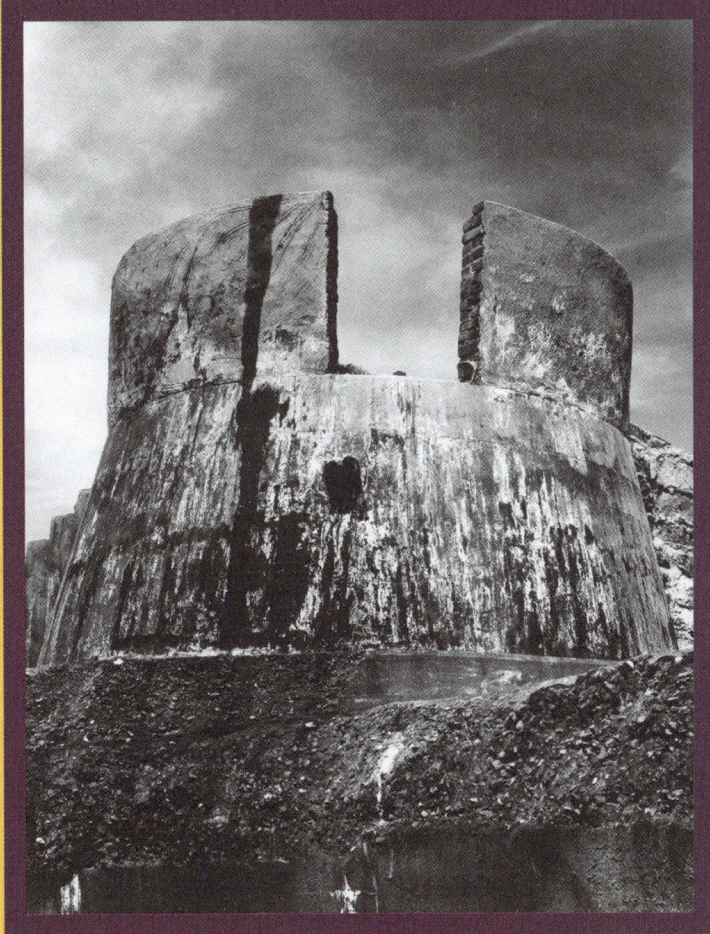
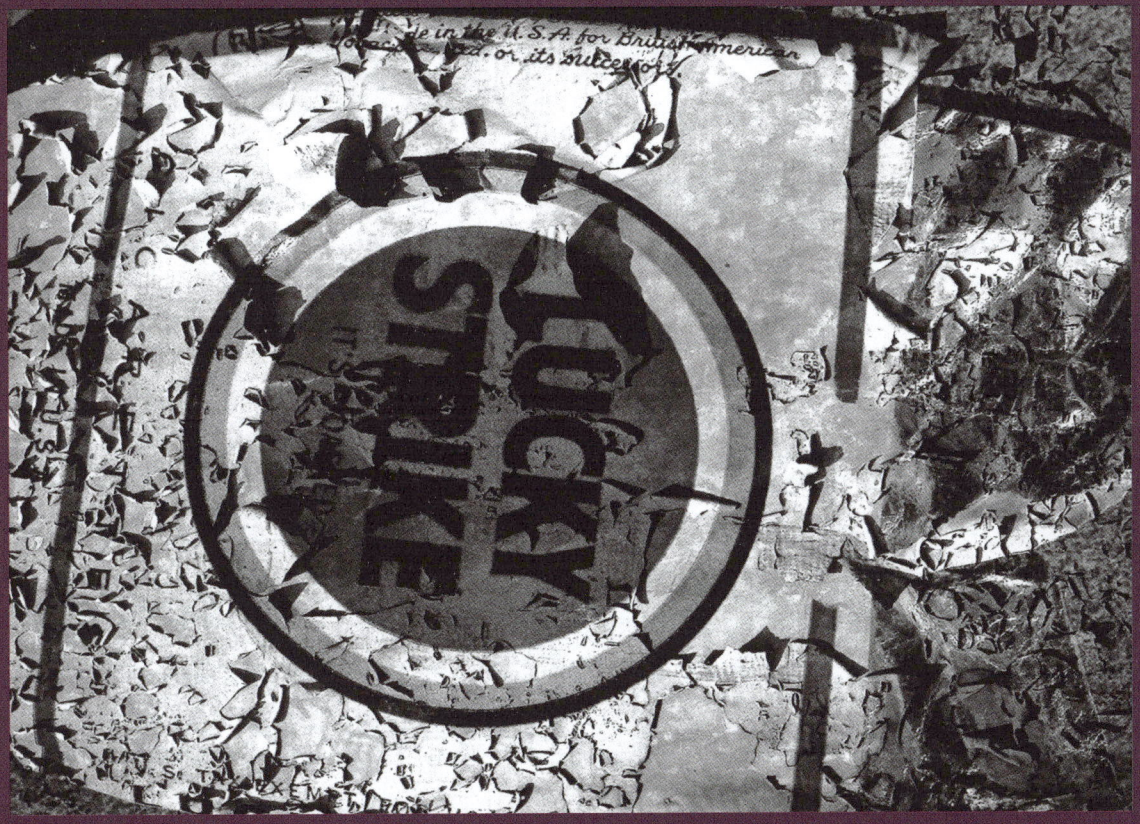

THE MAP CHIZU

川田喜久治

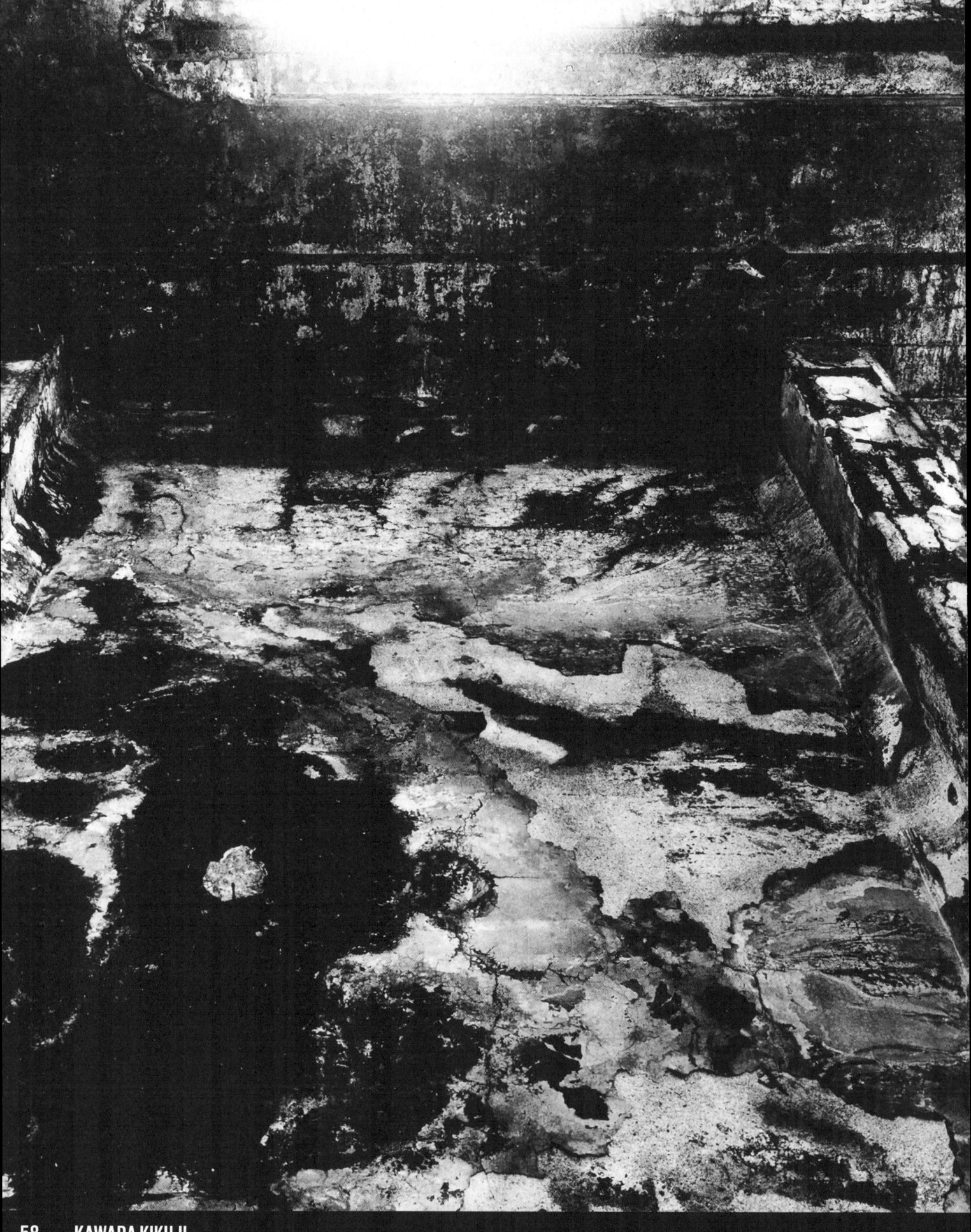

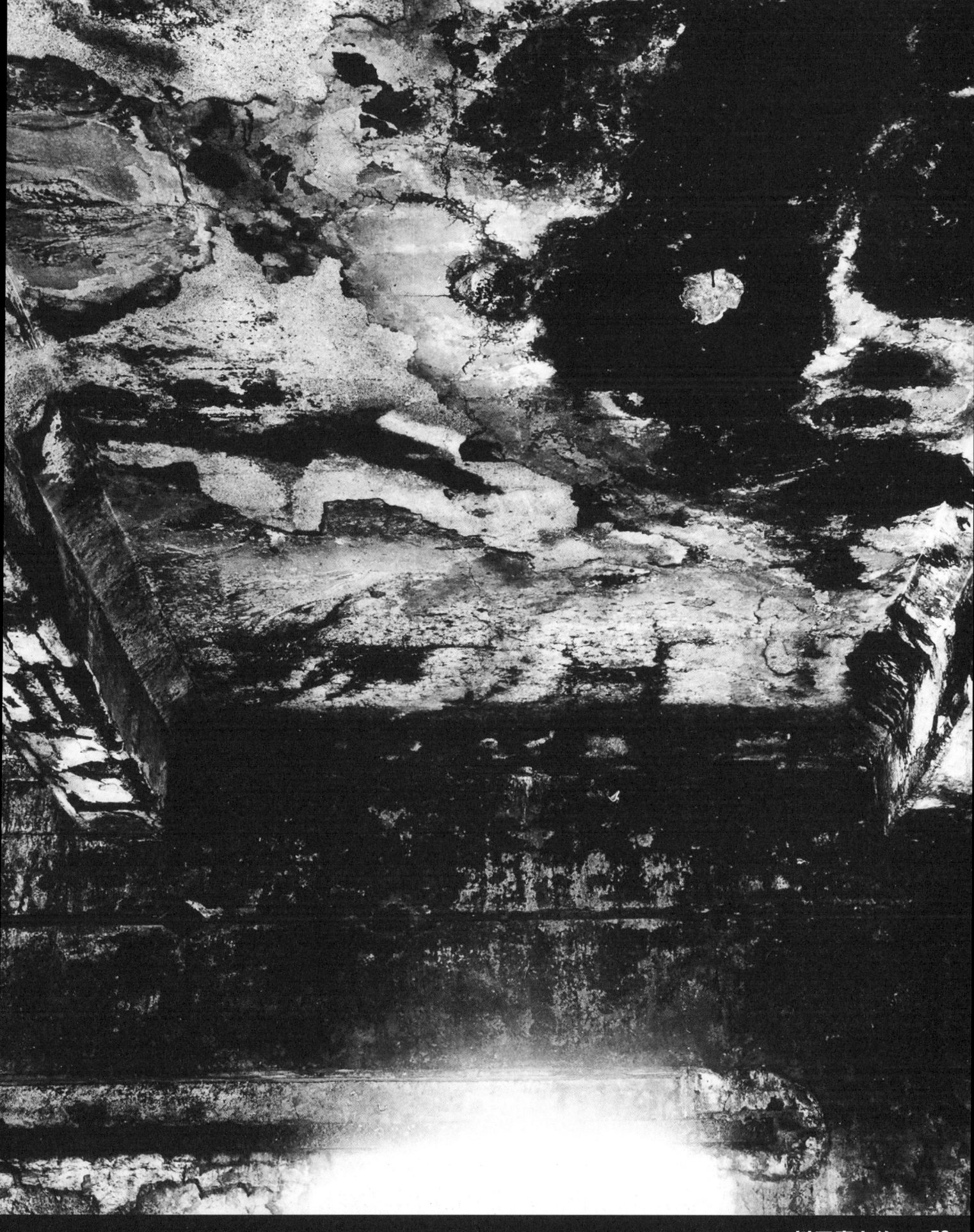

Kawada Kikuji published one of the most important photobooks of the 20th century, *The Map*, which presents photographs he took from 1960 until 1965.

The photographs range from close-up shots of a Japanese flag that he found on the ground after student demonstrations, to close-up photographs of Coca-Cola bottles or Lucky Strike cigarette packaging, to photographs of the Hiroshima Atomic Dome. For him, they represent the scars of Japan after the war. Of course, *The Map* also deals with national identity, so issues between Japan and the US at the time.

LENA FRITSCH

I would say that this is the most insane photobook there is out there. I think there really is such a thing as a photo collection that transcends words.

This is firstly about looking at the photobook, so first taking the package out of its box, opening the package, then turning the first page and then on and on, opening the spread, closing the spread, turning the next page...

KANEKO RYŪICHI

pp. 58–59: **Kawada Kikuji**, *The A-Bomb Memorial Dome, Ceiling, Stain and Flaking-Off*, from the series *The Map* (*Chizu*), 1960–65, gelatin silver print.

Opposite: **Kawada Kikuji**, *A Memorial Decoration from the Shōwa Emperor*, from the series *The Map* (*Chizu*), 1960–65, gelatin silver print.

Overleaf: **Kawada Kikuji**, *Iron Scraps*, from the series *The Map* (*Chizu*), 1960–65, gelatin silver print.

I was shocked when I first saw *The Map*. There was a certain similarity to the monochrome I was doing, but when I first saw it I didn't recognize that it was Hiroshima.

It was beautiful. It's just an abandoned monochrome but there's this sense of beauty. I hadn't seen the photobook so I went to his house to see it. I said, 'Please allow me to see it.' It was Art. This photobook taught me what Art is.

ISHIUCHI MIYAKO

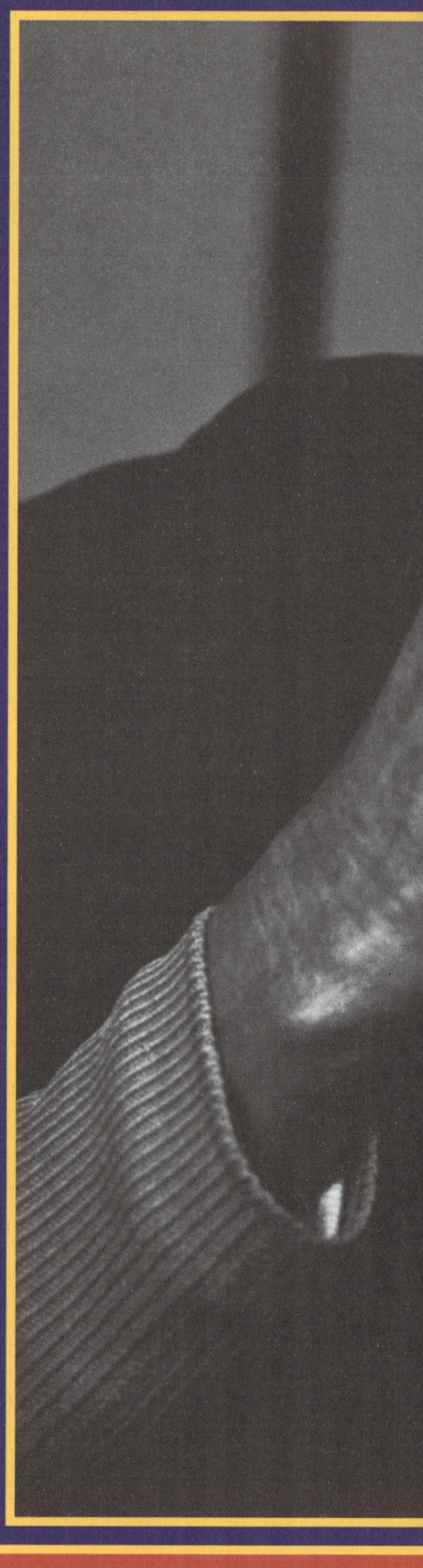

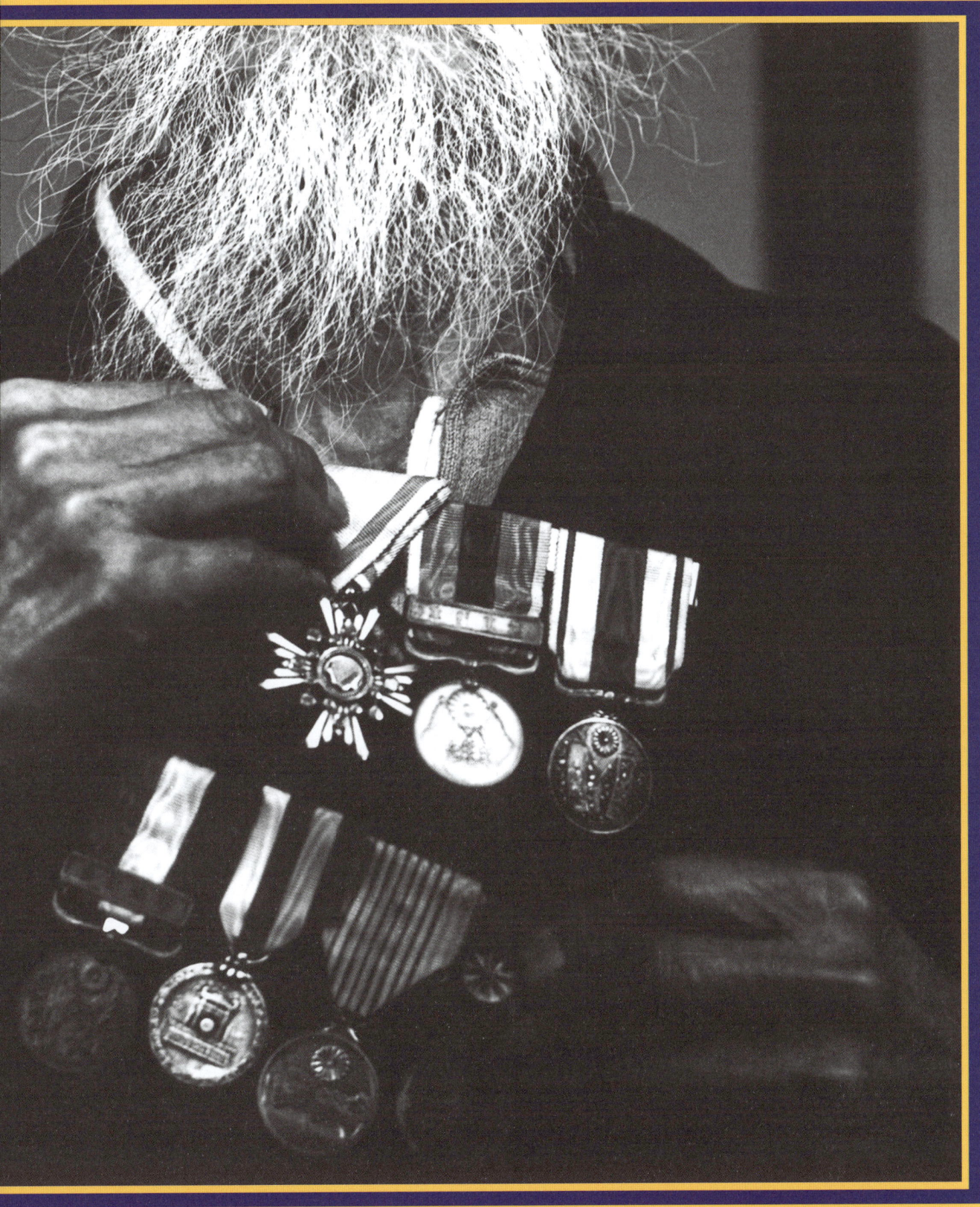

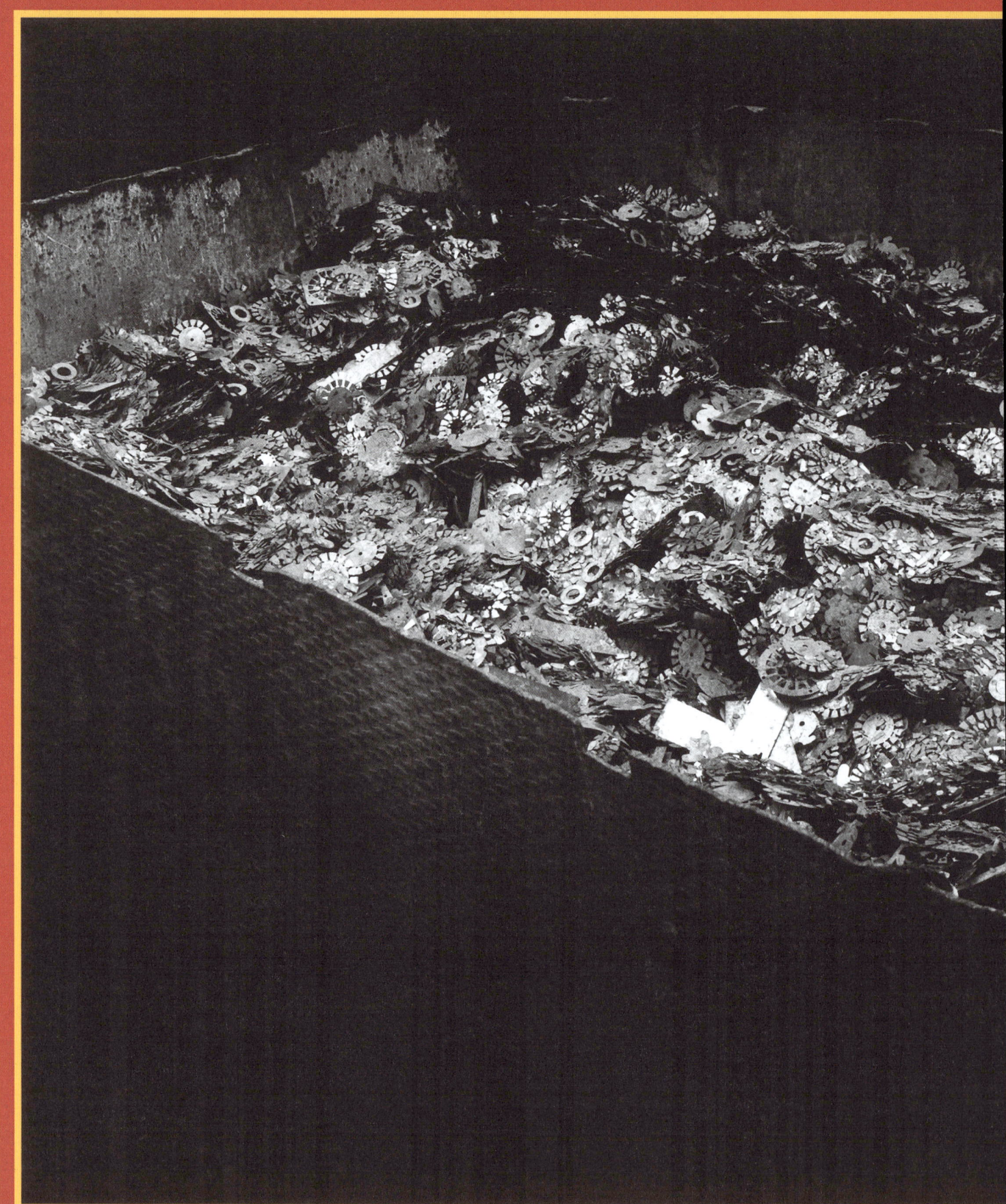

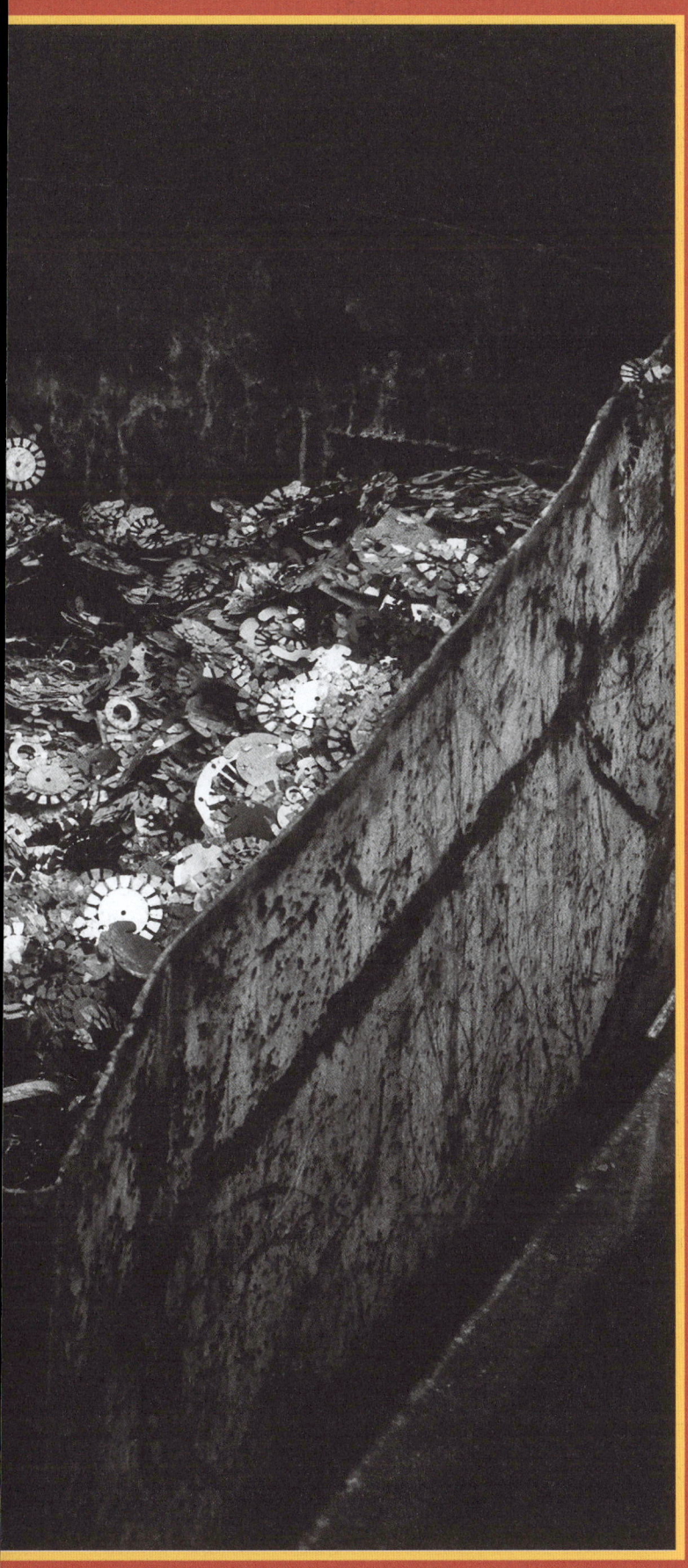

'The structure of the book was designed by Sugiura Kōhei, a genius designer. One night, we were drinking together and he said he wanted to make my photobook. I had accumulated a lot of photographs for *The Map*, so I agreed.

All the publishers we took the book to said it was splendid. They said, 'if we publish such an amazing book, we will never work again', so they all ran away from it.

If we divide *The Map* into sections, the first was the post-war Japanese economic development, and the objects that were thrown away in reaction to that, and the second revolved around the nuclear dome in Hiroshima. The third part was about Japanese soldiers and their fortresses, which were used by the US military.

I found the stain in the basement of the Atomic Bomb Dome. There were stairs going down. When I looked up, the stain looked like the shape of clouds. My eyes got used to the darkness and I looked around the room.

It was astonishing. This was where the atomic bomb was experienced. I felt this world was proliferating in front of me like an amoeba, and I lost myself trying to capture it. The truth really resonated with me emotionally. The patterns of the growing stains reflected the fear and horror of the post-war experience.

There was also a sense of danger or a sense of the end. Through photography, I learned for the first time that beautiful things can be terrifying. This kind of beauty is unworldly; in English, sublime.'

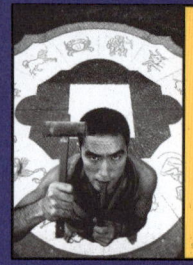

HOSOE EIKŌ
1933–2024

细江英公

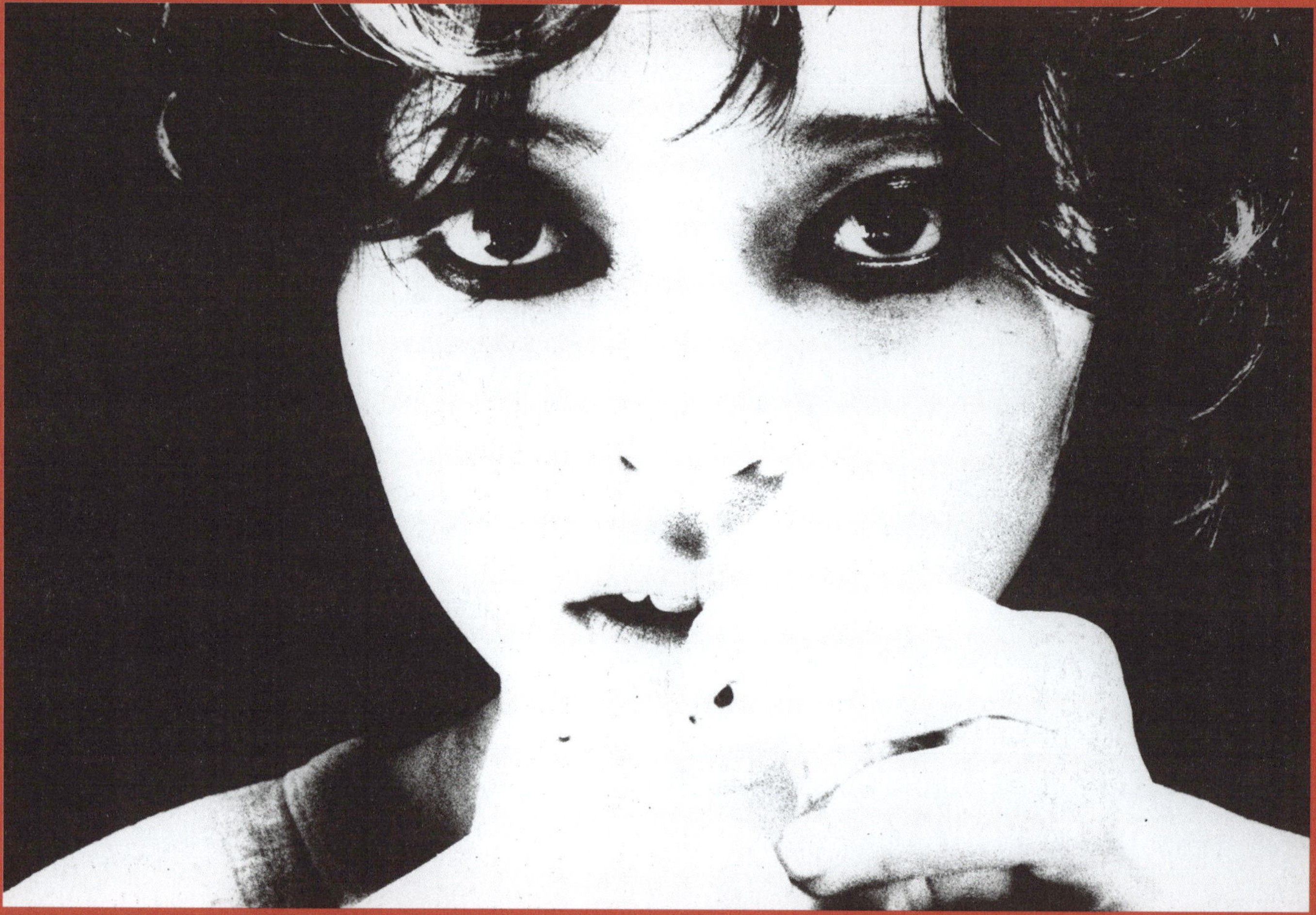

Above and opposite (above left): Photographs from **Hosoe Eikō**, *Man and Woman* (1960).

Opposite (above right): **Hosoe Eikō**, *Ordeal by Roses #22*, 1963, gelatin silver print.

Opposite (below): **Hosoe Eikō**, *Man and Woman #24*, 1960, gelatin silver print.

Hosoe partnered with leading members of the avant-garde to deliver extended portraits that attain a unique performative equilibrium through their approach to collaboration. *Barakei, or Ordeal by Roses* (1961–63), was born out of Hosoe's relationship with the provocative writer Mishima Yukio, while *Kamaitachi* (1969) centred on the iconoclastic *ankoku butoh* dancer Hijikata Tatsumi.

LUCY FLEMING-BROWN

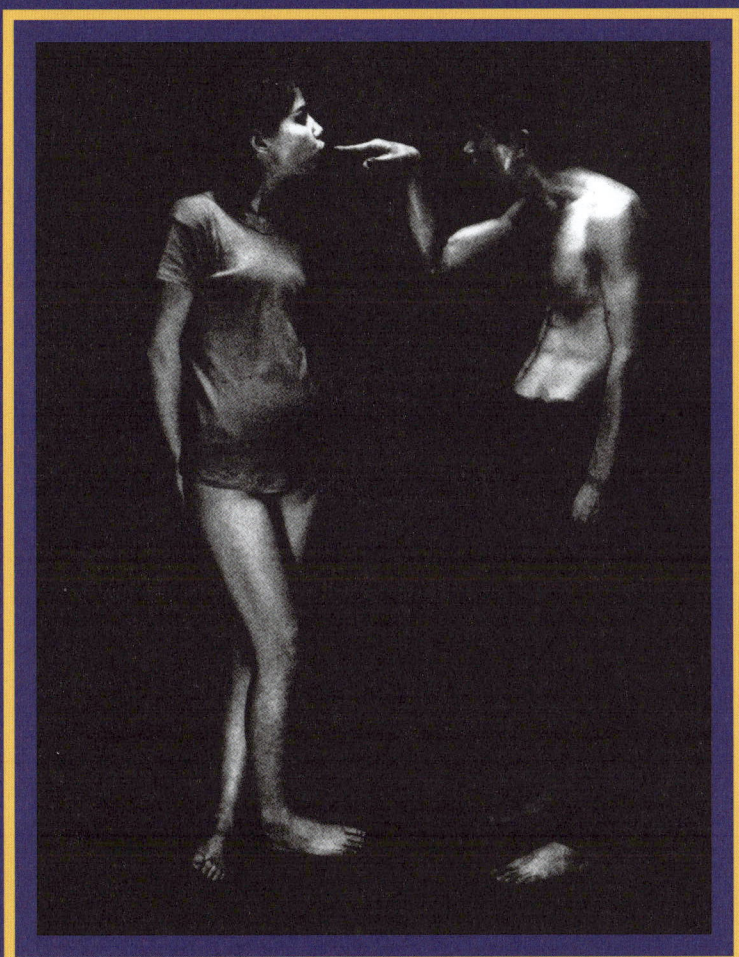
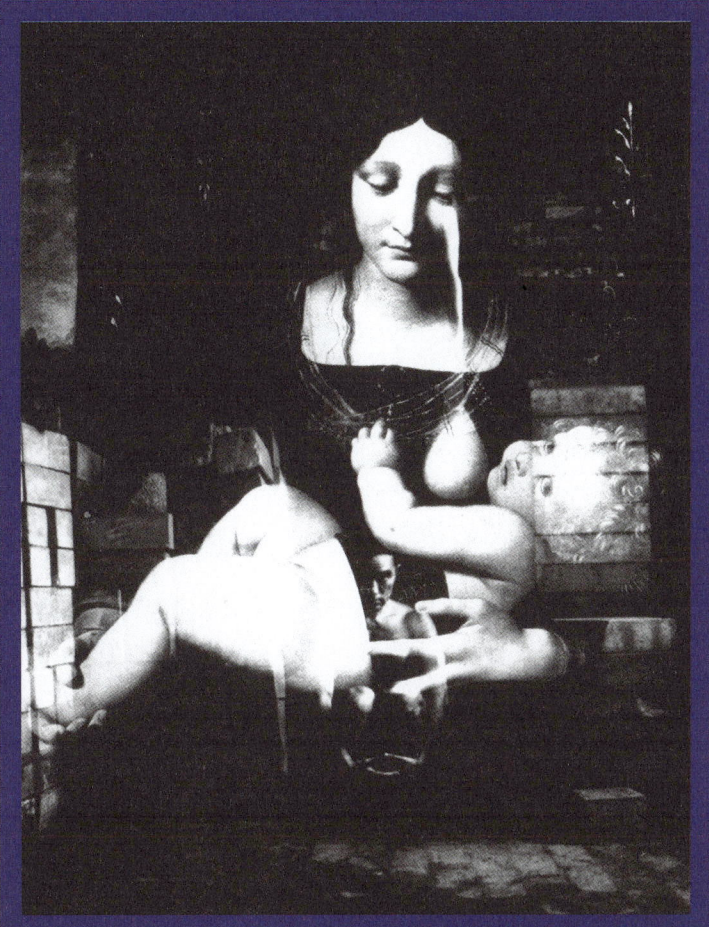

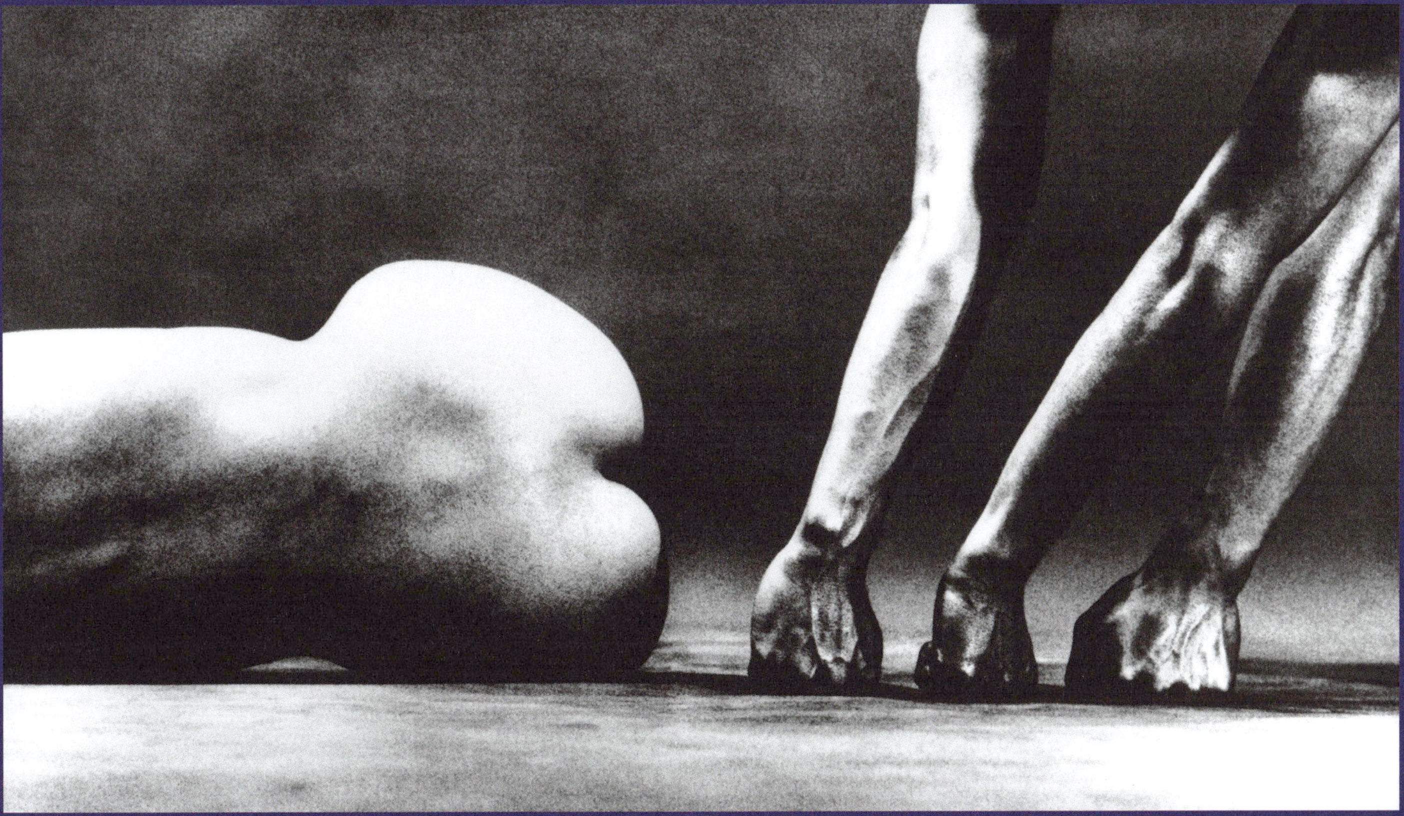

細江英公

'I was born in 1933. Then, during the war time between 1940 and 1945, I returned to my mother's home in Yamagata prefecture to escape from Tokyo. In Tokyo, every day B-29 bombers came and dropped many, many bombs, and most of the houses were burned.

When I was a high school boy, I used to go to the American soldiers' residence area in order to study English conversation. With me was my father's camera, and the next time I went, I gave those prints to little girls and boys playing over there.

"Oh, good. Come in! Do you like coffee?" What's coffee, what is coffee? I had never had a coffee before.'

Hosoe was fascinated by the post-war reality in which he came of age, and channelled his sensitivity to the changing times into a photographic vision that is now celebrated for its expressive use of aesthetics and pioneering attitude towards collaboration.

As a member of the legendary VIVO collective during the 1950s, Hosoe worked alongside artists including Tōmatsu Shōmei, Kawada Kikuji and Narahara Ikkō to pioneer new modes of photographic expression that confronted the transformation of Japanese society.

Hosoe was a committed member of pioneering avant-garde collectives like Demokrato and the Jazz Film Laboratory. He also played an important role in encouraging subsequent generations of photographers in Japan through his participation in initiatives including the independent WORKSHOP photography school, and his mentorship of artists such as Moriyama Daido.

Working together for years, and sometimes decades, Hosoe's subjects appear in different guises across his photographic series: the *Dance Experience* publications from the early 1960s feature Hijikata and Mishima as well as Ohno Kazuo, another renowned butoh dancer whom Hosoe would continue to shoot over the course of more than forty years, eventually resulting in *The Butterfly Dream* (2006).

Opposite: **Hosoe Eikō**, *Man and Woman #20*, 1960, gelatin silver print.

p. 69: **Hosoe Eikō**, *Ordeal by Roses #34*, 1961–62, gelatin silver print.

For the presentation of these photographs in book form, Hosoe worked extensively with several of the era's most renowned graphic designers, including Yokoo Tadanori and Sugiura Kōhei.

LUCY FLEMING-BROWN

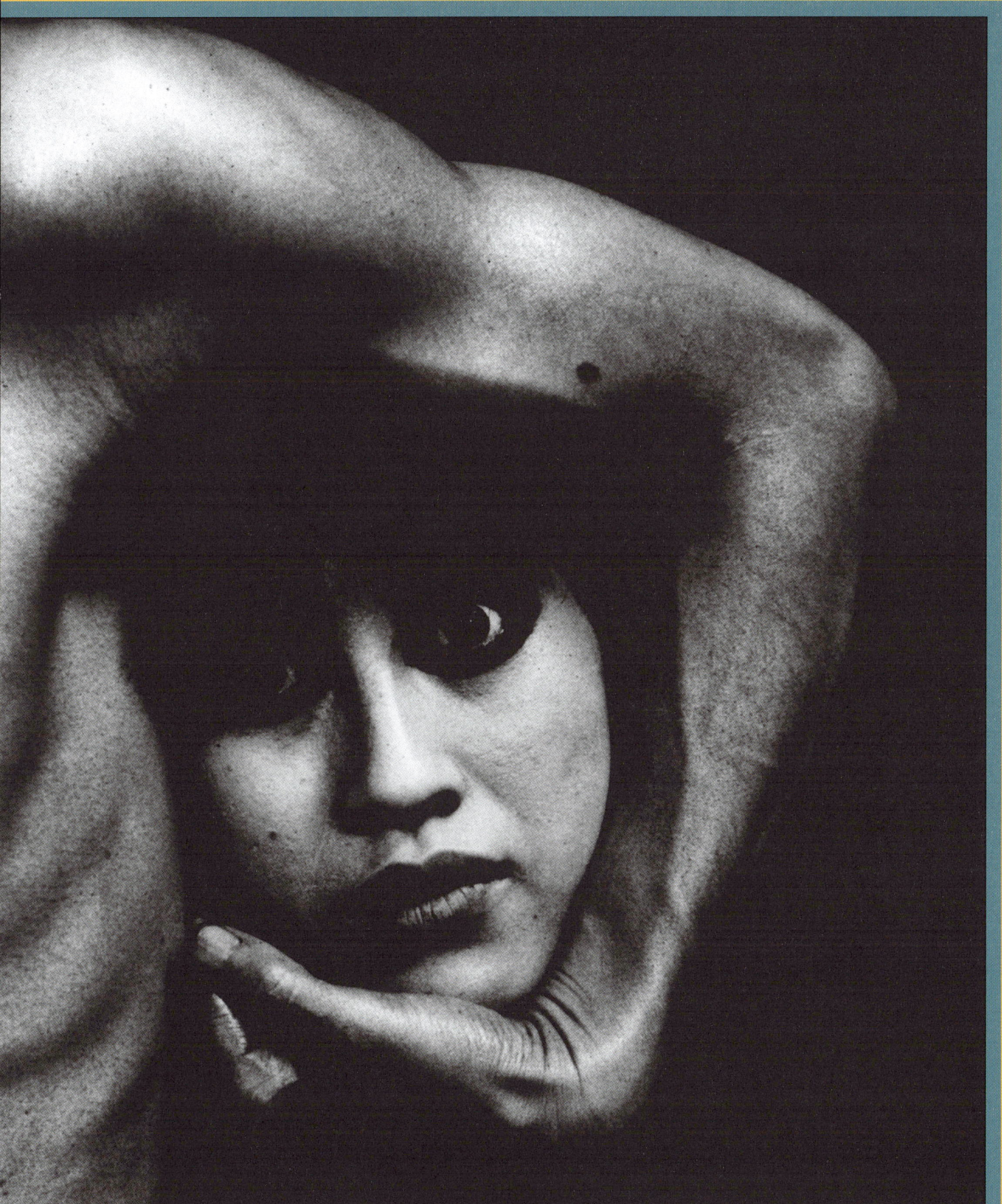

'YOU CAN EXPRESS YOUR IMAGES THROUGH THE CAMERA. THE APPEARANCE LOOKS REALISTIC. BUT THE PERSON WHO PUSHED THE SHUTTER IS A MAKER.

THROUGH THE CAMERA, YOU HAVE TO MAKE YOUR OWN WORK, PSYCHOLOGICALLY AND PHYSICALLY. THE PHOTOGRAPH IS NOT JUST THE PRODUCT OF PHYSICAL MOVEMENT, BUT OF PSYCHOLOGICAL WORK, BECAUSE THE CAMERA IS OPERATED BY A HUMAN BEING.

IT'S REFLECTED IN THE TRANSLATION OF PHOTOGRAPHY. IF "PHOTOGRAPHY" WAS TRANSLATED ACCORDING TO THE SIGNIFICANCE OF THE CHARACTER OR THE WORD, IT WOULD BE "KŌ-GA" – KŌ, PHOTO, GA, DRAWING: PHOTO-DRAWING. BUT IT'S TRANSLATED TO "SHASHIN", MEANING "REFLECTION OF THE TRUTH".'

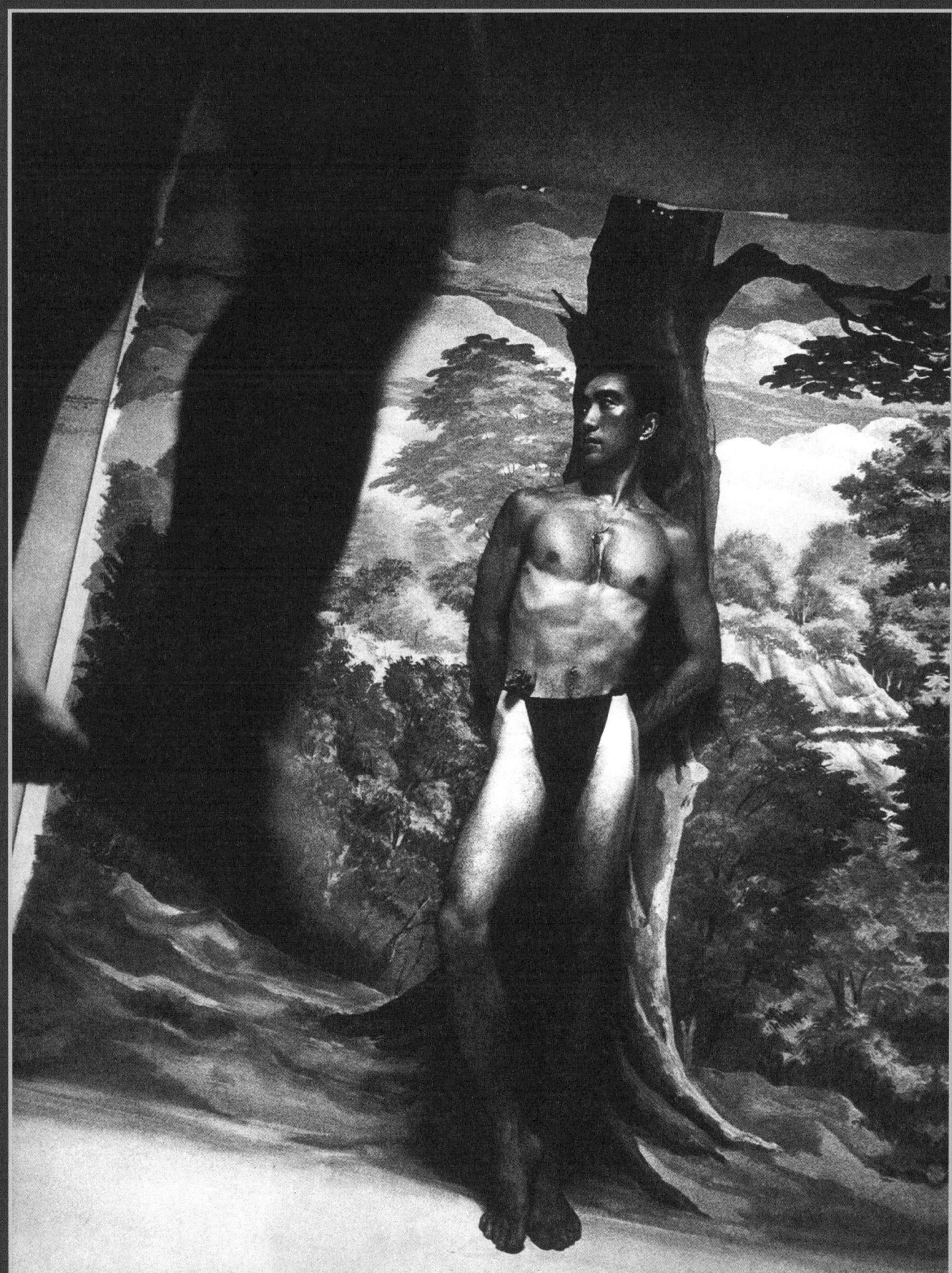

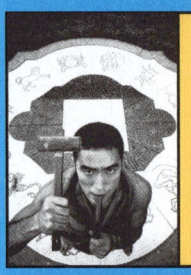

MISHIMA YUKIO
1925–1970

三島由紀夫

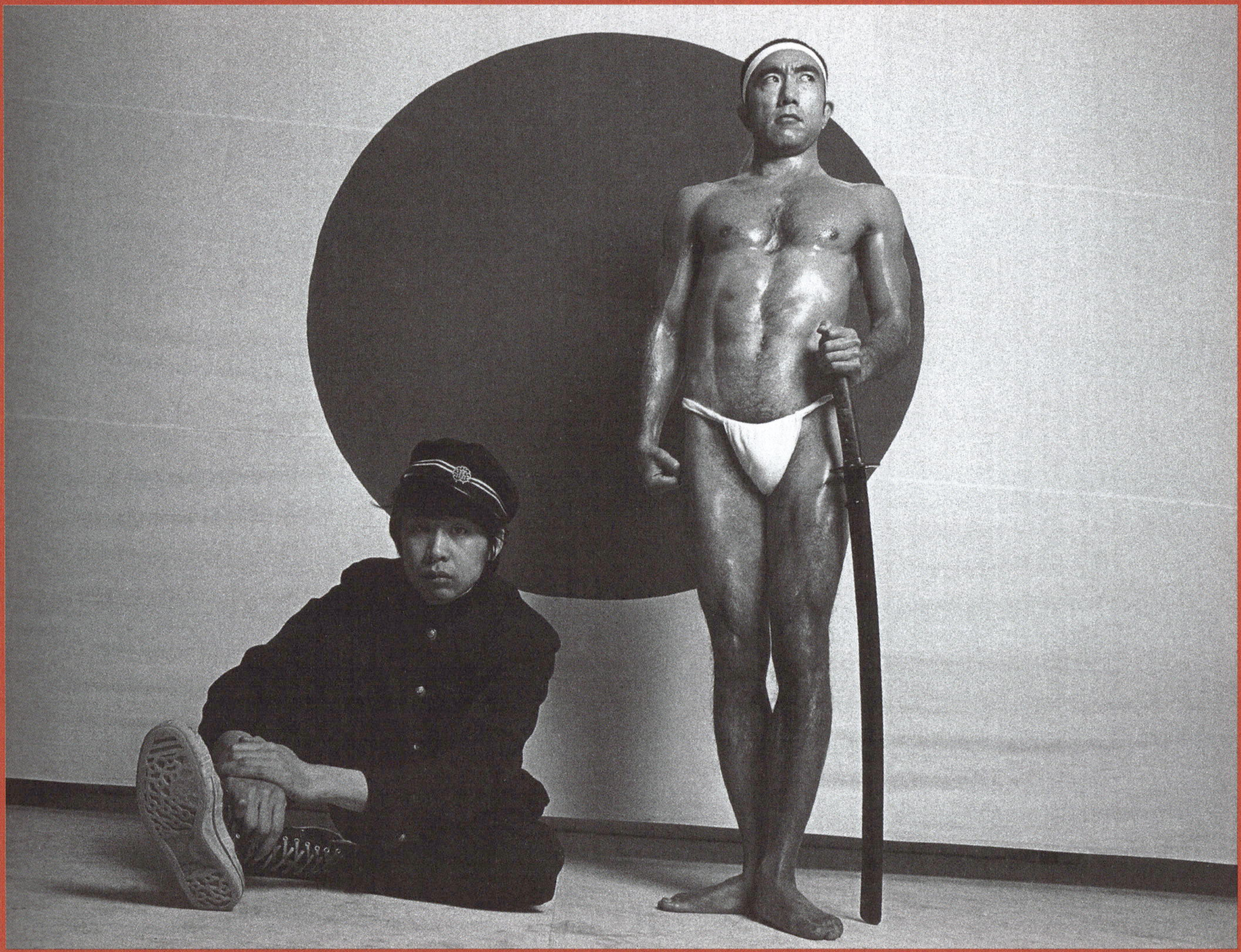

Above and opposite (above, left and right): Photographs from **Shinoyama Kishin and Mishima Yukio**, *The Death of a Man* (1970–2020).

Opposite (below): Photographs from **Hosoe Eikō**, *Ordeal by Roses* (*Barakei*, 1961–63).

'One day, Hosoe Eikō came and took my body away to a mysterious world. I had seen magical works produced by cameras before, but Hosoe's work was more in the nature of mechanical magic than witchcraft, an extremely anti-civilized use of this civilized precision machine.'

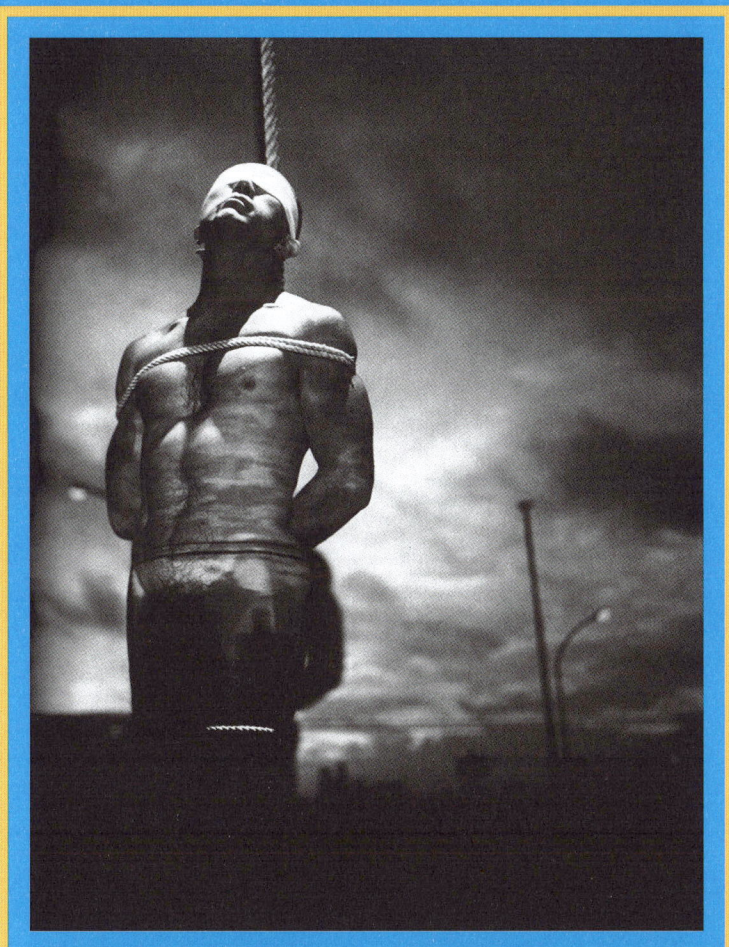
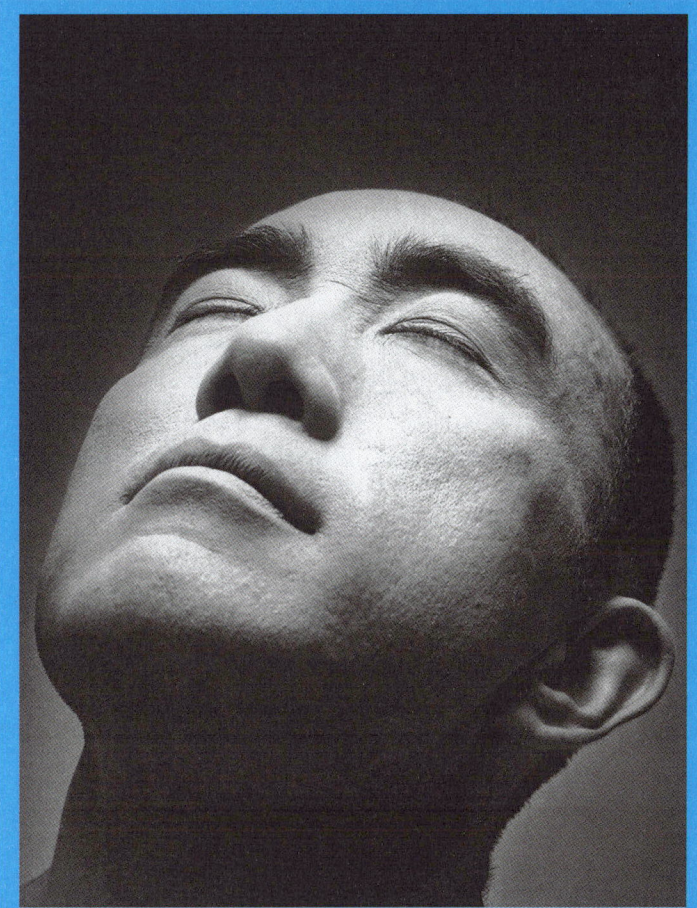

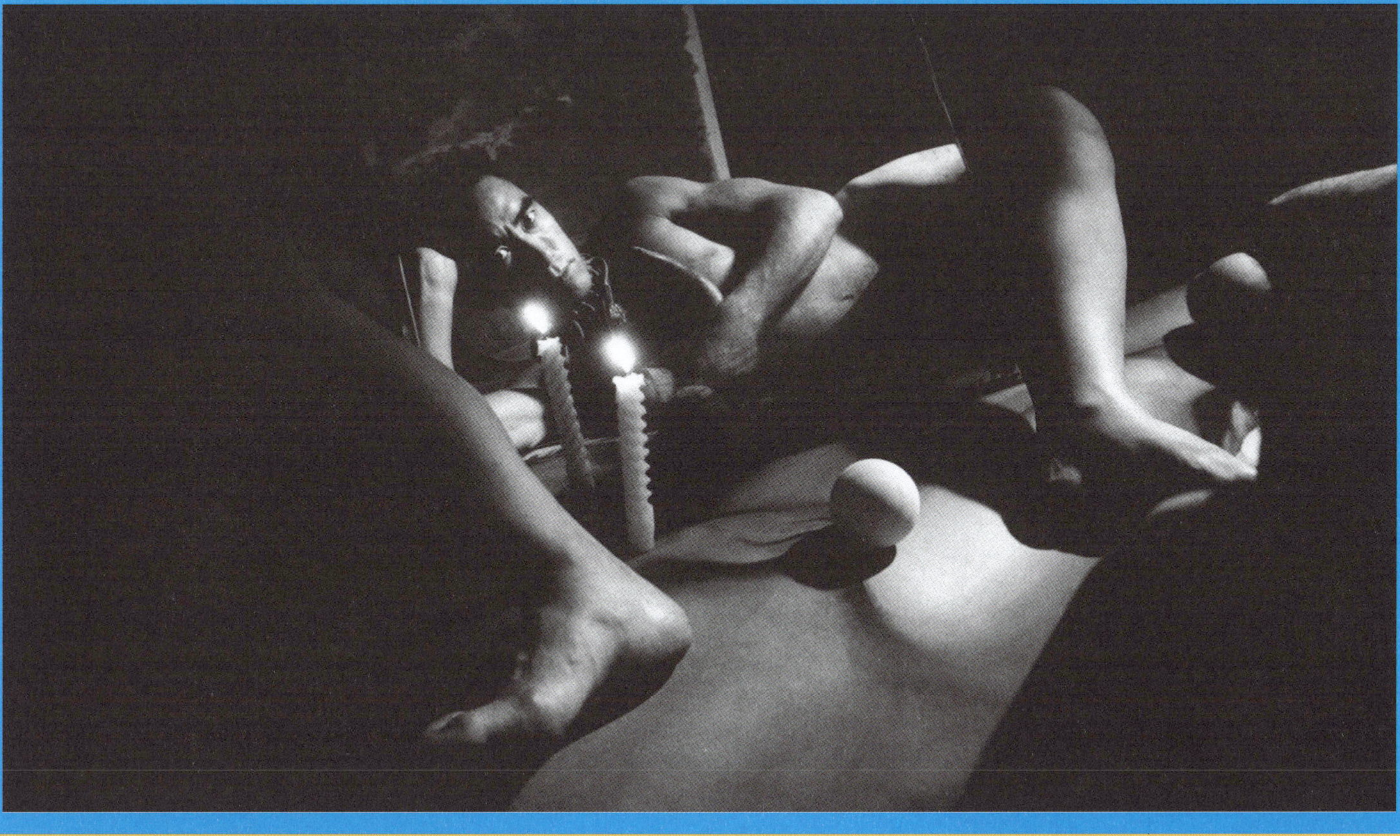

三島由紀夫

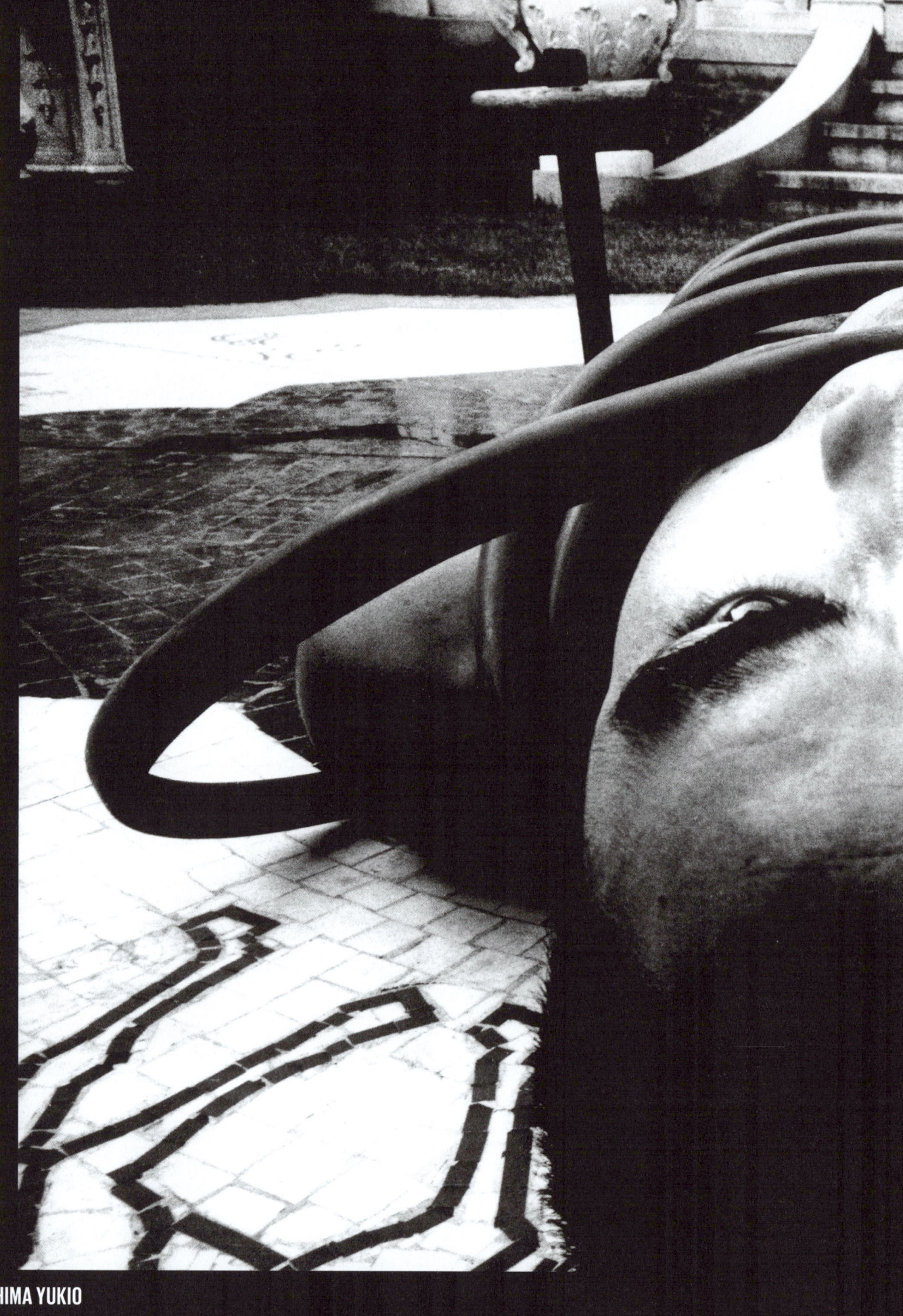

ORDEAL BY ROSES

薔薇刑

MISHIMA YUKIO

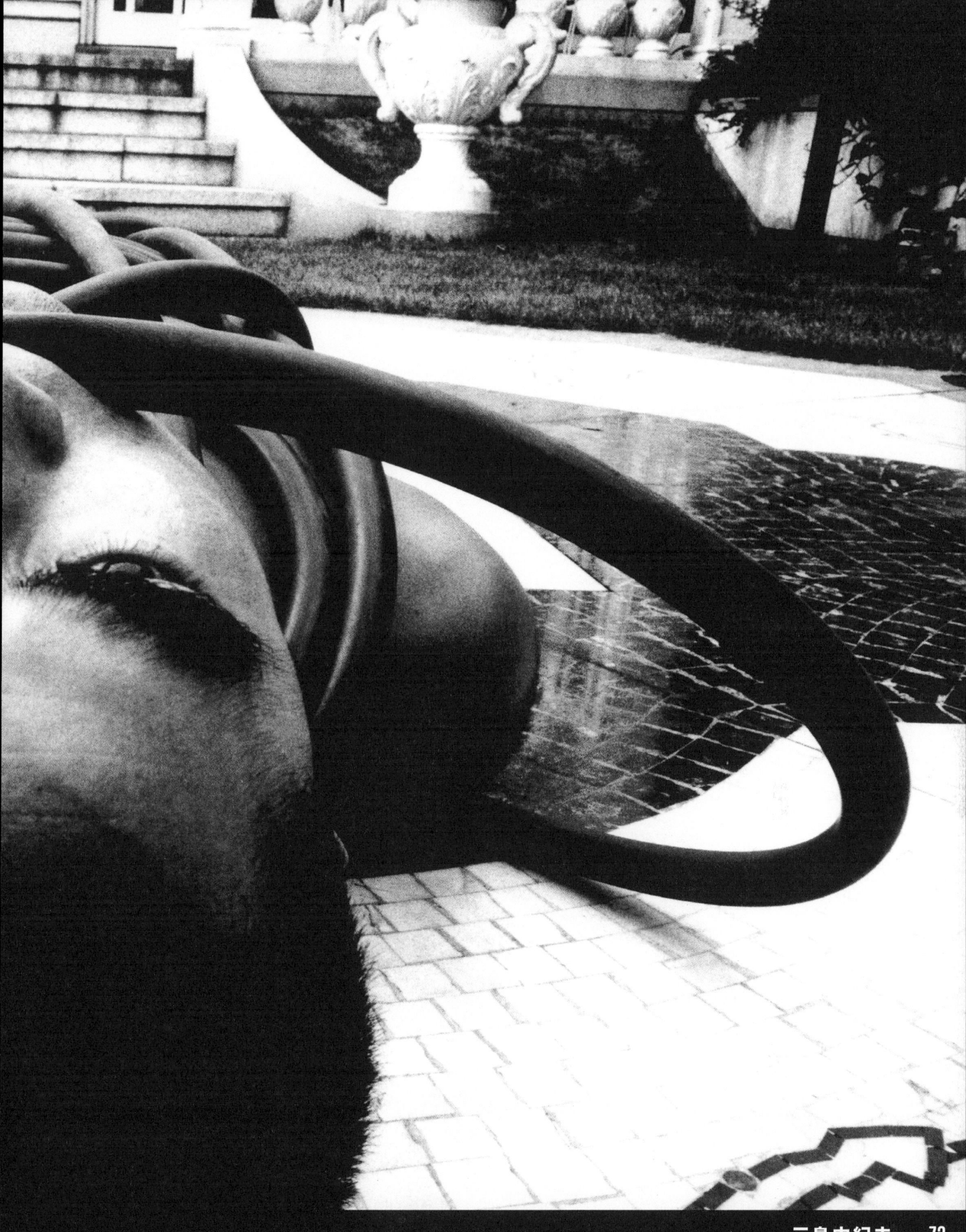

Mishima Yukio's sensuous craving for a forbidden erotic theatre of the naked male body was celebrated in Hosoe Eikō's photograph series *Ordeal by Roses* (1961–63).

Set in Mishima's Rococo-style house in Tokyo, this cumulative photographic portrait presents the bodybuilder author clad in *fundoshi*, a traditional male loincloth, and posing before reproductions of Renaissance paintings and gaudy European furniture.

ALEXANDRA MUNROE

In 1963, I had a visitor from Mishima's publisher. I was told that Mishima Yukio wanted me to photograph him. He was then a kind of god of literature. Why did Mr Mishima, such a great man, ask me to take a photograph of him? I was twenty-one or twenty-two. But I took the best photographs I have ever done.

'I want you to take my picture as you like,' he said. As you like! So I just said, take off your jacket, everything.'

There was a water hose because his father was watering the garden. So I went to his father. 'Mr Mishima, please. Can I use your water hose?' And he was watching and wondering what I was doing. I came back to him and told him to lie down.

Afterwards, he said, 'I have never been photographed like that.' He'd never been treated in such a way by somebody else.

HOSOE EIKŌ

pp. 72-73: **Hosoe Eikō**, *Ordeal by Roses #6*, 1961, gelatin silver print.

Opposite: **Hosoe Eikō**, *Ordeal by Roses #5*, 1961, gelatin silver print.

Overleaf: **Hosoe Eikō**, *Ordeal by Roses #32*, 1961, gelatin silver print.

p. 78 (above and below): Illustrations from **Yokoo Tadanori**, *Ordeal by Roses* (*Barakei*, 1971).

p. 78 (middle): **Yokoo Tadanori and Mishima Yukio**, *The Aesthetics of End*, 1966, silkscreen print.

p. 79: **Yokoo Tadanori**, *Love of Death*, 1994, acrylic on canvas.

'IN FRONT OF MR HOSOE'S CAMERA, I FOUND THAT MY SPIRIT AND MIND WERE NOT NEEDED IN THE SLIGHTEST. IT WAS AN EXHILARATING EXPERIENCE, A SITUATION I HAD ALWAYS LONGED FOR.

JUST AS A NOVELIST USES WORDS AND A COMPOSER USES SOUND, HE USES THE CAMERA AS A MEDIUM TO CREATE VARIOUS COMBINATIONS OF THE SITUATIONS IN WHICH HIS SUBJECTS ARE PLACED, AND THE LIGHT AND SHADOW THAT MAKE THESE COMBINATIONS POSSIBLE.

IN OTHER WORDS, THE WORDS HE USED AND THE SOUNDS HE USED WERE THE BODY.'

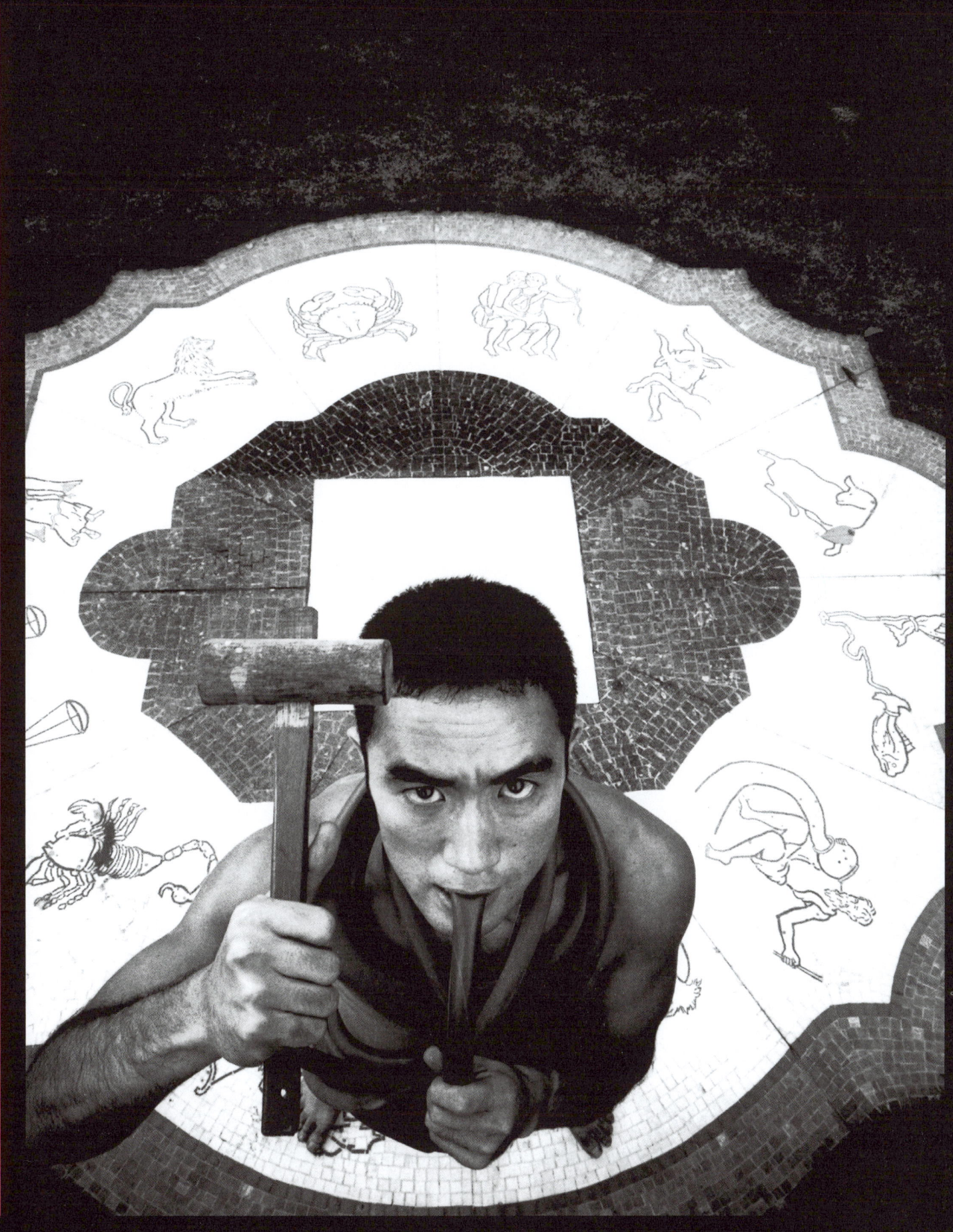

三島由紀夫

'THE WORLD TO WHICH I WAS ABDUCTED UNDER THE SPELL OF HOSOE'S LENS WAS ABNORMAL, WARPED, SARCASTIC, GROTESQUE, SAVAGE AND PROMISCUOUS.

IT WAS, IN A SENSE, THE REVERSE OF THE WORLD WE LIVE IN, WHERE OUR WORSHIP OF SOCIAL APPEARANCES AND OUR CONCERN FOR PUBLIC MORALITY AND HYGIENE CREATE FOUL, FILTHY SEWERS WINDING BENEATH THE SURFACE.

YET IN ITS UNDERGROUND CHANNELS, THERE FLOWED INEXHAUSTIBLY A STREAM OF UNSULLIED FEELING.'

MISHIMA YUKIO

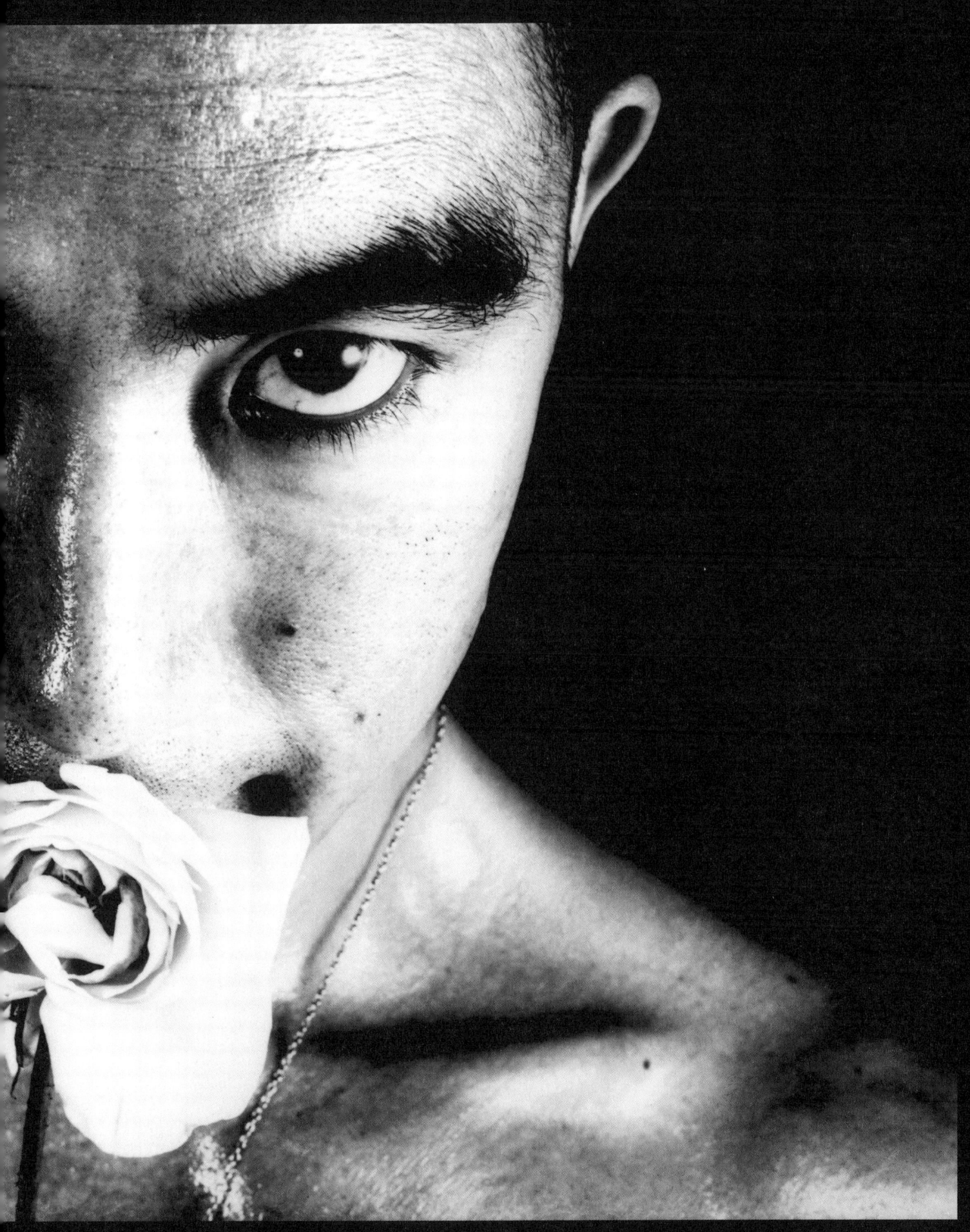

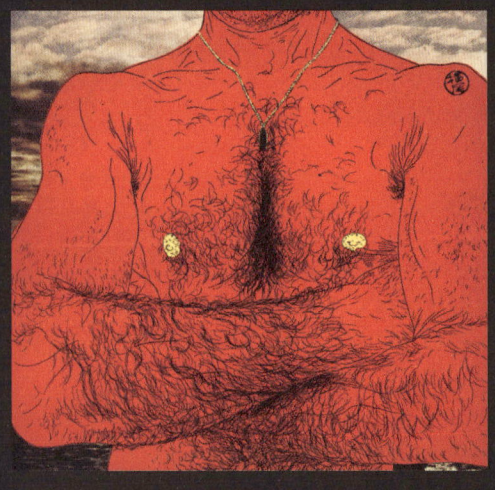

> I decided to make a book. The only thing I asked him was the title of the book, as a man of literature. He wrote me a postcard with ten titles. The last title was *Barakei* (*Ordeal by Roses*).
>
> HOSOE EIKŌ

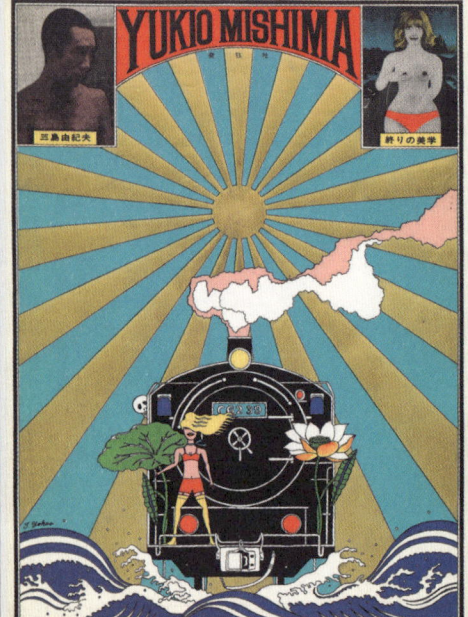

> When I came to Tokyo, I heard the news that Hosoe was going to make *Barakei* with Mishima, so I jumped into it. That was the beginning of my collaborations with Mishima. After that, Mishima asked me to write various essays, and to design covers for books and posters for his theatre.
>
> I drew a big picture on the cover, and I asked Mishima to be the model for it. I took a photo of him in the pose of an odalisque, I combined it with an Indian god and I made the painting. That was in 1970.
>
> A few days after seeing the picture, Mishima committed suicide by *seppuku*. It was a crazy time. I think that experience may have been one of the reasons I moved out of design and stepped into the world of art.
>
> YOKOO TADANORI

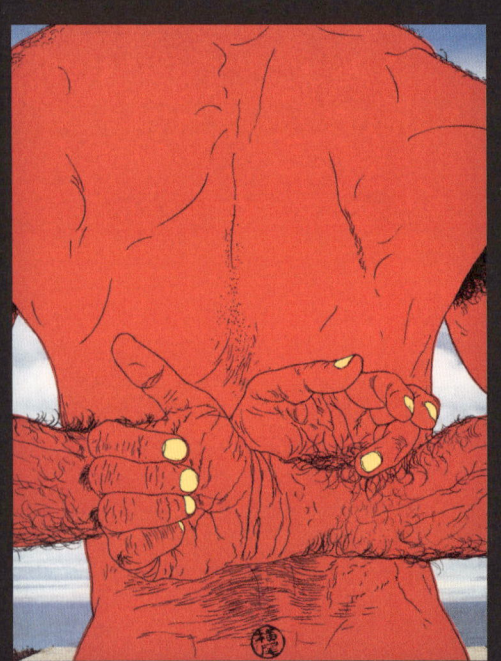

> In 1970, Mishima shocked Japan with his dramatic ritual suicide. After a failed coup in which he led a private militia to the Self-Defence Force's Tokyo headquarters, the writer publicly disembowelled himself (*seppuku*) in ultimate sacrifice to his nationalist ideals.
>
> In the months leading up to this incident, Mishima had worked closely with Hosoe Eikō and Yokoo Tadanori to produce a completely redesigned second edition of *Barakei* (1971).
>
> In keeping with Mishima's longstanding desire for mastery over his own image, his efforts in the run-up to the book's release suggested to Hosoe that this publication was intended by Mishima as a kind of requiem.
>
> LUCY FLEMING-BROWN

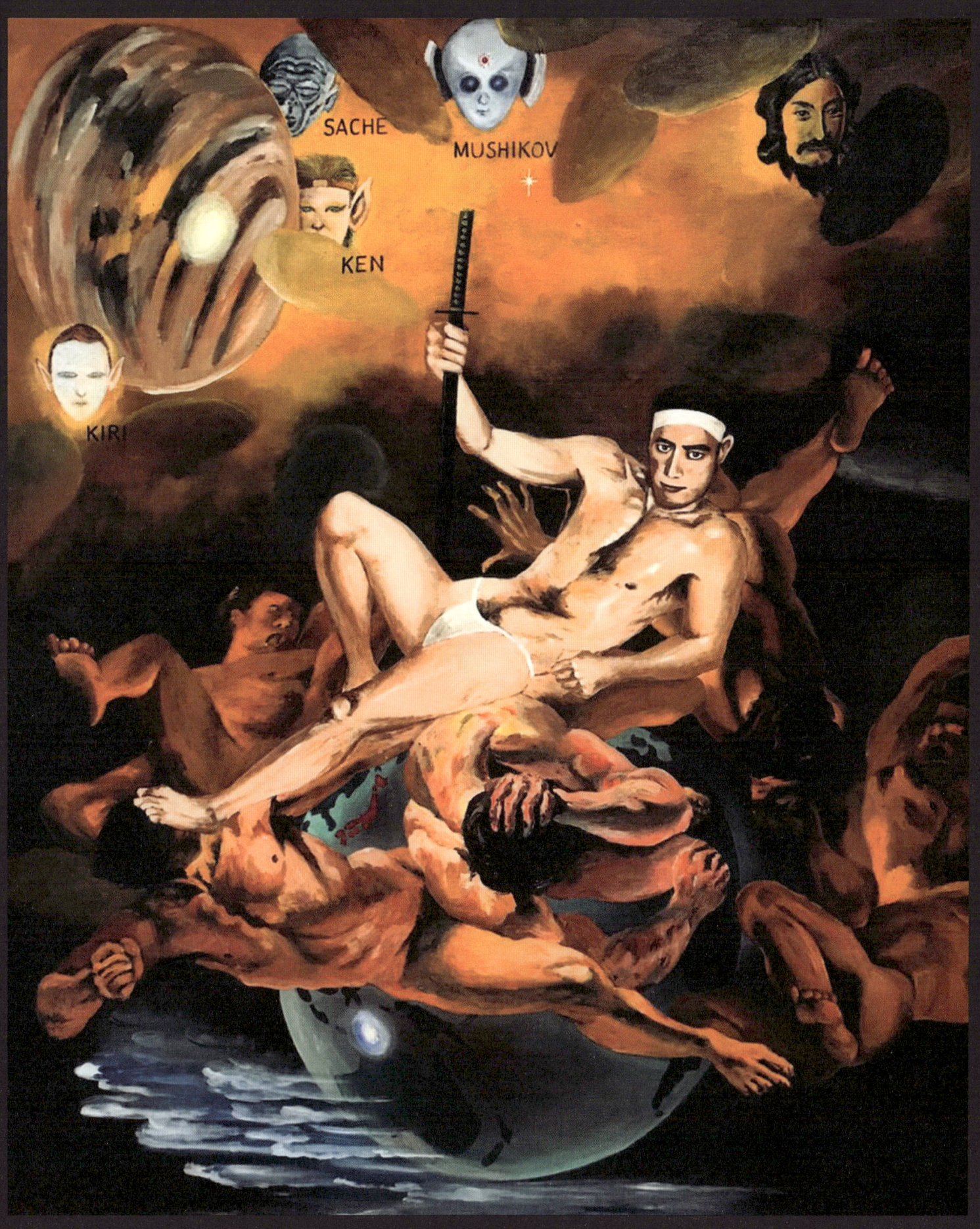

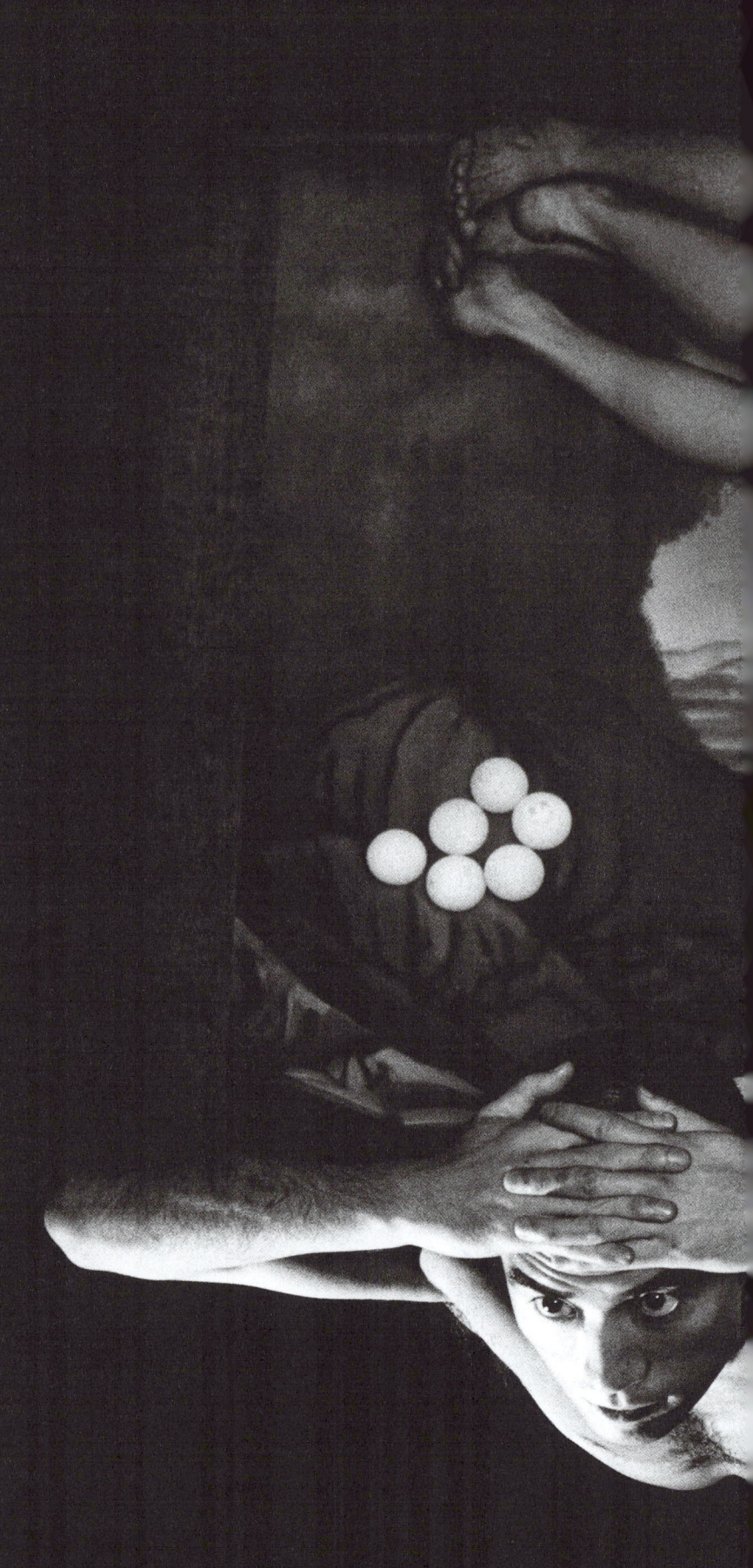

'THE AGONY OF THE SLOW EXECUTION OF THE ORDEAL OF ROSES AWAITS.

HERE THE SYMBOL OF THE ROSE WITH ITS CRUEL THORNS COMES TO THE FORE, AND TORTURE AND ENDLESS SLOW DEATH ARE PREPARED.

AND WITH DEATH AND THE ASCENSION INTO THE DARK SUN, THE COLLECTION COMES TO A CLOSE.'

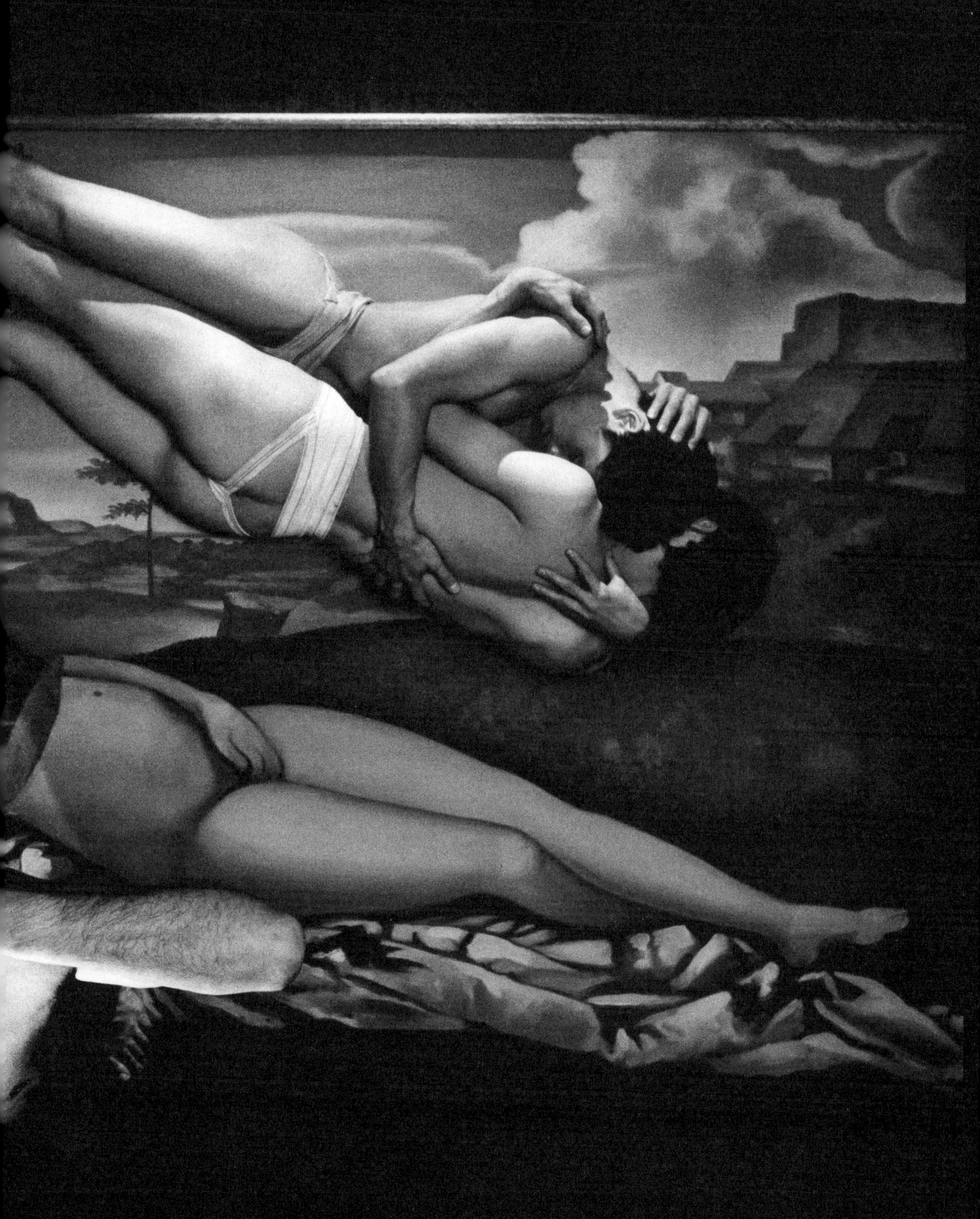

三島由紀夫

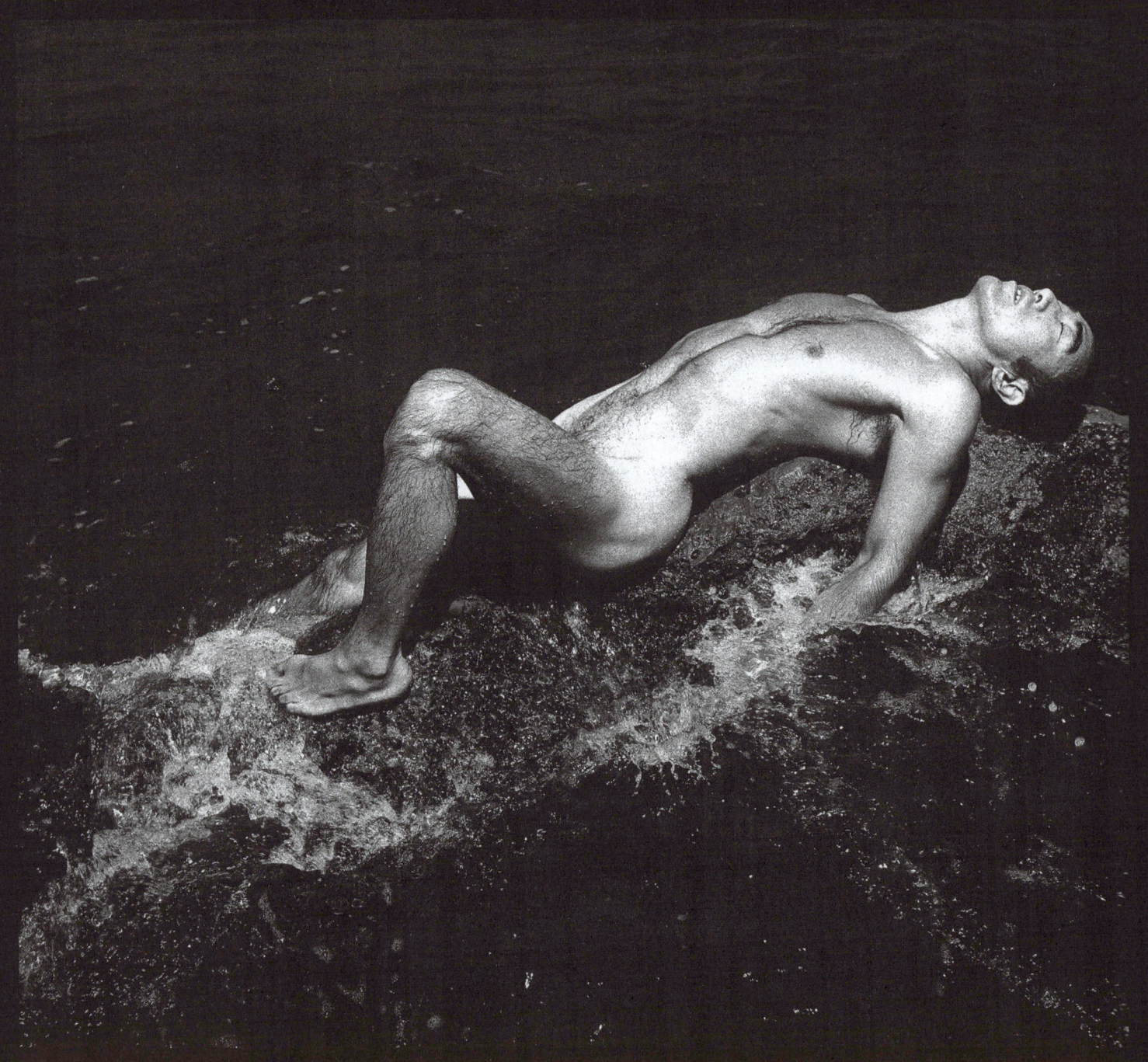

pp. 80-81: **Hosoe Eikō**, *Ordeal by Roses #16*, 1963, gelatin silver print.

Above and opposite: Photographs from **Shinoyama Kishin and Yukio Mishima**, *The Death of a Man* (1970–2020).

Overleaf: Photographs from **Shinoyama Kishin and Mishima Yukio**, *The Death of a Man* (1970–2020).

Mishima was interested in exploring sexual psychology, however perverse, and glorifying death with an obsession that led to his sensationalist suicide by *seppuku* in 1970, to illuminate the primordial darkness seething beneath the surface of human imagination.

One photograph from Shinoyama Kishin shows Mishima assuming the posture from Guido Reni's painting of St Sebastian being martyred, standing *contrapposto* with his hands tied above his head, a symbol of sacrifice.

ALEXANDRA MUNROE

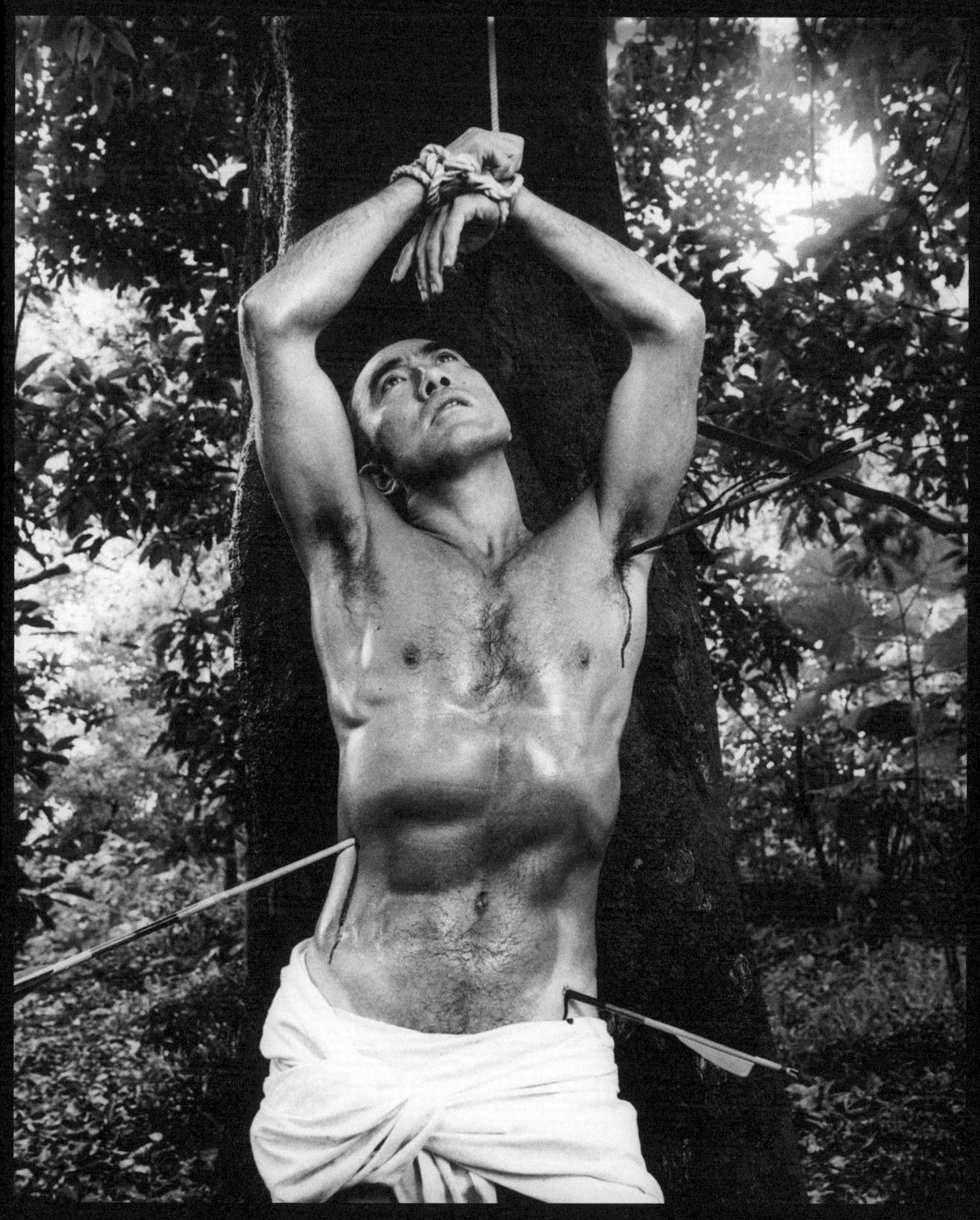

三島由紀夫　83

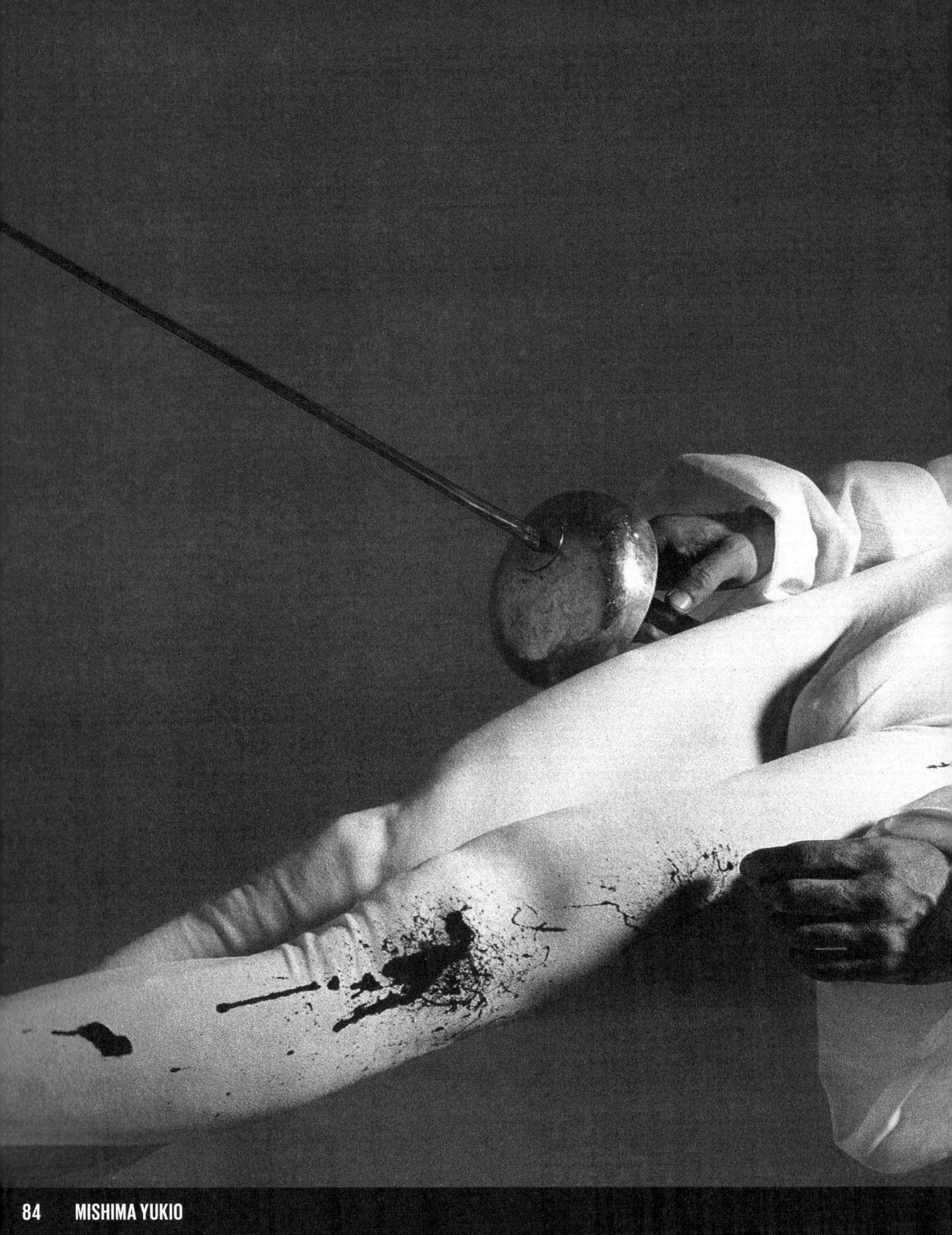

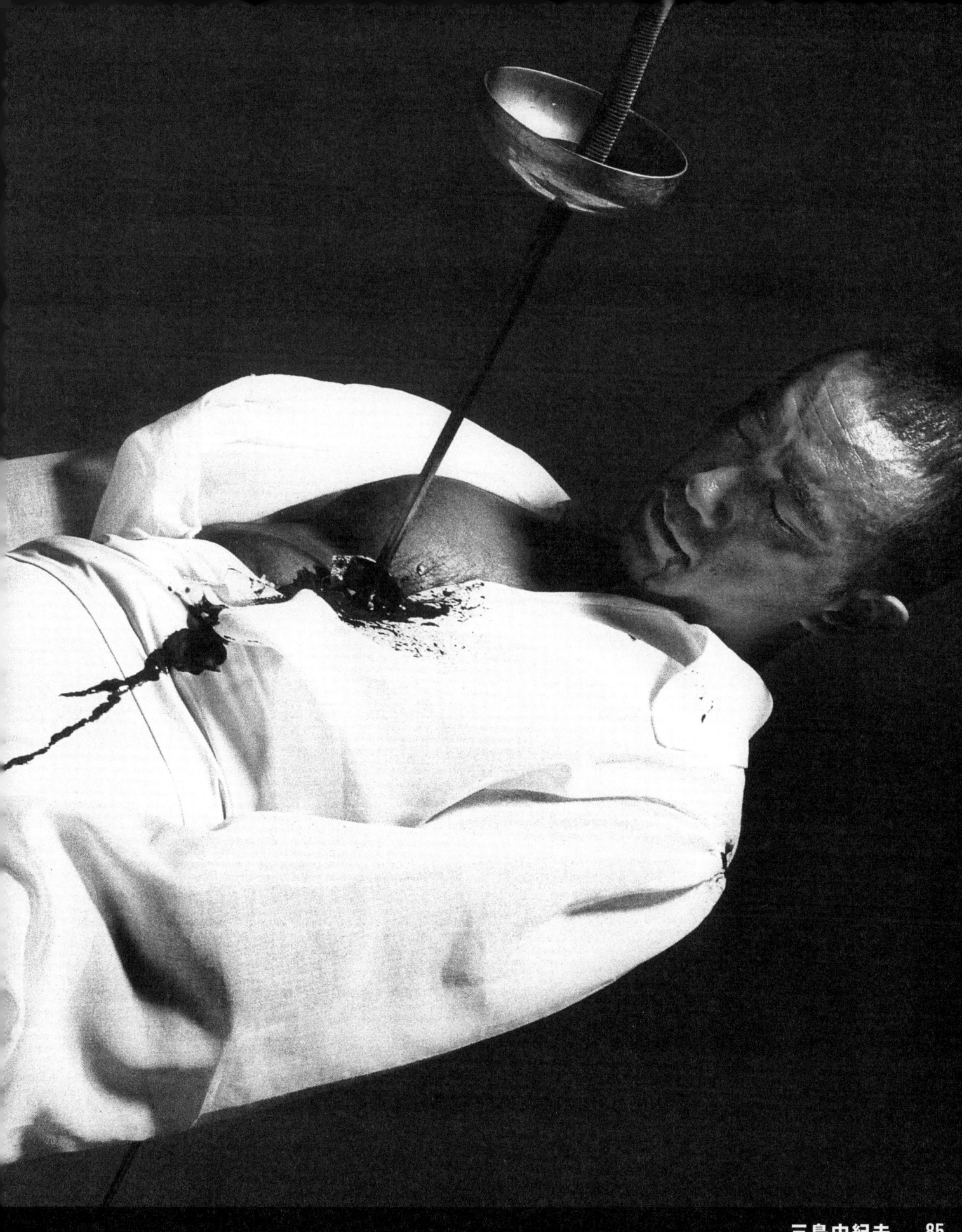

三島由紀夫

YOKOO TADANORI
横尾忠則
1936—

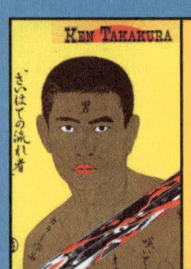

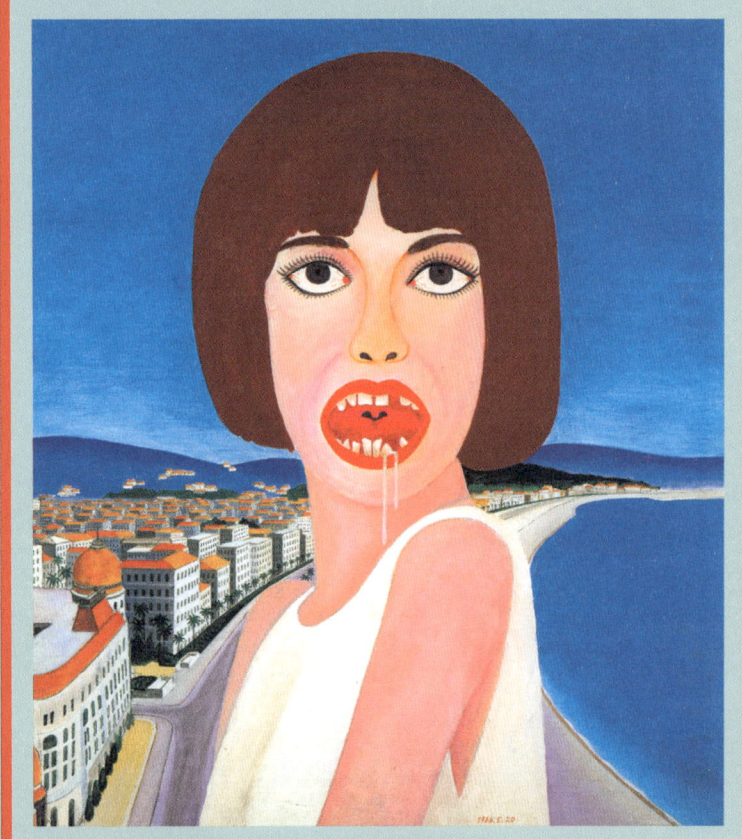

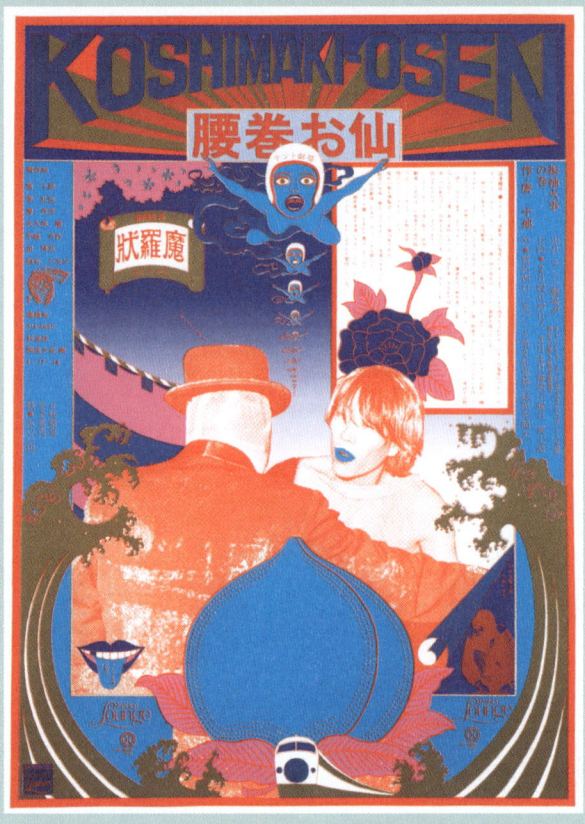

Above (left): **Yokoo Tadanori**, *Drooling*, 1966, acrylic on canvas.

Above (right): **Yokoo Tadanori**, *Koshimaki-Osen*, 1966, silkscreen.

Opposite (above left): **Yokoo Tadanori**, *Razor*, 1966, acrylic on canvas.

Opposite (above right): **Yokoo Tadanori**, *Mona Lisa*, 1966, acrylic on canvas.

Opposite (below): **Yokoo Tadanori**, *Blue Wonderland*, 1973, silkscreen.

'During the avant-garde period of the '60s, something new was created and broken down every day. It was a very energetic period. I think the desire to destroy the established rule is what constructed those avant-garde art movements. This culture did not end there, and the experience still lives within us today.'

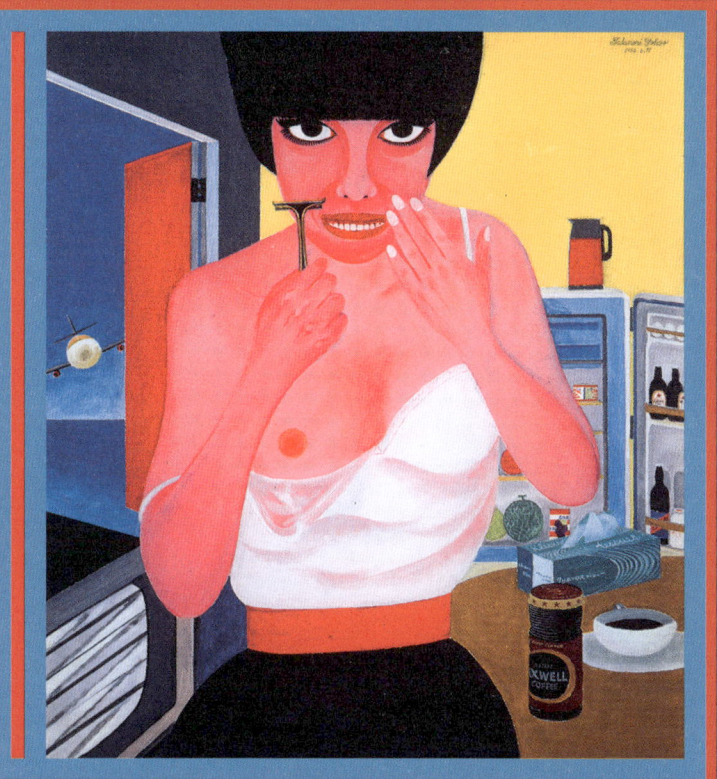
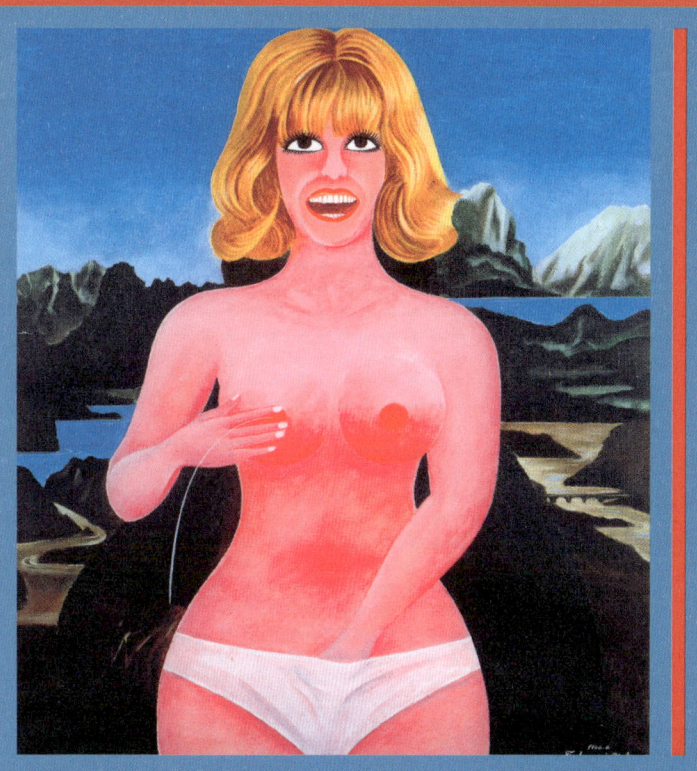

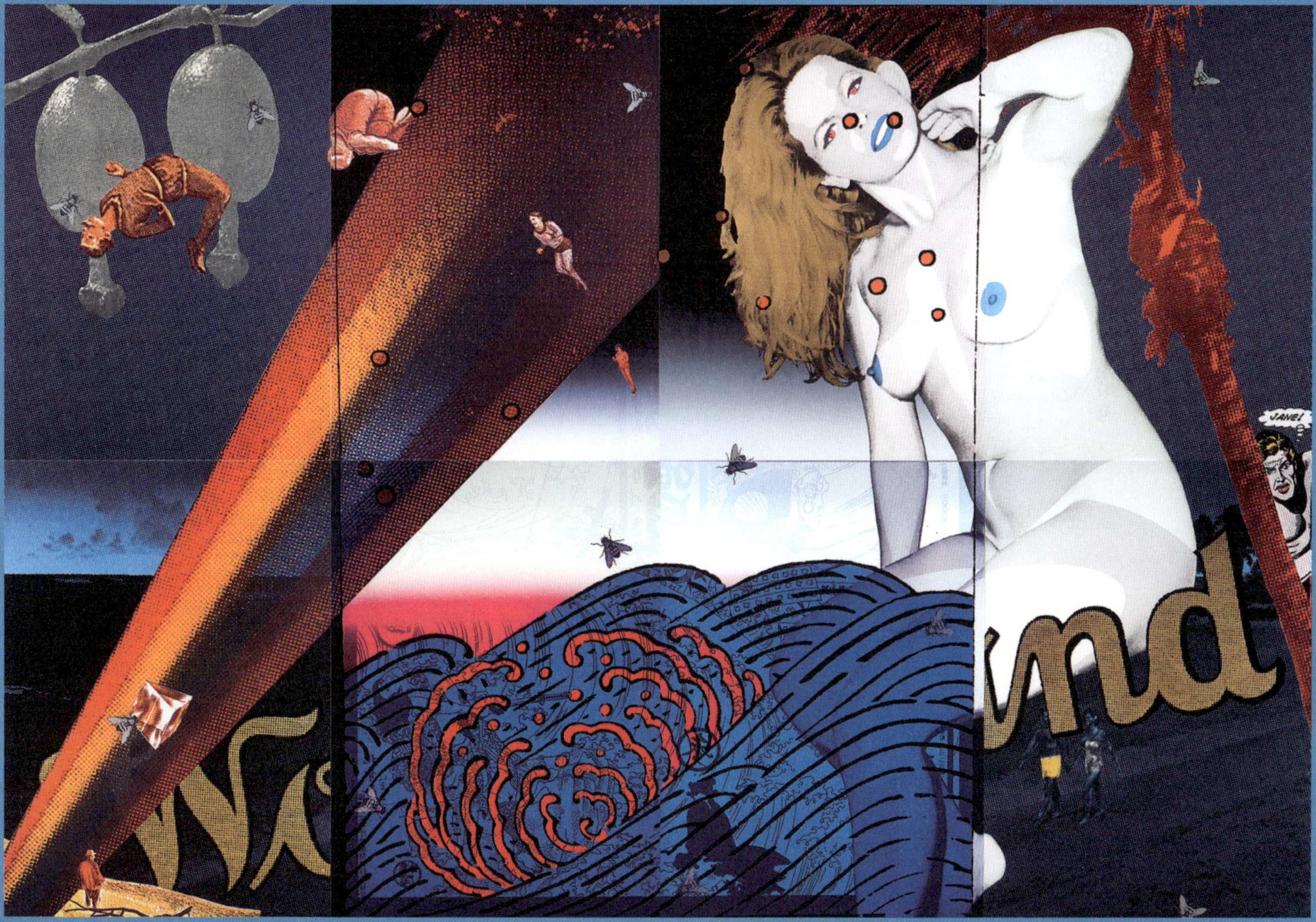

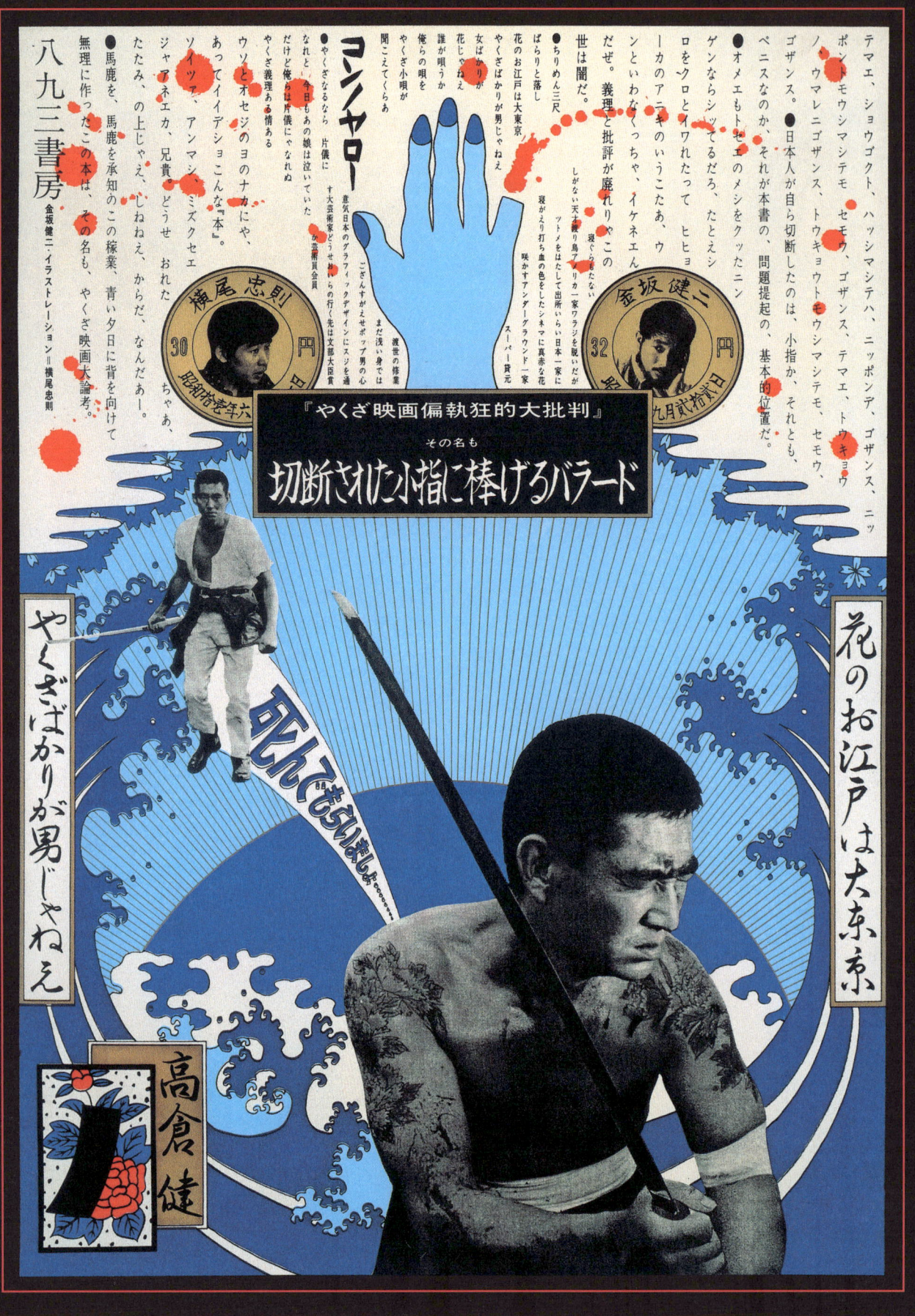

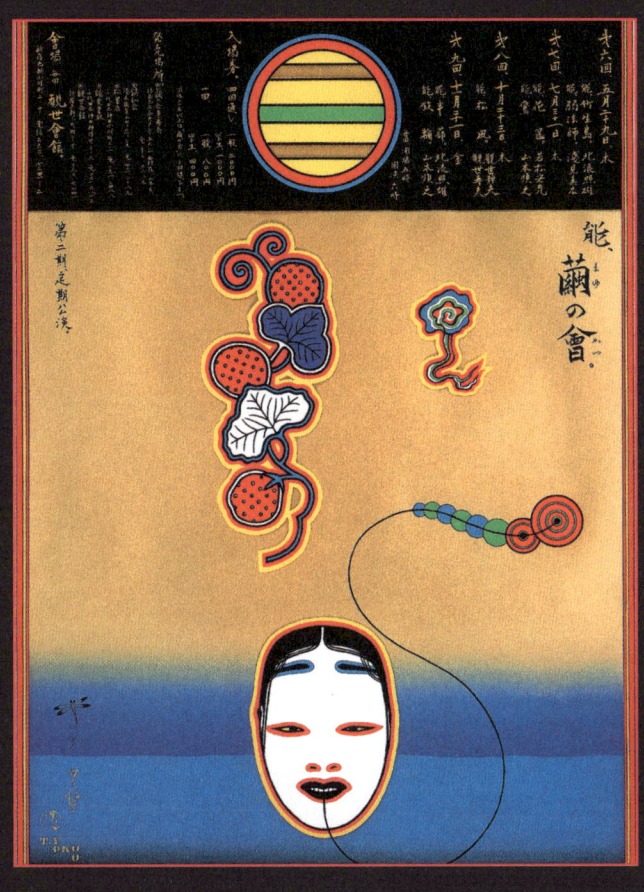

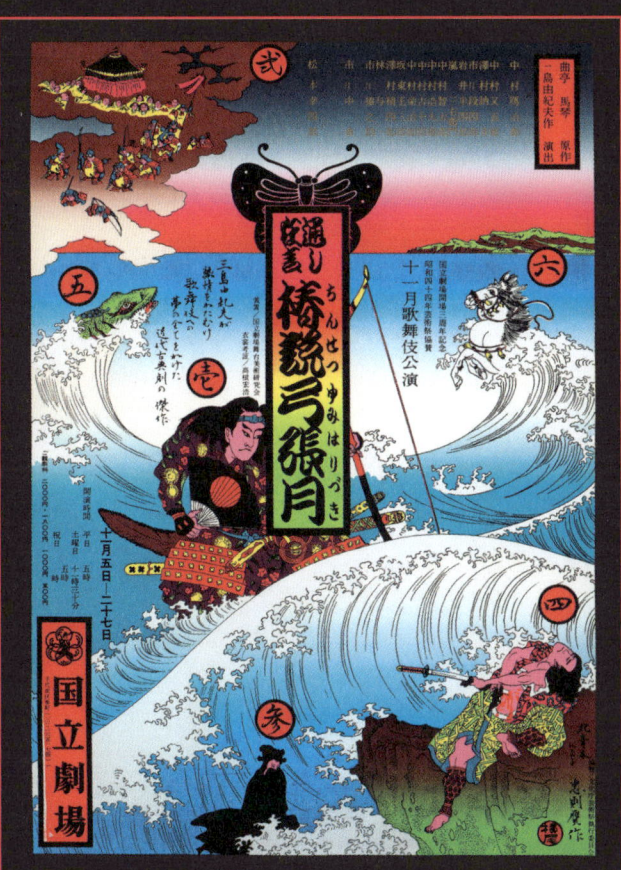

'WHEN THE PACIFIC WAR HAPPENED, SUDDENLY, GRUMMAN FIGHTER PLANES FROM THE USA ATTACKED US DURING THE MORNING ASSEMBLY IN THE SCHOOLYARD. I WASN'T SHOT SO I SURVIVED IT, BUT IT GAVE ME A VERY REAL FEAR OF DEATH.

WE WERE NOT IN A SIMULATION, WE CONFRONTED DEATH DIRECTLY IN FRONT OF US. THAT'S WHY MY ART HAS IMAGES OF DEATH, AND SOMETIMES SHOWS CONFLICTS AND WAR. THAT FEAR HAS REMAINED INGRAINED IN MY BODY AS A MEMORY EVER SINCE. THOSE MEMORIES STILL MOTIVATE MY PAINTINGS TODAY.

I THINK MAKING THINGS IS AN ACT OF CONSTRUCTION AND DESTRUCTION. WAR IS ABOUT DESTRUCTION, ISN'T IT? IT'S NOT ABOUT CREATION.

BUT BECAUSE OF THE DESTRUCTIVE ACT THAT THE WAR INFLICTS ON US, THE DESIRE TO CREATE IS EVEN STRONGER.

IN THE 1960S, THERE WERE MANY PEOPLE WHO EXPERIENCED WAR, AND I THINK THIS CULTURE WAS CREATED BY THEM.'

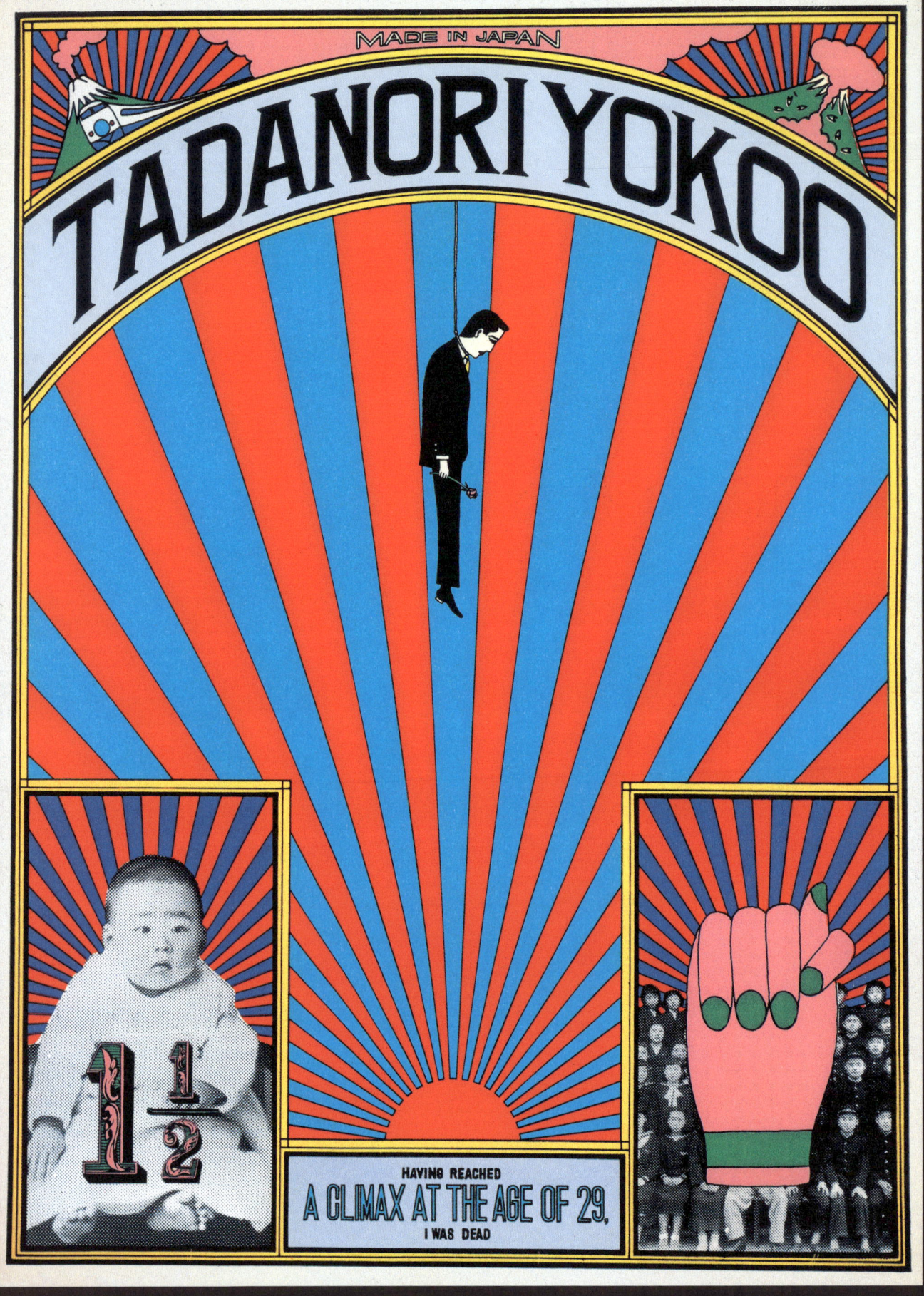

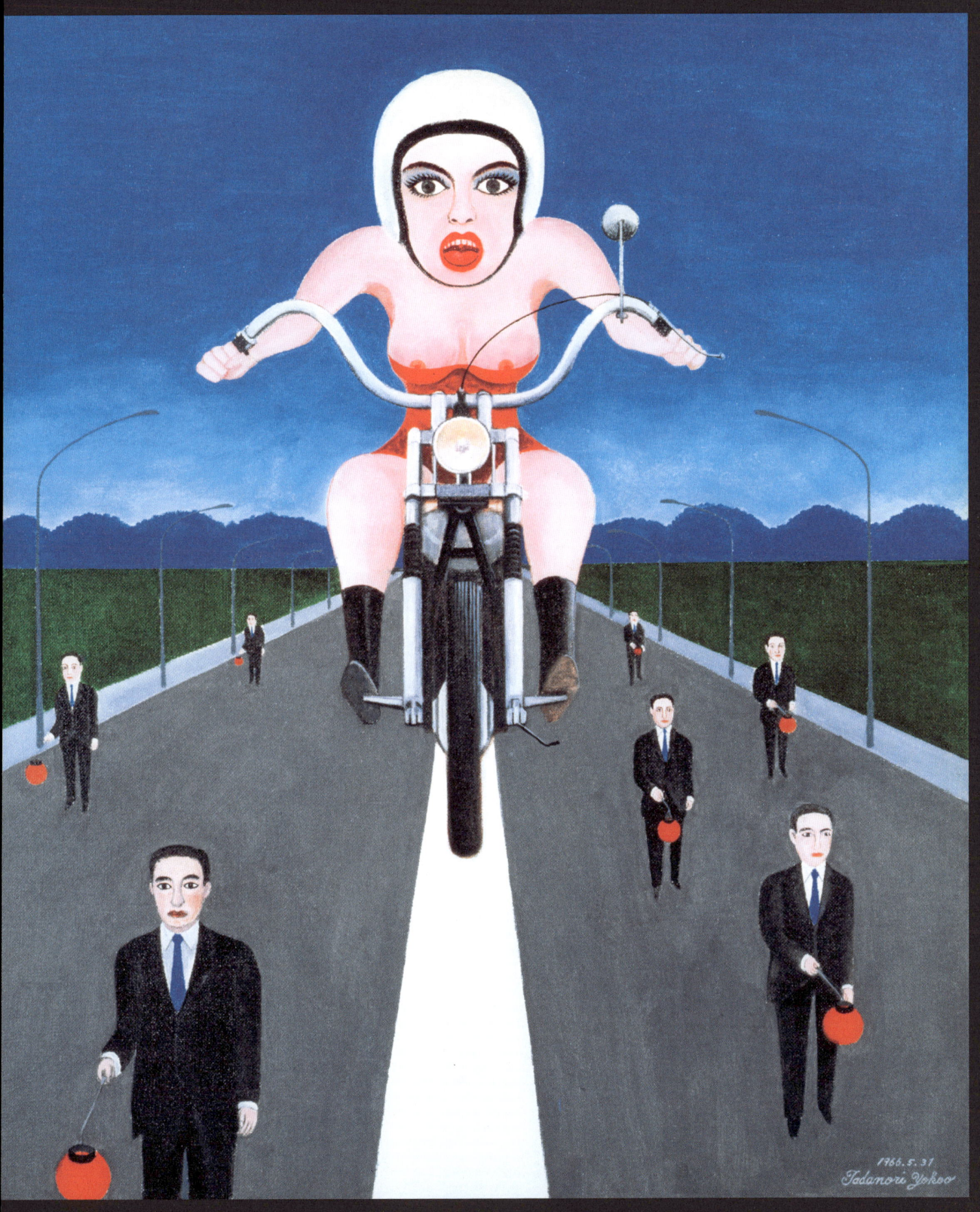

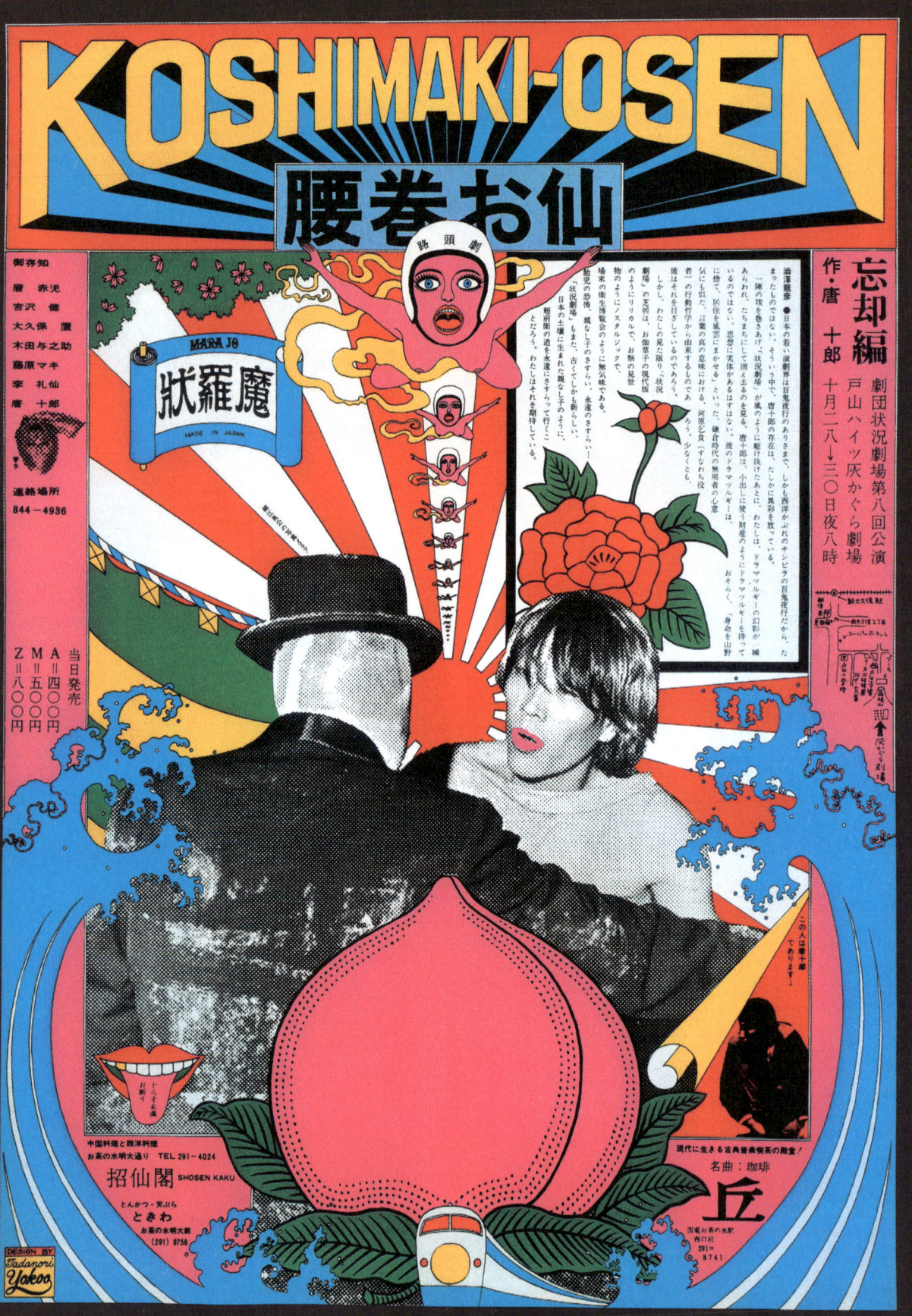

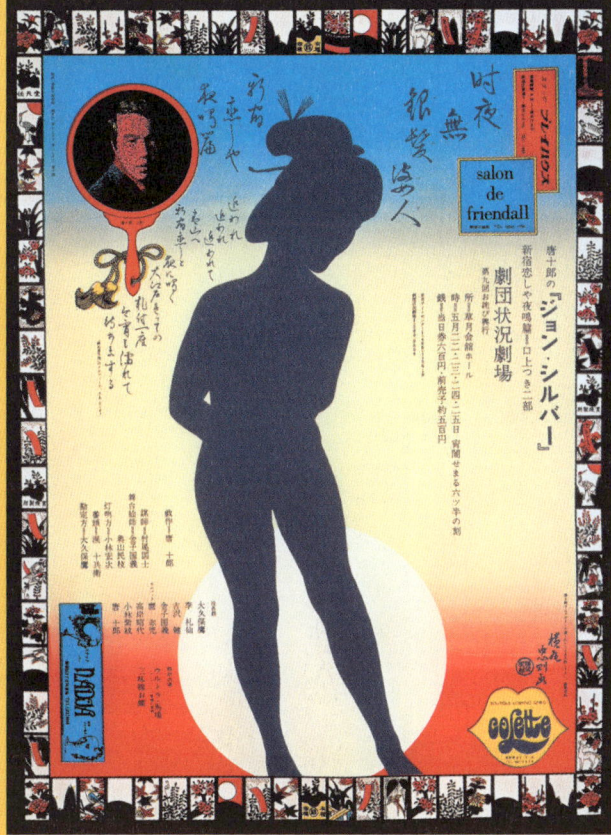

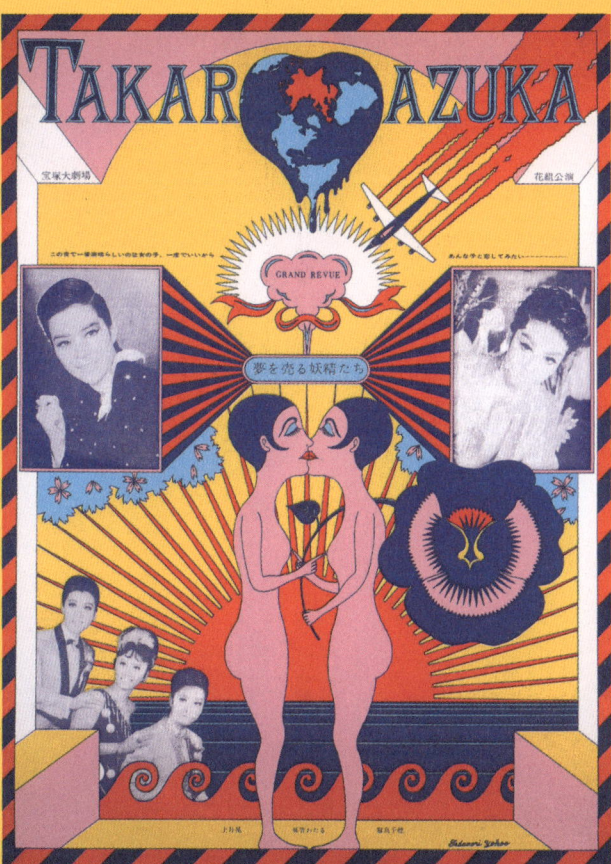

In the flattened cultural landscape of post-war Japan, where high art and popular entertainment collided to form a new avant-garde, posters gained currency as an innovative medium for the dissemination of ideas and information. With their intense colours and irreverent, often surreal iconography, the posters were designed to make an immediate impression on Tokyo's busy streets. They testify to an atmosphere of radical enthusiasm and creative liberty at this moment of political instability.

The boundaries between art, graphic design and illustration were relatively fluid in Japan at this time, and icons of the counterculture such as Yokoo Tadanori and Aquirax Uno rose to prominence with posters that explored the shared ground between these art forms.

The posters were designed to spread the word about underground performances and events that proliferated across Tokyo during the 1960s and '70s.

The *angura* scene, which encompassed experimental theatre, dance and film, attracted many artists who went on to participate in different aspects of production, including the creation of posters.

Yokoo Tadanori is perhaps the most widely recognized poster artist of his generation, and his Pop vision inspired long-term collaborations with some of the era's most famous artists, both in Japan and internationally.

Yokoo's early screen-print posters combined media samples with the influence of traditional ukiyo-e woodblock prints, translated into Pop art's bold palette with an emphasis on graphic humour and explicit content.

LUCY FLEMING-BROWN

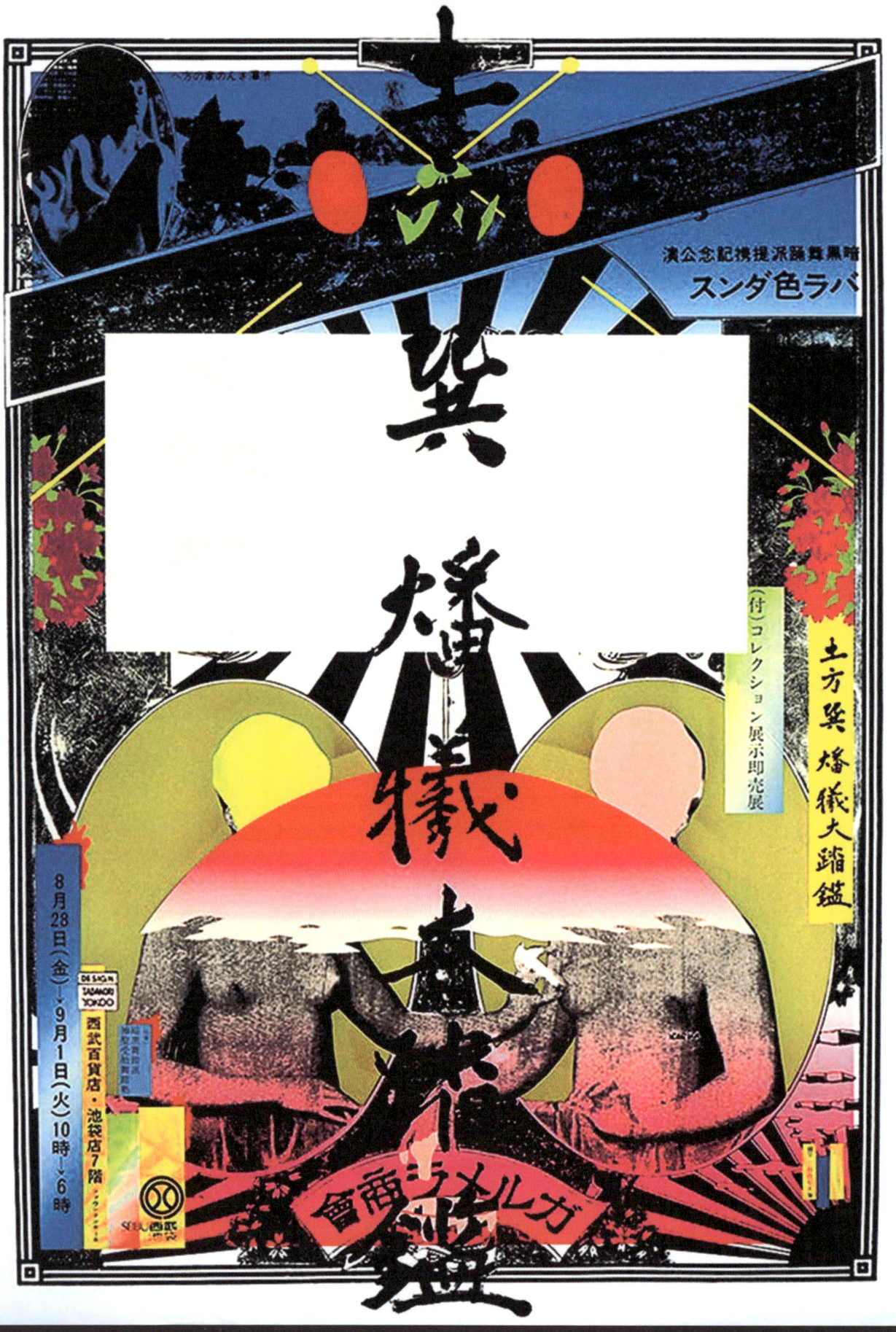

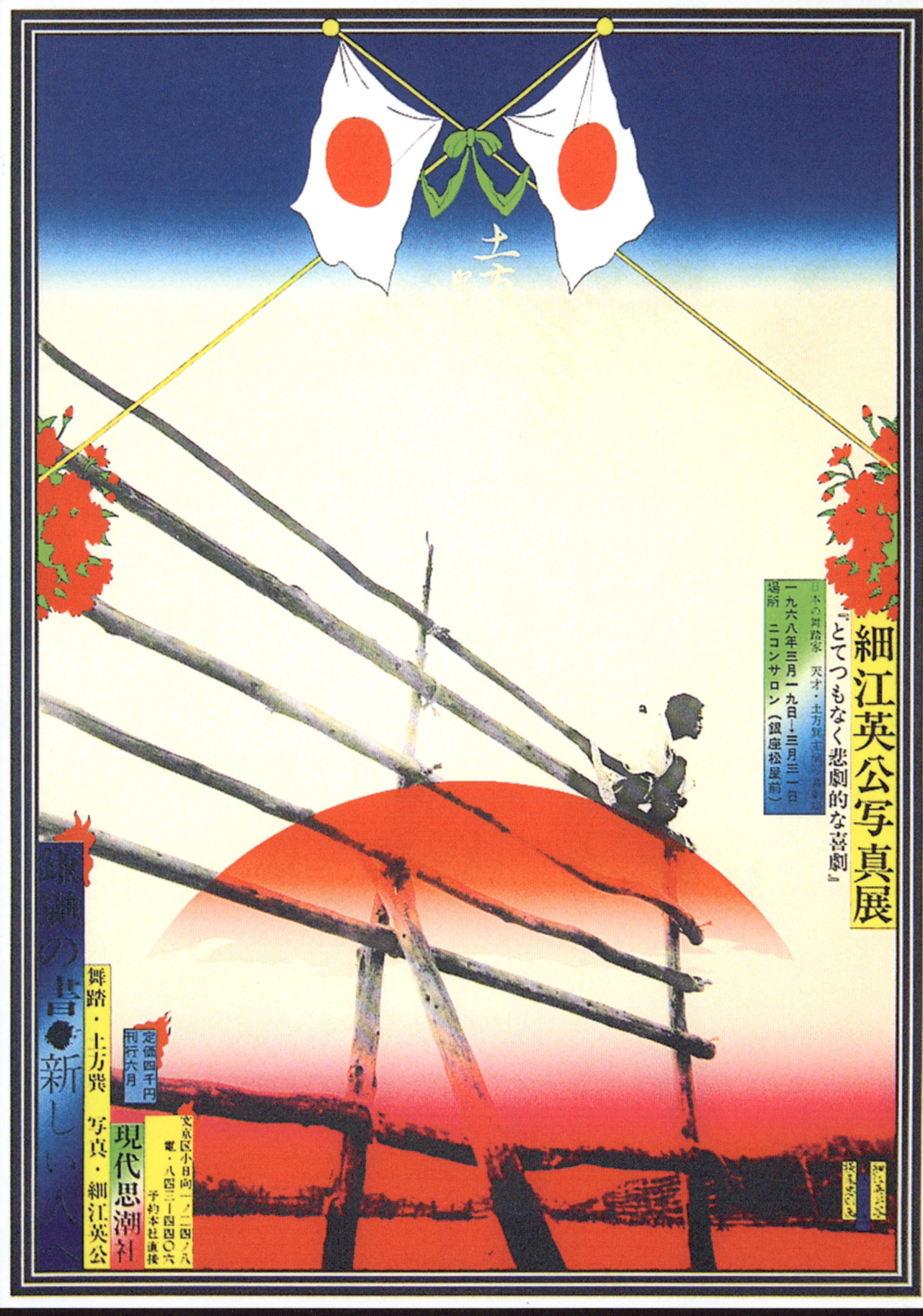

p. 88: **Yokoo Tadanori**, *Ballad for the Cut-Off Little Finger*, 1966, silkscreen on paper.

p. 89 (above): **Yokoo Tadanori**, *Poster for a Noh Play*, 1969, silkscreen.

p. 89 (below): **Yokoo Tadanori**, *The Kabuki Play Chinsetsu Yumihari-zuki (National Theatre)*, 1969, silkscreen on paper.

pp. 90 and 102 (detail): **Yokoo Tadanori**, *Tadanori Yokoo*, 1965, silkscreen on paper.

p. 91: **Yokoo Tadanori**, *Motorcycle*, 1966, acrylic on canvas.

p. 92: **Yokoo Tadanori**, *Koshimaki-Osen (Gekidan Jōkyō Gekijō)*, 1966, silkscreen on paper.

p. 93 (above): **Yokoo Tadanori**, *John Silver (Gekidan Jōkyō Gekijō)*, 1967, silkscreen on paper.

p. 93 (below): **Yokoo Tadanori**, *Takarazuka, Grand Revue*, 1966, silkscreen on paper.

p. 94: **Yokoo Tadanori**, *Hijikata Tatsumi, Mirror of Sacrificing Great Dance*, 1970, silkscreen on paper.

p. 95: **Yokoo Tadanori**, *Rose-Colored Dance Poster*, 1965, silkscreen on paper.

Above (left): **Yokoo Tadanori**, *Poetry by Mutsuo Takahashi*, 1966, silkscreen on paper.

Above (right): **Yokoo Tadanori**, *Recruiting Members for Tenjō Sajiki*, 1967, silkscreen on paper.

Opposite: **Yokoo Tadanori**, *À La Maison de M. Civeçawa (Garumera Shōkai)*, 1965, silkscreen on paper.

'*Angura* is the Japanese word for "underground". People like Terayama Shūji, Kara Jūrō, Hijikata Tatsumi, Ōshima Nagisa and others interacted and became famous. From knowing Terayama, Hosoe Eikō and Mishima, works in the fields of theatre, film and music were created during that period. I felt a strong sense of fate. It wasn't that I had planned everything, reached out to those people, and deliberately decided to work with them.

In Surrealism, there is a term called "dépaysement", which refers to the unexpected and mysterious encounter of things that are not inherently related. I feel like something similar happened within human relationships at that time. And without those encounters, that era itself might never have come into being.'

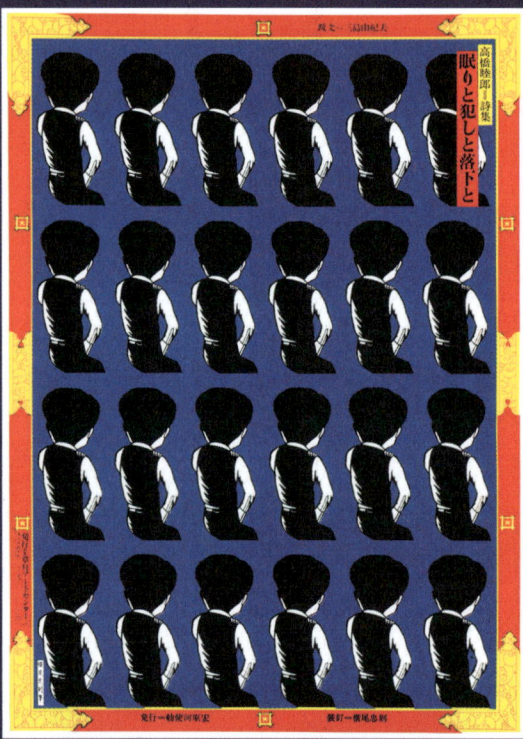

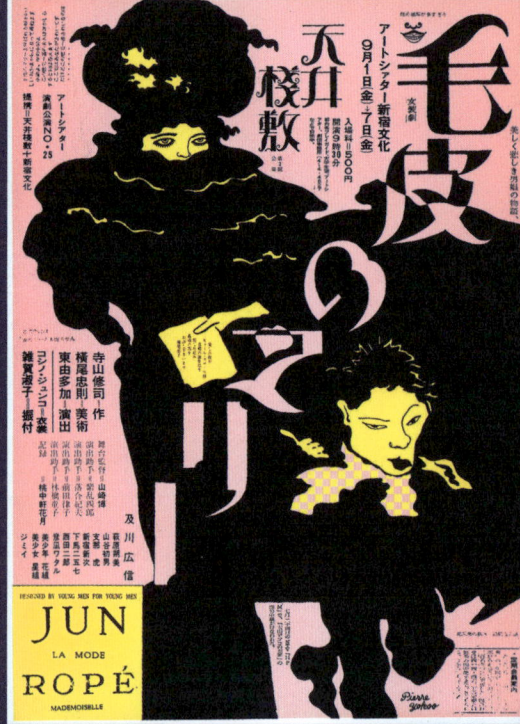

Yokoo Tadanori designed the poster for Hijikata Tatsumi's *Rose-Colored Dance*, and this was very impactful. Yokoo imagined things like bullet trains out of Hijikata's dance or a pattern of the Japanese rising sun, and he kept accumulating images. The posters became the witnesses of an era. Theatre is known as a mirror to the times already, so it follows that the posters would also reflect the times. They provided the space where the most creativity could happen.

SASAME HIROYUKI

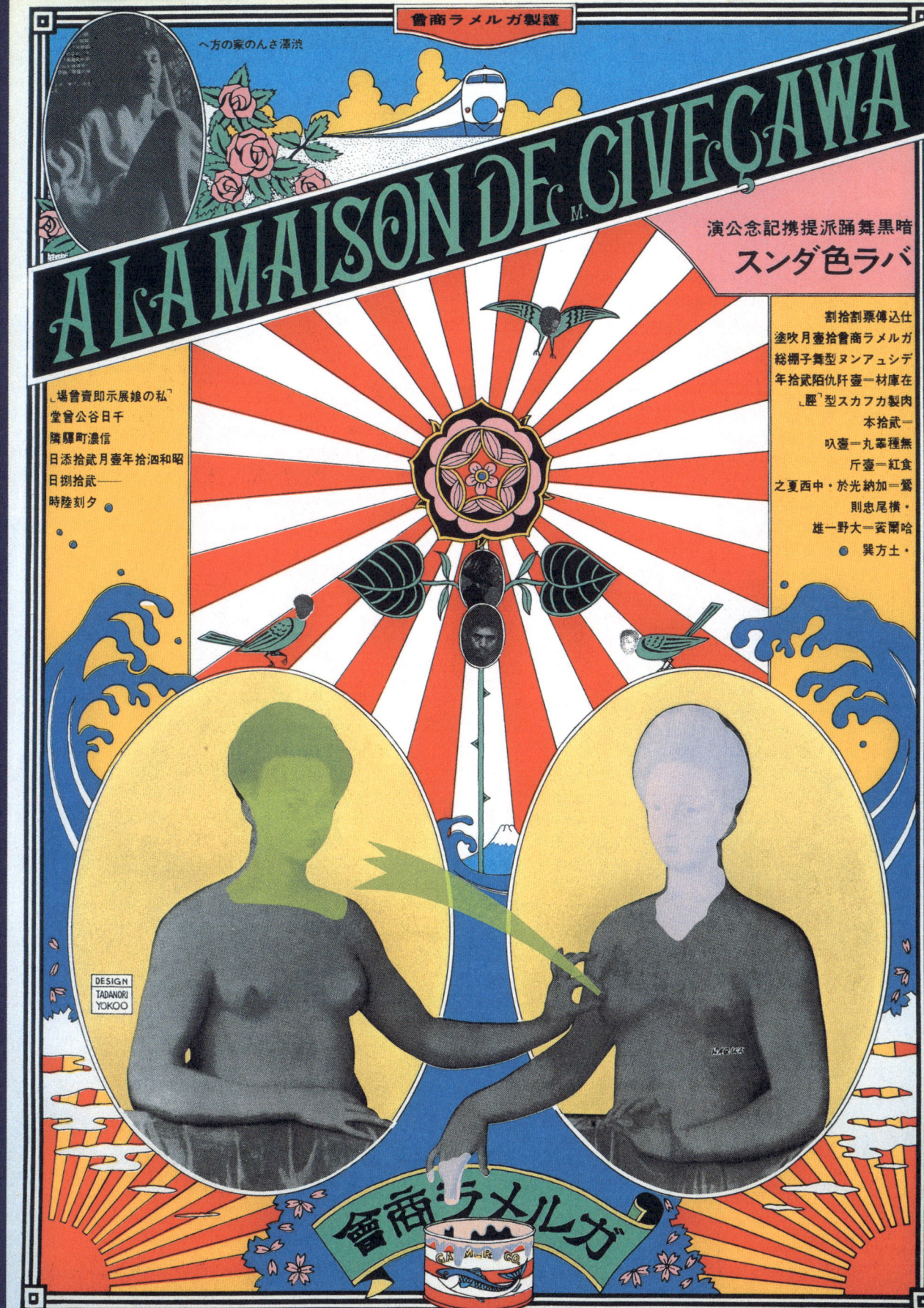

'My inspiration comes from everyday life, or it might come from the world of death, or from experiences gained from multiple reincarnations. These experiences might appear as imagination when I'm drawing. I think they come from all possible realms.

I was born in a textile town, so as a child, I went to the fields and rice paddies, where I experienced the colourful scenery of dyed threads and cloth hung out to dry in nature. I remember experiencing landscapes with these beautiful colours, such as red, yellow, blue, green and purple. I have a longing for such vivid colours, I think they are the colours inside me. I am influenced by the colours of different places in the world, and they come out naturally in me through my subconscious.'

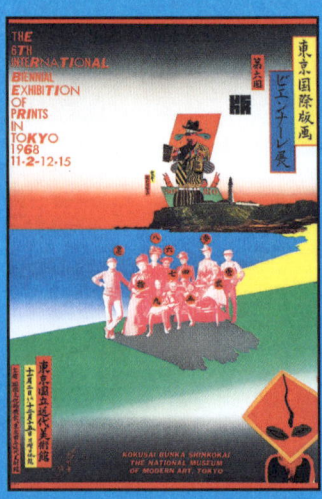

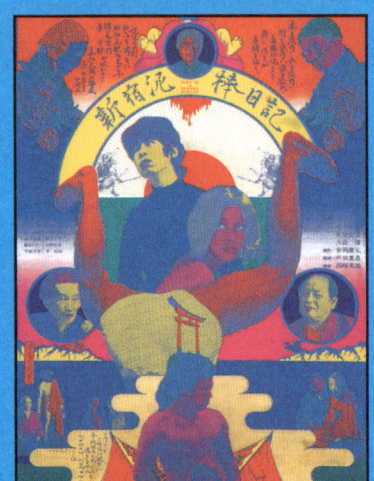

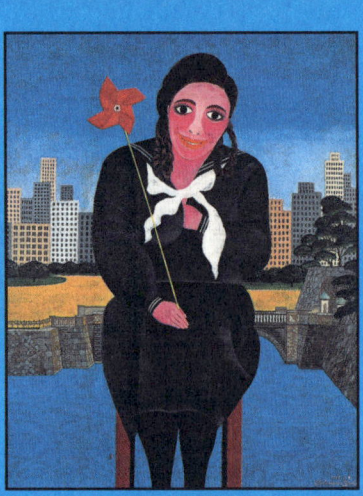

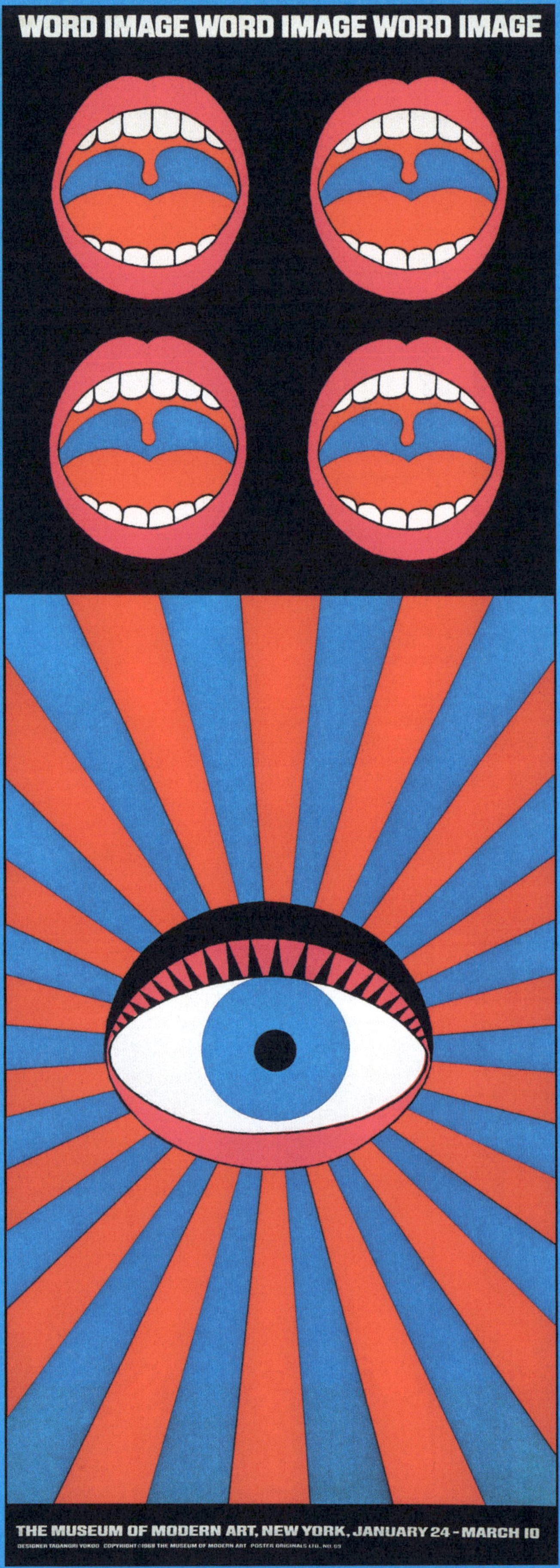

Above (left): **Yokoo Tadanori**, *The 6th International Biennial Exhibition of Prints in Tokyo*, 1968, silkscreen.

Above (right): **Yokoo Tadanori**, *Diary of a Shinjuku Burglar*, 1968, silkscreen.

Right: **Yokoo Tadanori**, *Pinwheel*, 1966, acrylic on canvas.

Far right: **Yokoo Tadanori**, *Word and Image*, 1968, silkscreen.

'In Japan, there was no drug culture in the 1960s. There was a bit of it in the entertainment industry, but not in the arts. Among artists and creators, drugs were nonexistent. That's why artists expressed their visions purely through their art, without the external influences that shaped psychedelic art movements in the West.

The term "psychedelic" as a cultural concept originates from the West and is tied to their cultural expressions. That's why my work ended up being labelled as part of that movement. But in reality, I never considered my work to be "psychedelic" in the way it is understood in the West.

I first went to New York in 1967. At that time, I held an exhibition at a gallery there, showcasing a series of my works that I had created in 1965, including pieces related to theatre.

Meanwhile, the American psychedelic movement didn't start until 1966 or 1967, so there's a significant gap in time between my work and the rise of psychedelic art in America. That's why, even now, it feels strange to hear people assume that my art was a product of that movement.'

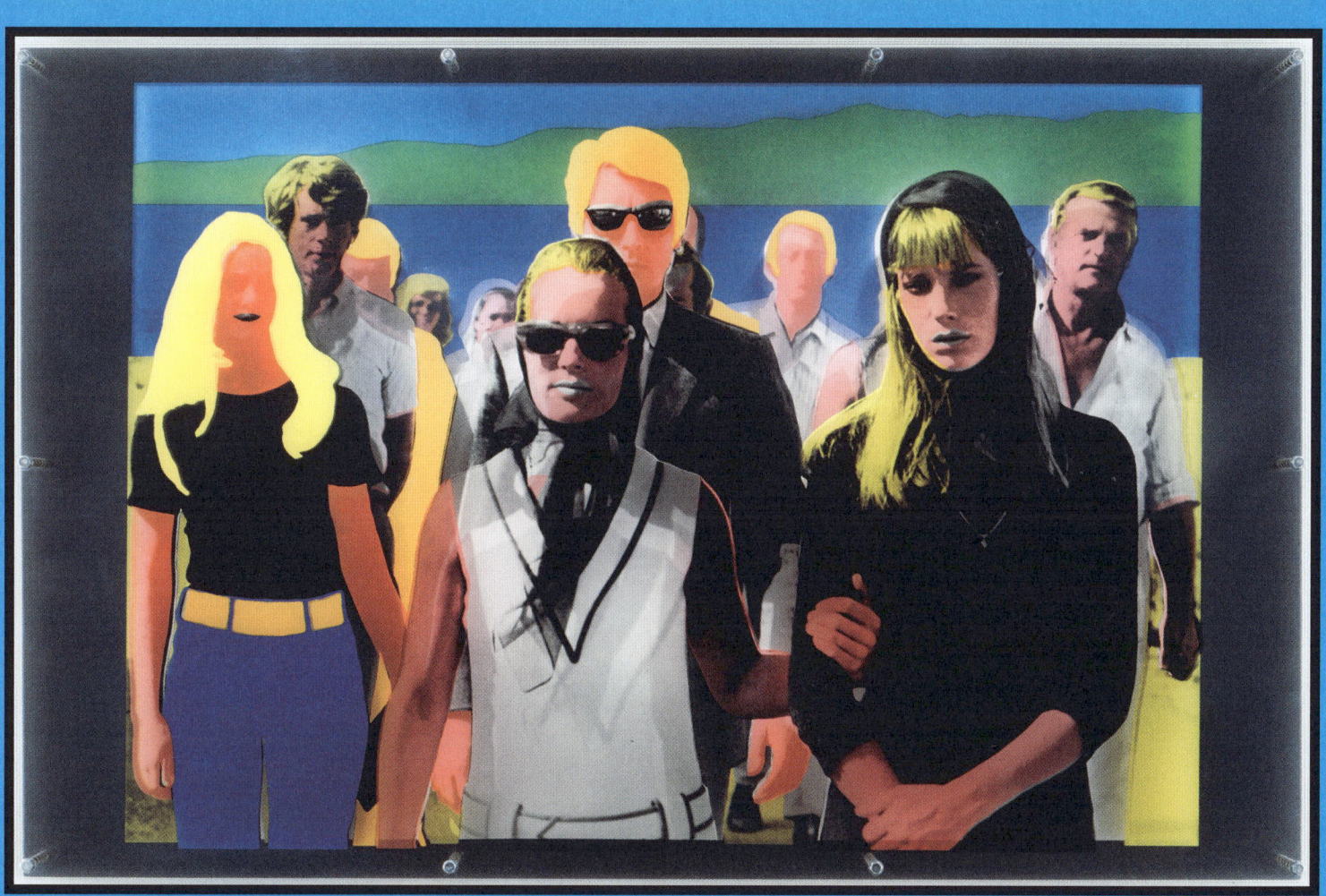

WHAT YOKOO DID WAS NOT TO GET MINUS BY MULTIPLYING PLUS, BUT TO GET PLUS BY MULTIPLYING MINUS. IT WAS A SPIRITUAL EXCHANGE THROUGH DAMP AND SHADY CHANNELS HIDDEN DEEP INSIDE OF MEN'S HEARTS. IT WAS THE OPPOSITE OF SO-CALLED INTERNATIONAL FRIENDSHIP, TOURISM, WORLD TRENDS, INDUSTRIALIZED SOCIETY, URBANIZATION, AND MASS SOCIETY.

THE WARMTH AND DARKNESS UNIQUE TO YOKOO'S ART IS THEREFORE SPIRITUAL. BECAUSE IT WAS BASED ON COMMUNICATION BETWEEN MINDS, IT IS CALLED SPIRITUALISM, WHICH IS THE MOST ADVANCED COMMUNICATION METHOD IN THE 20TH CENTURY.

MISHIMA YUKIO

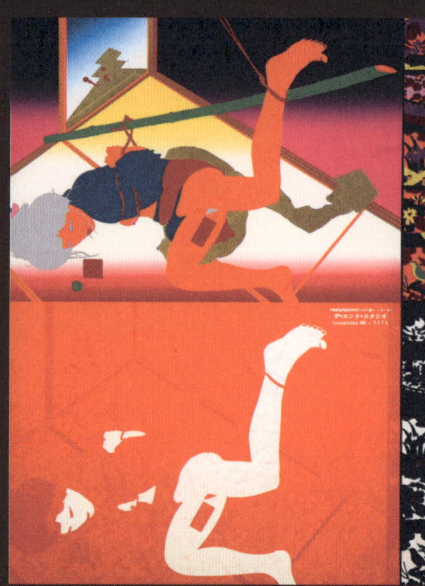

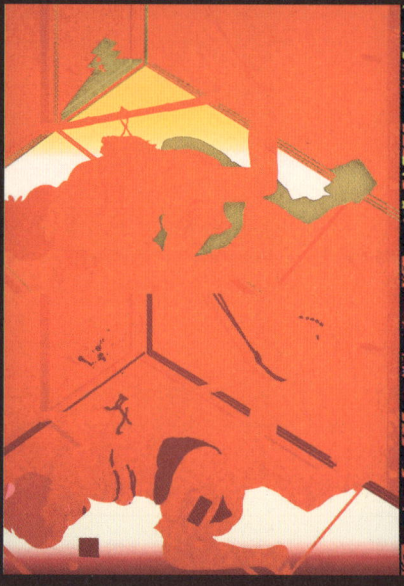

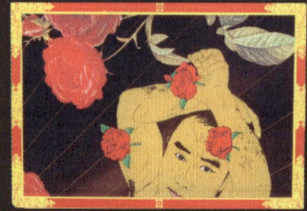 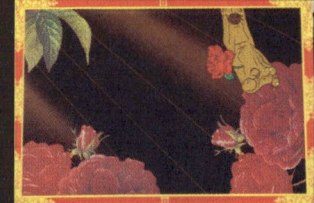

p. 99: **Yokoo Tadanori**, *Funeral Procession II*, 1969–85, silkscreen.

Far right (above): **Yokoo Tadanori**, *Torture A*, 1969, silkscreen on paper.

Far right (middle): **Yokoo Tadanori**, *Torture B*, 1969, silkscreen on paper.

Far right (below): **Yokoo Tadanori**, *Torture C*, 1969, silkscreen on paper.

Right: **Yokoo Tadanori**, *Ordeal by Roses*, new edition (Shueisha, 1971), bookbinding.

Opposite: **Yokoo Tadanori**, *Stranger from the Wilderness*, 1967, offset lithograph.

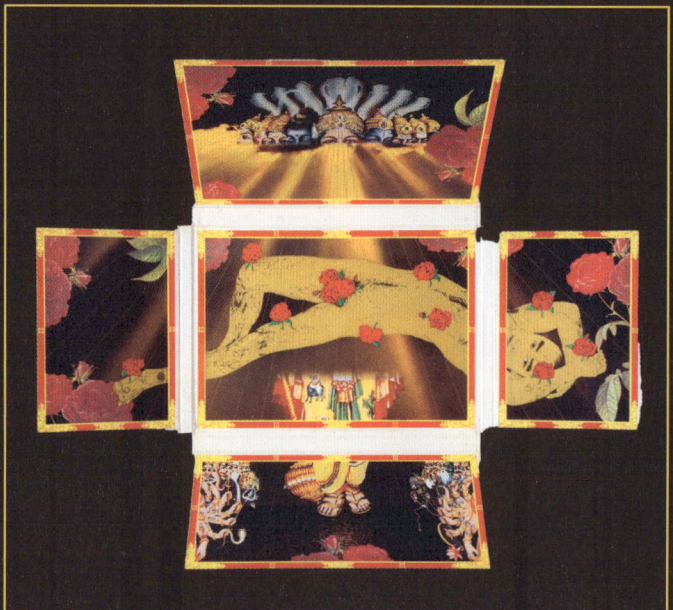

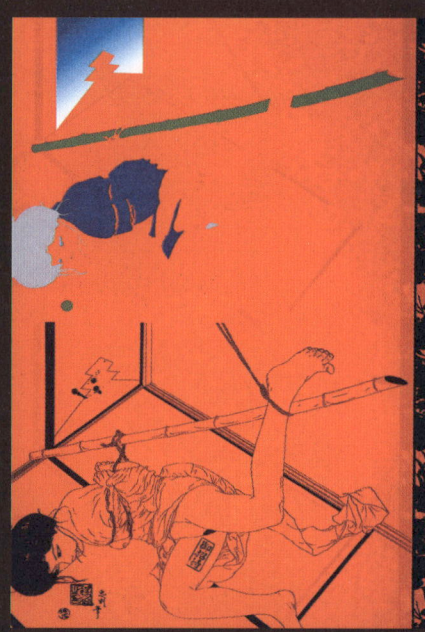

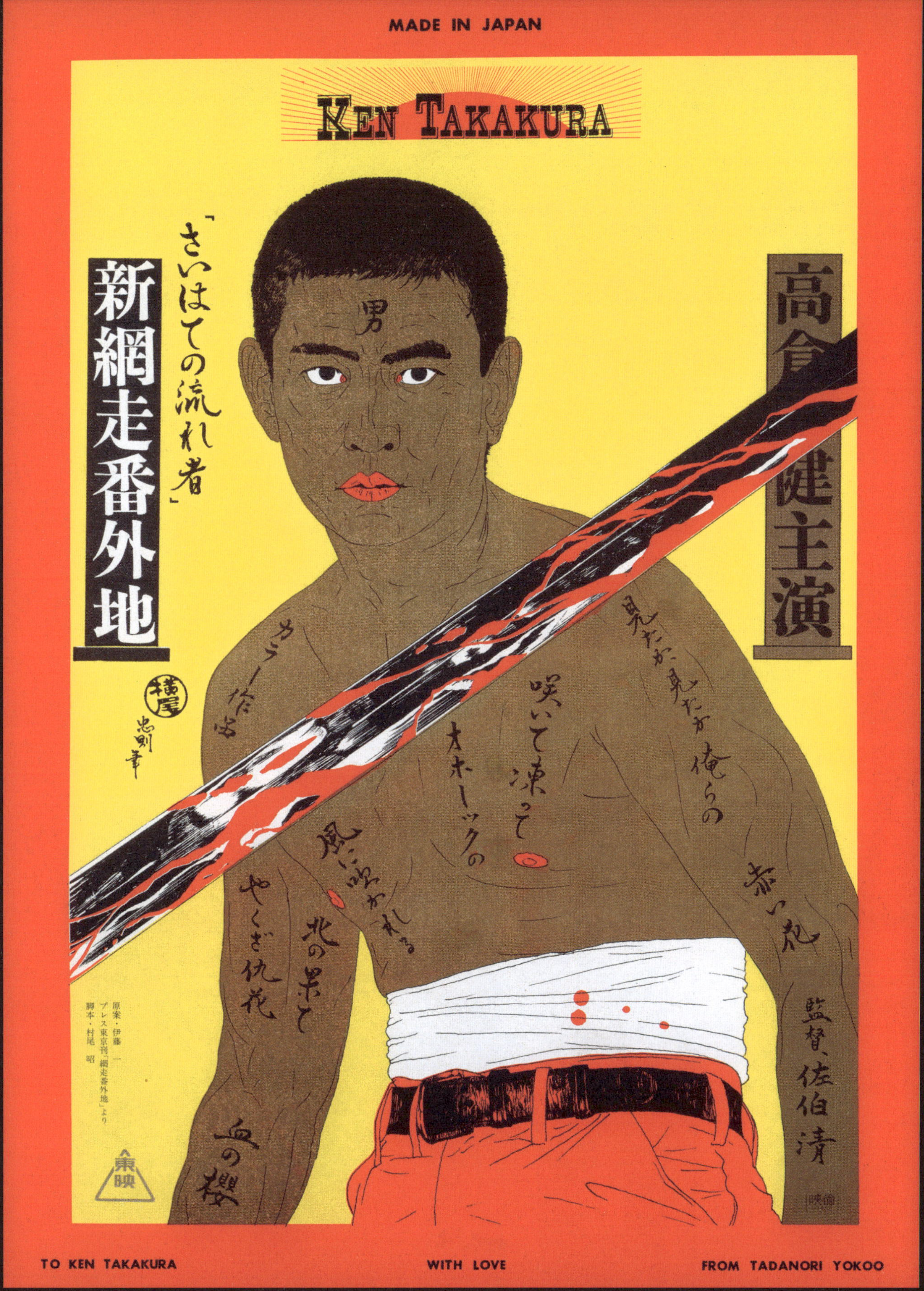

MADE IN JAPAN

KEN TAKAKURA

「さいはての流れ者」
新網走番外地

高倉健主演

監督・佐伯清

原案・伊藤一
プレス東京刊「網走番外地」より
脚本・村尾昭

TO KEN TAKAKURA　　　WITH LOVE　　　FROM TADANORI YOKOO

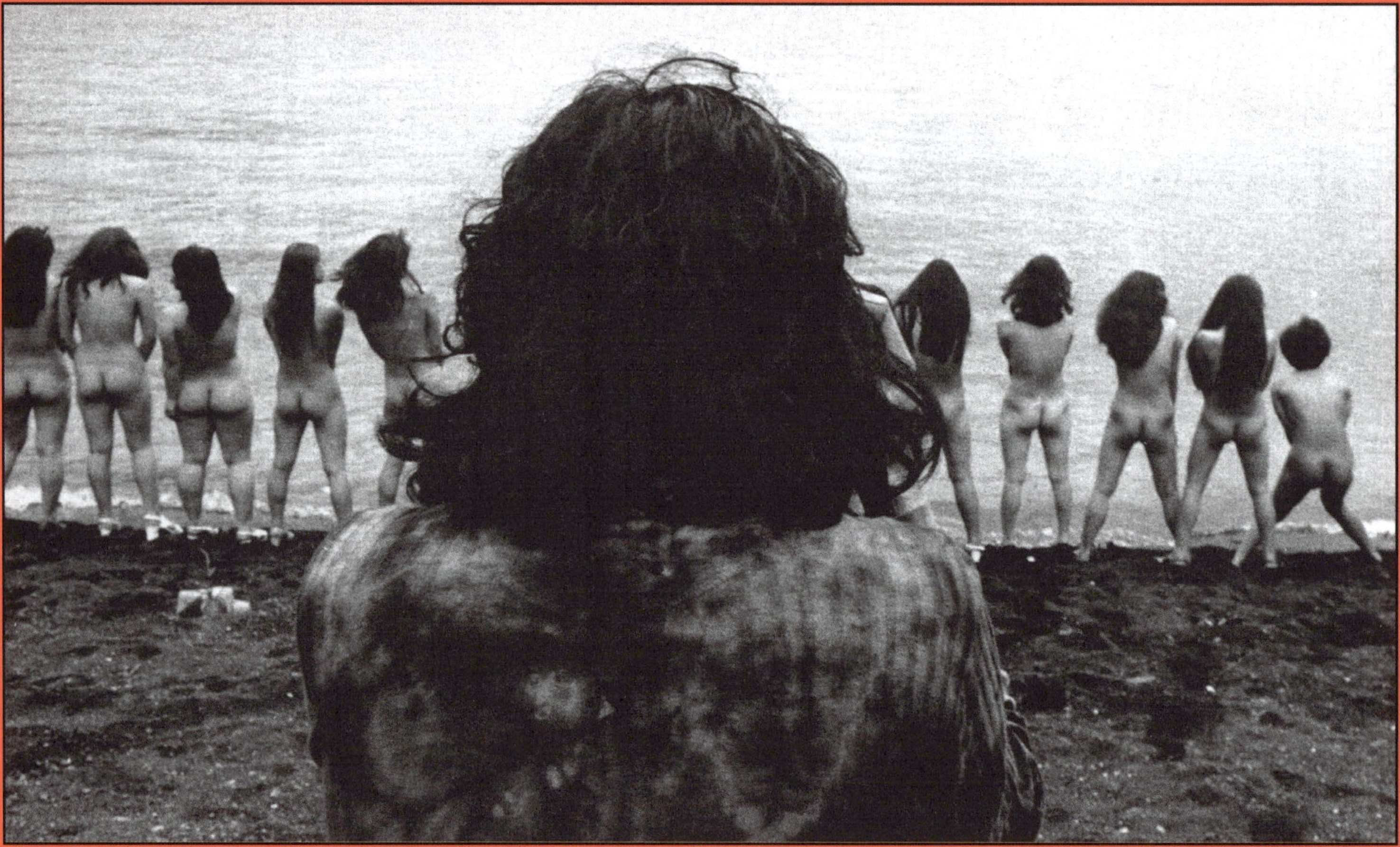

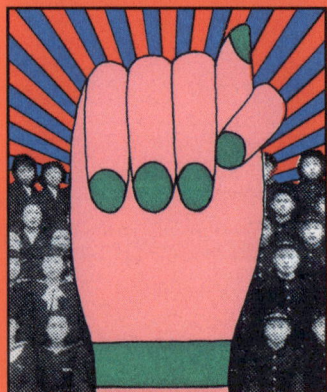

Above and right: **Yokoo Tadanori**, Photographs from *The Complete Tadanori Yokoo Book*, 1971.

Opposite: **Yokoo Tadanori**, *Seni-kan pavilion, Expo '70, Osaka*, 1970.

p. 104: **Yokoo Tadanori**, *Hong Kong*, 1997, acrylic and oil on canvas.

p. 105: **Yokoo Tadanori**, *Bride*, 1966, acrylic on canvas.

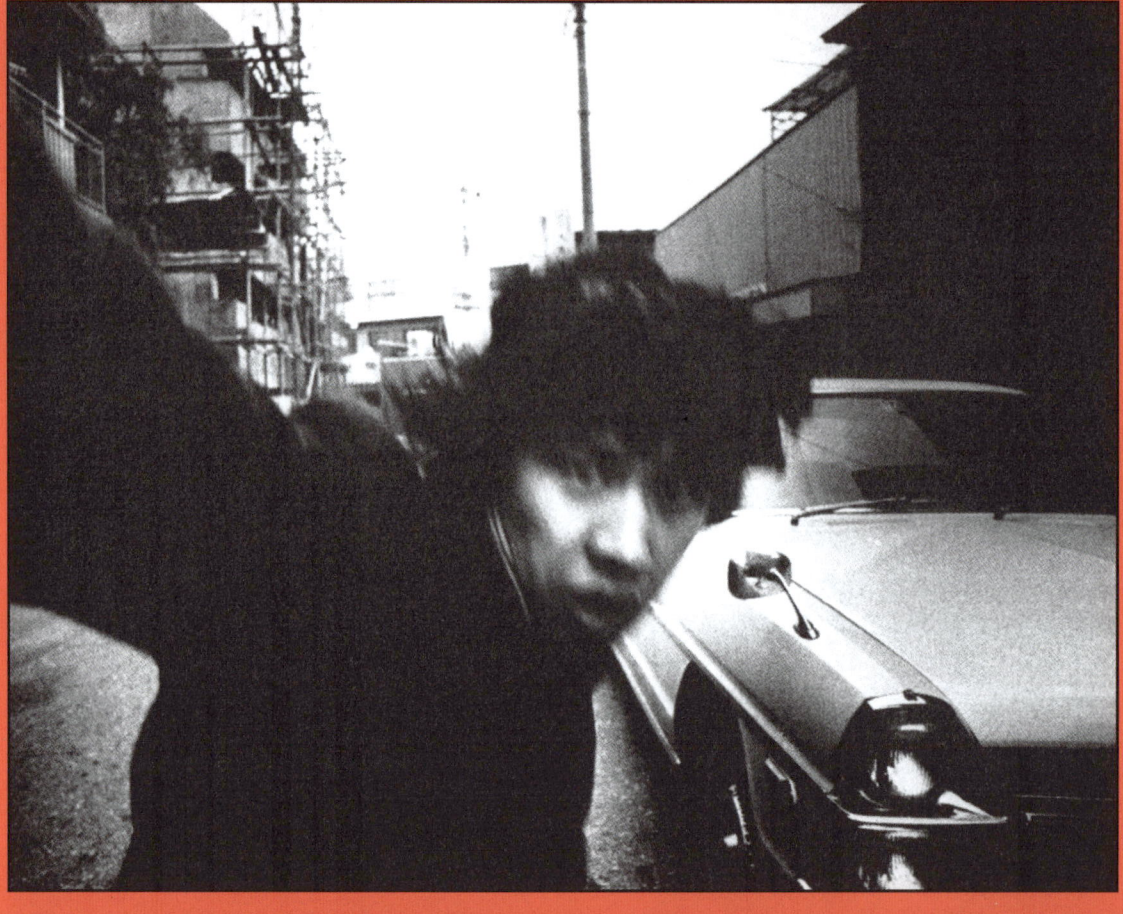

EXPO '70, OSAKA

At Expo '70 in Osaka, Yokoo Tadanori was responsible for the architectural design of the Seni-kan pavilion. During a site visit while the dome was still under construction, he noticed the scaffolding surrounding the structure. At that moment, he wondered: 'Would it be possible to leave this scaffolding in place and complete the building in an unfinished state?'

Despite strong opposition, he pushed forward with this idea, resulting in an unprecedented pavilion that became a major topic of discussion.

This 'unfinished art' with its bright red scaffolding was a direct expression of Yokoo's lifelong artistic philosophy – that the creativity of art is best expressed through incompleteness. Additionally, his approach of perceiving art as a process and dynamic movement resonated with the international contemporary art trends of the late 1960s, demonstrating Yokoo's pioneering vision.

MINAMI YUSUKE

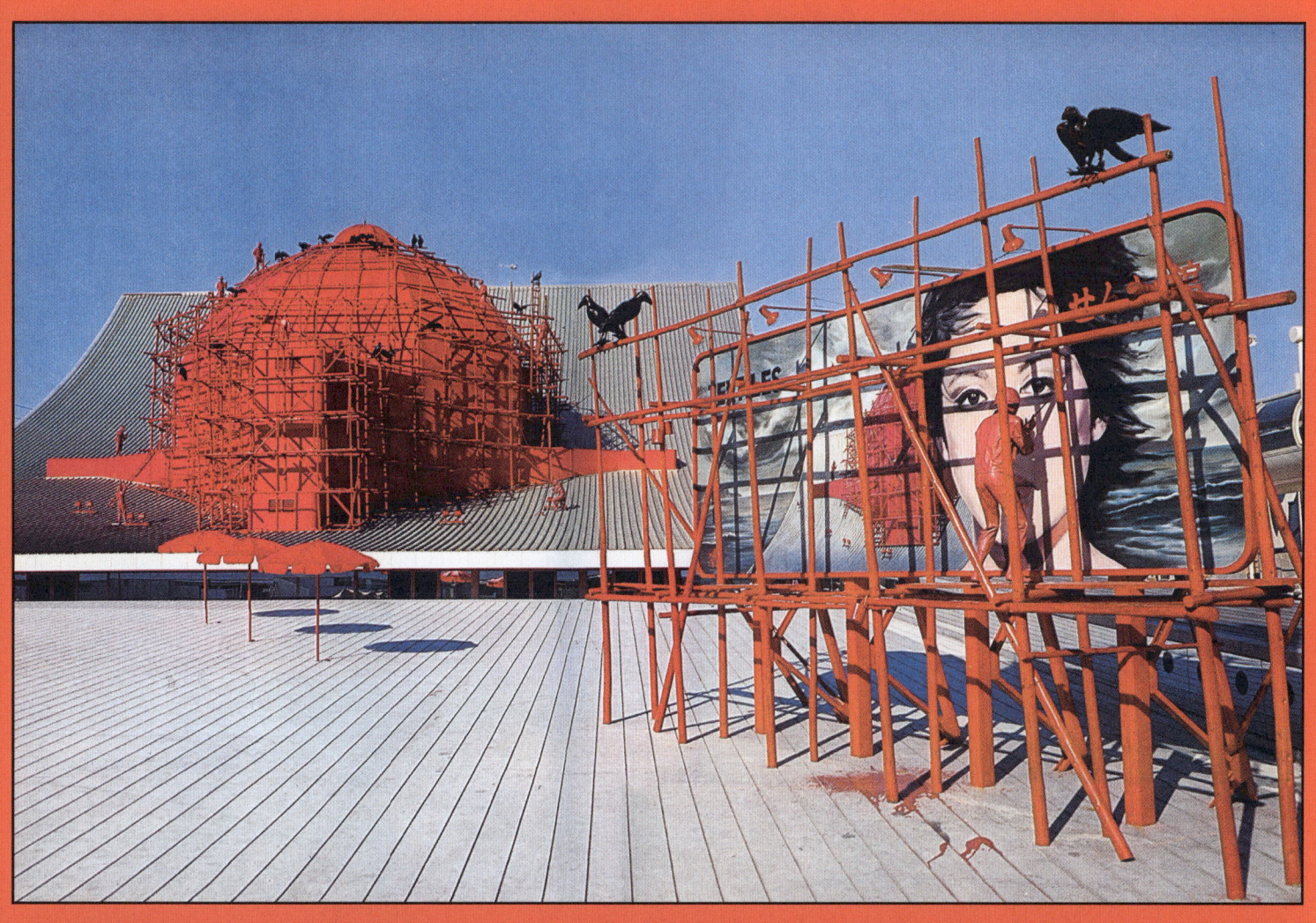

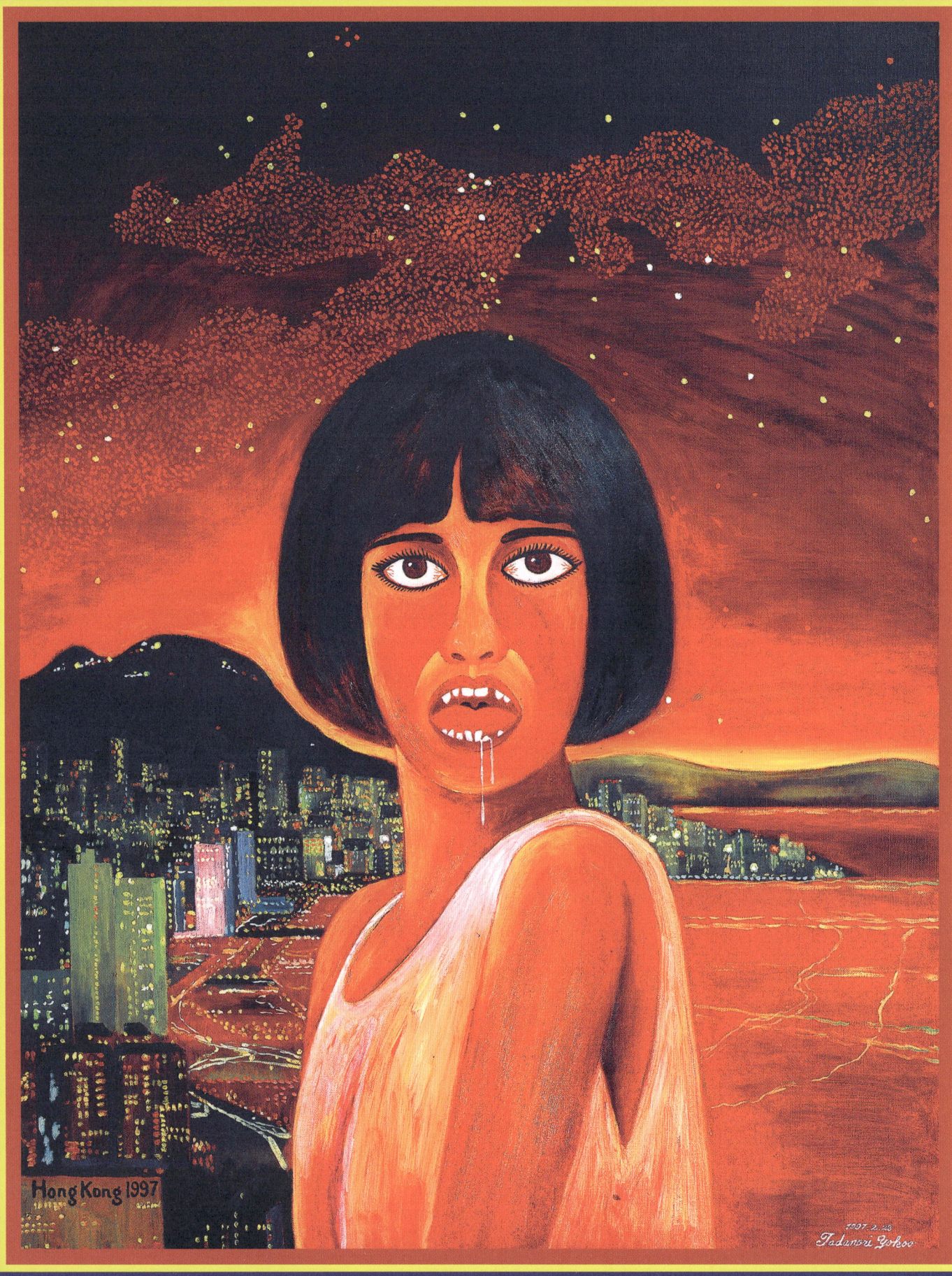

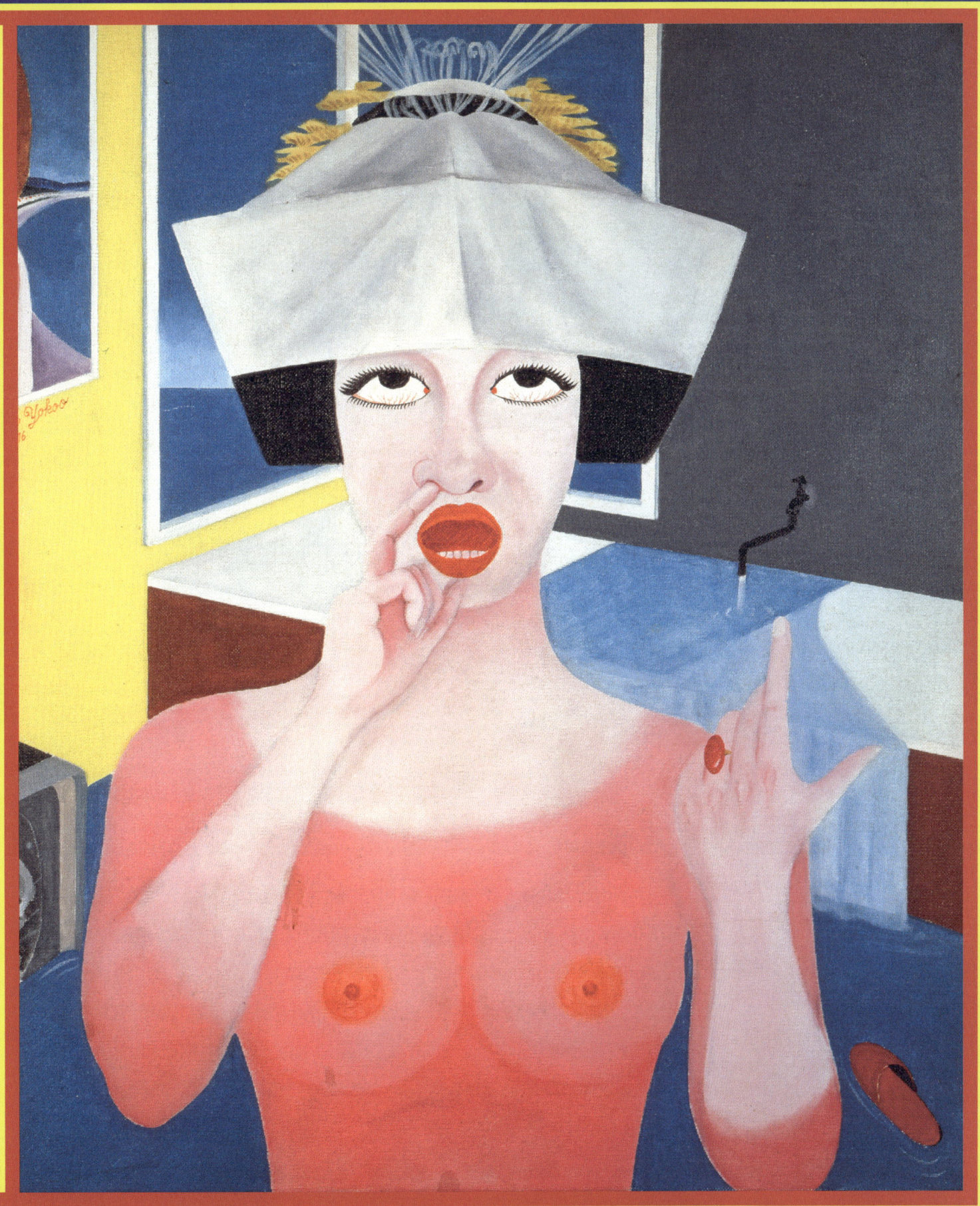

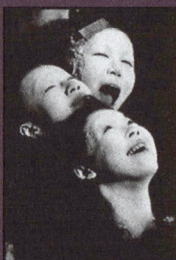

BUTOH
1959

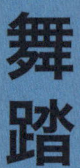

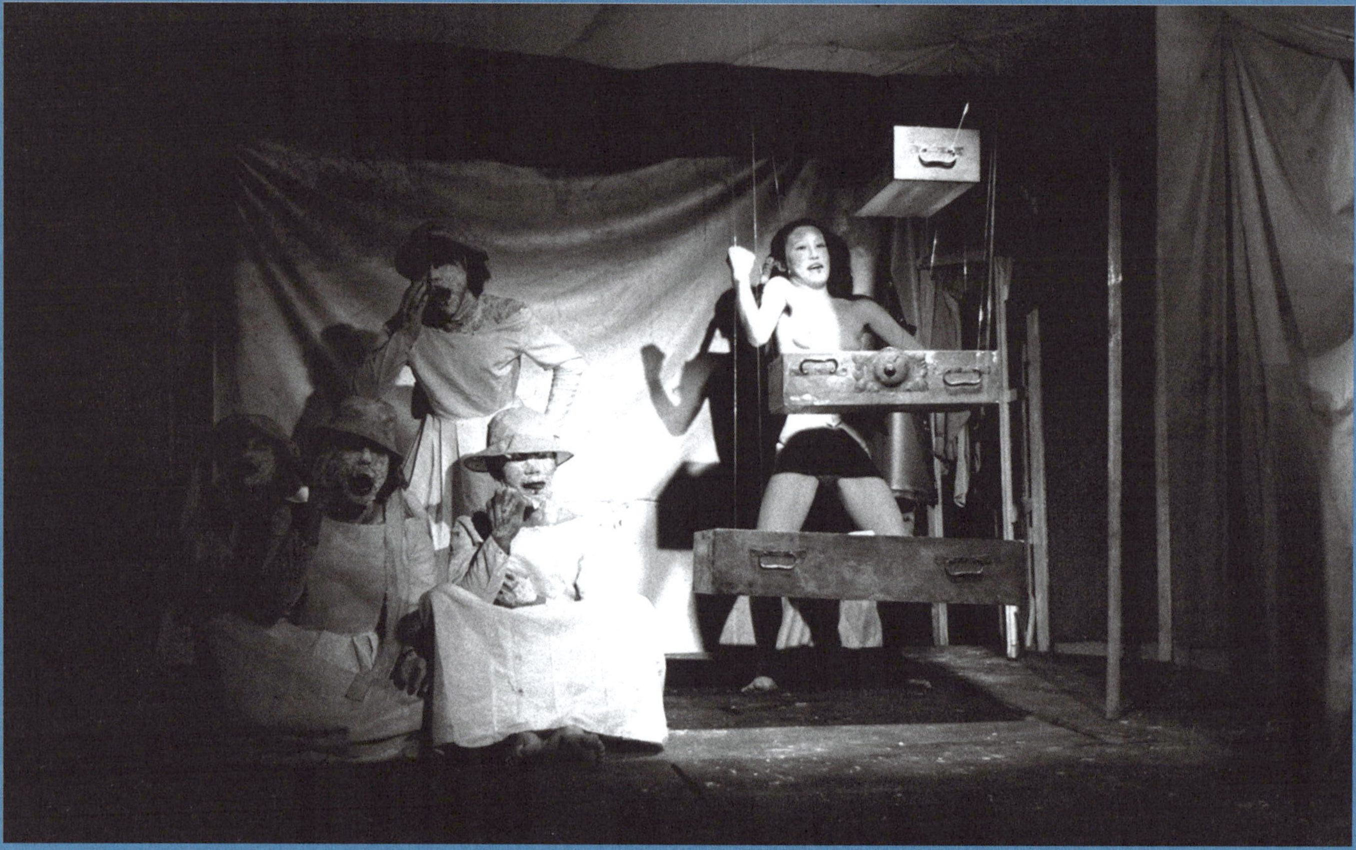

Nakatani Tadao, *Note of Regret (Zannenki)*, 1971, gelatin silver print.

Opposite (above left): **Nakatani Tadao**, *Mitsutaka Ishii Butoh with a Hose*, 1966, gelatin silver print.

Opposite (above right): **Nakatani Tadao**, *An experimental photograph at the Asbestos Studio*, 1970, gelatin silver print.

Opposite (below): **Hanaga Mitsutoshi**, *Ariadone Society*, 1970s, gelatin silver print.

The *ankoku butoh* movement originated on 24 May 1959, with Hijikata Tatsumi's first major performance, *Forbidden Colours (Kinjiki)*. In its representation of perverse savagery, primitive sacrifice and homosexual passion, Hijikata's expressionistic performance aimed to uncage a primal energy at the core of man's physical being. An energy suppressed and forgotten in modern society.

ALEXANDRA MUNROE

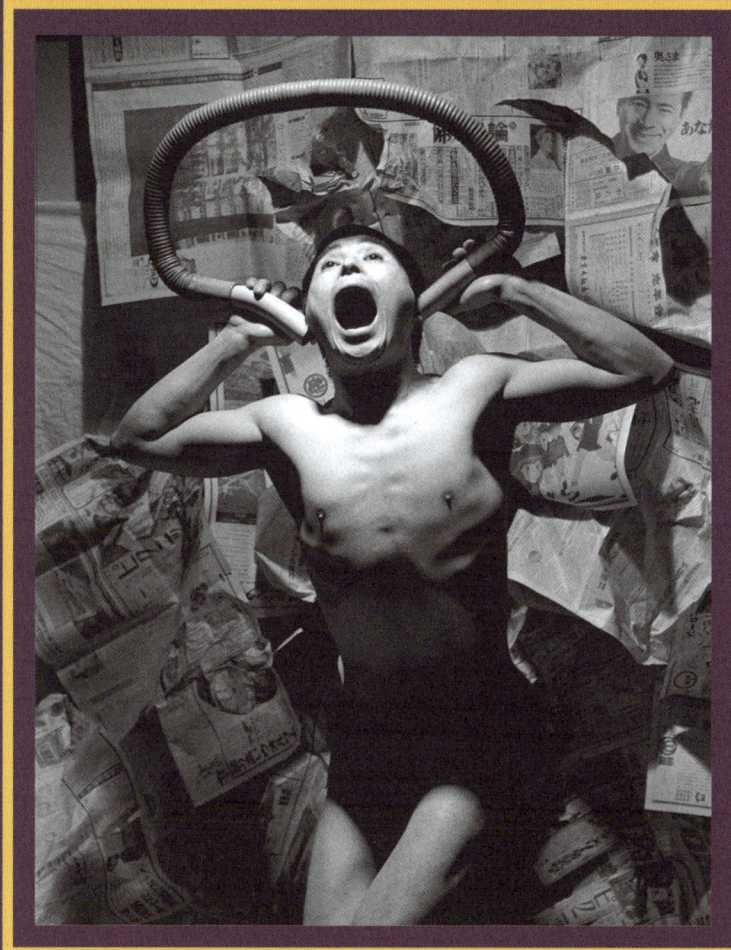
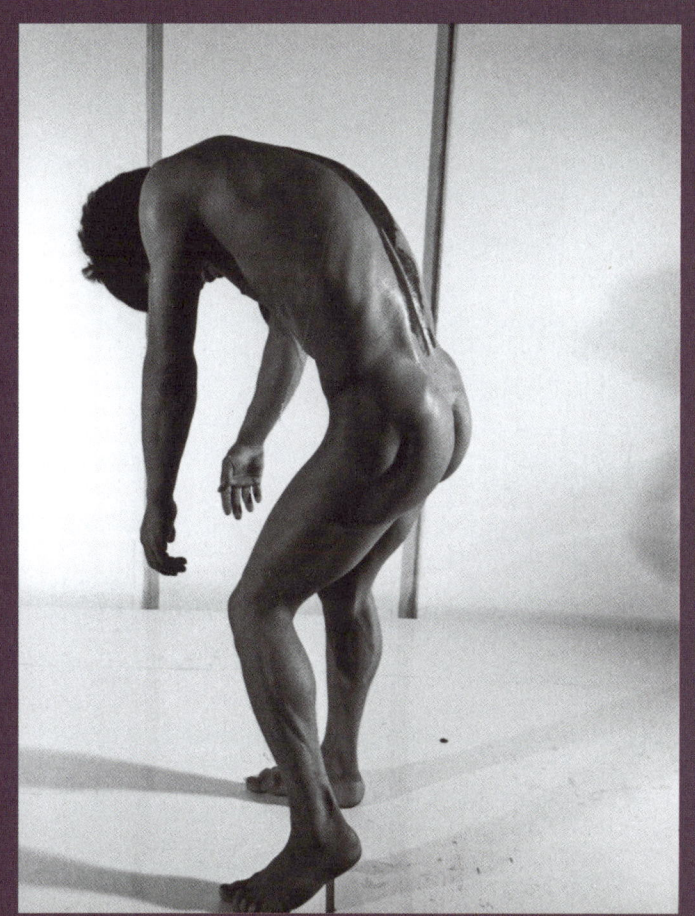

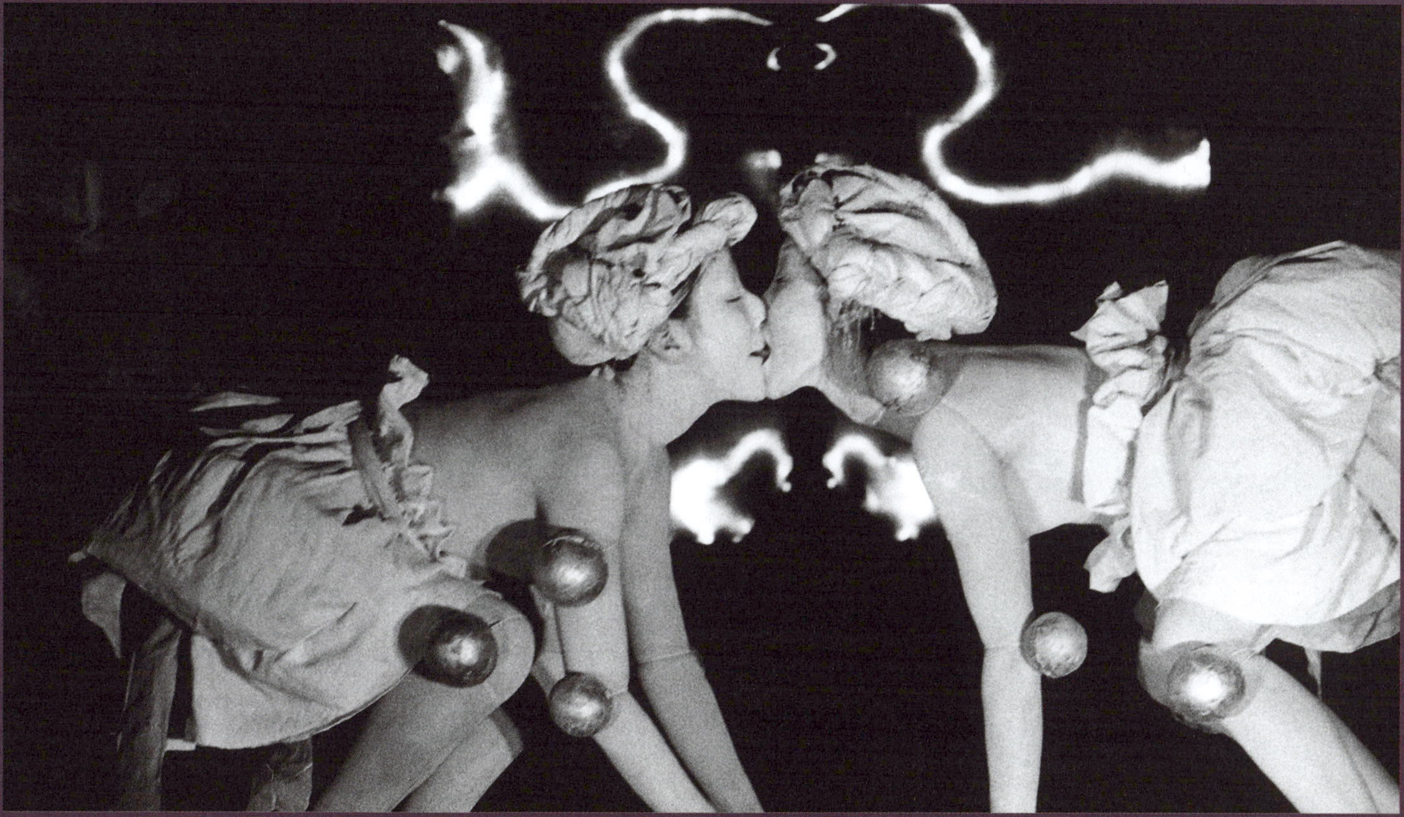

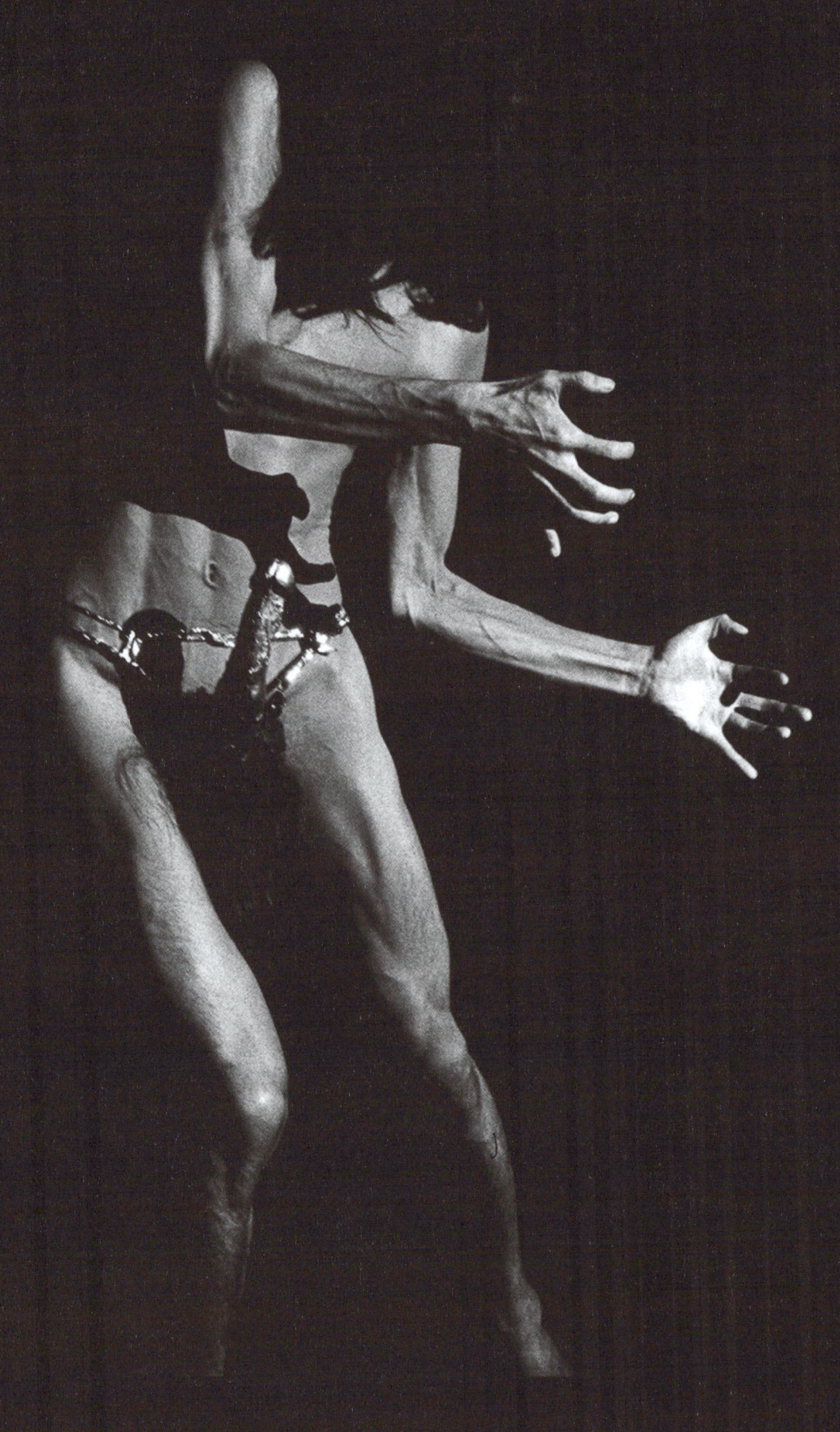

Torii Ryōzen, *Revolt of the Body, Tatsumi Hijikata Wearing a Golden Phallus*, 1968, gelatin silver print.

Opposite (left): **Hanaga Mitsutoshi**, *Ariadone Society, Zarathustra, Sogetsu Hall*, 1980, gelatin silver print.

Opposite (above right): **Hanaga Mitsutoshi**, *Tamano Koichi, Harupin-ha*, date unknown, gelatin silver print.

Opposite (below right): **Torii Ryōzen**, *Gibasan of Twenty-Seven Nights for Four Seasons*, 1972, gelatin silver print.

p. 110: **Nakatani Tadao**, *An experimental photograph at the Asbestos Studio*, 1968, gelatin silver print.

p. 111: **Hanaga Mitsutoshi**, *Ariadone Society*, date unknown, gelatin silver print.

p. 112: Stills from **Iimura Takahiko**, *Cine-Dance: The Butoh of Tatsumi Hijikata – Anma (The Masseurs)* (1963), short film.

p. 113: Stills from **Ouchida Keiya and Hijikata Tatsumi**, *A Story of Smallpox (Hōsōtan*, 1972), short film.

There was a direct correlation between Hijikata's conception of the unthinkable and his experiences as a Japanese man who had grown up during the war, survived the war and was coming to terms with what atomic annihilation was all about.

ALEXANDRA MUNROE

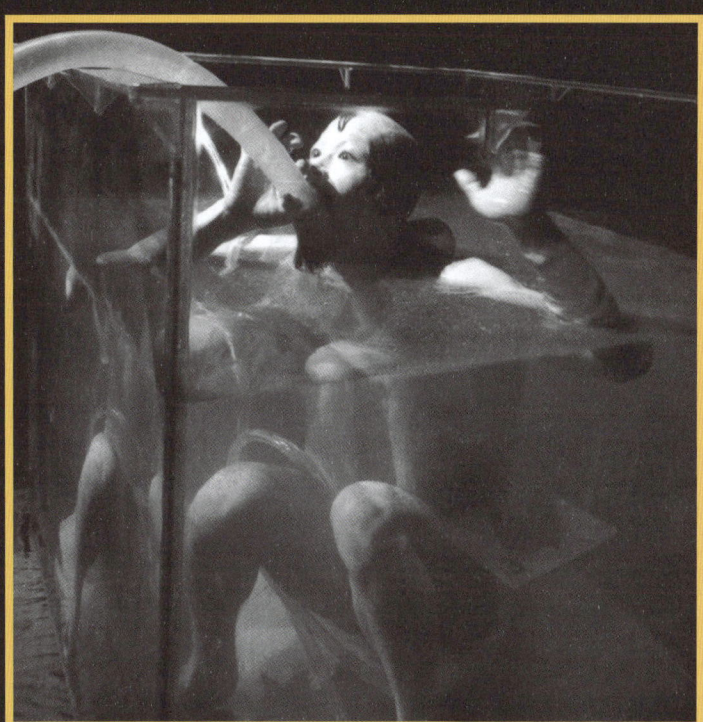

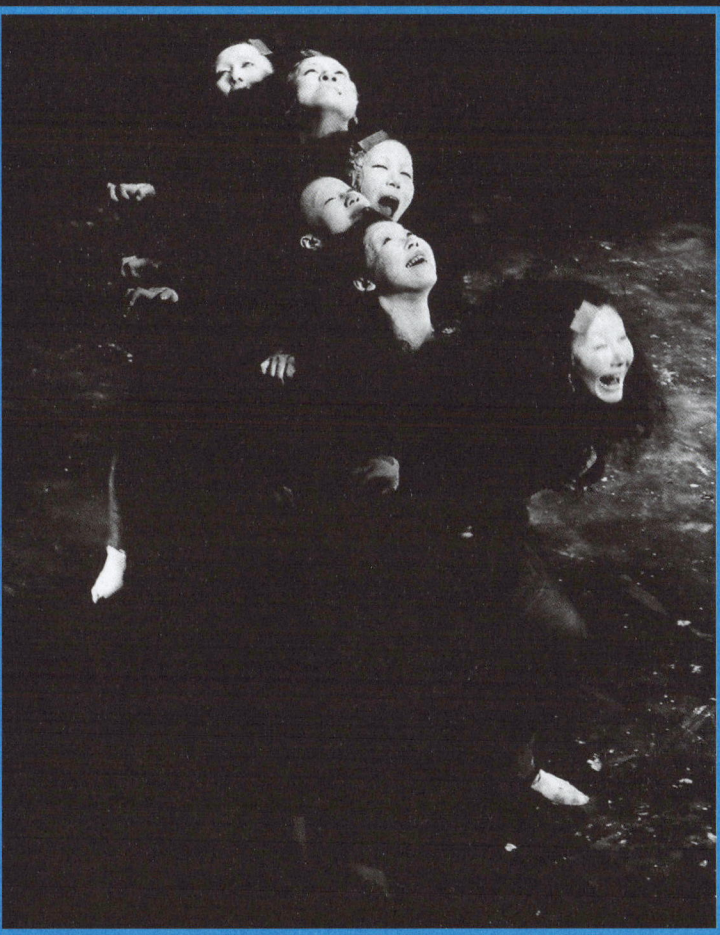

It was not something I had ever come across before. Something unimaginable appeared before my eyes.

You could say butoh is a dance, but I don't think I thought of it as such back then. It was a form of impact.

MIZOHATA TOSHIO

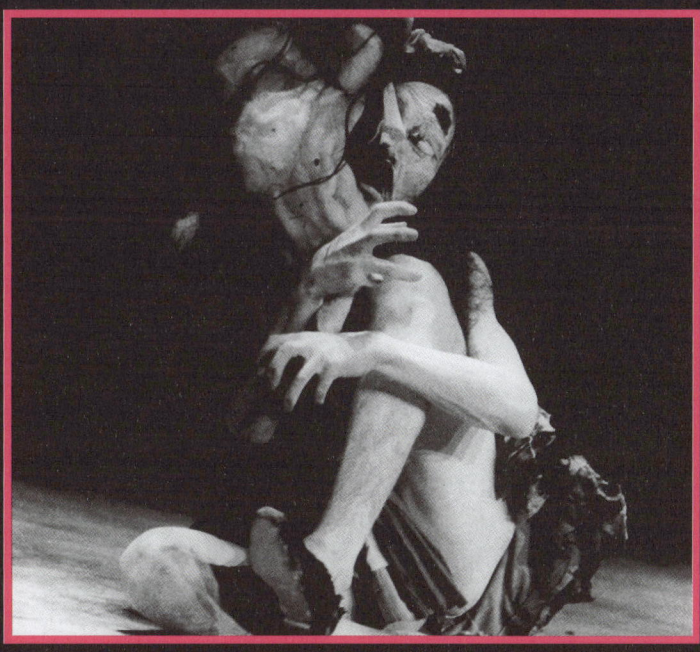

Butoh isn't really about works but more about a way of living or a way of seeing. It crosses many genres and propagates.

Hijikata's butoh exceeds the genre of dance by including art, photography, film, literature, music and philosophy, by being connected to different forms of art.

MORISHITA TAKASHI

舞踏 109

BUTOH IS AN EXPRESSION OF THE FLESH BY THE FLESH – EROTICISM, VIOLENCE, LIFE AND DEATH. EVERYTHING THAT HAS TO DO WITH THE HUMAN BODY.

MORISHITA TAKASHI

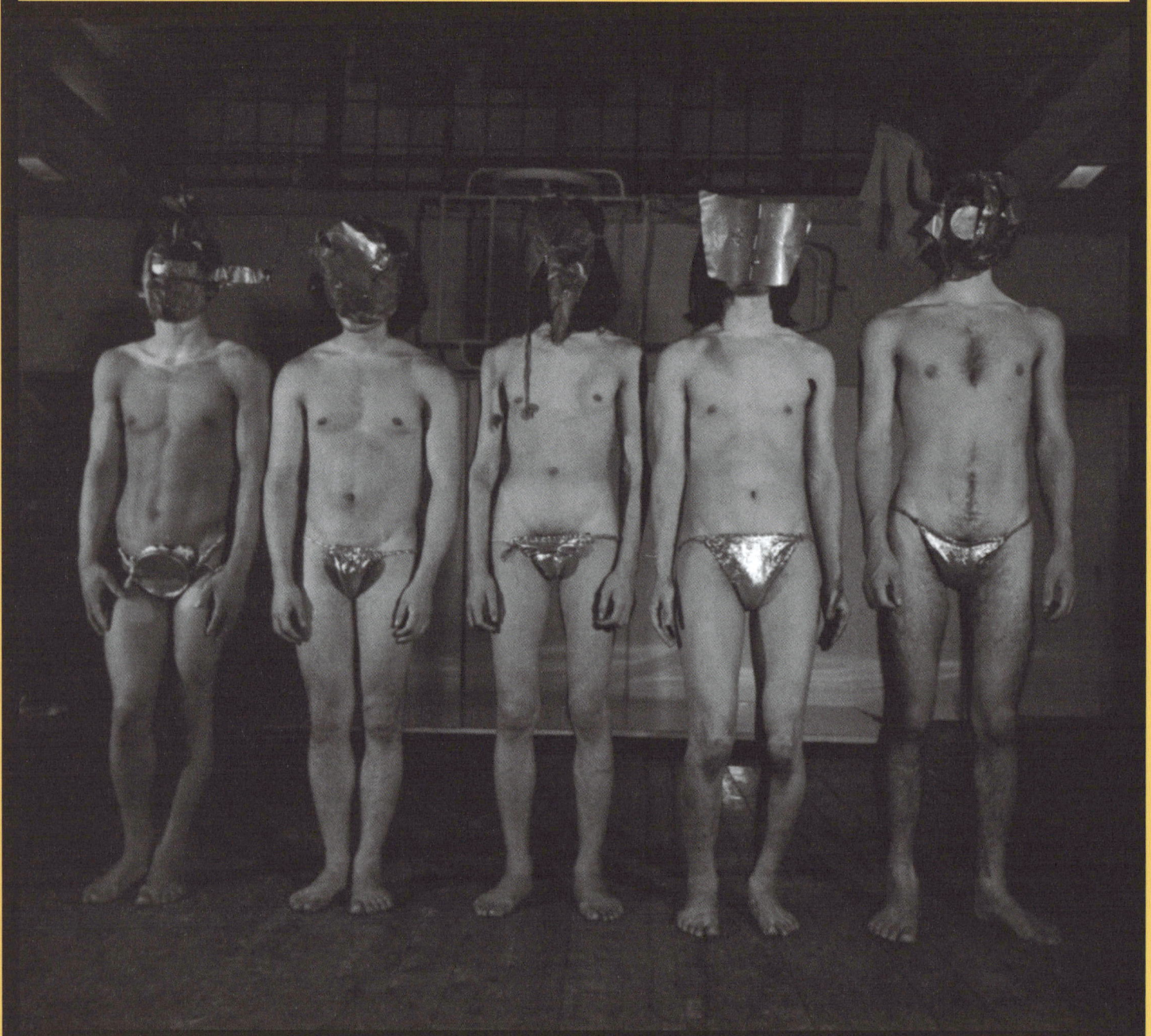

BUTOH IS STAGED IN THE AFTERLIFE, BUT IT'S THE AFTERLIFE OF THE APOCALYPSE.

ALEXANDRA MUNROE

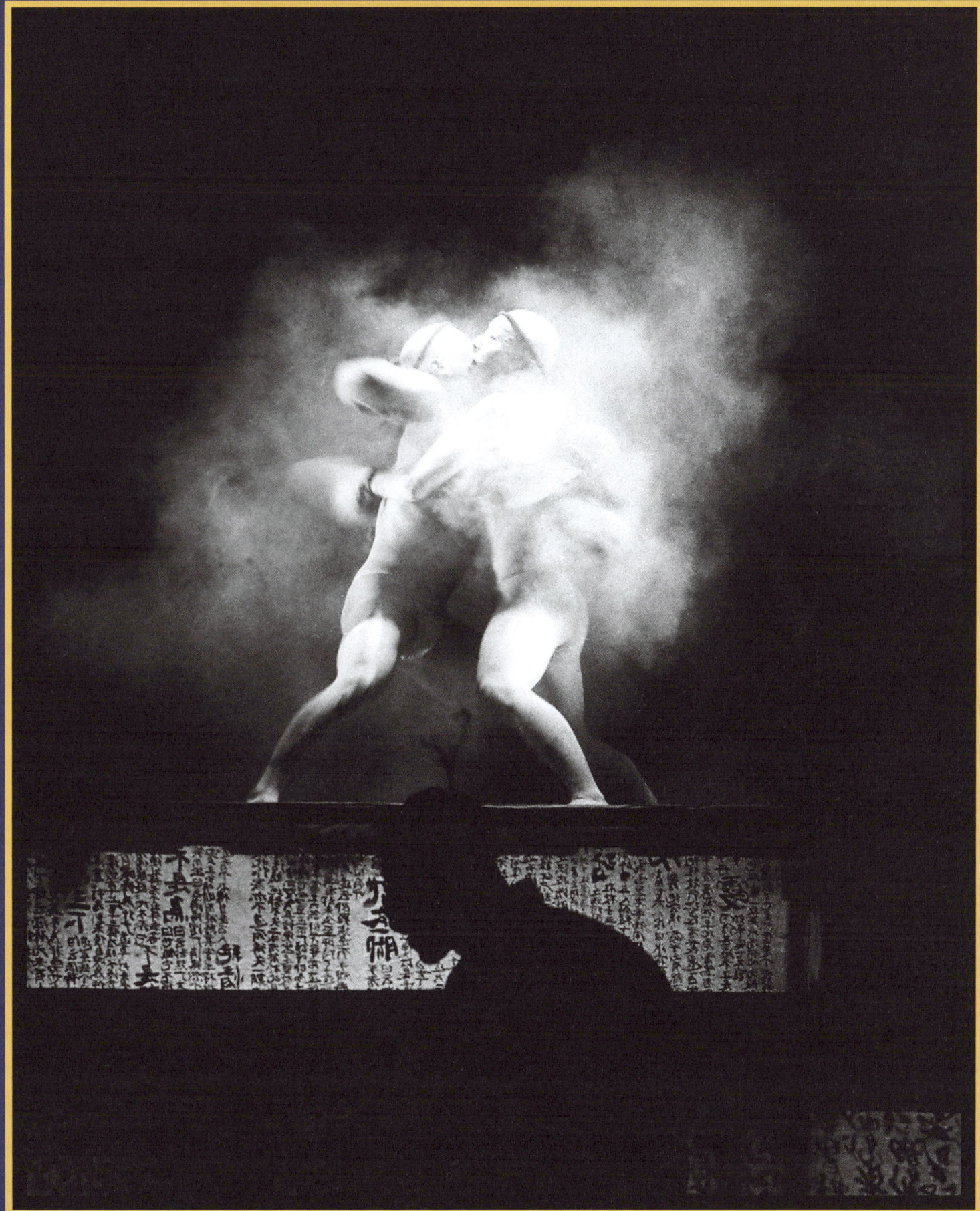

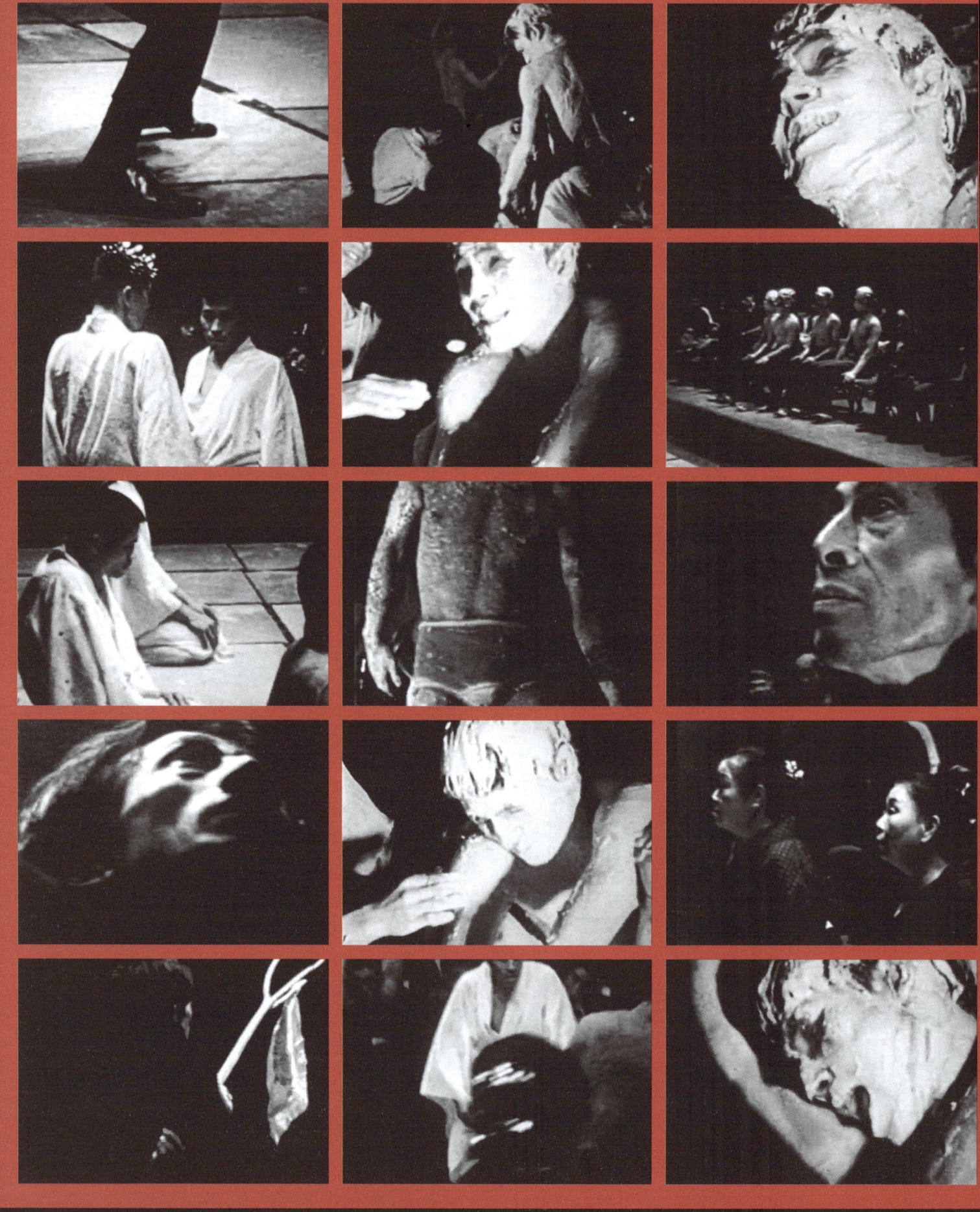

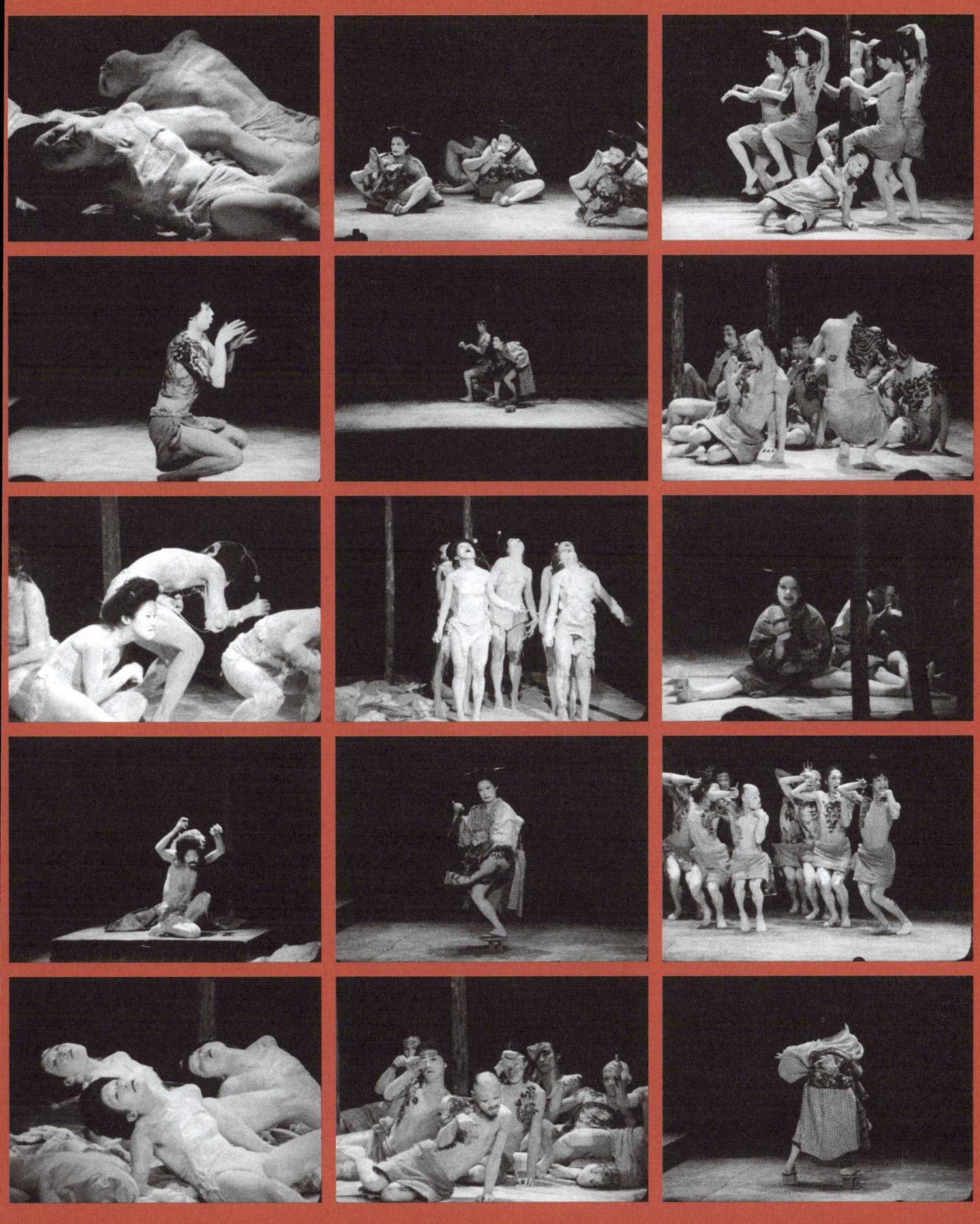

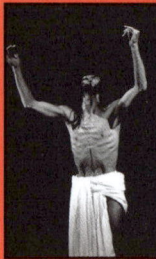

HIJIKATA TATSUMI
1928–1986

土方巽

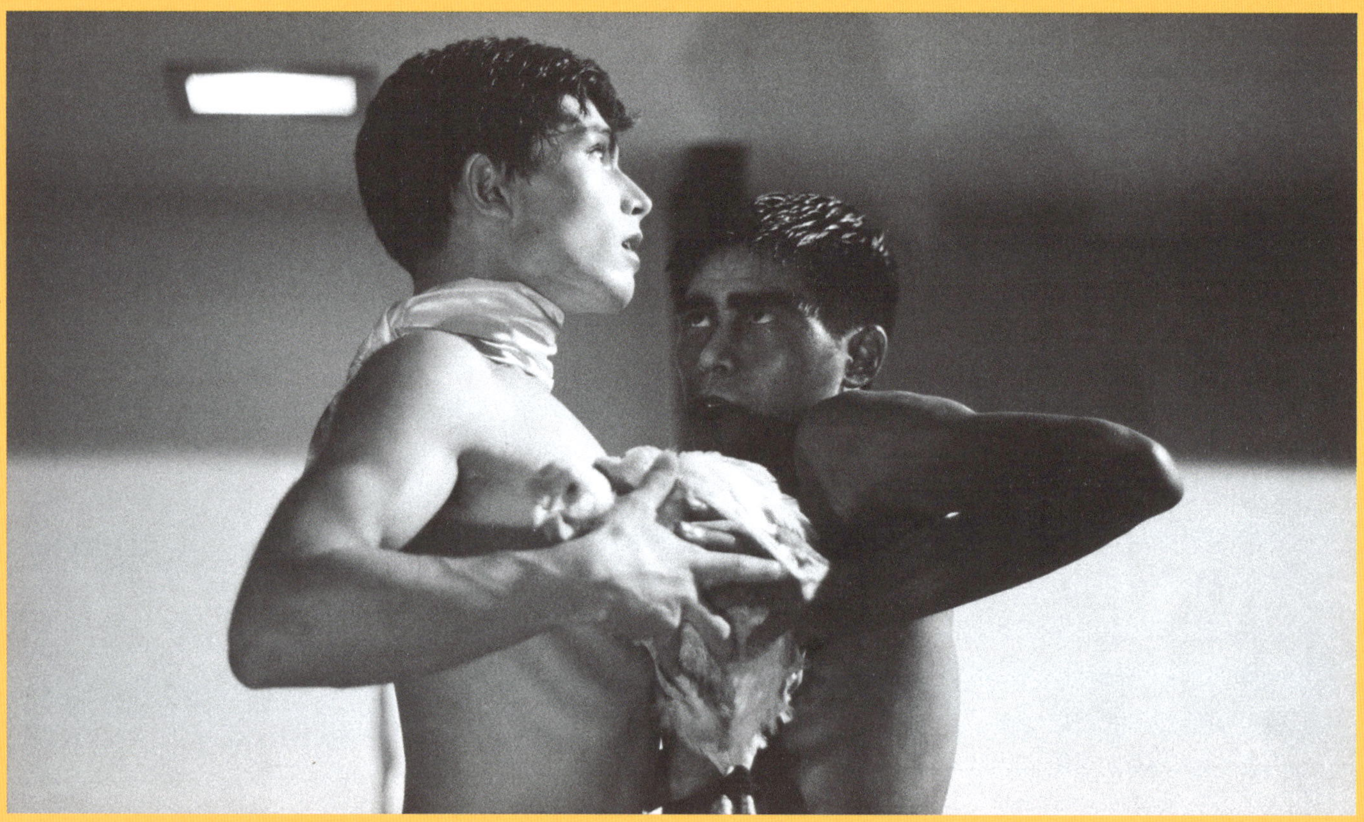

Ōtsuji Kiyoji, *Ōno Yoshito and Hijikata Tatsumi rehearse 'Kinjiki'*, 1959, gelatin silver print.

Opposite (above left): **Nakatani Tadao**, *Rebellion of the Body, Hijikata Tatsumi Wearing a White Suit*, 1968, gelatin silver print.

Opposite (above right): **Nakatani Tadao**, *Gibasan*, from *Twenty-Seven Nights for Four Seasons*, 1972, gelatin silver print.

Opposite (below): **Nakatani Tadao**, *Rebellion of the Body, The Last Scene*, 1968, gelatin silver print.

> There is a great propensity, in certain elements of the Japanese artistic imagination, of the grotesque. Part of that embrace of the grotesque is an encounter and a kind of overt dealing with sex, madness and death. I think butoh is an extraordinary example of this.
>
> ALEXANDRA MUNROE

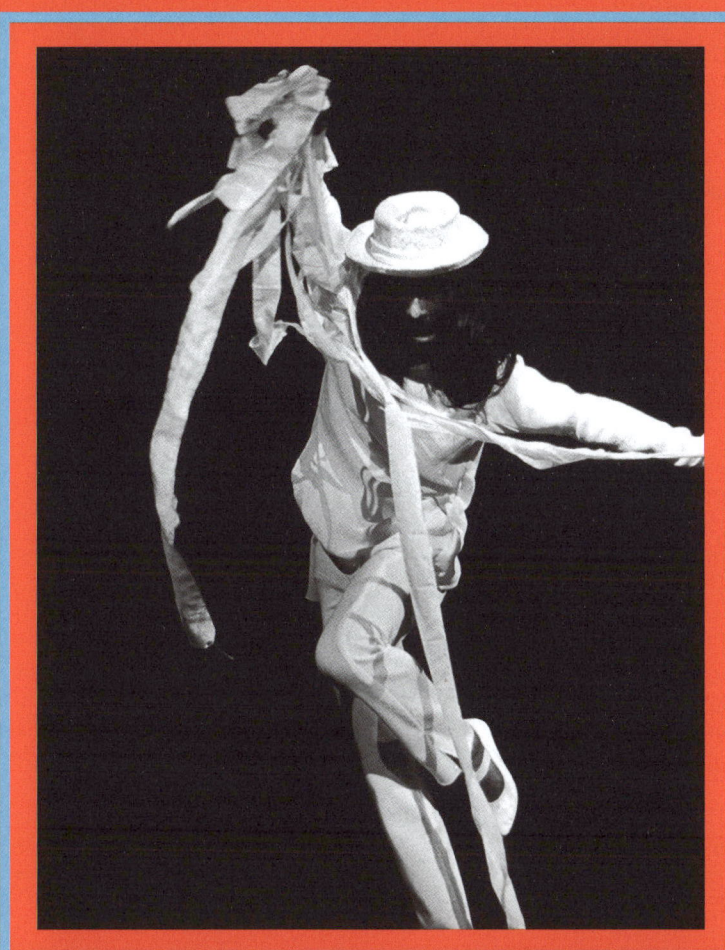
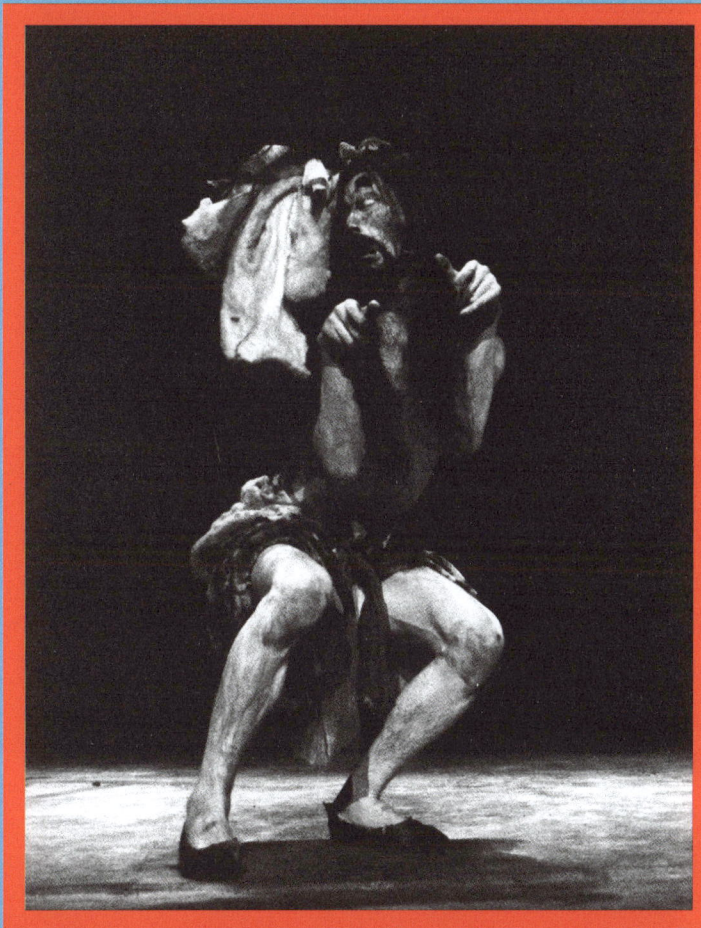

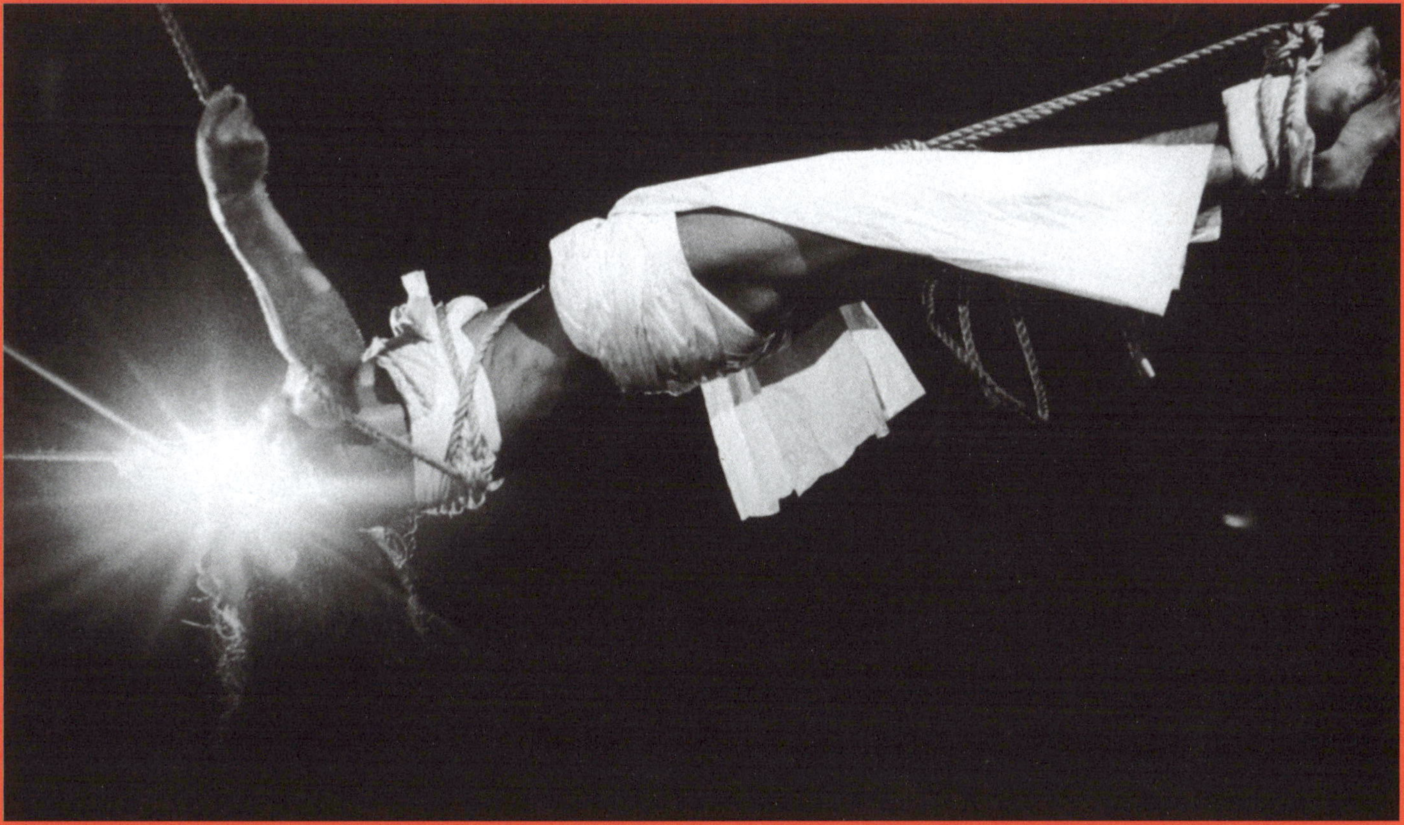

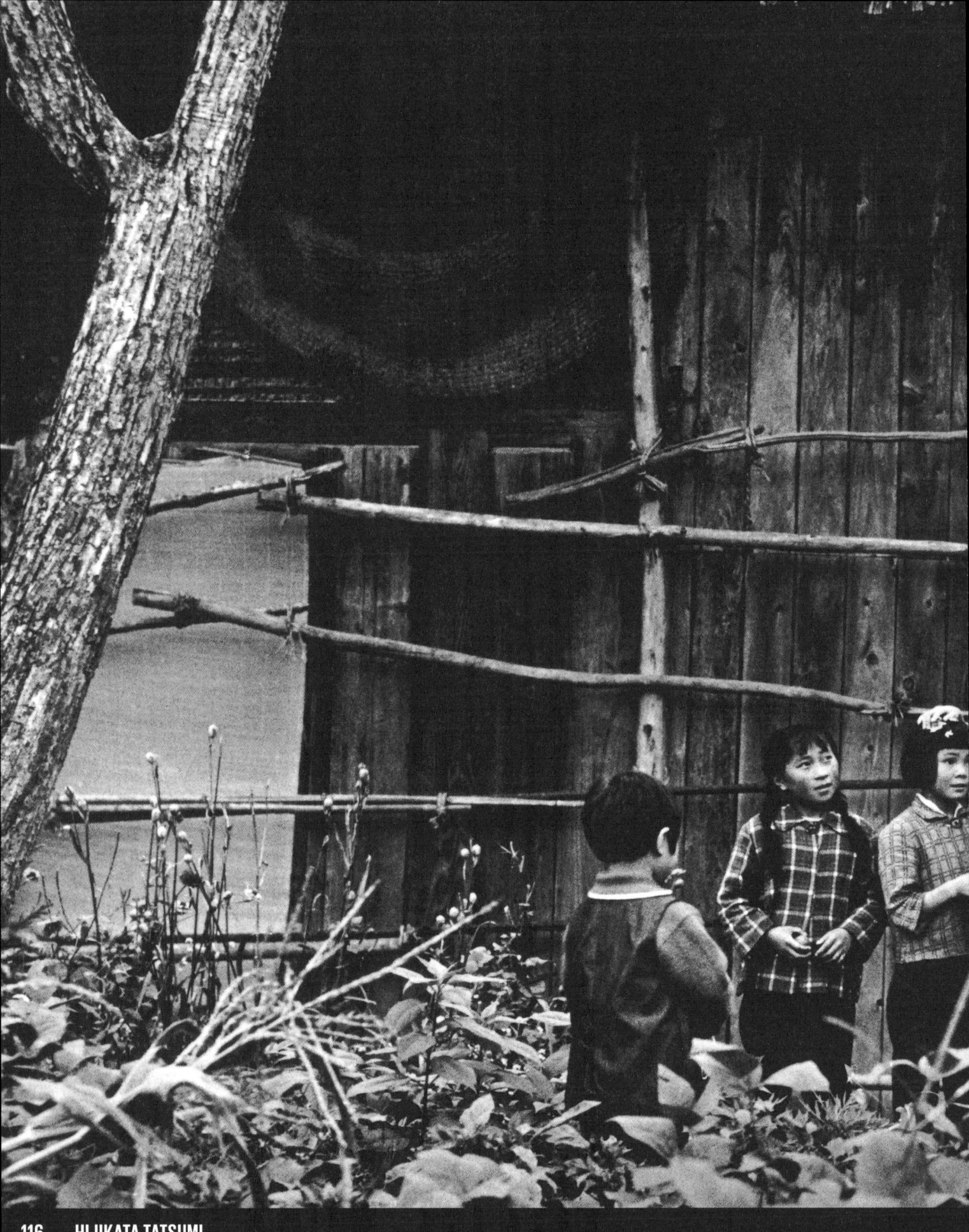

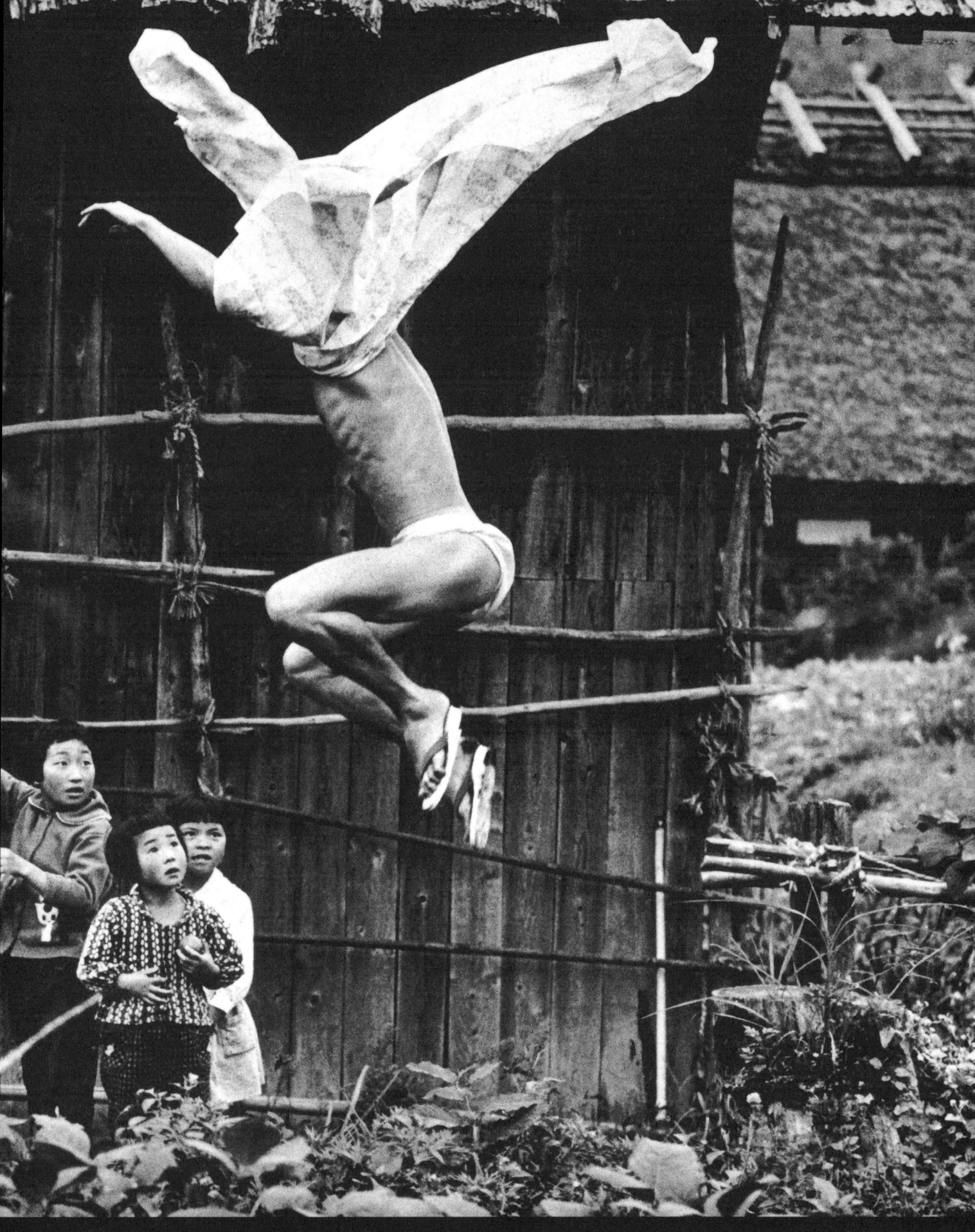

土方巽

THERE WAS A CONSTANT SEARCH FOR THE LIGHT WITHIN THE DARKNESS OF THE SOUL.

MORISHITA TAKASHI

Hijikata Tatsumi was one of my best friends. He created the word 'butoh'. The sense of butoh became a kind of a controlled movement, not with the movement of ballet dance, or American modern dance, but more Japanese.

'Free' means not only the physical, but a free spirit. It contains everything. He's a genius man, genius dancer. He expresses his dance in many ways. Sometimes he looks like a giant ghost. He has everything in himself.

HOSOE EIKŌ

While the darkness he expresses is fear and angst, in parallel there is softness, perhaps humour and laughter, pleasure, so one can find multiple aspects. The word *ankoku* can also mean 'darkness against light'. The darkness in *ankoku butoh* is more like a black hole, where everything can co-exist.

If there is light and dark, which comes first? Hijikata would say, darkness comes first. Light is born from darkness. There is no right answer, it is more of a philosophy that darkness is the original source.

MIZOHATA TOSHIO

pp. 116–17: **Hosoe Eikō**, *Kamaitachi #17*, 1965, gelatin silver print.

Opposite: **Nakatani Tadao**, *Rebellion of the Body (Finale)*, 1968, gelatin silver print.

Overleaf: **Hosoe Eikō**, *Kamaitachi #39*, 1965, gelatin silver print.

Hijikata studied French literature and considered how to express the eroticism he found there. He focused on the theme of same-sex love, but I think there are some differences in the way the Japanese think about it, and the way Christianity sees it. Hijikata himself was not gay. So what does it mean when someone who is not attracted to the same sex represents someone who is?

Historically, Japan has had a very open approach to sexual freedom. This differs greatly to the Christian world. Hijikata was expressing human life and death. By exploring these fundamental things, he reconsiders how one should live life.

MORISHITA TAKASHI

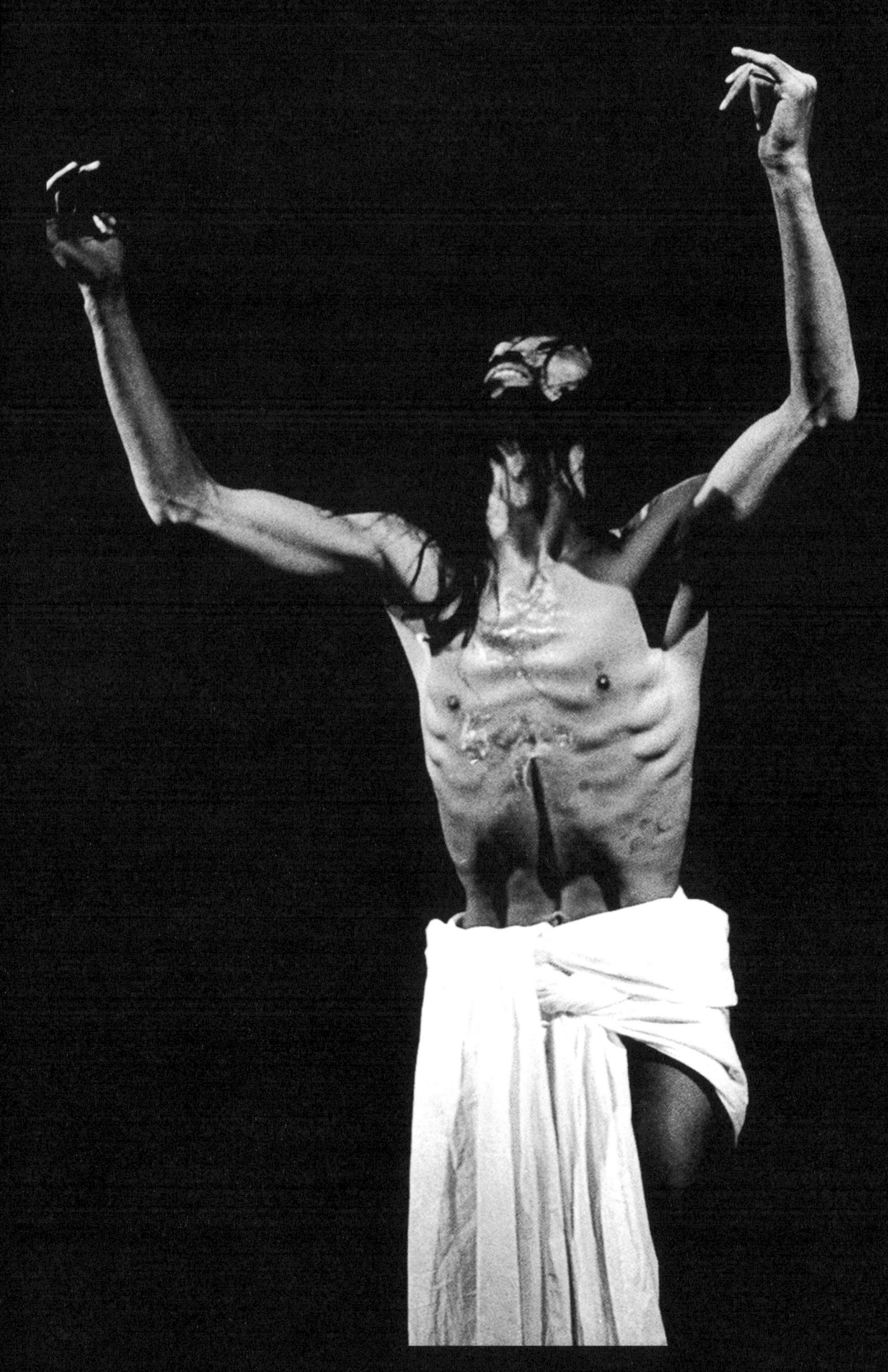

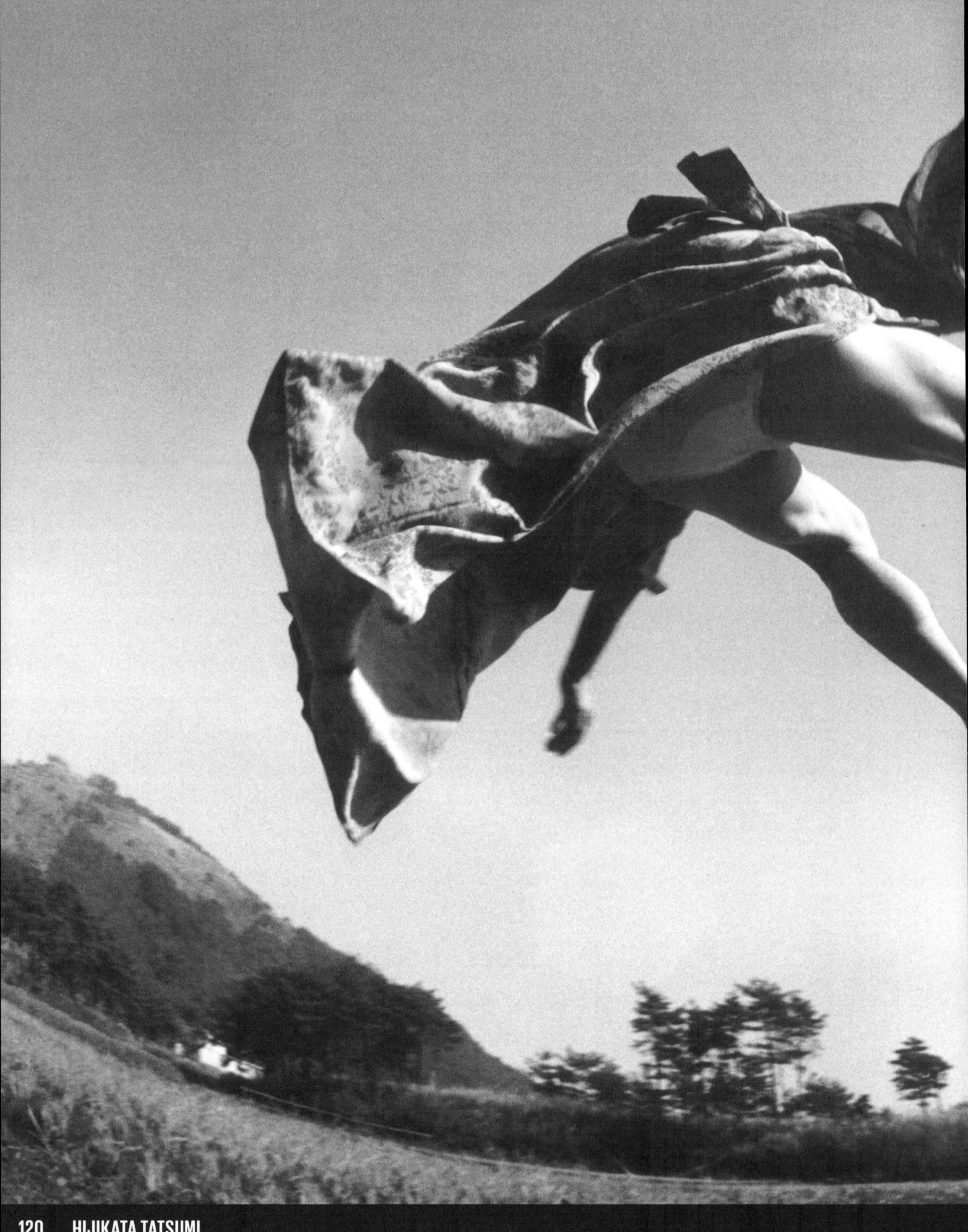

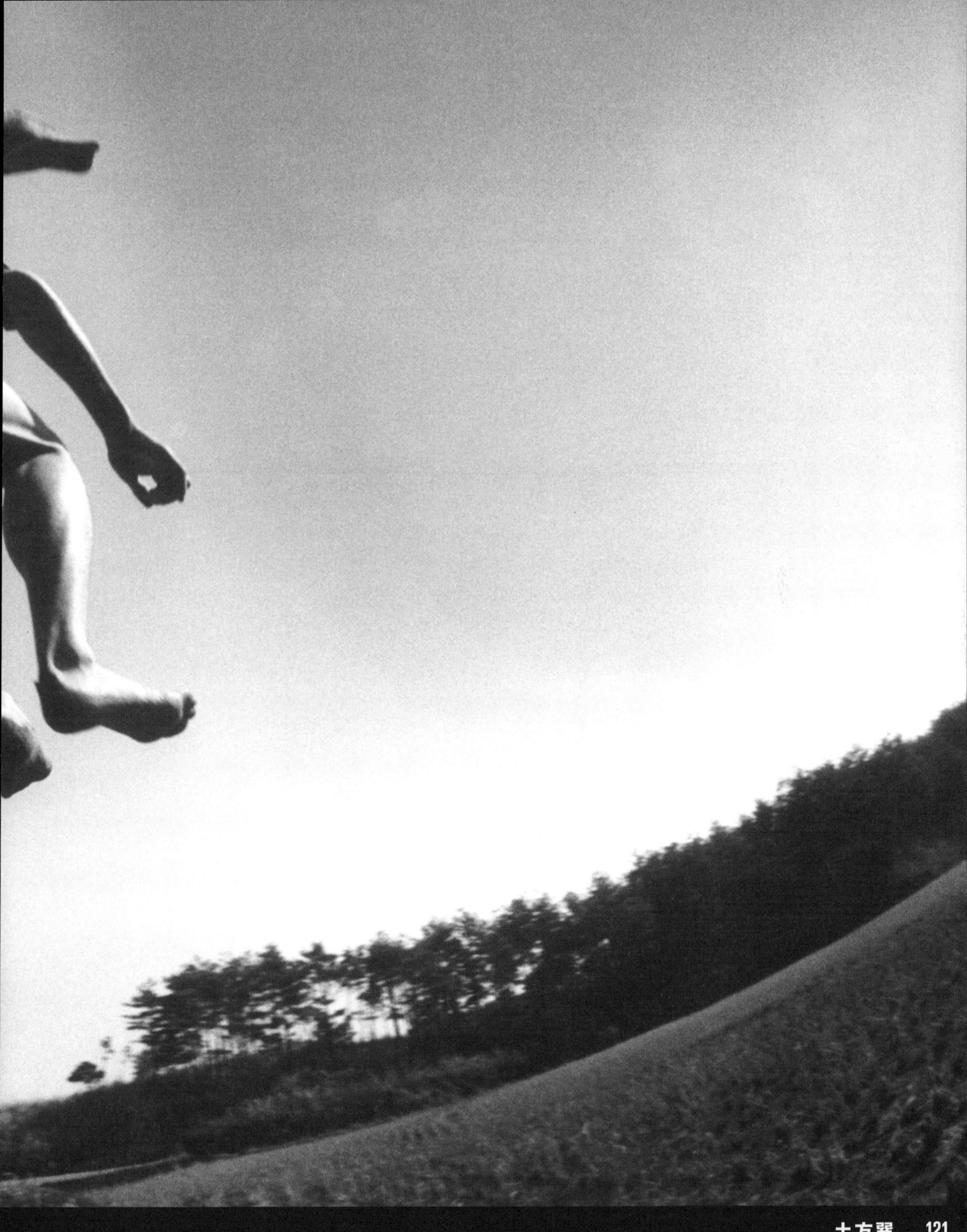

土方巽

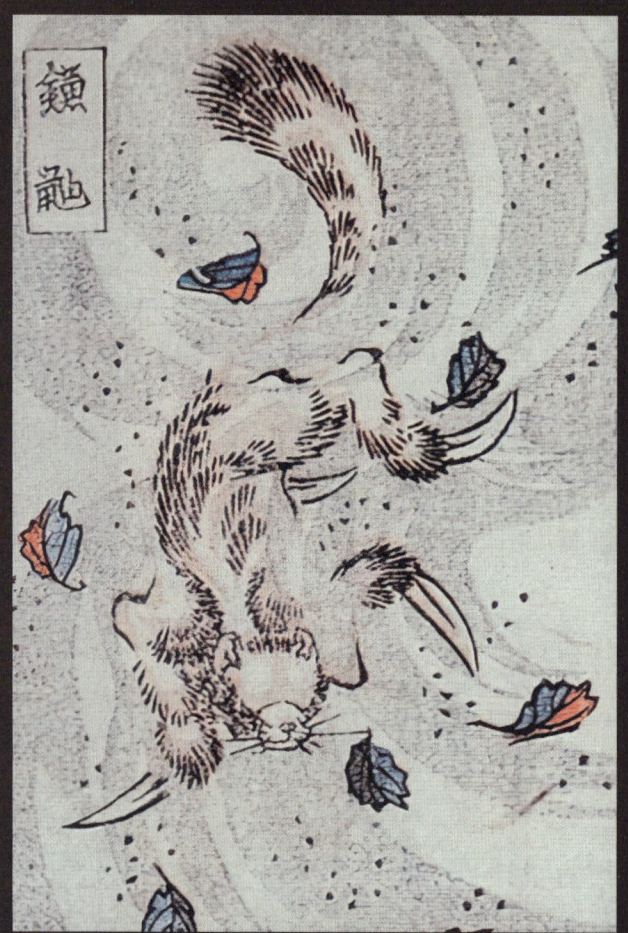

Hijikata Tatsumi... I was afraid of him at first because he looked very dark. Quiet. No smile. But soon we became very friendly, because we were from almost the same area of the north of Japan.

I said to him that I wanted to photograph him in his birthplace. So we went to Akita. I photographed him, and finally, I made a book titled *Kamaitachi*. Kamaitachi is a fictional creature: 'Kama' means sickle, 'itachi' means animal. His existence is Kamaitachi. It has some sort of humorous touch – not the safe humour, but the dangerous humour.

People were very much afraid. He did something erotic or something humorous. There were local people working in the fields there, and he was a star among ordinary actors and actresses.

HOSOE EIKŌ

Above: **Masasumi Ryūkansaijin**, *Kamaitachi*, from *Kyōka hyaku monogatari* (1853).

Opposite: **Hosoe Eikō**, *Kamaitachi #40*, 1968, gelatin silver print.

Overleaf: Photograph from **Hosoe Eikō**, *Kamaitachi #14*, 1965, gelatin silver print.

Kamaitachi developed out of the photographer Hosoe Eikō's long-term collaborative relationship with the *ankoku butoh* dancer Hijikata Tatsumi. Hosoe began to work with Hijikata after having witnessed his legendary experimental dance performance *Forbidden Colours* in 1959, but *Kamaitachi* was the first project in which Hosoe focused on Hijikata exclusively.

Mining Hijikata's rich memories of growing up in Tōhoku and the wild folkloric imagery which persisted in this part of northern Japan, they created a dance drama at once cinematic and intensely physical.

The title *Kamaitachi* refers to a weasel-like demon that allegedly haunted local rice fields, slashing at unlucky wanderers. Drawing on these associations of speed and violence, Hijikata danced through the landscape of his youth to create a series of unique portraits for Hosoe's camera.

LUCY FLEMING-BROWN

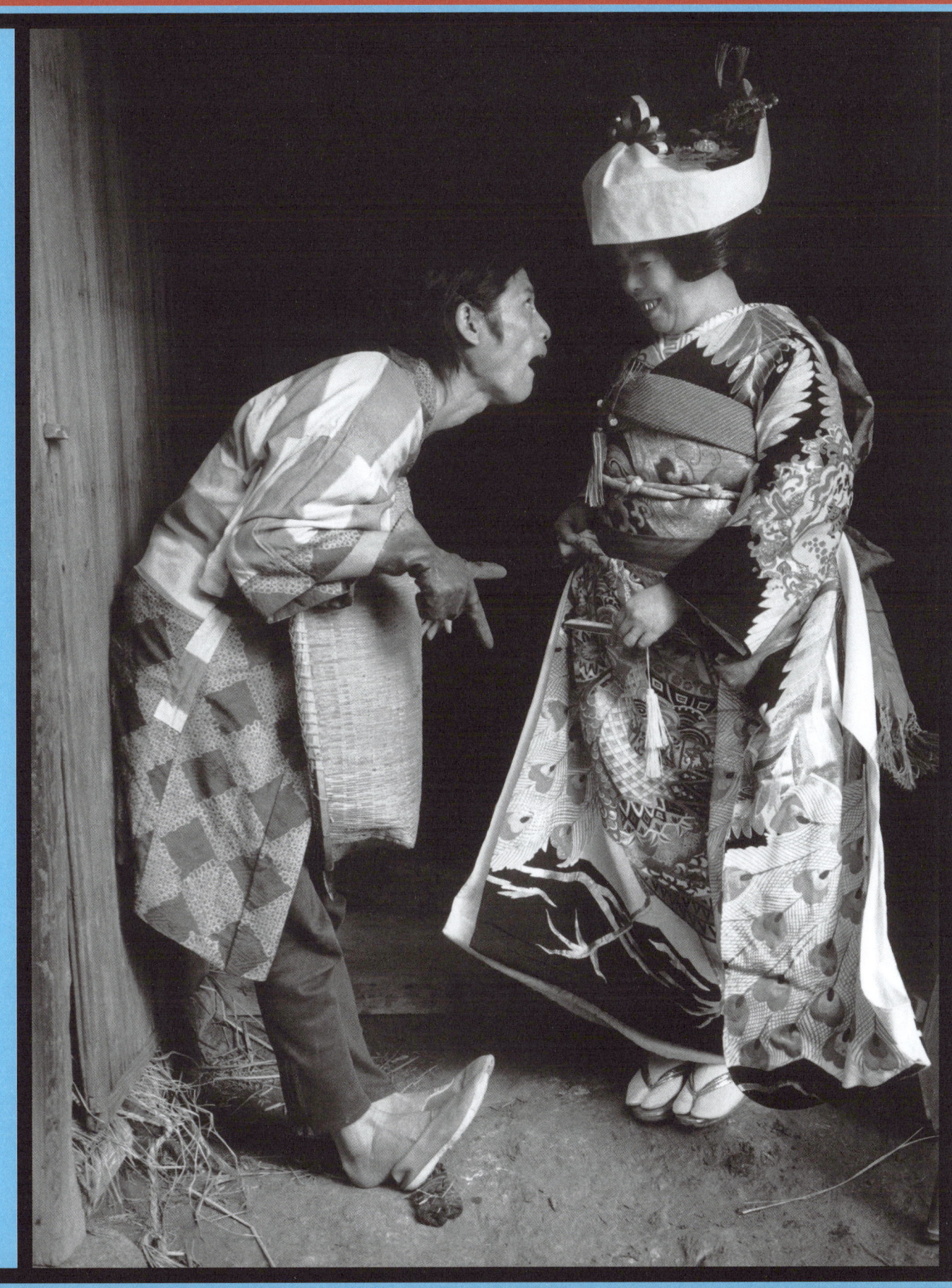

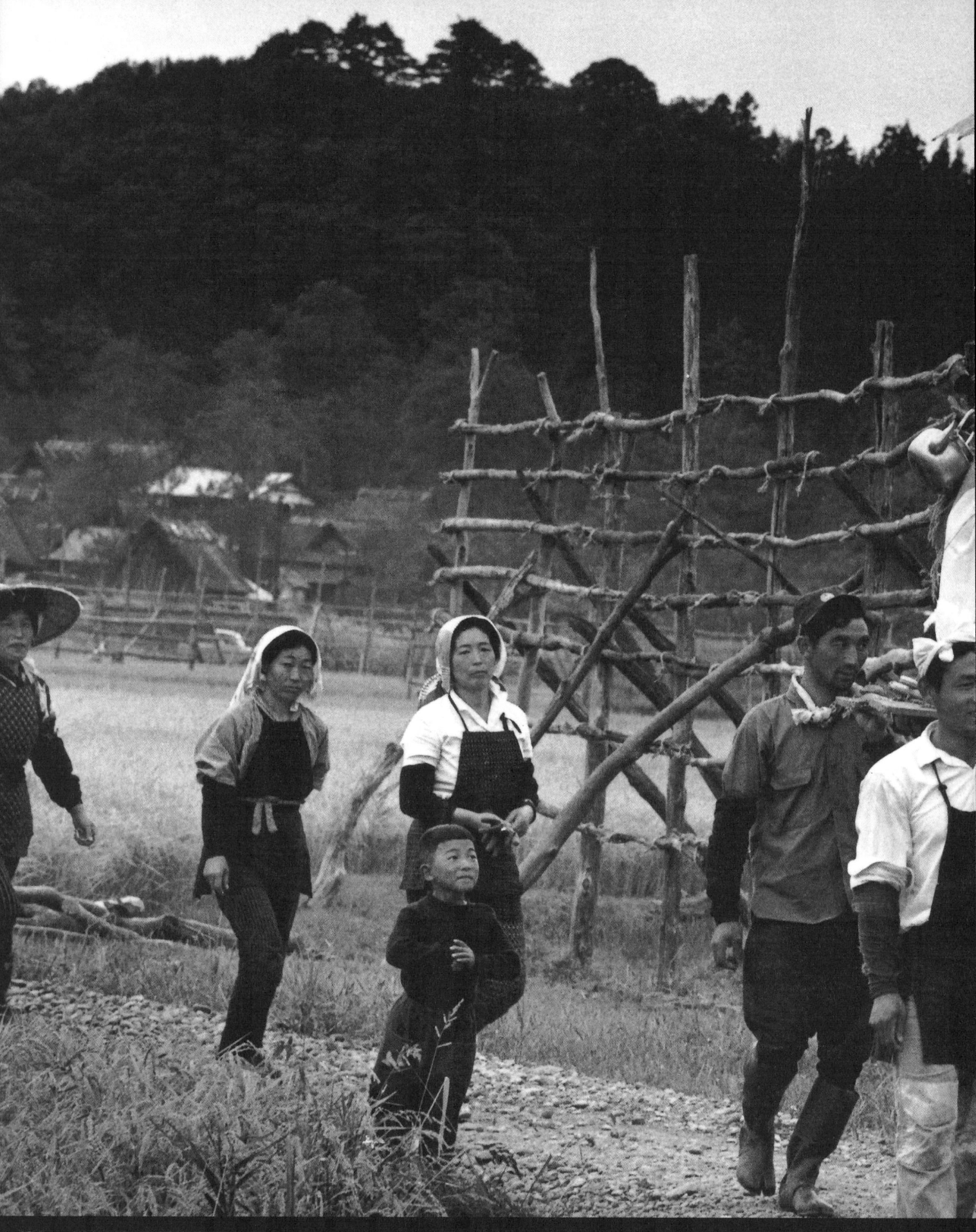

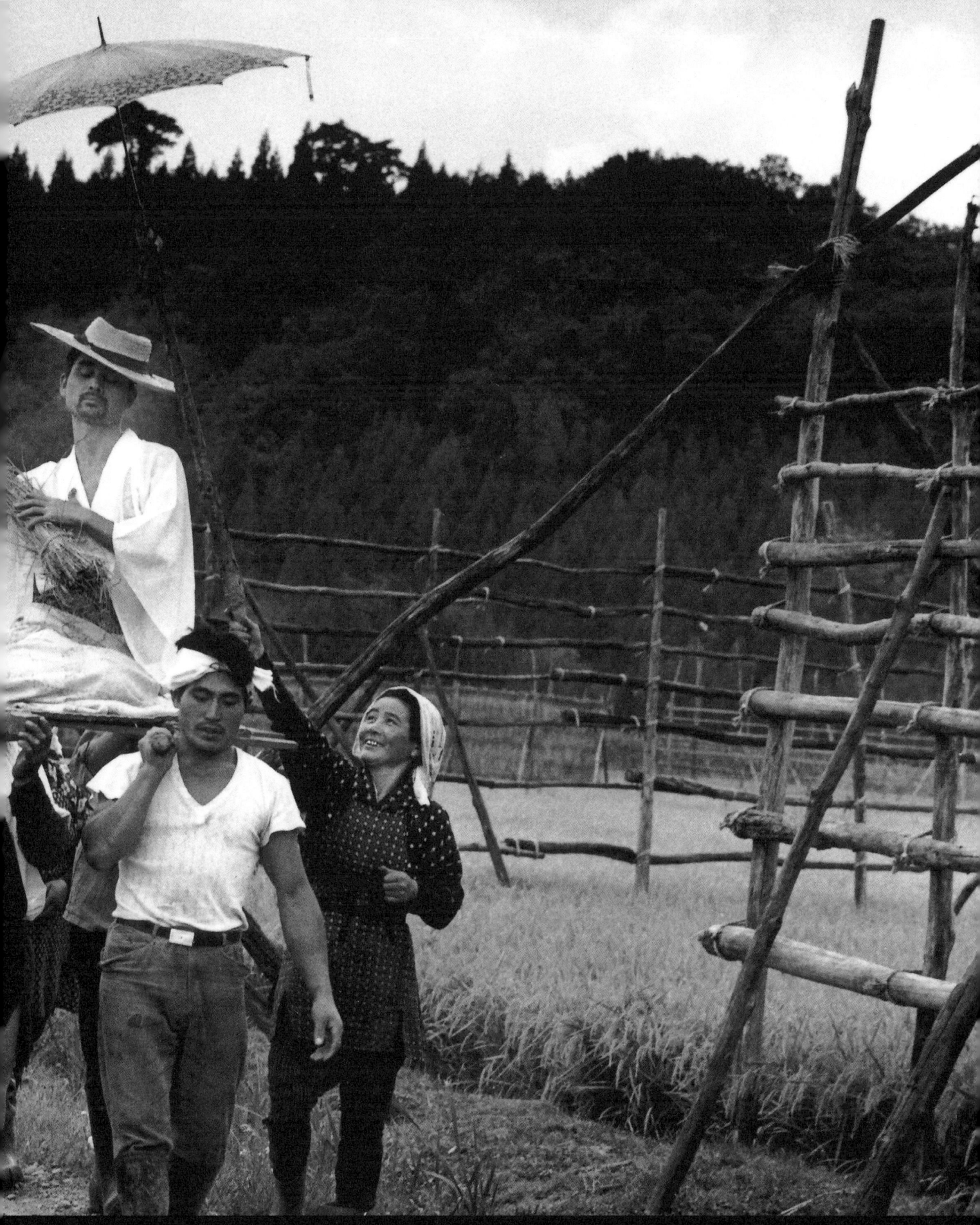

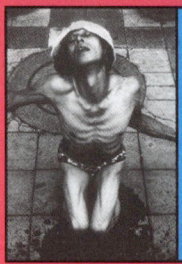

OHNO KAZUO
1906–2010

大野一雄

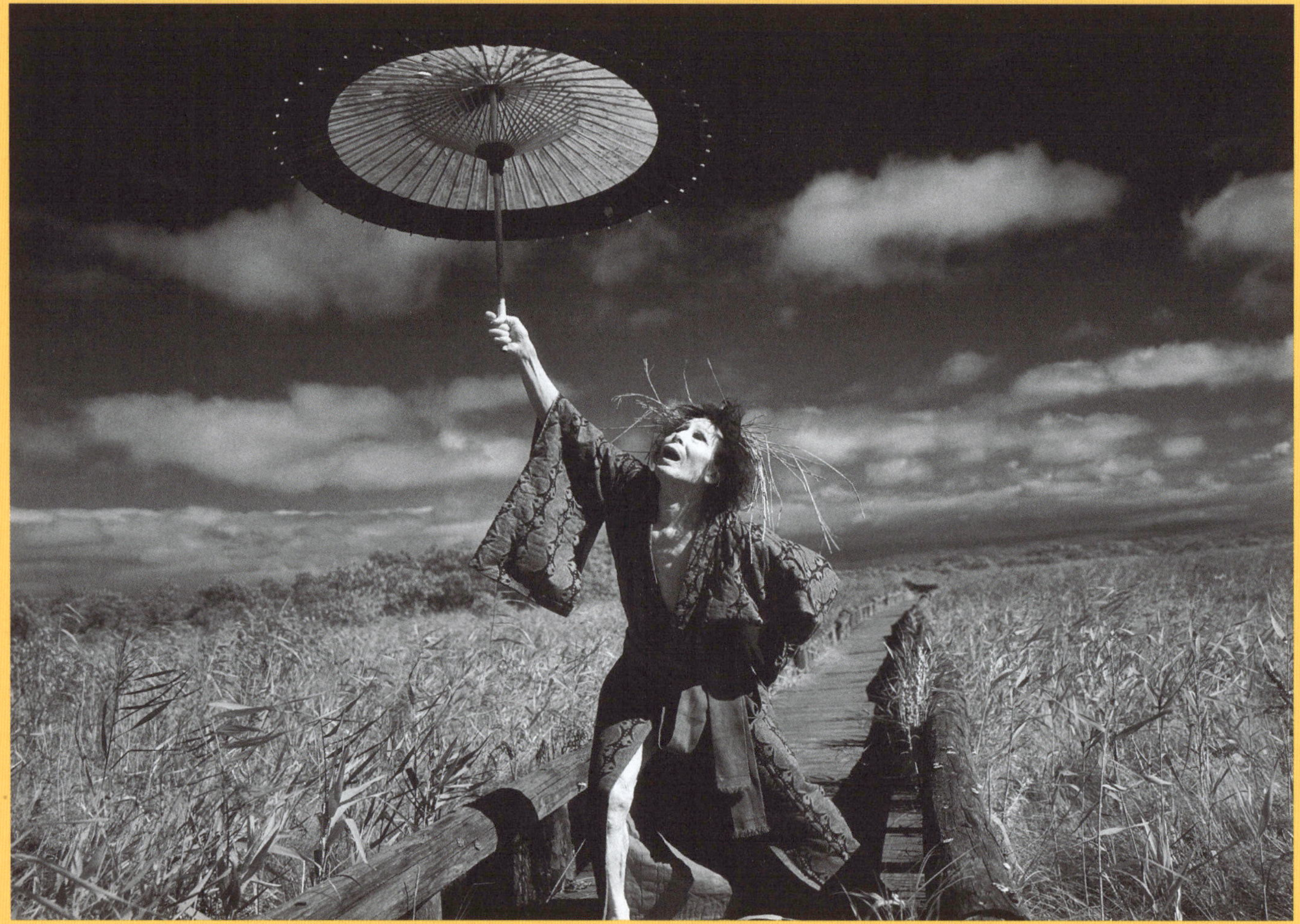

Hosoe Eikō, *Butterfly Dream #5*, 1994, gelatin silver print.

Opposite (above right): **Ikegami Naoya**, *Admiring La Argentina*, Daiichi Seimei Hall, Tokyo, 1977, gelatin silver print.

Opposite (above left and below): **Ikegami Naoya**, *The Dead Sea*, Yurakucho Asahi Hall, Tokyo, 1985, gelatin silver print.

'What do you want to say with butoh?' Ohno Kazuo would be asked this kind of question constantly and he would always answer, 'I want to convey the importance of life.' You often hear Ohno Kazuo's dance being described as a spiritual dance, or that the spirit takes form first and the dance follows suit.

MIZOHATA TOSHIO

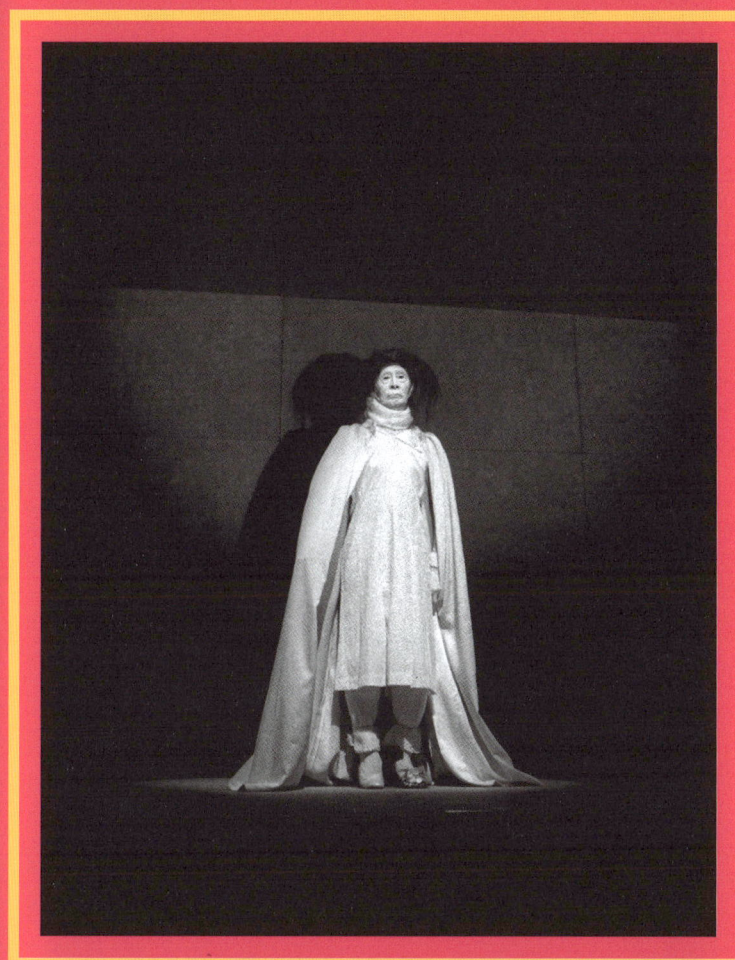
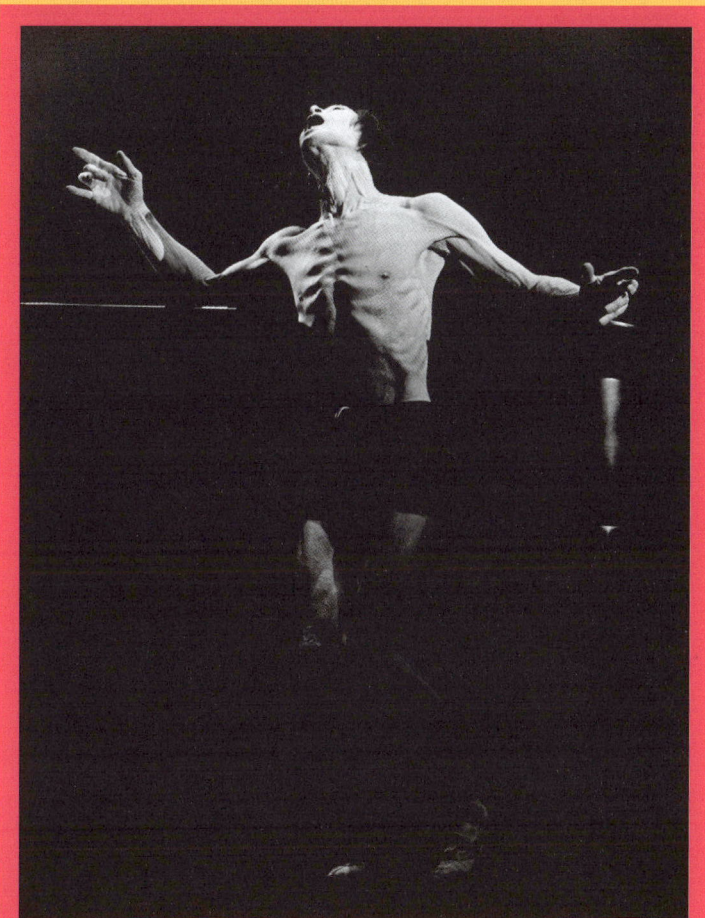

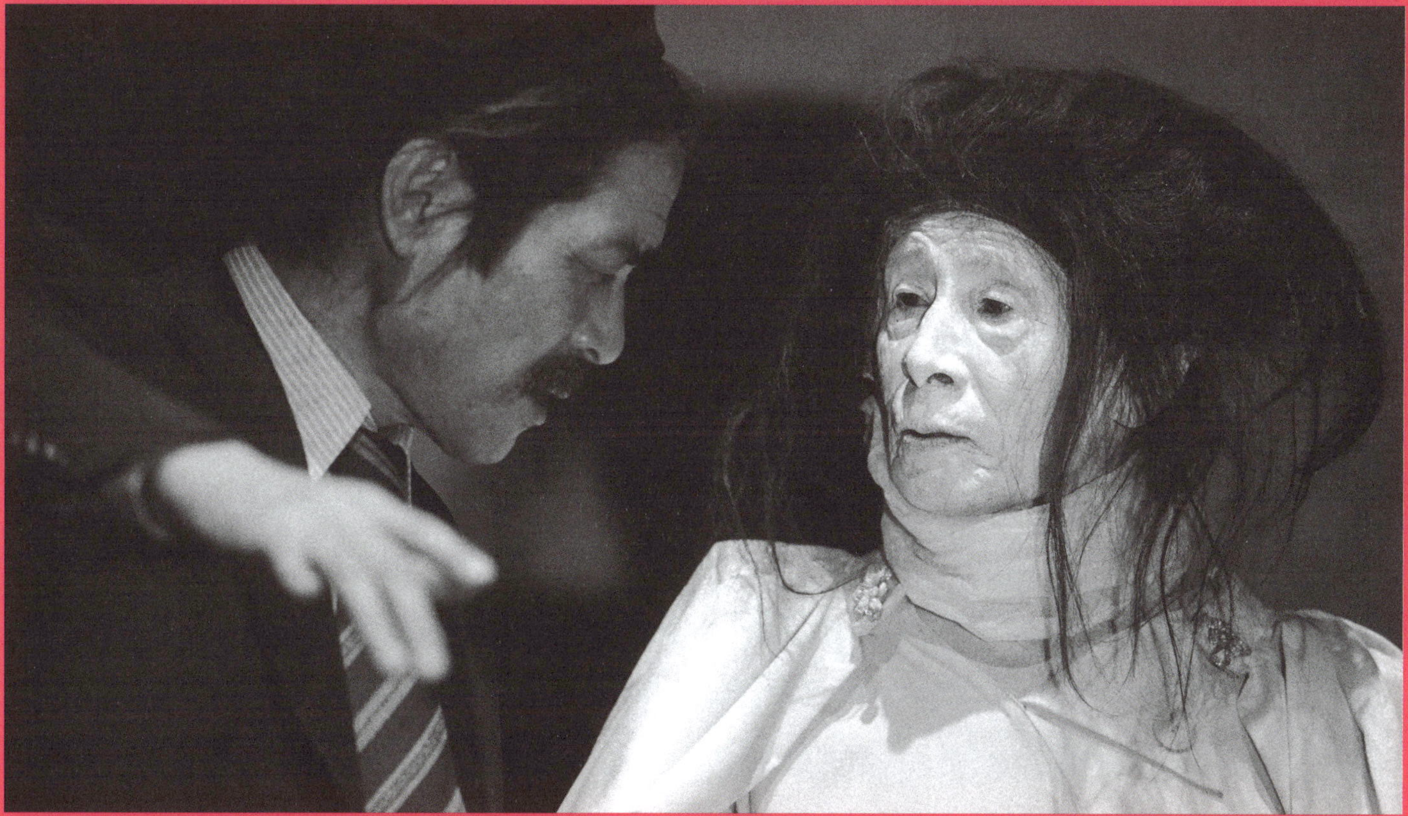

大野一雄

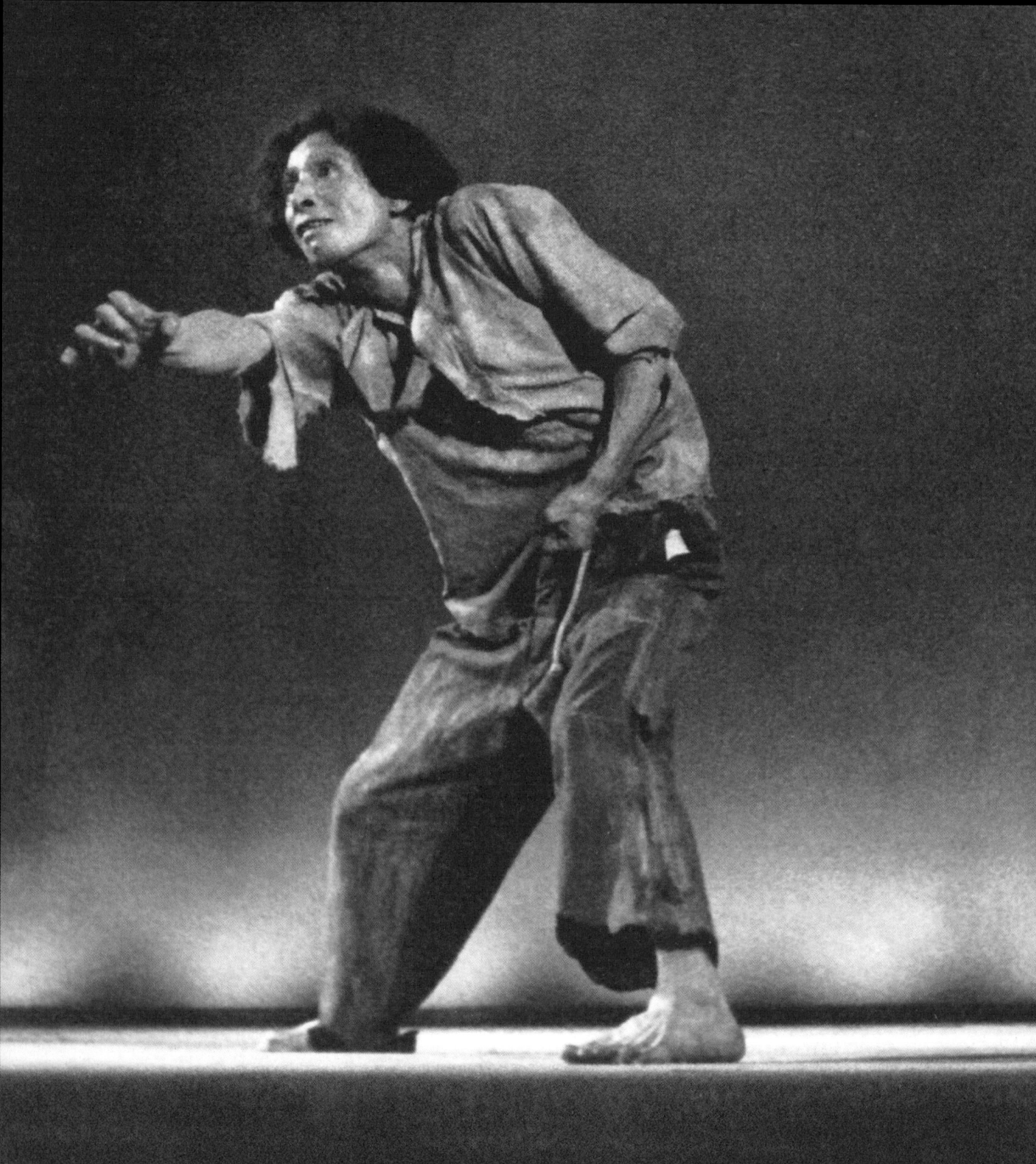

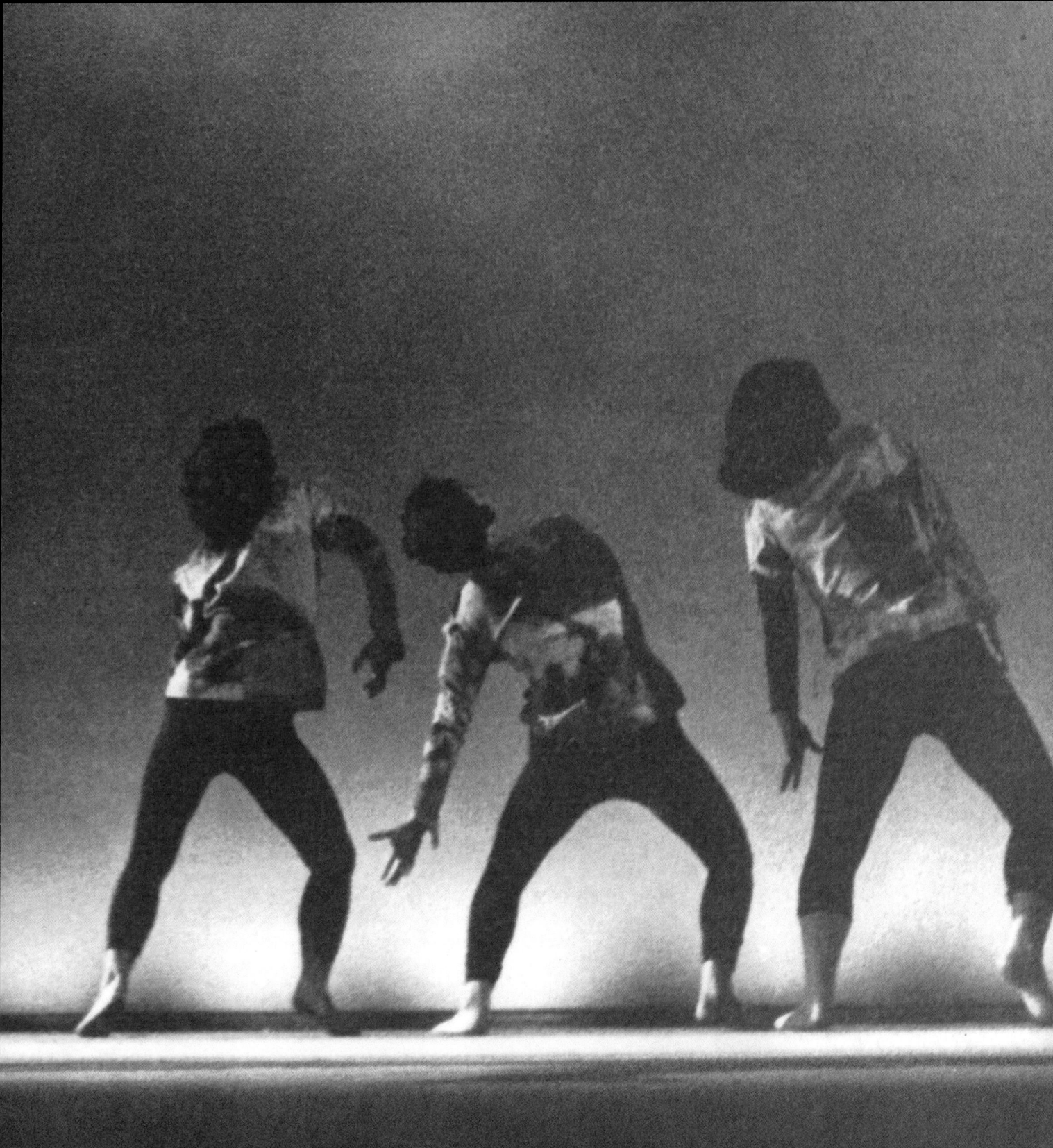

Ohno Kazuo was born in 1906 and started dancing in the 1930s. Japan was about to enter a long period of war. For nine years from 1938, a very long period, he served in the Japanese army. During the fighting in Papua New Guinea, people experienced the horrors of war: death, illnesses and hunger. Ohno experienced something like hell there. Having experienced all this, he wanted to communicate the preciousness of life.

MIZOHATA TOSHIO

Hosoe Eikō was very interested in butoh dance and in butoh dancers and their bodies. He was introduced to Ohno Kazuo and he started taking photographs of him. It became a long project, over a period of multiple decades, where he took photographs really focusing on Ohno's beautiful, stylized dance movements. He even took photographs of Ohno just before he passed away.

LENA FRITSCH

Butoh emphasizes dancers' physicality and dynamic movement. Hosoe's photographs of Ohno Kazuo resonate with these values while adopting a radically different timeframe to that of a typical performance. In a collaboration that continued for more than forty years, Hosoe set out to capture the transformation of Ohno's body over time, explored through his dance practice. Ohno was renowned for his grasp of the body's expressive potential, and these pictures chronicle the evolution of his performance style with age, as well as testifying to the enduring strength of his relationship with Hosoe.

LUCY FLEMING-BROWN

There is a work by Jean Genet called *Our Lady of the Flowers* (1943) where a character called Divine, an ageing male prostitute, perishes in a spectacular death. Hijikata asked Ohno Kazuo to play Divine. At first glance, it seems unthinkable, but Ohno Kazuo accepted it all and entered the role. Hijikata Tatsumi enormously respected Ohno and yet he asked him to do crazy things.

MIZOHATA TOSHIO

pp. 128–29: **Ohno Kazuo**, *The Old Man and the Sea*, Daiichi Seimei Hall, Tokyo, 1959, gelatin silver print.

Opposite: **Hosoe Eikō**, *Butterfly Dream #1*, 1960, gelatin silver print.

Hijikata would make rather cruel demands of Ohno sensei, but Ohno Kazuo would answer his demands, and he continued to perform as a butoh dancer. At first glance, Hijikata was the 'evil' one, and Ohno Kazuo the 'good' one. Especially as Ohno was Christian, but really it could be the other way around, Ohno could be 'evil' and Hijikata may be 'good'.

MORISHITA TAKASHI

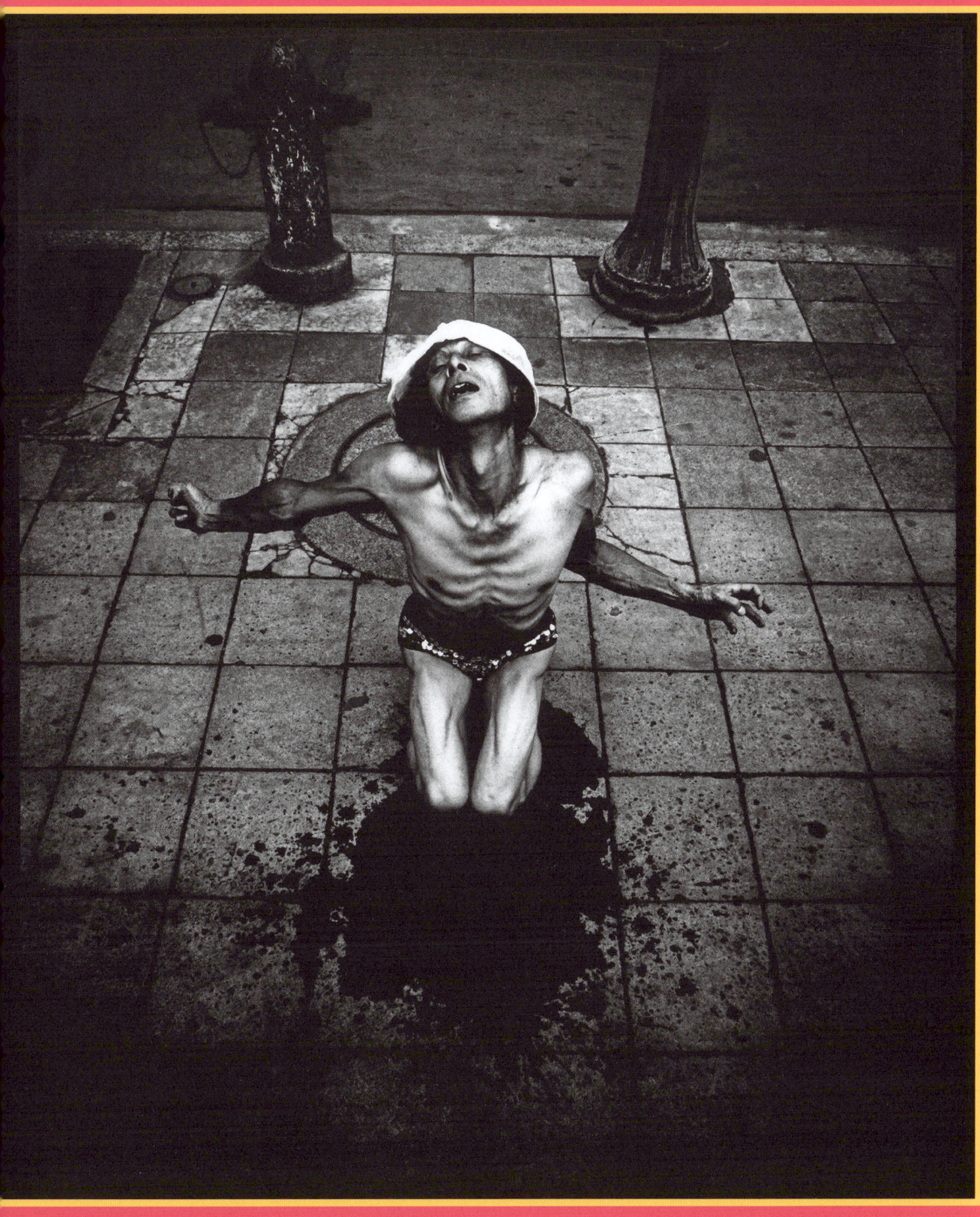

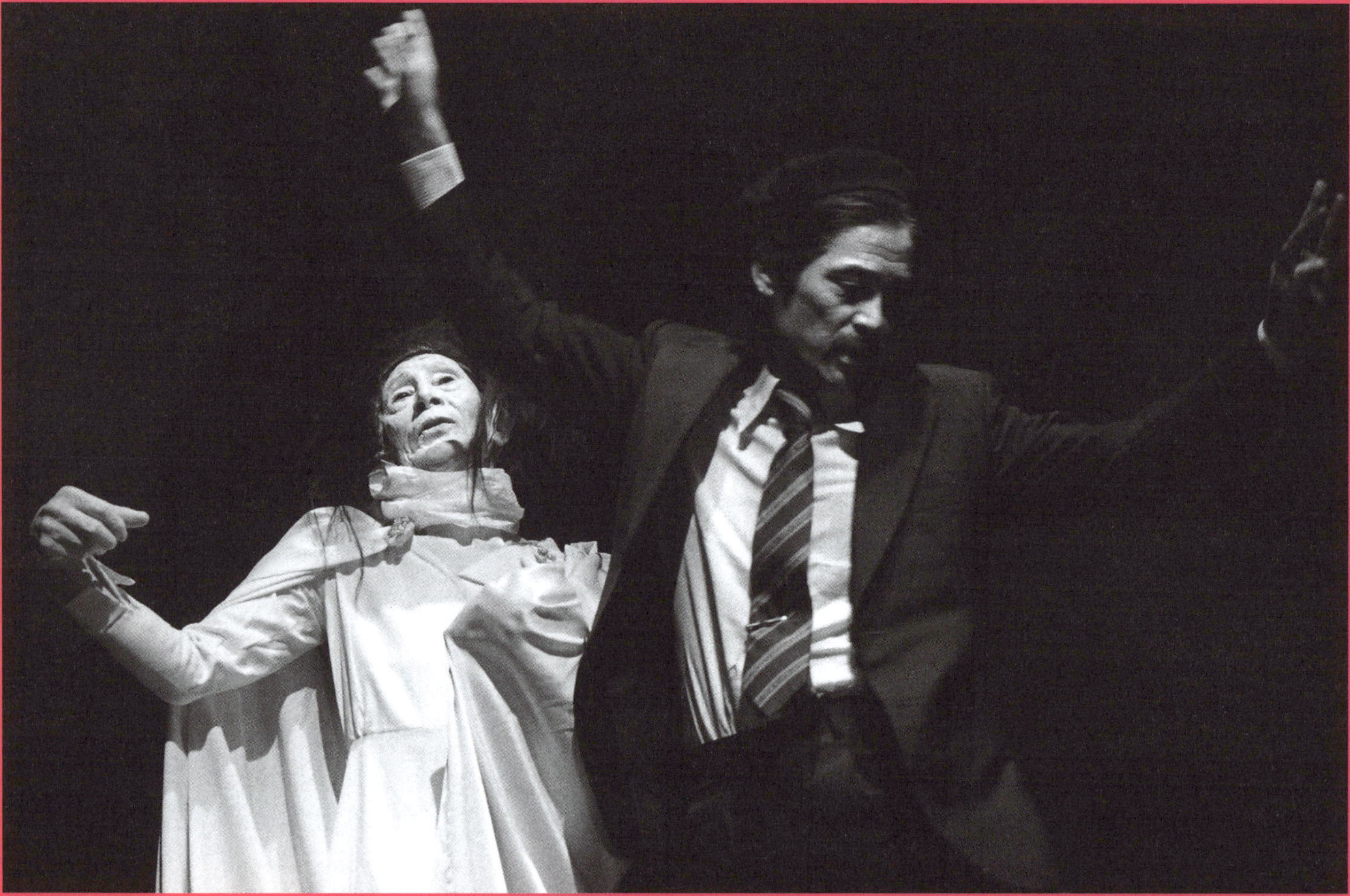

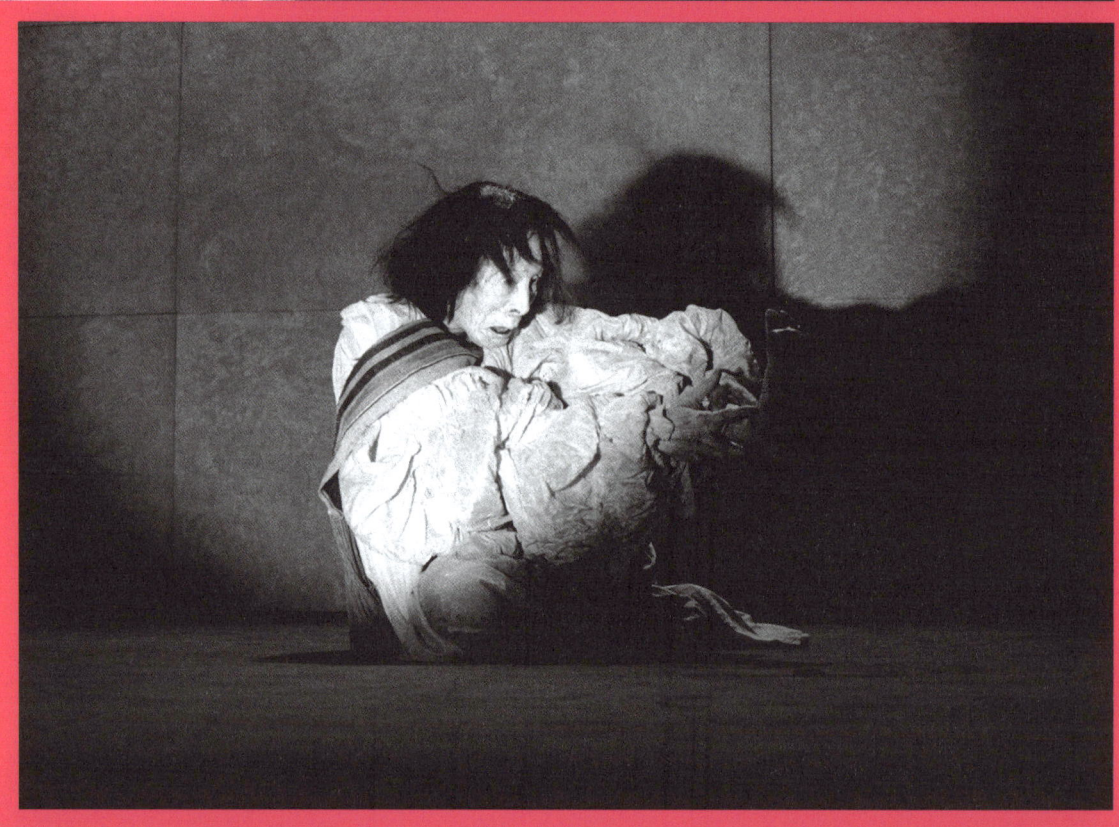

Ikegami Naoya, *The Dead Sea*, 1985, gelatin silver print.

Opposite (above, left and right): **Ikegami Naoya,** *Admiring La Argentina*, 1977, gelatin silver print.

Opposite (above middle): **Ikegami Naoya,** *My Mother*, Daiichi Seimei Hall, Tokyo, 1981, gelatin silver print.

Opposite (below left): **Ikegami Naoya,** *Admiring La Argentina*, 1977, gelatin silver print.

Opposite (below right): **Ikegami Naoya,** *The Dead Sea*, 1985, gelatin silver print.

Overleaf: **Kamiyama Teijirō,** *My Mother*, Ohno Kazuo Dance Studio, Kanagawa, 1981, gelatin silver print.

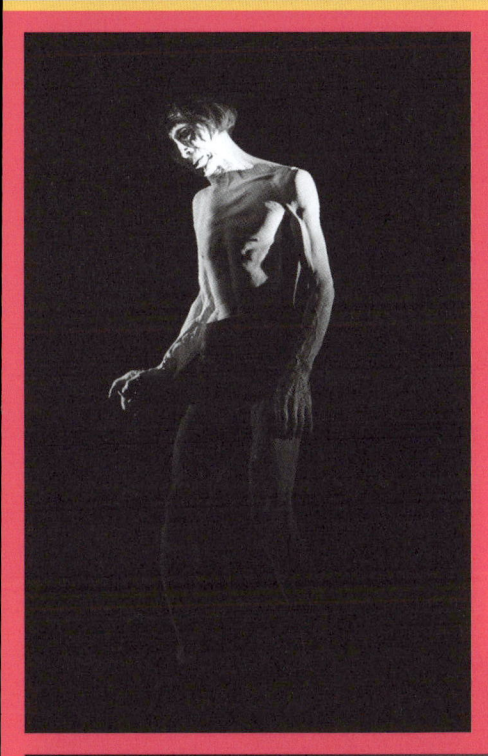
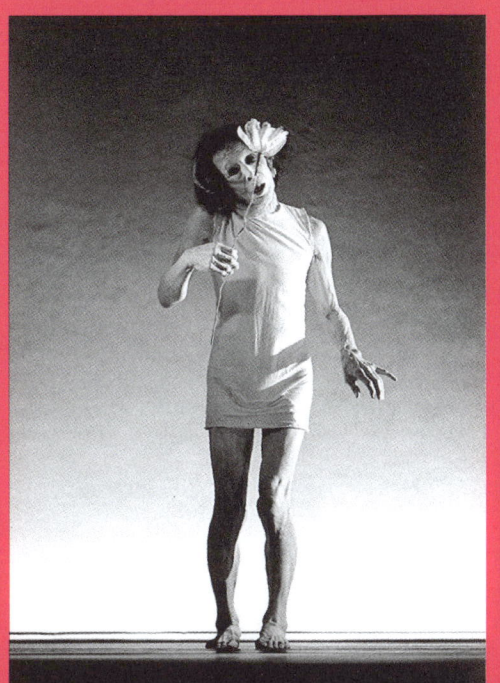
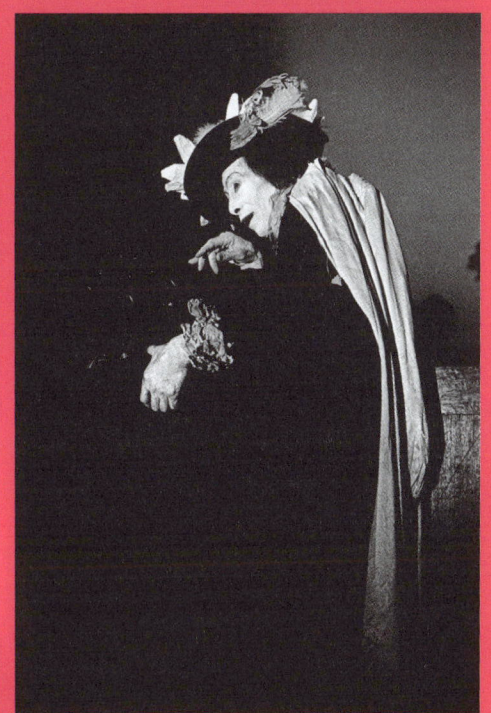
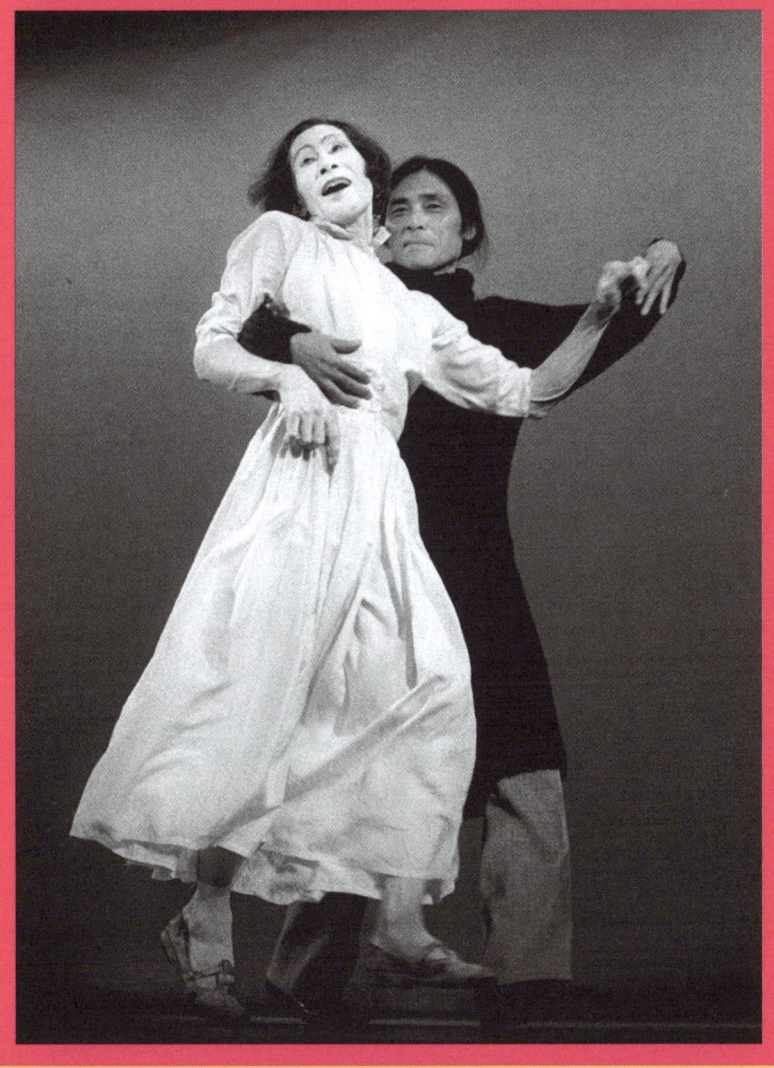
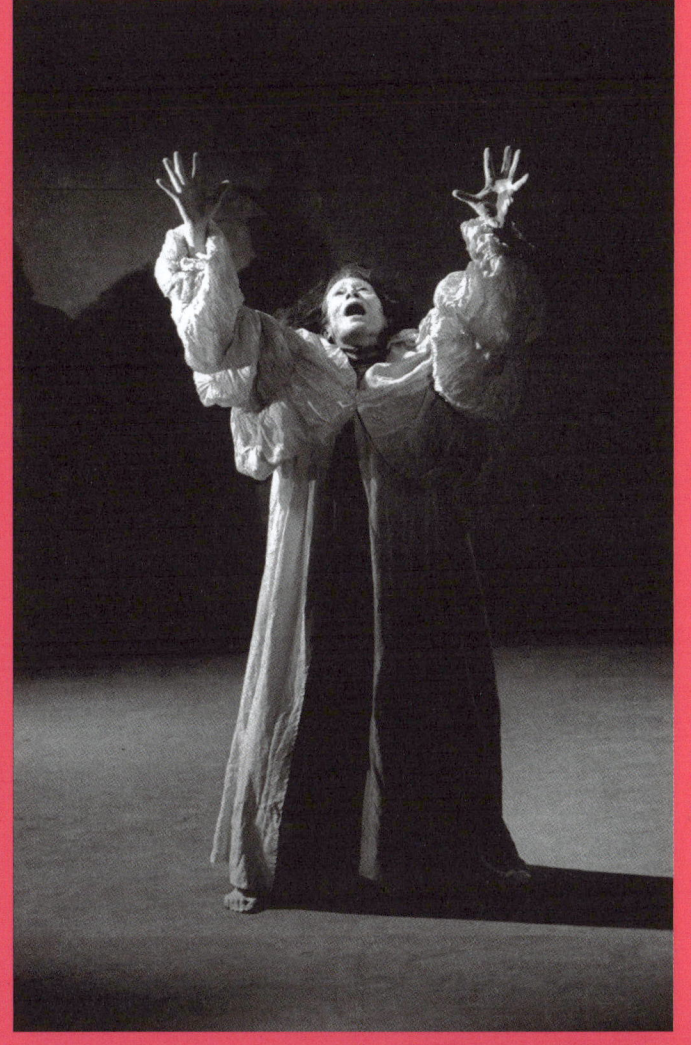

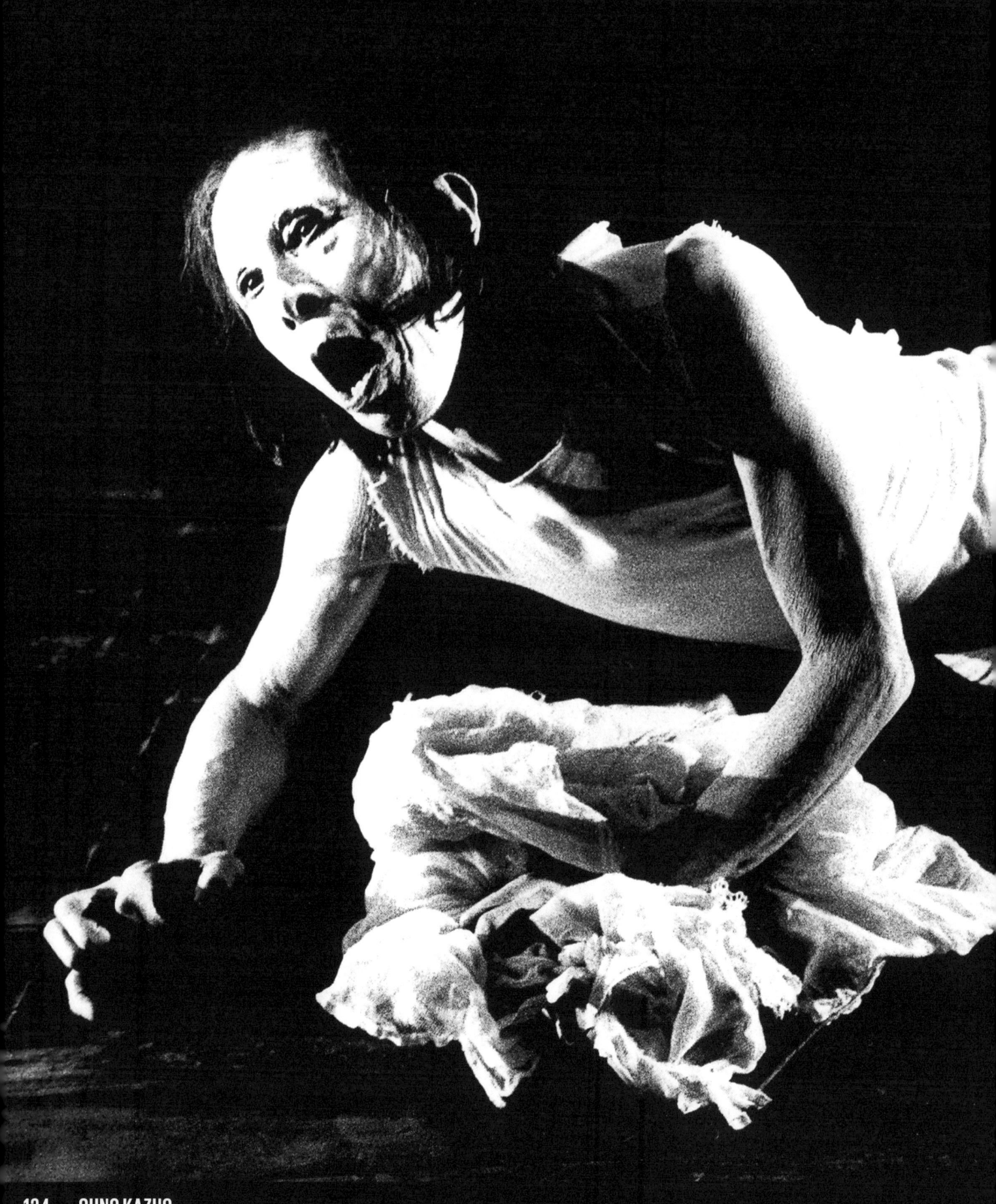

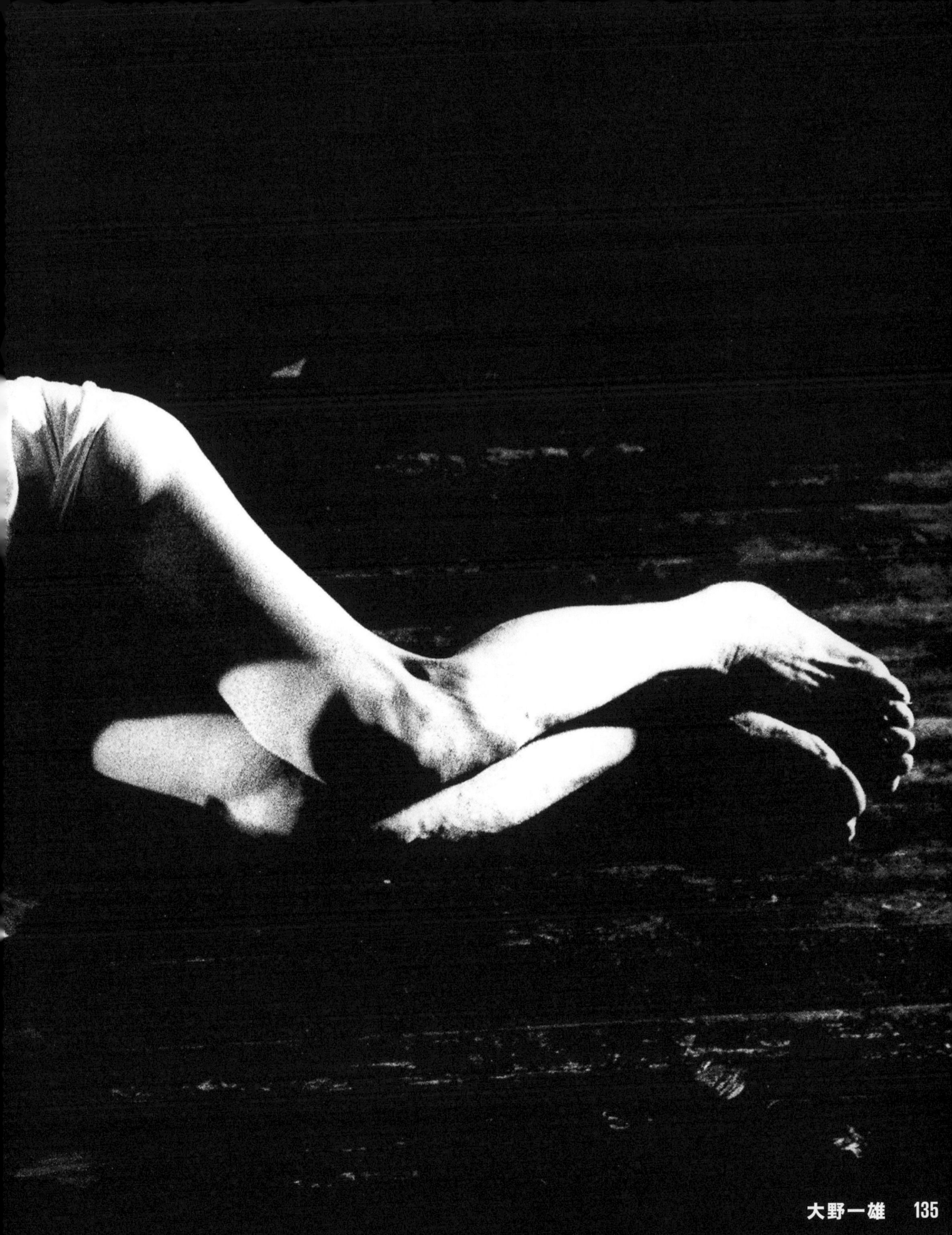

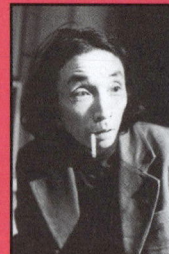

AWAZU KIYOSHI

粟津潔

1929–2009

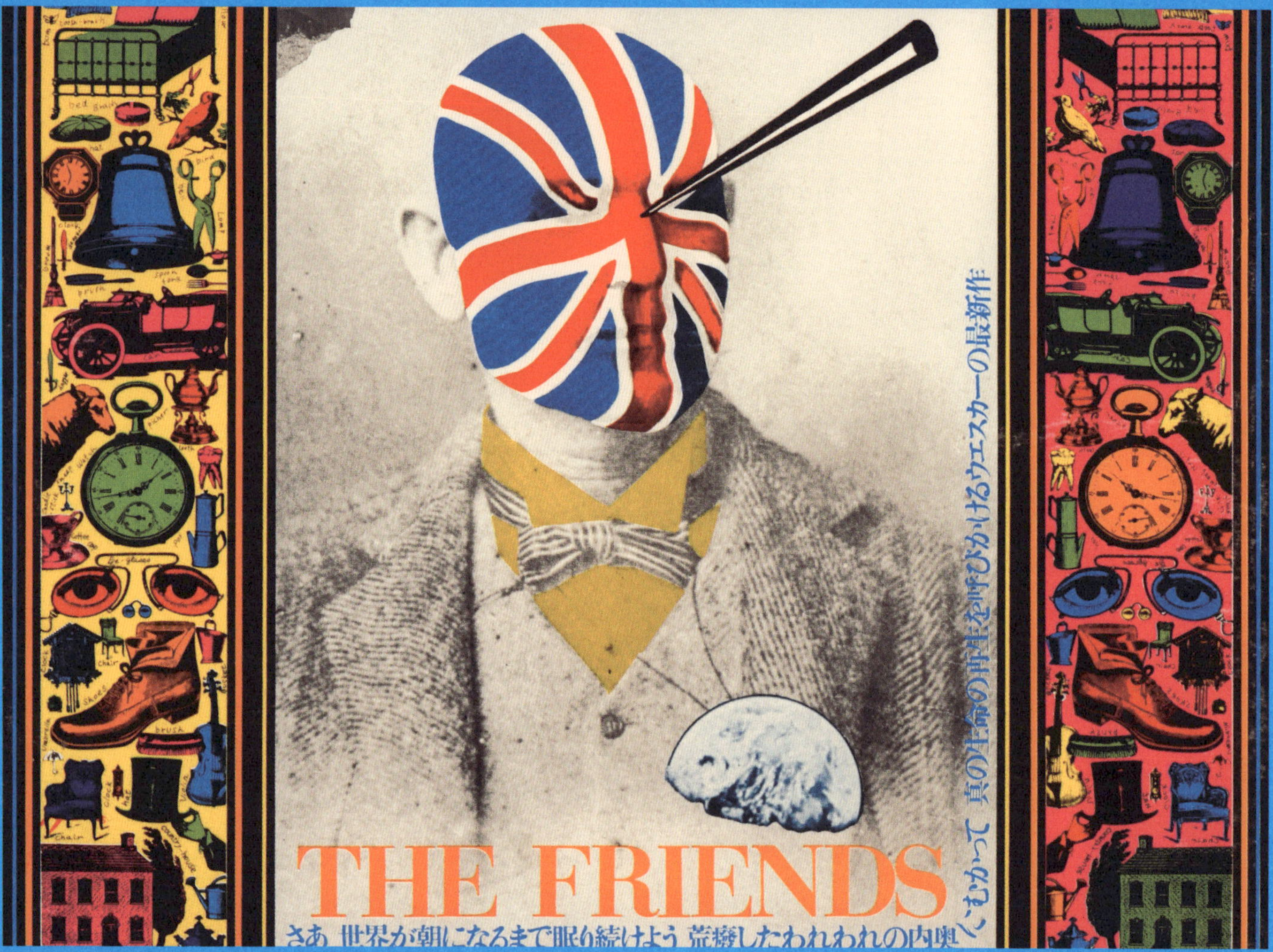

Awazu Kiyoshi, *The Friends* (detail), 1969, offset lithograph.

Opposite (above left): **Awazu Kiyoshi,** *Kikan geijutsu,* vol. 4, no. 2 (Spring 1970), cover.

Opposite (above right): **Awazu Kiyoshi,** *The 6th Exhibition of Contemporary Japanese Sculpture, Ube City, Japan,* 1975, poster.

Awazu Kiyoshi was a self-taught designer whose posters for theatrical performances, films, magazines, political campaigns and exhibitions helped to define the visual culture of the underground scene.

LUCY FLEMING-BROWN

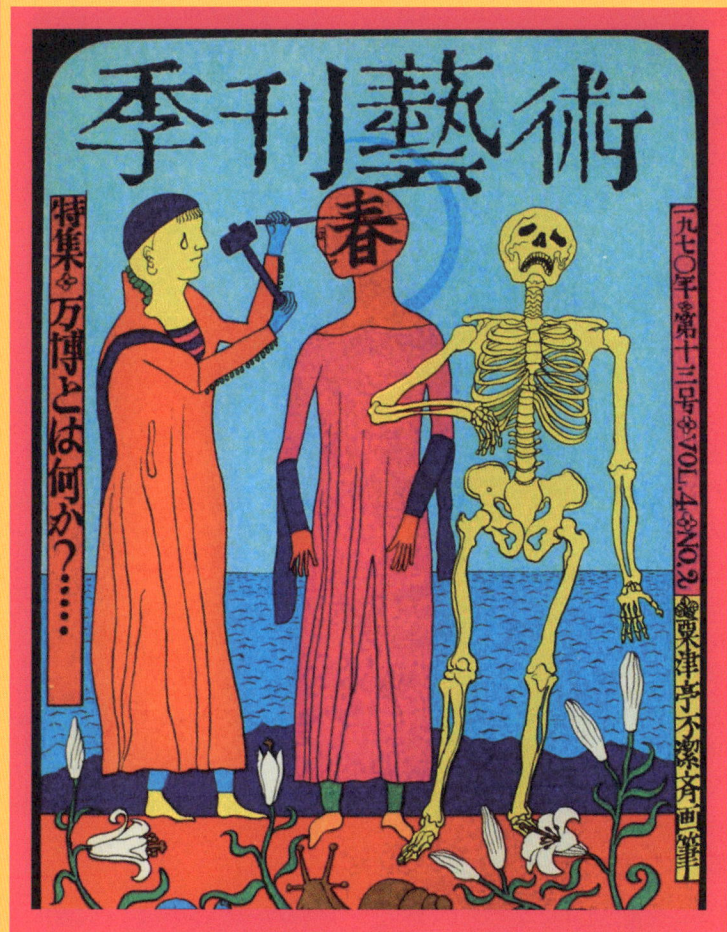
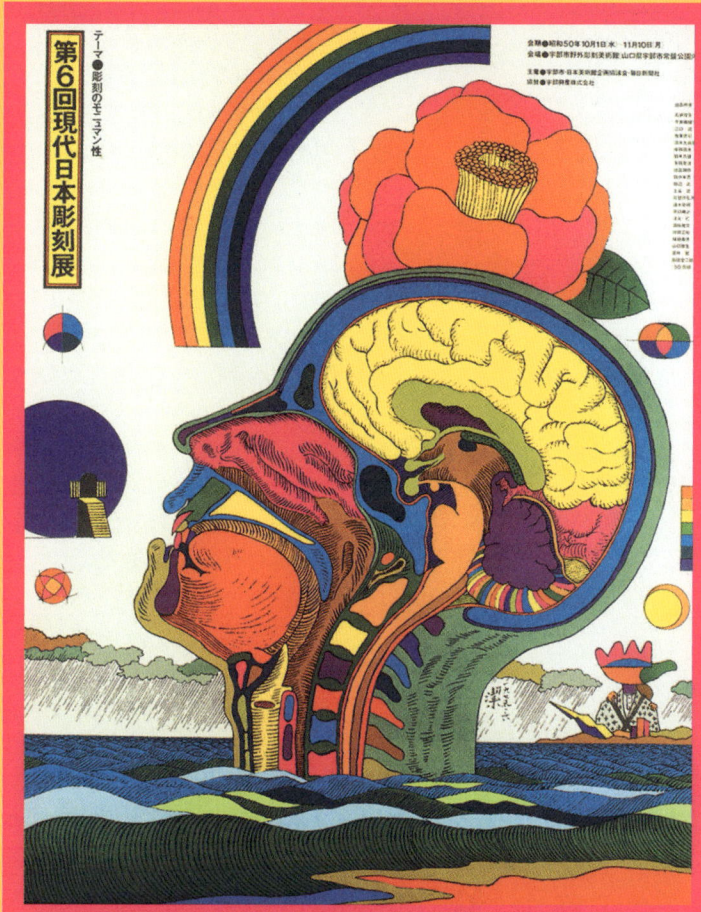

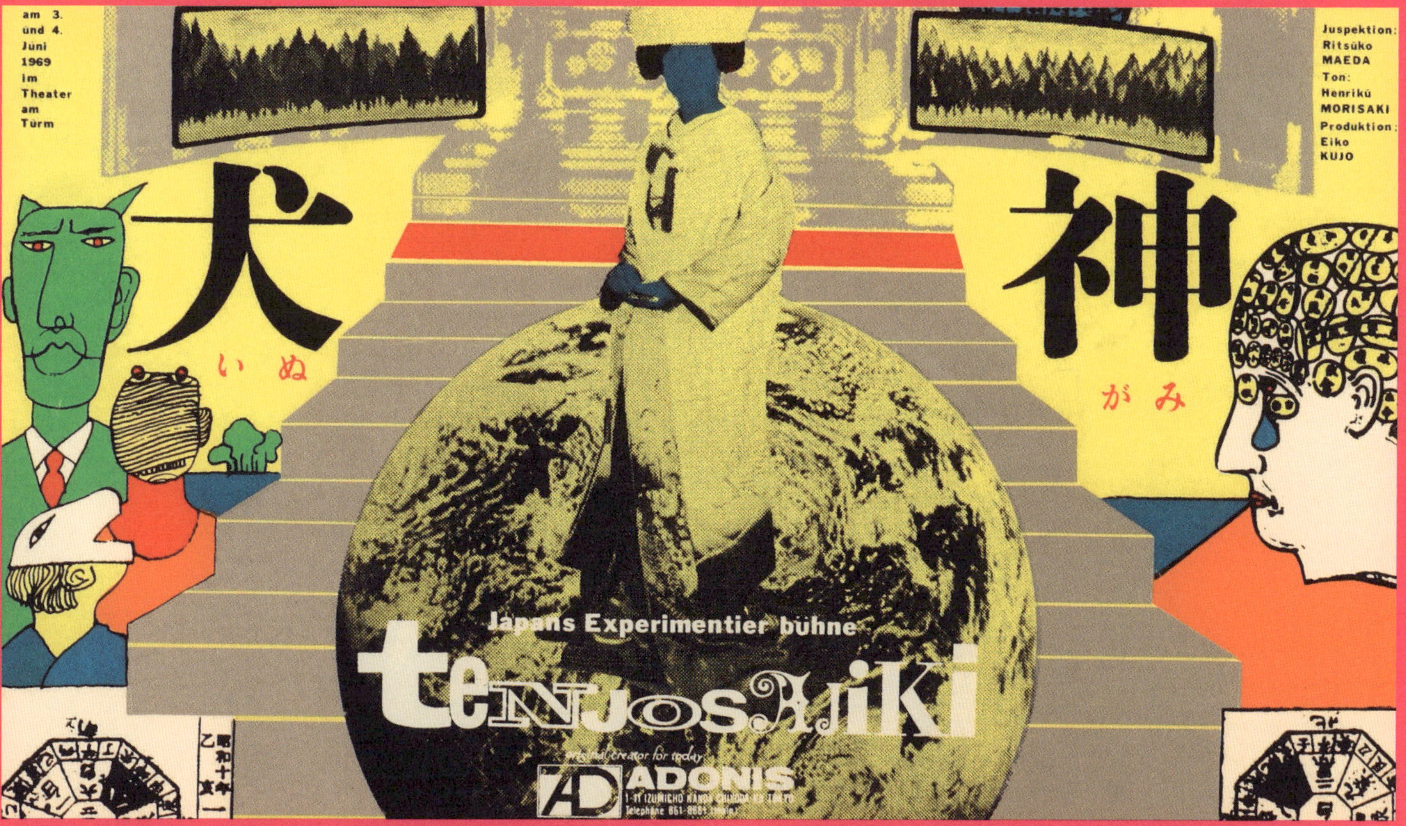

AWAZU KIYOSHI

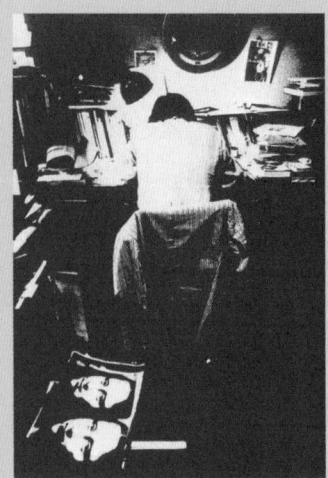

Drawn to posters as a medium that functions in the public realm, Awazu made art that was informed by a strong sense of social responsibility and an interest in the new politics of communication prompted by the nascent age of mass media communication and technological reproduction. His understanding of design was not limited to the graphic arts, and during the 1970s Awazu also collaborated with proponents of Metabolist architecture to explore the possibilities of 'environmental design'.

Awazu was born in Tokyo, and his schooling was interrupted by the intensive bombing raids which destroyed the city towards the end of the Pacific War (1941–45). During this period he was exposed to the socialist realist approach of the artist Ben Shahn, as well as the Bauhaus-trained aesthetics of graphic designer Herbert Bayer, and these influences progressed Awazu's socially engaged attitude to design. Awazu's breakthrough came in 1955, when he was awarded the Japan Advertising Artists' Club's Grand Prize for his poster *Give Our Sea Back*. This design was created to raise awareness of the plight of fishermen whose livelihoods were threatened by the destruction of fishing grounds in Chiba prefecture, cleared to make way for a US military firing range.

Awazu's graphic style, exemplified by his designs for Terayama Shūji's Tenjō Sajiki theatre troupe, combines expressive hand-drawn illustrations with a strikingly surreal and often playful inflection. He rejected the cold formalism of international modernism to make use of folkloric imagery and symbols from popular culture.

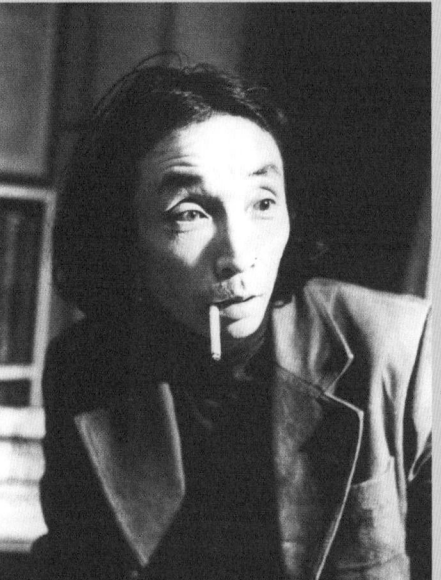

This distinctive visual language imbues his designs with a local potency, rooted in a far-reaching sensitivity to Japanese aesthetics drawn from his own historical context and beyond.

LUCY FLEMING-BROWN

p. 137 (below): **Awazu Kiyoshi**, *Tenjō Sajiki: Inugami* (detail), 1969, poster.

Above and below: Photographs of **Awazu Kiyoshi** from *Scrapbook* (1974).

Opposite: **Awazu Kiyoshi**, *Himiko/Hyogensha Co. Ltd, The Japan Art Theatre Guild*, 1974, poster.

Overleaf: Illustrations from **Awazu Kiyoshi**, *Scrapbook* (1974).

p. 142: **Awazu Kiyoshi**, *Onnatachi: Kumehachi ichiza no hitobito/Bungakuza*, 1977, offset print.

p. 143: **Awazu Kiyoshi**, *Chi no mure/Bungakuza*, 1970, offset print.

p. 144: **Awazu Kiyoshi**, *Inugami/Tenjō Sajiki*, 1969, silkscreen print.

p. 145: **Awazu Kiyoshi**, *Hanaoka Seishū no tsuma/Bungakuza*, 1970, poster.

pp. 146–47: Images from **Awazu Kiyoshi**, *Scrapbook* (1974).

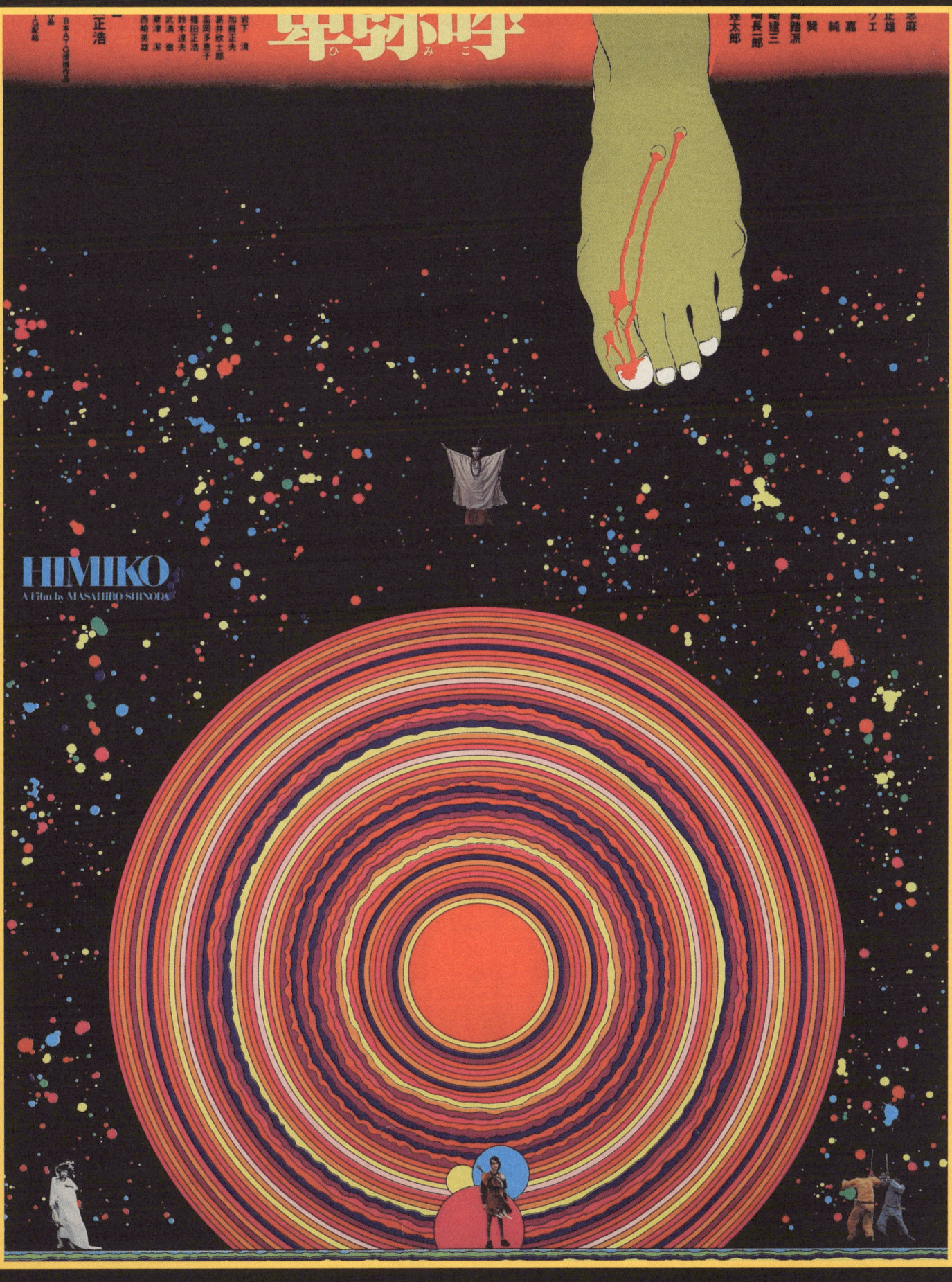

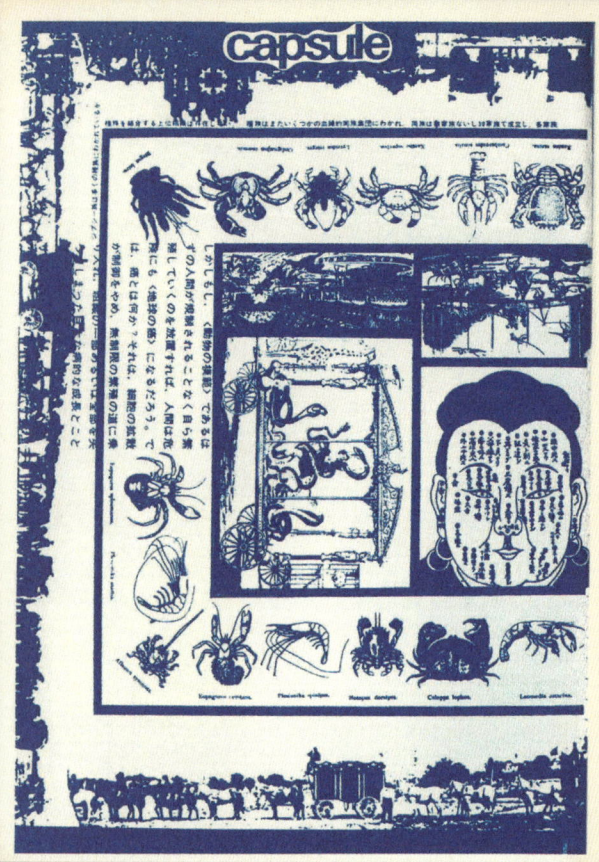
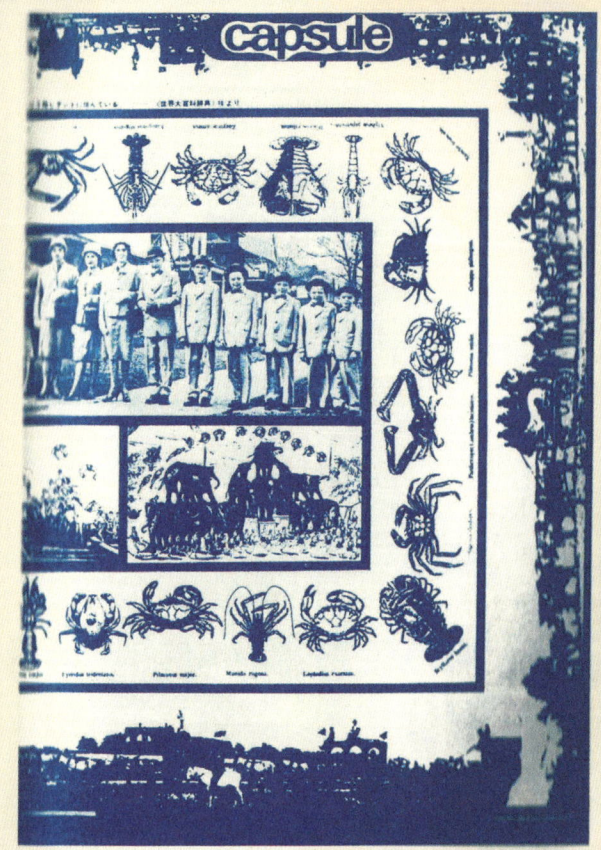
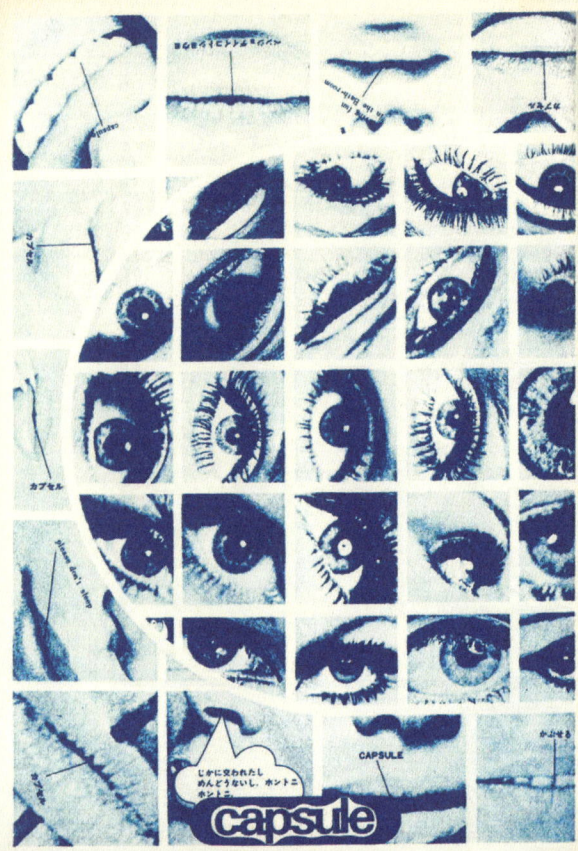
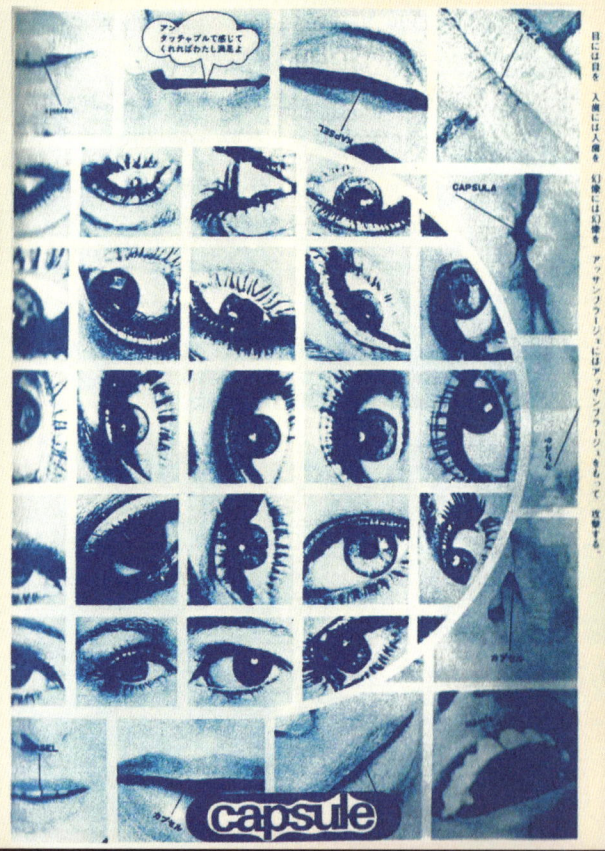

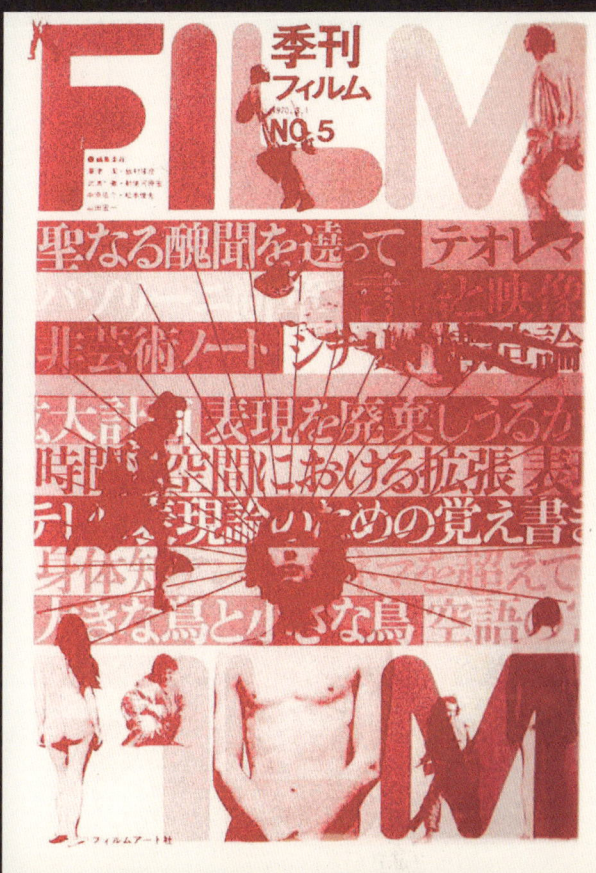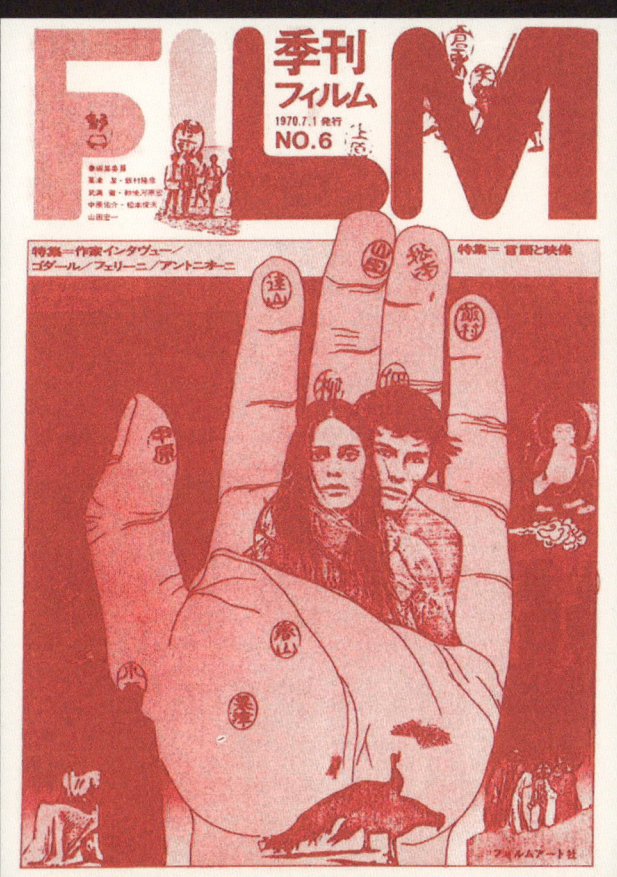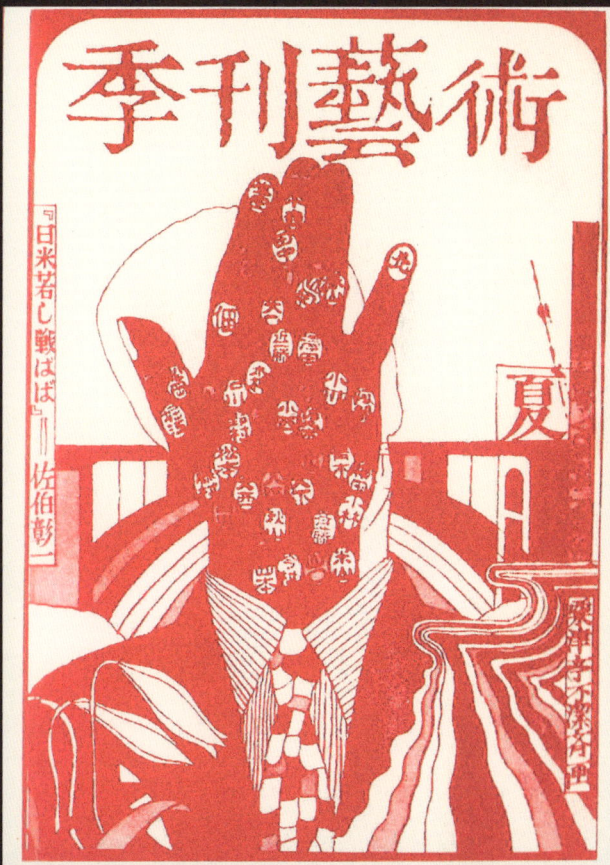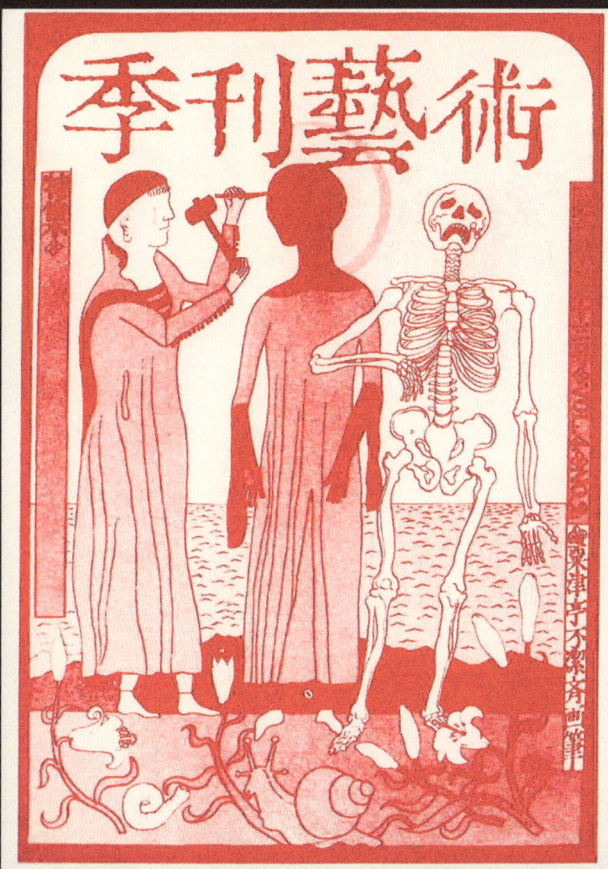

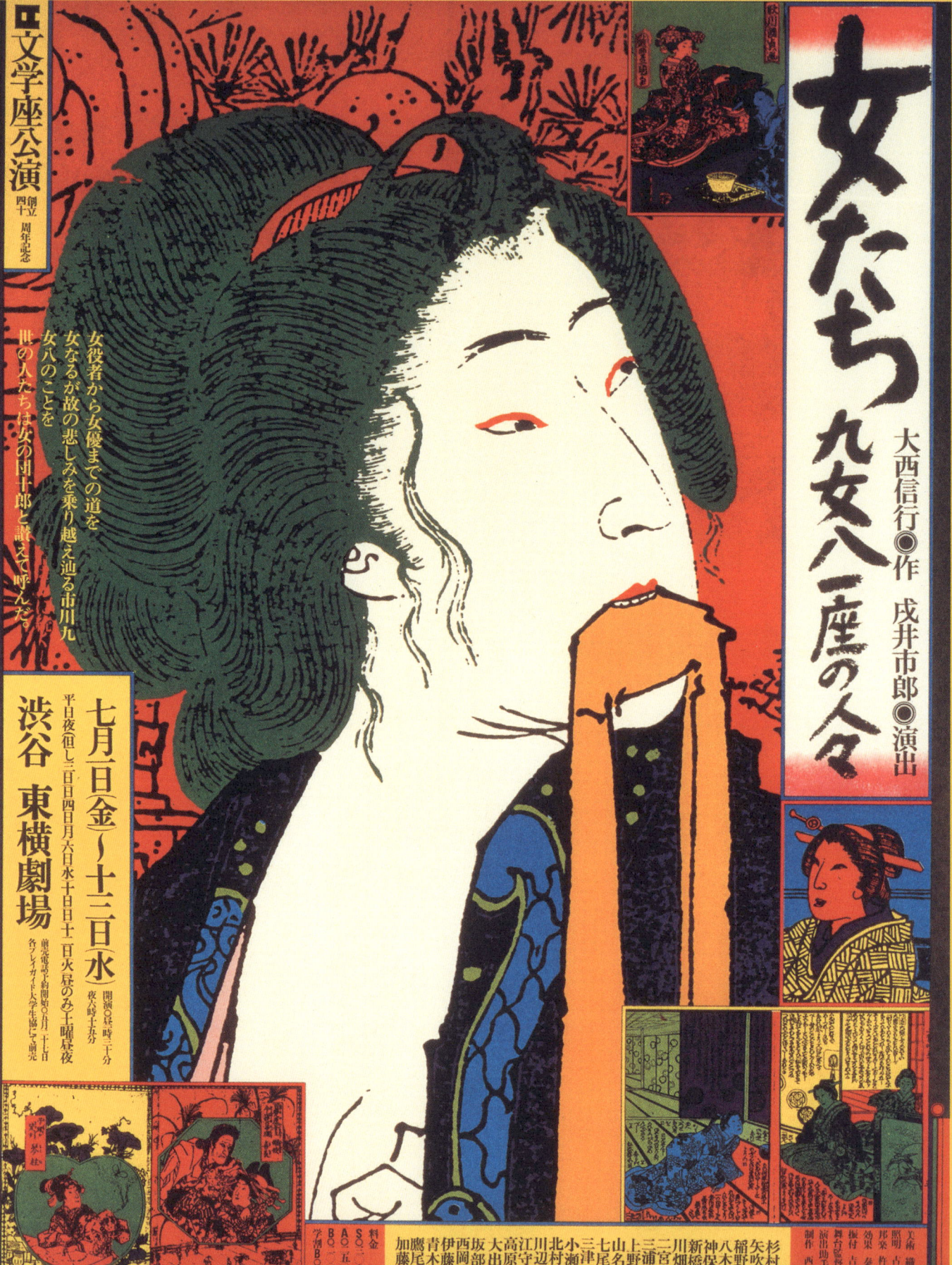

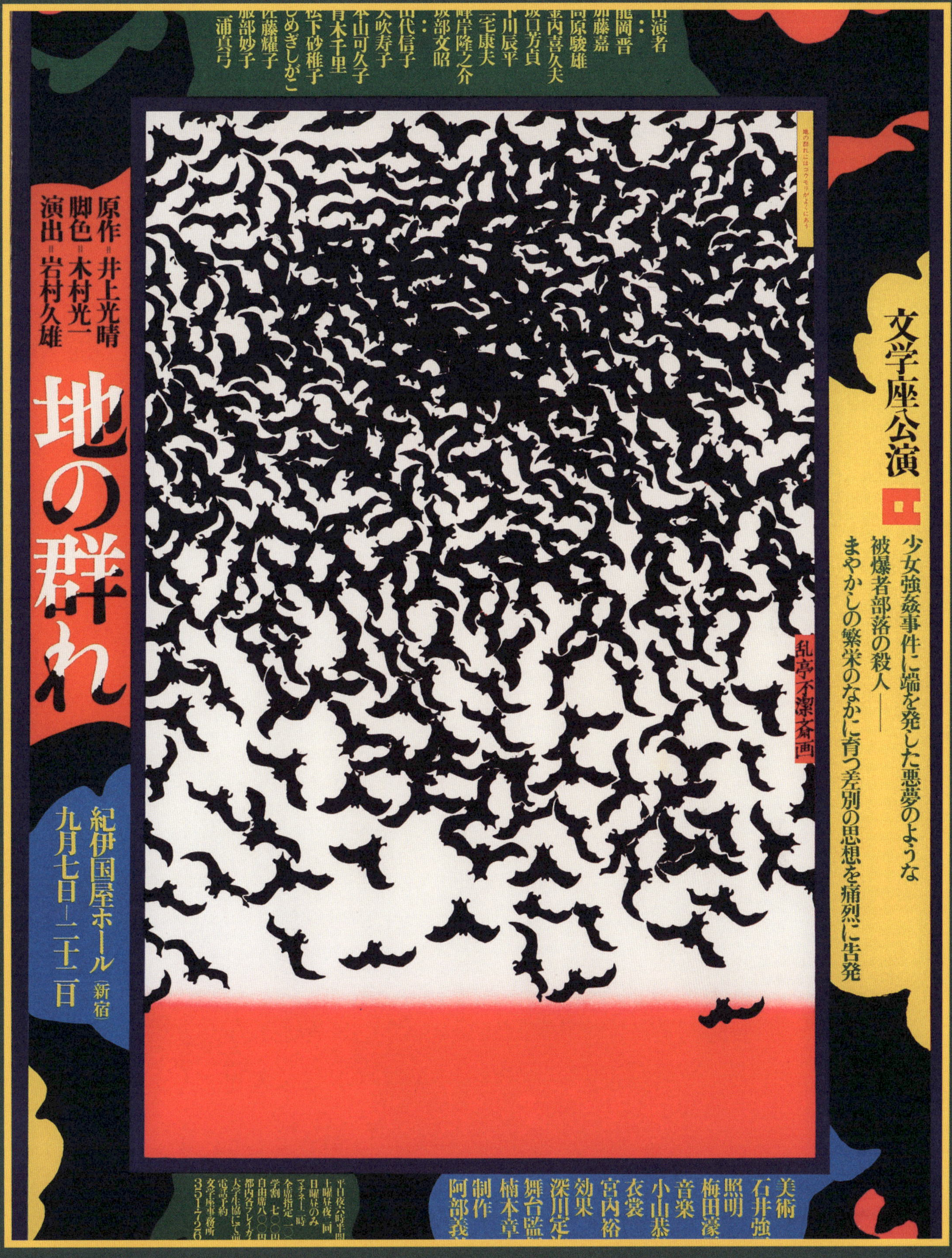

文学座公演

地の群れ

原作＝井上光晴
脚色＝木村光一
演出＝岩村久雄

紀伊国屋ホール〈新宿〉
九月七日―二十一日

少女強姦事件に端を発した悪夢のような
被爆者部落の殺人――
まやかしの繁栄のなかに育つ差別の思想を痛烈に告発

出演者
龍岡晋　加藤嘉　金内喜久雄　同原駿雄　坂口芳貞　戸川辰平　三宅康夫　峯岸隆之介　坂部文昭　田代信子　大吹寿子　本山可久子　青木千里　松下砂稚子　ひめぎしがこ　佐藤耀子　服部妙子　浦真弓

地の群れにはコタクなりようにあみ

乱亭不潔斎画

美術＝石井強
照明＝梅田濠
音楽＝宮内裕
効果＝深川定
衣裳＝小山恭
舞台監督＝楠本章
制作＝阿部義

平日夜＝六時半開演
土曜昼夜＝二回
日曜昼夜＝のみ
マチネー＝一時
全席指定　一〇〇〇円
学割　七〇〇円
自由席八〇〇円
都内各プレイガ
イド・生協にてお
求め下さい
文学座事務所
電話＝
351-7265

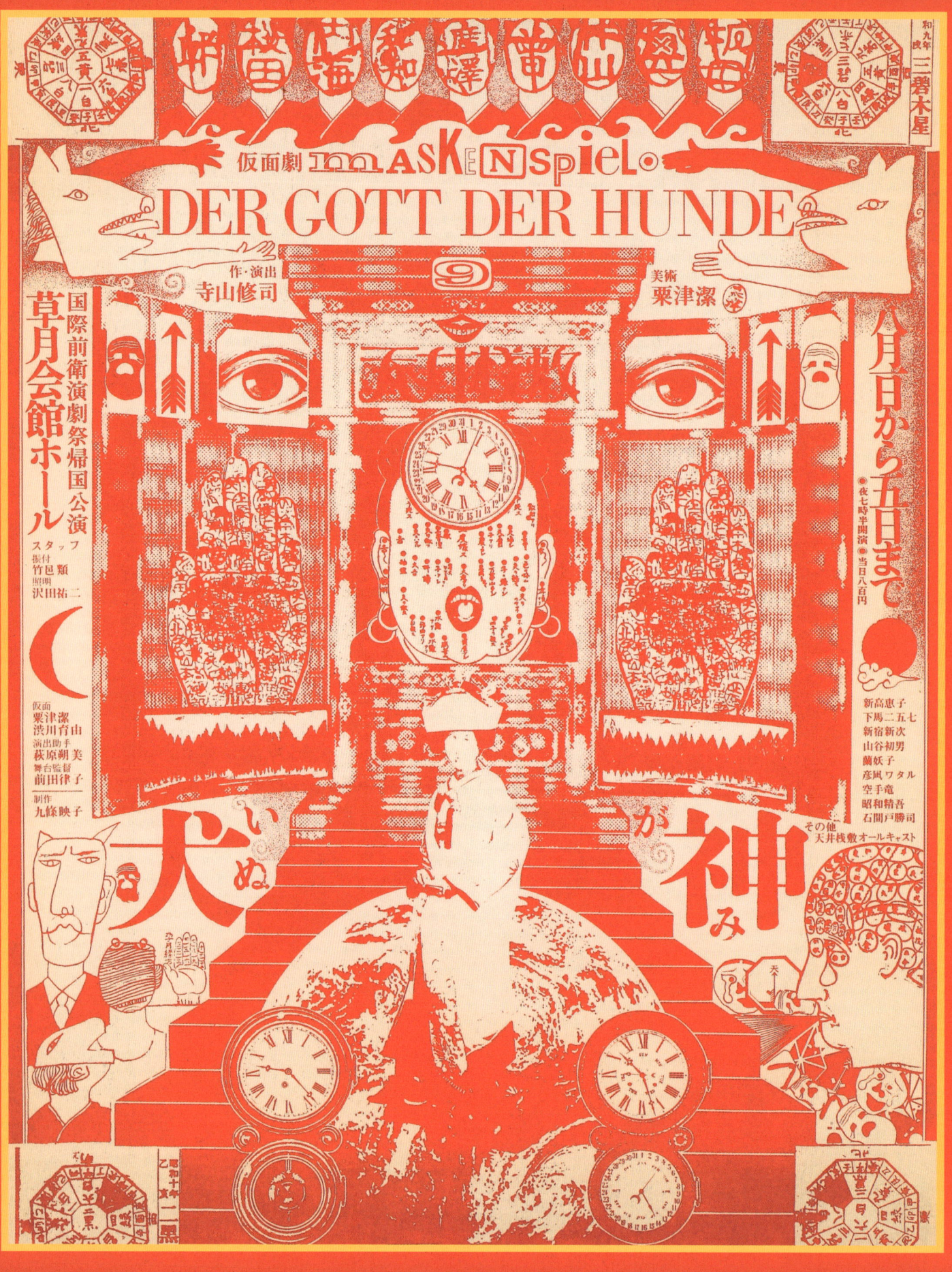

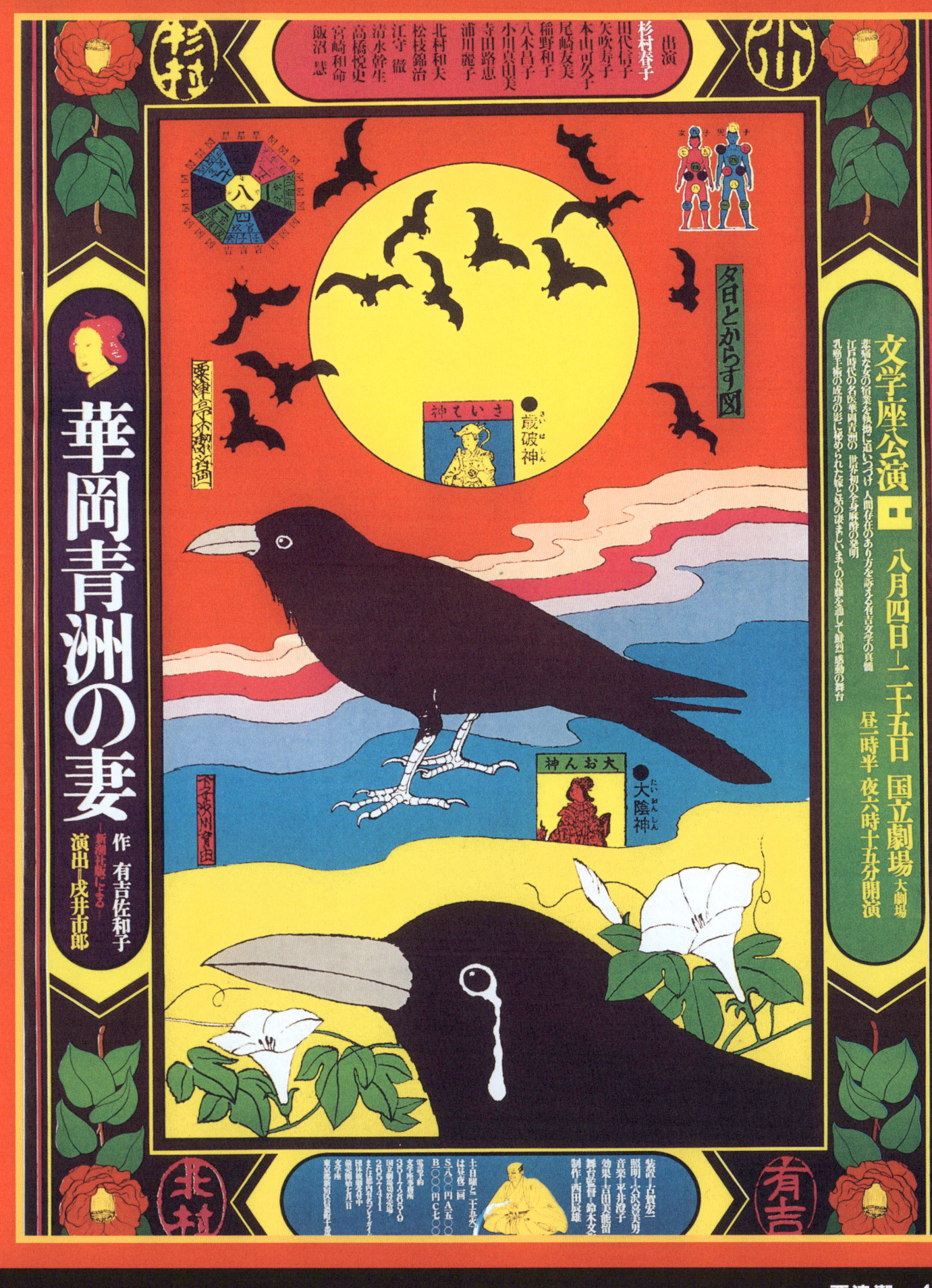

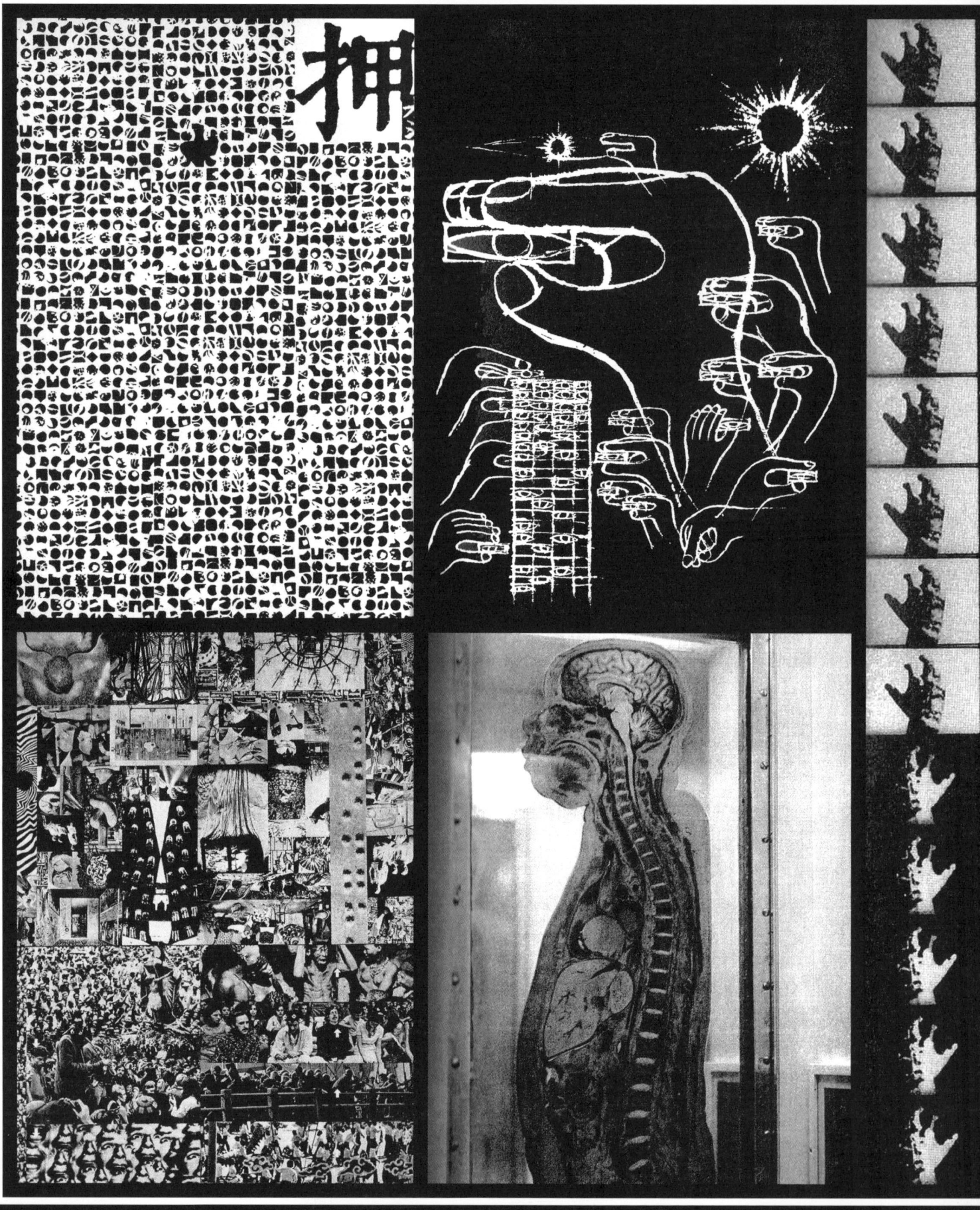

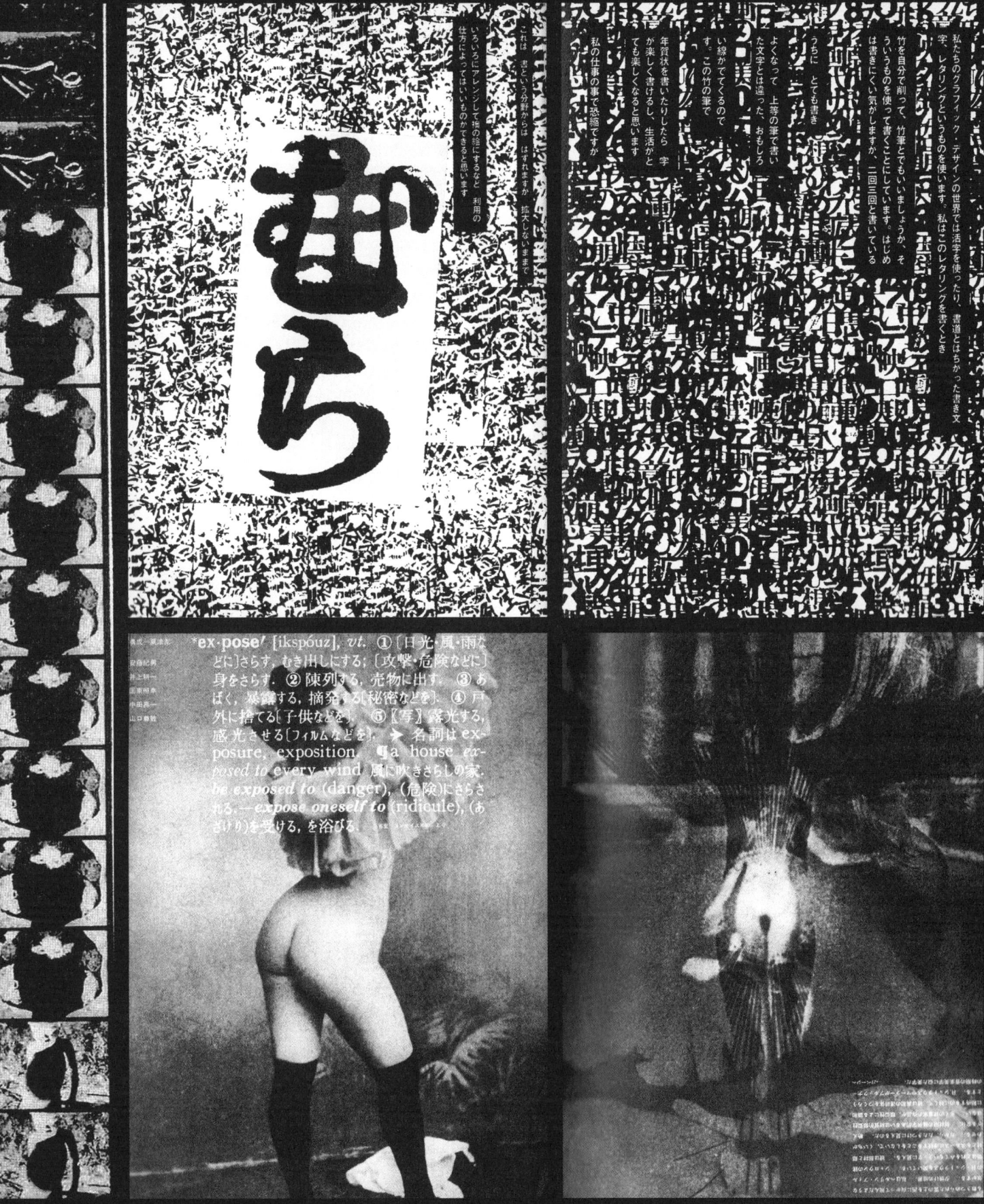

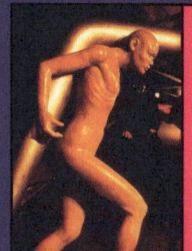

TERAYAMA SHŪJI

1935–1983

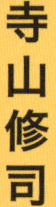

寺山修司

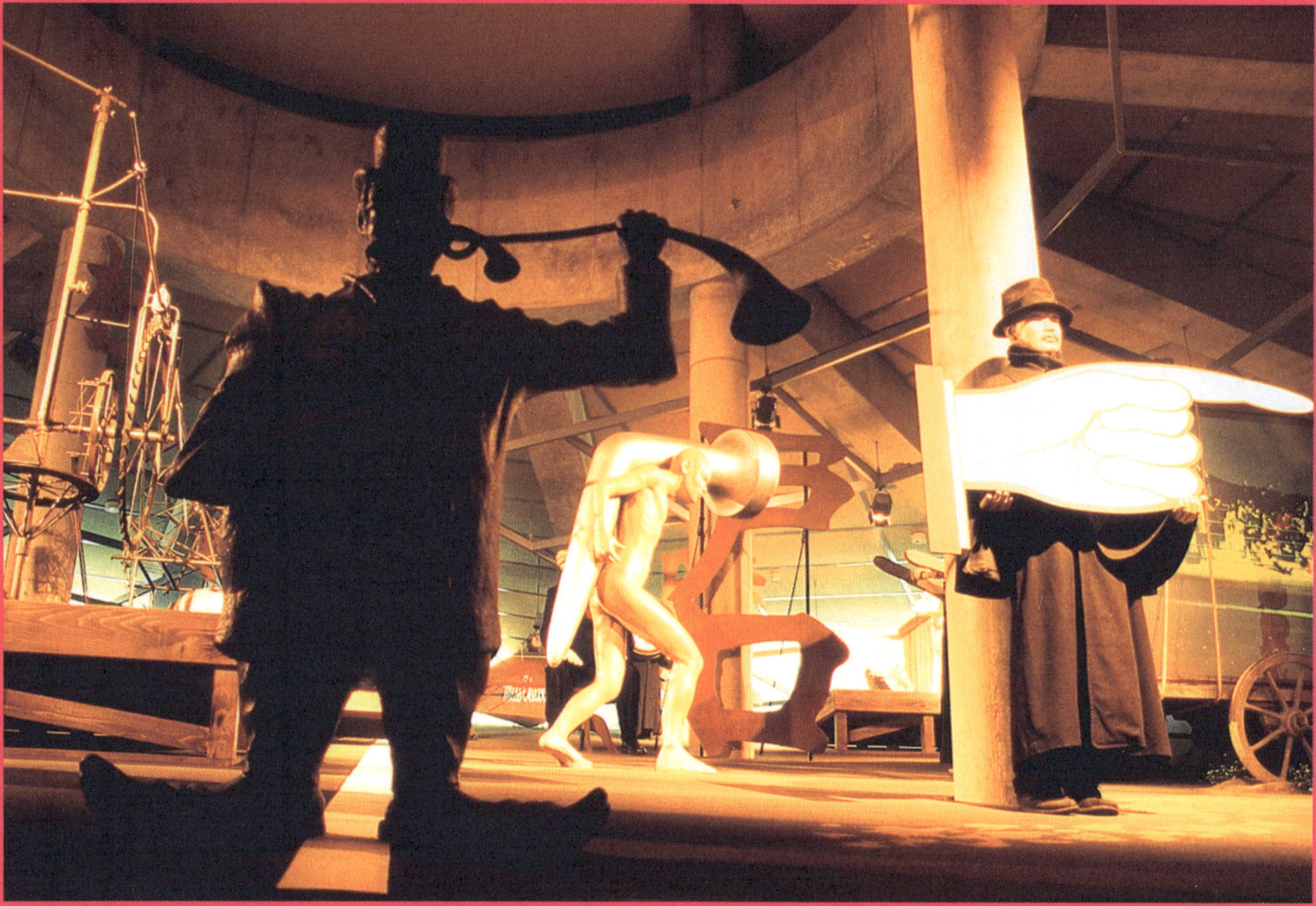

Photograph from **Terayama Shūji**, *The Terayama Shuji Theatre Museum: 1935–2008* (2008).

Opposite (above, left and right): Photographs from **Terayama Shūji**, *Photothèque imaginaire de Shuji Terayama* (1975).

Opposite (below): Photograph from **Terayama Shūji**, *Terayama Shūji no kamen gahō* (1978).

'The very first thing we tried to do with theatre was to create a cultural scandal. At the beginning, we were doing something similar to circuses or freak shows, where dwarfs and giants went on stage with circus people to accuse society. Society was in a period of upheaval in the 1960s, and the student protests were just beginning. I wanted to shake up the inertia of the everyday lives of Japanese citizens through theatre.'

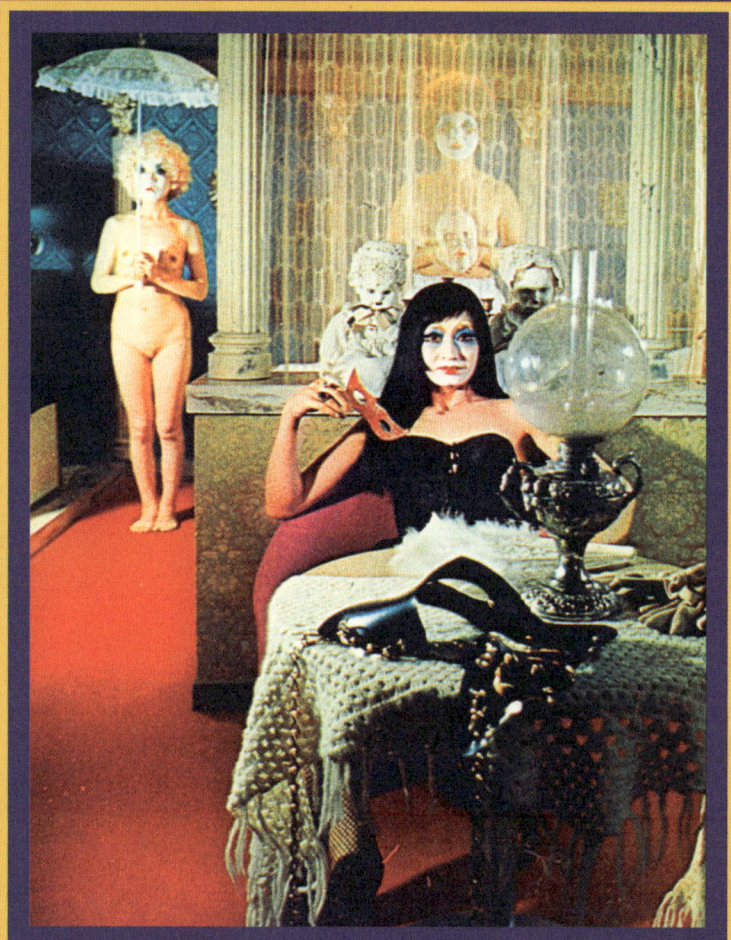
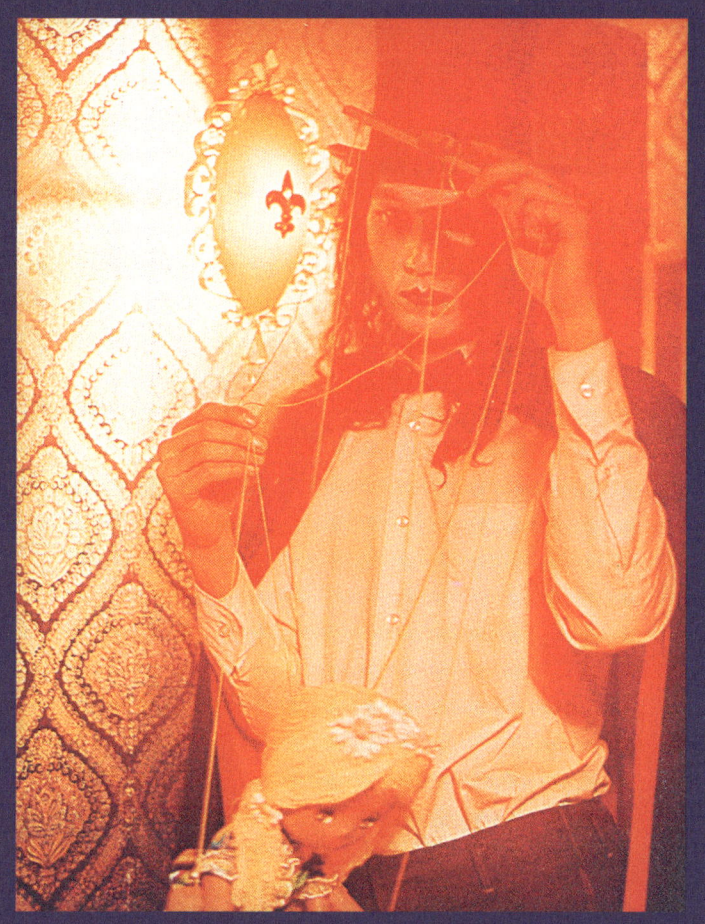

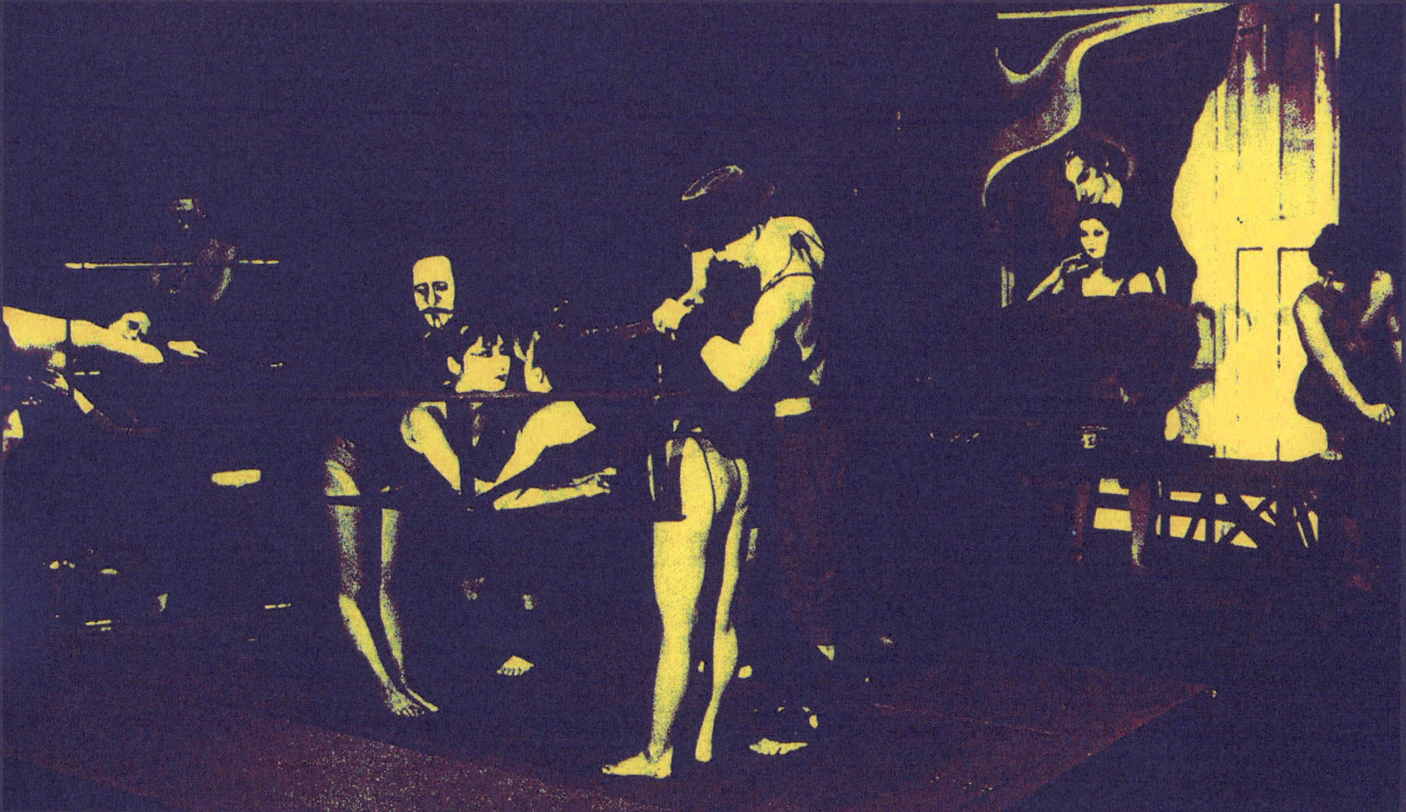

寺山修司　149

'I THINK PLAYS SHOULD SHOW THINGS THAT PEOPLE CANNOT SEE IN REALITY, LIKE THE WORLD BEFORE BIRTH, OR THE WORLD AFTER DEATH – SOMETHING THAT WOULD NEVER HAPPEN. I THINK SOMETHING FANTASTIC AND BIZARRE IS MORE INTERESTING.'

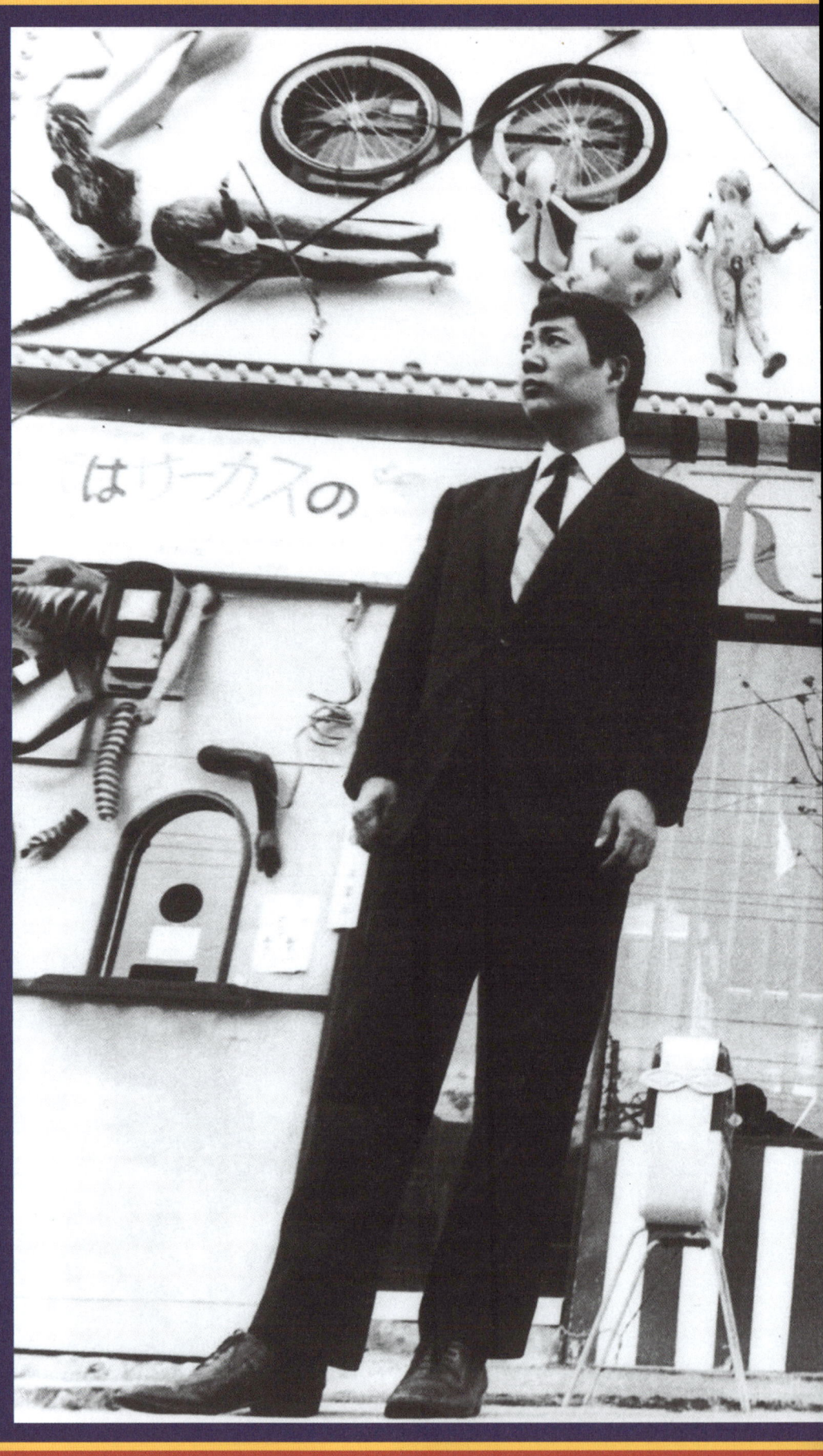

Photograph from **Terayama Shūji**, *The Terayama Shuji Theatre Museum: 1935–2008* (2008).

Overleaf (left): Stills from **Terayama Shūji**, *The Cage* (1964) short film.

Overleaf (right): Stills from **Terayama Shūji**, *Butterfly* (1974), short film.

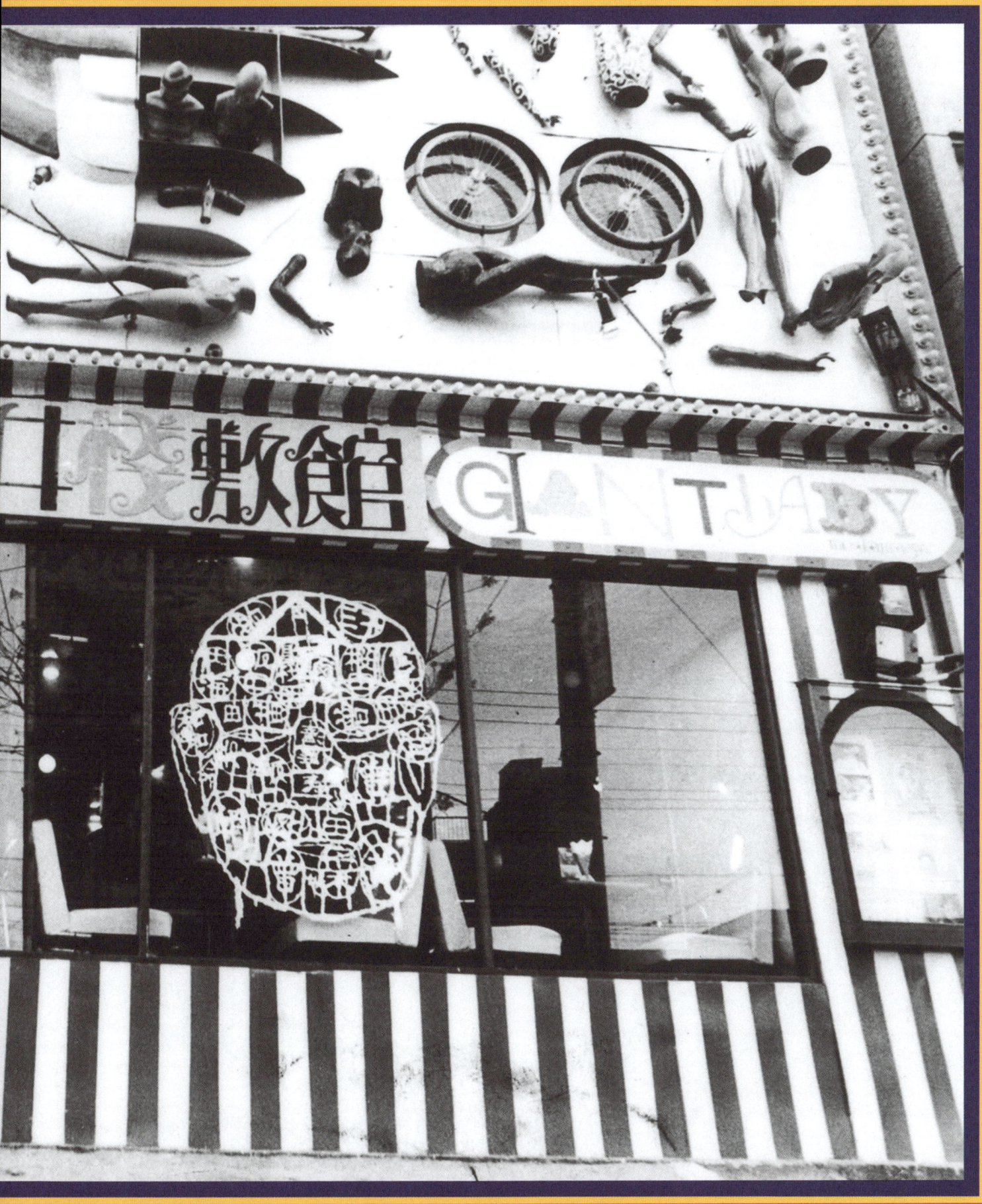

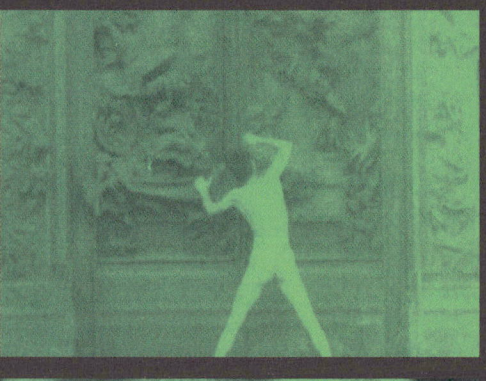
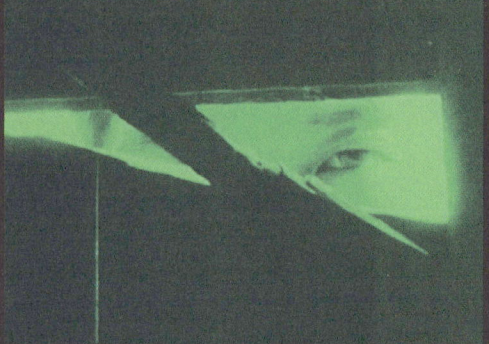
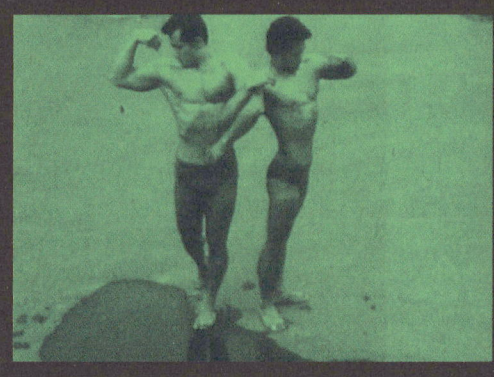
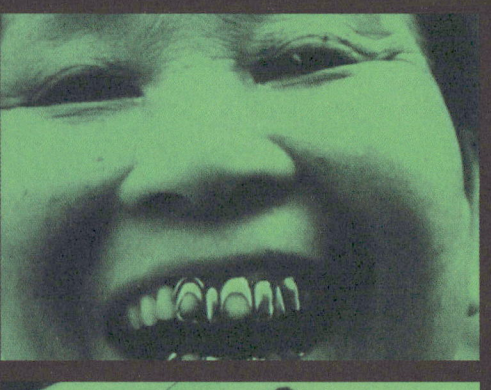

'When reality takes hold as another illusion, which runs into another reality, there will be an infinite conflict between reality and imagination. In *Ekibyō ryūkōki* (*Journal of the Plague Year*), we set up curtains in the auditorium, making the play visible and invisible. A person in seat A and a person in seat B would see completely different things, so the play was constructed by the imagination of each.'

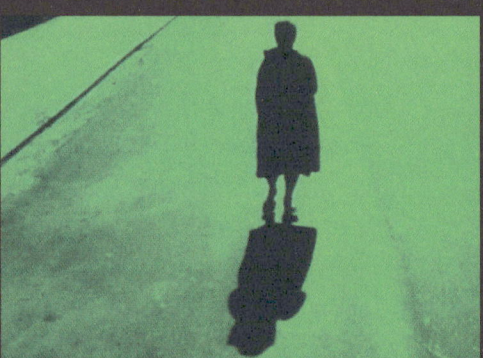
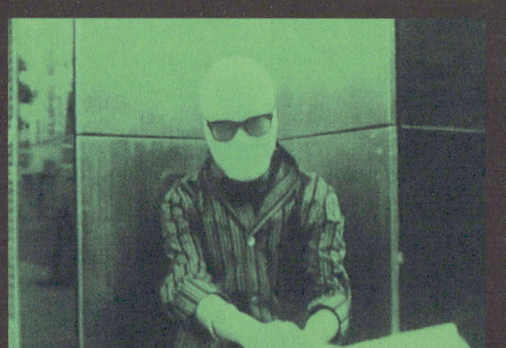
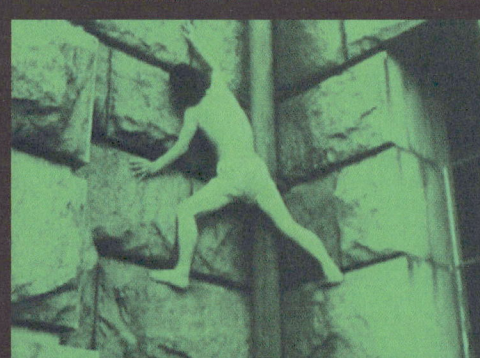

'It's the bizarre department of the human museum. Within the grotesque fiction of what appear to be disgraceful exhibitions, we catch a glimpse of hell and thereby open our eyes to the harmony of everyday reality. Instead of enjoying illusions as illusions, people have poured their energies into making a giant illusion of reality.'

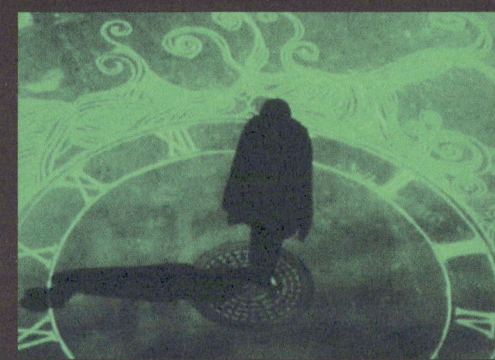
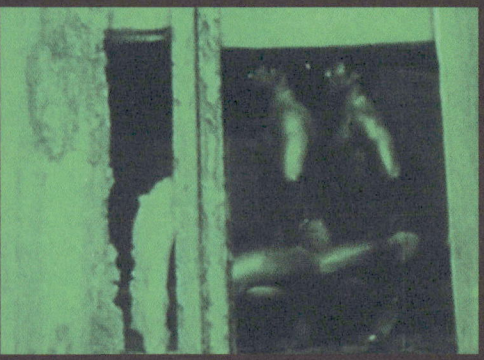
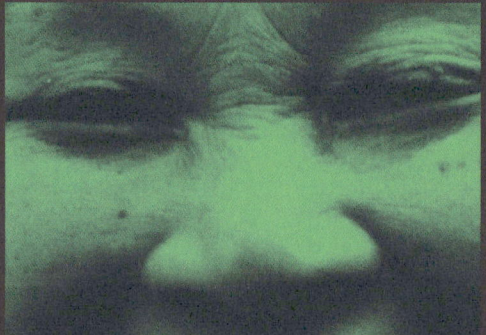
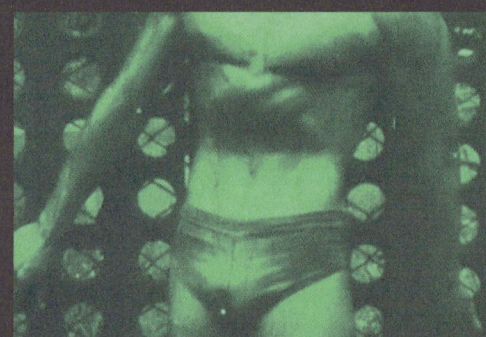

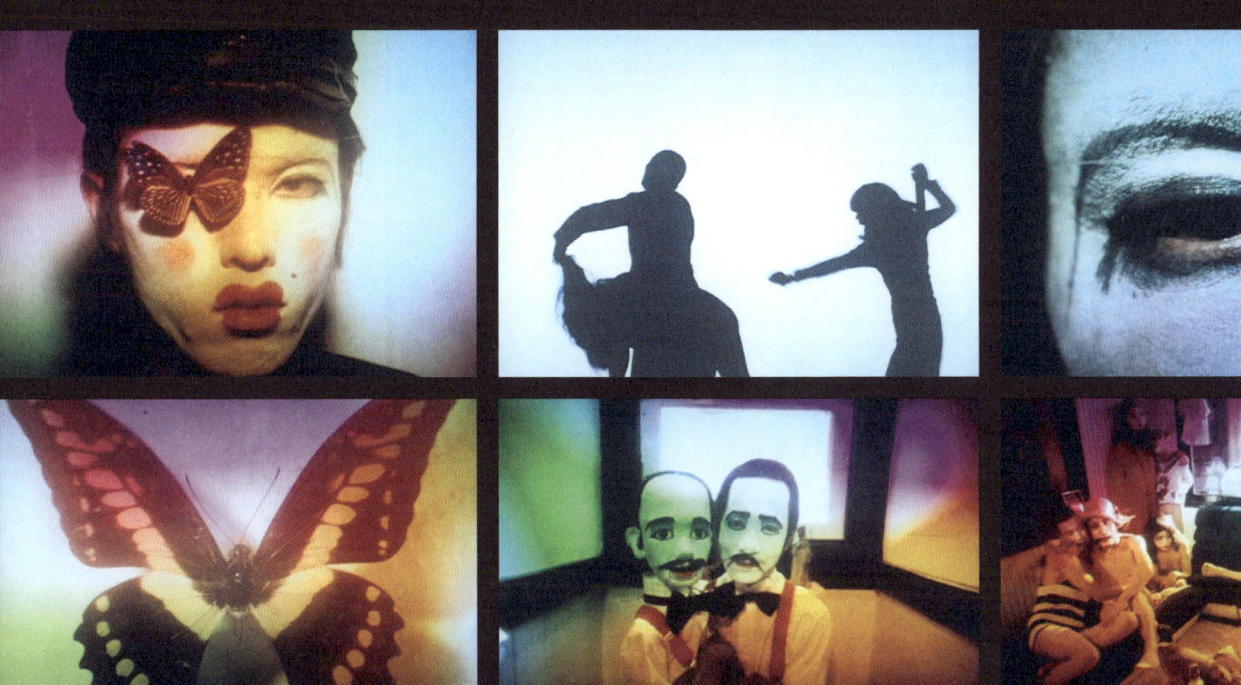
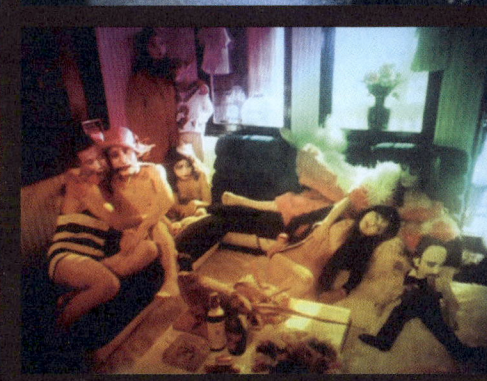
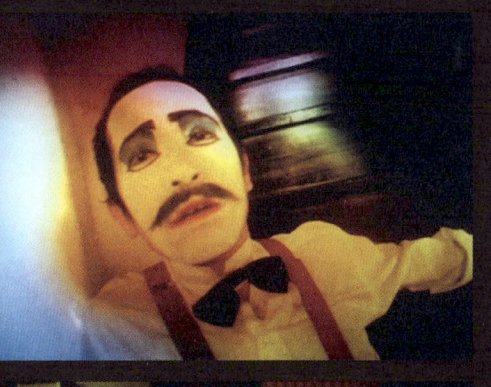

Terayama read non-mainstream European literature – Surrealism, Artaud, Bataille, Lautréamont … He was very influenced by Dalí and Buñuel too. He had a number of themes in his work, the most important being how you can create your own reality through your imagination. And that's the dreamy element of it. Is this a dream? Is it reality? What is this?

PETER TASKER

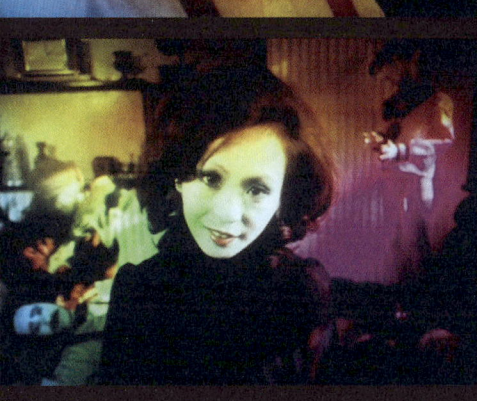
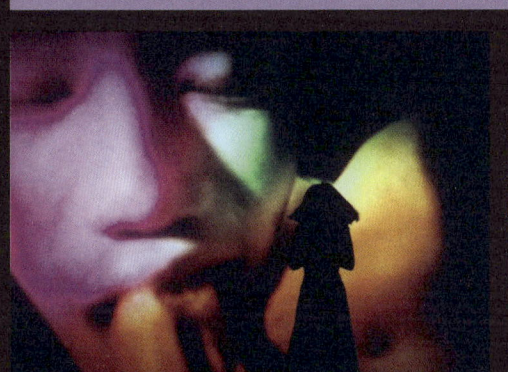
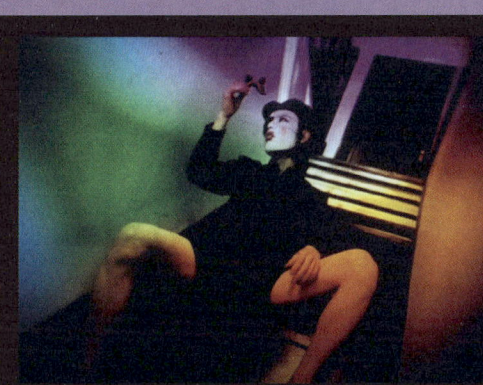

Terayama was very interested in my regional work. He was from Aomori, so he had the spirit of the Tōhoku region. I'm from the Kansai region, and when we met, the spirit of the west and the spirit of the north connected. That was already very theatrical. He was thinking of reviving freak shows with Tenjō Sajiki.

YOKOO TADANORI

> For Terayama, the only real revolution was in the imagination, and this essentially non-political position alienated him from many of his peers in the increasingly fractured and contested political landscape at the beginning of the 1970s. Terayama's vision resisted orthodoxies of both left and right, maintaining an anarchic, deeply held belief in the potential of art to bring about personal transformation.
>
> LUCY FLEMING-BROWN

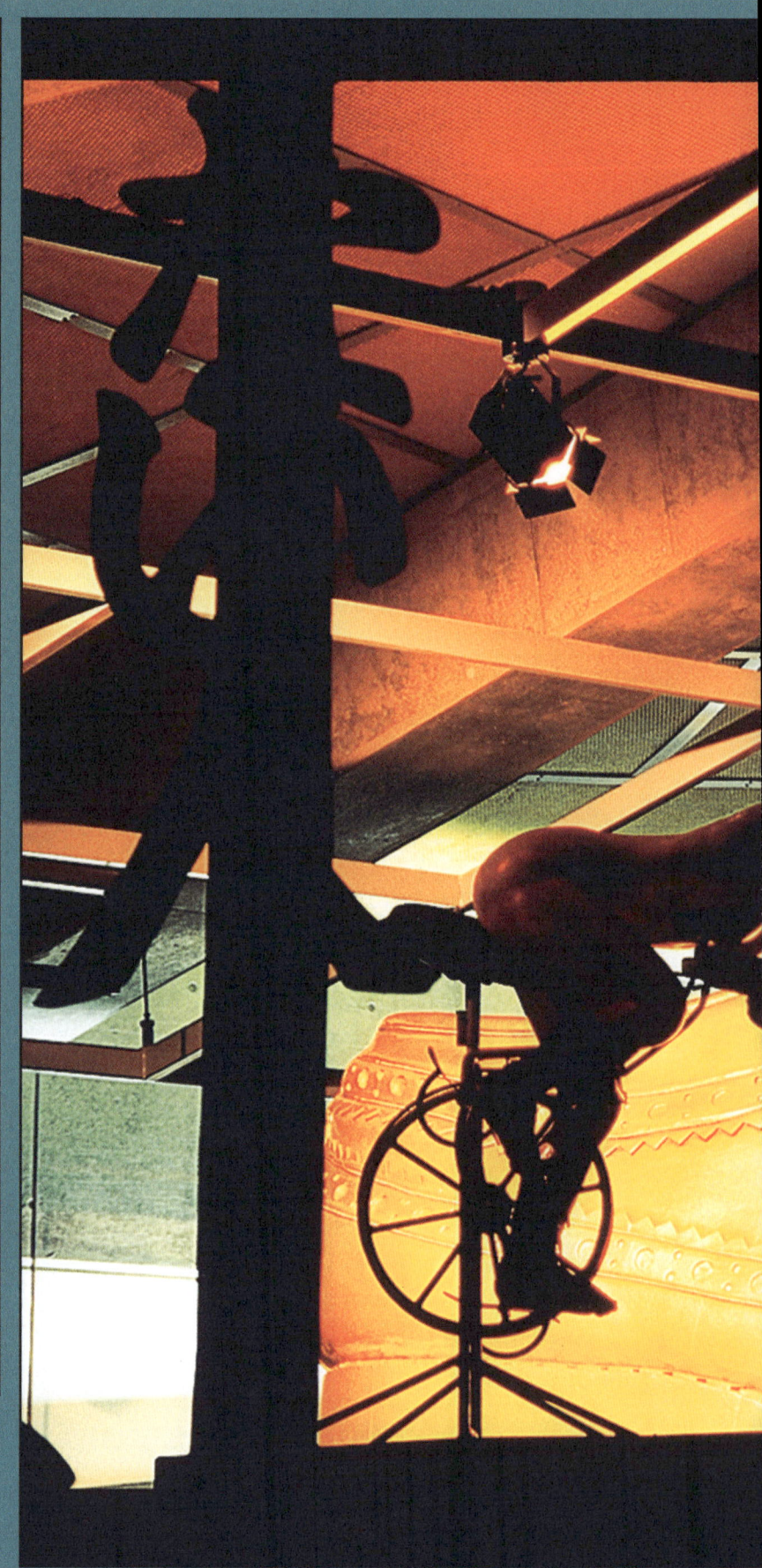

Photograph from **Terayama Shūji**, *The Terayama Shuji Theatre Museum: 1935–2008* (2008).

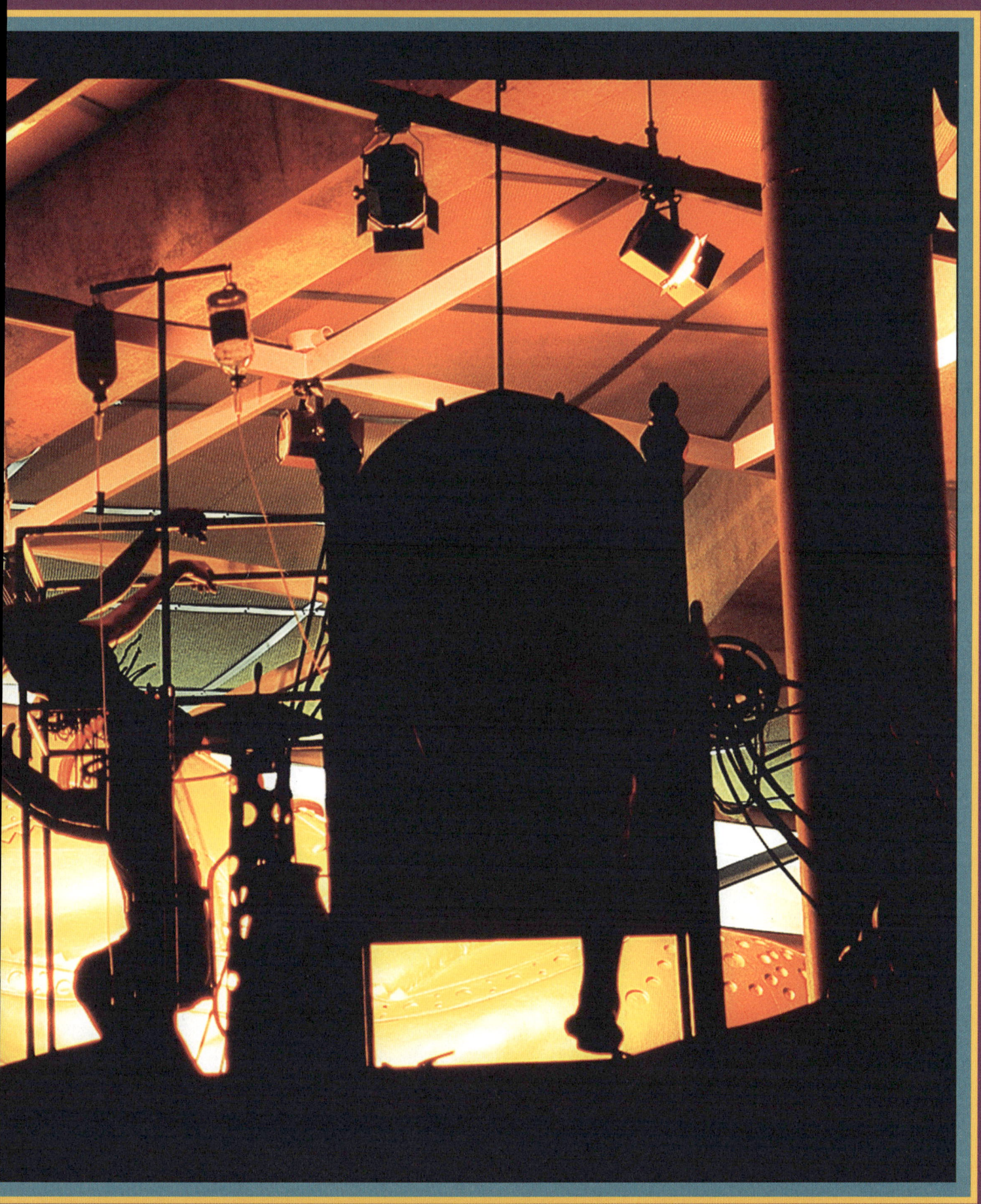

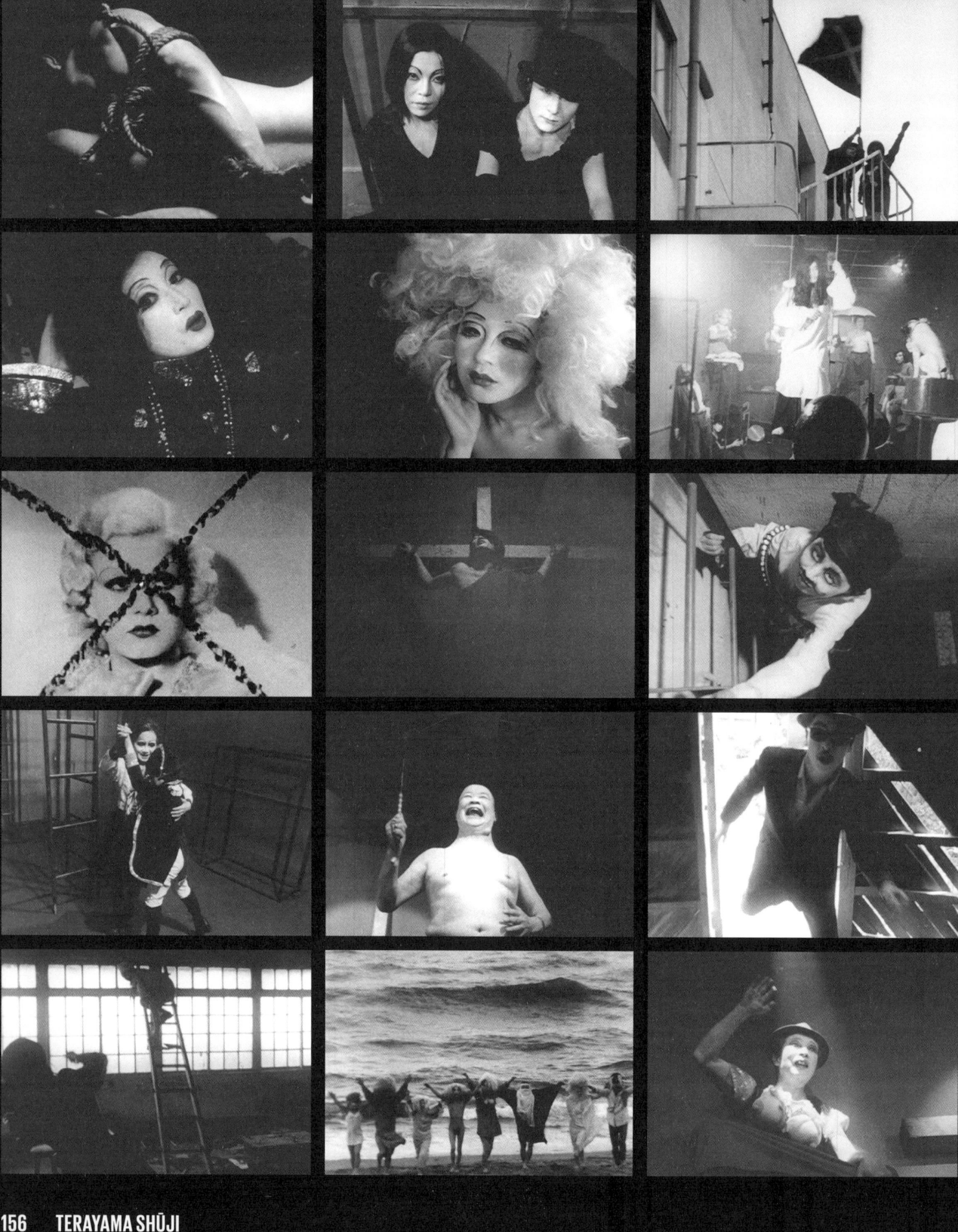

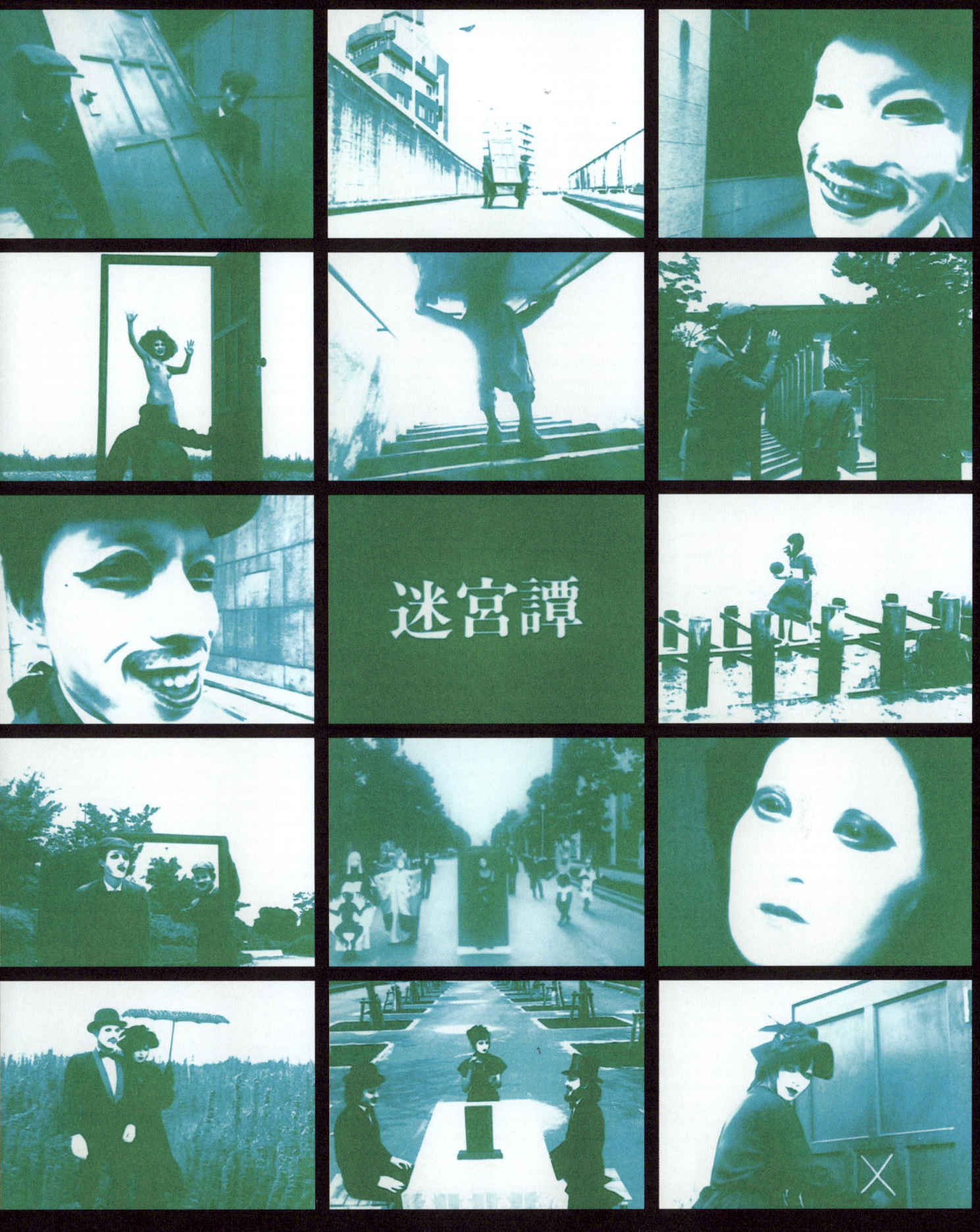

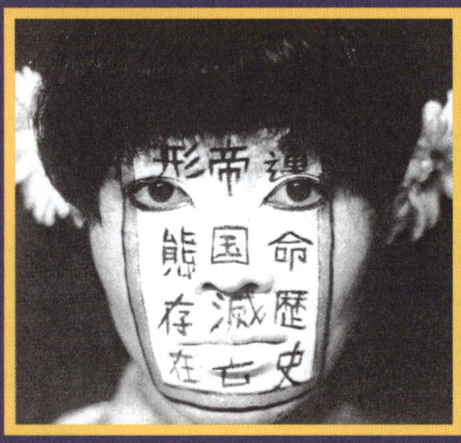 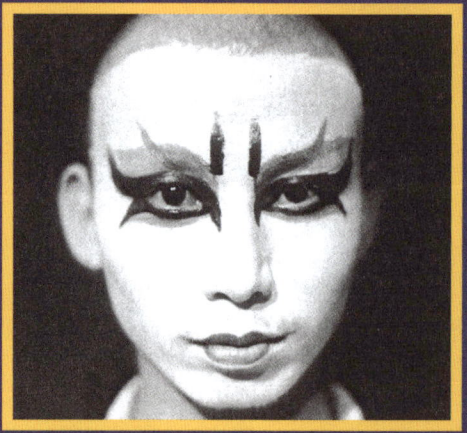 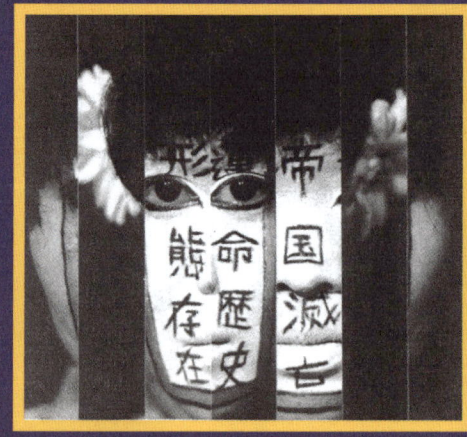

Tenjō Sajiki, meaning the cheapest seats in the theatre, or 'the gods' in English, was from Tokyo. The founder and director Terayama Shūji, an aloof but charismatic figure, was a poet, playwright, essayist, novelist, photographer and filmmaker, who functioned as a kind of Pied Piper in Tokyo, gathering around him a shifting retinue of runaways, misfits and eccentrics who acted as living props in his surreal theatrical fantasies. What astonished me about Tokyo on first sight in the fall of 1975 was how much it resembled a Tenjō Sajiki theatre set. I assumed that Terayama's spectacles were the madly exaggerated, surreal fantasies of a poet's feverish mind. To be sure, I did not come across ventriloquists in 19th-century French clothes being whipped by leather-clad dominatrices, but there was something theatrical, even hallucinatory about the cityscape itself, where nothing was understood.

Seeing the Tenjō Sajiki for the first time was like squinting through the keyhole of a grotesque peep show full of extraordinary goings on. I had never seen anything remotely like it. The public was led by a succession of guides into different rooms decorated with old Japanese movie posters, blown up details of erotic woodblock prints, lurid comic books and props seemed to have been lifted from a 1920s whorehouse. Naked girls were displayed in a variety of peculiar poses and ventriloquists in chalky kabuki makeup spoke through dolls dressed like Toulouse-Lautrec. Kimonoed ogres from ancient Japanese ghost stories mingled with men in women's makeup. It was deeply weird, over-the-top, largely unintelligible, perversely erotic and totally unforgettable.

IAN BURUMA, *A TOKYO ROMANCE* (2018)

p. 156: Stills from **Terayama Shūji**, *Emperor Tomato Ketchup* (1971), short film.

p. 157: Stills from **Terayama Shūji**, *The Labyrinth Tale* (1975), short film.

pp. 158–63: Images from **Terayama Shūji**, *Photothèque imaginaire de Shuji Terayama* (1975).

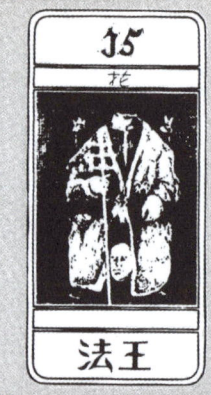 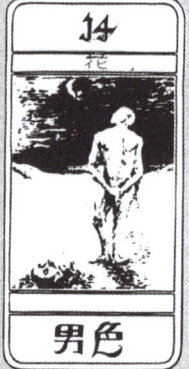 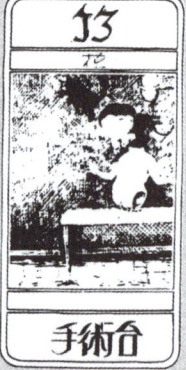 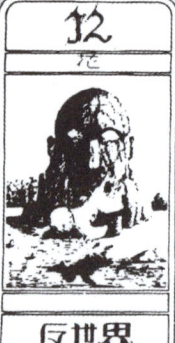 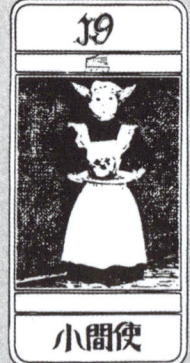

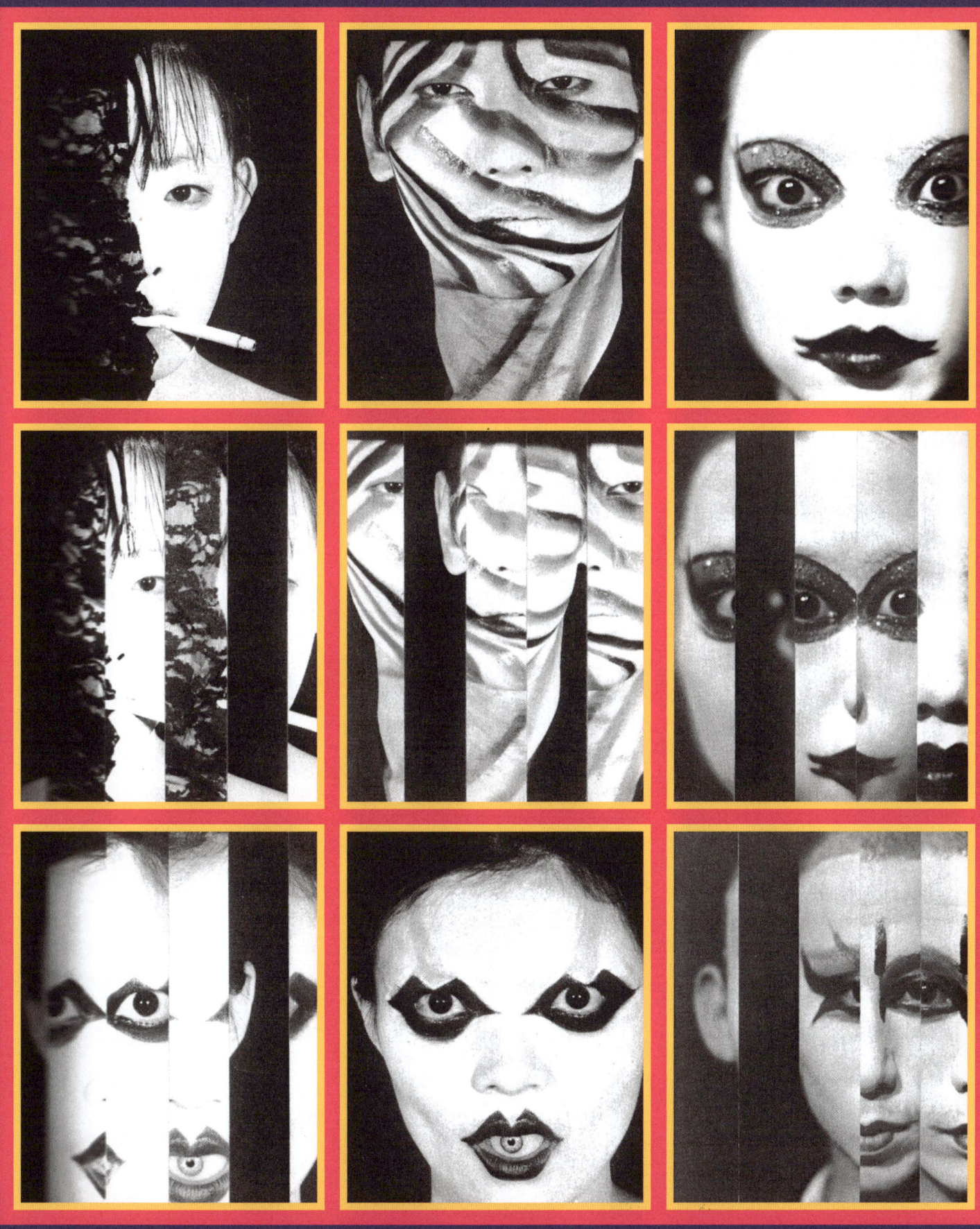

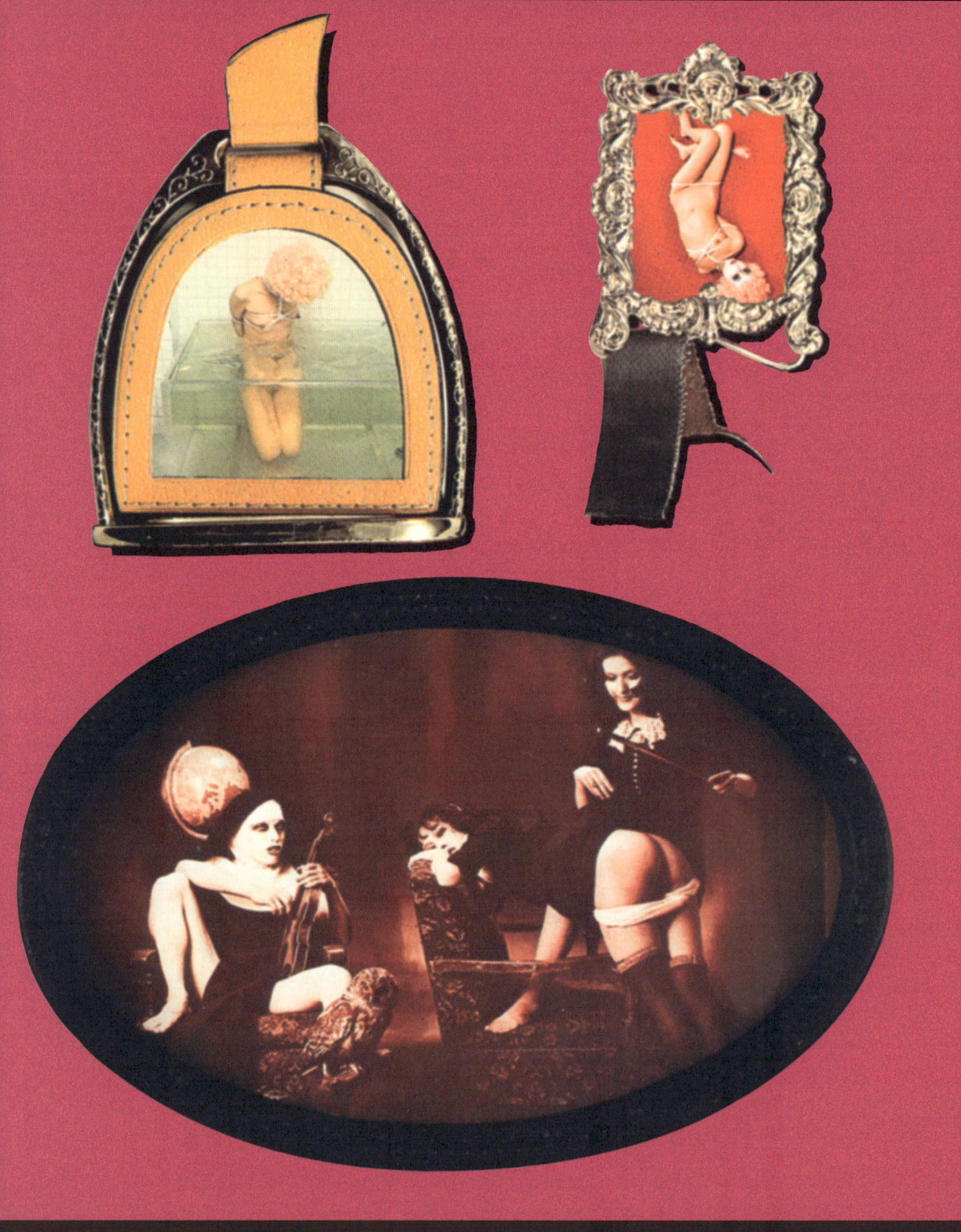

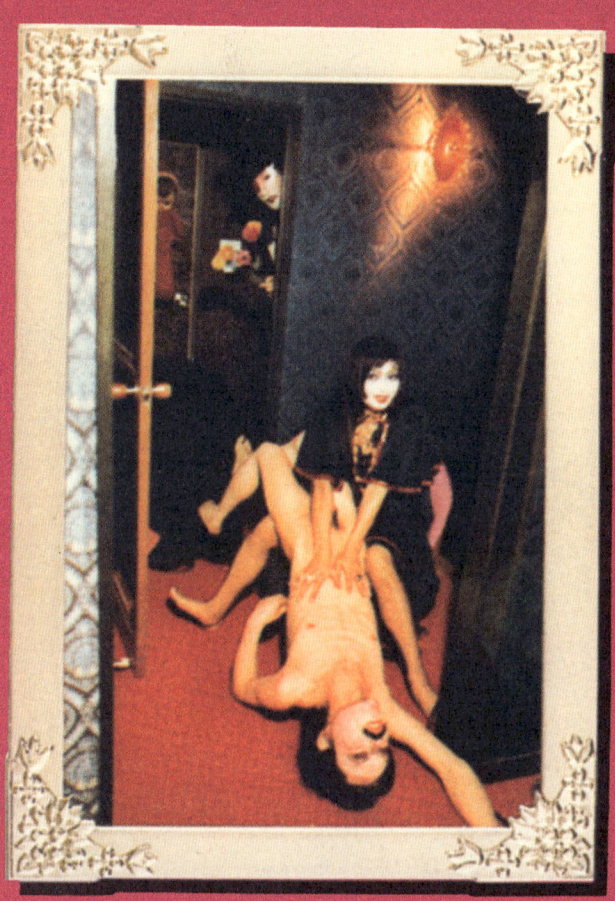
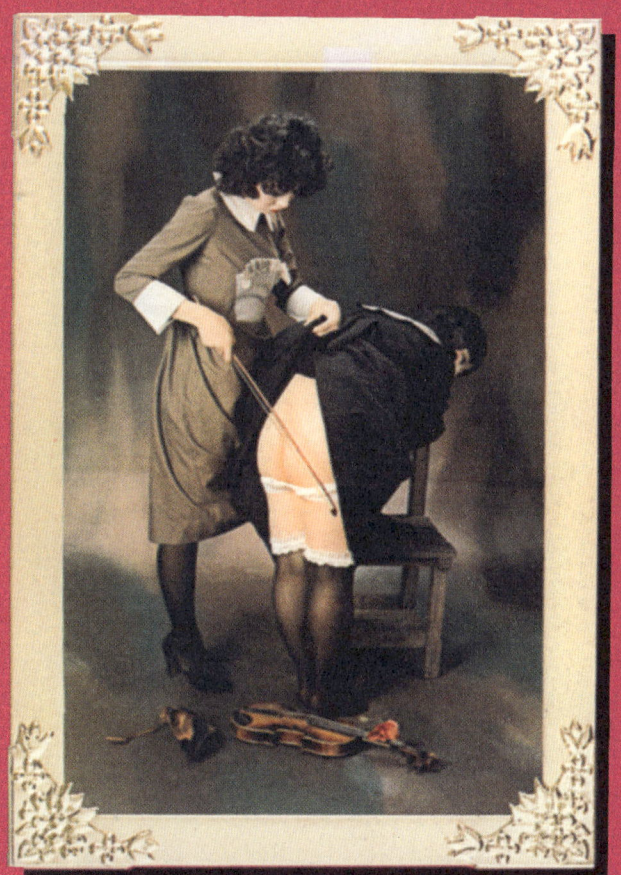

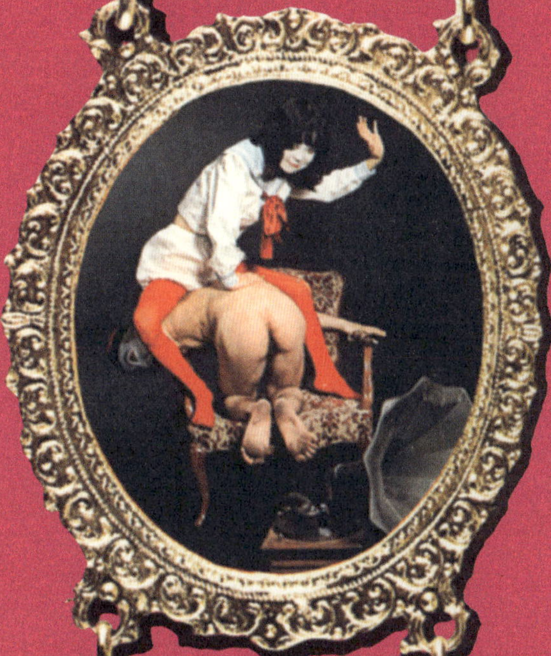

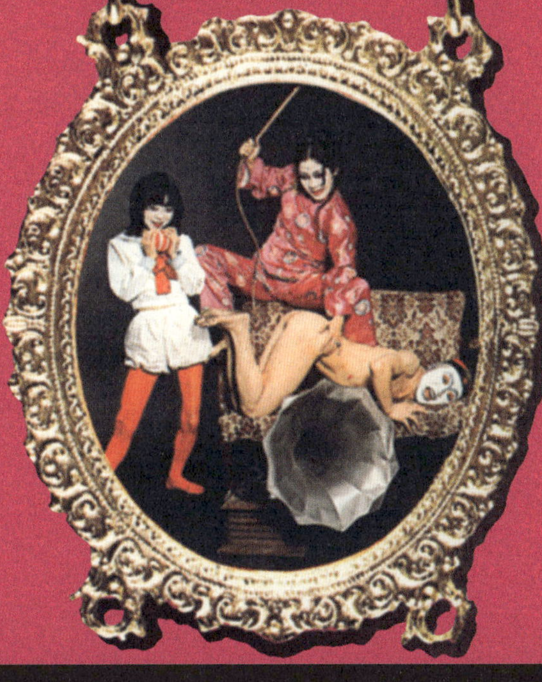

寺山修司

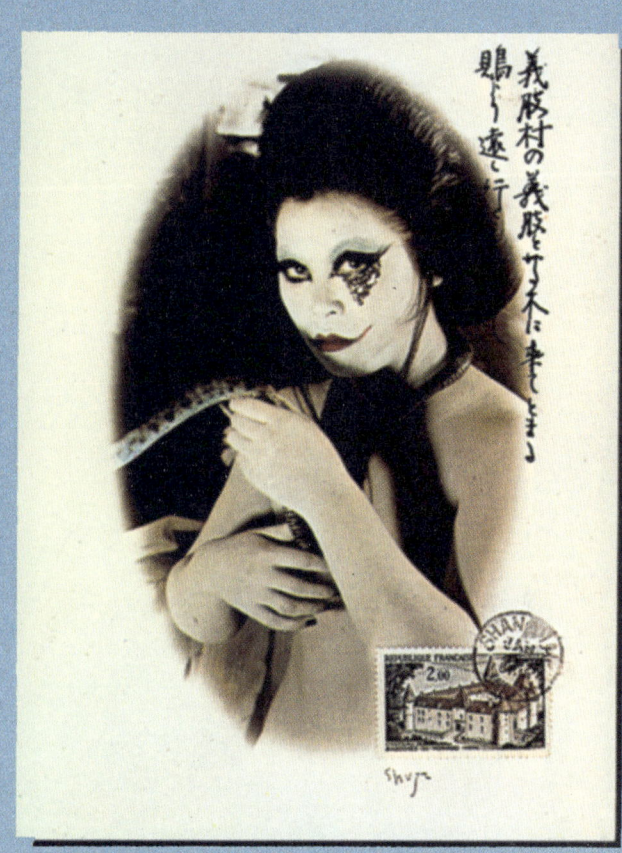
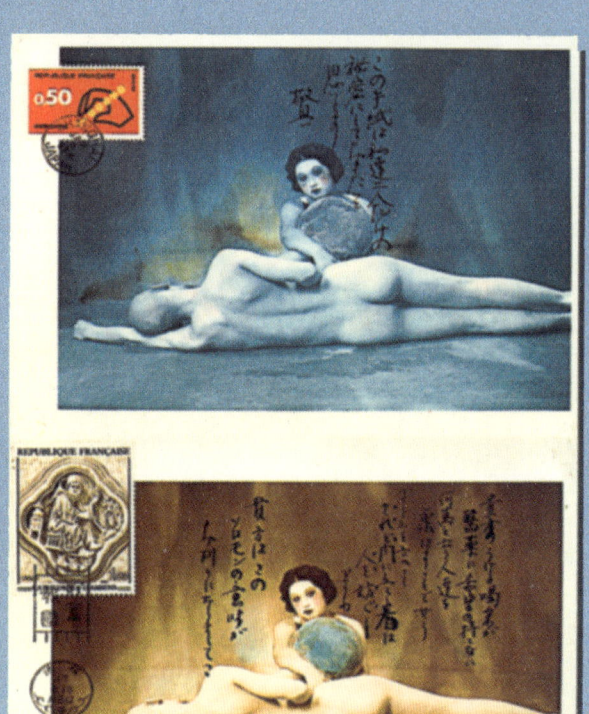

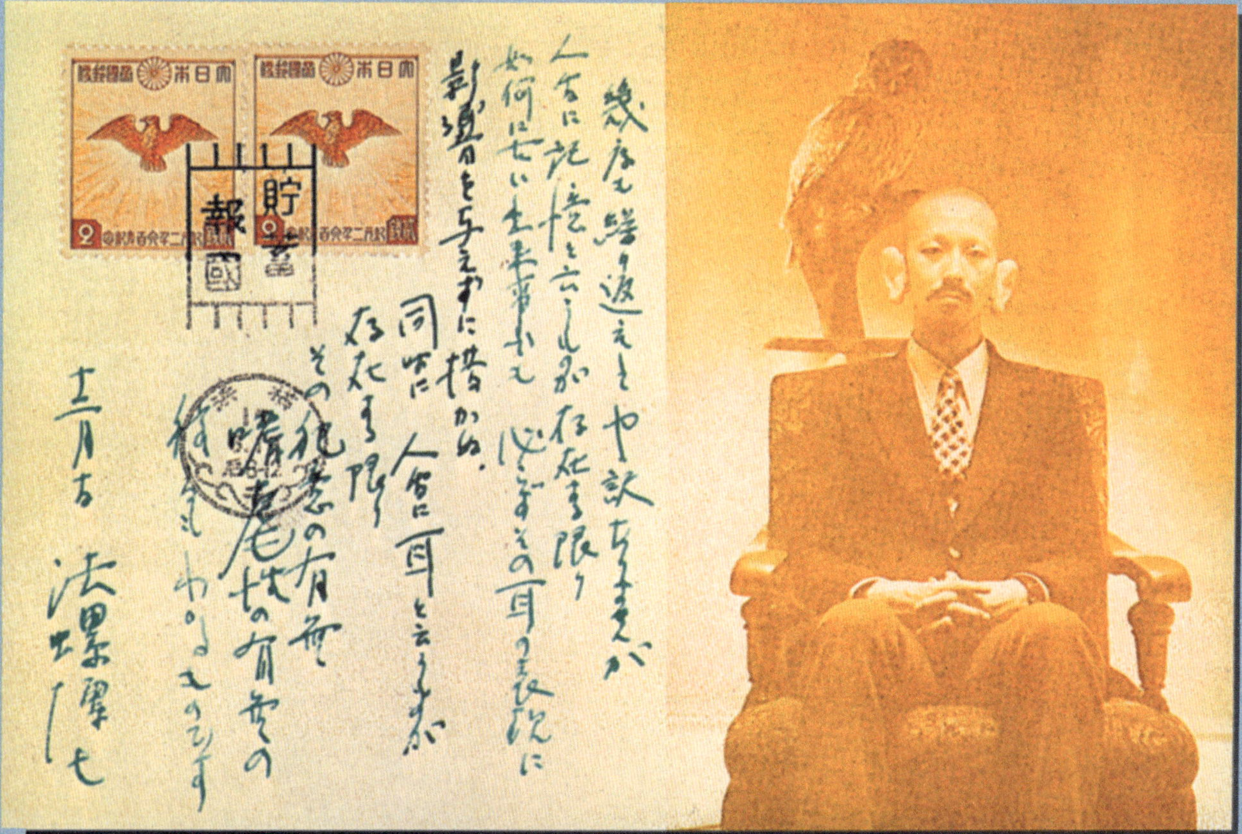

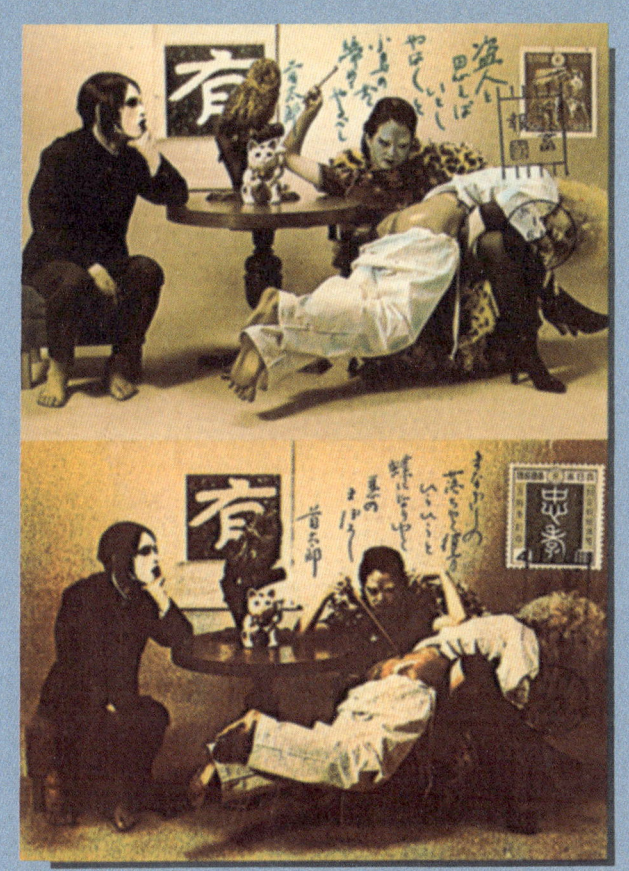
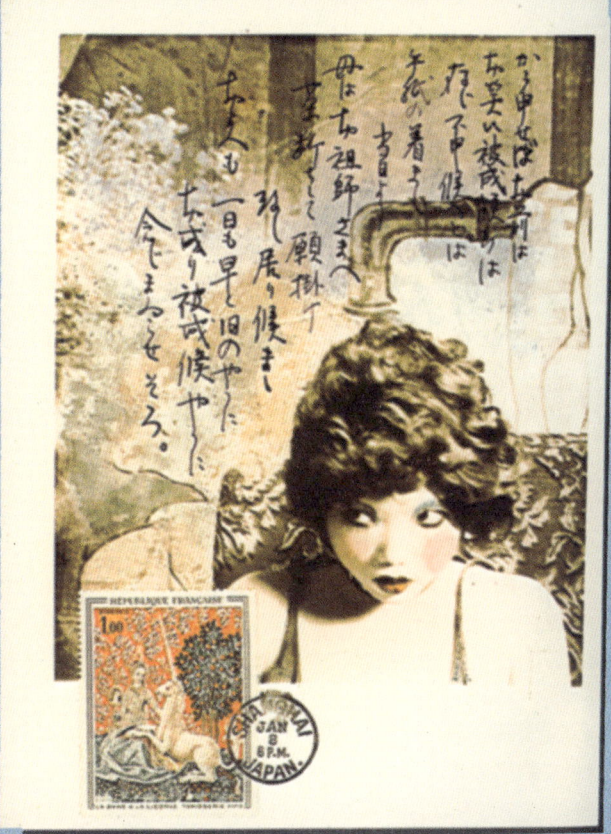
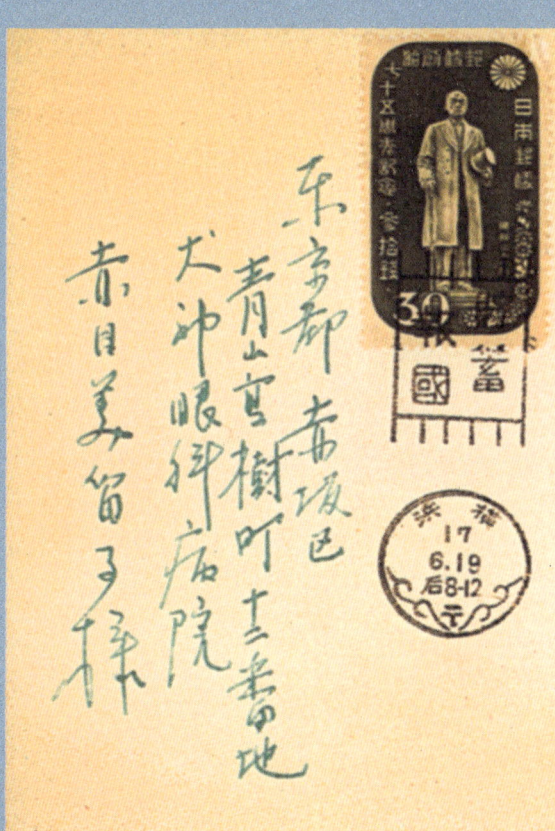
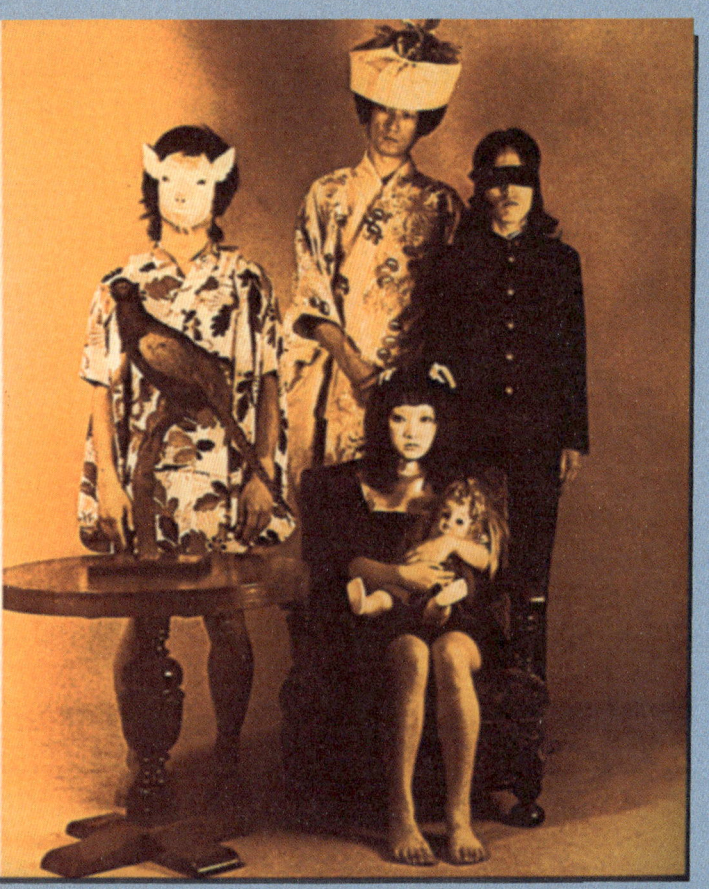

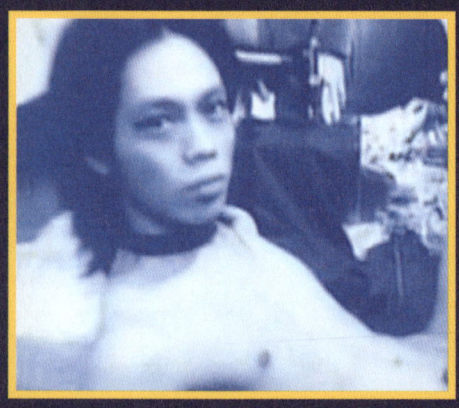 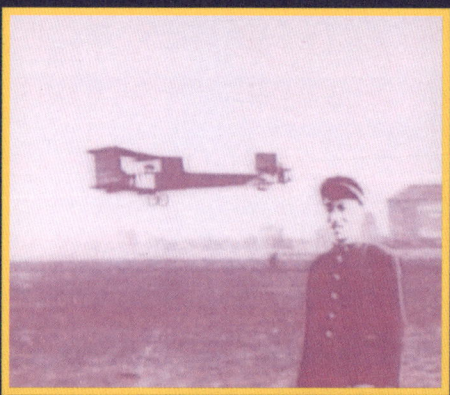 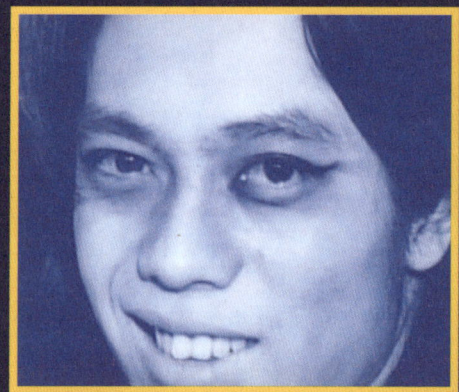

Terayama's experimental films contain some of his most potent and iconic images. The human sundial in *Ori* (*The Cage*, 1964), for example, juxtaposes a dog casually strolling through town with a man imprisoned in the cage of a clock chalked onto the pavement, keeping time for us and himself with his shadow. Wall clocks, representing centralized power across Terayama's work, are thrown from windows to reorientate liberation towards freedom from regulated temporality.

Chōfuku-ki (*Butterfly*, 1974) was released internationally as '16 +/– 1', apt for a 16mm film where shadows of people and butterflies cover a portion of the image, subtracting it from view. This expanded cinema project also requires accomplices to add shadows to the projected image with paper butterflies on sticks, which combined with the celluloid shadows call into question the status (plus or minus) of each shadow-image.

Emperor Tomato Ketchup (1971) is a farce about a revolution of elementary school children against adult society. The film, an expansion of Terayama's 1960 radio drama *Otona-gari* (*Adult-Hunting*), parodies the moral panic around student activism while simultaneously challenging the youth movement to grapple with its 'don't trust anyone over thirty' ethos – the Emperor is deposed the moment he grows his first beard.

Shinpan (*The Trial*, 1975) likely draws its name from Kafka's novel and depicts a similarly vague sense of persecution, in this case by all manner of nails and hammers. One man carries a giant nail larger than himself. Another is stricken with action-at-a-distance pain as another pounds nails elsewhere. When exhibited as intended, the audience is invited to pound nails into the wooden screen upon which the film has been projected while the film still rolls, mixing real nails with nail-images in a joint production.

Meikyū-tan (*The Labyrinth Tale*, 1975) is a meditation on doorways, both real and imagined. Doors and their frames are transported through urban space, then placed to create portals to other realms. But these efforts to delineate real from imaginary space with the portable threshold are continually thwarted by the lack of walls surrounding the doorway. The film (which is intended to be projected onto an actual door used as a screen) closes with a circus-like cast parading past the door placed in the middle of a road.

STEVE RIDGELY

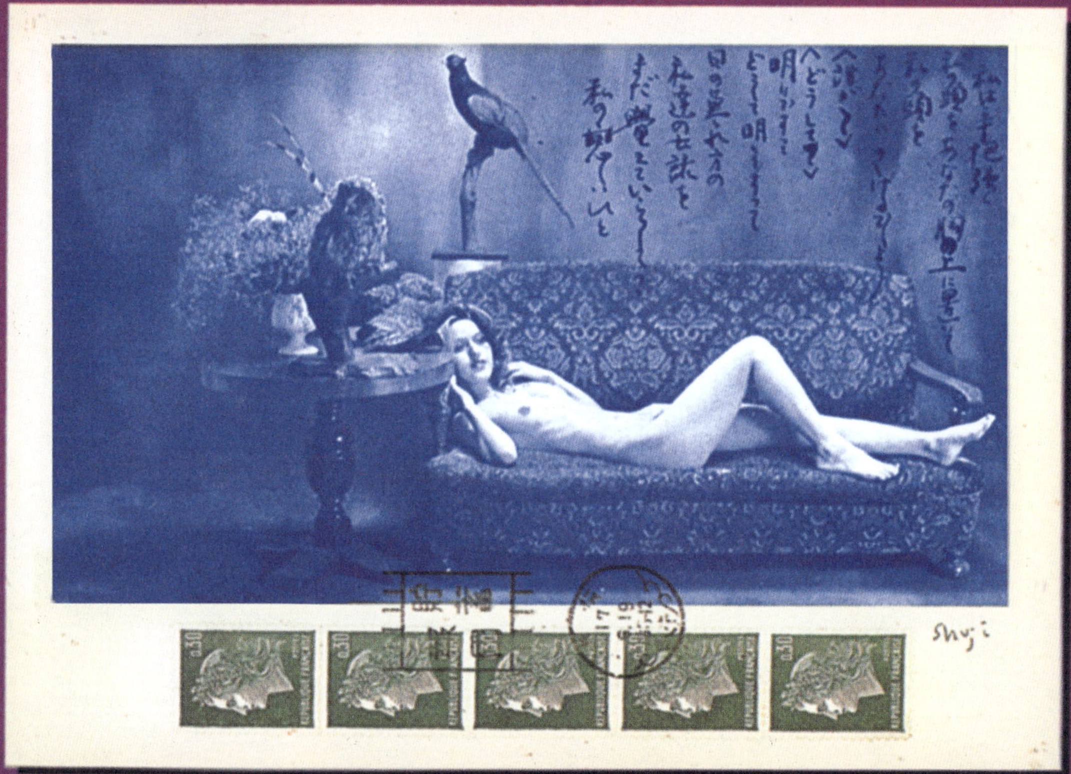

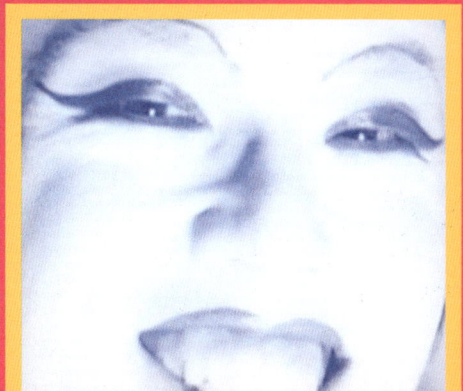
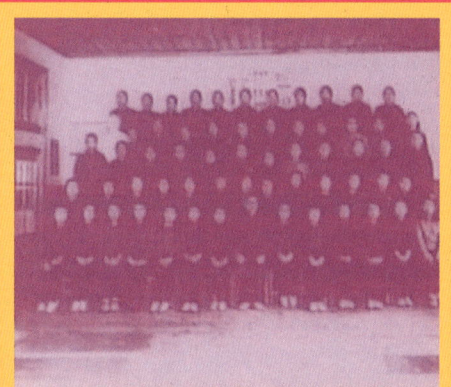
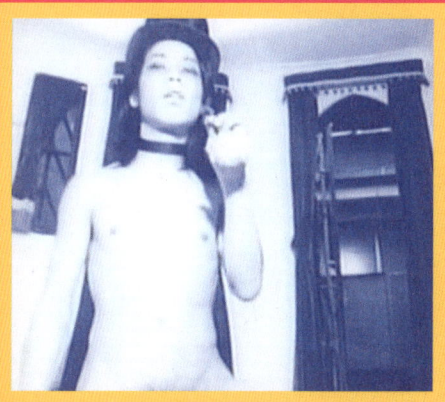
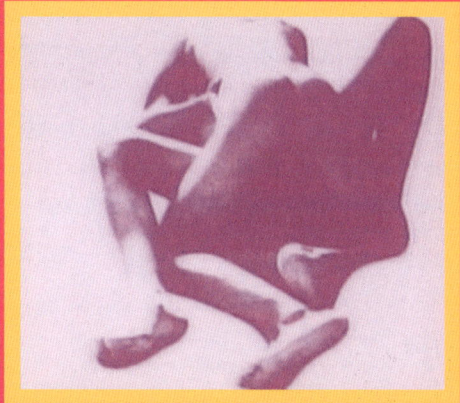
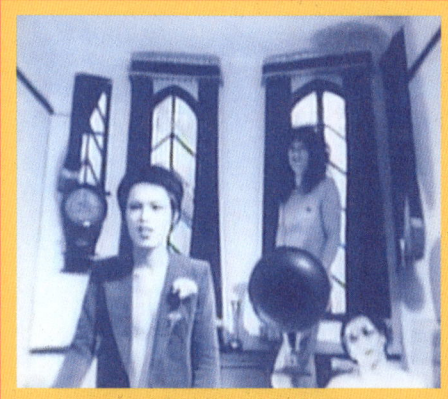
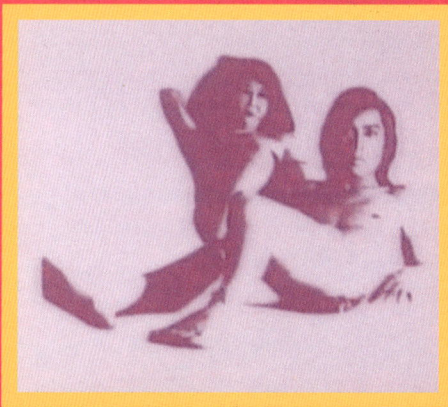

寺山修司

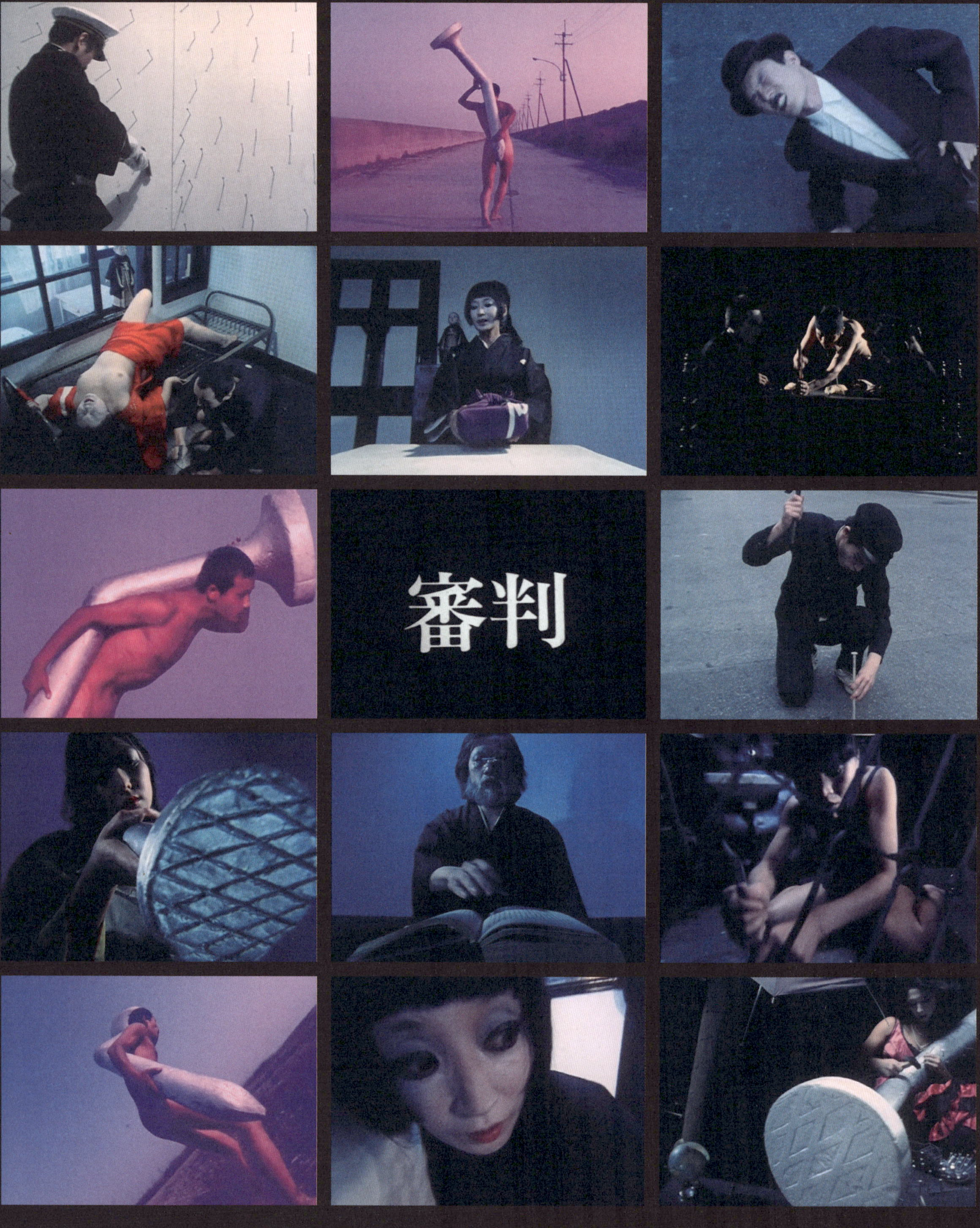

審判

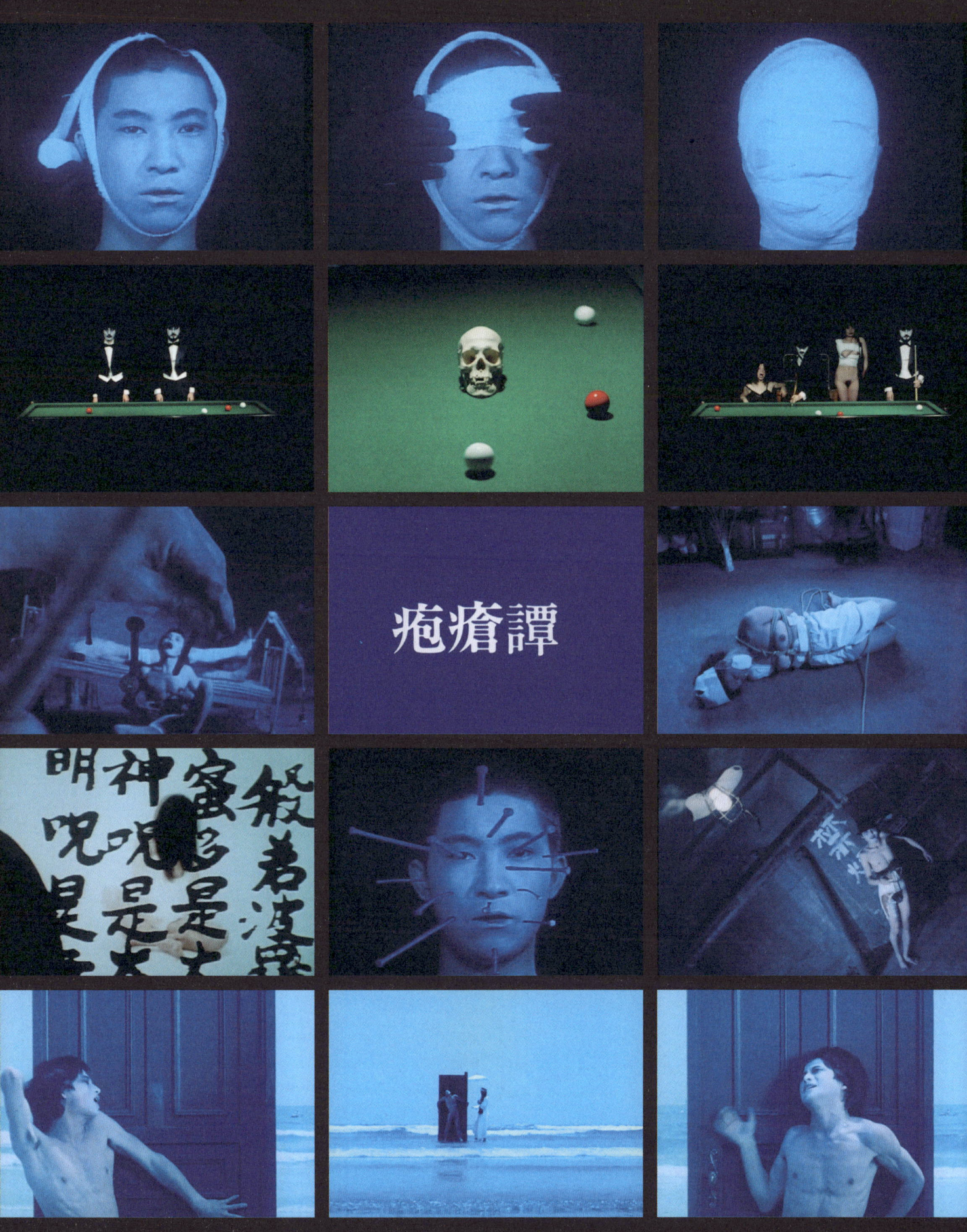

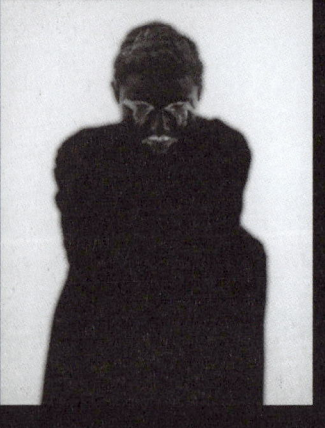

In 1968, I heard that Terayama Shūji was building the Tenjō Sajiki building in Shibuya. We planned the building with Awazu Kiyoshi, who gave us free rein to do our things. I was nineteen then.

From then on, the underground theatre started, and Terayama gave me work for books as well as in film. He was such an interesting person, I was never bored. I think everyone had fun at work.

ENOMOTO RYOICHI

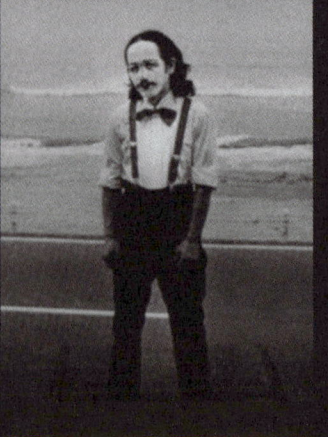

I had failed my university exams and I was taking a gap year, and then I encountered Terayama Shūji's play *Lemming, Take Me to the End of the World*. The words uttered by Terayama cut through me like a knife. From the next day, I would follow him everywhere, and this one piece of work completely transformed my life.

Terayama's idea was to put on stage people who are rejected from society. His first play was called *The Hunchback of Aomori*. It starred disabled people, dwarfs and people from *misemono* (freak show). There was also a snake lady who came from a circus, and she performed with them.

He also put untrained, normal people on stage who don't normally belong there. These kinds of people were more interesting to him. Back then, poets and artists were often seen as crazy, and he also shone a light on those outsiders of society.

He was kind of treading ahead of the LGBT culture. He was posing the questions as to why some people are discriminated against. Everything is normal, also in terms of sexuality.

Prejudice is gradually changing now, and he really put the focus on it in this way.

SASAME HIROYUKI

pp. 164 and 165 (below): Stills from **Terayama Shūji**, *A Young Person's Guide to Cinema* (1979), short film.

p. 165 (above): Image from **Terayama Shūji**, *Photothèque imaginaire de Shuji Terayama* (1975).

p. 166: Stills from **Terayama Shūji**, *The Trial* (1975), short film.

p. 167: Stills from **Terayama Shūji**, *A Tale of Smallpox* (1975), short film.

Above and opposite: Images from **Terayama Shūji**, *Photothèque imaginaire de Shuji Terayama* (1975).

pp. 170–73: Images from **Terayama Shūji**, *Photothèque imaginaire de Shuji Terayama* (1975).

He respected and enjoyed various subcultures and lifestyles of all sorts. He thought that they were more authentic and they were more interesting. Gay people, Koreans, boxers, long-distance truckers, gamblers, *pachinko* players, all kinds of people who were marginalized.

PETER TASKER

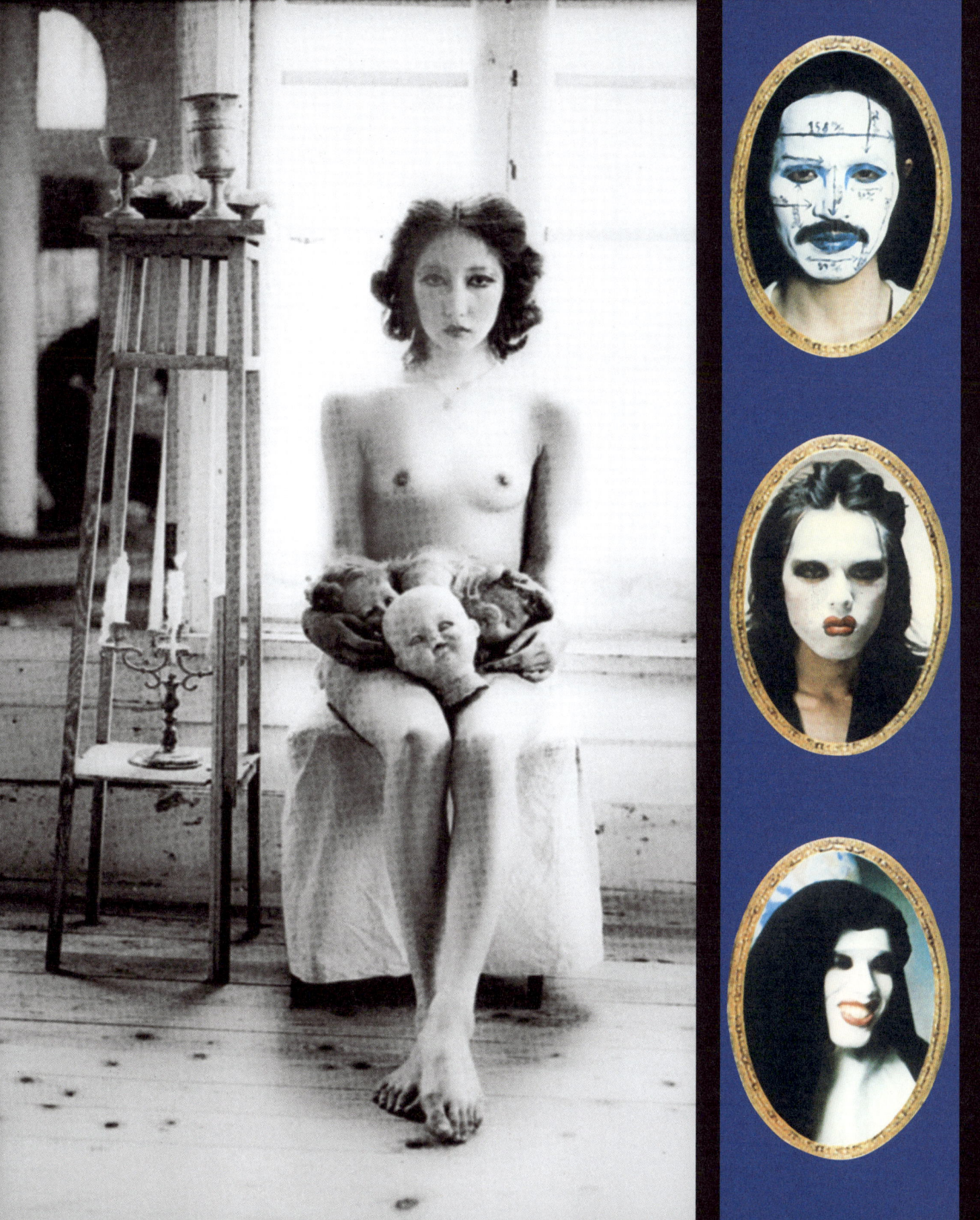

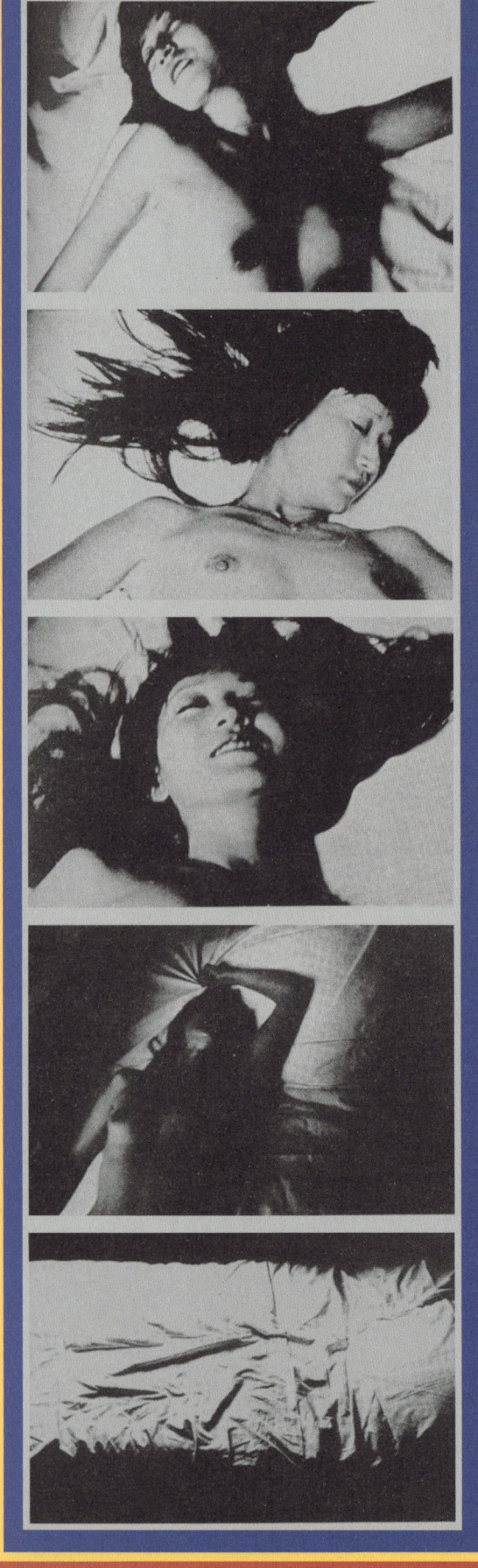

Eroticism is part of the package that Terayama took from the Surrealists and Dalí in particular. Eroticism was part of the armoury of transgression and pushing boundaries of the era. He had male and female gay scenes, orgies... It's very different from pornographic pictures of that era, which show women in positions of submission and sometimes being brutalized.

Terayama wanted his work to be handmade, what we might call these days a punk ethic, though he started before there were punks. He was already a theatre producer and writer of plays, and a kind of impresario of avant-garde theatre.

Then he went into experimental films, feature films, journalism and what you might call happenings or events, or street theatre.

At the age of about thirty-four or thirty-five, he decided that he wanted to become a photographer. So he became the disciple of the famous photographer Araki.

Terayama suffered from nephritis, a disease of the kidneys, which finally killed him in 1983 at the age of forty-nine. In that short life, he was tremendously prolific. He had enormous flexibility, ambition and drive, boundless creativity. Did he ever sleep? I wonder sometimes.

PETER TASKER

Araki was having difficulties at the time finding nude models, so some of the Tenjō Sajiki actors crossed over with Araki. Terayama also became a student of his, so some of his photos are a bit Araki in style, although Araki doesn't deal in false realities.

Terayama created this world where we don't know what is real; he played with truth and illusion. Like in his photobook *Inugamikeno-hitobito* (*Photothèque imaginaire*), he created such a motif, inventing fake costumes for made-up family photographs.

SASAME HIROYUKI

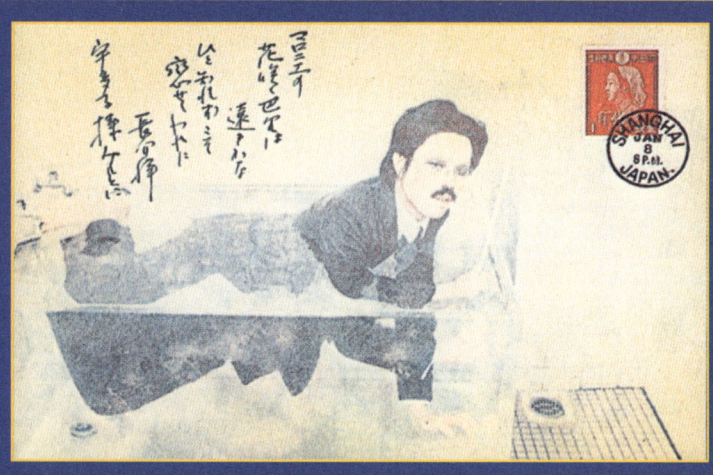
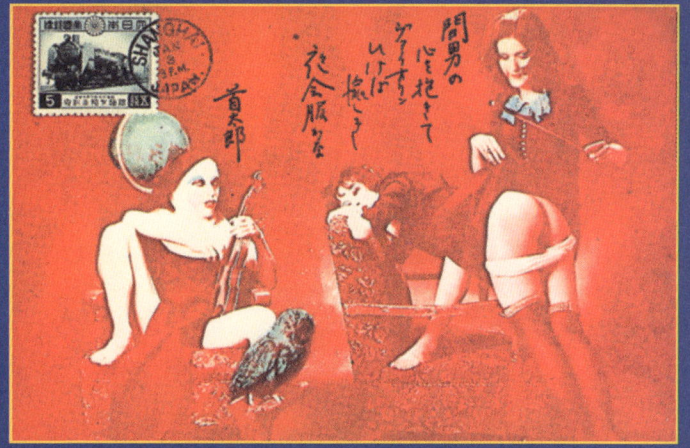

'MOST HUMAN MISTAKES IN HISTORY HAVE BEEN MADE BY REASON. IT WAS REASON, NOT MADNESS, THAT CREATED THE ATOMIC BOMB. WE MADE A PLAY CALLED *AHOU BUNE*, WHICH WAS CREATED BY A GROUP OF PEOPLE THINKING ABOUT REASON AND MADNESS. IN THE 15TH CENTURY, PEOPLE WHO WROTE POETRY OR DRANK ALCOHOL WERE TREATED AS MADMEN, PUT ON A SAILING SHIP AND WASHED OUT TO SEA, SO THE CATEGORIES OF REASON AND MADNESS WERE COMPLETELY DIFFERENT DEPENDING ON THE PERIOD.'

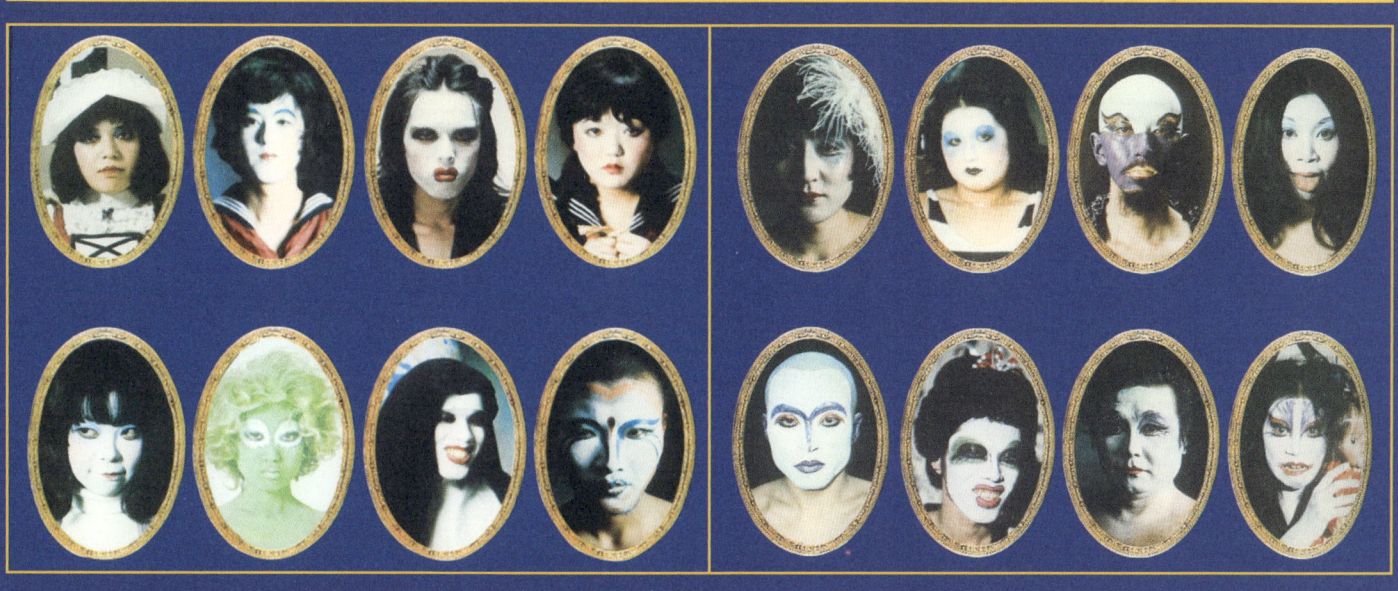

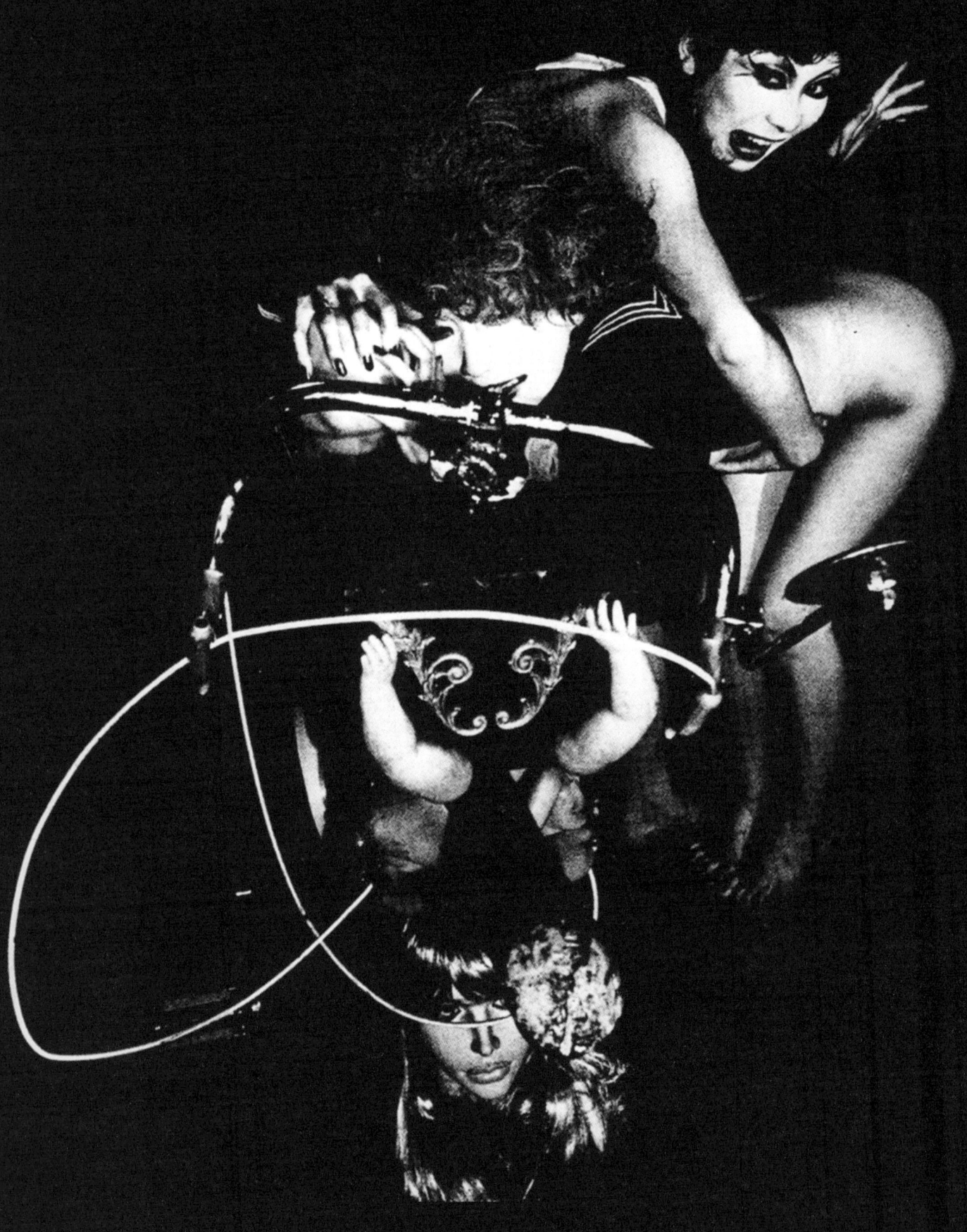

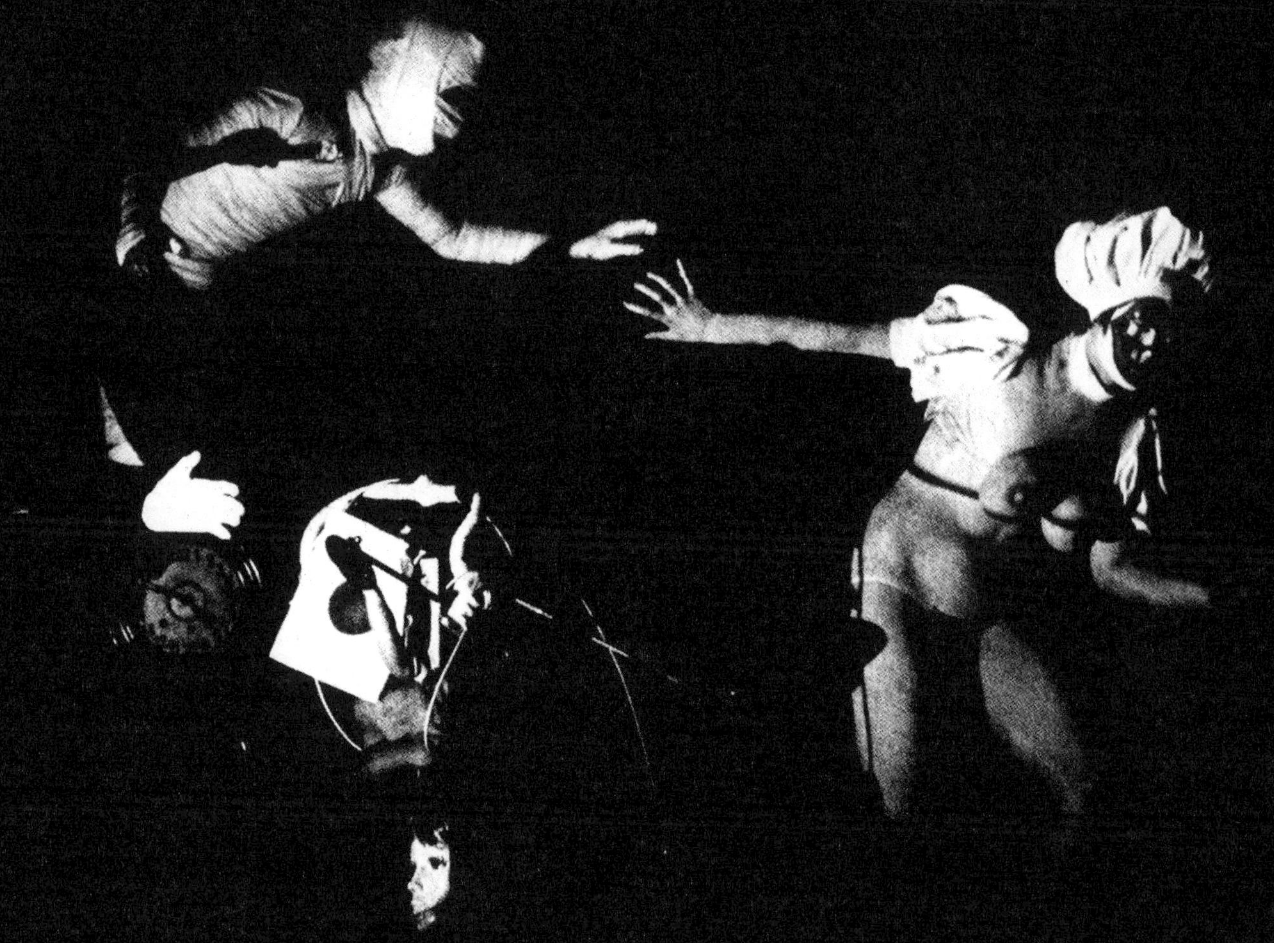

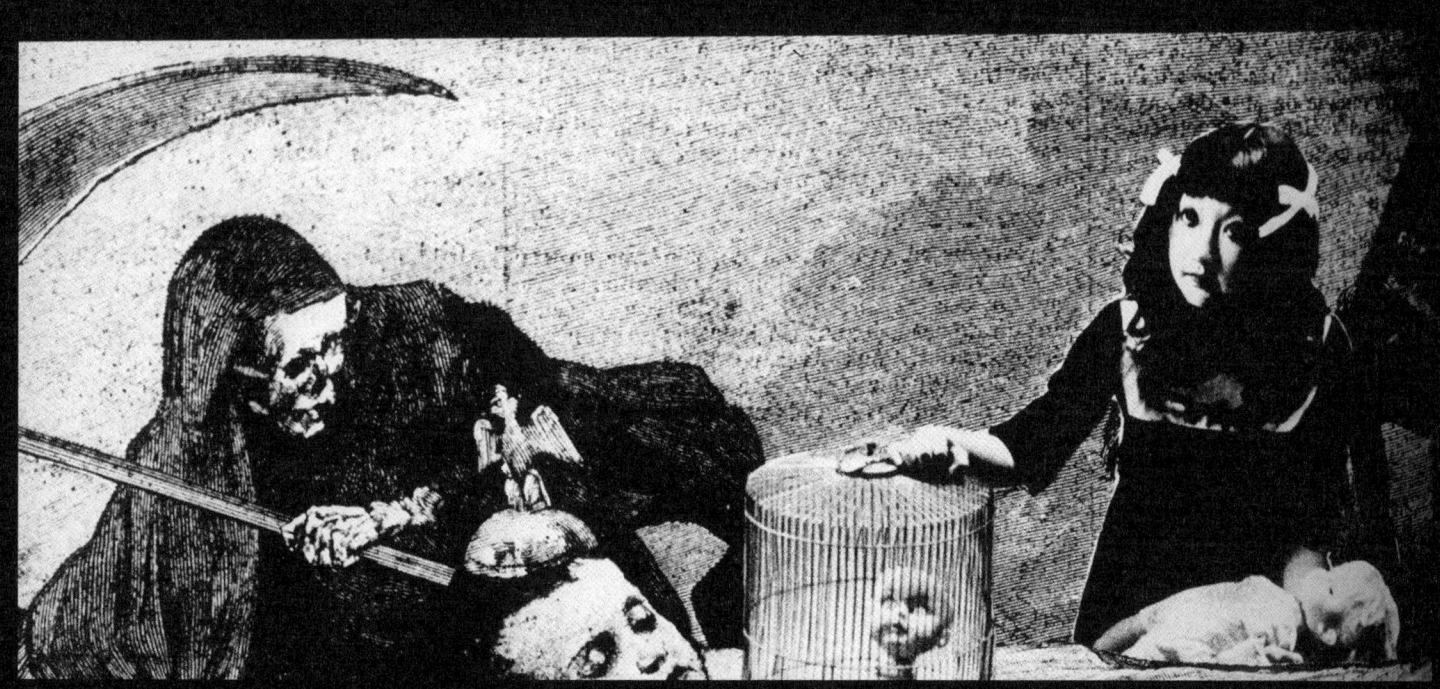

寺山修司

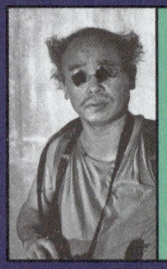

ARAKI NOBUYOSHI
1940–
アラーキー

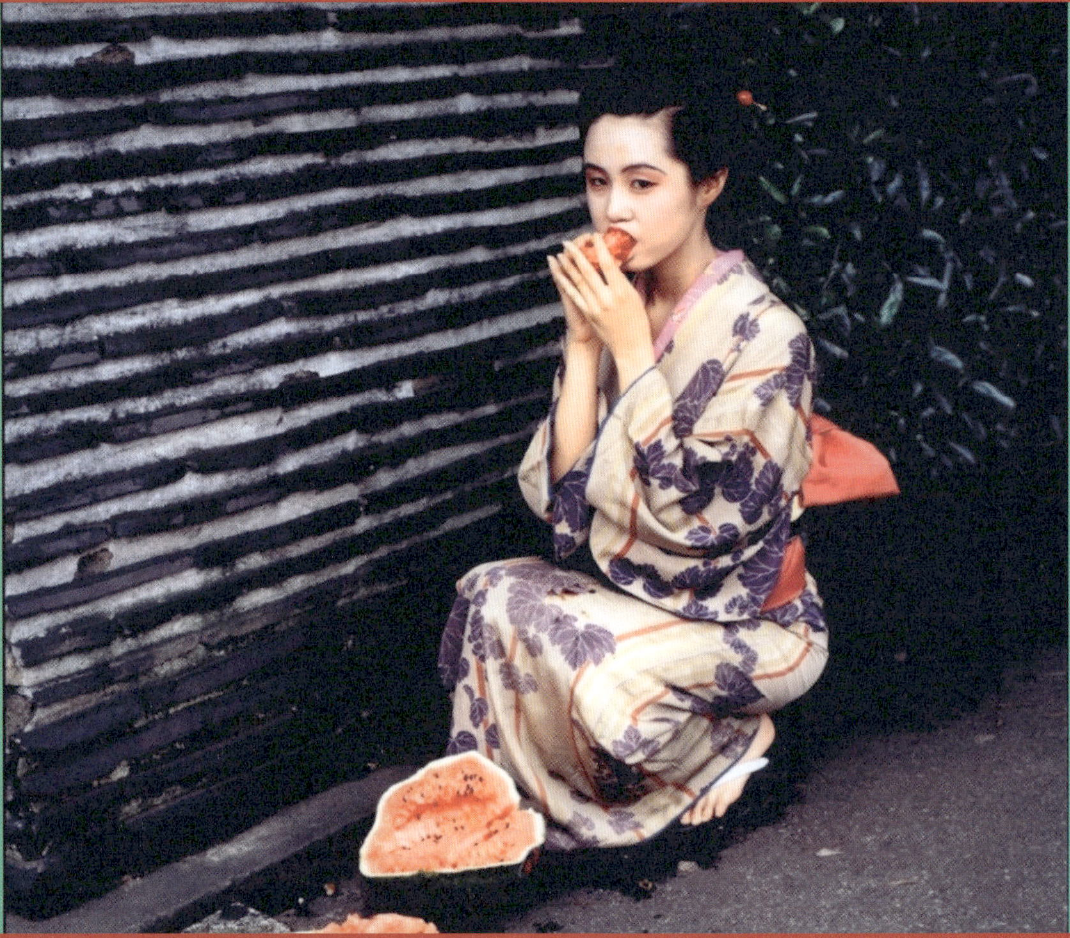

Araki Nobuyoshi, *Geisha Girl with Watermelon*, 1991, C-type print.

Opposite (above left): **Araki Nobuyoshi**, *Bondage*, 1994, gelatin silver print.

Opposite (above right): **Araki Nobuyoshi**, *Bondage, Art Edition C*, 1994, digital C-type print.

Opposite (below): **Araki Nobuyoshi**, *Kakyoku*, 1997, metallic print.

Araki was everywhere in the 1970s, making the rounds of the tiny bars in Shinjuku or the raunchiest cabarets, giggling and chattering non-stop as he snapped away anything that caught his fancy on the seamy side of Tokyo nightlife. Cabaret hostesses cavorting in the nude amid drunken punters in suits ... He was the Toulouse-Lautrec of contemporary Ero Guro Nansensu [erotic grotesque nonsense].

IAN BURUMA, *A TOKYO ROMANCE* (2018)

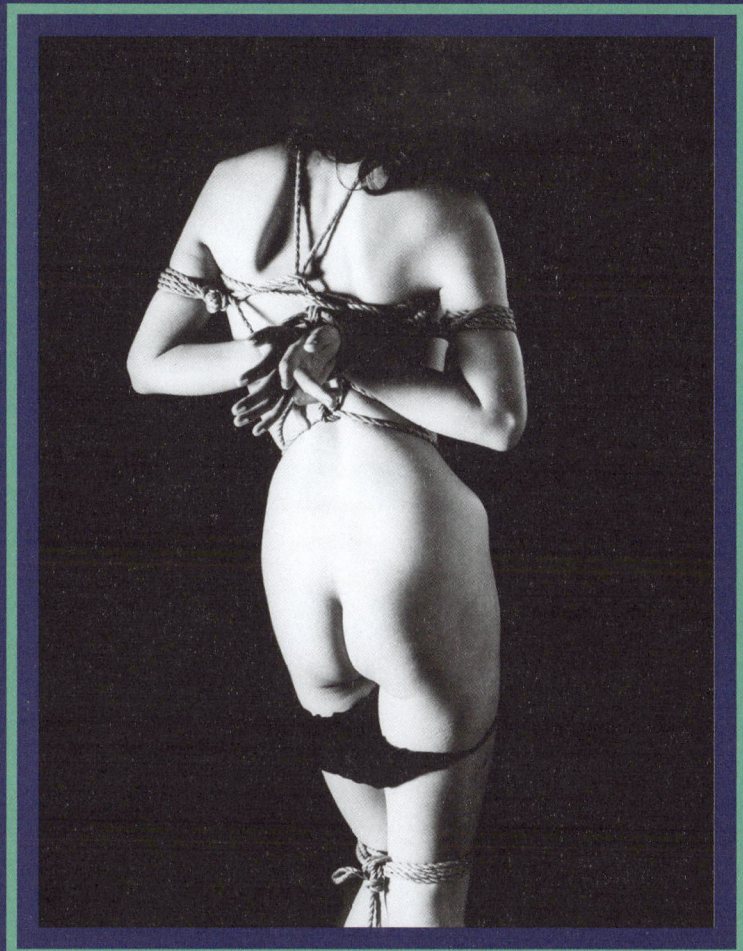
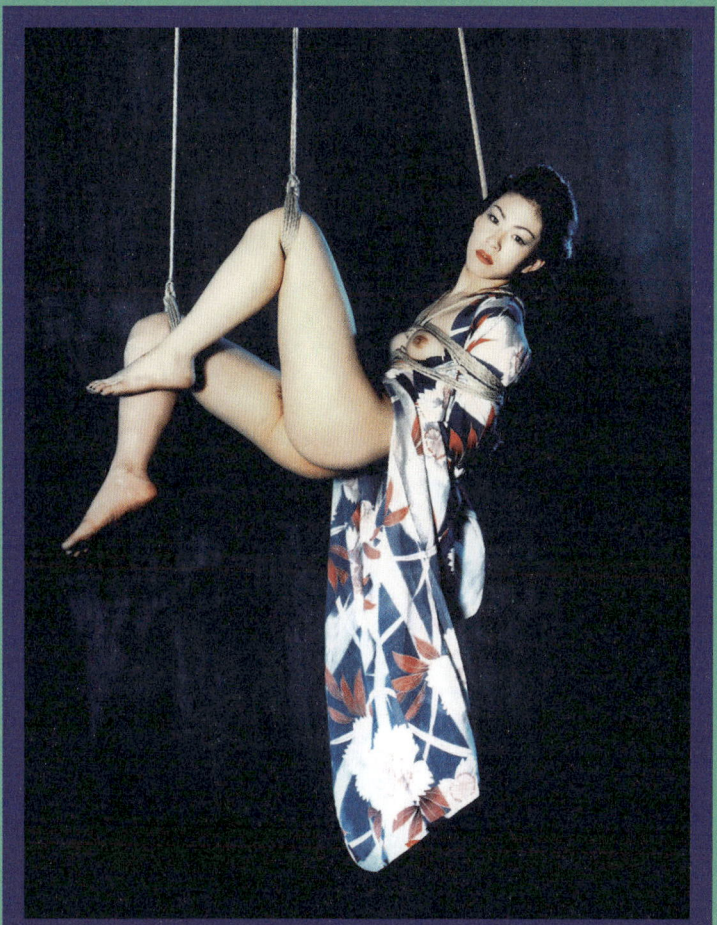

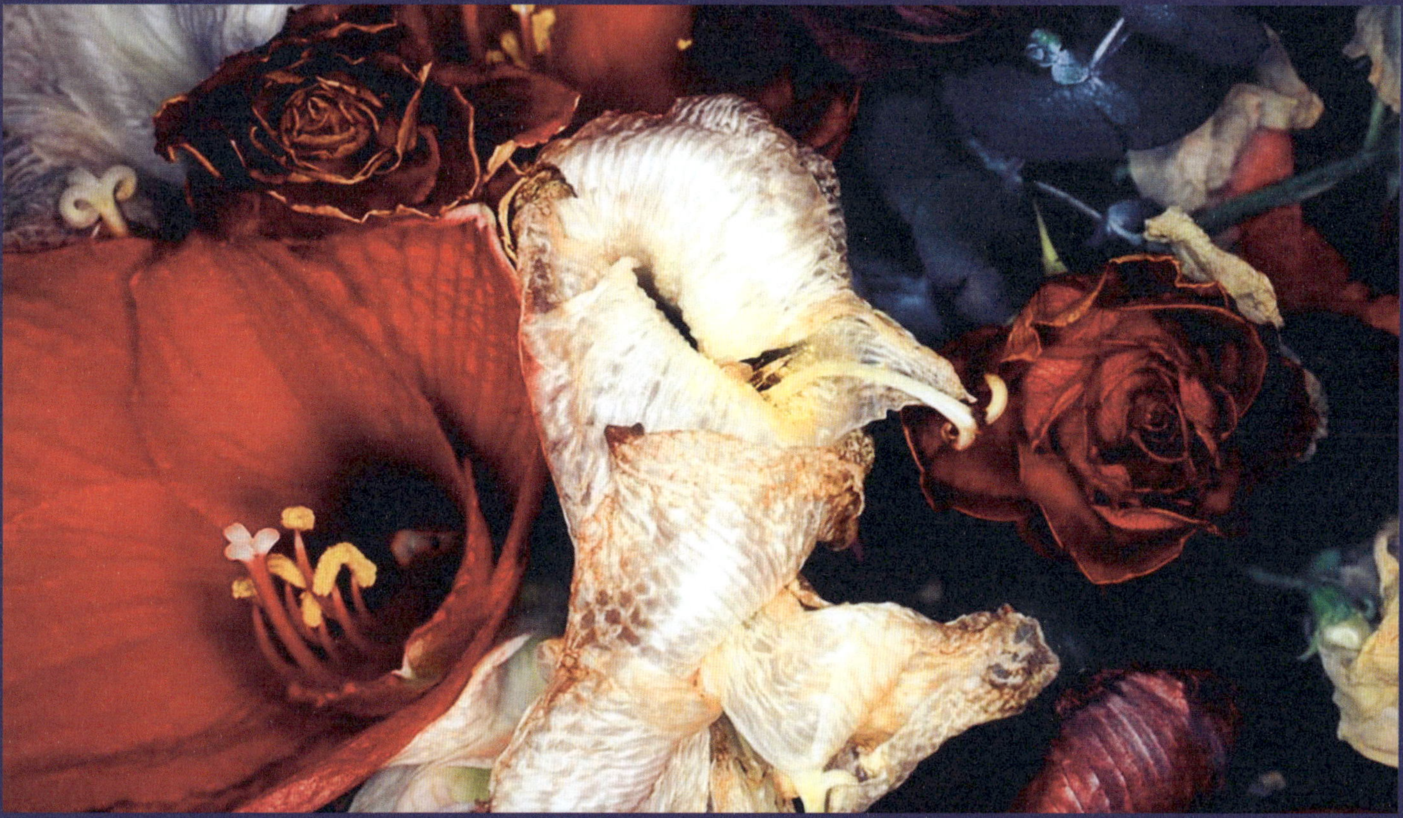

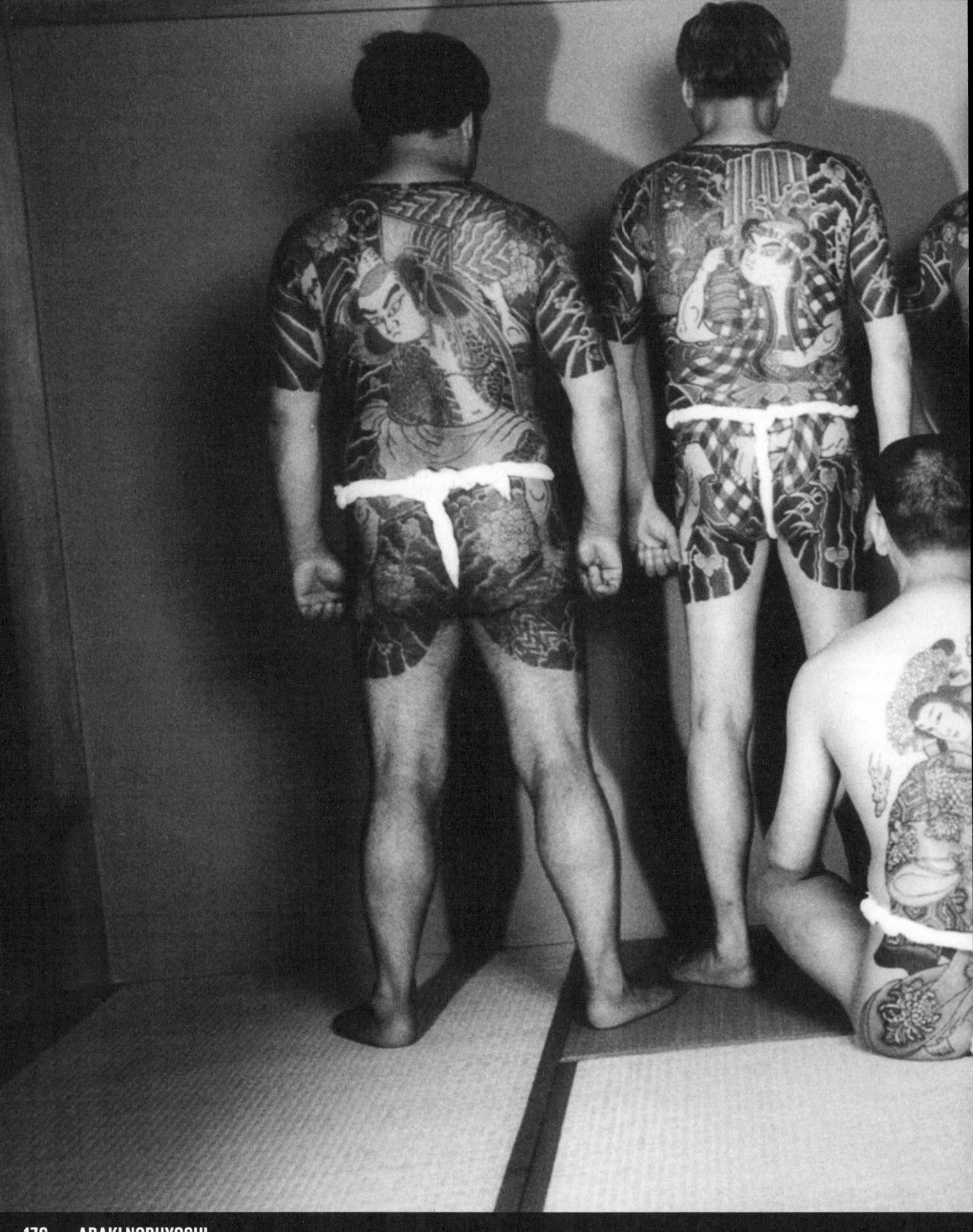

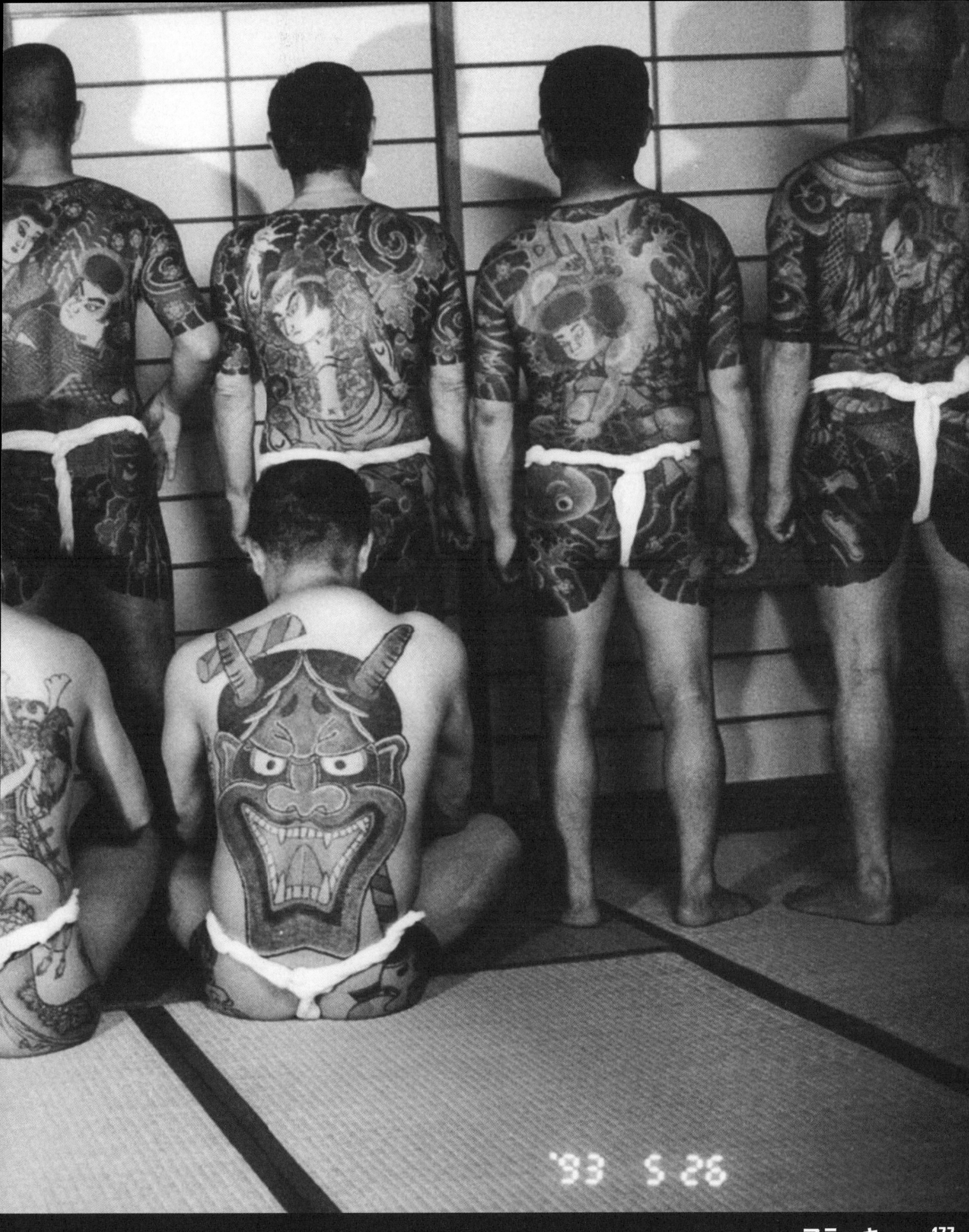

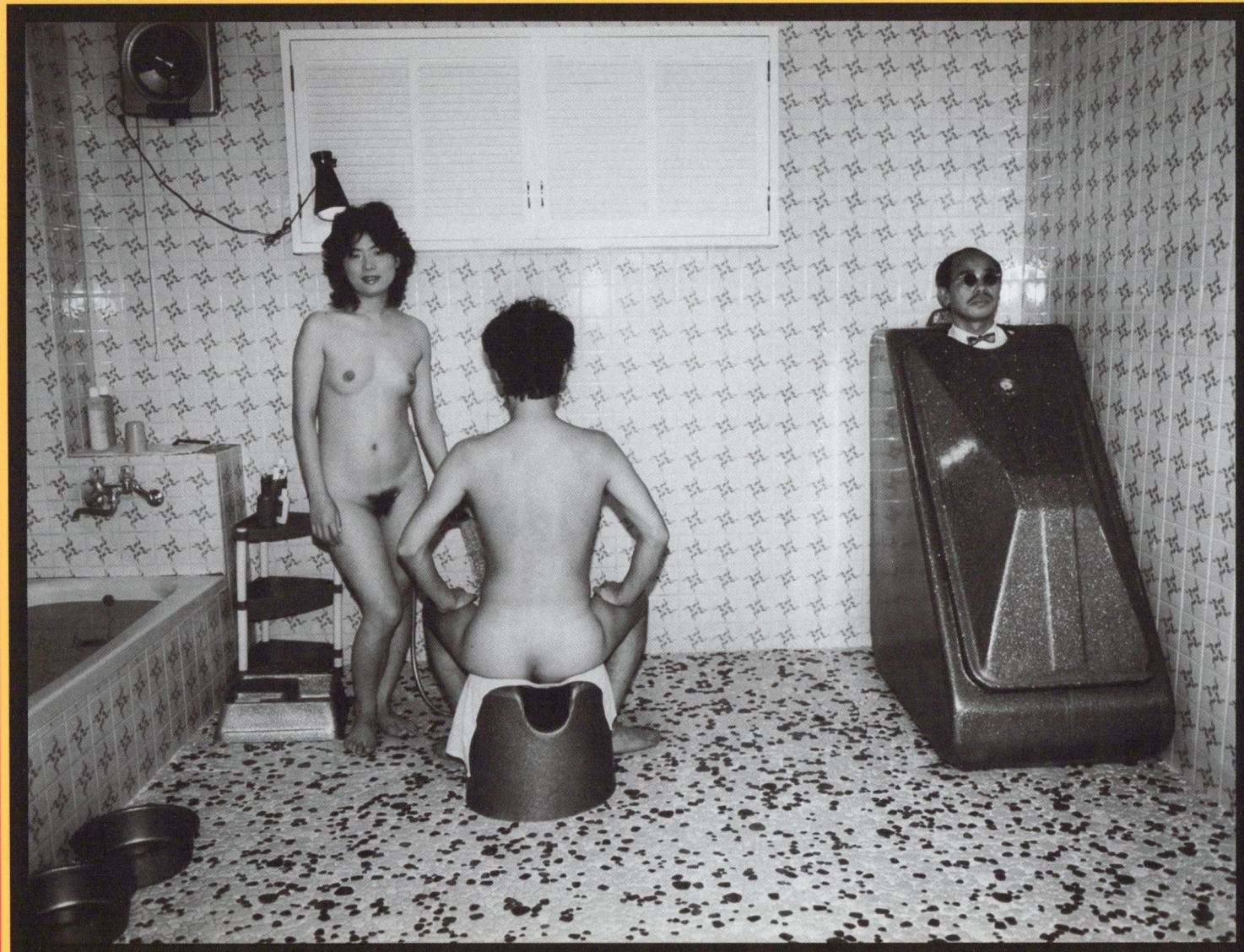

'I don't "think" about what I want to capture, I let the camera guide me to what I "feel" I want to take. You have to have noise, even in photography. People have been trying to eliminate excess things to make photography look neat and tidy. They "frame-out" the noise. Sometimes, you're ready to shoot, but extra elements enter the picture. They link the outside world to the inside, and that's what makes it fun for the photographer.

When I'm framing my picture, my subject may not be at the forefront and something could obstruct the image, or I could be pushed and fall. I put it all into my photograph. I don't aim for perfection. If you don't capture the spontaneous moment, your pictures lose life.'

pp. 176–77: **Araki Nobuyoshi**, *Past Tense – Future 2*, 1979–2011/12, gelatin silver print.

Above: **Araki Nobuyoshi**, *Untitled, Tokyo*, 1985, gelatin silver print.

Opposite: **Araki Nobuyoshi**, *Past Tense – Future*, 1979–2011/12, gelatin silver print.

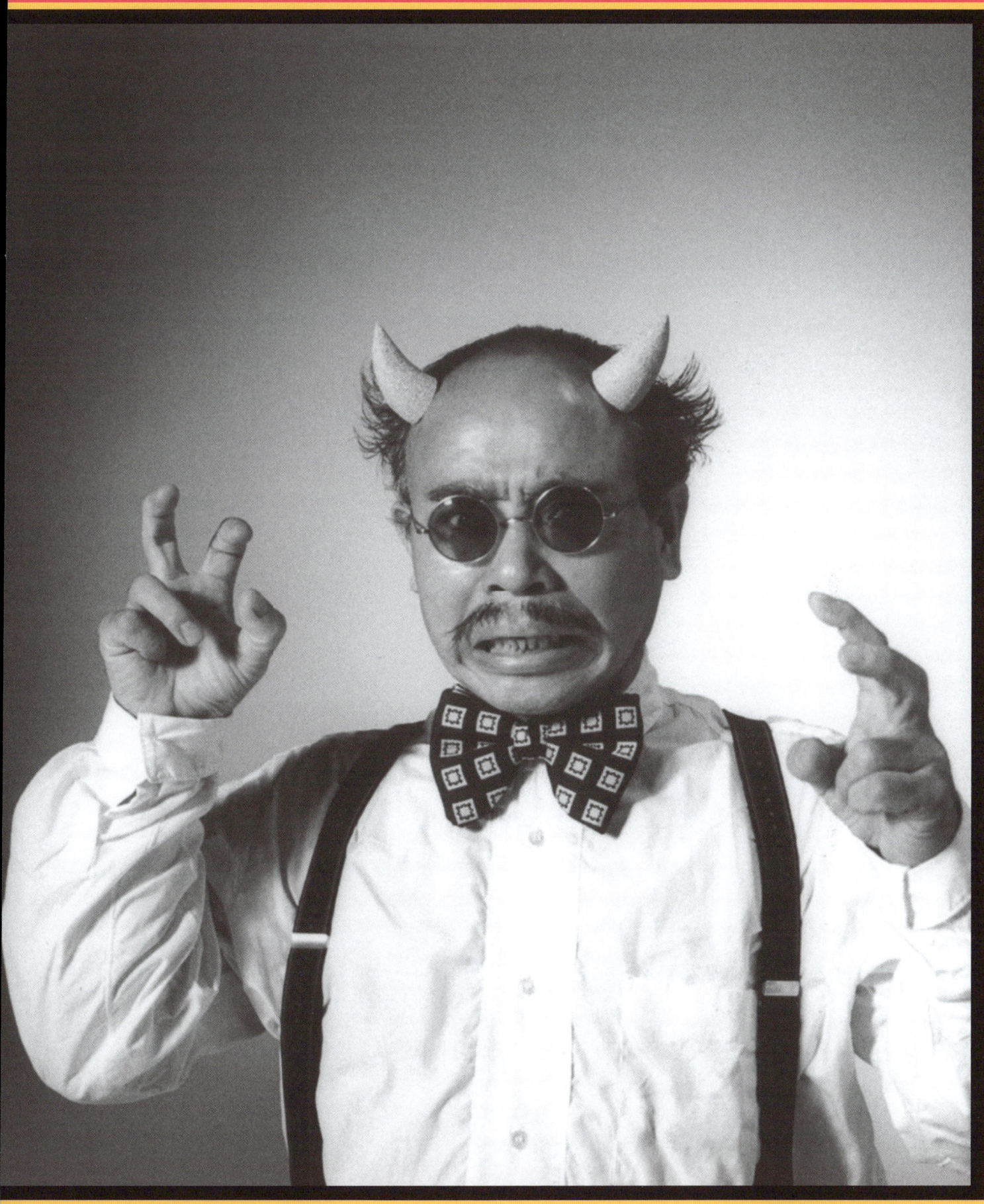

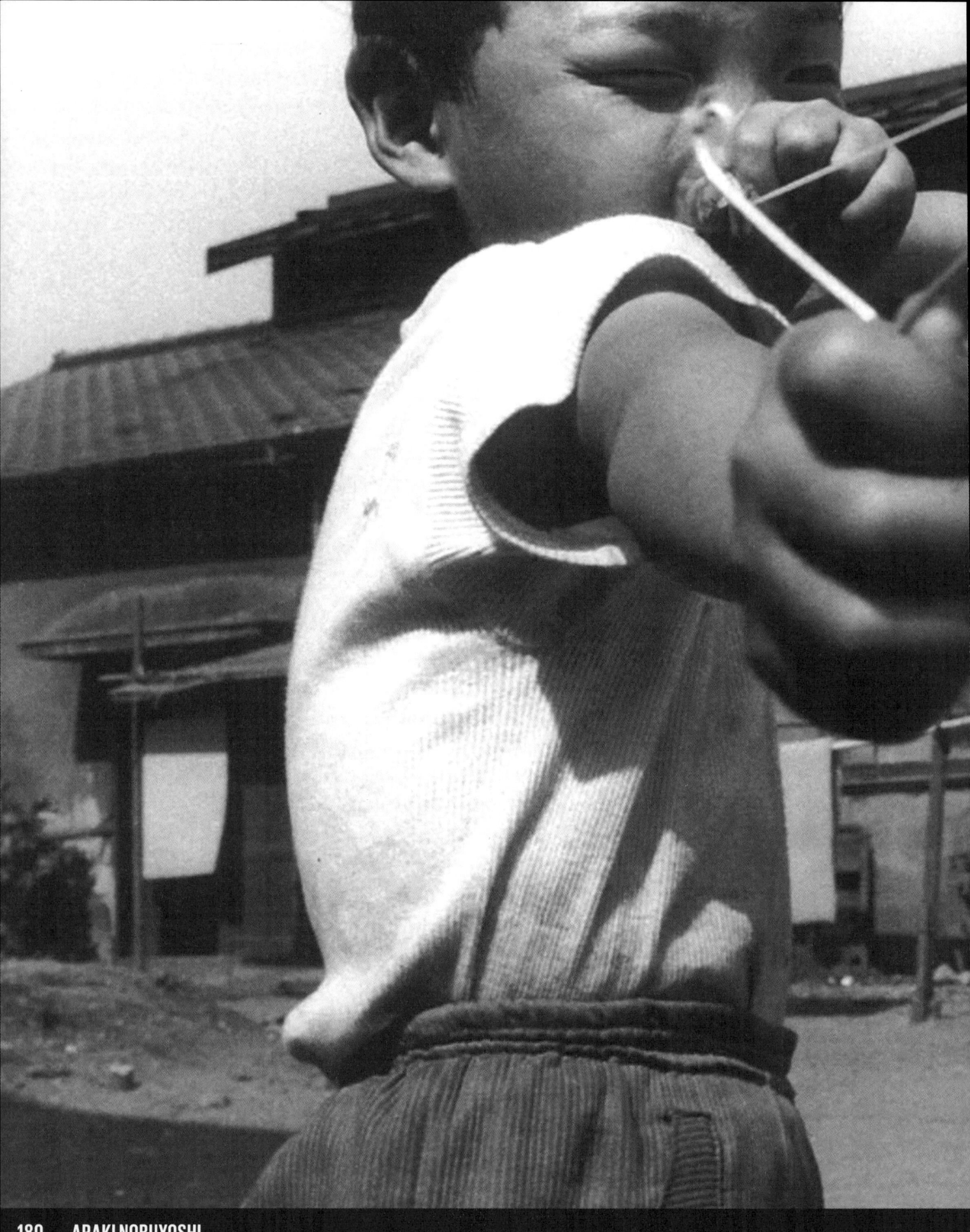

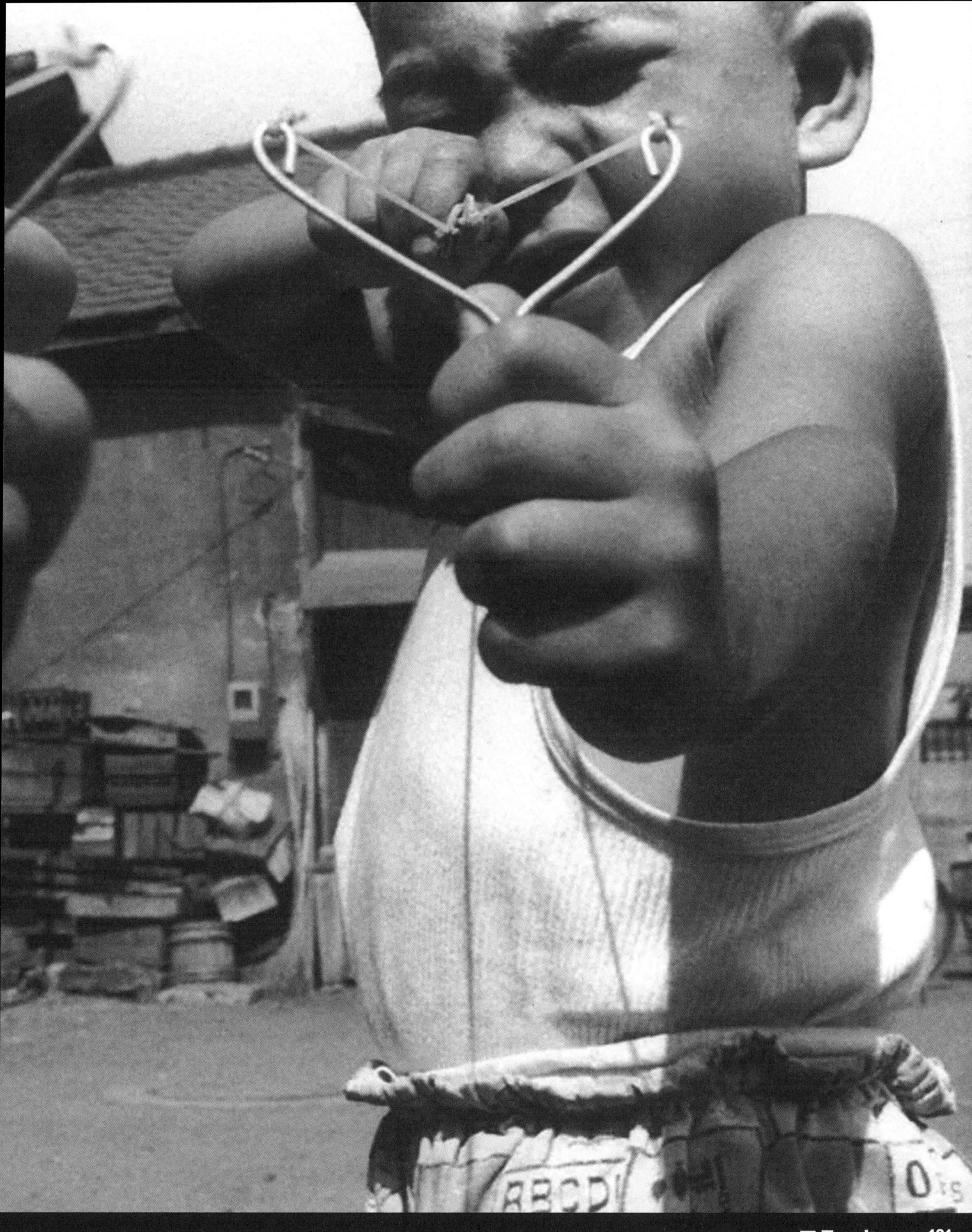

'I TAKE A LOT OF LIFE AND DEATH PICTURES. I DELIBERATELY SET MYSELF IN THE AFTERLIFE TO TAKE PICTURES. THE *PSEUDO-REPORTAGE* PHOTOGRAPHS WERE SPECIAL BECAUSE THOSE PICTURES ARE CLOSELY RELATED TO LIFE AND DEATH. I'M KIND OF PLAYING AROUND WITH IT, BUT THOSE PICTURES RELATED TO DEATH CLEARLY HAVE AN IMPACT ON ME. PICTURES THAT UNINTENTIONALLY CAPTURE A SENSE OF LONELINESS ARE SPECIAL TOO.'

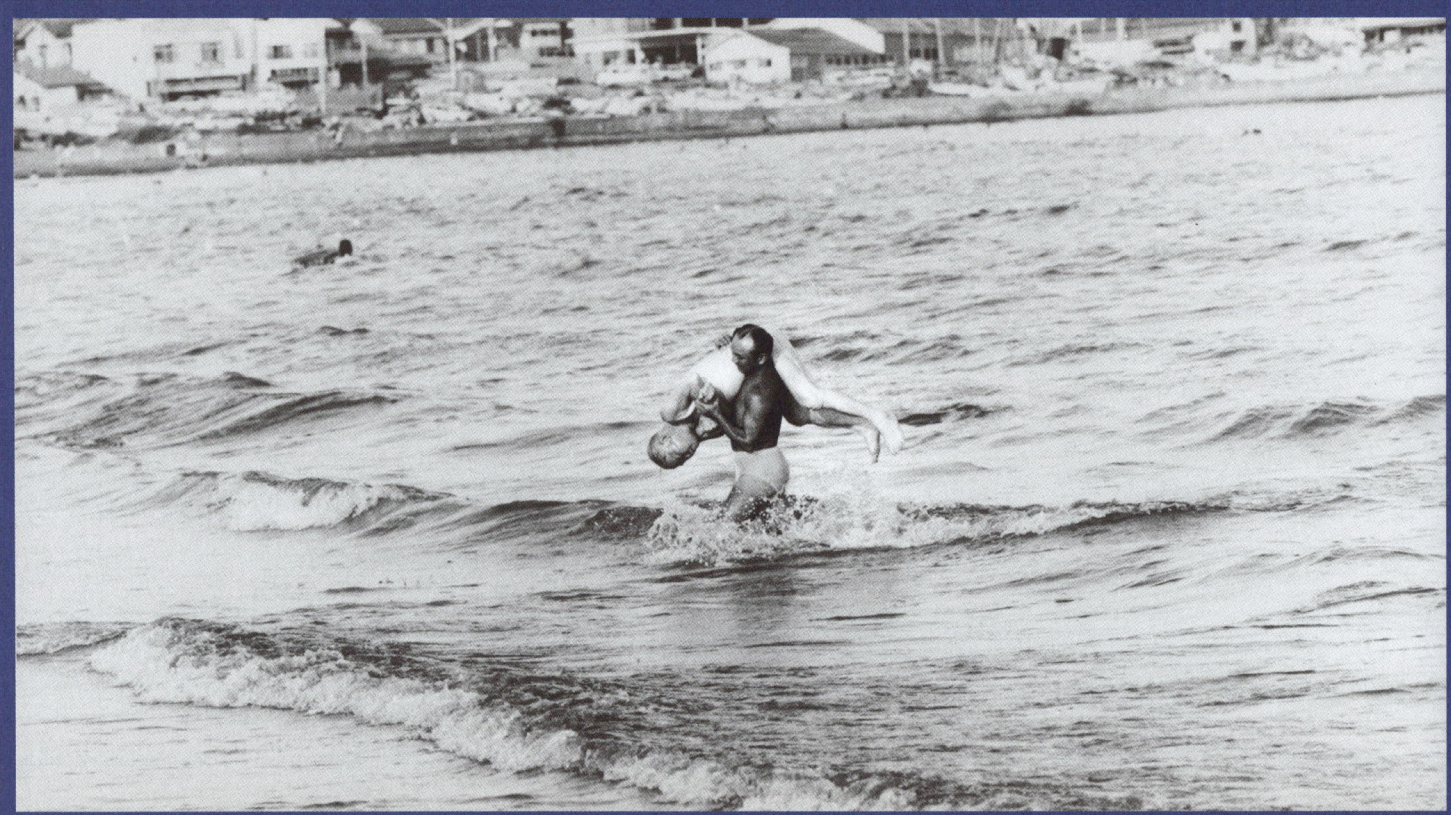

pp. 180–81: **Araki Nobuyoshi**, *Sachin and his Brother Mabo*, 1963, gelatin silver print.

Above: **Araki Nobuyoshi**, *Pseudo-Reportage*, 1977, gelatin silver print.

Opposite: **Araki Nobuyoshi**, *Personal Sentimentalism in Photography*, 1981, gelatin silver print.

Araki is interested in photography's ambivalent claim to representing reality. His *Pseudo-Reportage* series (1980) brought together images of female boxers and sex clubs, as well as pictures shot during photoshoots and romantic encounters from throughout the 1970s. These were presented with a text that blended autobiography and fiction, in spite of its documentary tone. In *Pseudo Diary* (published in the same year), Araki would render this mismatch graphically by playing with the date-stamp function of his camera. The book presents a single dated snapshot on each page in chronological progress, however some of the photographs purport to have been shot after the date of publication, according to their date stamps.

LUCY FLEMING-BROWN

When I asked Araki about what photography means to him, he said, 'It's like breathing in and breathing out.' It's really part of his life. It's part of his own body. He just takes as many photographs as possible. He produces so many photobooks, he's published over 500 photobooks to date. His approach is very diaristic. He takes photographs of everything that he experiences and encounters.

LENA FRITSCH

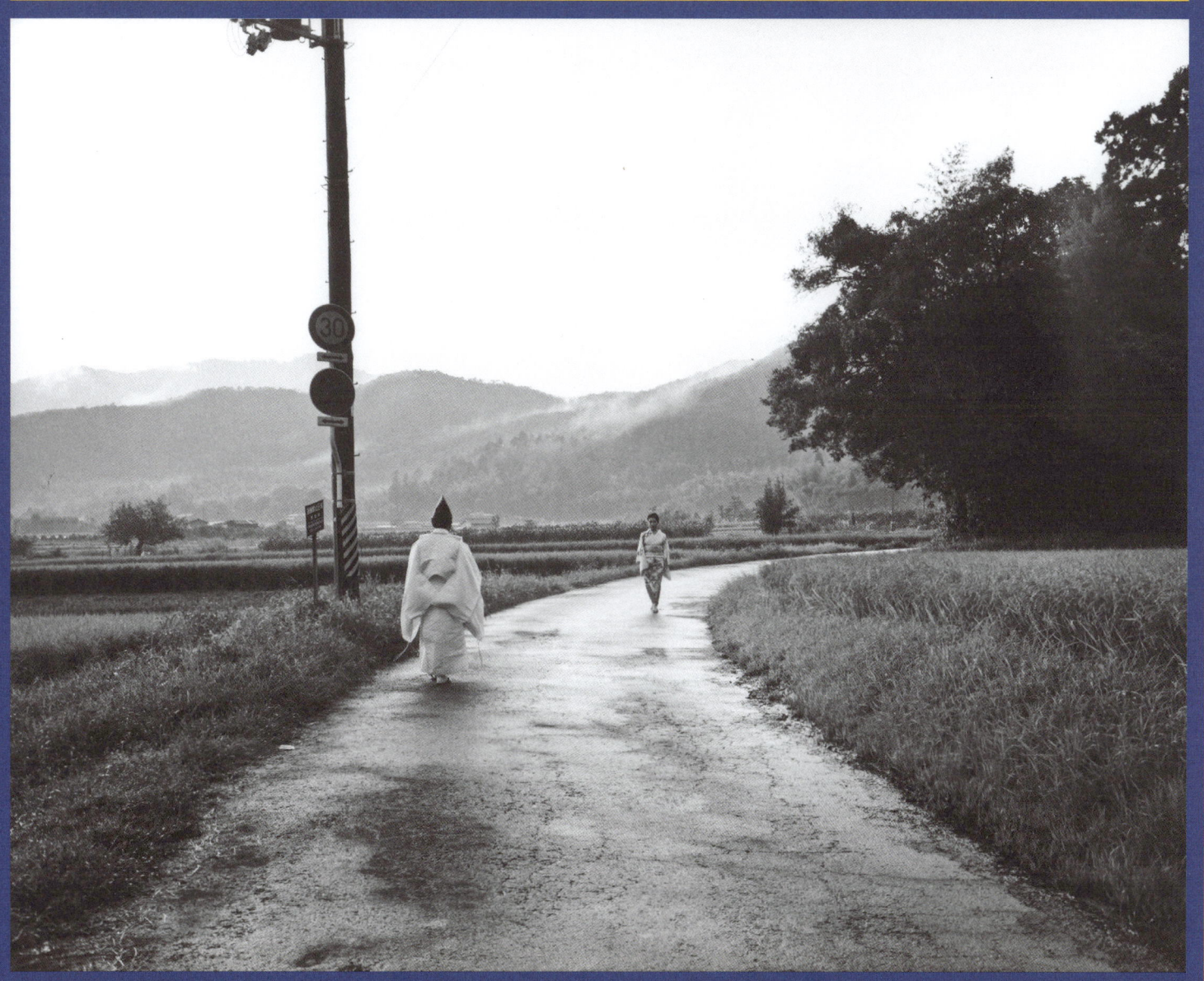

'YOU KNOW HOW PEOPLE SAY THAT PHOTOS DON'T LIE? WELL, THAT'S NOT TRUE. EVERYTHING IS A LIE. THE CAMERA ITSELF IS A LIAR IN A WAY. I FEEL THAT THE REAL TRUTH IS NOT SOMETHING THAT'S EASY TO UNDERSTAND. SO THEN, WHY NOT LIE FROM THE BEGINNING?'

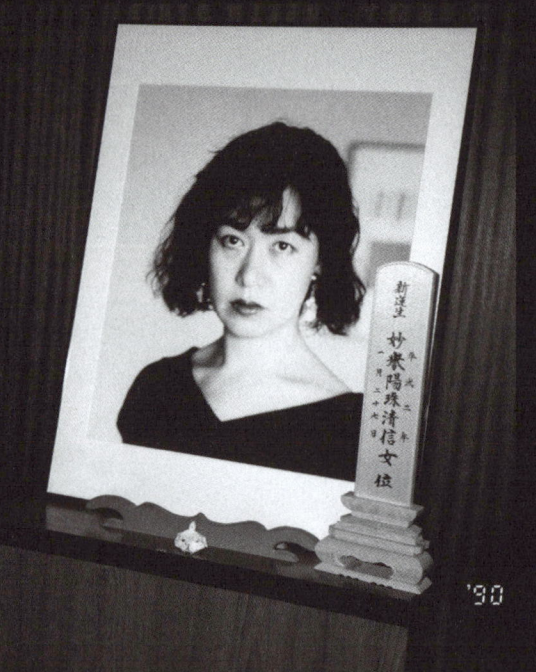

Araki termed his confessional mode of diaristic photography 'I-photography' (*shi-shashin*), in punning reference to the autobiographical literary genre known as *shi-shōsetsu*, or 'I-novel'.

This approach is exemplified in the series *Sentimental Journey* (1971) and *Winter Journey* (1989–90), in which Araki used his camera to reveal moments in the life he shared with his wife that would usually be treated as private.

Recording their honeymoon alongside dinner menus, and his wife's struggle with cancer beside the changing seasons of his hometown, Araki's appetite for exposing these experiences together is at once shocking and intimately familiar.

LUCY FLEMING-BROWN

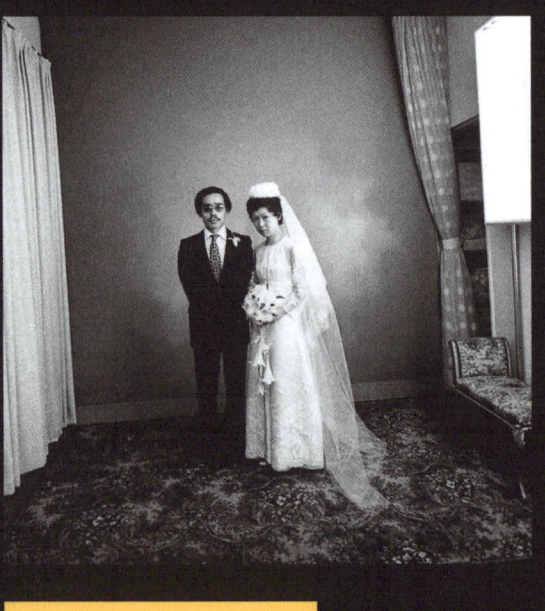

Top and above: Photographs from **Araki Nobuyoshi**, *Sentimental Journey* (1971).

Right: Negative from **Araki Nobuyoshi**, date unknown.

Opposite (above): Photograph from **Araki Nobuyoshi**, *Winter Journey*, (1989–90).

Opposite (below): Photograph from **Araki Nobuyoshi**, *Sentimental Journey* (1971).

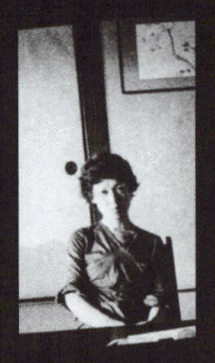

'I took many pictures of my wife, and people ask me which one I like the most. Those pictures are so precious to me. "Love" is one of the most important factors in my photography. But no matter how much I loved my wife, she's the only one in the picture. Because in the end, the camera lens is like a mirror reflecting yourself. And it's hard to connect your feelings and the picture. I feel the camera obstructs our true feelings, preventing us from making a connection.

Sentimental Journey was a photobook of my honeymoon. Marriage and life were a sentimental journey. Living is a journey, and taking photographs was part of mine. This combined journey was sentimental for me. When taking a photo of life, you can sometimes see death in it, which makes you appreciate being alive. I reflected that in *Sentimental Journey* and *Winter Journey*.

I was at a starting point, ready to live my life. But when the photobook was printed even at that time, I felt that it wasn't a journey to happiness, but already a journey to death. After that, when my wife died, I put it together with *Journey of Death*, which contains pictures I took of her from while she was sick until she died. When she died, we put her in a coffin and she was cremated, and in those moments, I was feeling that this is what it means "to live".'

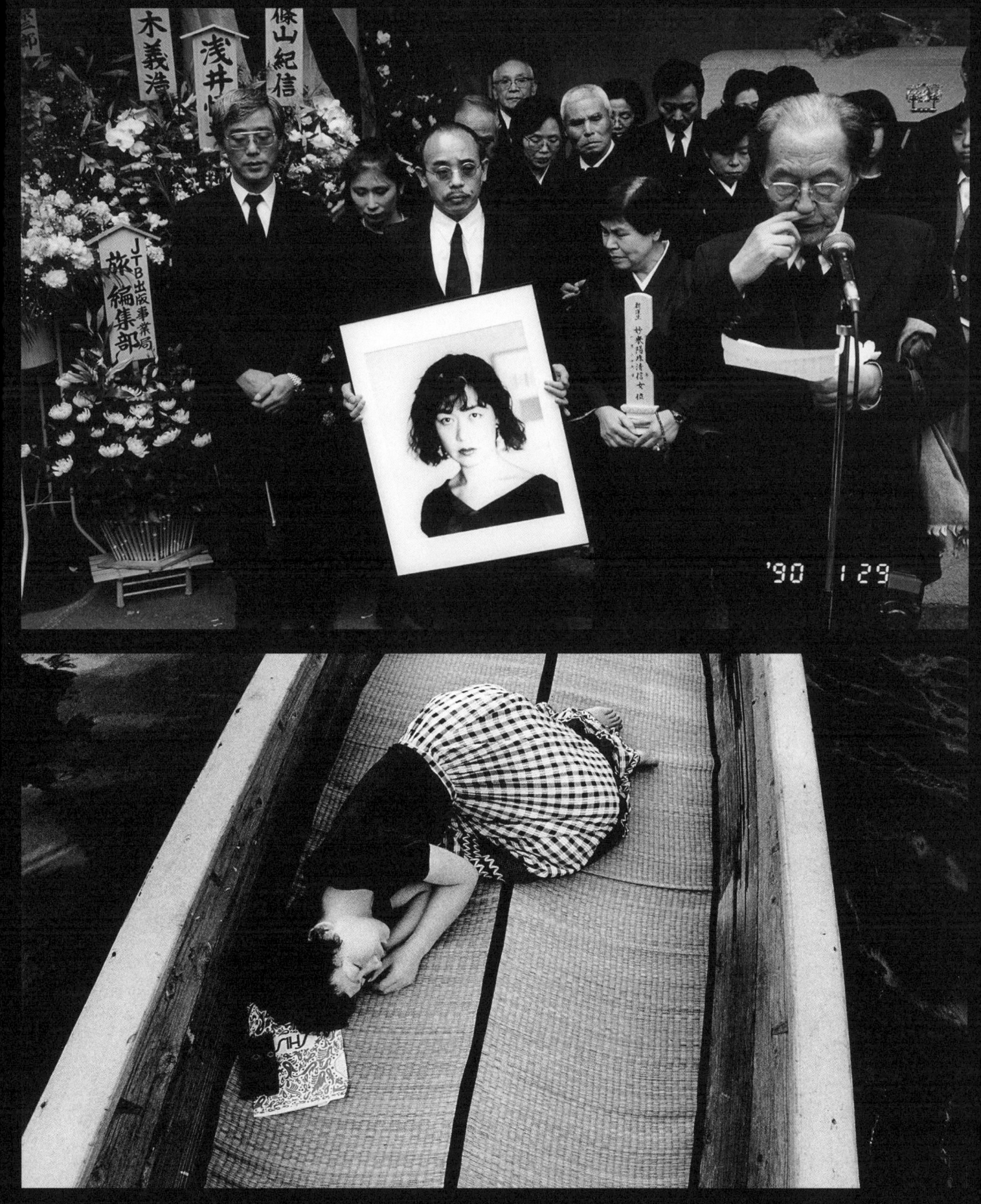

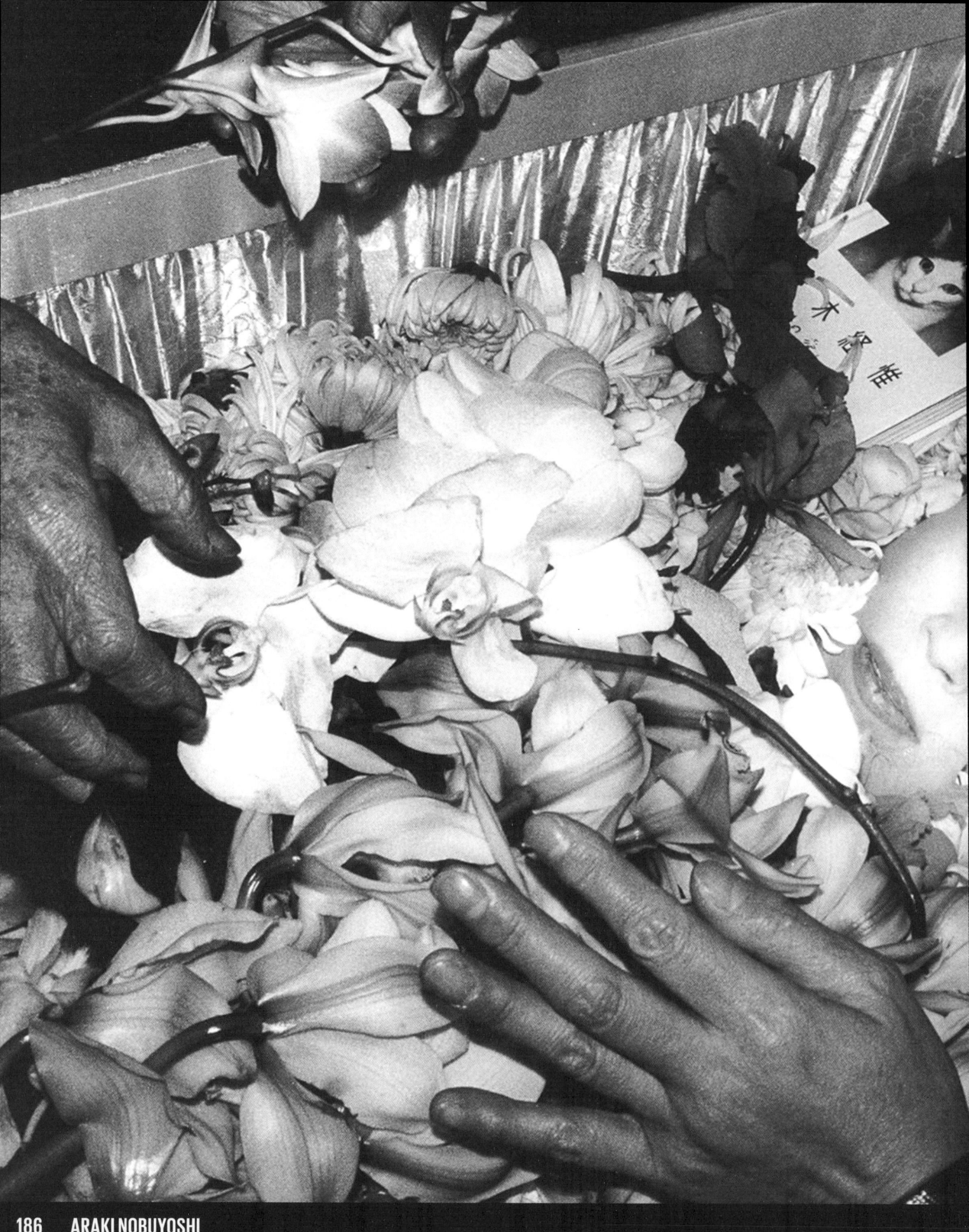

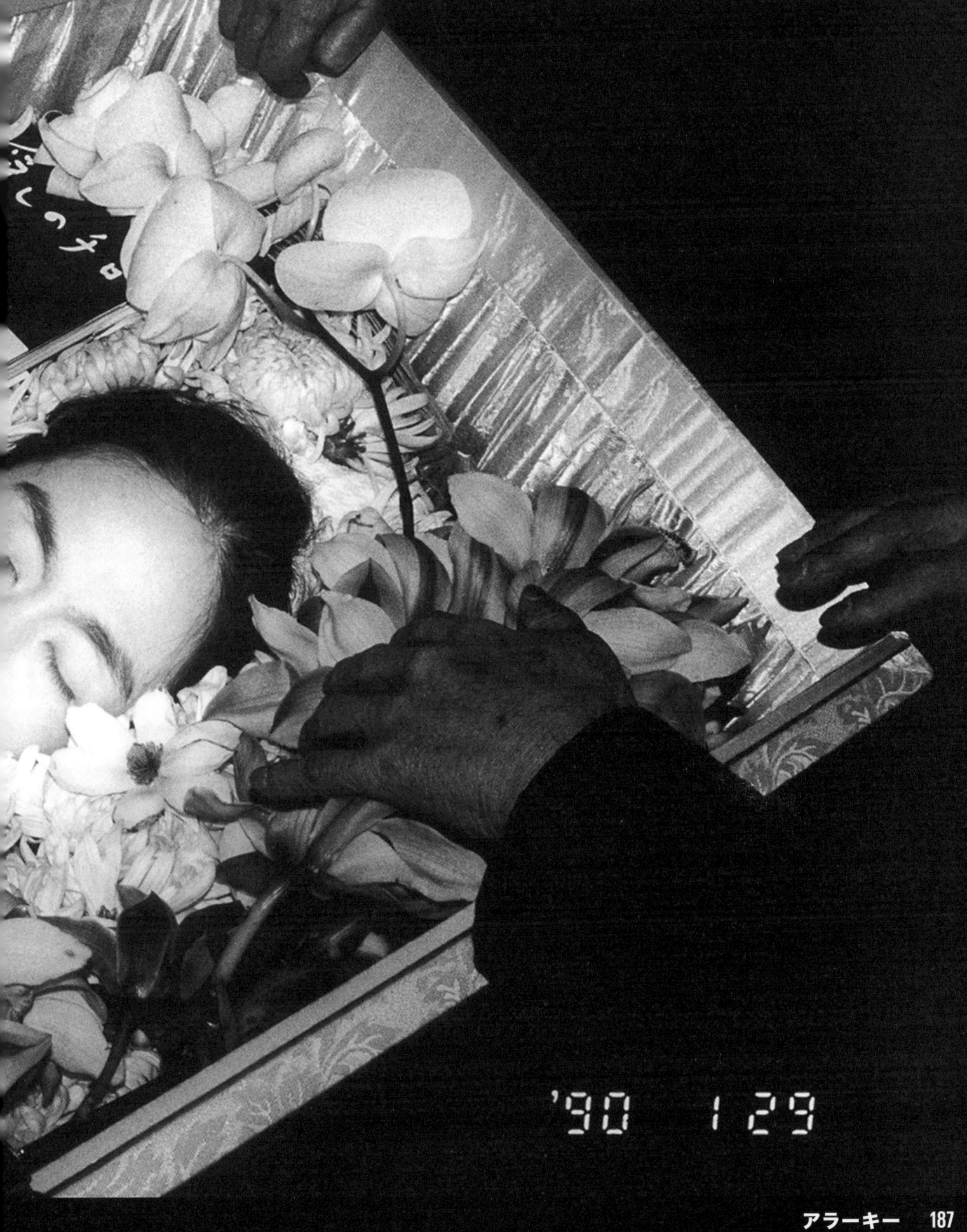

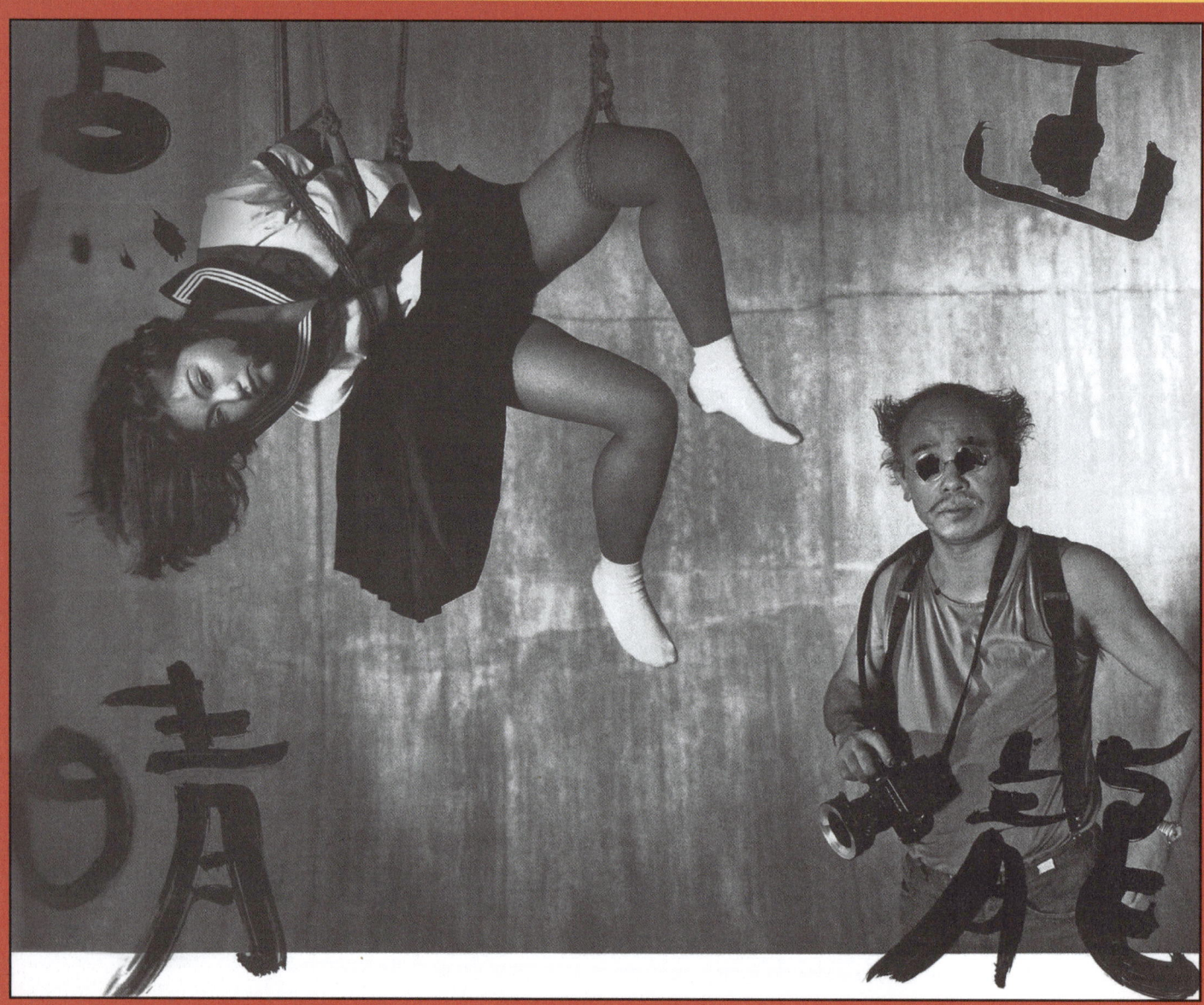

pp. 186–87: Photograph from **Araki Nobuyoshi**, *Winter Journey* (1989–90).

Above: **Araki Nobuyoshi**, *Journal intime*, 1994, gelatin silver print.

Opposite: **Araki Nobuyoshi**, *Untitled*, 2000, gelatin silver print.

From his serialization of photographs in pornographic magazines during the 1970s to his retrospective at New York's Museum of Sex in 2018, Araki has consistently embraced the controversy that accompanies his bodies of explicit work. These range from spontaneous point-and-shoot images of scenes in hotels, clubs and brothels to elaborately staged pictures in which women have been tied up, ornamented with props and toys or otherwise erotically posed to create tableaux. His work has consistently challenged Japanese obscenity legislation, for example in its representation of pubic hair, but Araki has refused to reform any aspect of his practice, despite public outcry and interventions by the police.

LUCY FLEMING-BROWN

'ISN'T IT NATURAL TO PHOTOGRAPH WHAT YOU LOVE THE MOST? IT'S THAT SIMPLE. WOMEN HAVE A LOT OF EMOTIONS AND THEY HAVE SO MUCH MEANING TO THEM. HOW THEIR MIND AND BODY INTERTWINE, THAT'S WHY I AM ATTRACTED TO THEM.'

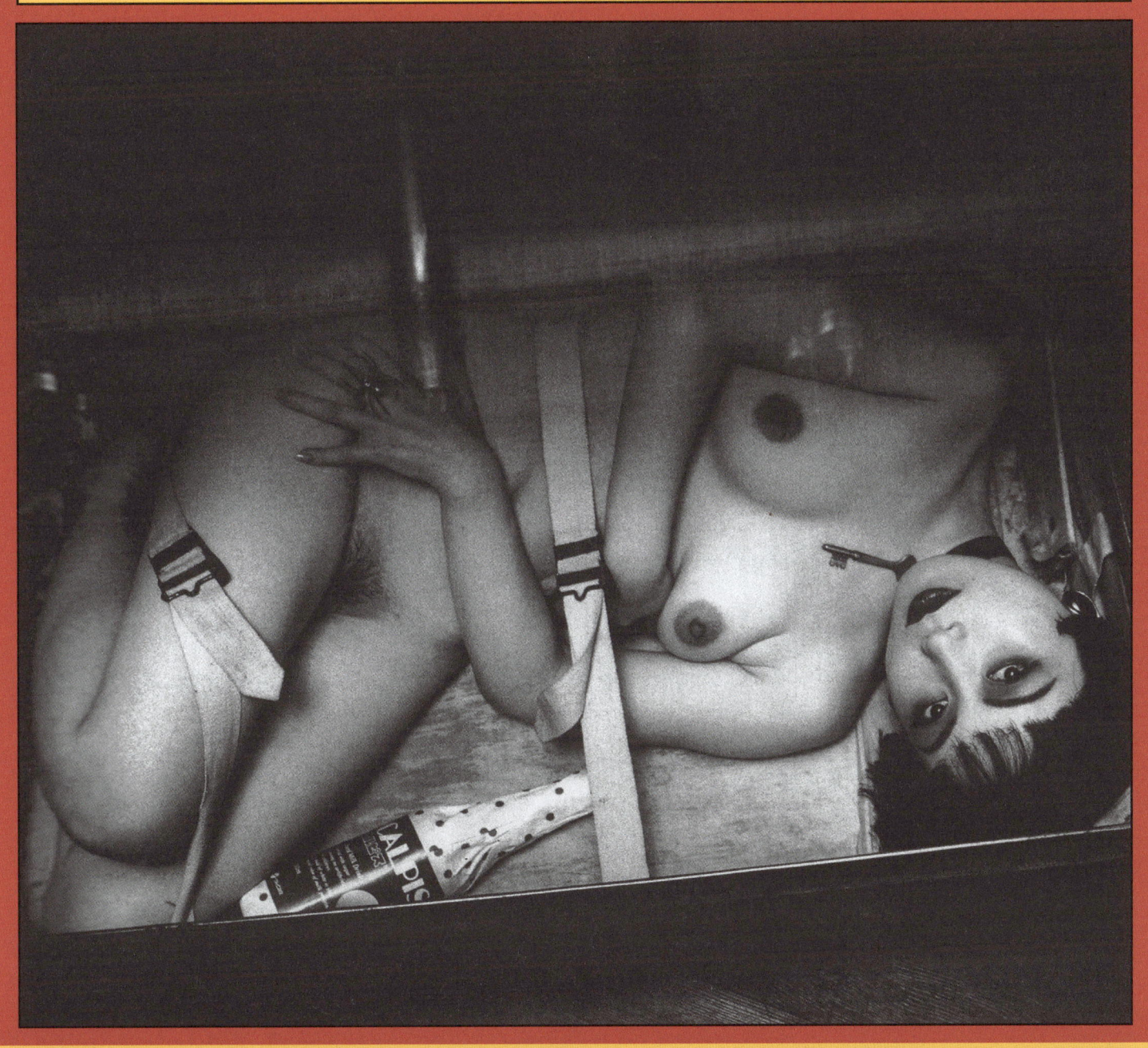

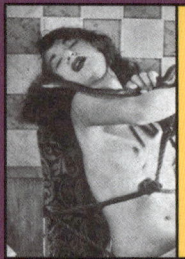

KINBAKU

1952

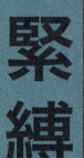

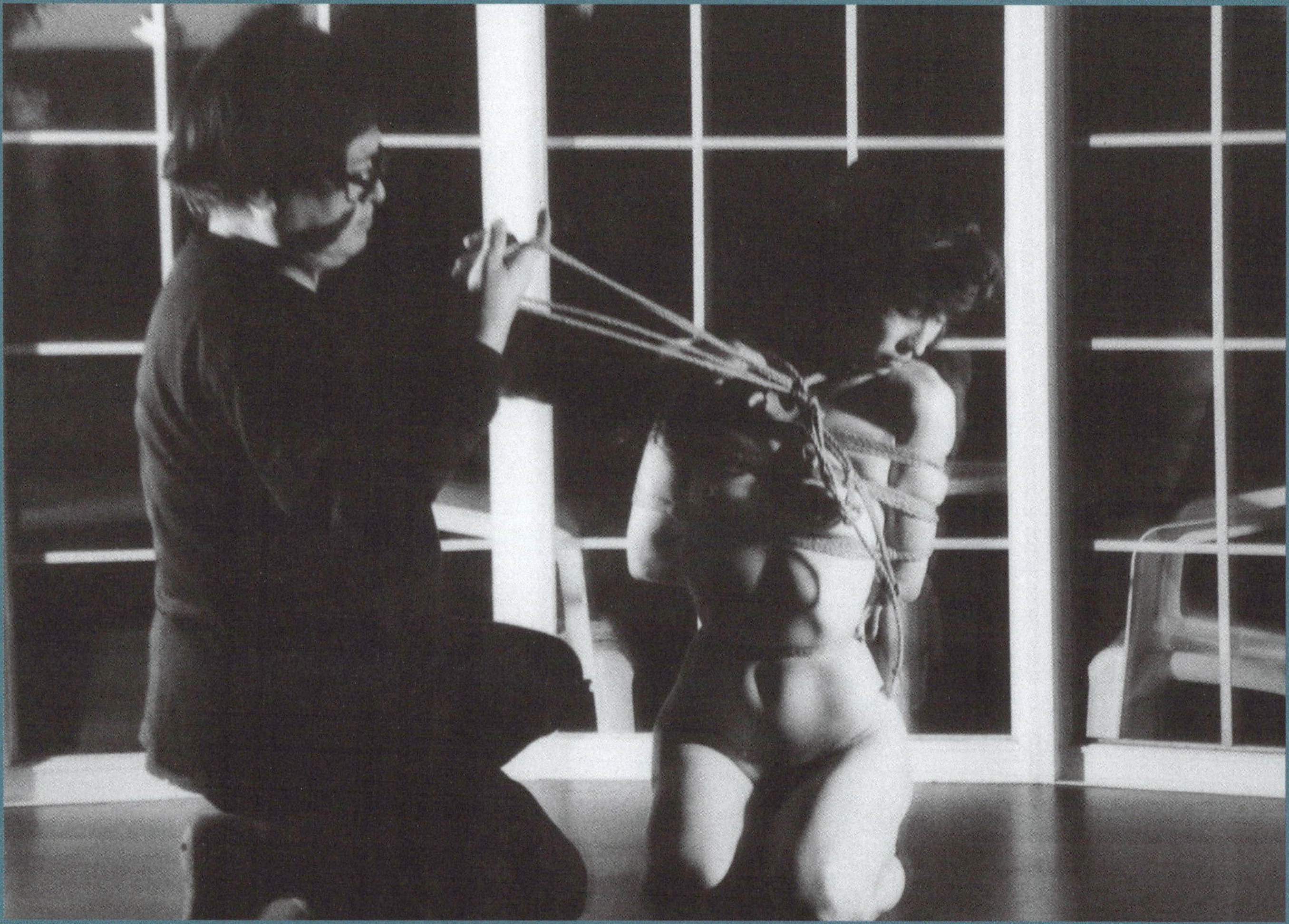

Fuji Akio (attrib.), *Nureki Chimuo Tying a Model*, early 1980s, materials unknown.

Opposite (above left): Photograph from *Kitan Club* (1962).

Opposite (above right): Photograph from *Kitan Club* (1961).

Opposite (below): Photograph from *Kitan Club* (1963).

The use of rope symbolically and religiously in Japan has been the norm for hundreds, if not thousands of years. Japan is, in many ways, a rope-based society. From a philosophical standpoint, it is a wonderful subject, if you want to look deeply into aspects of Japanese culture that go back hundreds and hundreds of years.

MASTER K

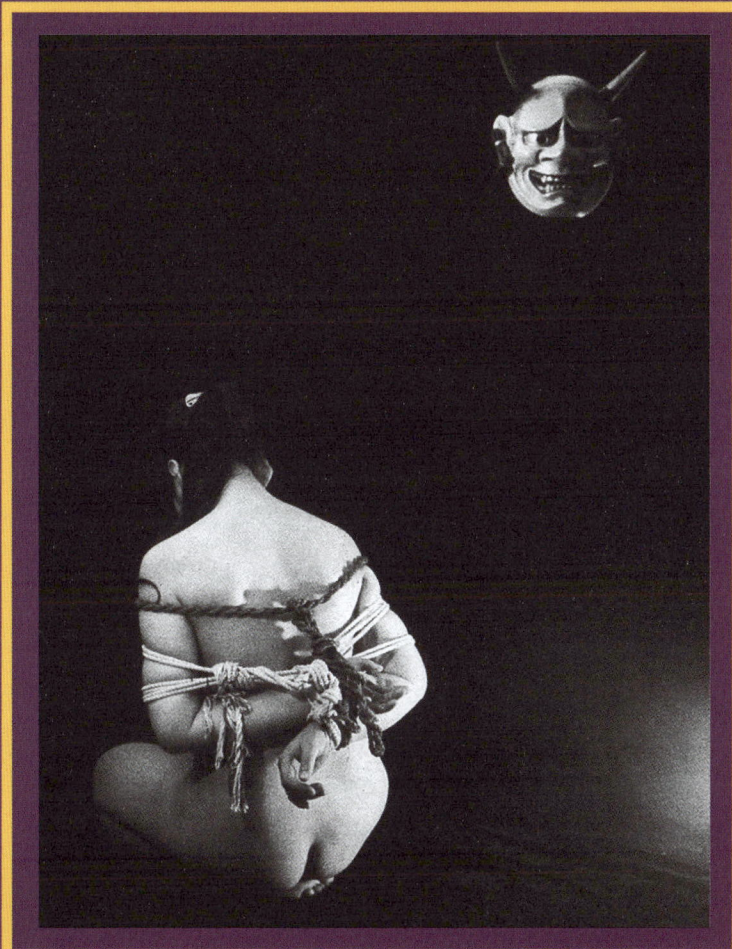
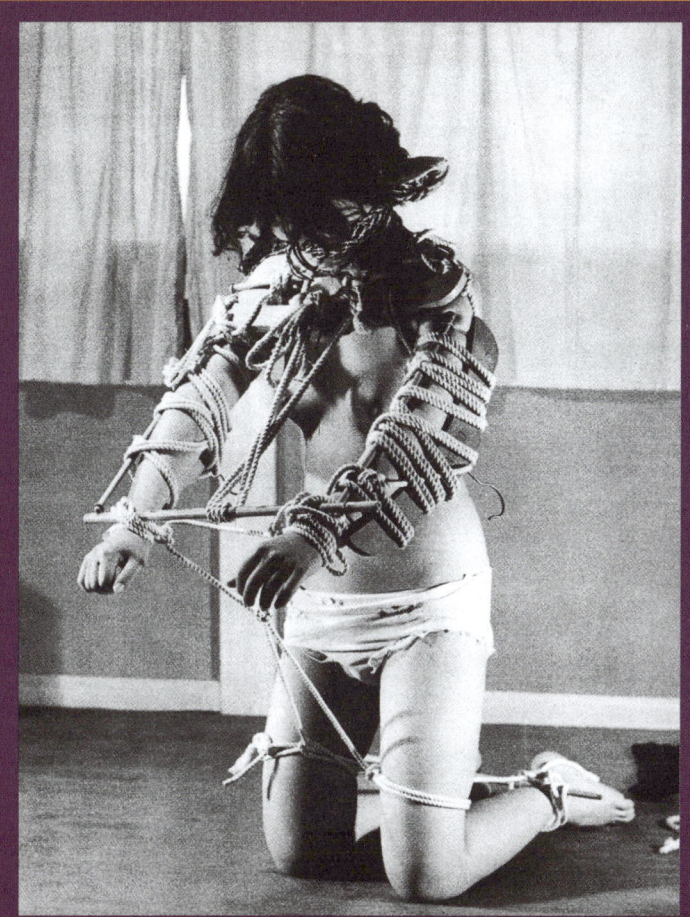

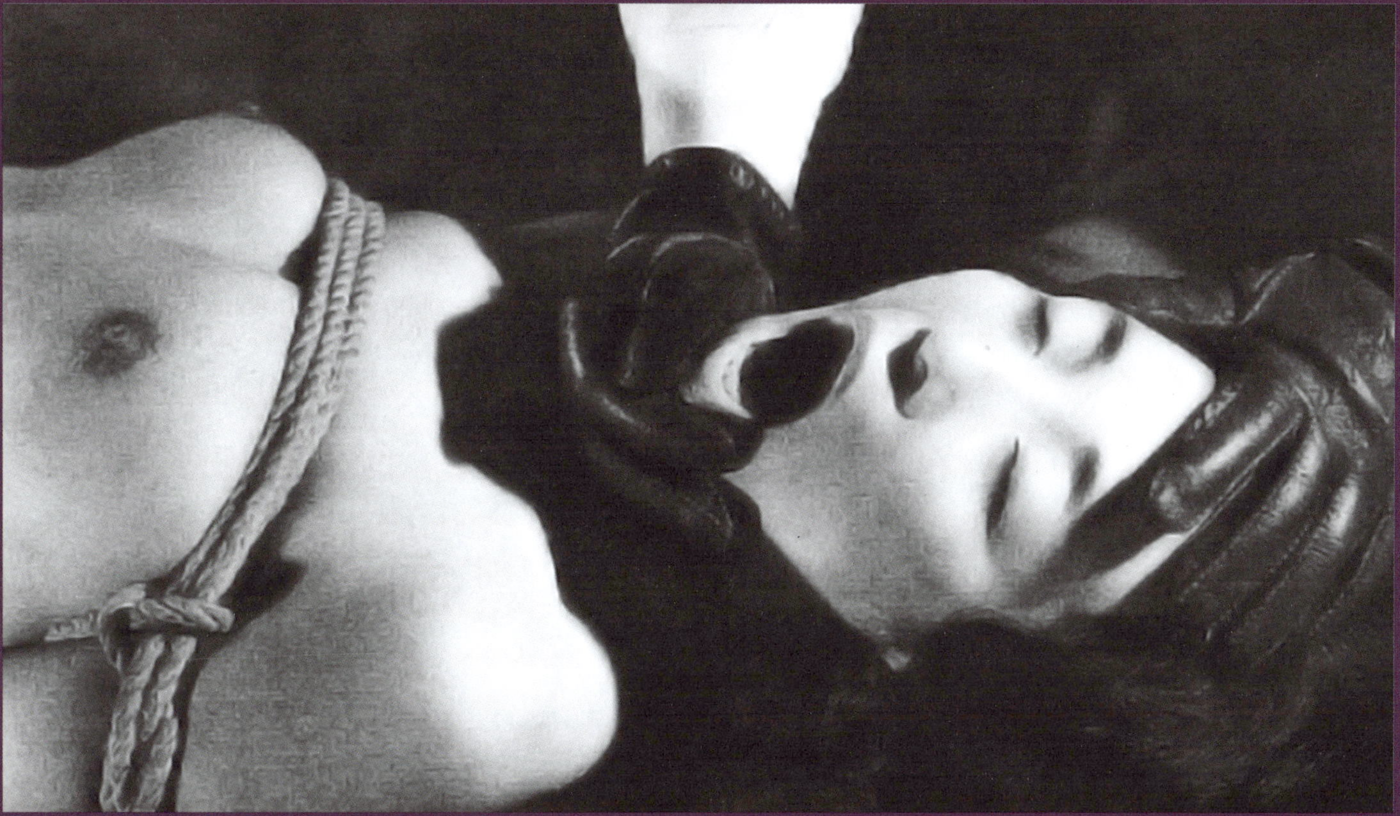

緊縛 191

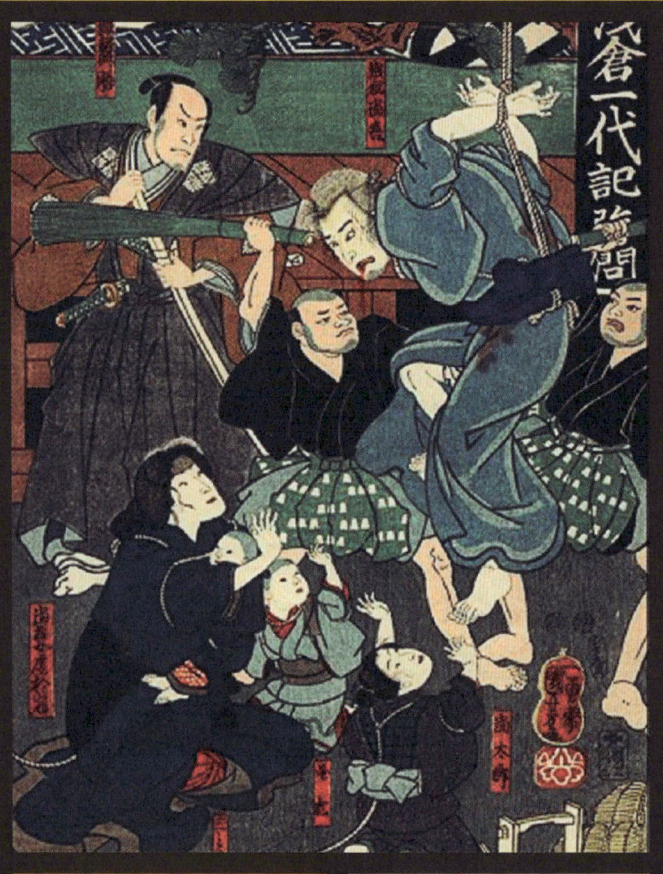
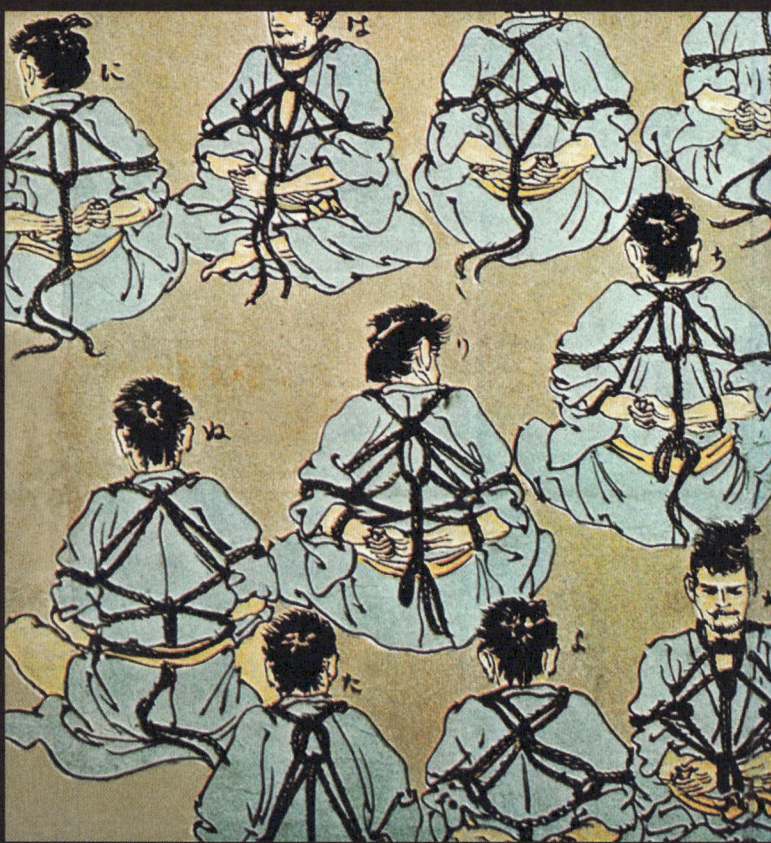

Above (left): *The Life of Asakura*, 1851, painting.

Above (right): *Tokugawa Bakufu keiji zufu* (1893).

Right: **Shimooka Renjō (attrib.)**, *A Prisoner in Court*, 1863, hand-coloured photograph.

Far right: *Battle at Amagasaki*, from *Taiheiki Amagasaki gassen*, 1861, woodblock print.

Opposite (above): **Itō Seiu**, *Art of Knots and Ropes*, 1930s, ink and colour on paper.

Opposite (below left): **Itō Seiu**, *Bamboo Torture Wheel*, 1920, woodblock print

Opposite (below right): **Kusakabe Kimbei**, *A dōshin, Edo period police officer, and a captured criminal*, 1860, coloured photograph.

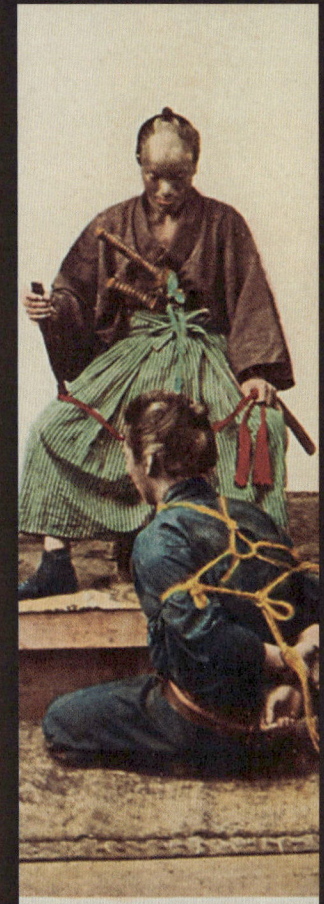
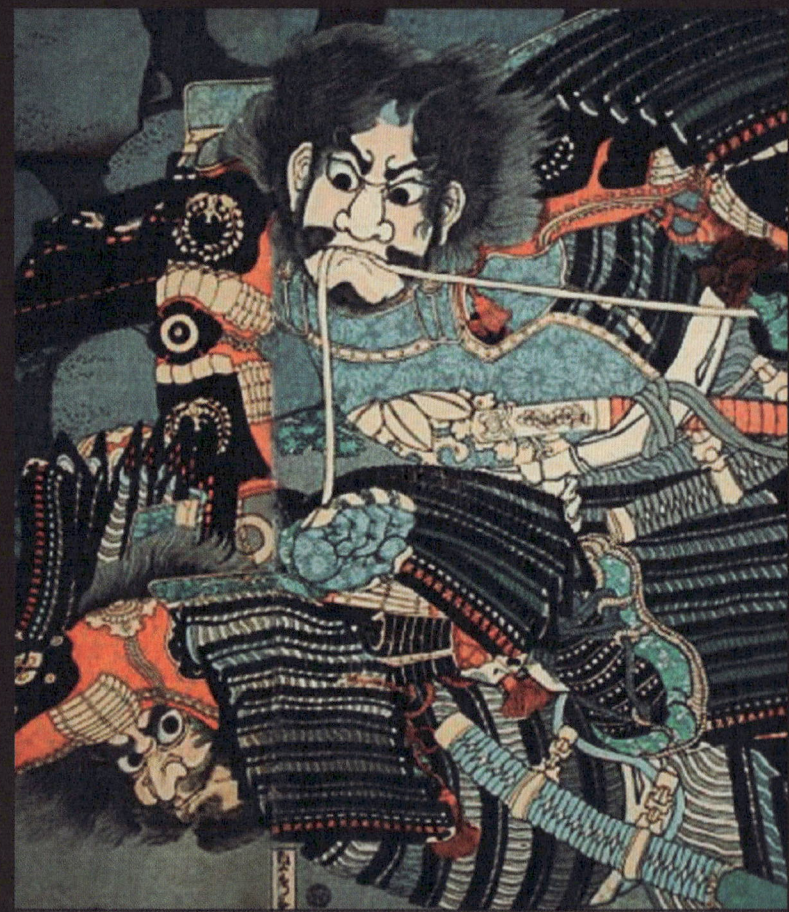

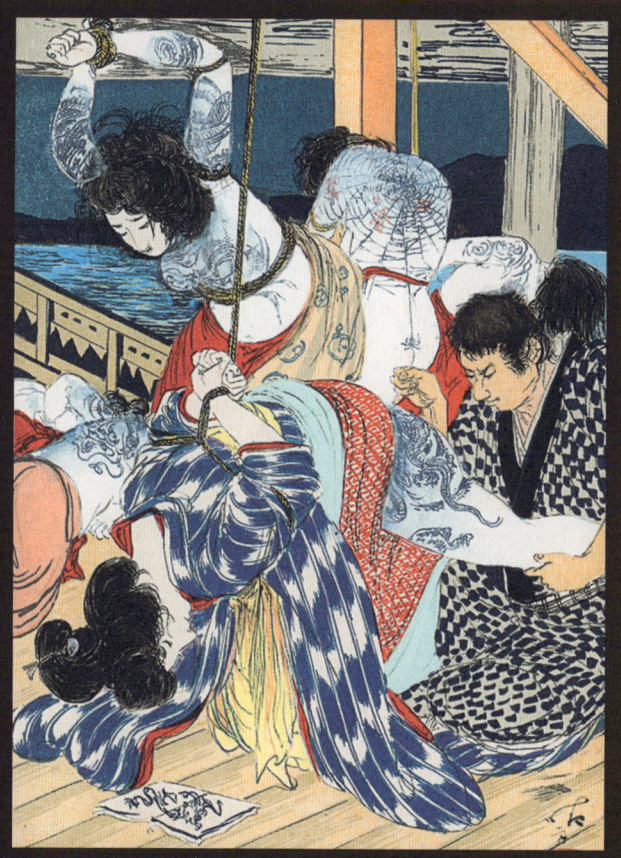

In the Shinto religion, when they want to create a sacred space, they put a rope around it. In the Buddhist religion, which is the second most prevalent religion in Japan, there is something known as the endless knot. For the military, samurai armour is tied onto the warrior.

Kinbaku as an actual practice started with the martial art *hojōjutsu*. *Hojōjutsu* was one of the eighteen martial arts that a samurai had to learn before they were considered a samurai and would go into battle. After 1600, the use of *hojōjutsu* became a policing matter – it was used for capturing prisoners. And just from the tie, an official could tell what the crime was, the class of the prisoner and their punishment. You would never tie a samurai the way you would tie a peasant, it would be a great insult to the samurai, even if he was being brought to trial.

MASTER K

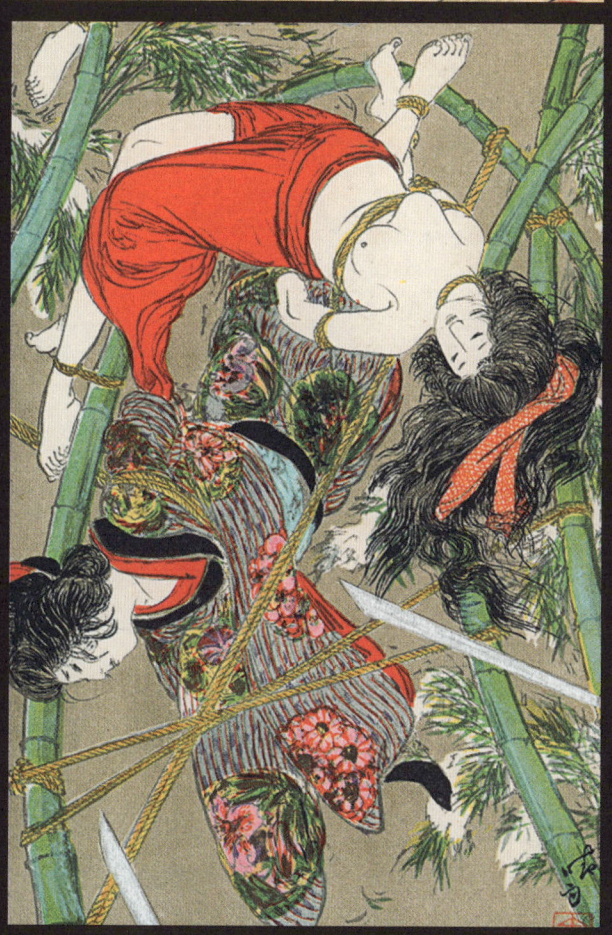

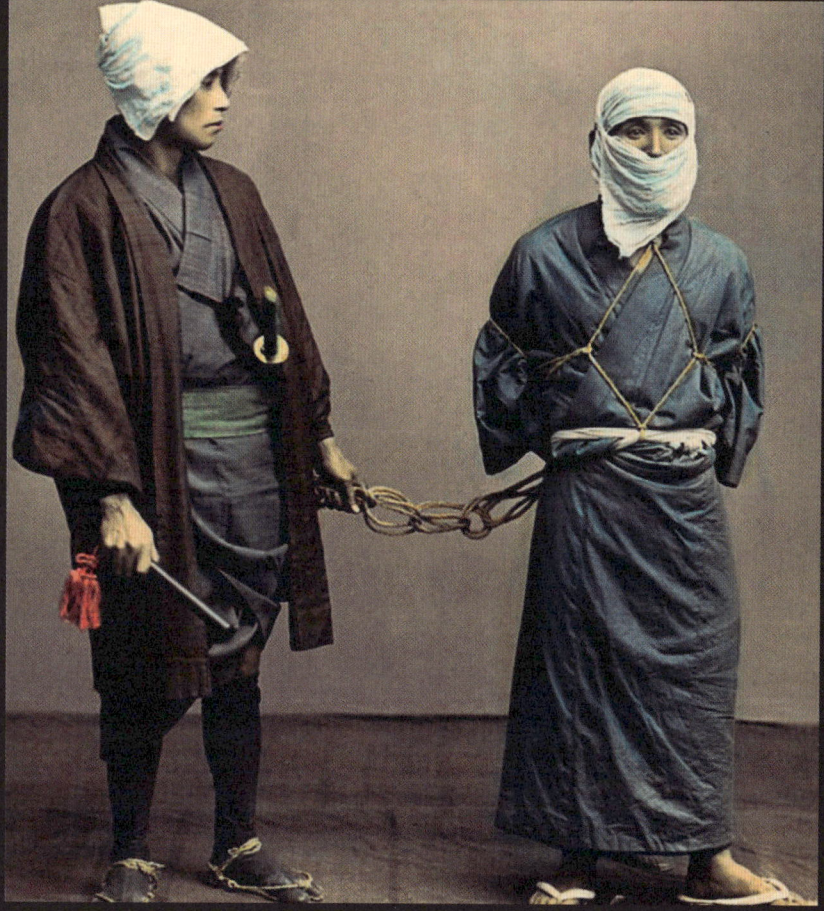

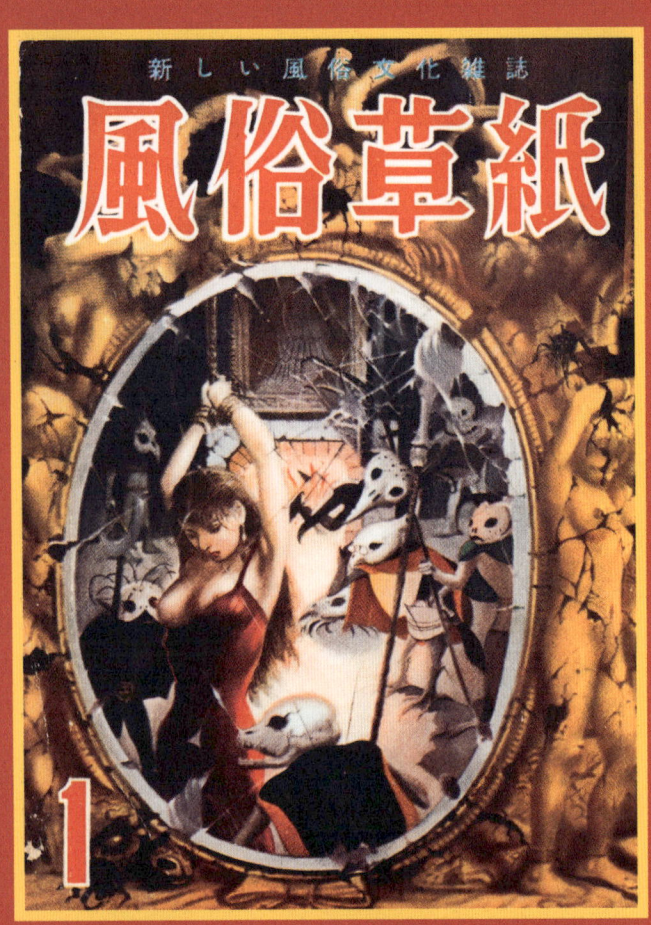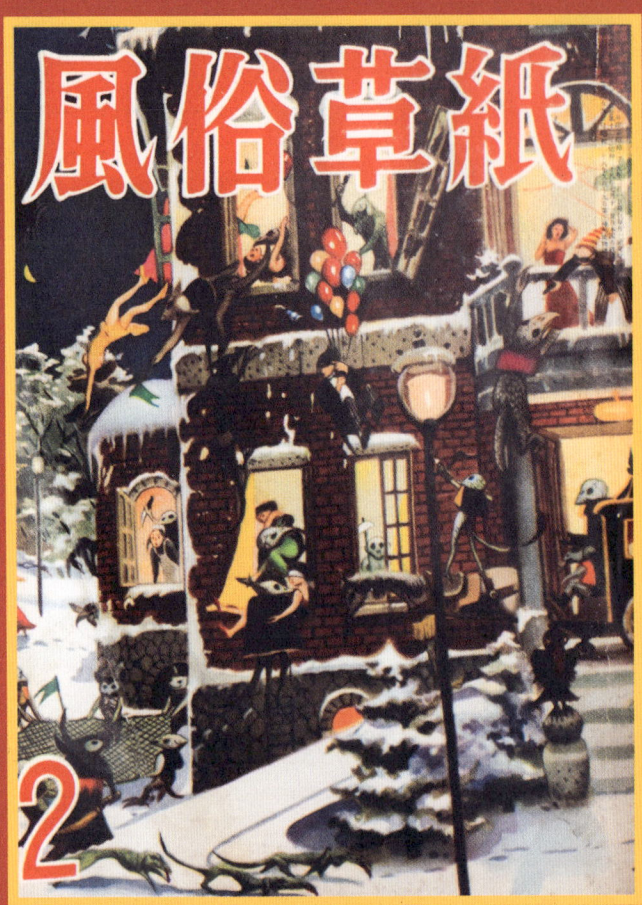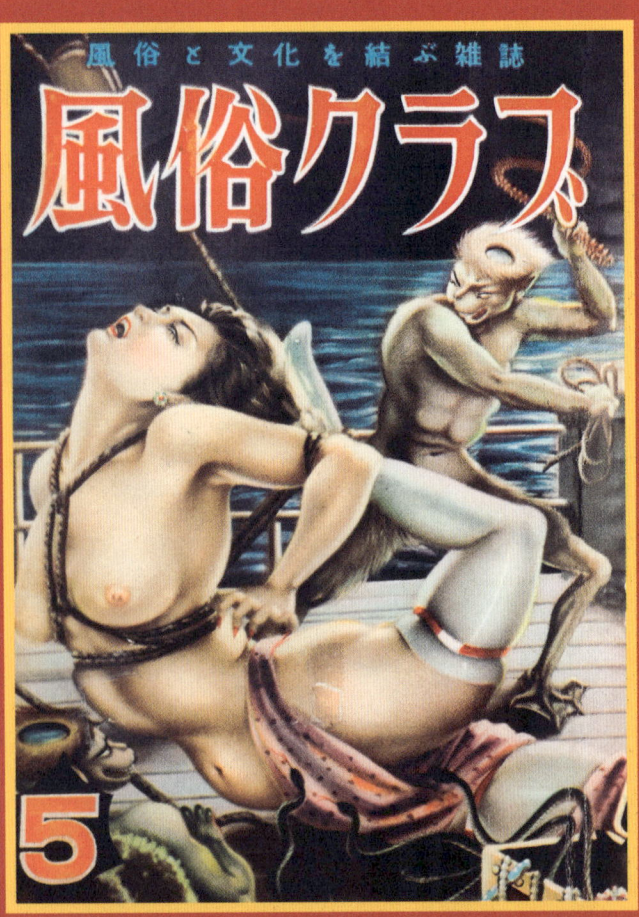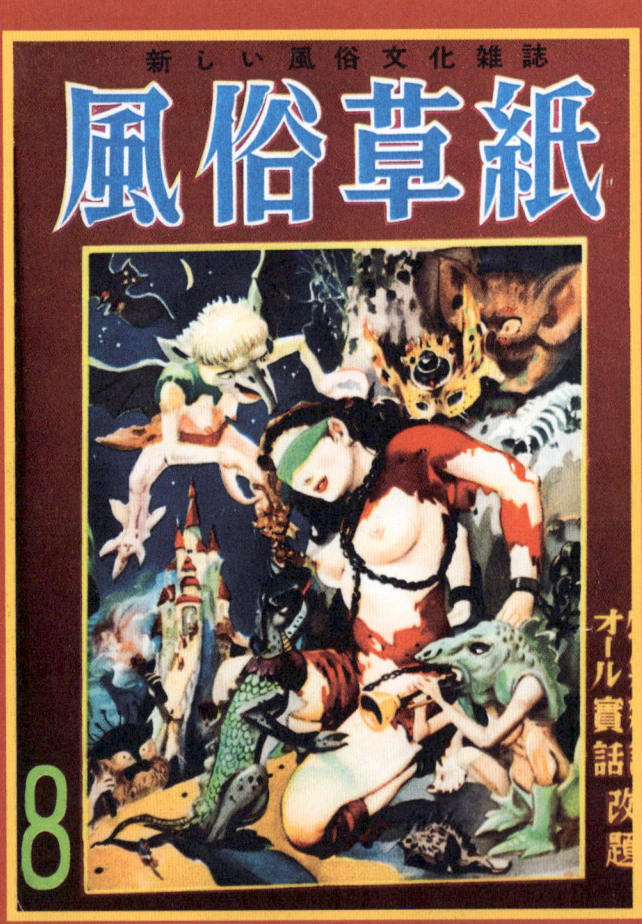

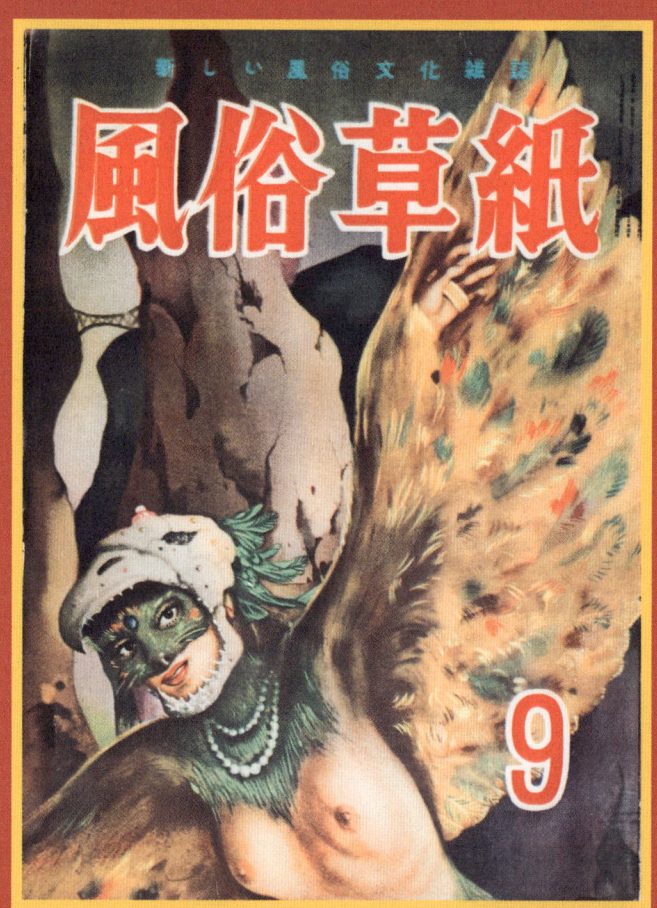
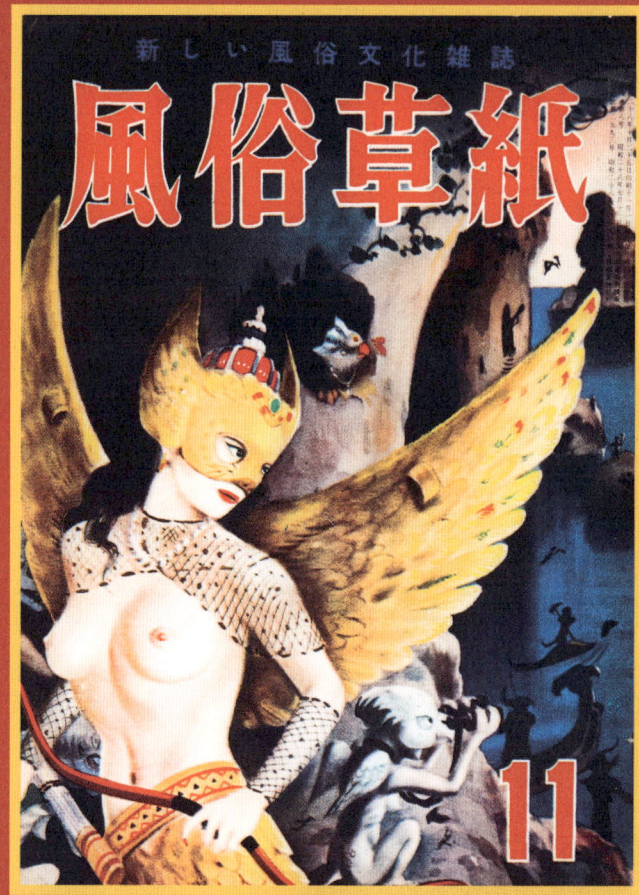
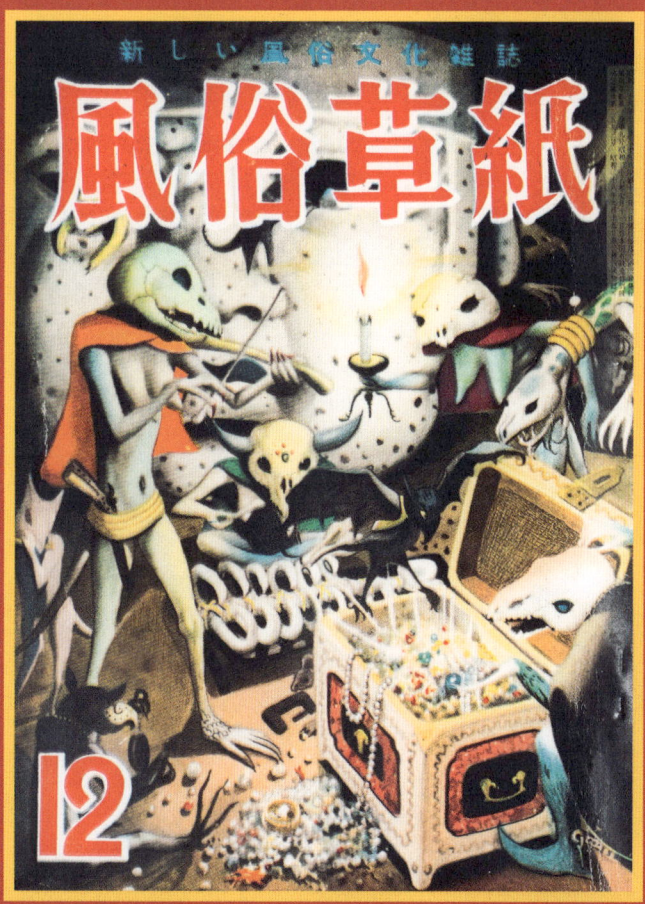
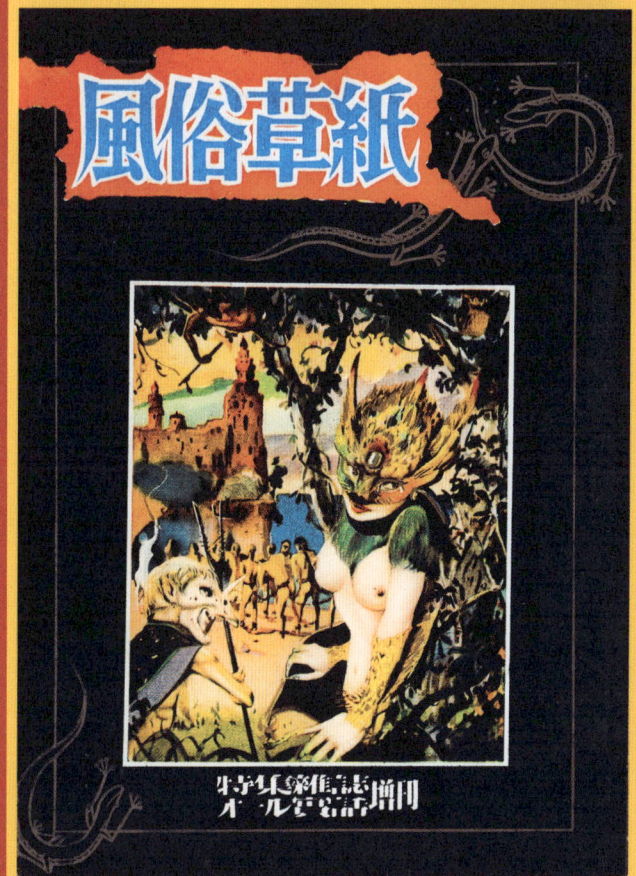

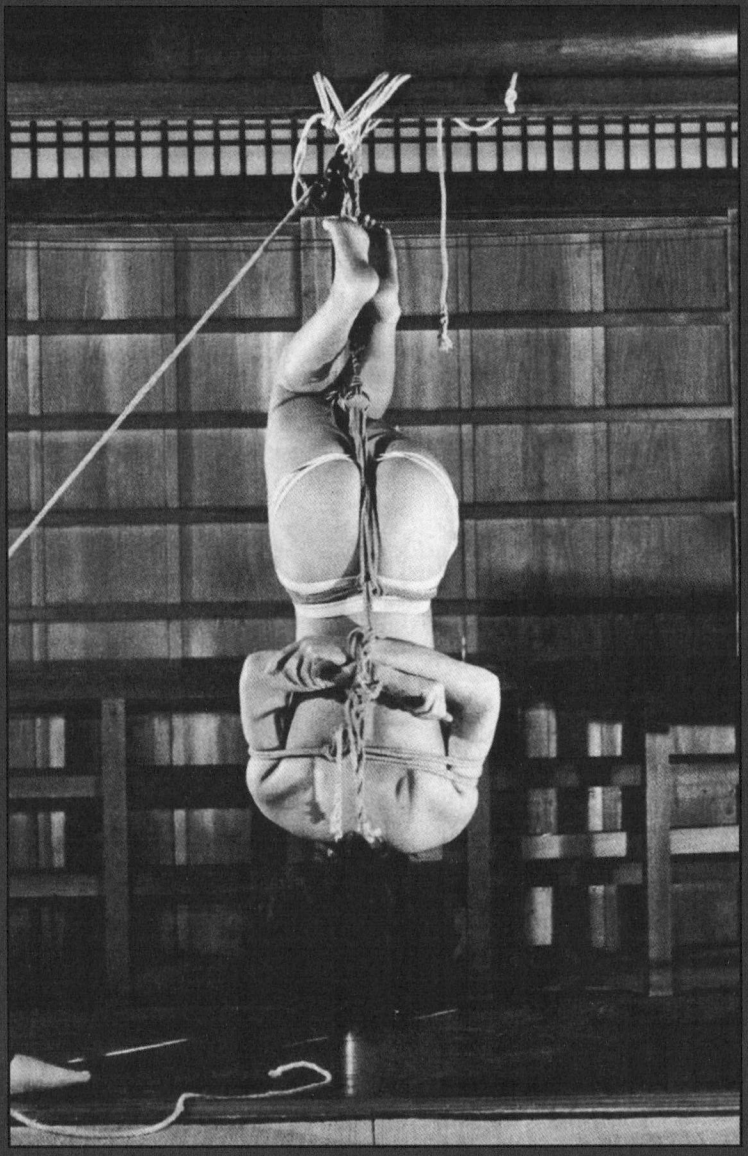

The word *kinbaku* is actually a modern word. It was coined in 1952 for the magazine *Kitan Club*, when they were looking for a specific term that defined Japanese-style erotic bondage.

There are three ways of thinking about *kinbaku*: there is the doing of it; there is the philosophical examination of Japan, and its sociology and history; and then there's the artistic side of it.

It includes such erudite and sophisticated themes as *wabi-sabi*, an artistic philosophy which talks about the impermanence and transient nature of things. One of the wonderful things about *kinbaku* is that it is completely ephemeral. Like the theatre, when the curtains come down, that session is over and it will never happen again.

The Japanese have a wonderful attitude in that, as long as you don't disturb the *wa*, the calm of society, you can do anything you like.

In Japan, there's a very famous expression, 'it's the protruding nail that gets the hammer'. It's when you are noticed, or when you are causing embarrassment to the collective, that there is a problem. Now of course, this does not include antisocial behaviour, violence or cruelty.

The Japanese also have a much more mature understanding of sex. Japan is the only industrialized power that does not have a Judeo-Christian background.

Their background is Buddhist and Shinto, for the most part, and neither of those religions demonize sexuality.

MASTER K

pp. 194–95: Covers from *Fusoku Soshi* (1953–54).

Photographs from *Kitan Club* (1961, above, and 1963, right).

Opposite (above left): Photograph from *Kitan Club* (1961).

Opposite (above right): Photograph from *Kitan Club* (1962).

Opposite (below): **Moriyama Daido**, *Mayfly*, 1972, photogravure.

Overleaf: Photographs from *Kitan Club* (1961–62).

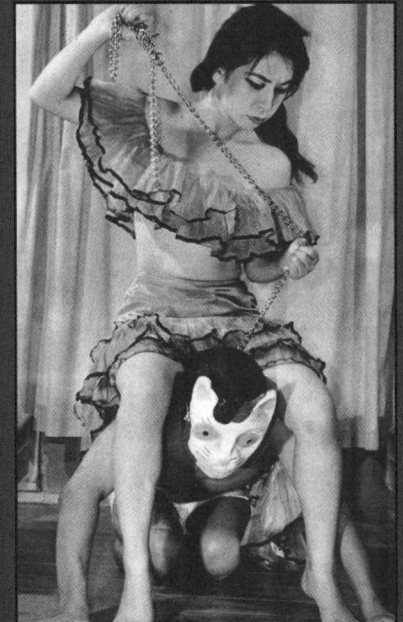

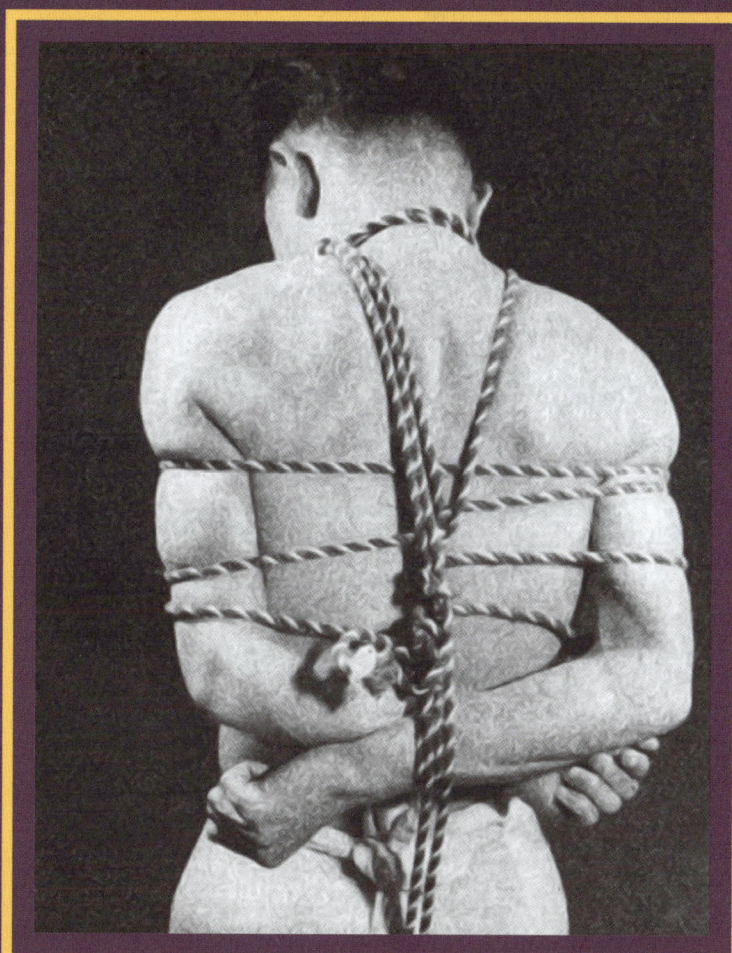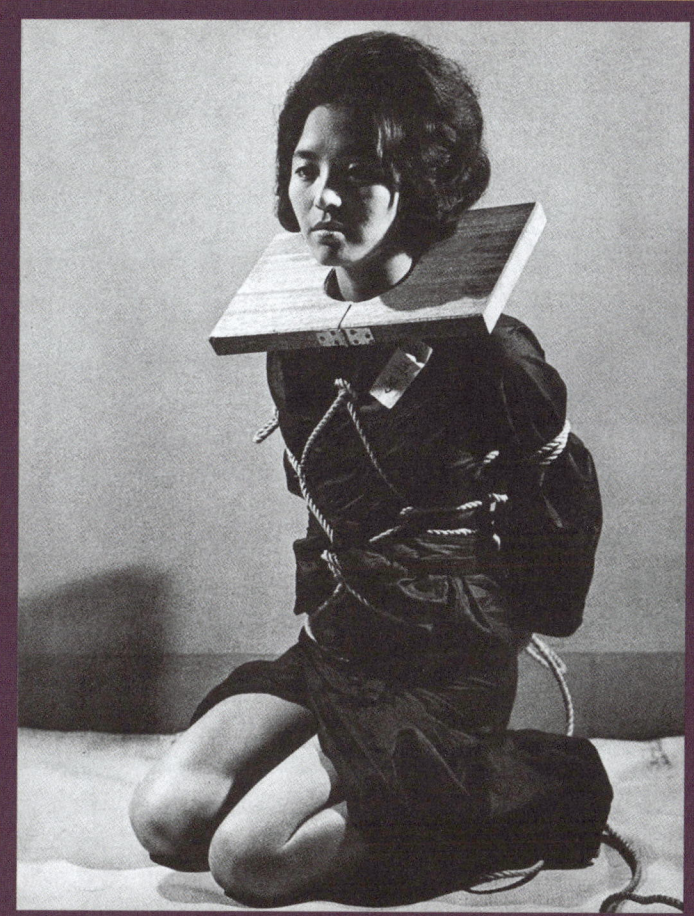

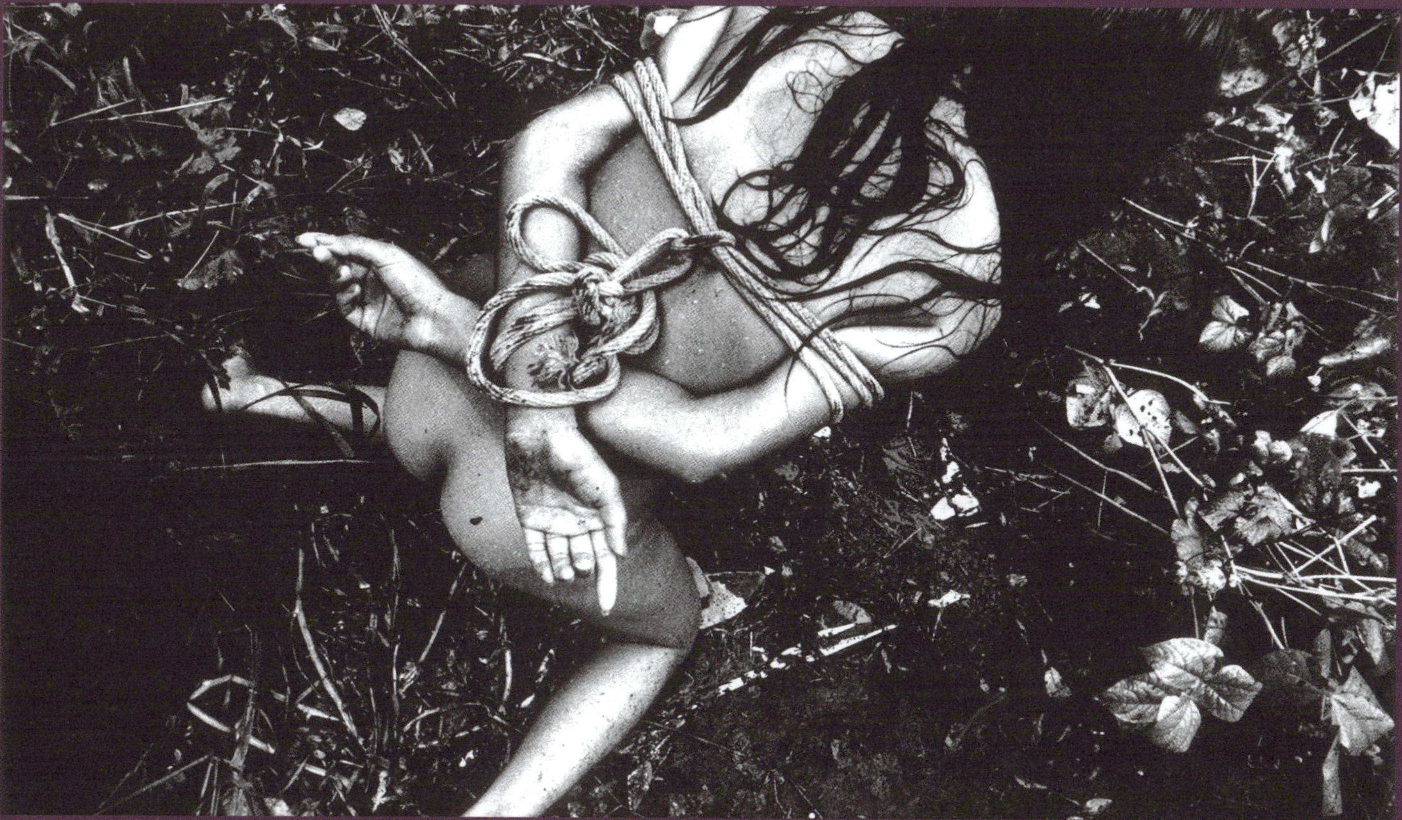

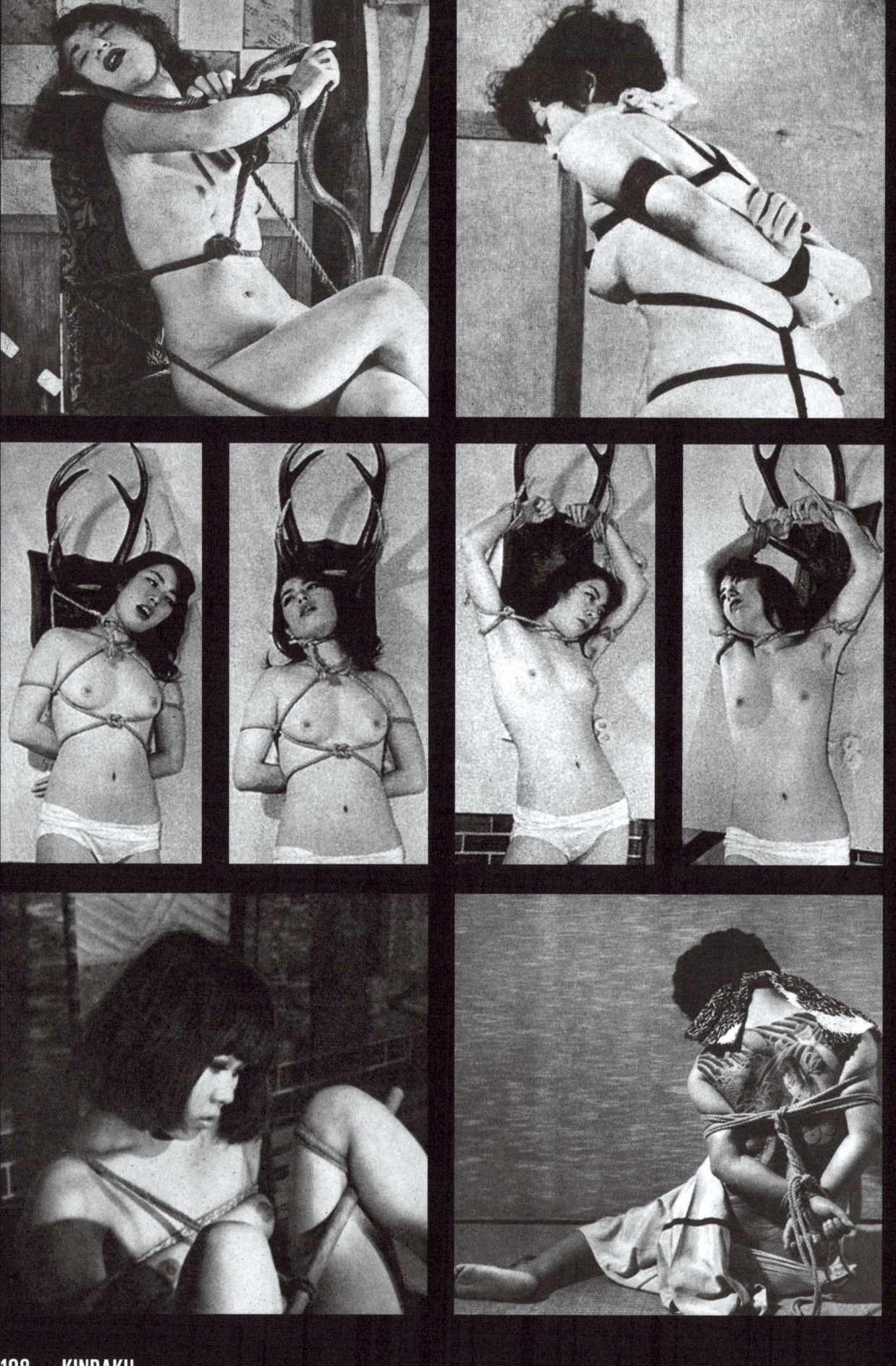

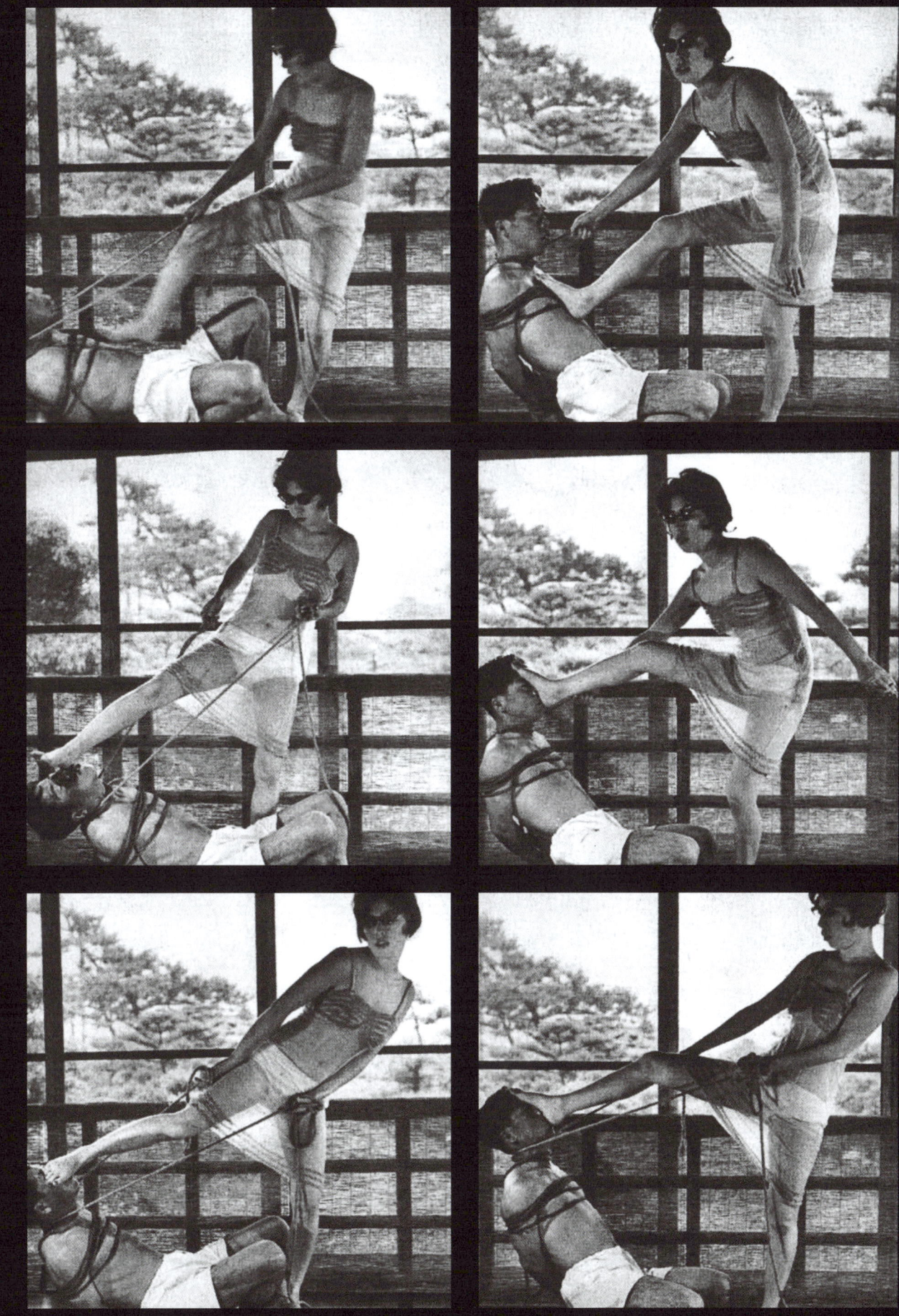

緊縛

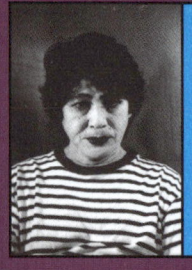

MORIYAMA DAIDO
1938–
森山大道

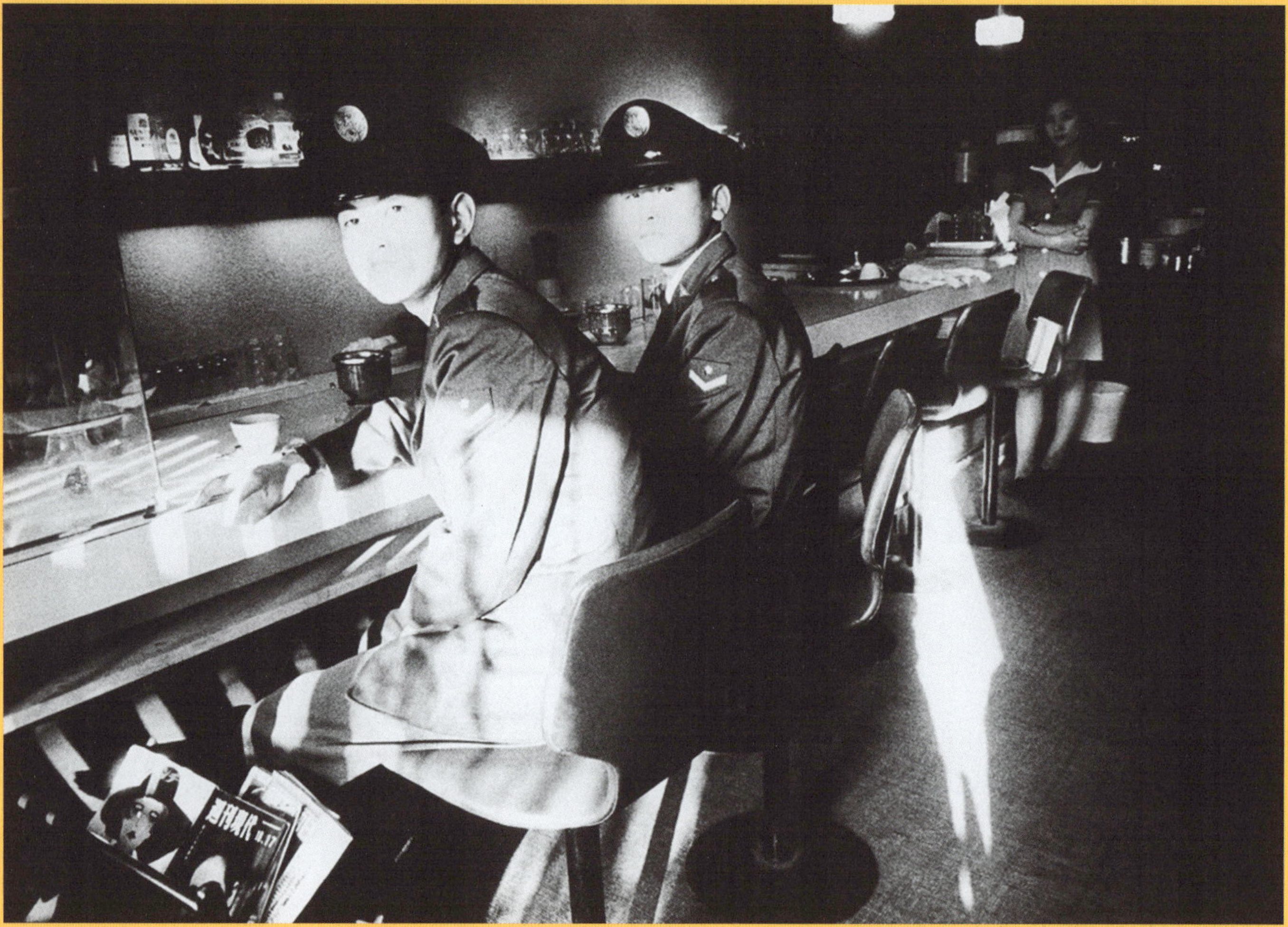

Moriyama Daido, *Soldiers, Hamamatsu*, 1968, gelatin silver print.

Opposite (left): **Moriyama Daido**, *Dog and Mesh Tights*, 2015, gelatin silver print.

Opposite (right): **Moriyama Daido**, *RECORD No.36*, 2017, gelatin silver print.

'The war ended when I was in first grade. Japan was under occupying army in the years that followed, and there were many Americans in our daily lives. During the Vietnam and Korean wars, there were so many US bases, and jet planes flew around all day. I felt that the USA was very much immersed in our daily lives.'

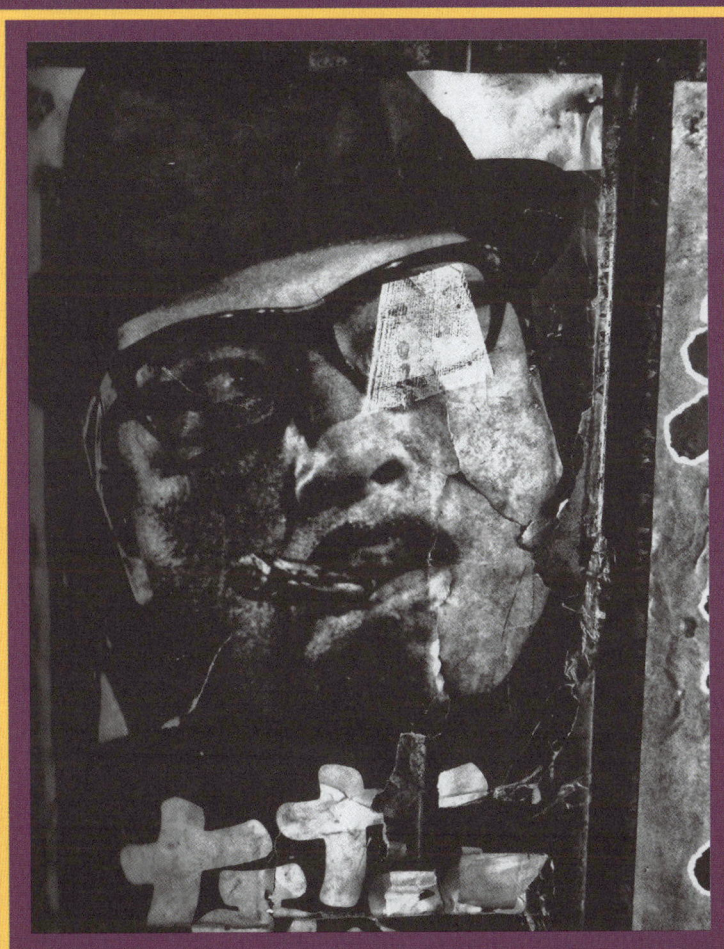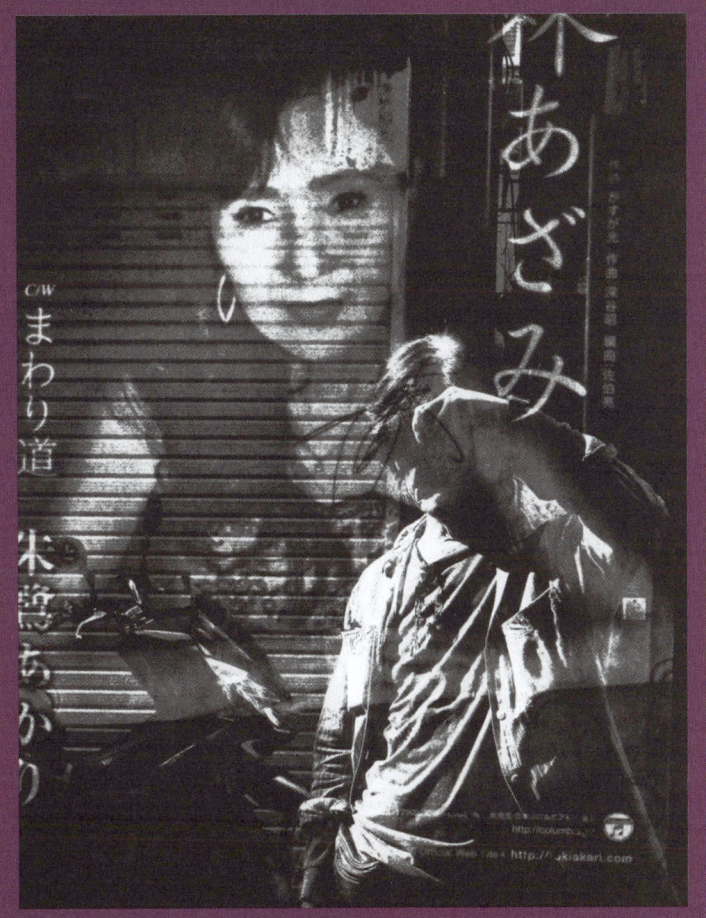

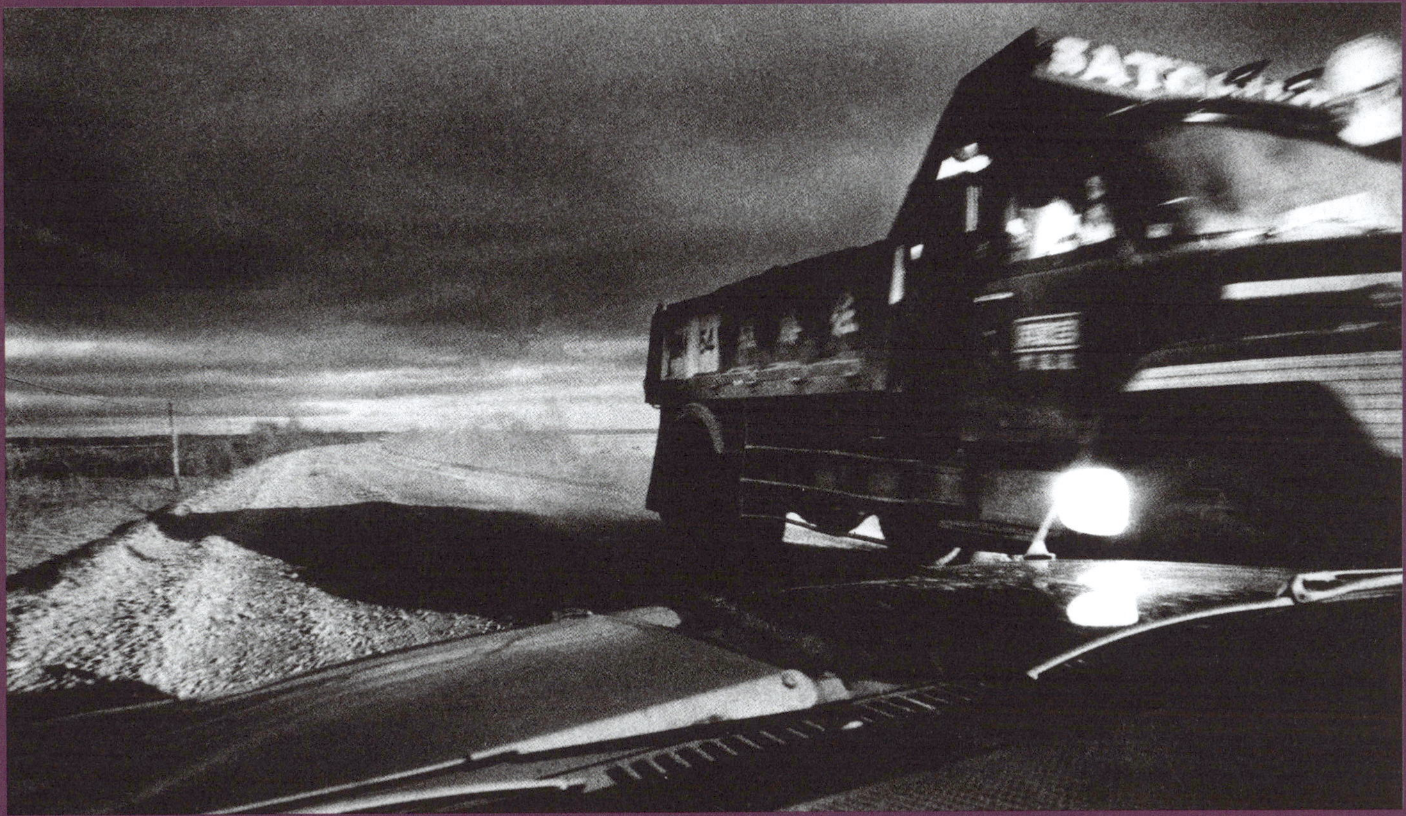

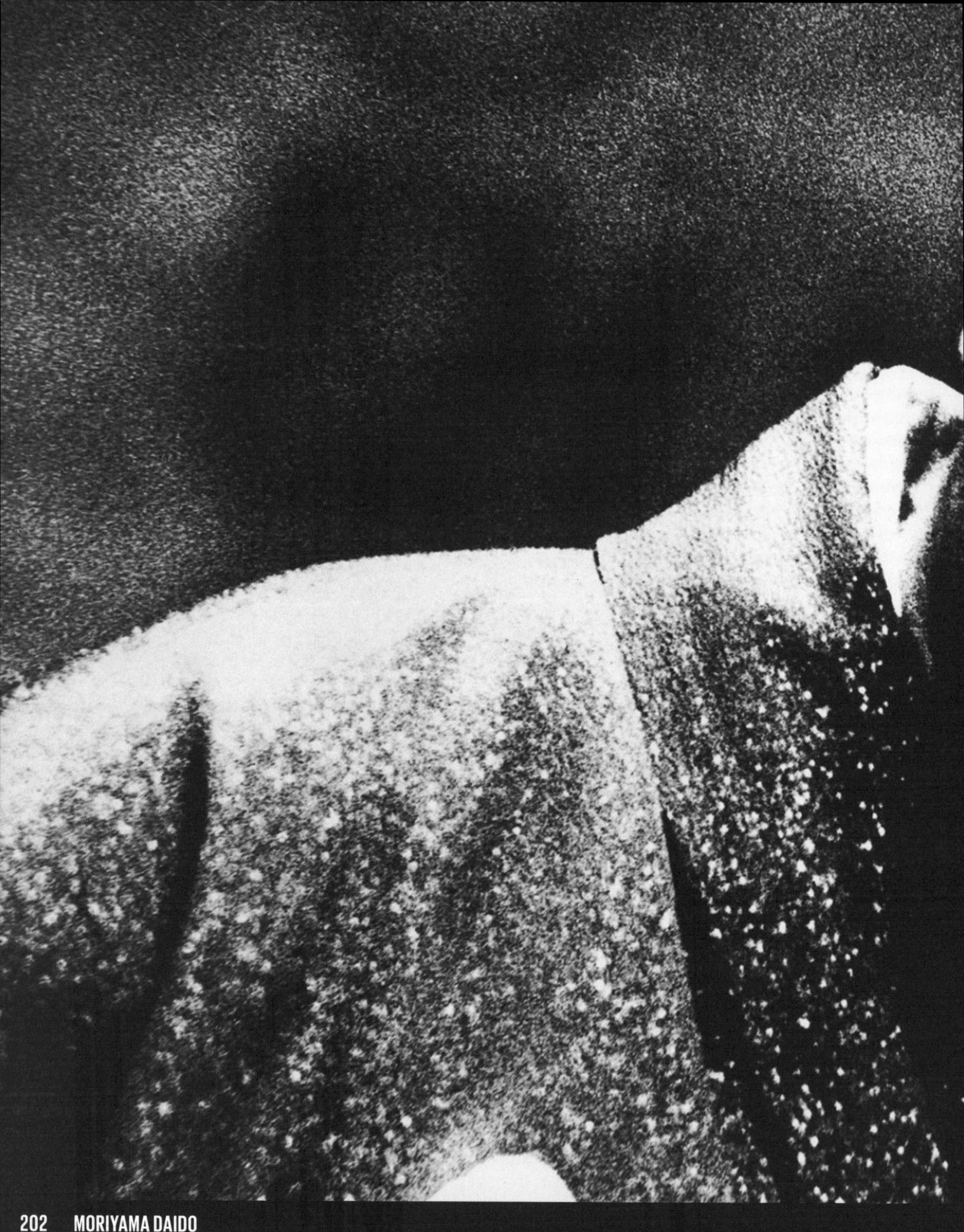

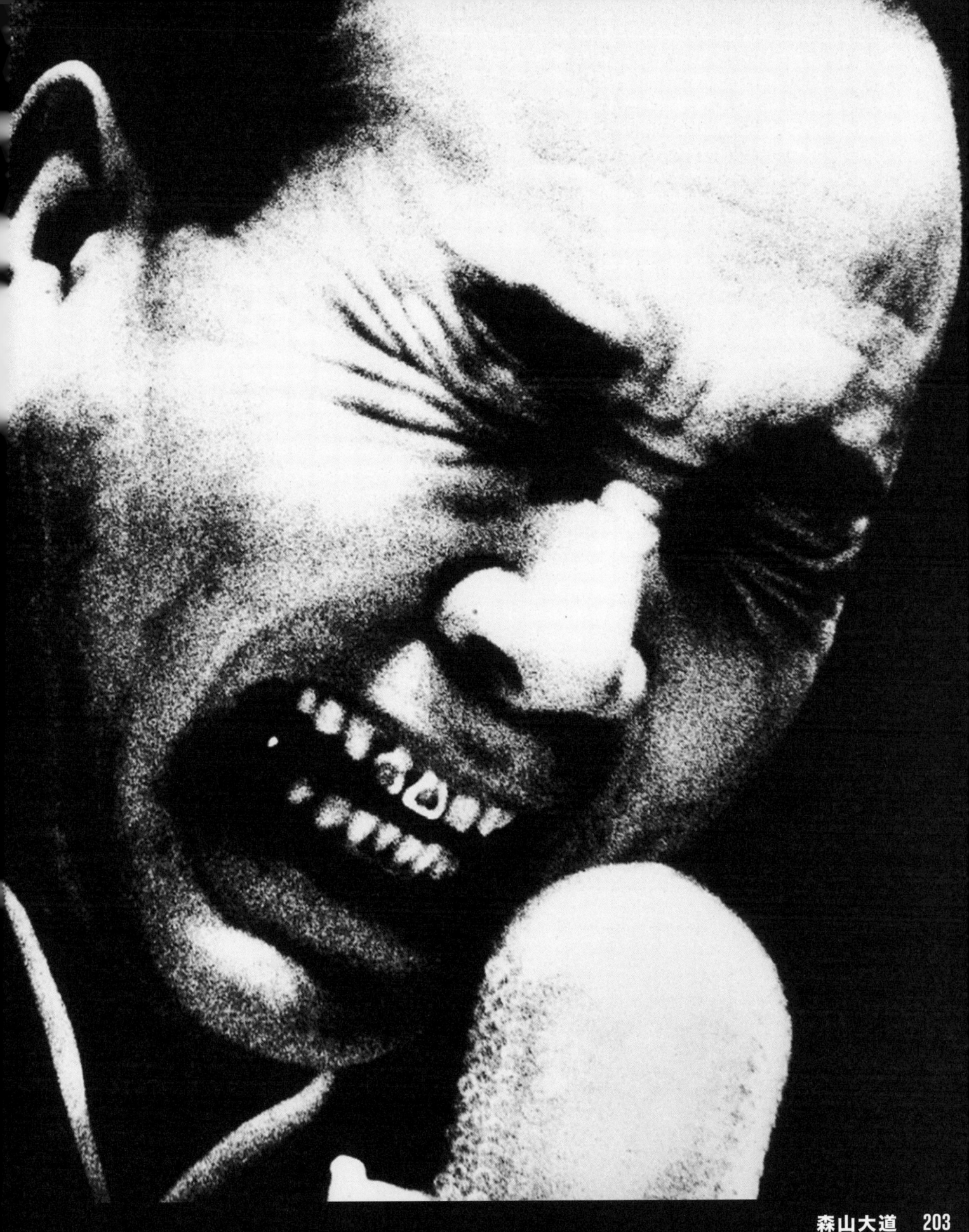

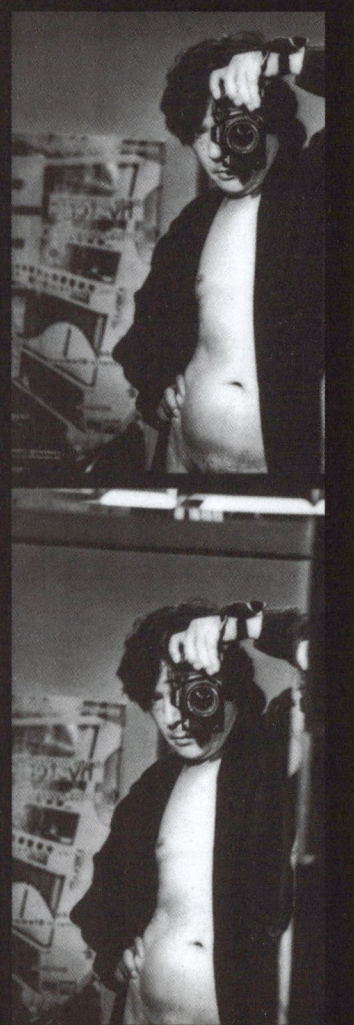

'I FIRST STARTED TAKING STREET SNAPSHOTS AT THE US NAVAL BASE IN YOKOSUKA. IT ALL STARTED THERE. I HAD ALWAYS BEEN INTERESTED IN THE US BASE. I WAS VERY IMMATURE BACK THEN, SO IT WAS A REALLY PURE FEELING OF ADORATION AND INTEREST. FROM THE TIME THAT I BEGAN TO SHOOT YOKOSUKA UP UNTIL 1970, ALL OF JAPAN BECAME VERY POLITICAL. THERE WERE MANY GENRES OF EXPRESSION, BUT EVERYONE SEEMED TO BE REBELLIOUS, FIGHTING AGAINST THEIR GENRE, THE WORLD, AND ANYTHING POLITICAL. YOUNG PEOPLE USED THAT FEELING AS MOTIVATION TO EXPRESS THEMSELVES.

WHEN I CAME TO TOKYO, I ENCOUNTERED AMERICAN LITERATURE AND ART, WHICH REALLY INTERESTED ME. WHEN I SAW ANDY WARHOL'S CATALOGUE FROM AN EXHIBIT HE PUT ON IN NORTHERN EUROPE, I WAS DEEPLY SHOCKED. I THINK THE ESSENCE OF PHOTOGRAPHY IS THE CONCEPT OF COPYING, OR DUPLICATION. WARHOL COPIES PHOTOGRAPHS OF VARIOUS SCENES AND PRODUCES HIS WORKS FROM THEM. AND THEN HE MAKES COPIES OF THOSE WORKS. THAT CONCEPT IS REALLY CLOSE TO WHAT I THINK THE ESSENCE OF PHOTOGRAPHY IS.'

p. 201 (below): **Moriyama Daido**, *Hokkaido, Japan, Northern Series*, 1978, gelatin silver print.

pp. 202–3: **Moriyama Daido**, *Entertainer on Stage, Shimizu*, 1967, gelatin silver print.

Above: **Moriyama Daido**, *Self-Portrait*, 1997, gelatin silver print.

Opposite (above): **Moriyama Daido**, *Farewell Photography*, 1972, gelatin silver print.

Opposite (below): **Moriyama Daido**, *Farewell Photography*, 1972, gelatin silver print.

Overleaf: **Moriyama Daido**, *Color*, 2012, gelatin silver print.

Moriyama Daido was interested in creative developments occurring outside Japan, and he was particularly drawn to America's counterculture. Jack Kerouac's era-defining Beat novel *On the Road* (1957) inspired Moriyama to set out on his own journey across Japan during the 1970s, capturing recently constructed national highways without any obvious endpoint in sight. When he visited New York with Yokoo Tadanori in 1971, Moriyama made a point of seeking out Andy Warhol and his circle.

Moriyama's attitude went beyond the more overtly critical stance of artists like Tōmatsu Shōmei and Kawada Kikuji, who had begun creating photobooks more than a decade earlier. For these photographers, the influx of American consumer culture during the Occupation period (1945–52) was charged with the burden of post-war hardship, represented in influential bodies of work including Tōmatsu's *Chewing Gum and Chocolate* (originally *Occupation*, 1960) and *The Map* (1965) by Kawada.

LUCY FLEMING-BROWN

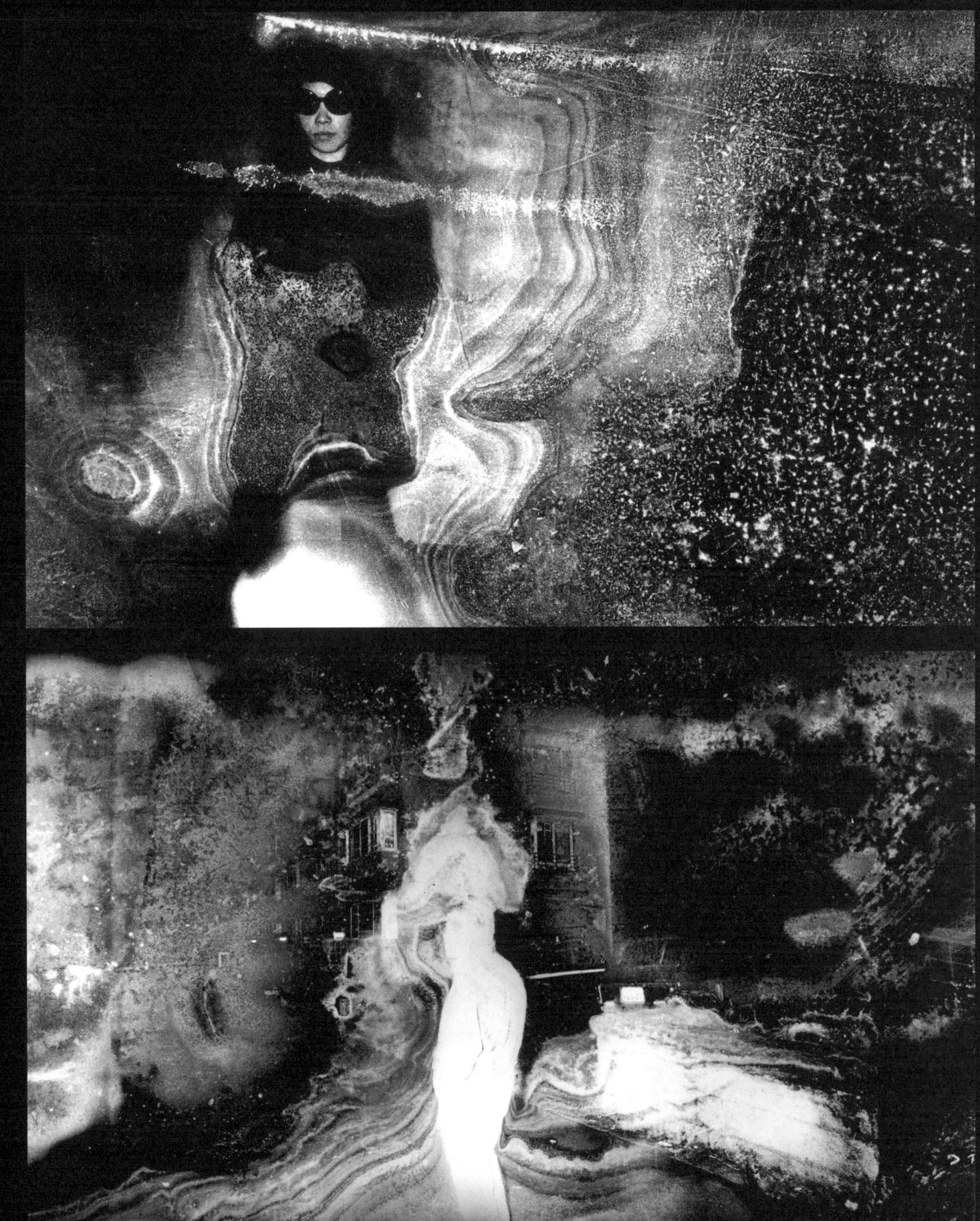

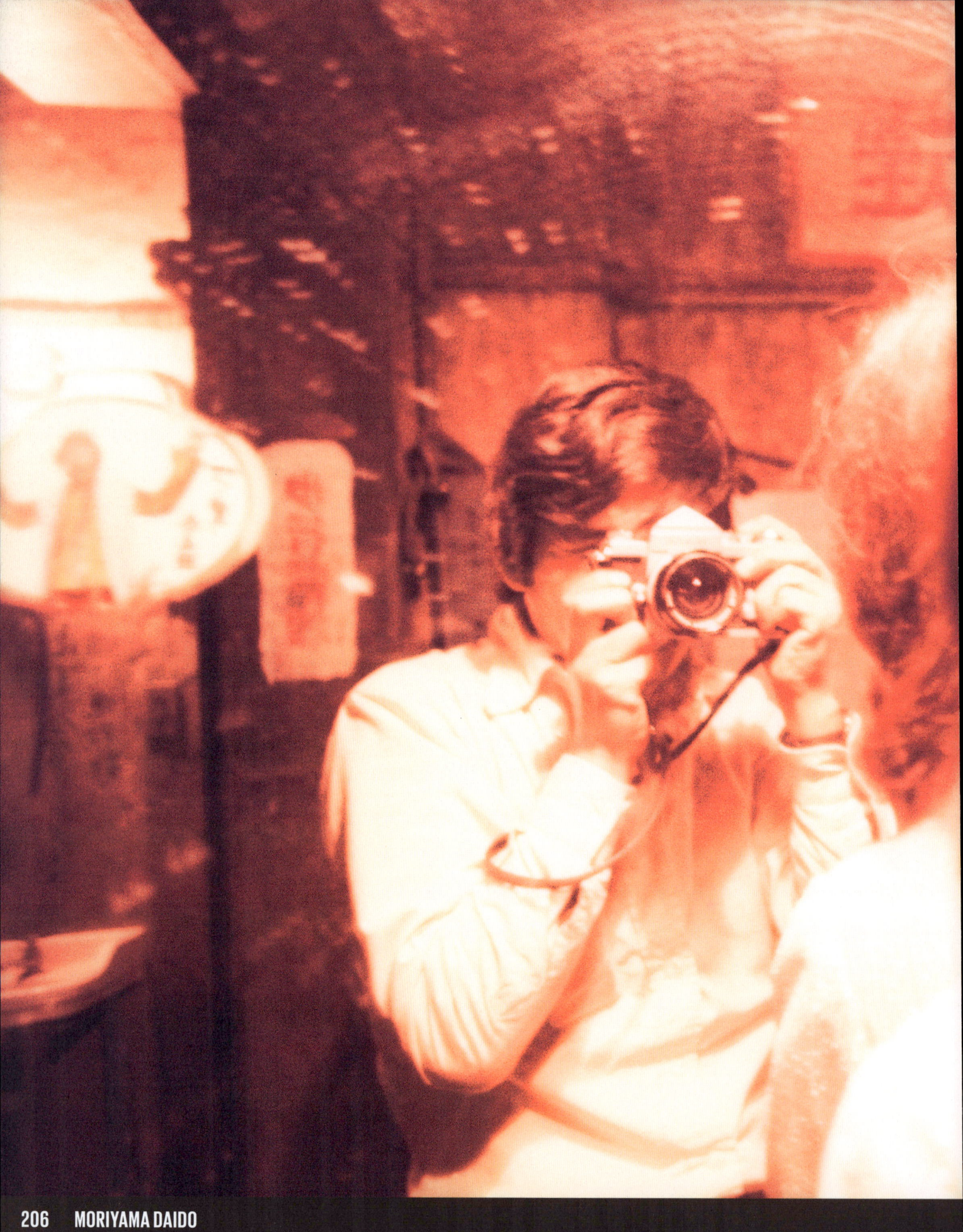

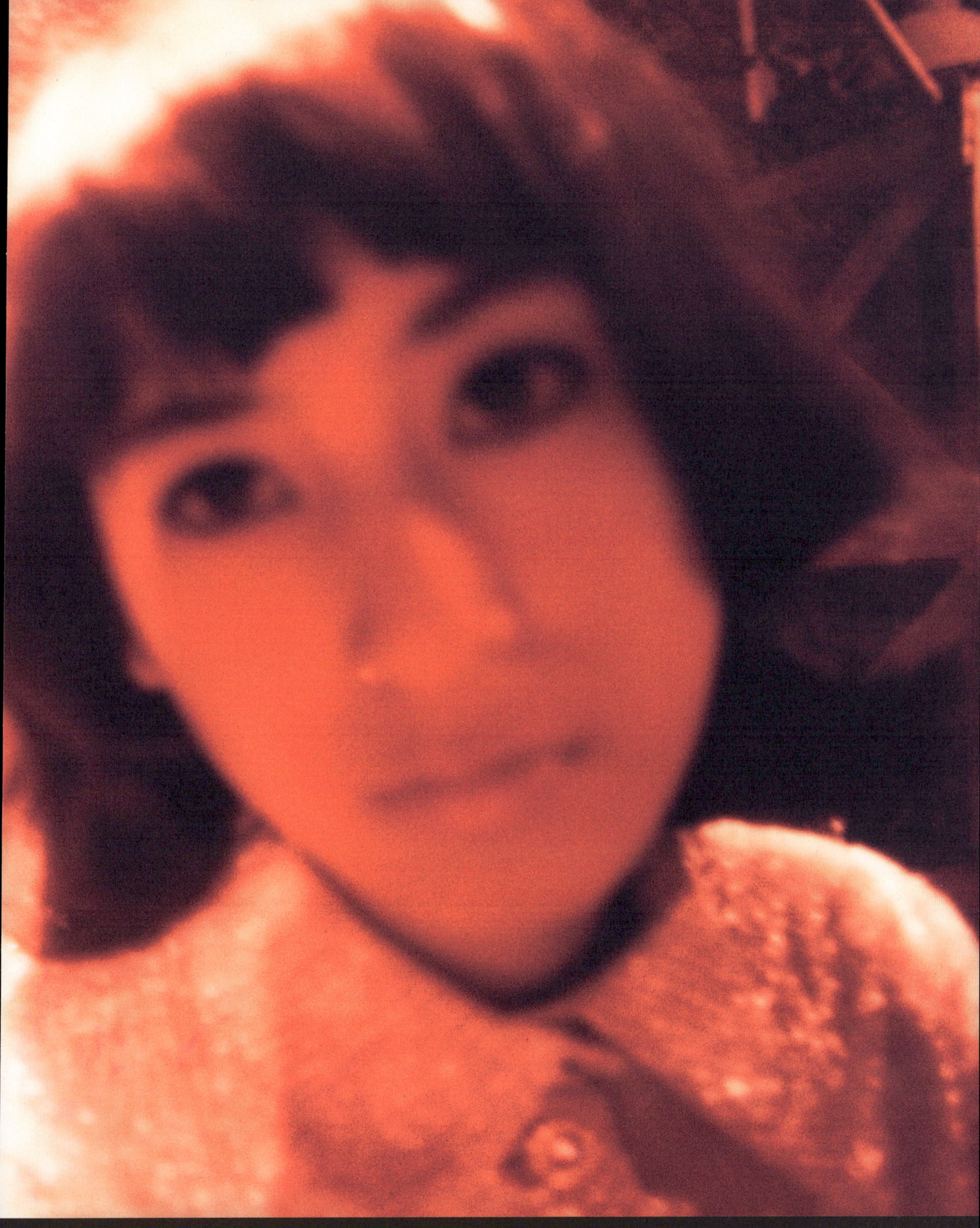

At the invitation of Terayama, Moriyama began taking photographs of Tokyo that captured the diverse intensity of this period of post-war transformation. These photographs developed into Moriyama's first photobook, *Japan: A Photo Theater* (1968), in which scenes from traditional performing arts and underground theatre were juxtaposed against the drama playing out on the streets of the city.

LUCY FLEMING-BROWN

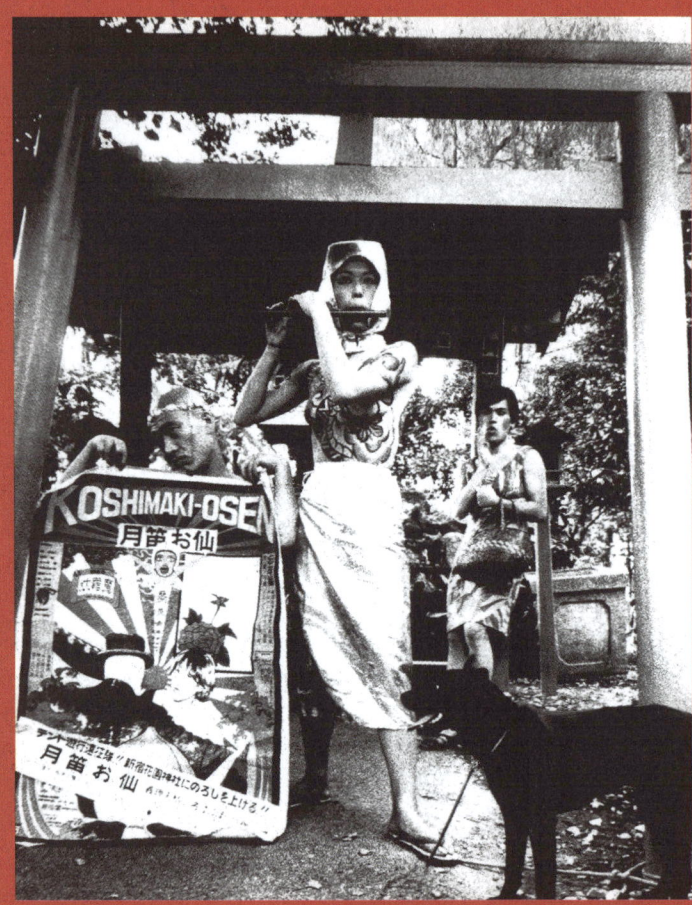 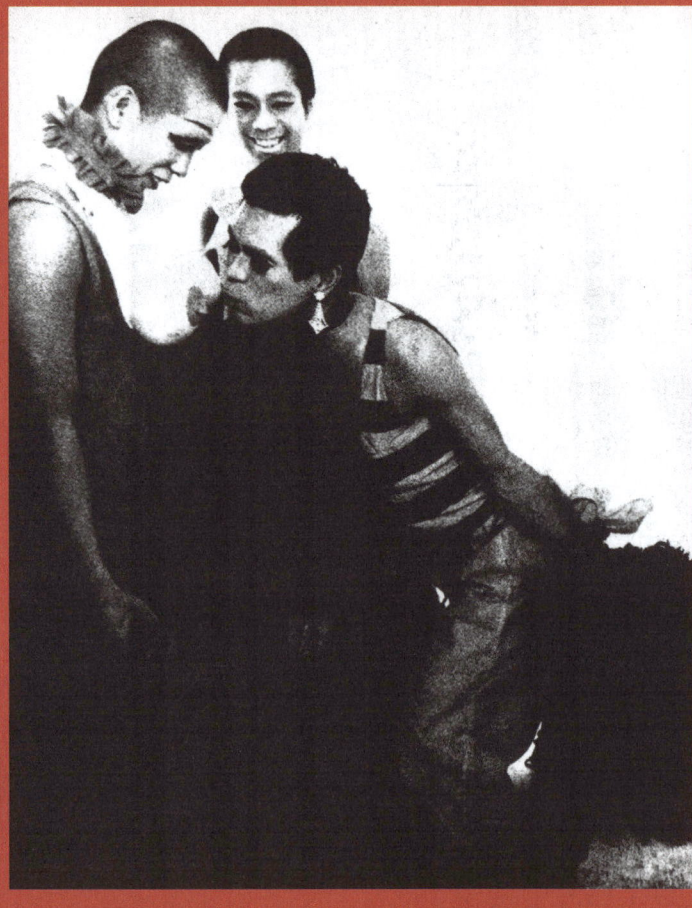

Above (left): **Moriyama Daido**, *Japan: A Photo Theater*, 1968, gelatin silver print.

Above (right): **Moriyama Daido**, *Japan: A Photo Theater*, 1968, gelatin silver print.

Opposite: **Moriyama Daido**, *Kariudo (Hunter)*, 1970, gelatin silver print.

This world of local folks, such as popular theatre, was only a part of the photobook. Much more significant were the many photos of the streets, so-called street snapshots. So what was it he was trying to capture? Because these were mundane and everyday scenes which have no value in themselves to shoot.

This work was precisely questioning what photography is. Moriyama Daido would say that this is the new significance of photography, to take objects that in themselves have no value.

KANEKO RYŪICHI

'I JUST WALK AROUND THE CITY EVERYDAY AND SHOOT WHATEVER I SEE. AND THEN I WORK WITH WHAT I'VE CAPTURED TO MAKE A BOOK. WITH PHOTOGRAPHY BOOKS, I CONSIDER IT TO BE MY PLACE, OR TIME, OR SPACE, WHERE I CAN THINK ABOUT PHOTOGRAPHY IN THE MOST INTENSE WAY. ON THE OTHER HAND, I THINK OF EXHIBITS AS A SHOW, ON HOW MUCH IMPACT YOU CAN HAVE ON THE AUDIENCE THROUGH DRAMATIC DISPLAY.'

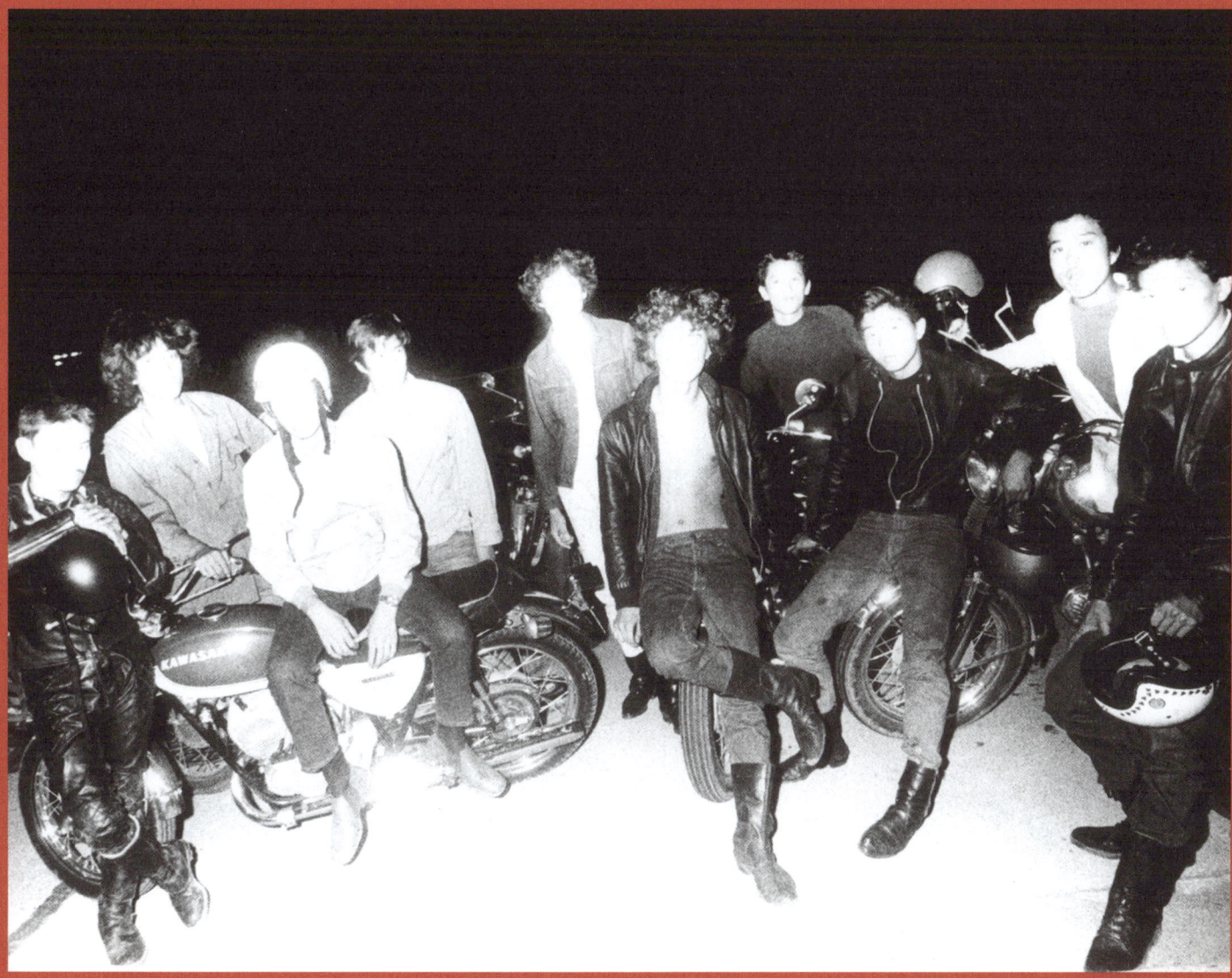

にっぽん劇場写真帖

JAPAN: A PHOTO THEATER

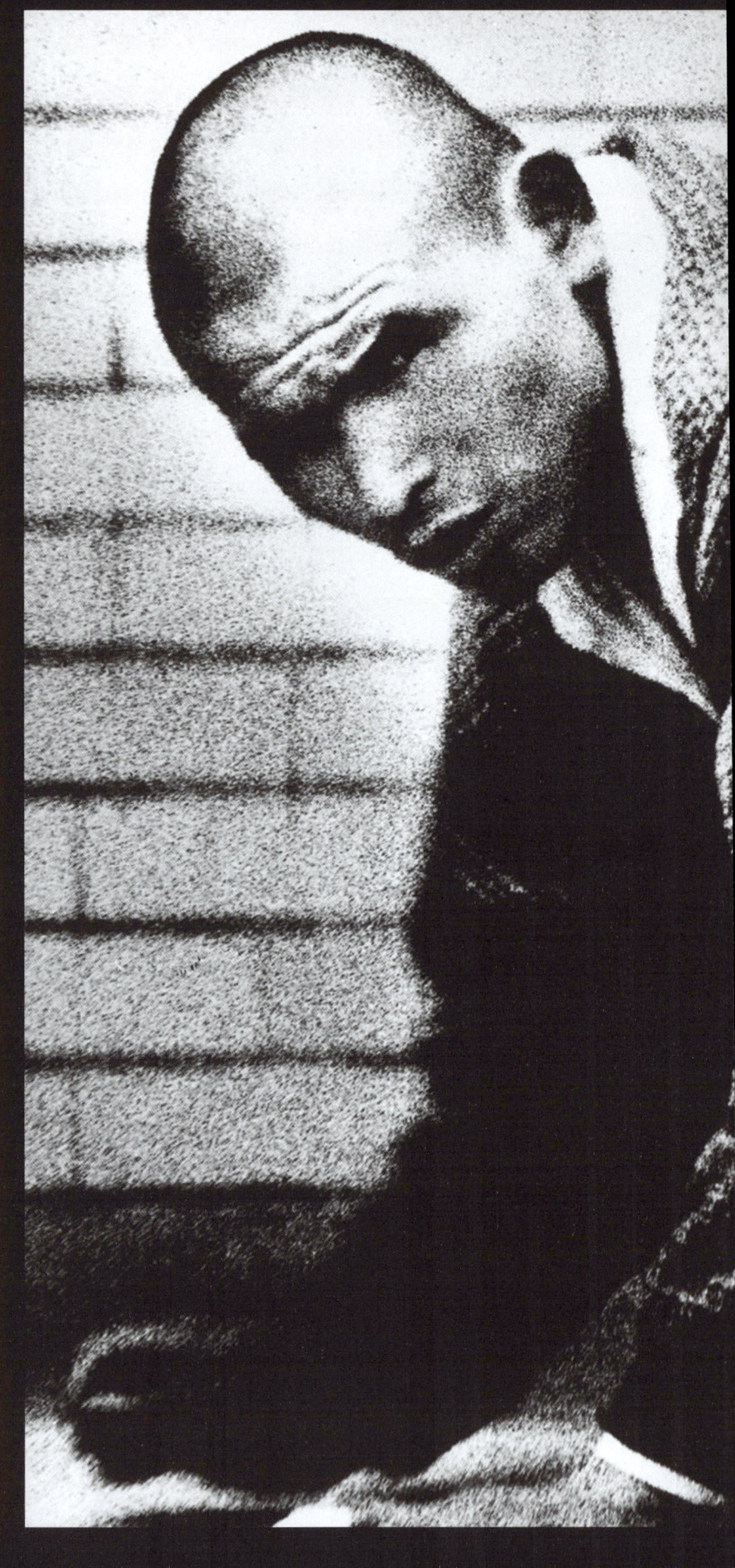

What's really interesting about his work is the concept of equivalence.

He would say, it doesn't really matter what you photograph, you just photograph everything.

It's about recording his own time. He would try to overcome the border between himself as a photographer and photography – the photograph itself.

LENA FRITSCH

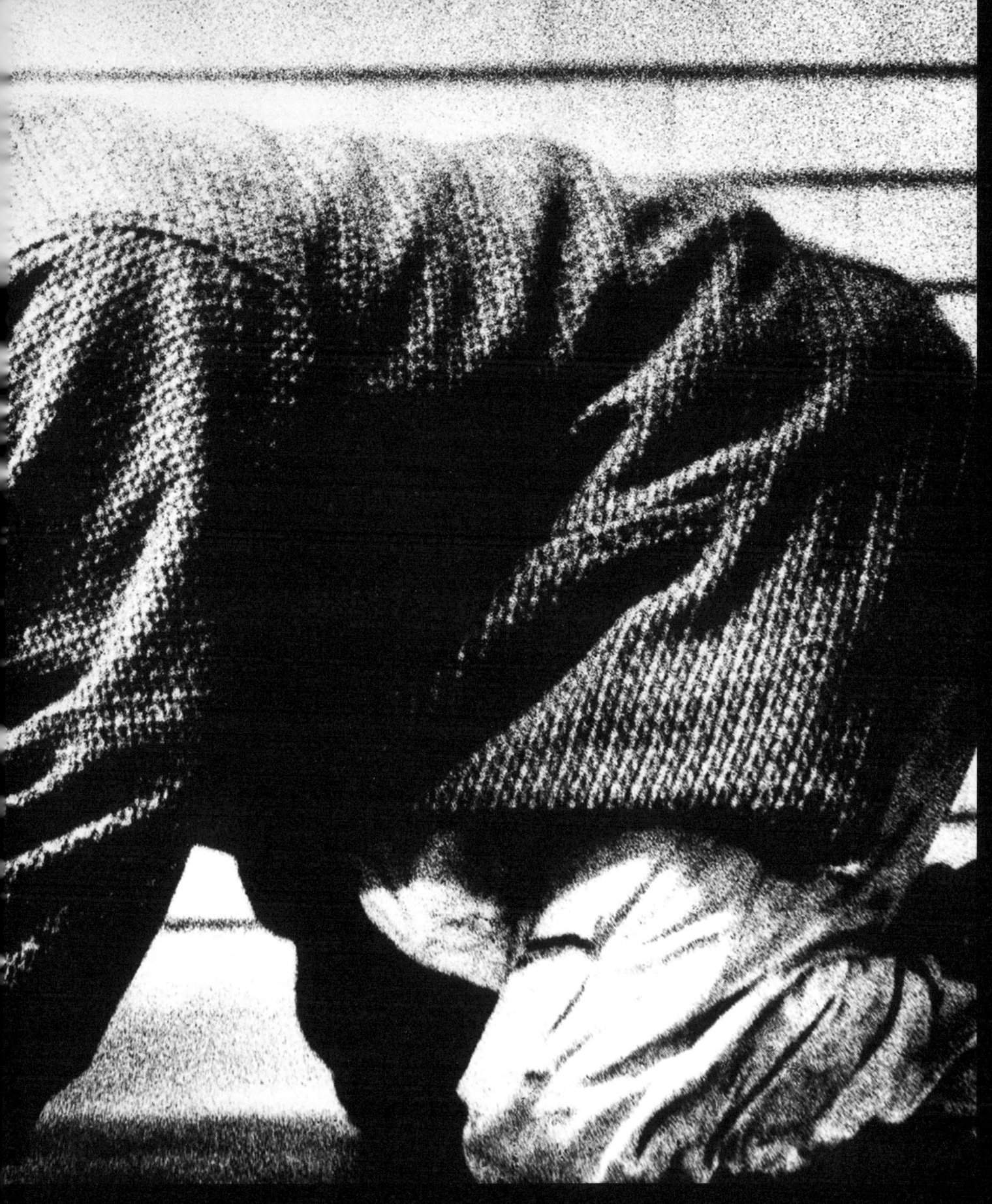

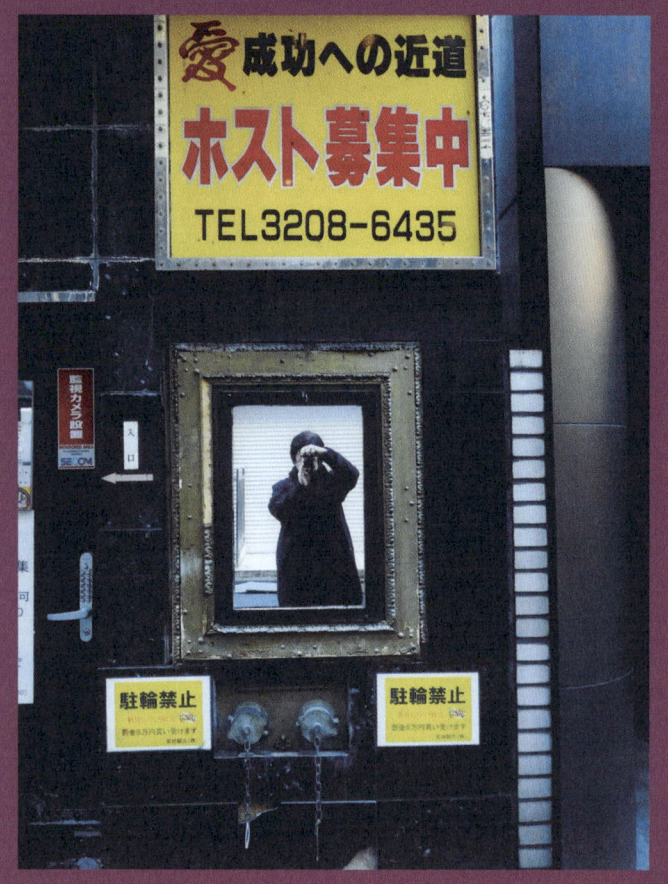

'THE CHAIN OF EXTRAORDINARY IS CALLED EVERYDAY LIFE.'

pp. 210–11: **Moriyama Daido**, *Crippled Beggar, Tokyo*, 1965, gelatin silver print.

Above: **Moriyama Daido**, *Boku*, 2019, gelatin silver print.

Right: **Moriyama Daido**, *Whore, Yokosuka*, 1970, gelatin silver print.

Opposite (above left): **Moriyama Daido**, *Dog and Mesh Tights*, 2015, gelatin silver print.

Opposite (above right): **Moriyama Daido**, *Dog and Mesh Tights*, 2015, gelatin silver print.

Opposite (below): **Moriyama Daido**, *Lips*, 2018, gelatin silver print.

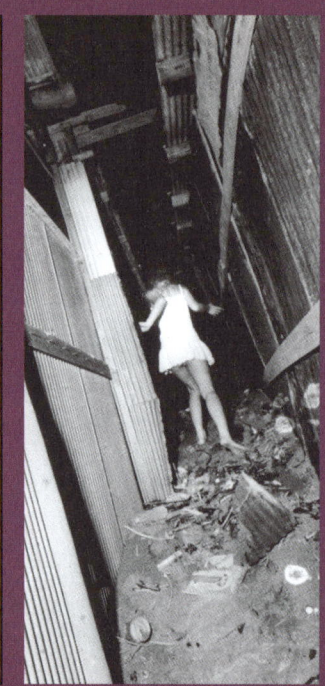

'When you're working on a new photography book, several things race through your mind. What do I want to do with photography? What is photography? How do I see the outside world? So I begin to have a better understanding of my current state of mind. I was convinced that what was beautifully shot was not true photography. So that's why I captured shots that deviated from that idea. I wanted to deconstruct photography. But in the end, I was the one who was deconstructed.

Whether TV screens or posters in the city, everything is the same to me. Shooting the TV picture tube is just another subject in my point of view, that also includes the city, cars, people, posters, film screens…

When I shoot, I'm driven by my interests, my physical reactions, memories and all kinds of other elements. Every day is extraordinary. The chain of extraordinary is called everyday life. In everyday life, there are slits, and beyond that, you can always see a different world. That's how I feel when I take pictures.

Every day is different, but basically, I want to shoot every day, and I actually do, all the time.'

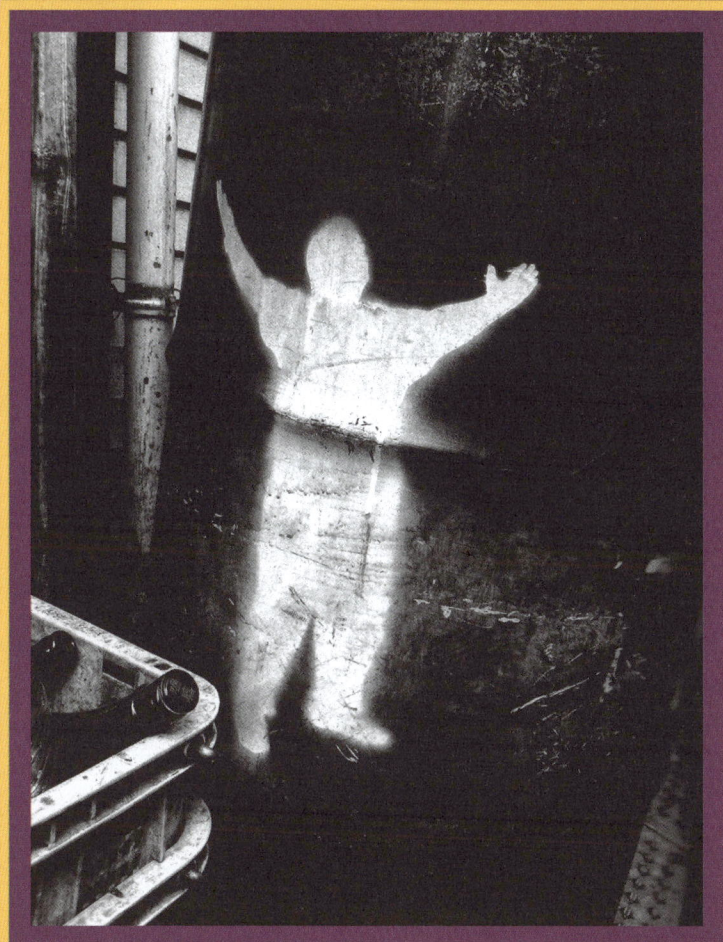
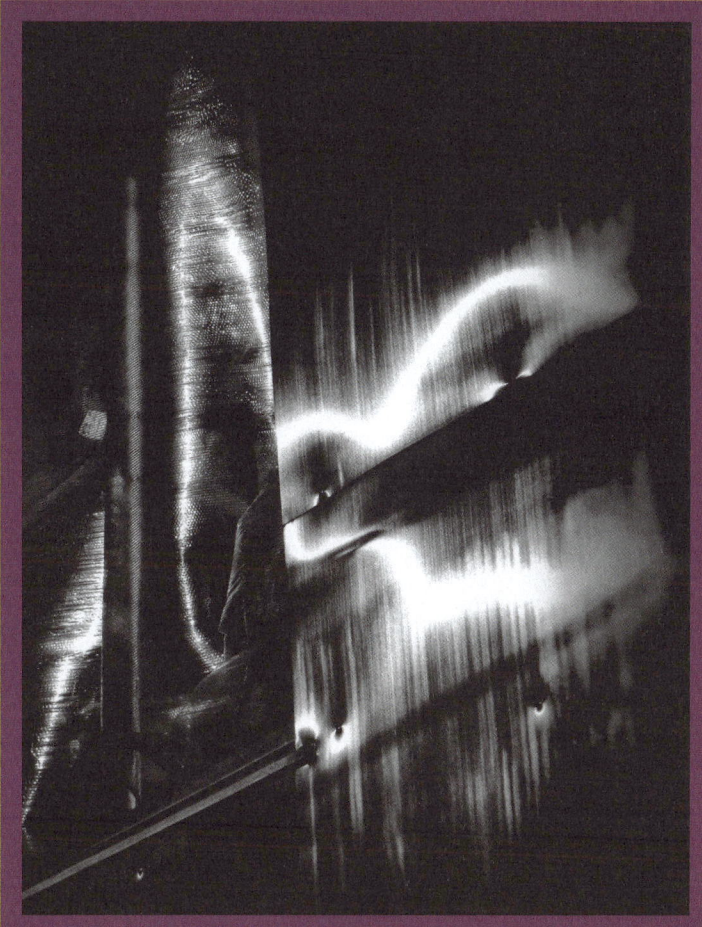

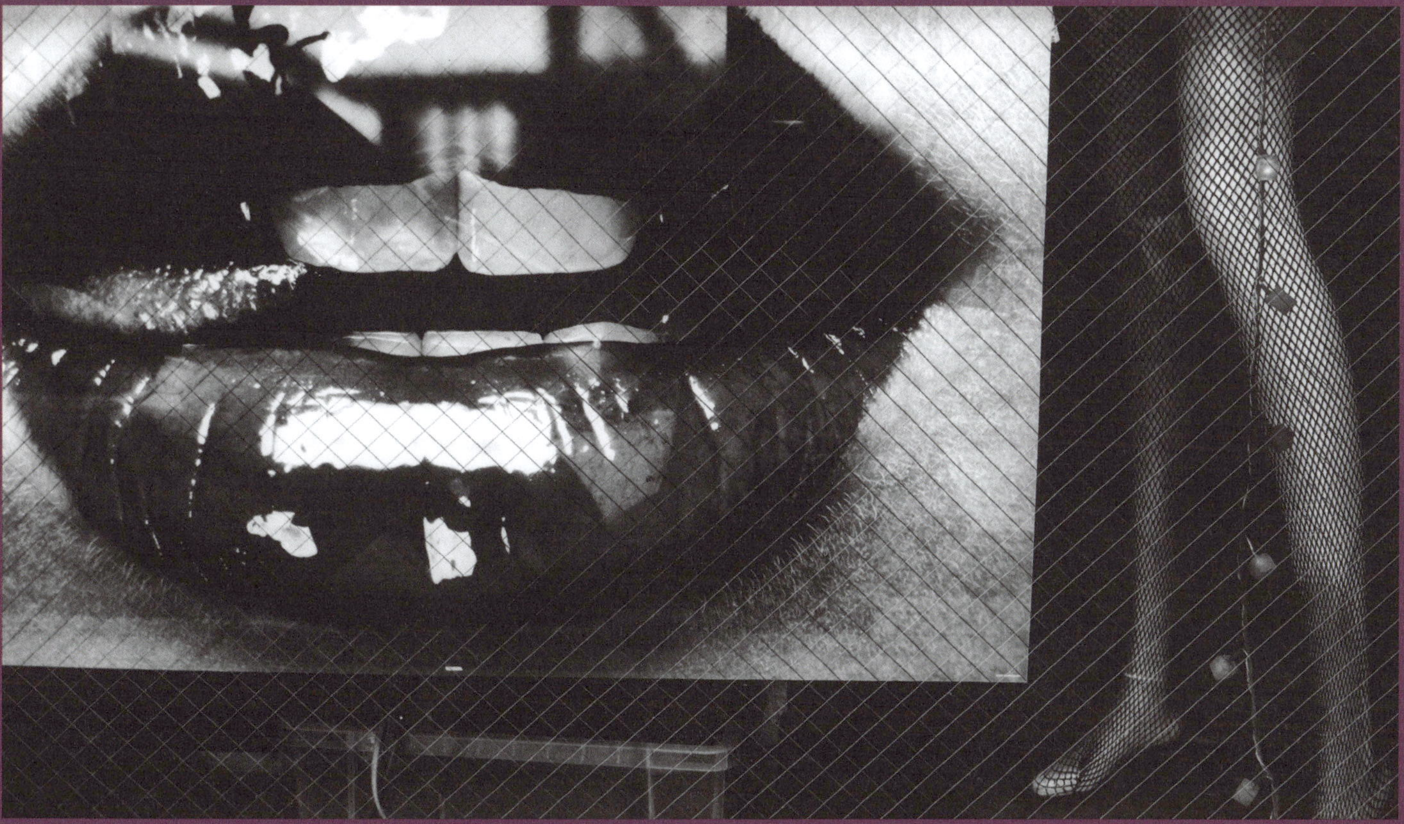

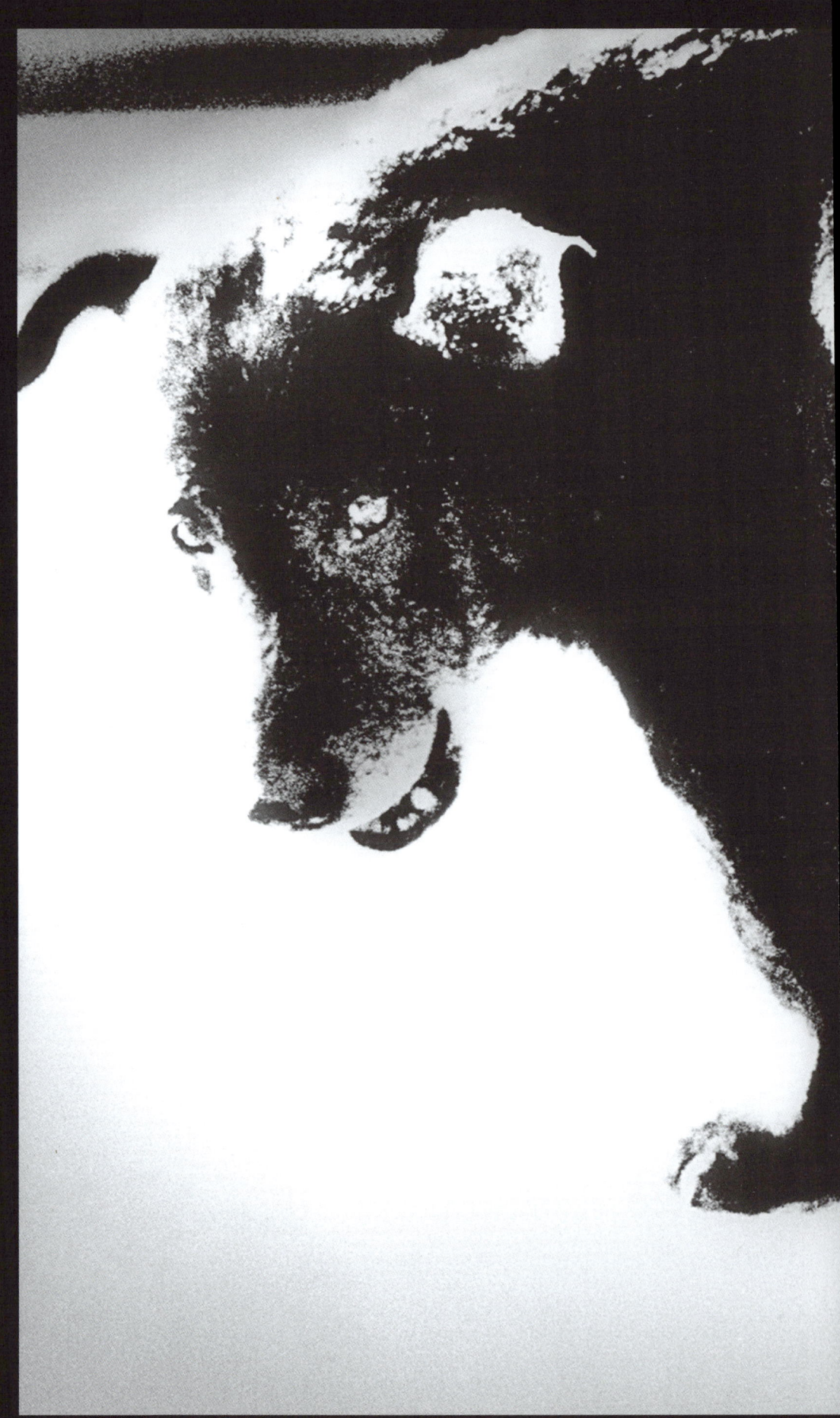

Moriyama takes photographs instinctively and compulsively, sometimes without using the viewfinder.

This approach is reflected in the response he wishes his photography to provoke in his audience.

LUCY FLEMING-BROWN

'GOING HAND-IN-HAND WITH THE CAMERA, THAT'S MY LIFE.

AS LONG AS I'M ALIVE, I WANT TO SHOOT AND CAPTURE AS MANY MOMENTS AS I CAN.'

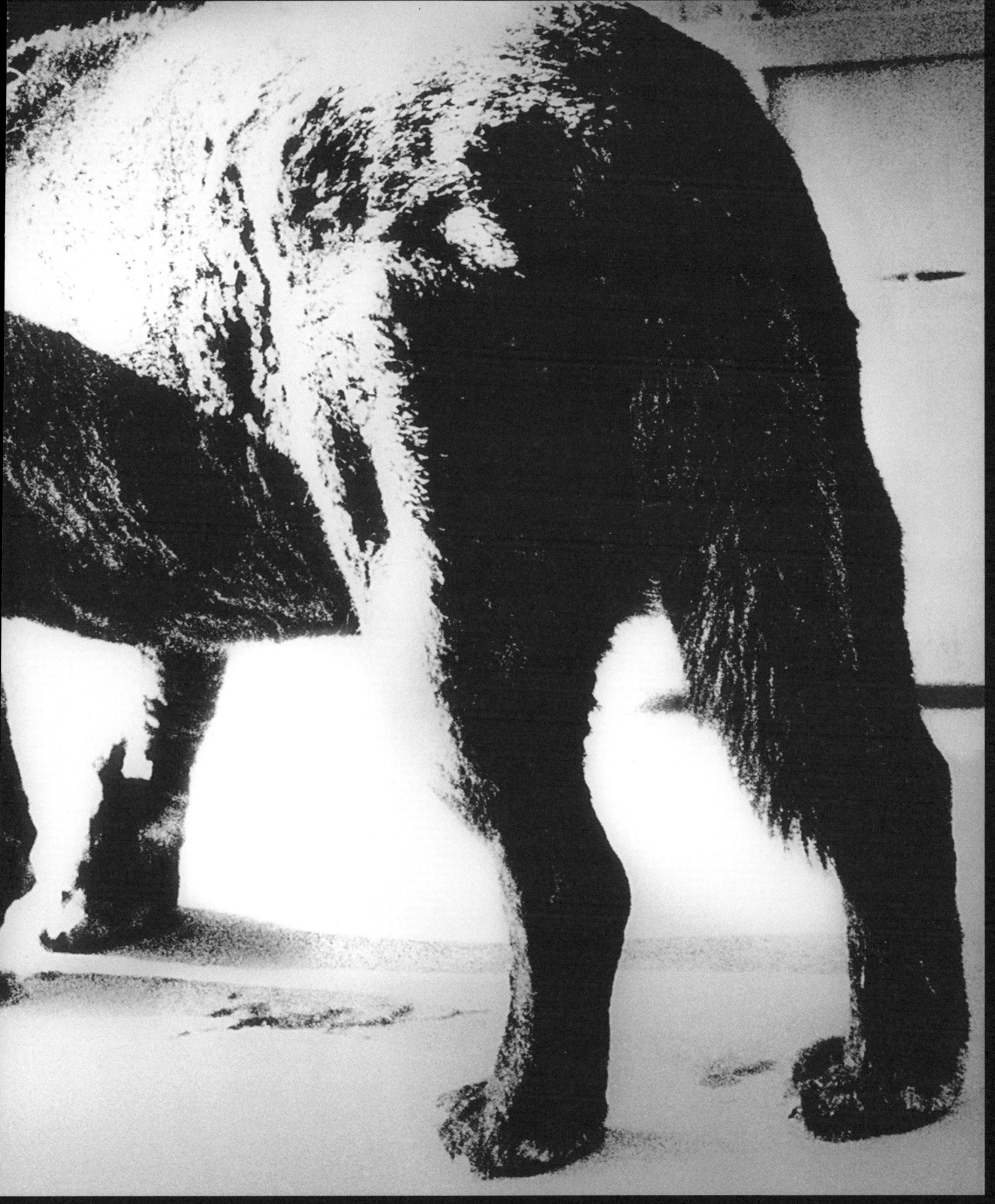

ACCIDENT

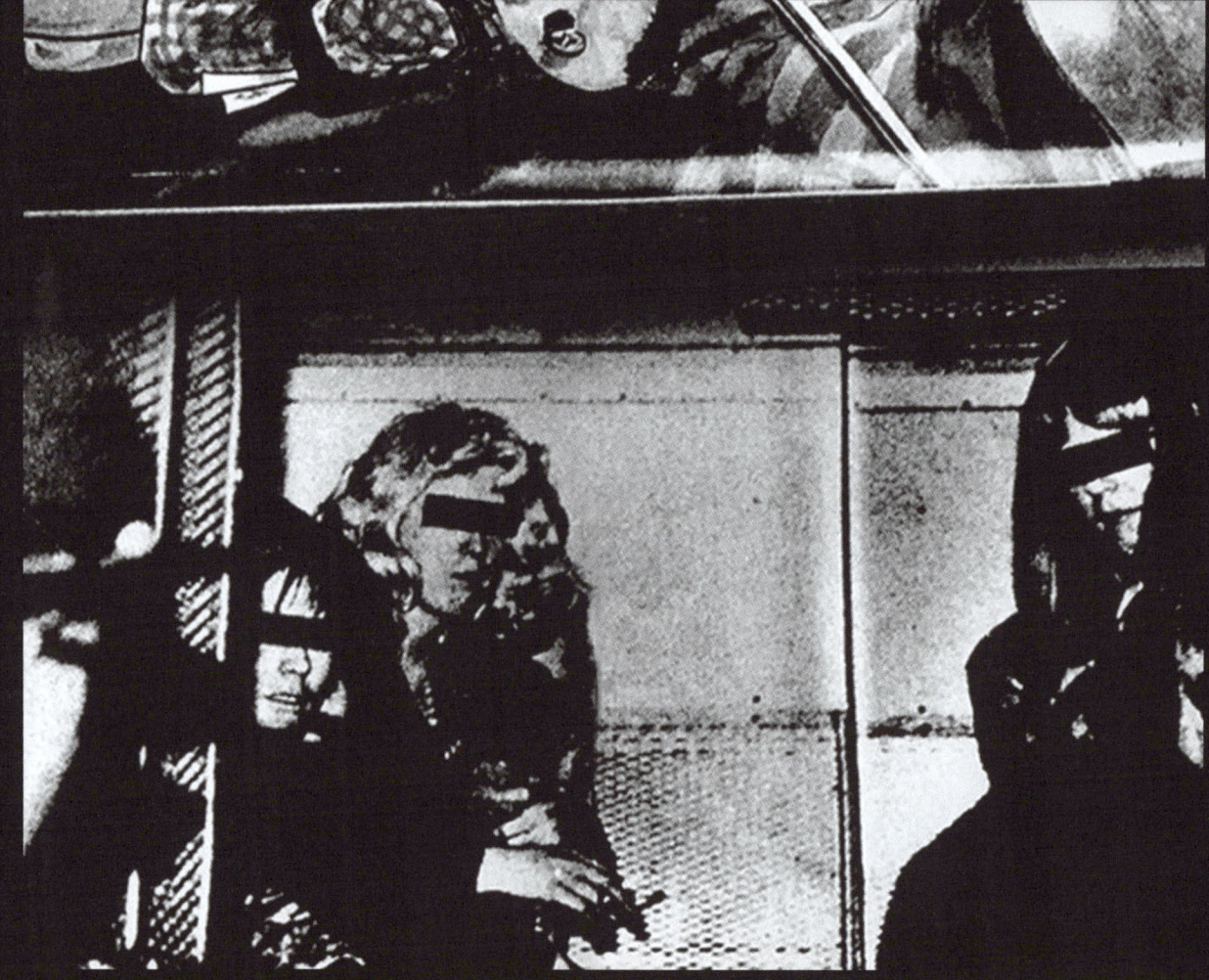

Moriyama Daido is a conceptual artist disguised as a street photographer. His obsessions and fetishes led him to walk thousands of kilometres across cities to find the perfect photographic expression of the combination of anguish and enthusiasm that dominated post-war Japan, when traditional values were consumed by the fire of capitalist freedom. Through his extraordinary photographs, Moriyama also presented us with a sombre and tilted world, from which we heard a long, tormented howl. The series *Accident, Premeditated or Not*, published in 1969 in the magazine *Asahi Camera*, is a profound conceptual investigation into photography.

ACCIDENT

pp. 214–15: **Moriyama Daido**, *Misawa*, 1971, gelatin silver print.

Above and opposite: **Moriyama Daido**, *Accident*, 1969, gelatin silver print.

Overleaf: **Moriyama Daido**, *Midnight Accident, Tokyo*, 1969, gelatin silver print.

Over the course of a year, in monthly chapters, Moriyama infiltrated a mass media outlet to ask questions about the role of photography within the press: the distance between facts and news, the use of sensationalism and other people's suffering to enrich media companies, the different perceptions of time and the relationship between the advancement of optical technologies and a surveilled society.

The courage to keep asking these fundamental questions led him to the masterpiece *Farewell Photography* (1972), in which he exposed all his scepticism towards photography's pretension to change the world, until he faced his own existential void. Moriyama obscured our vision so that we could look inside ourselves.

By superimposing the scenes in front of him with images he found in the territory of his mind, Moriyama invented a new kind of photography where the real world and his memories collide. His is a long and prolific career, but Moriyama has never been afraid to challenge his certainties.

While seeking to strip photography of all its artifice, he continues to show us that a direct and prosaic reproduction of the world is photography's most radically original contribution to art.

THYAGO NOGUEIRA

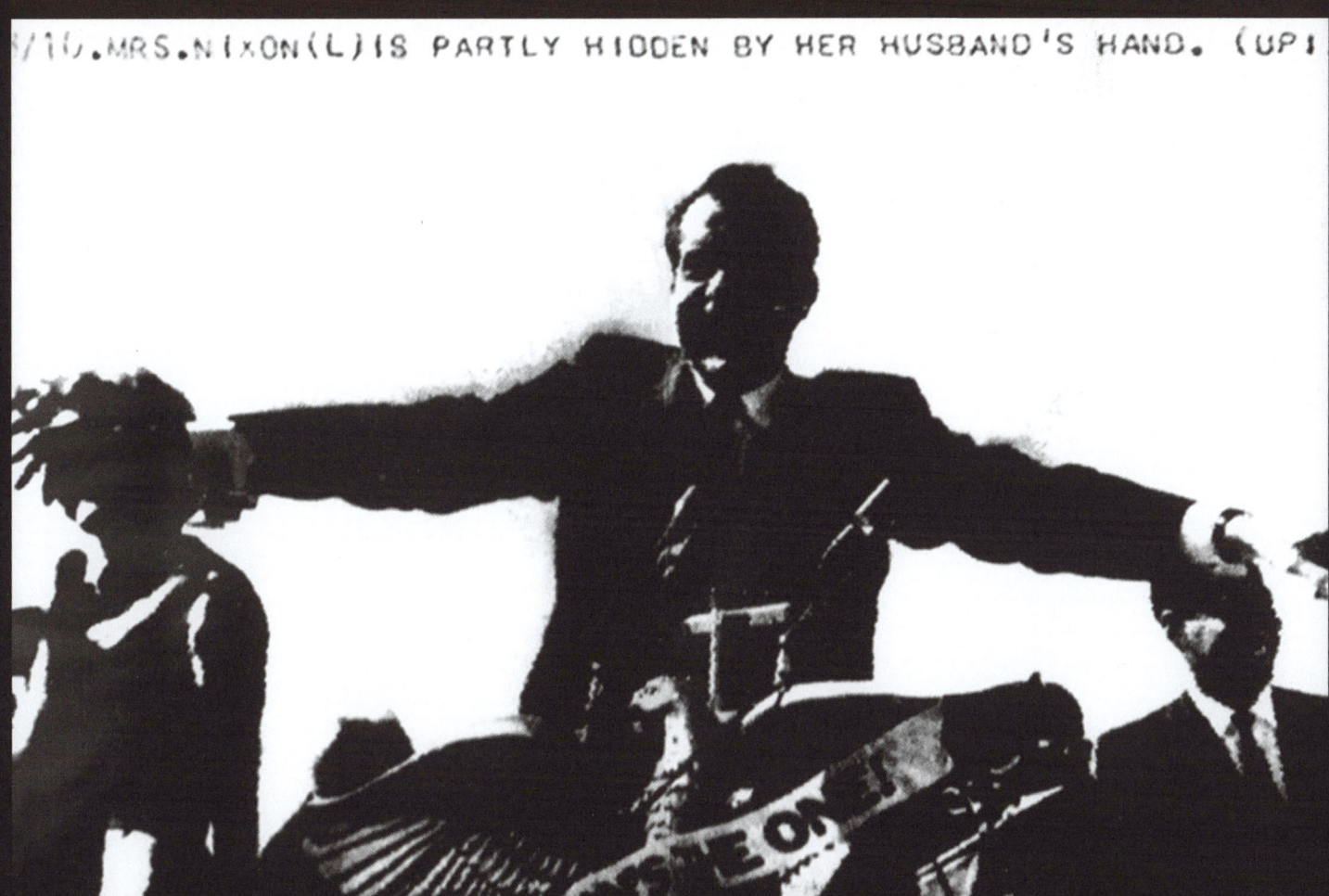

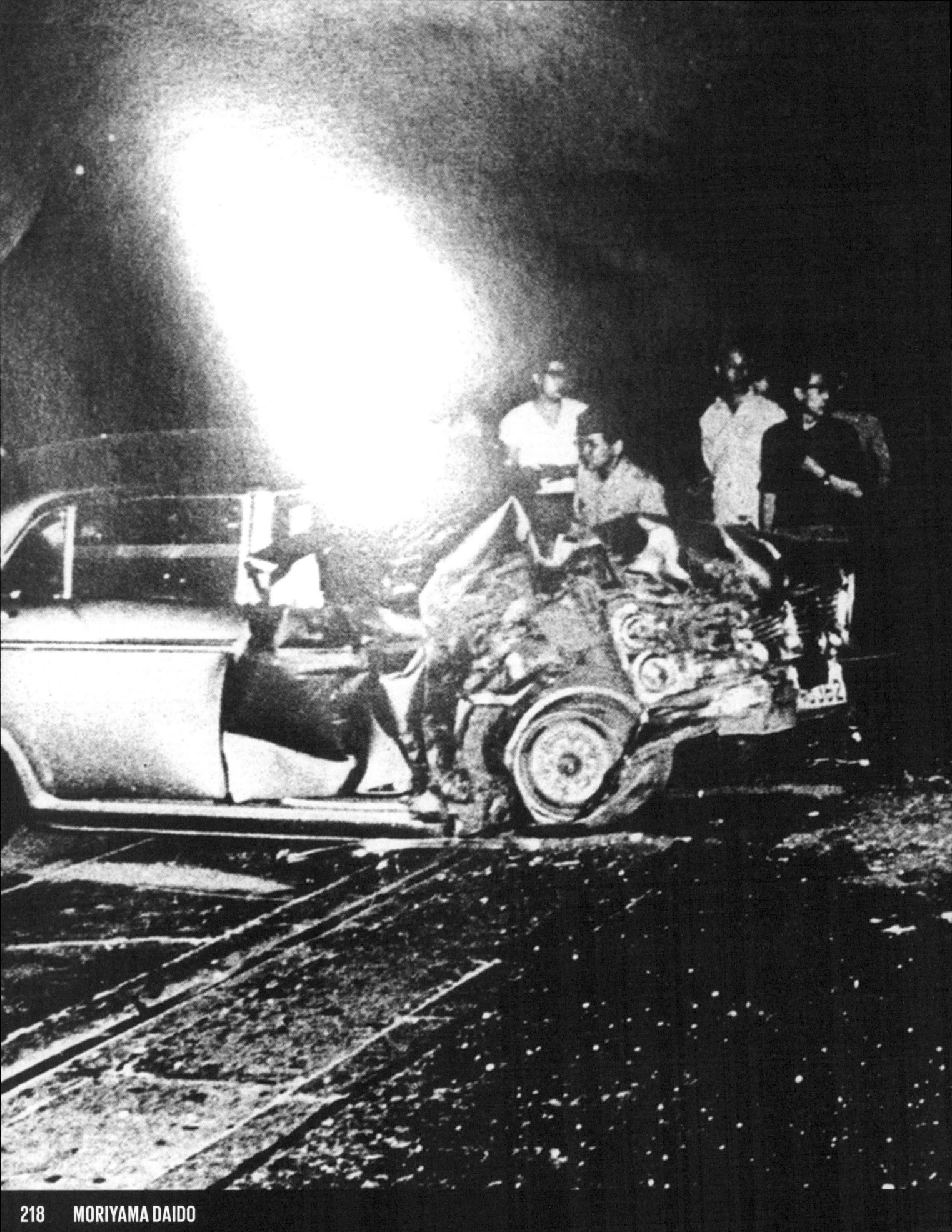

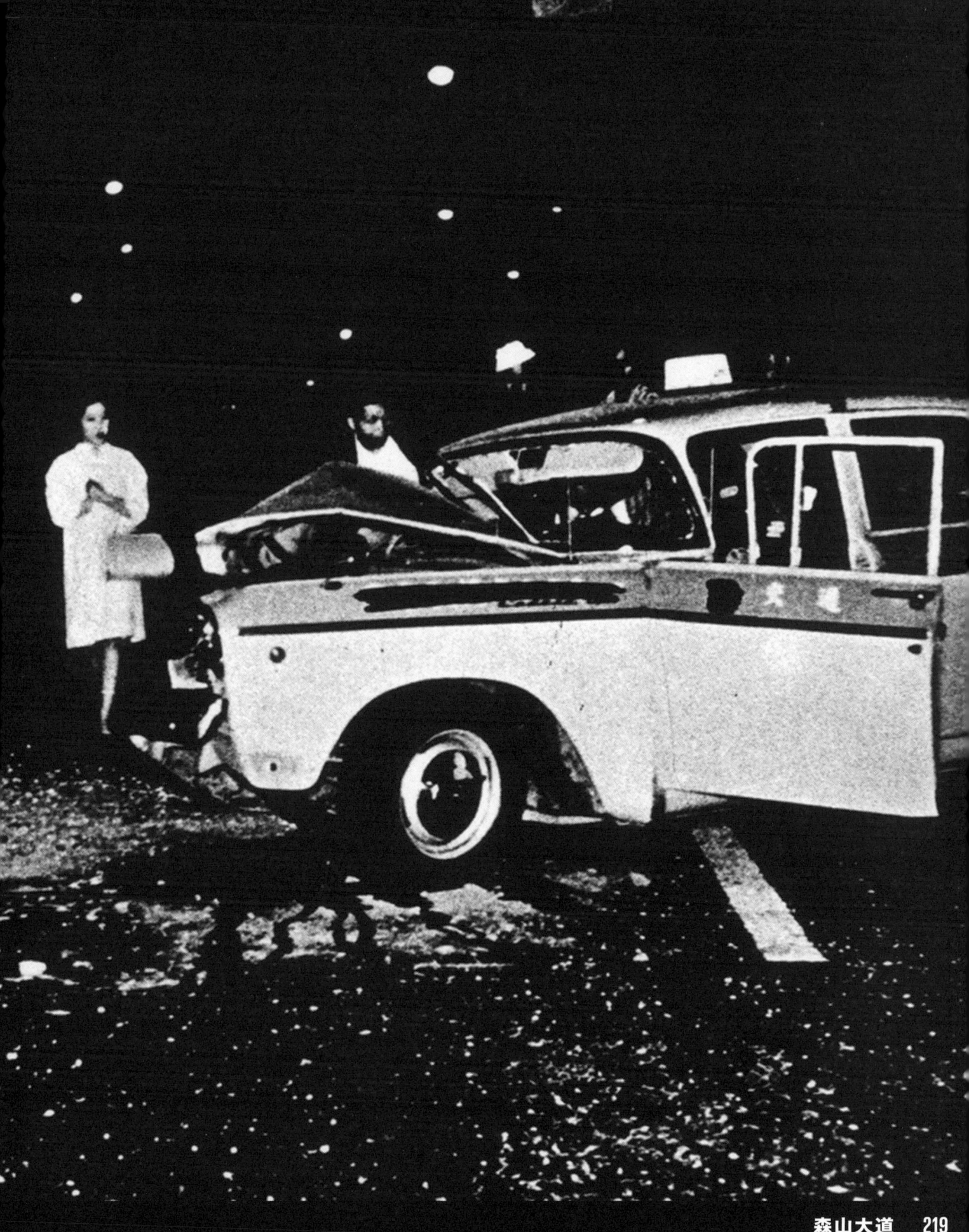

PROVOKE
1968—69
プロヴォーク

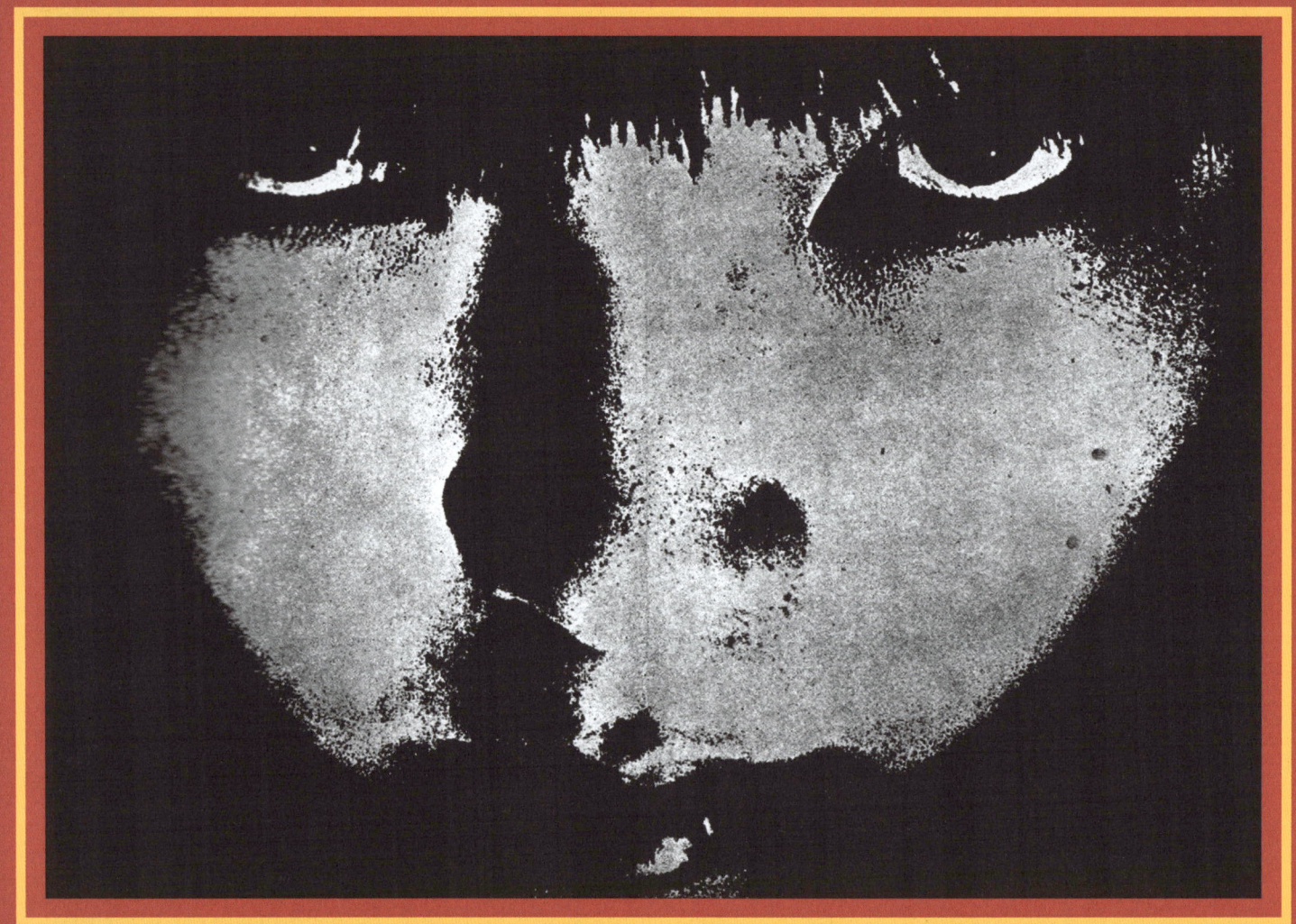

Photograph by **Taki Kōji**, from *PROVOKE*, no. 3 (1969).

Opposite (above, left and right): Photographs by **Taki Kōji**, from *PROVOKE*, no. 3 (1969).

Opposite (below): Photograph by **Taki Kōji**, from *PROVOKE*, no. 1 (1968).

Provoke was a destruction of what was considered 'proper'. I was attracted to the young, fresh energy, and personally, I don't care much about ideology and expression styles. What I felt was a break from the ordinary. I felt they were trying to tell us to stop living a bland, ordinary life through the photographs.

ARAKI NOBUYOSHI

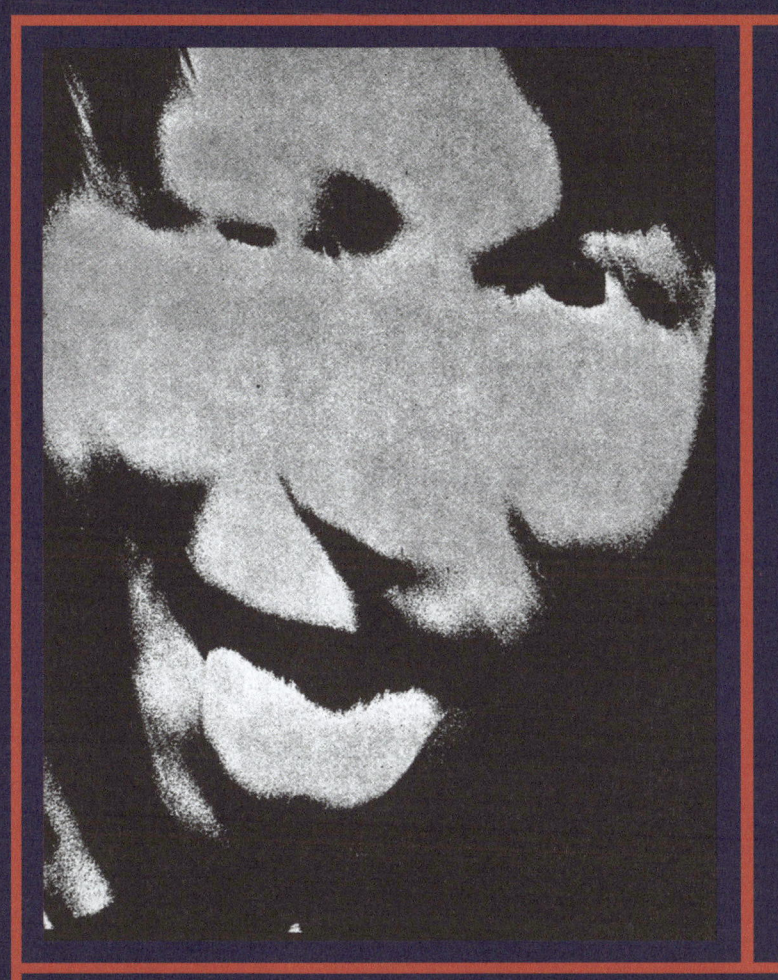
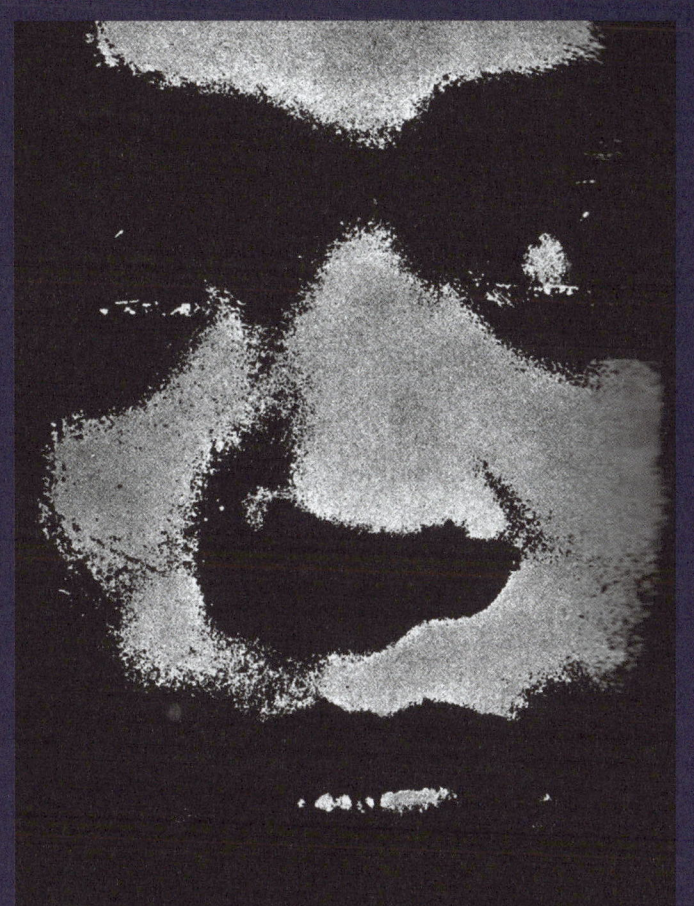

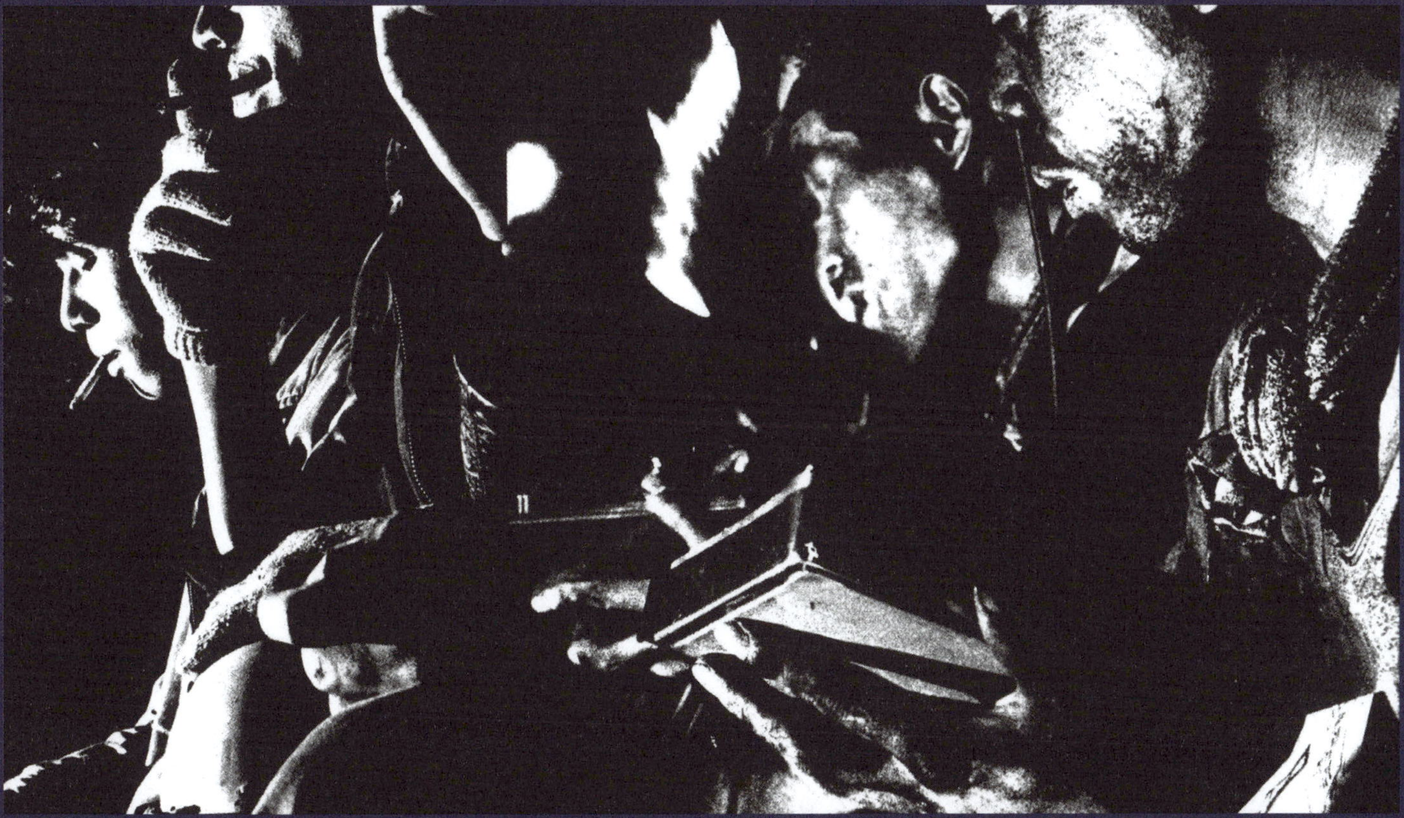

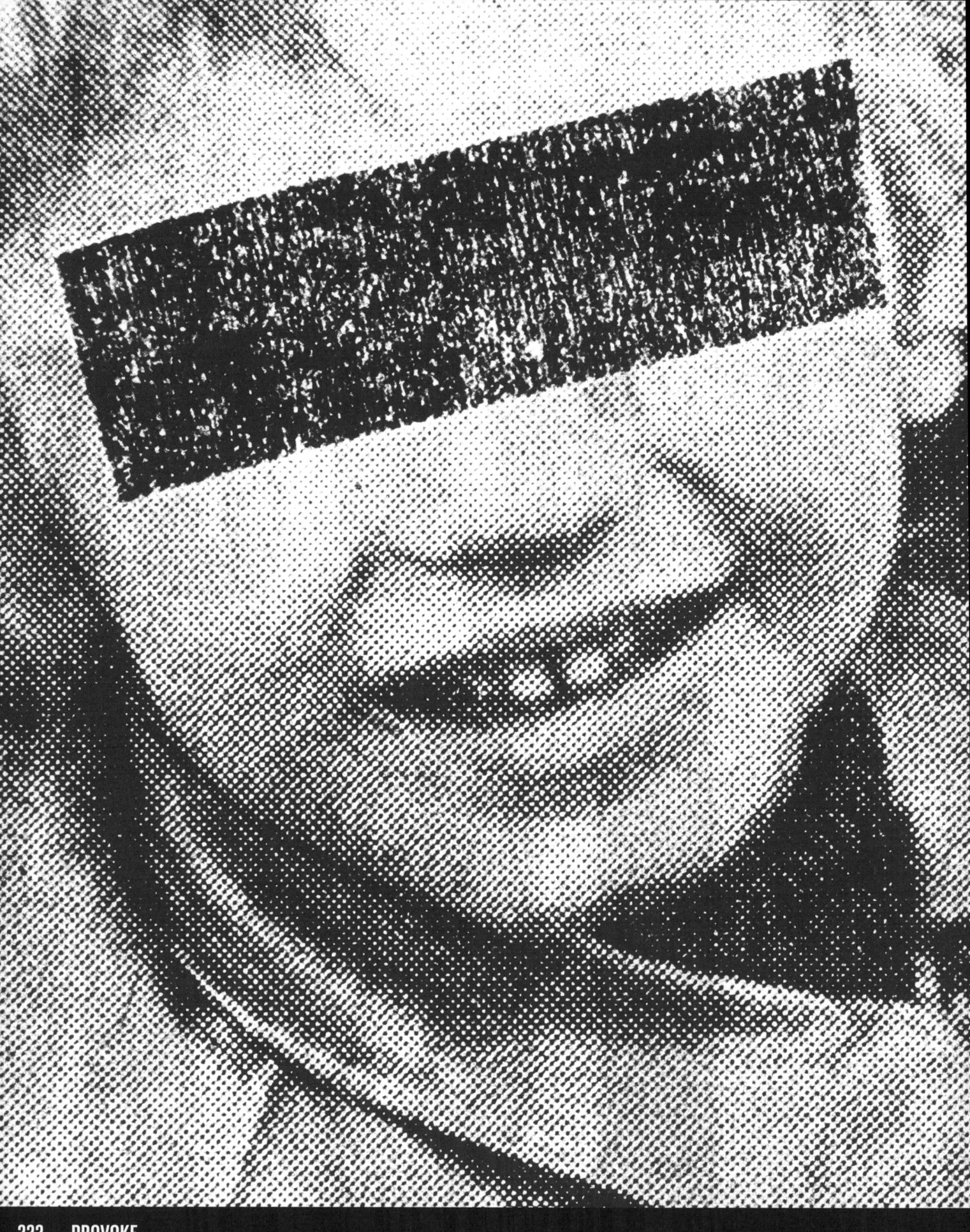

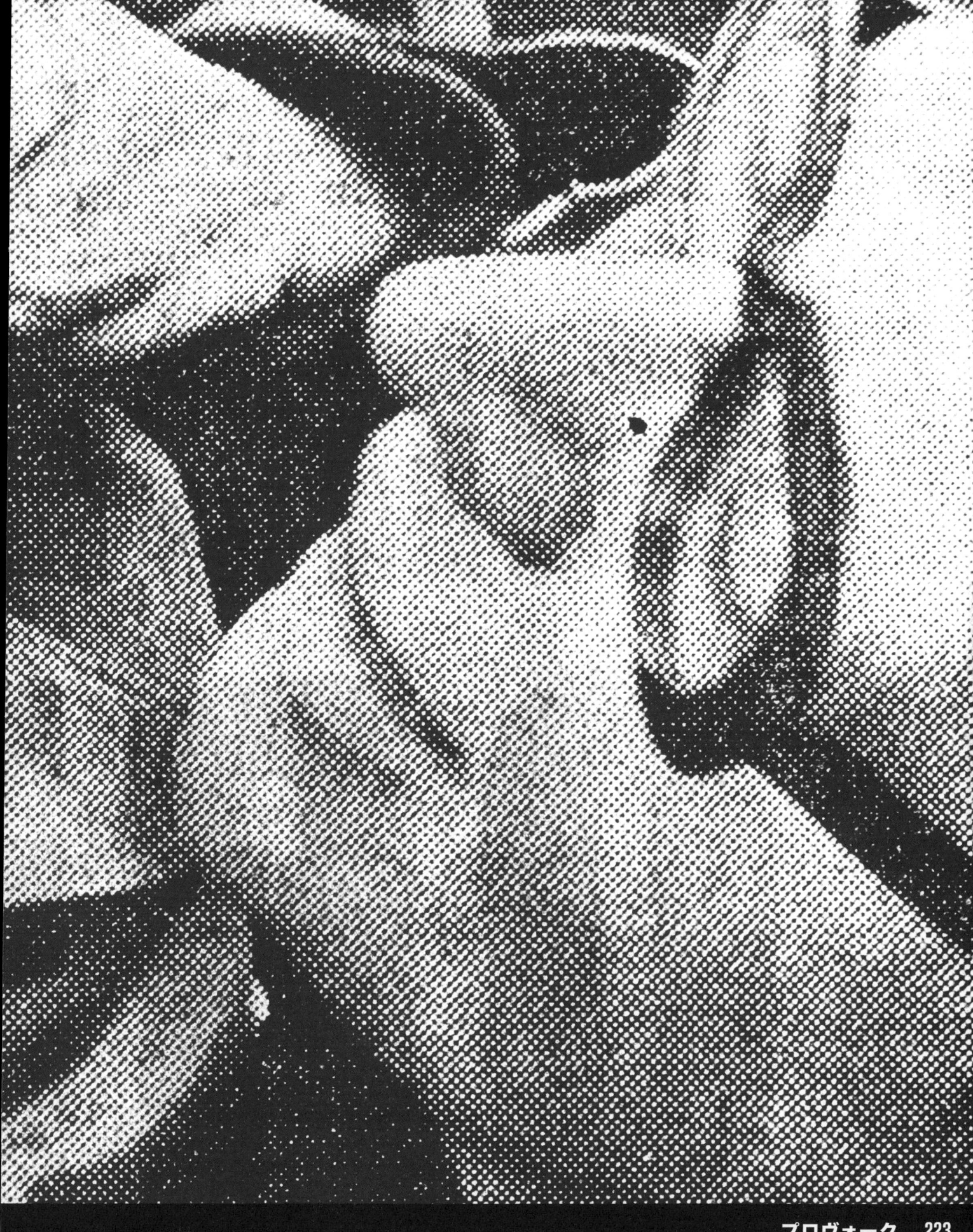

In 1968, Taki Kōji, Nakahira Takuma, Okada Takahiko and Takanashi Yutaka, and from the second edition, Moriyama Daido, who brought it its current fame, started a publication called *Provoke*, born out of the chaotic movement of the same name.

The expression *are-bure-boke* – 'rough, blurred and out of focus' – reversed from its roots the notion that photography must always reflect something.

KANEKO RYŪICHI

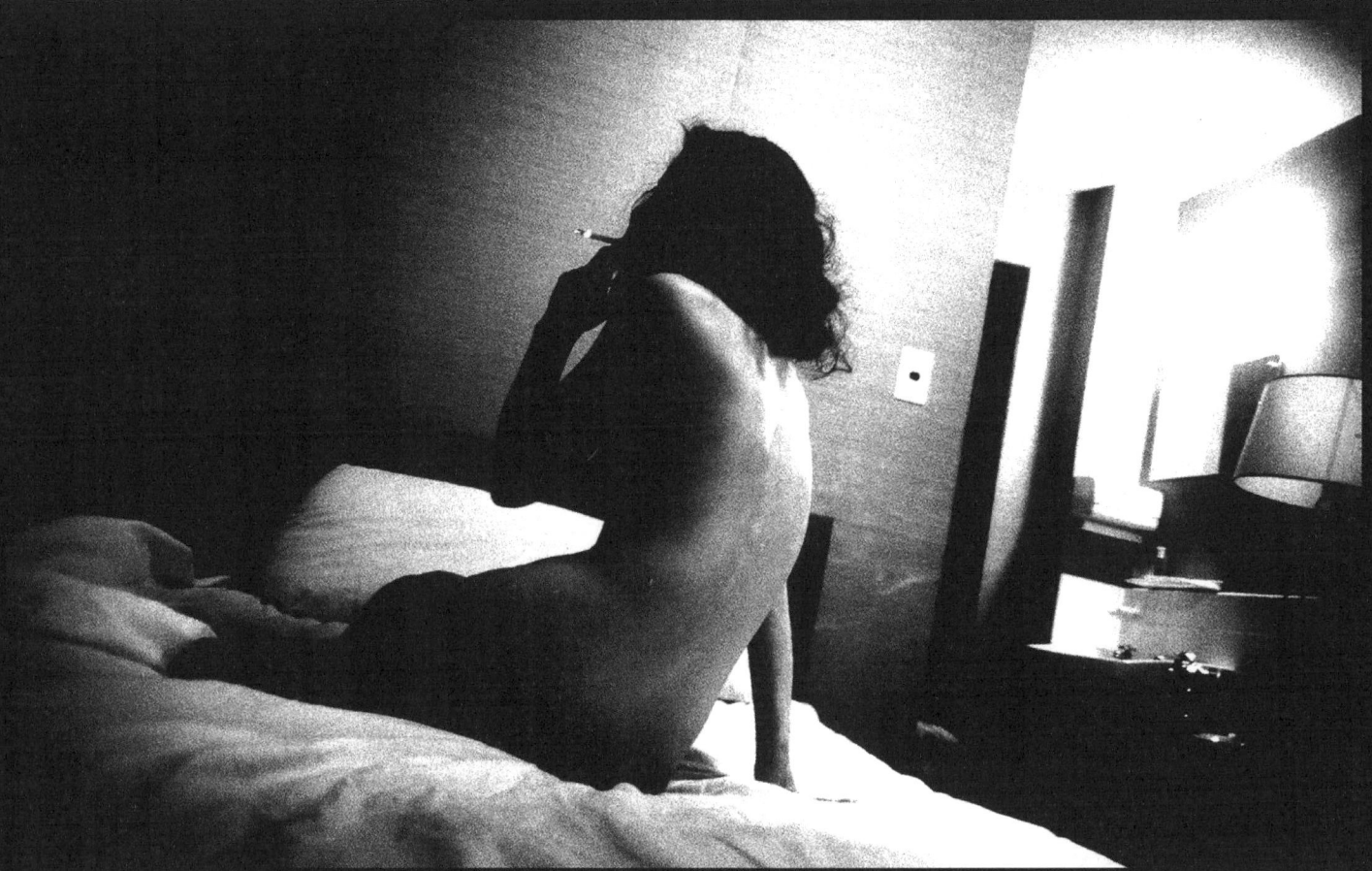

Provoke was originally formed by philosopher and critic Taki Kōji, and my friend who had just started photography, Nakahira Takuma. Both Taki and Nakahira considered words to be very important, but I wanted to express myself through visual images rather than words.

pp. 222–23: **Nakahira Takuma**, *Circulation: Date, Place, Events*, 1971, gelatin silver print.

Above: Photograph by **Moriyama Daido**, from *PROVOKE*, no. 2 (1969).

The magazine lasted for a short term of only two years. It was the most political and radical time. Our space was the secret base for the Zengakuren All-Japan Federation of Student Self-Government Associations and all types of artists and creators.

MORIYAMA DAIDO

PROVOKE MANIFESTO

THE IMAGE BY ITSELF IS NOT A THOUGHT. IT CANNOT POSSESS A WHOLENESS LIKE THAT OF A CONCEPT. NEITHER IS IT AN INTERCHANGEABLE CODE LIKE LANGUAGE. YET ITS IRREVERSIBLE MATERIALITY – THE REALITY THAT IS CUT OUT BY THE CAMERA – CONSTITUTES THE OPPOSITE SIDE OF LANGUAGE, AND FOR THIS REASON AT TIMES IT STIMULATES THE WORLD OF LANGUAGE AND CONCEPTS. WHEN THIS HAPPENS, LANGUAGE TRANSCENDS ITS FIXED AND CONCEPTUALIZED SELF, TRANSFORMING INTO A NEW LANGUAGE, AND THEREFORE NEW THOUGHT.

AT THIS SINGULAR MOMENT – NOW – LANGUAGE LOSES ITS MATERIAL BASIS – IN SHORT ITS REALITY – AND DRIFTS IN SPACE. WE PHOTOGRAPHERS MUST GO ON GRASPING WITH OUR OWN EYES THOSE FRAGMENTS OF REALITY THAT CANNOT POSSIBLY BE CAPTURED WITH EXISTING LANGUAGE, ACTIVELY PUTTING FORTH MATERIALS AGAINST LANGUAGE AND AGAINST THOUGHT. DESPITE SOME RESERVATIONS, THIS IS WHY WE HAVE GIVEN *PROVOKE* THE SUBTITLE 'PROVOCATIVE MATERIALS FOR THOUGHT'.

DRAFTED BY NAKAHIRA TAKUMA AND TAKI KŌJI, 1968

NAKAHIRA TAKUMA

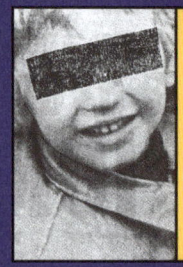

中平卓馬

1938–2015

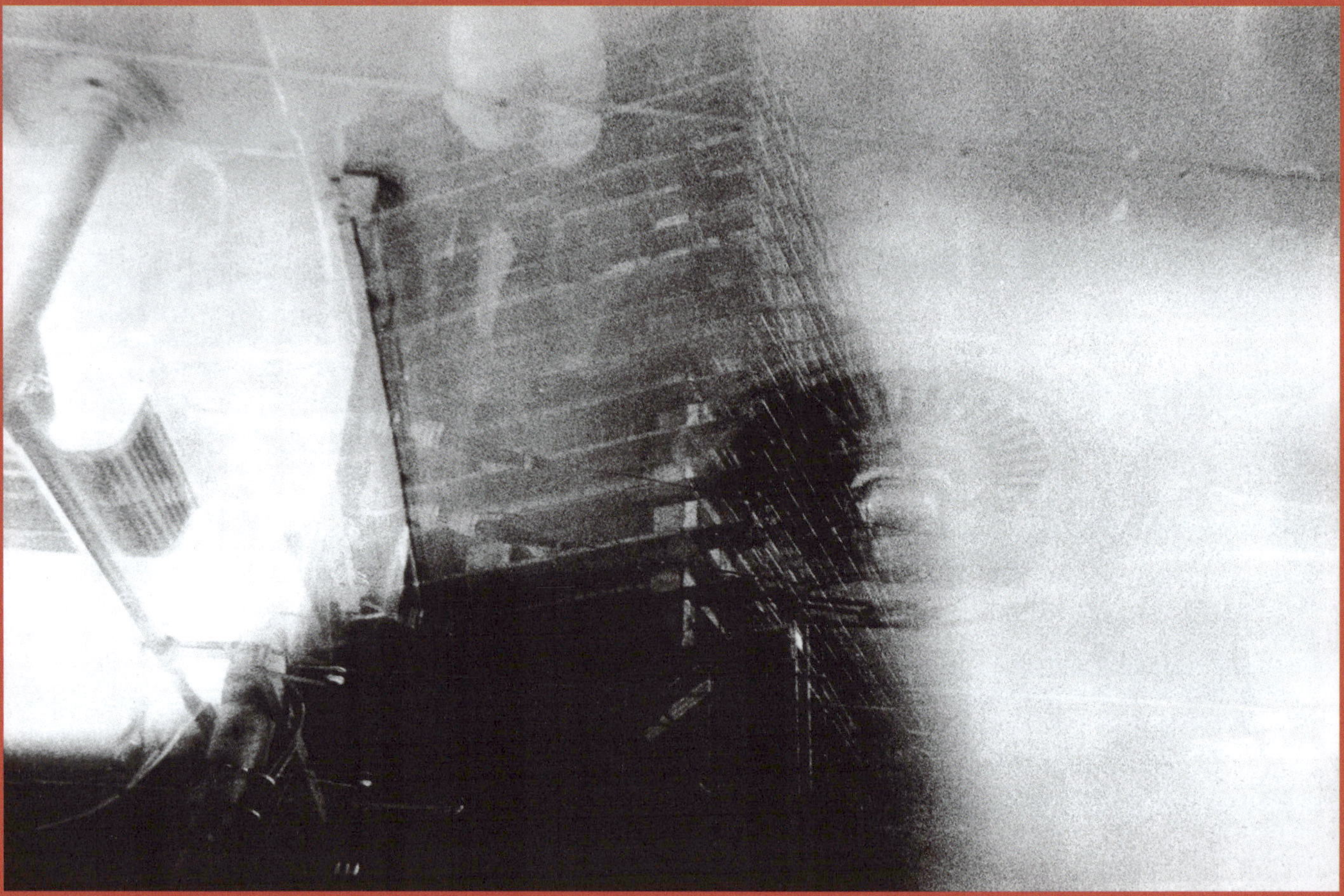

Photograph by **Nakahira Takuma**, from *For a Language to Come* (1970).

Opposite (above, right and left): Photographs by **Nakahira Takuma**, from *PROVOKE*, no. 2 (1969).

Opposite (below): Photograph by **Nakahira Takuma**, from *PROVOKE*, no. 1 (1968).

Overleaf: **Nakahira Takuma**, *Circulation: Date, Place, Events*, 1971, gelatin silver print.

'With the camera as the superb product of modernity, the world can be controlled based on a single-point perspective. The camera unilaterally restricts the act of seeing to the eye. As a result, the camera is an embodiment of an ideology of humanity as operator of the world. If that is the case, then isn't the camera, by its very nature, a method that cannot totalize the world?'

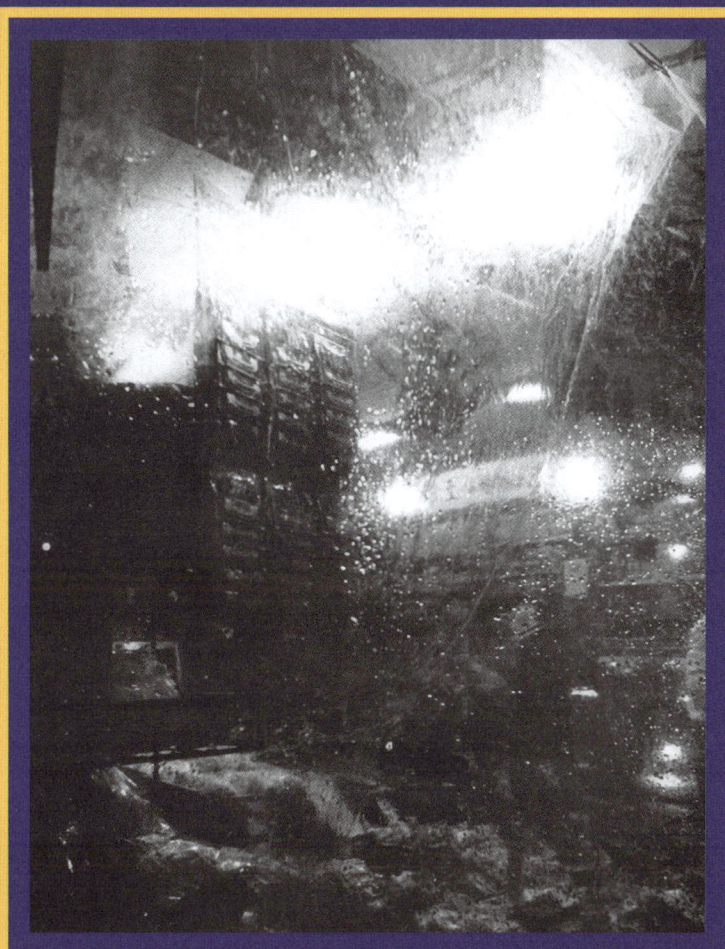
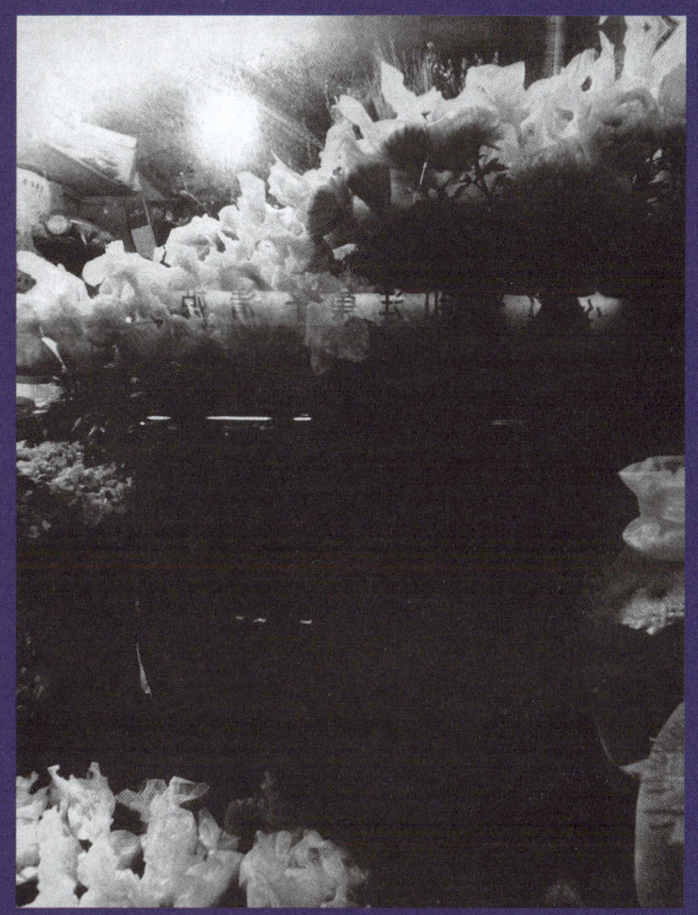

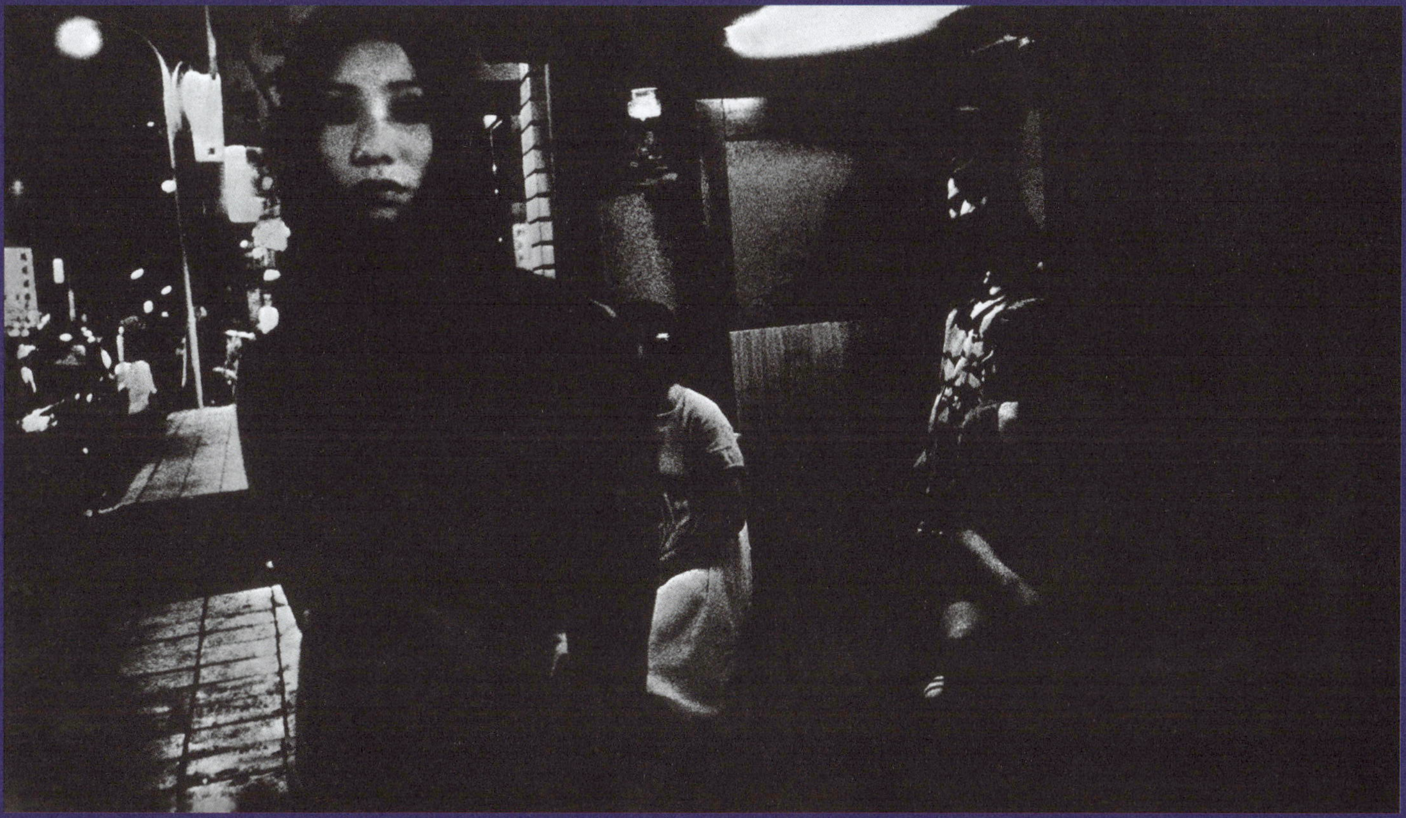

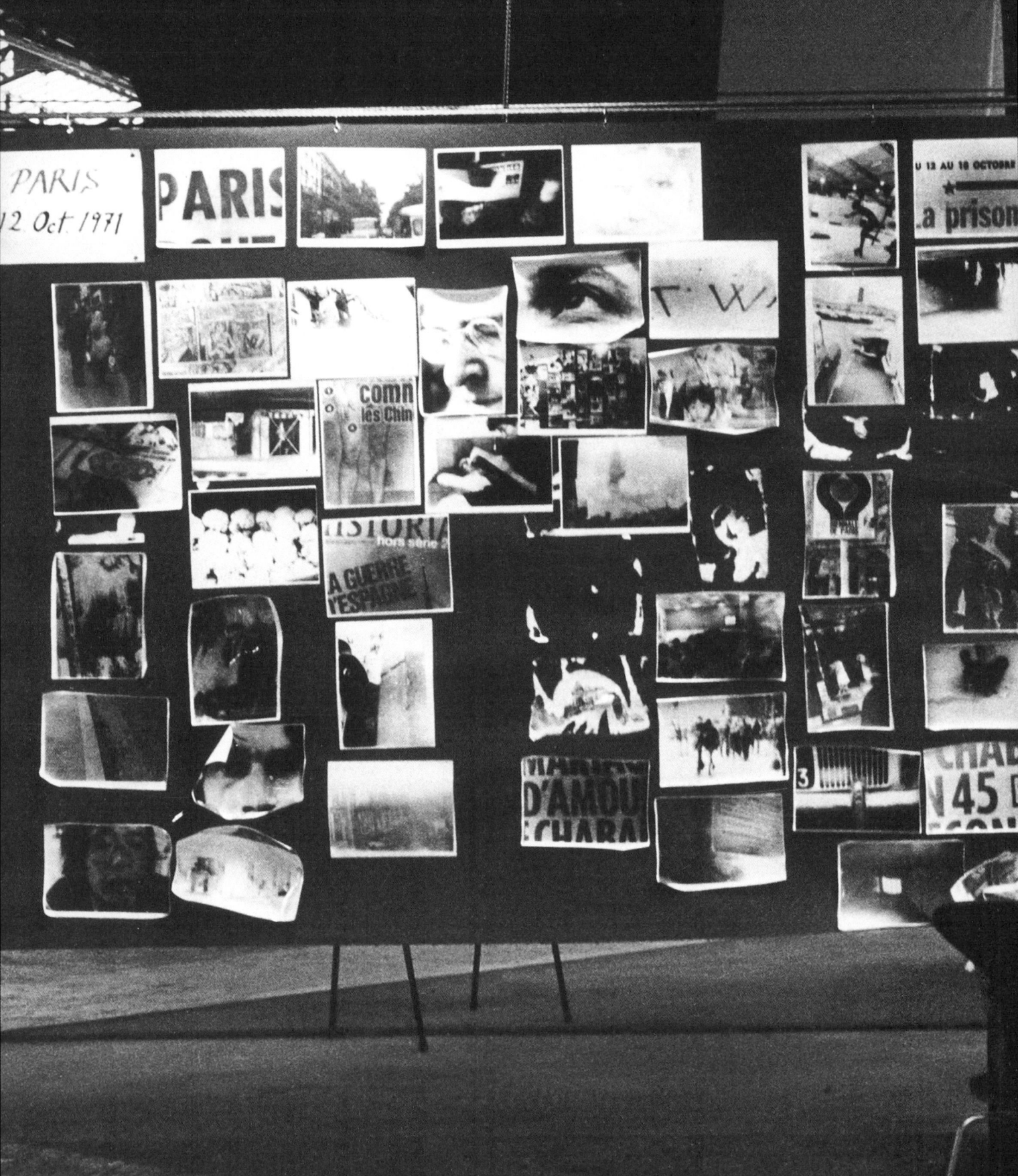

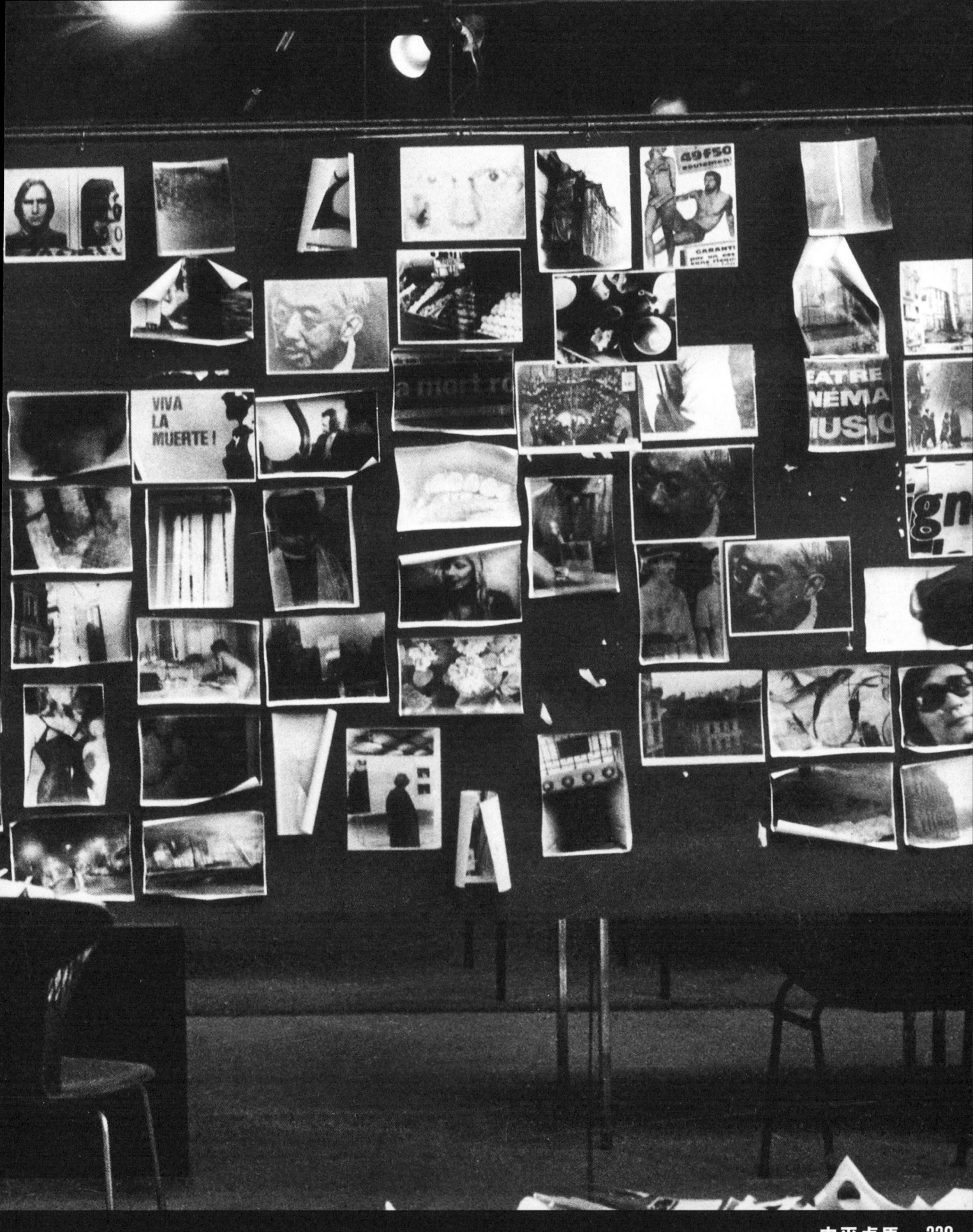

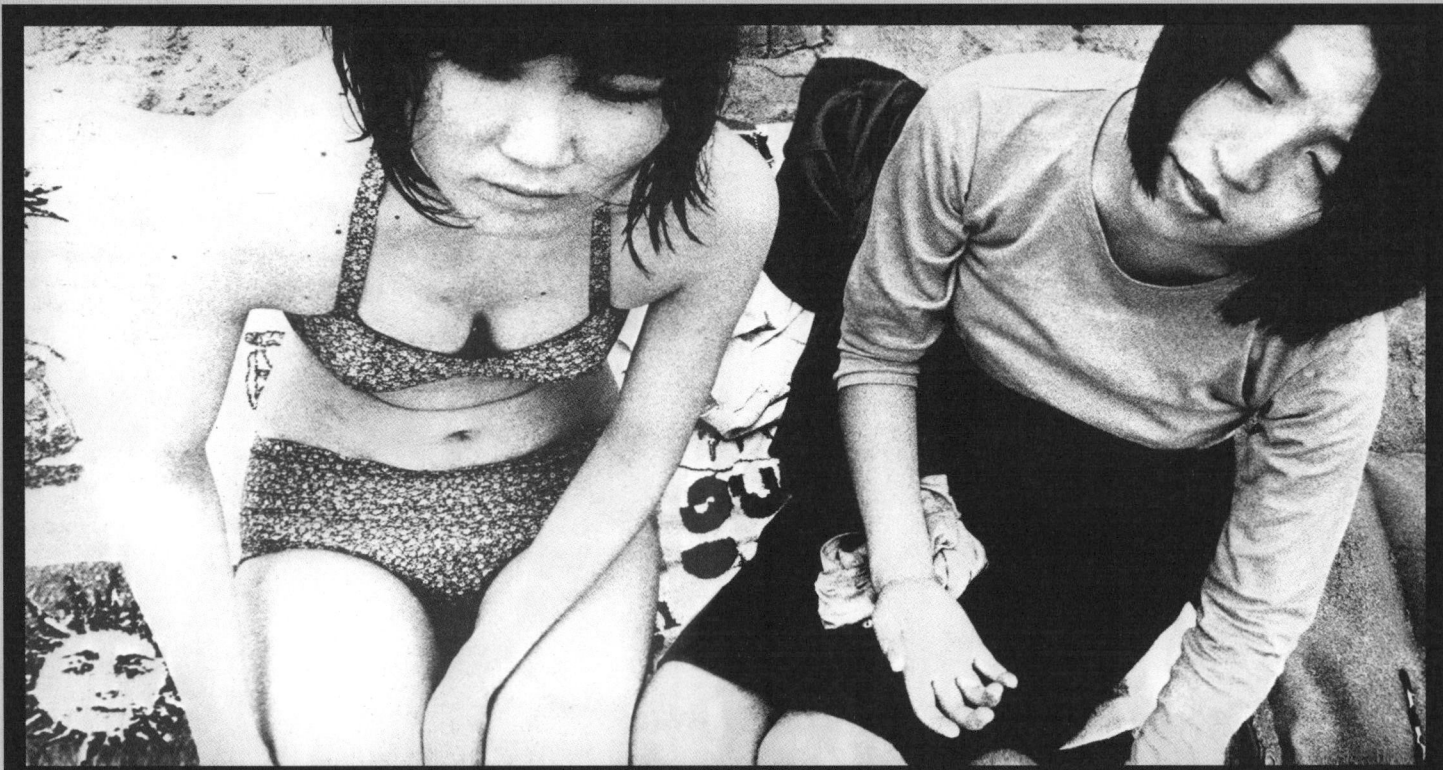

Nakahira Takuma was a photographer and critic whose life changed in 1977, when he suffered substantial memory loss; he would not publish any more critical essays for the rest of his life. Up until this point, however, he engaged keenly with current affairs, and it is his unusual position at the centre of both Japanese public intellectual life and Tokyo's politically sensitive avant-garde that renders his attitudes of particular interest when assessing the cultural climate at this moment of transition in Japanese politics.

Following the collapse of popular support for the dissenting activities in Tokyo at the end of the 1960s, and the subsequent splintering of the Japanese left wing into different factions, Nakahira developed new political vocabularies in response to an emergent discourse surrounding the term *fūkei* (landscape). Explored through his photography and writing, these varied efforts include his participation in the legendary, short-lived journal *Provoke* and his debut photobook *For a Language to Come* (1970).

Photograph by **Nakahira Takuma**, from *PROVOKE*, no. 1 (1968).

Opposite: **Nakahira Takuma**, *Untitled*, 1968–70, gelatin silver print.

pp. 232–33: **Nakahira Takuma**, *Untitled Work*, 1968, gelatin silver print.

They constitute Nakahira's contribution to wider attempts to probe the frustration and disappointment experienced by many who had lost faith in public protest as a mechanism by which to bring about lasting, systemic change. Like many of his peers who endeavoured to identify new means of resistance by which to move beyond this impasse, Nakahira went on to leave the city behind during the 1970s, to seek out new grounds for intervention through his travels in Okinawa. Nakahira's critical stance was rooted in his perception of Japan as undergoing a transformation, most obviously represented by the post-war developments occurring in media and infrastructure.

He recognized the dramatic changes as directed by the agendas of Japanese industry and political elites, who sought to maximize economic efficiency and concentrate authority through encouraging the centralization of production and political agency.

Nakahira's restless experimentation with different forms across his critical, journalistic and creative activities testifies to an enduring preoccupation with identifying the presence of structural powers at play in Japanese society. Determined to analyse the mechanisms by which such forces are engendered and perpetuated, Nakahira took his cue from the writings of Frantz Fanon and was driven by the ultimate aim of resisting the influence of such dynamics within Japan and further afield.

Coming of age in the era of popular television, student revolutionaries of the 1960s had learned to express their dissent through staging public acts and referencing symbols that translated their ideological positions into an iconic visual rhetoric for the mass media's waiting cameras. At the other end of the political spectrum, governmental agencies were exploring the potential of media manipulation and advertising to refine their presentation of statistics and harness the impact of broadcasts screened live and in colour, directly into people's homes.

Nakahira's early work displays intensely personal reactions towards political situations and causes, however he does not valorize these experiences to directly compel audiences towards partisan sympathies. Instead, Nakahira's efforts strive towards a kind of raising of consciousness; he seeks to create encounters through which individuals might independently arrive at perspectives that bypass habitual ways of seeing the world.

LUCY FLEMING-BROWN

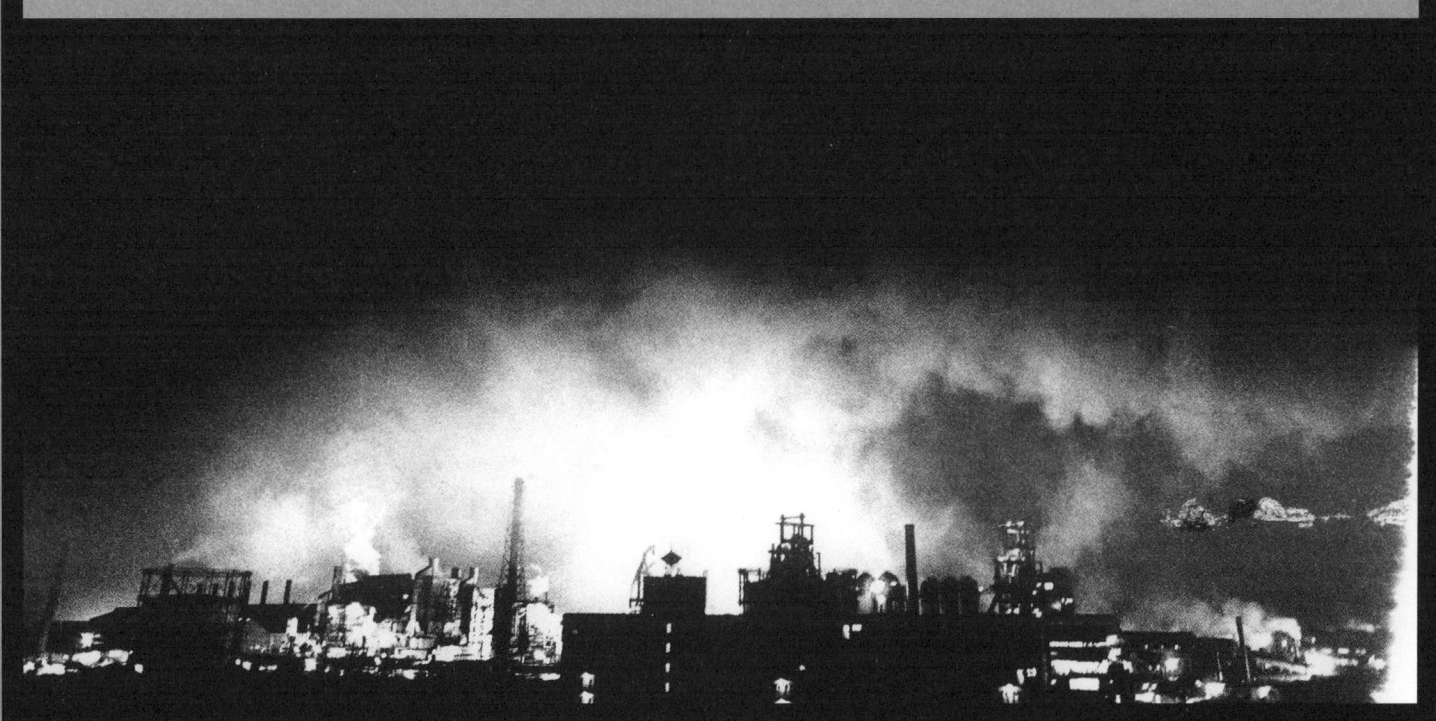

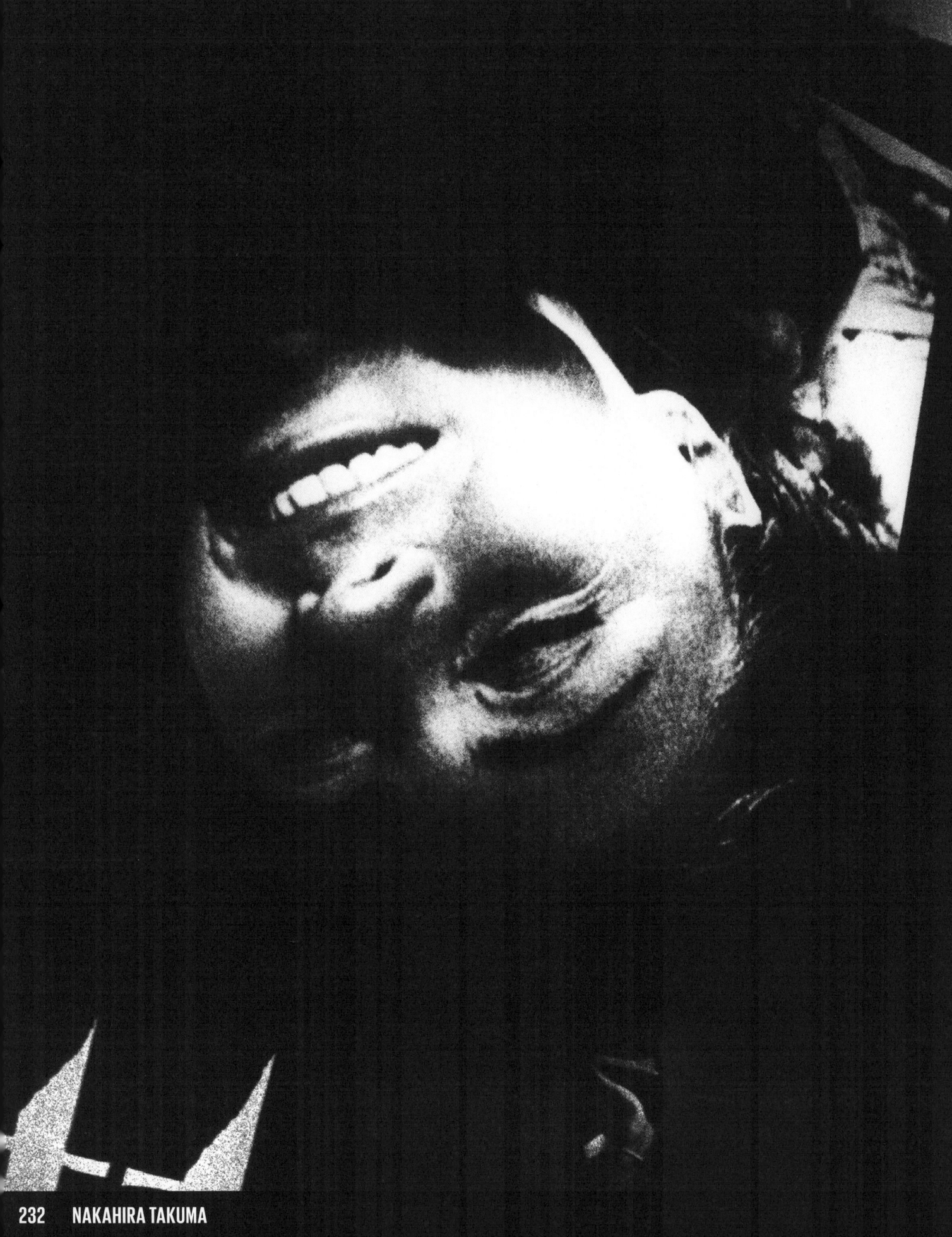

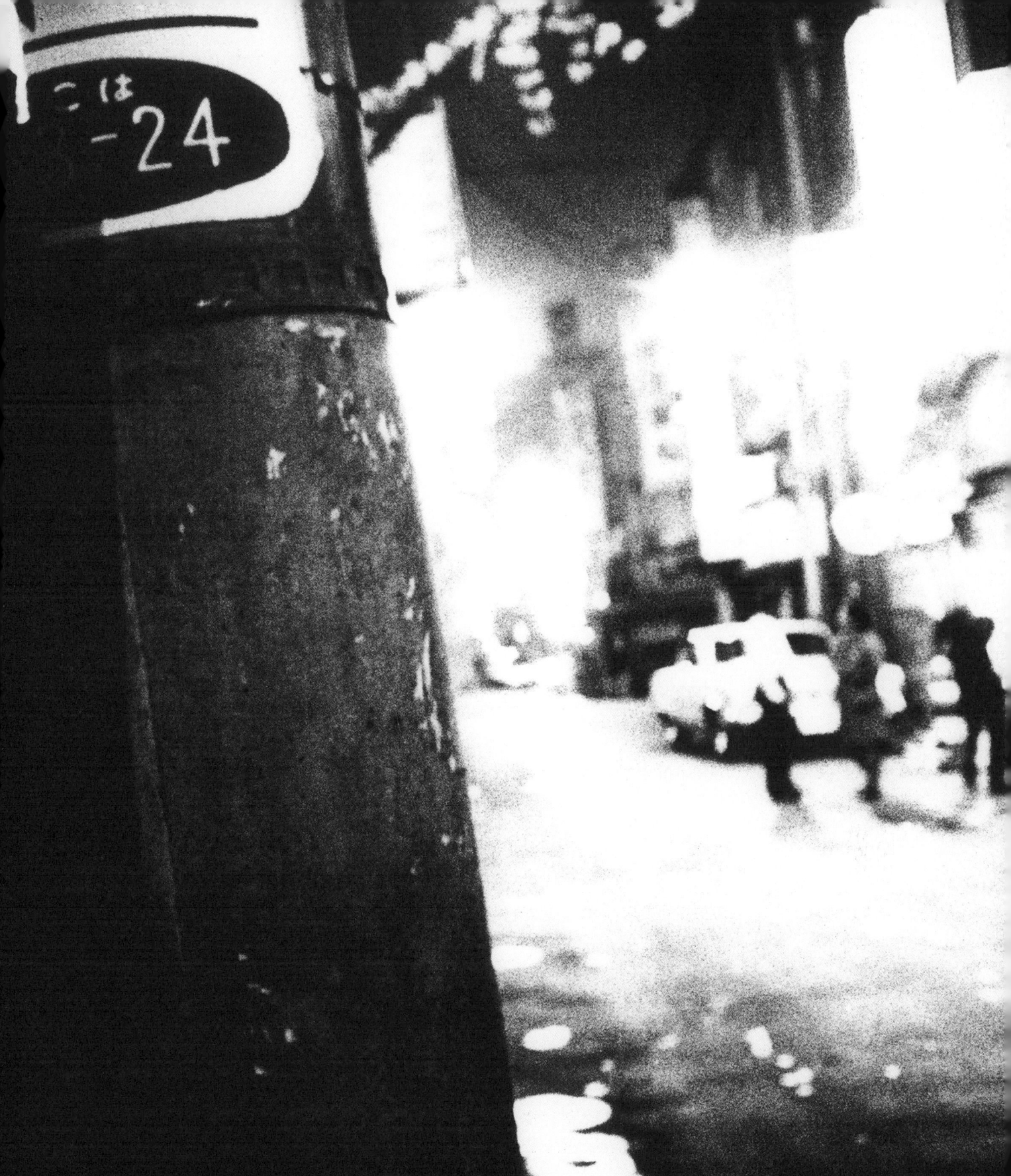

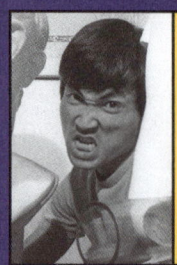

NEO-DADA ORGANIZERS
1960–62

ネオ・ダダ

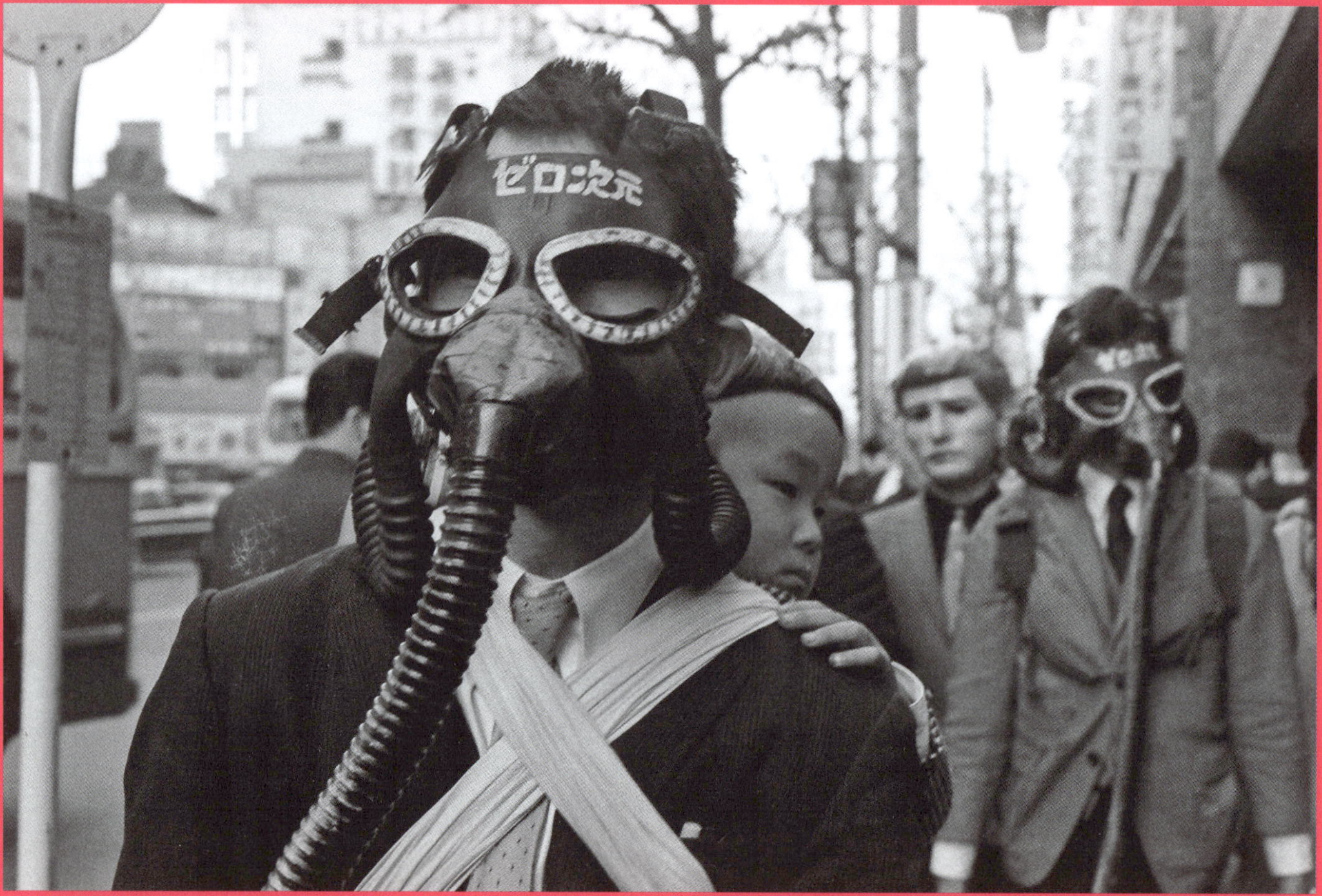

Hanaga Mitsutoshi, *Zero Dimension's Buck-Naked and Gas-Masked Walking Ritual*, 1967, gelatin silver print.

Opposite (above, left and right): Photographs by **Tanabe Santaro**, details and dates unknown.

Opposite (below): **Hanaga Mitsutoshi**, *Akasegawa Genpei Near his Residence in Tokyo*, 1967, gelatin silver print.

The Neo-Dada Organizers emerged in 1960 out of a group of young artists gathering around Shinjuku's legendary White House studio. In reaction to society's transition towards consumption-orientated lifestyles, members pursued alternative creative visions that attacked capital at the intersection of everyday life and State authority. The term 'anti-art' was coined by critic Tōno Yoshiaki in response to the diverse, iconoclastic practices generated during the movement's short-lived period of activity.

LUCY FLEMING-BROWN

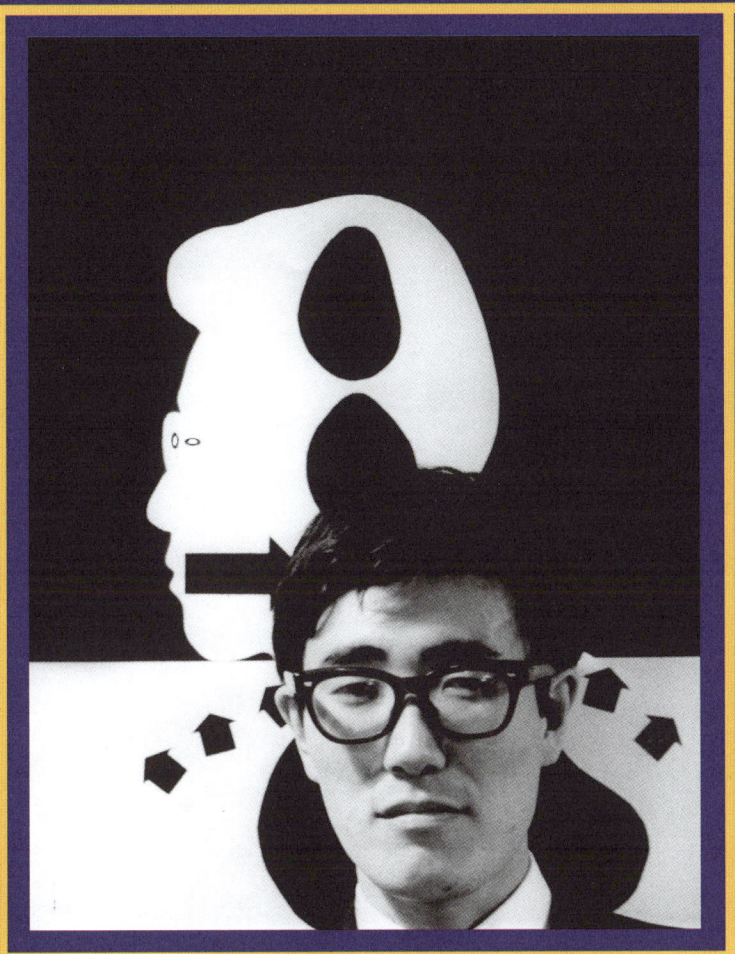
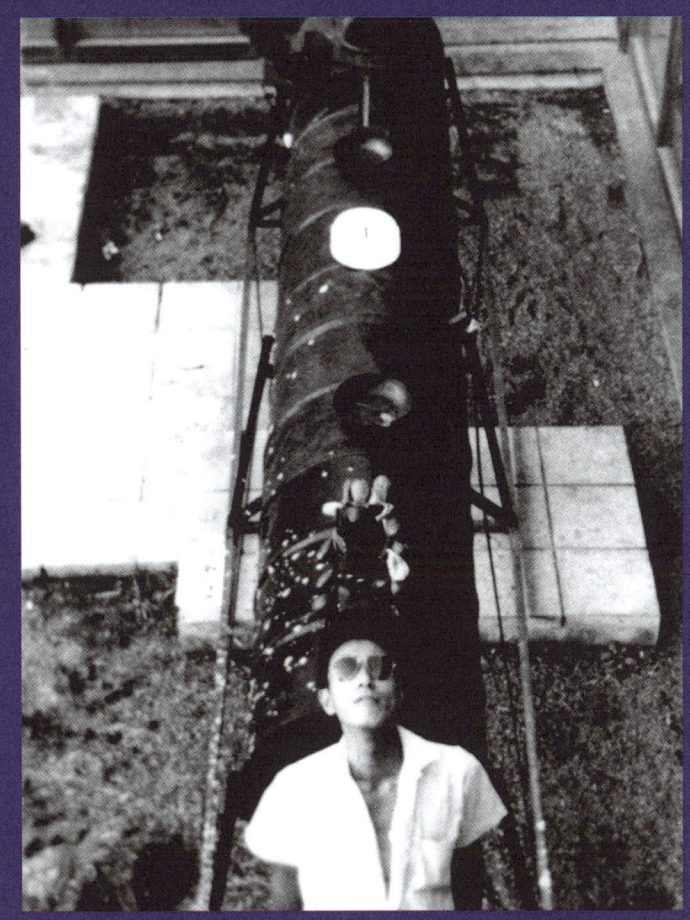

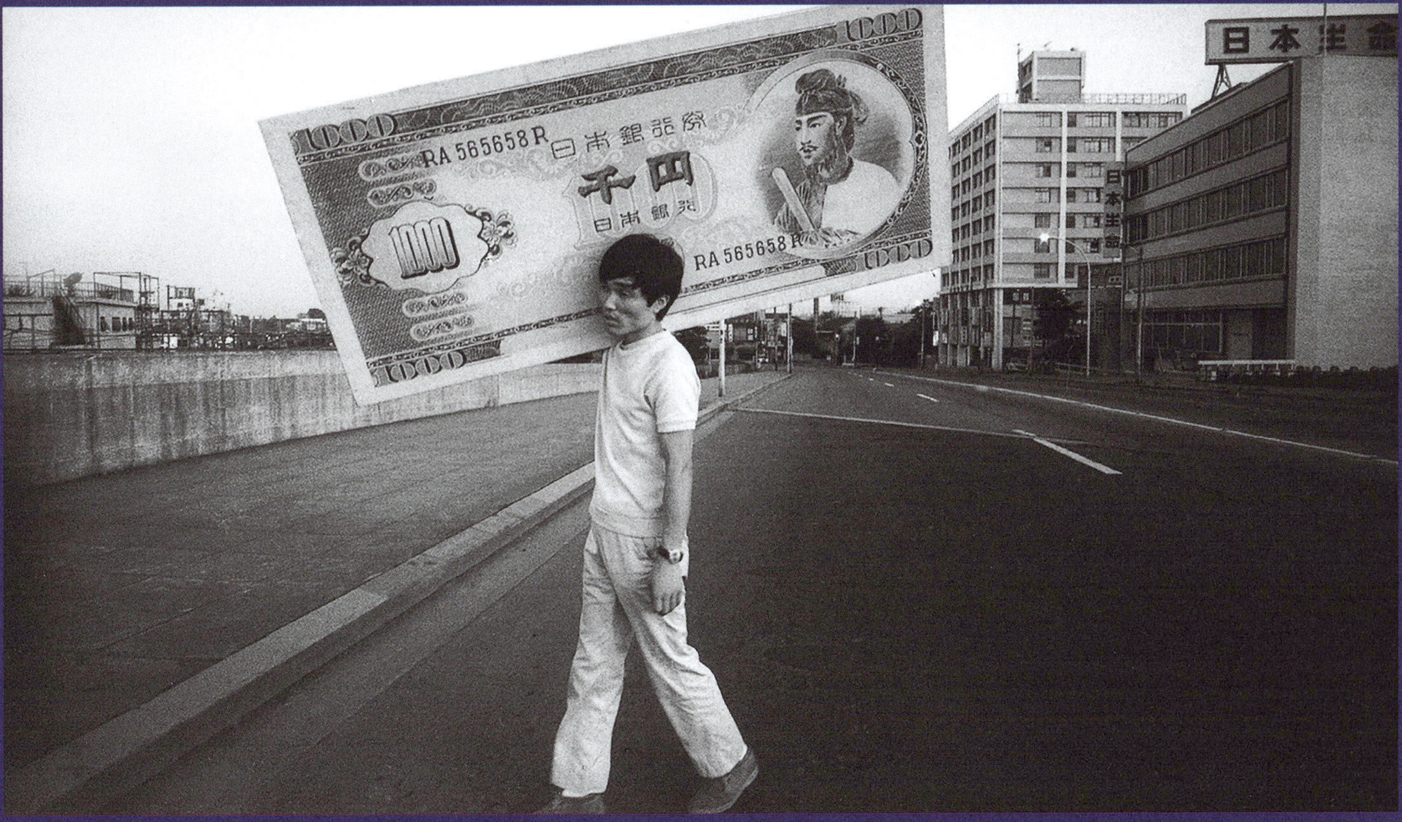

ネオ・ダダ　235

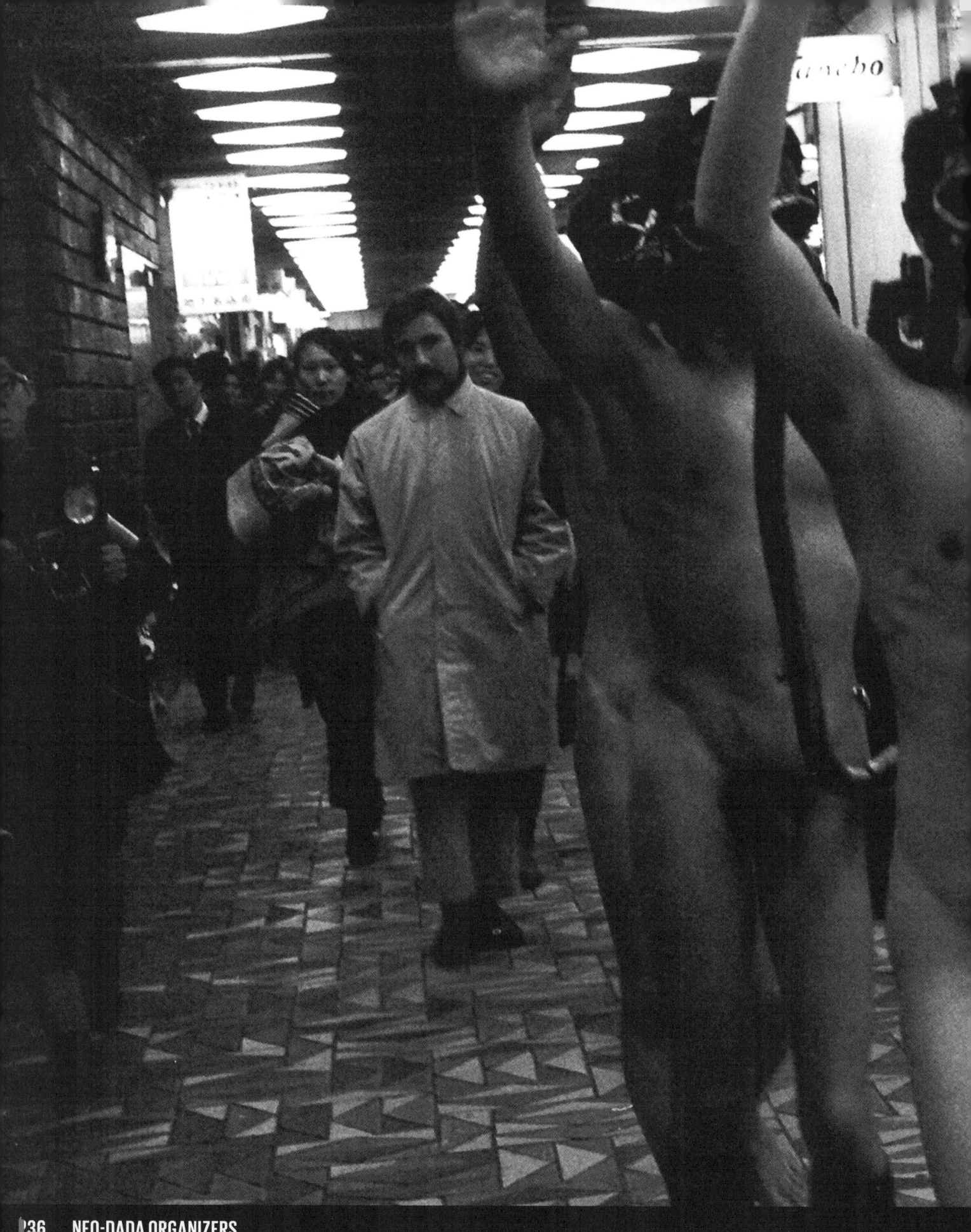

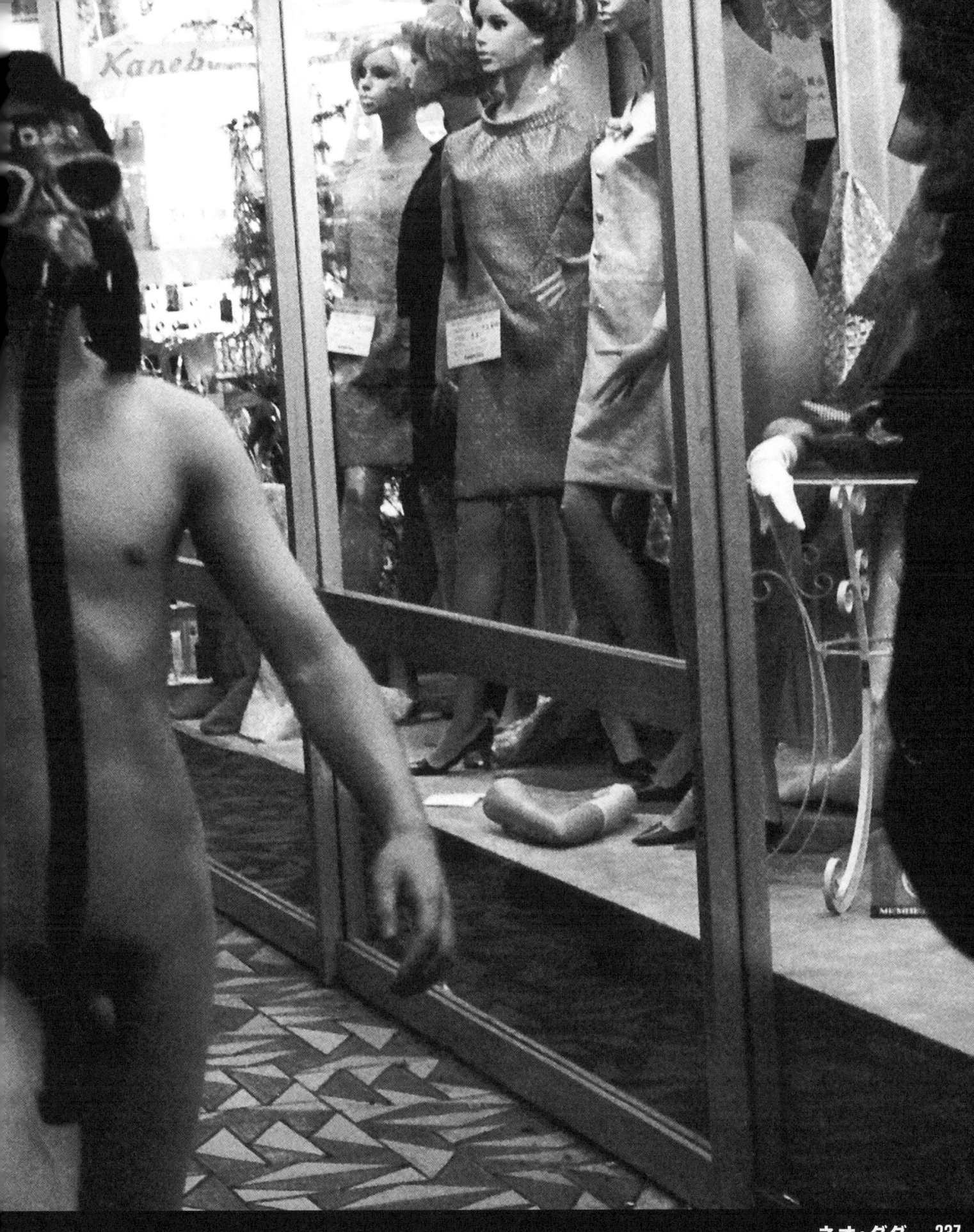

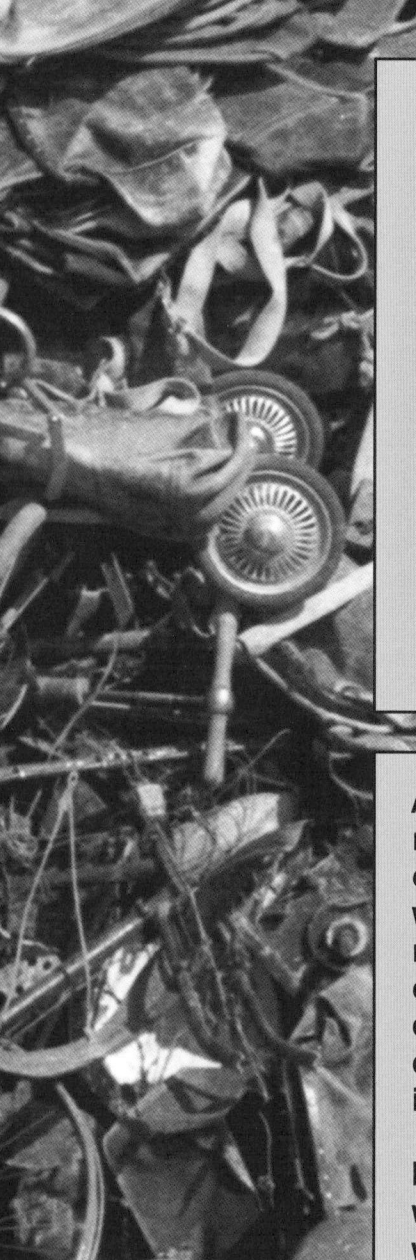

> ONE BY ONE, UNOBTRUSIVE ARTICLES OF DAILY LIFE BECAME REDOLENT WITH NEW SECRETS. AS I CLAMBERED UP THESE MOUNTAINS OF RUBBISH, I BEGAN TO FIND IN THEM OBJECTS WHICH HAD AN UNMISTAKABLE QUALITY OF THEIR OWN.
>
> AKASEGAWA GENPEI

Akasegawa Genpei moved to Tokyo to study art in 1955 and rapidly asserted himself as a leading figure in avant-garde circles. Following a host of frustrating experiences submitting works to juried group exhibitions that favoured socialist realist art, Akasegawa joined the Neo-Dada Organizers in the early 1960s. The movement formed out of a diverse group of artists with a shared sensitivity to the ongoing political unrest and an appetite for spontaneous, often irreverent creative intervention.

It was around this time that Akasegawa established contact with Takamatsu Jirō and Nakanishi Natsuyuki, with whom he would found Hi-Red Center in 1963. The group were interested in questioning the role of everyday objects and their own actions within larger systems, such as the judiciary, transportation and media networks, and initiatives perpetuated by the authorities, including policing and public sanitation. Akasegawa attained notoriety for his reproduction of Japanese currency as exhibition invitations in 1963, resulting in a long-running and highly publicized counterfeiting trial that he insistently treated as a kind of performance. While Hi-Red Center never formally disbanded, members of the group pursued increasingly individualized practices from 1964 onwards.

LUCY FLEMING-BROWN

pp. 236–37: **Hanaga Mitsutoshi**, *Rituals of Completely Naked Walks with Gas Masks*, 1967, gelatin silver print.

Hanaga Mitsutoshi, *Shinohara Ushio*, 1965, gelatin silver print.

Overleaf: **Hanaga Mitsutoshi**, *Shinohara Ushio*, date unknown, gelatin silver print.

I myself am a member of Neo-Dada, and I've learned various things from Neo-Dada. I was taught the passion of the heart. And because of that, I was able to break down my own sense of self. I was young, and there was a lot of energy, that sort of thing, and I struggled to process it inside of myself to the point that I needed to let my feelings out. I was in that state of mind.

I made drum cans in a junkyard in Tokyo. Back then, was it called the junk shop? Artists would go to places like the paint store to buy canvases and paints. But that did not excite me at all. For me, going to the junkyard was more exciting.

My dreams got bigger and bigger there. What comes to the junkyard is the junk that reflects the reality of the current social situation. I don't believe that art is just what's being shown in museums. I'm thinking of dismantling the idea that these art galleries, these museums, these 'castles', where one statically observes pieces, are art.

TANABE SANTARO

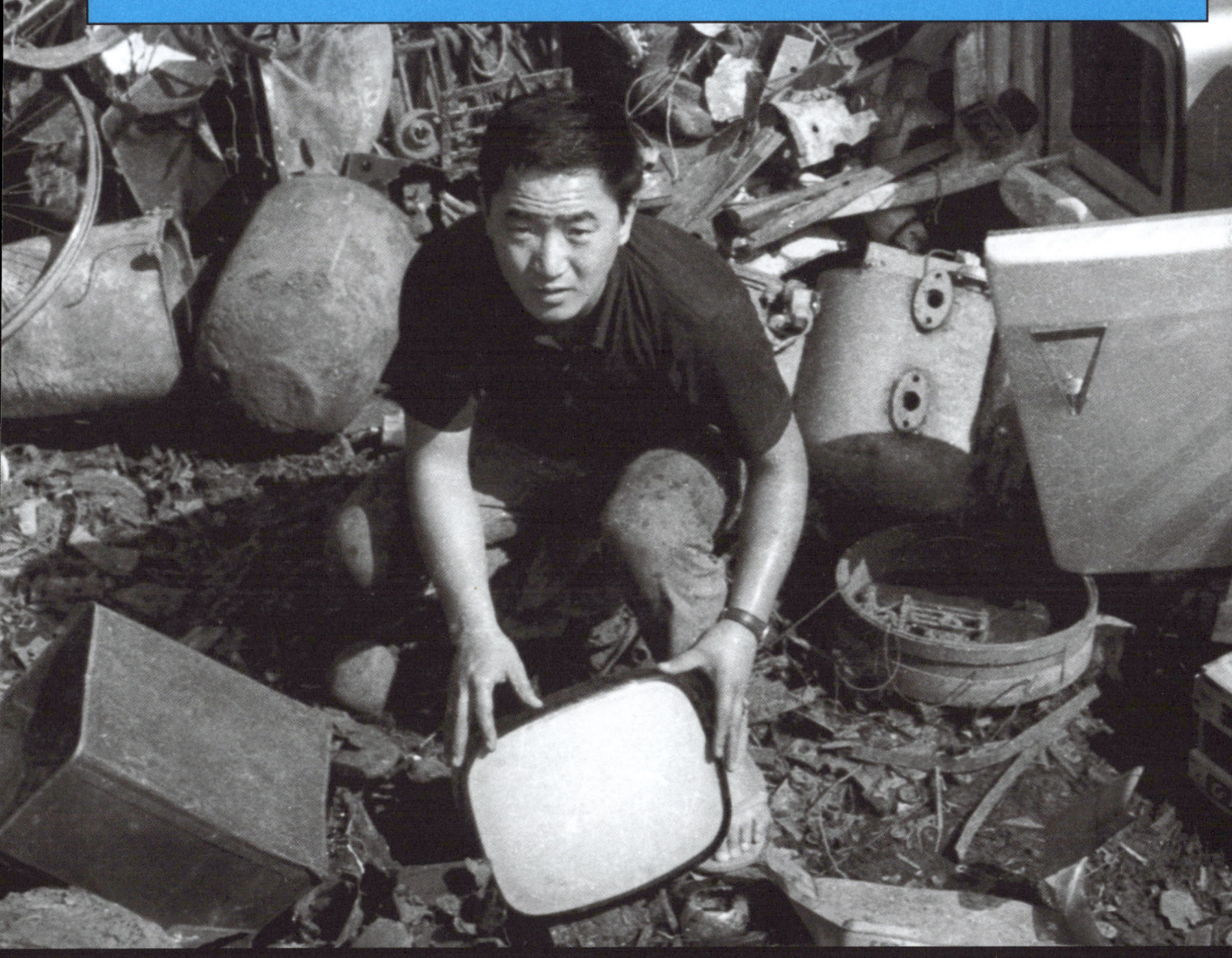

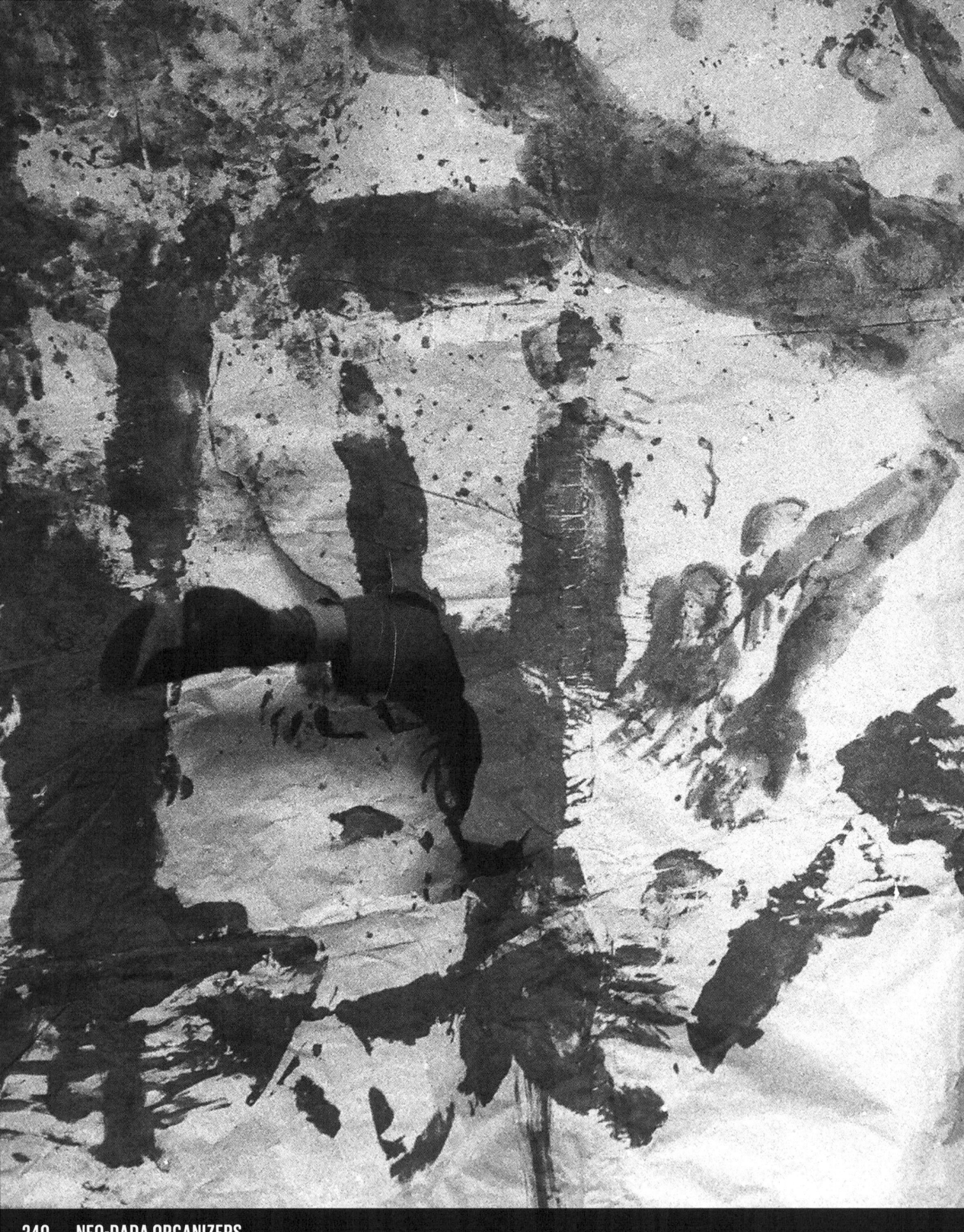

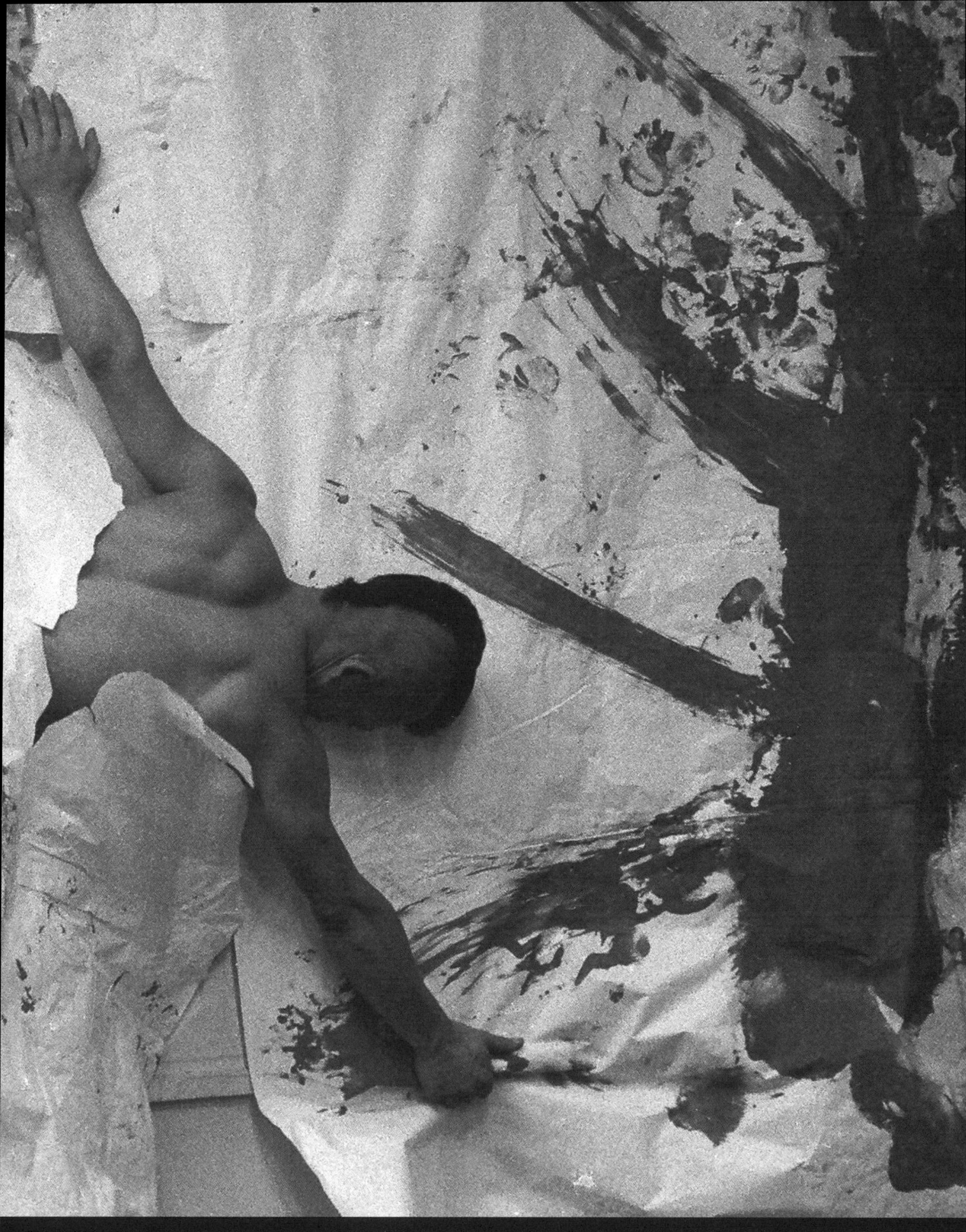

> THE NEO-DADA ORGANIZERS WERE A GROUP THAT WOULD METAPHORICALLY CRASH THEIR OWN BODIES INTO THINGS. THEY HAD NO MONEY, OR PLACE TO SHOW THEIR WORK, AND OF COURSE THEY COULDN'T SELL THEIR PAINTINGS, SO THEY ARE A VERY PARTICULAR ART GROUP, BORN OUT OF POVERTY.
>
> TANAAMI KEIICHI

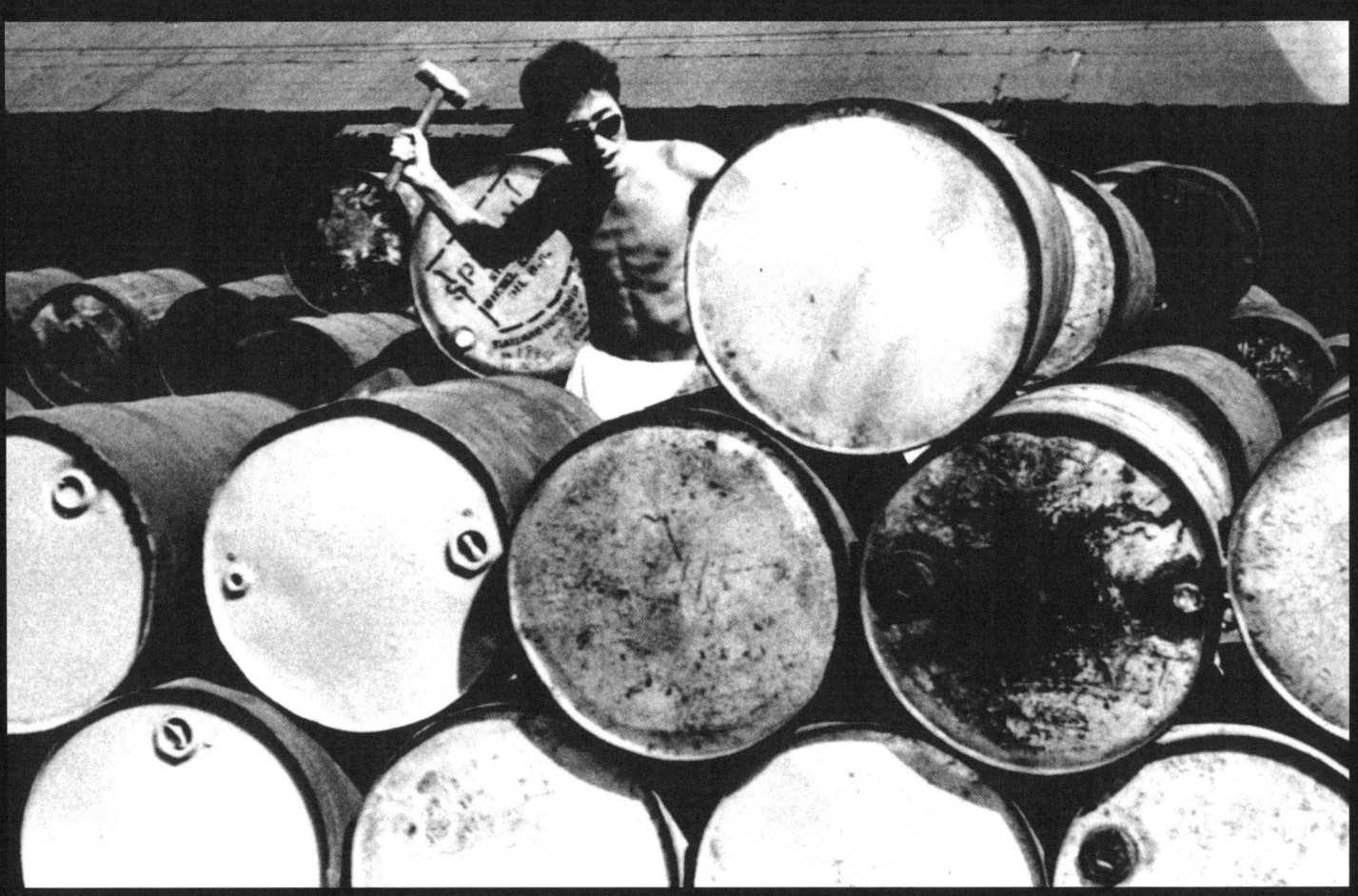

Above and opposite: Photographs by **Tanabe Santaro**, details and dates unknown.

Overleaf: **Hanaga Mitsutoshi**, *Shinohara Ushio*, date unknown, gelatin silver print.

> The thought that you could actually make an object of art that would have monetary value, and you could live on, was preposterous at that time. There was no support.
>
> So, of course, they were making stuff from junk and throwing it away after. They didn't have the means to store any of these rather large-scale, environmental works that they were staging at the Yomiuri Indépendant Exhibition, for example, and later in their own shows. It was just junk to them.
>
> ALEXANDRA MUNROE

NO MATTER HOW MUCH WE FANTASIZE ABOUT PROCREATION IN THE YEAR 1960, A SINGLE ATOMIC EXPLOSION WILL CASUALLY SOLVE EVERYTHING FOR US, SO PICASSO'S FIGHTING BULLS NO LONGER MOVE US.

AS WE ENTER THE BLOOD-SOAKED RING IN THIS 20TH CENTURY – A CENTURY WHICH HAS TRAMPLED ON SINCERE WORKS OF ART – THE ONLY WAY TO AVOID BEING BUTCHERED IS TO BECOME BUTCHERS OURSELVES.

SHINOHARA USHIO

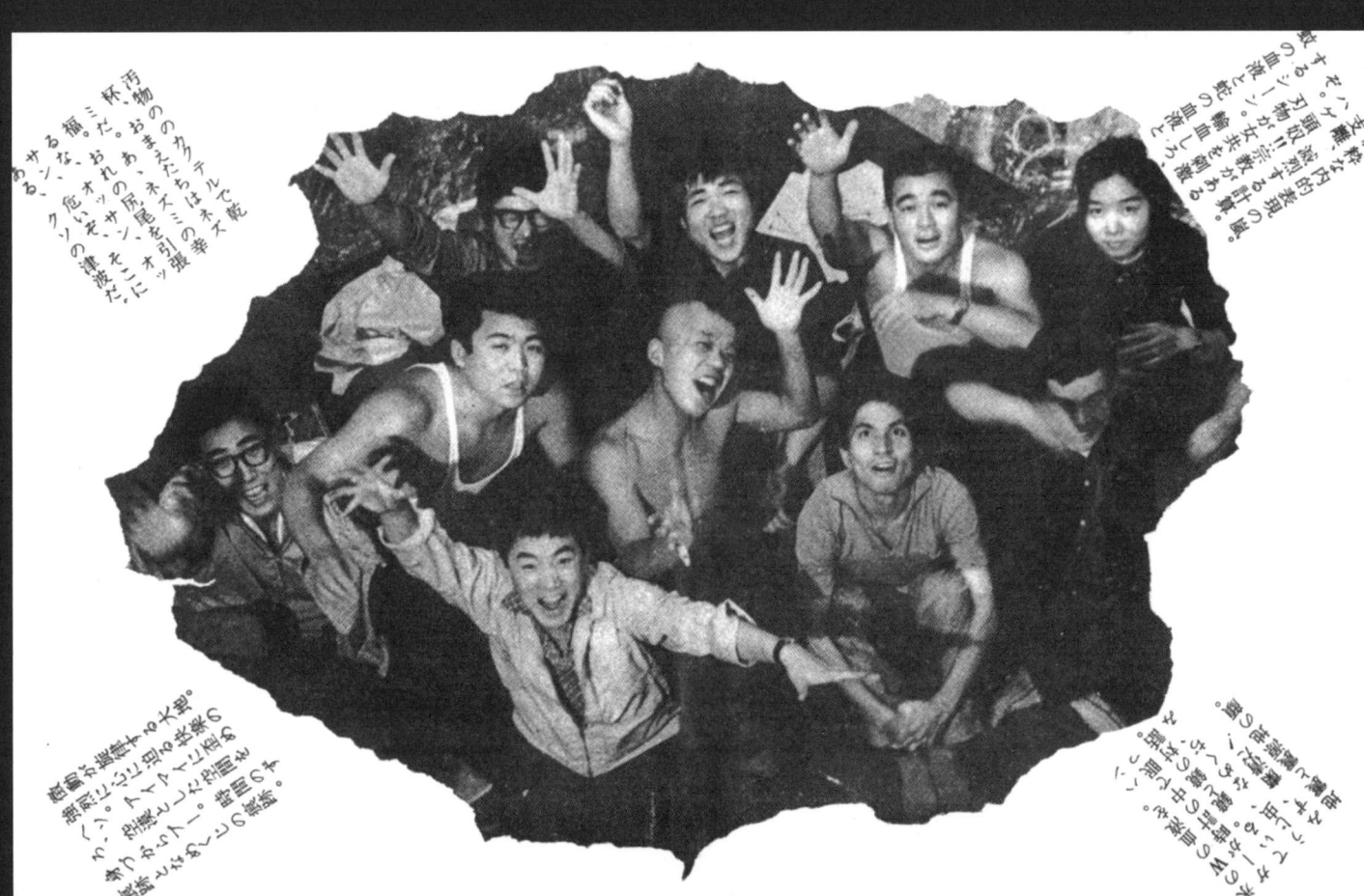

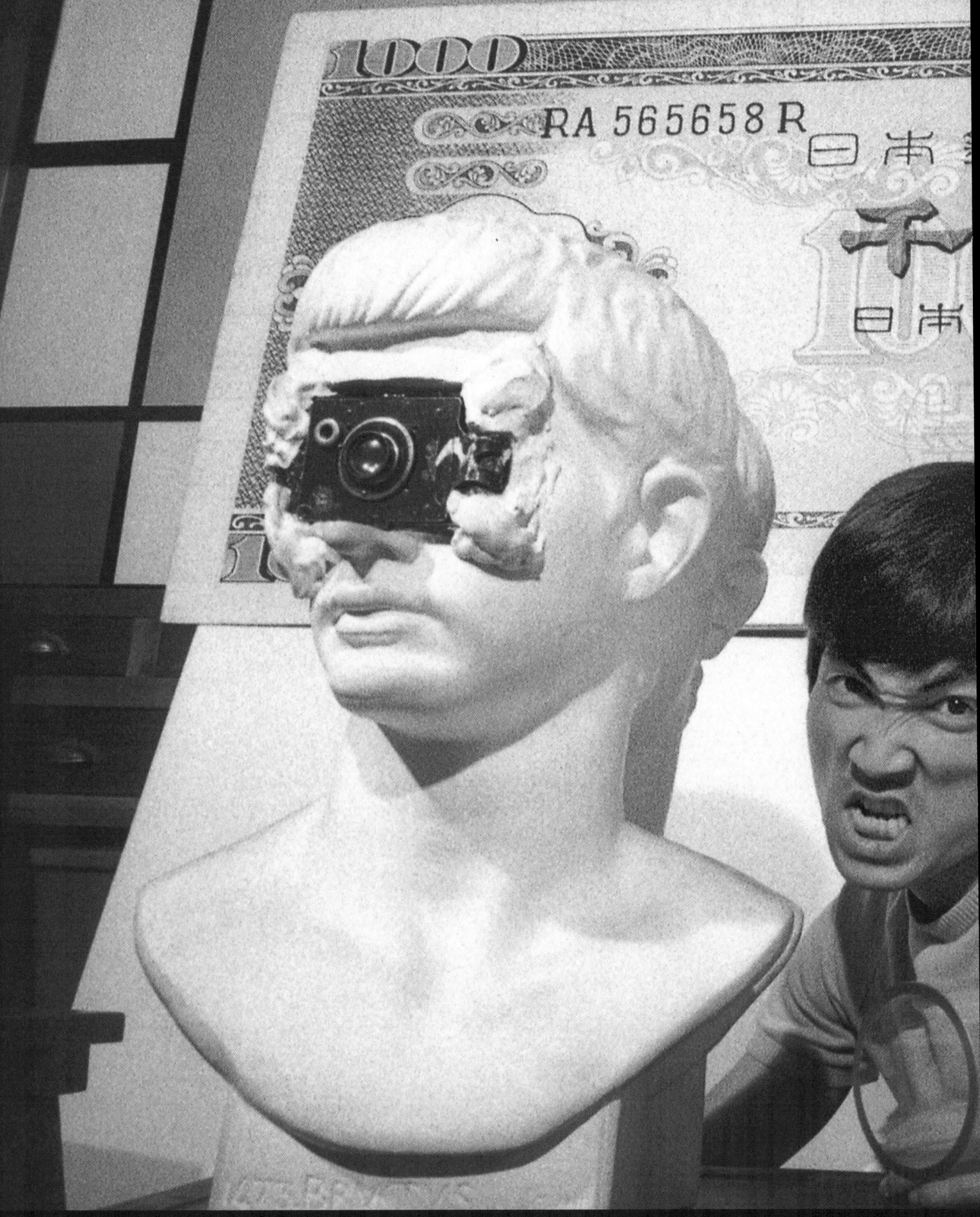

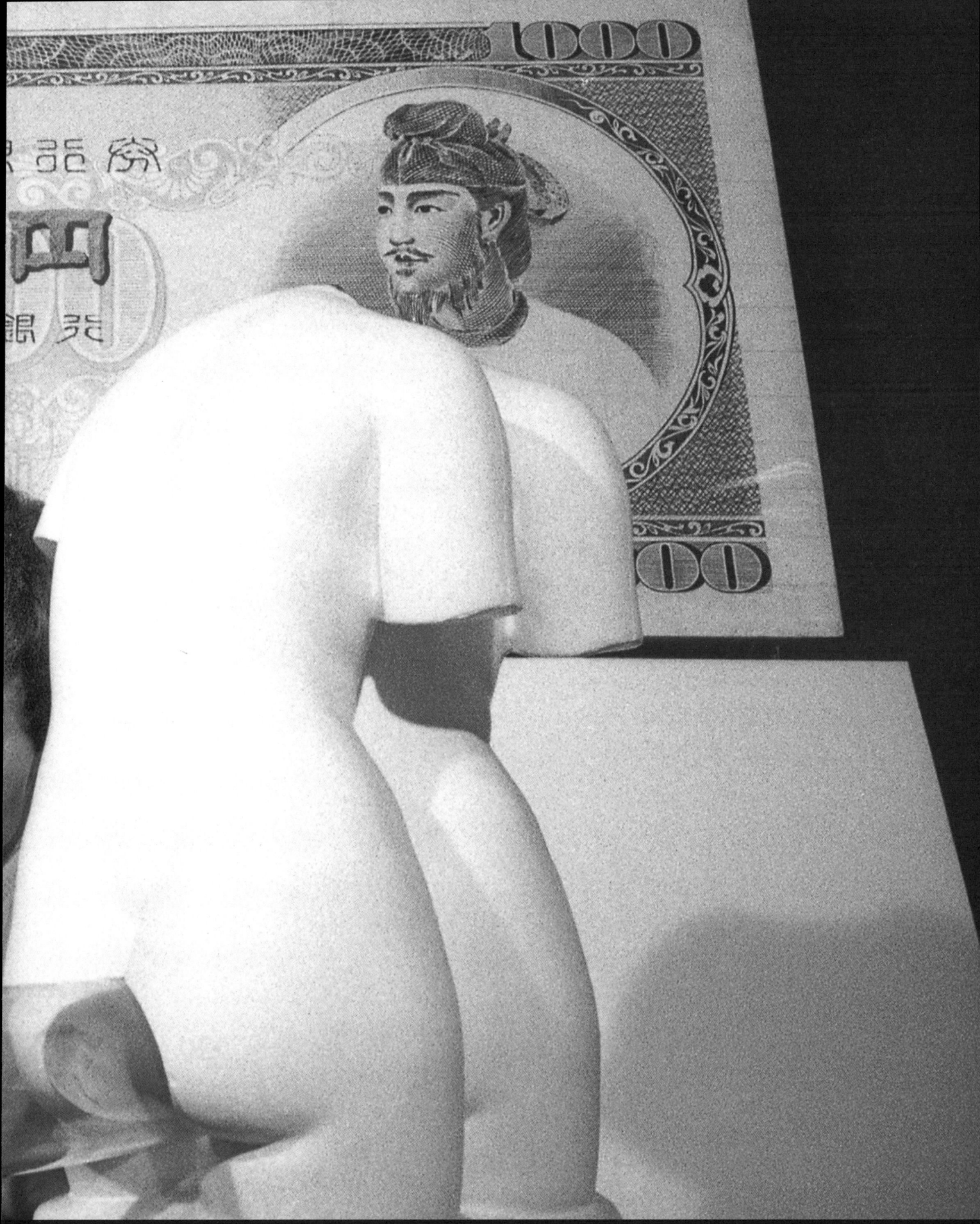

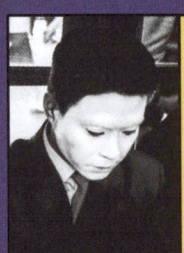

HI-RED CENTER
1963–64

・センター ハイレッド

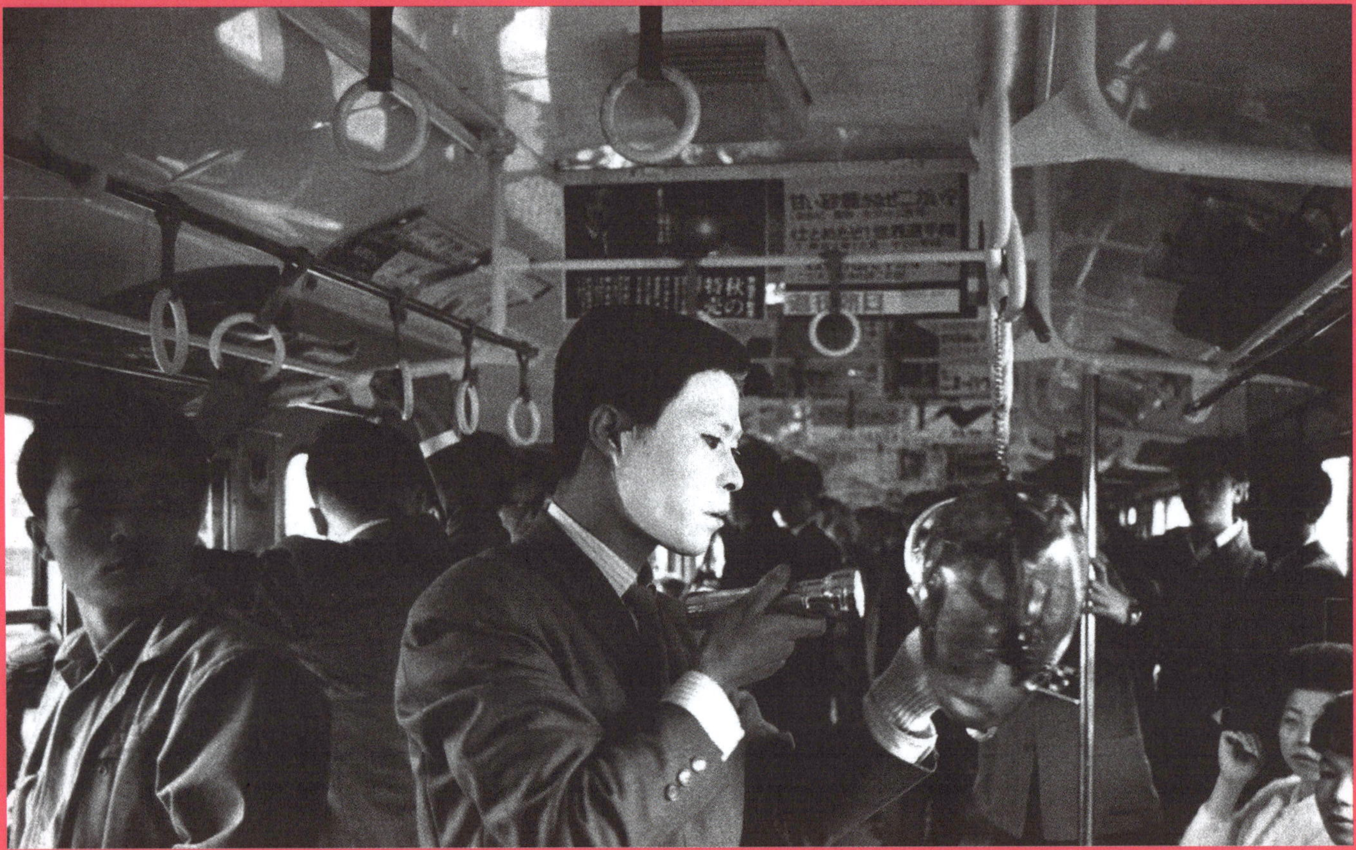

Above and opposite: Murai Tokuji and Hi-Red Center, *Nakanishi Natsuyuki with a Compact Object during the Yamanote Line Incident*, 1962, gelatin silver print.

Overleaf: Murai Tokuji and Hi-Red Center, *Nakanishi Natsuyuki with a Compact Object during the Yamanote Line Incident*, 1962, gelatin silver print.

Hi-Red Center's *chokusetsu kōdō* (direct action) philosophy was formulated in response to the heightened atmosphere of socio-political tension in Tokyo during the 1960s. The group's interventions, often held in public spaces across the city, testify to a powerfully anti-establishment, anti-commercial vision shared by founding members Takamatsu Jirō, Akasegawa Genpei and Nakanishi Natsuyuki.

LUCY FLEMING-BROWN

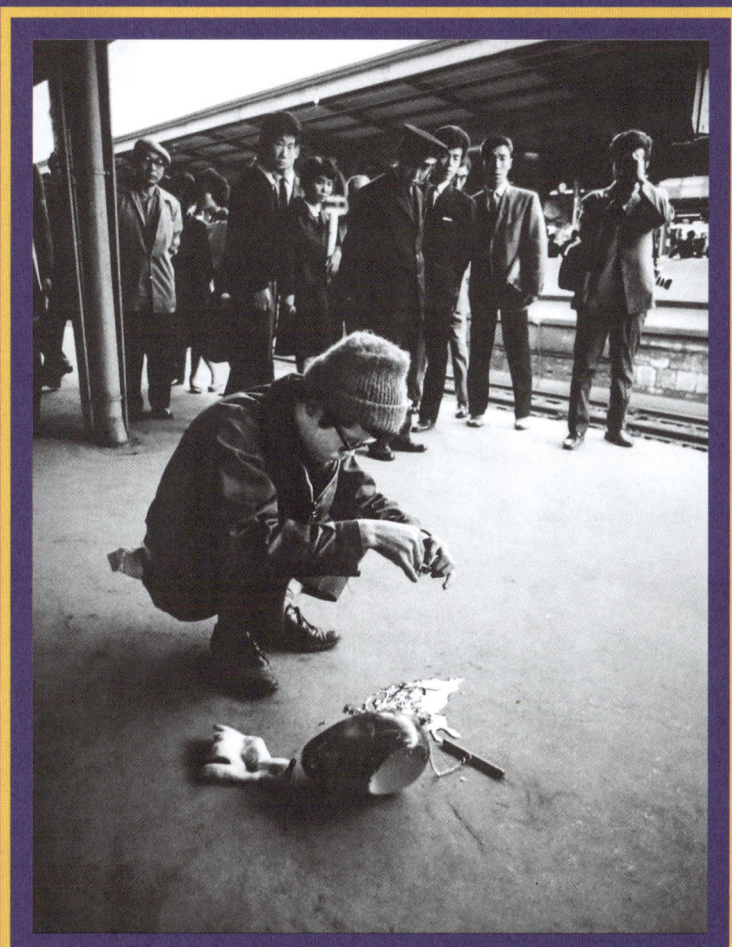
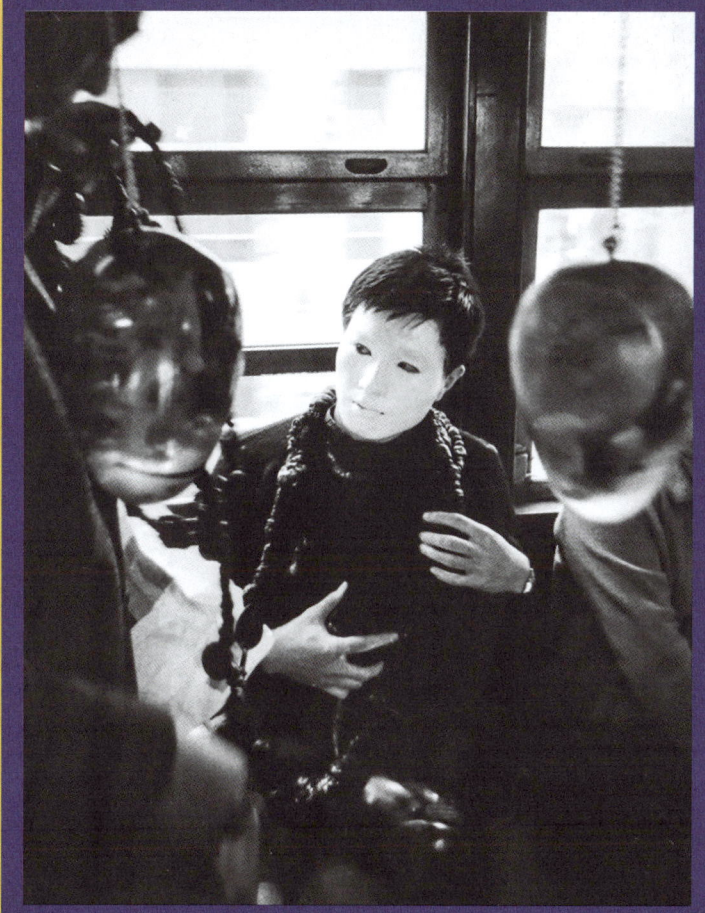

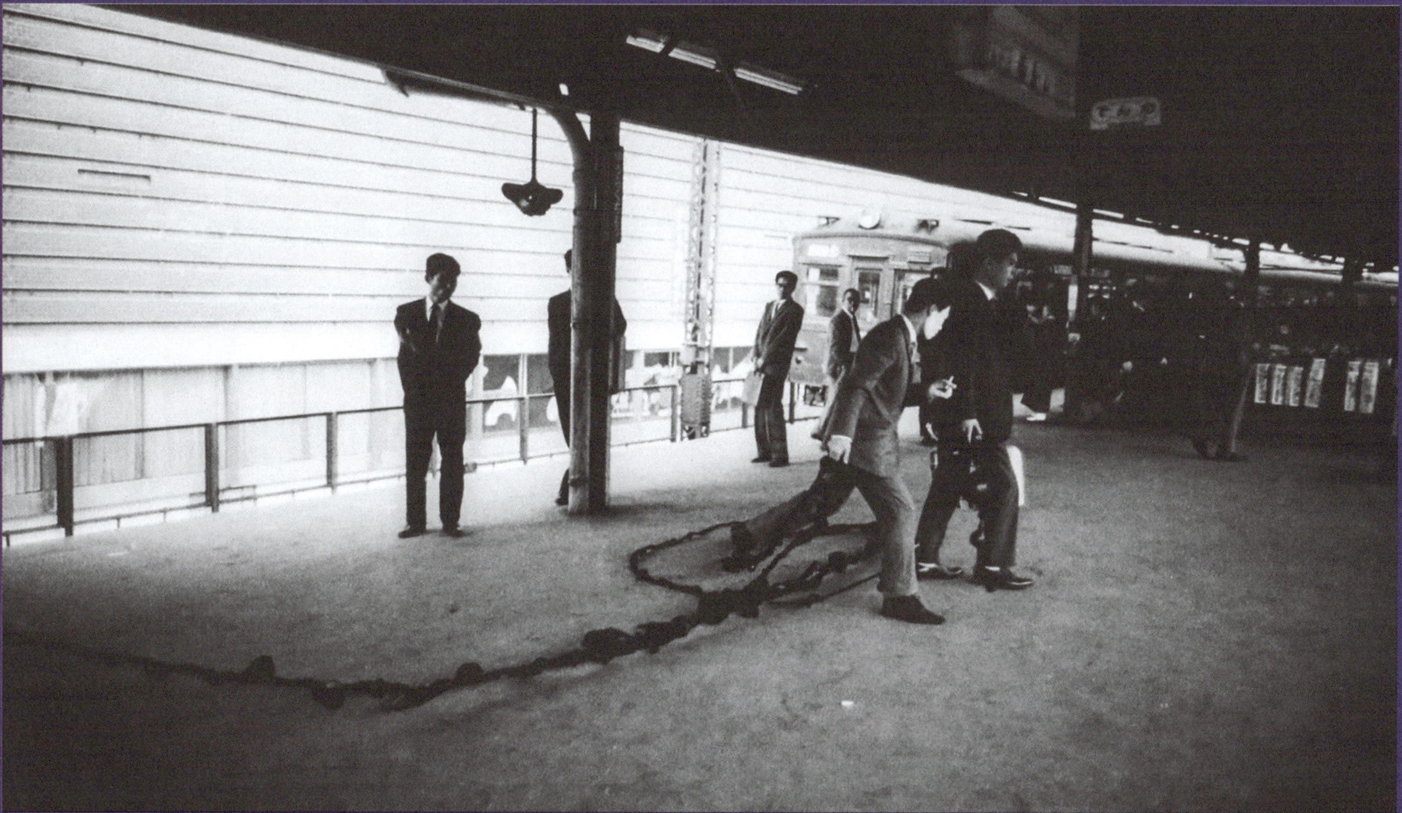

ハイレッド・センター

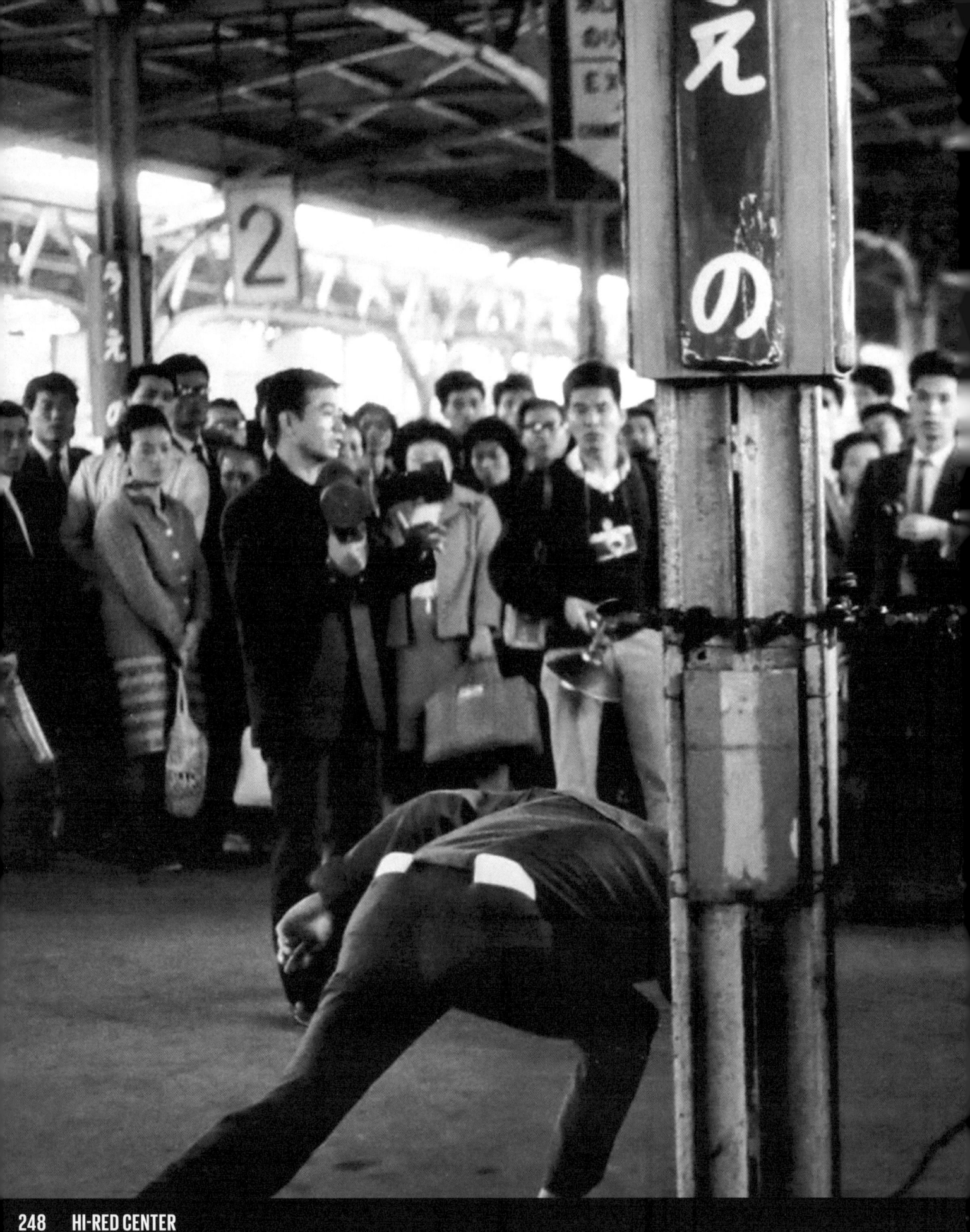

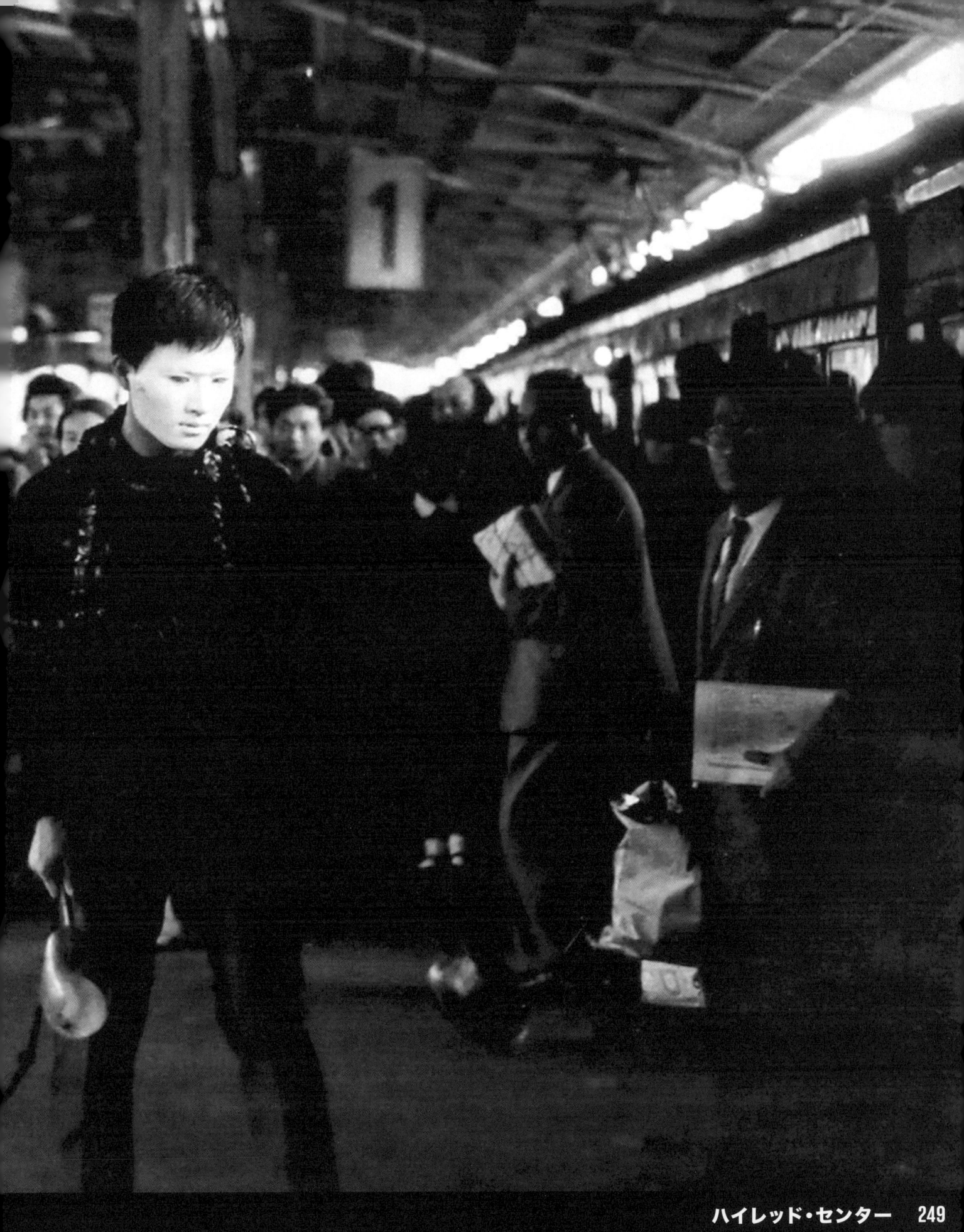

ハイレッド・センター 249

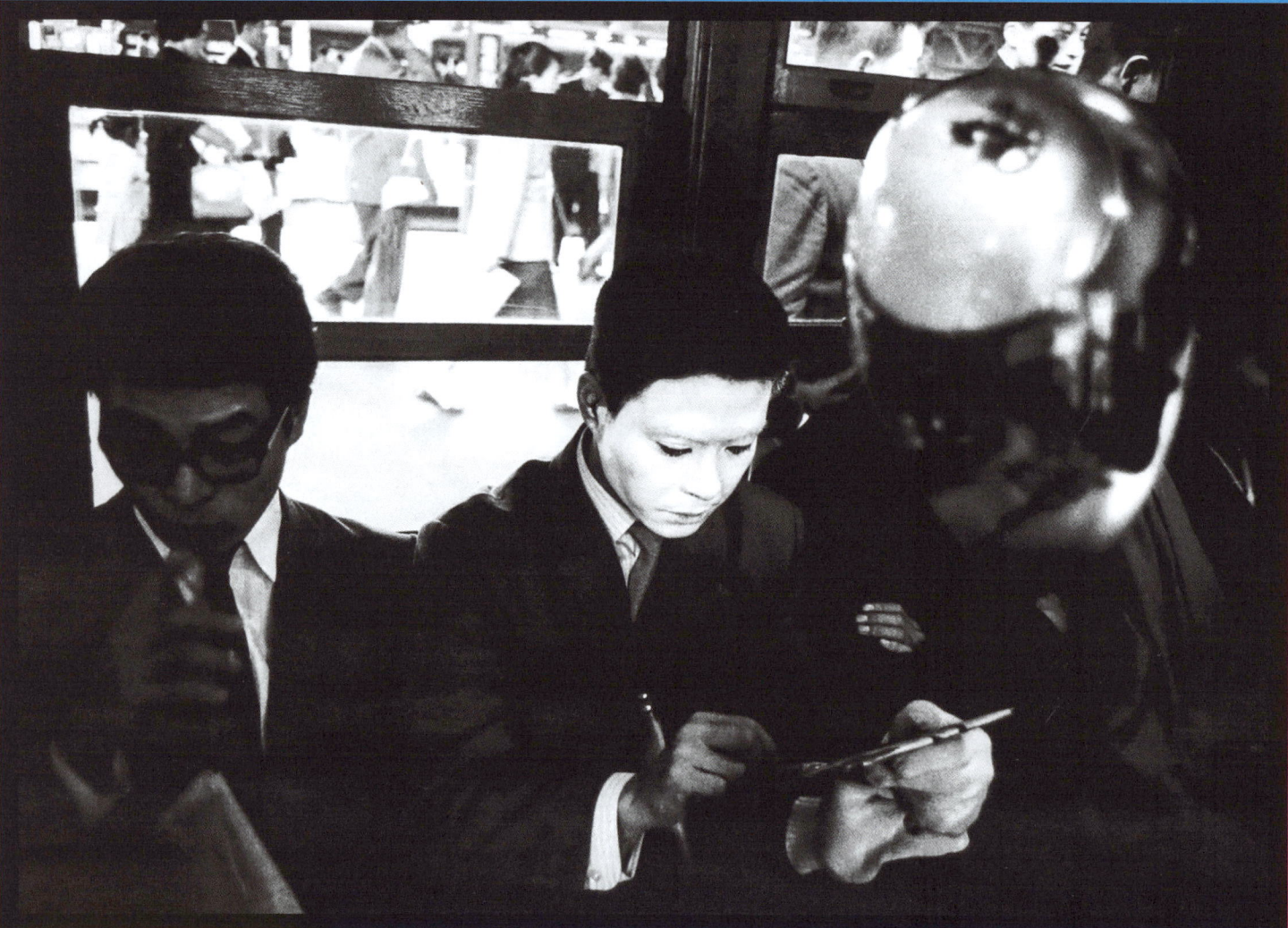

Above and opposite: **Murai Tokuji and Hi-Red Center**, *Nakanishi Natsuyuki with a Compact Object during the Yamanote Line Incident*, 1962, gelatin silver print.

Overleaf: **Murai Tokuji and Hi-Red Center**, *Nakanishi Natsuyuki with a Compact Object during the Yamanote Line Incident*, 1962, gelatin silver print.

pp. 254–55: **Murai Tokuji and Hi-Red Center**, *Documentation of Nakanishi Natsuyuki with a Compact Object during the Yamanote Line Incident*, 1962, gelatin silver print.

Hi-Red Center used satirical performances staged in public spaces to critique the mechanical banality and covert authoritarianism underlying Japan's mass capitalist society.

In the *Yamanote Line Incident* of October 1962, Nakanishi rode Tokyo's busiest train line carrying an egg-shaped 'compact object' composed of junk set in polyester, while Takamatsu dragged around a long black string attached to various everyday objects.

With his face painted white, Nakanishi crouched on a station platform and licked his compact polyester egg, then calmly boarded a train where he hung it from the hand straps and observed people's reactions with a flashlight. According to Akasegawa, Nakanishi and Takamatsu's purpose for using the train as a site for this event was to destroy the hierarchical status of art by bringing it into the space of daily activities.

ALEXANDRA MUNROE

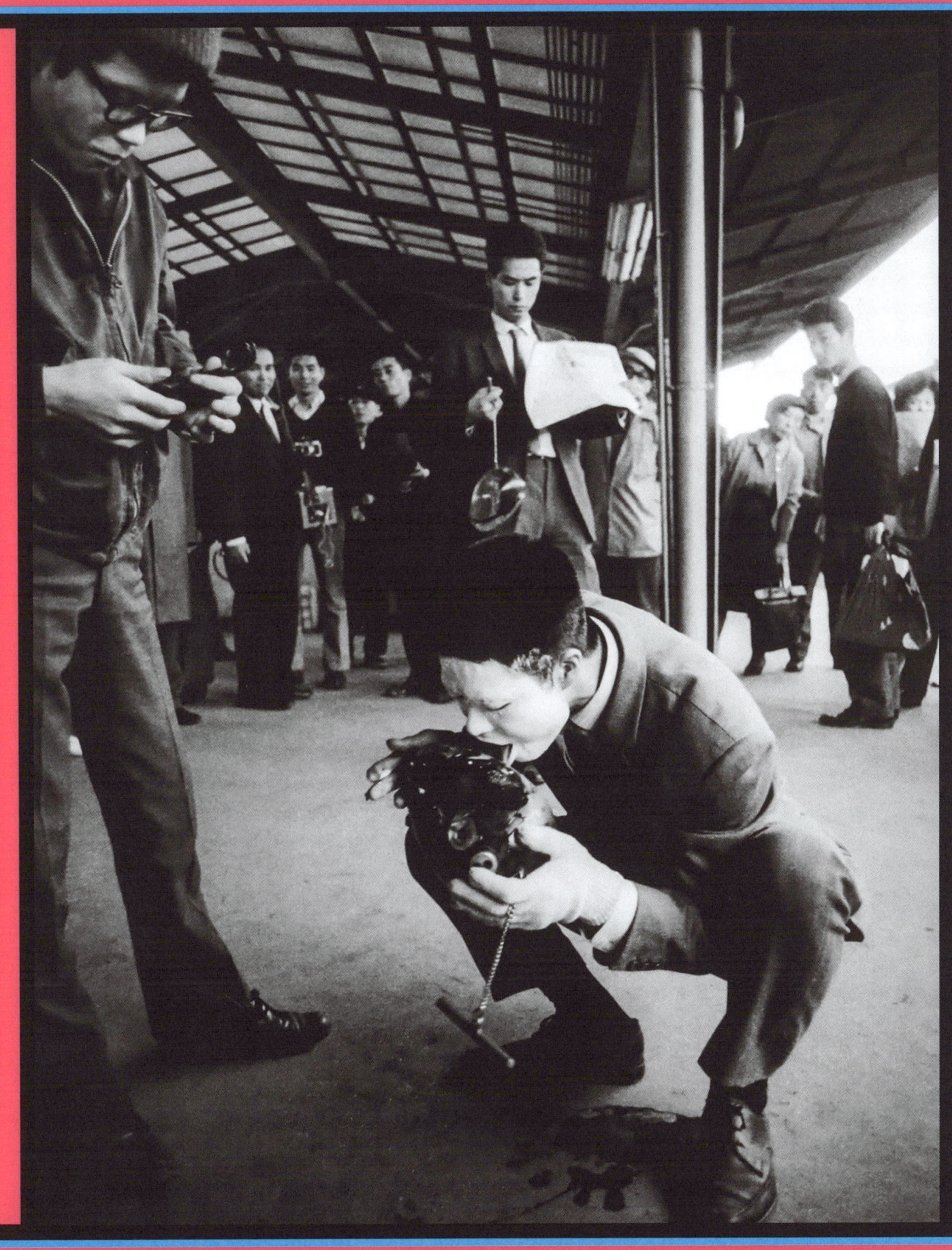

ハイレッド・センター

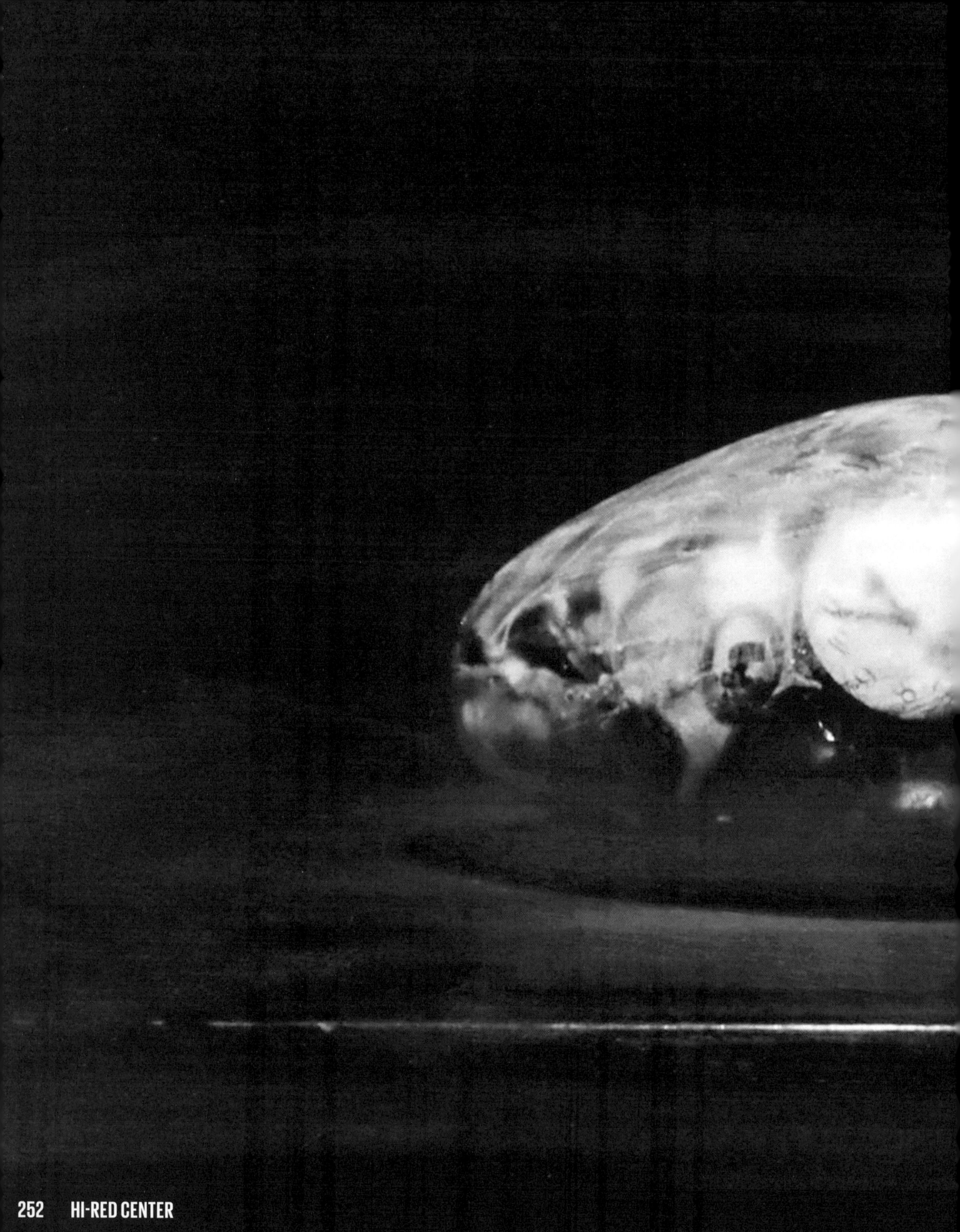

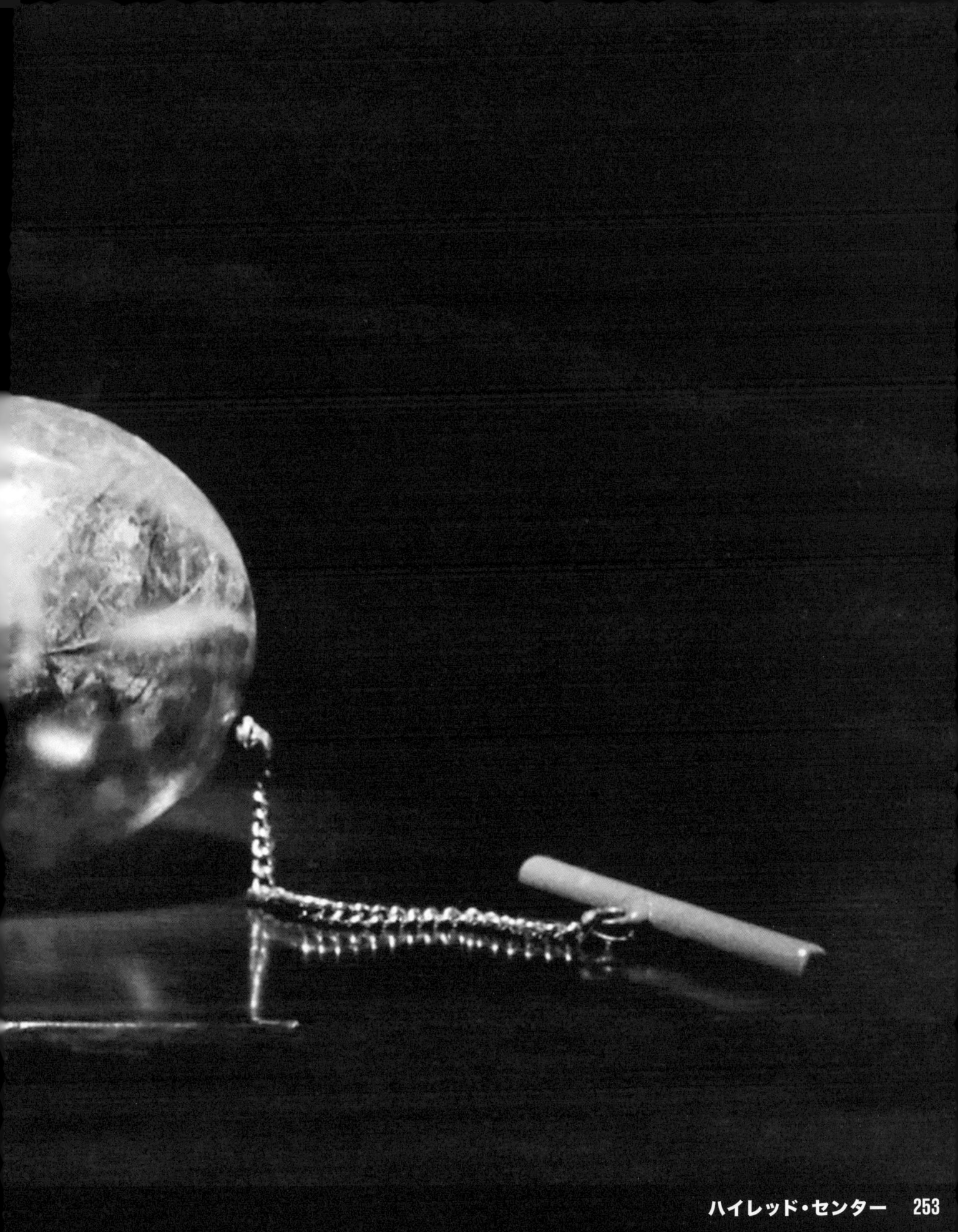

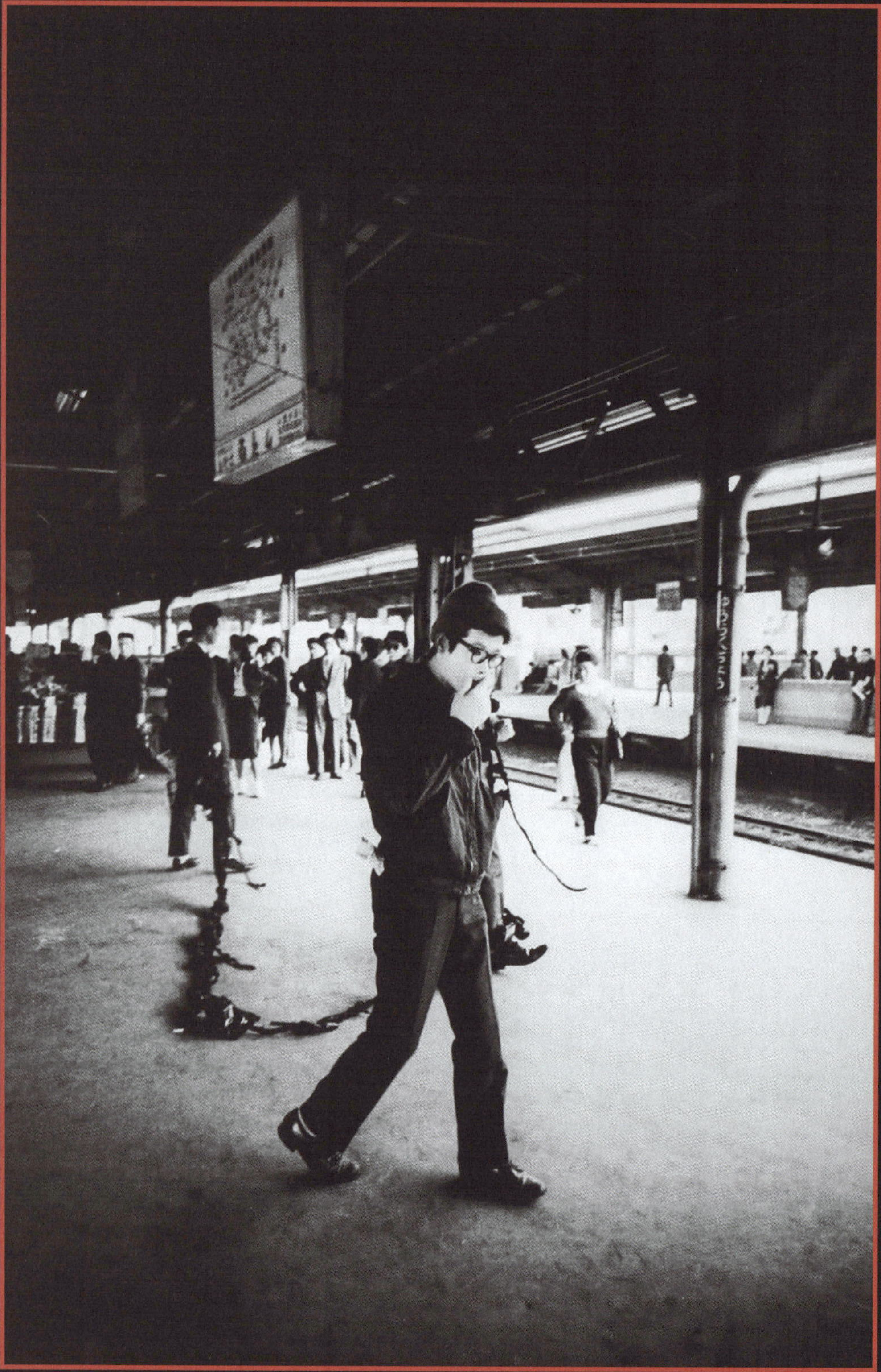

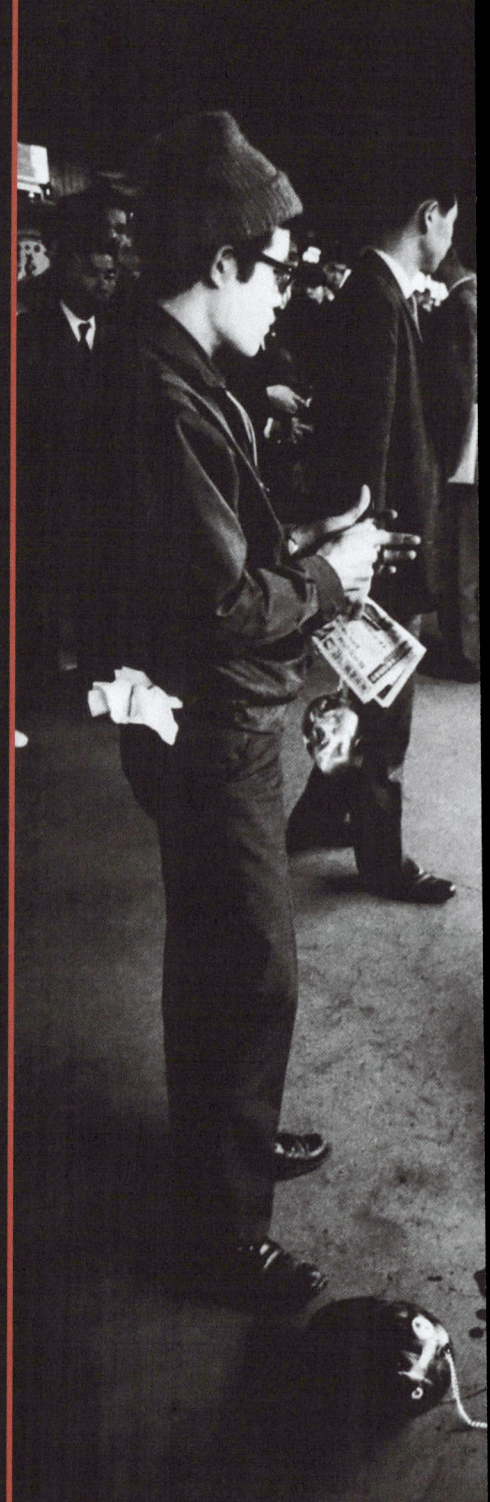

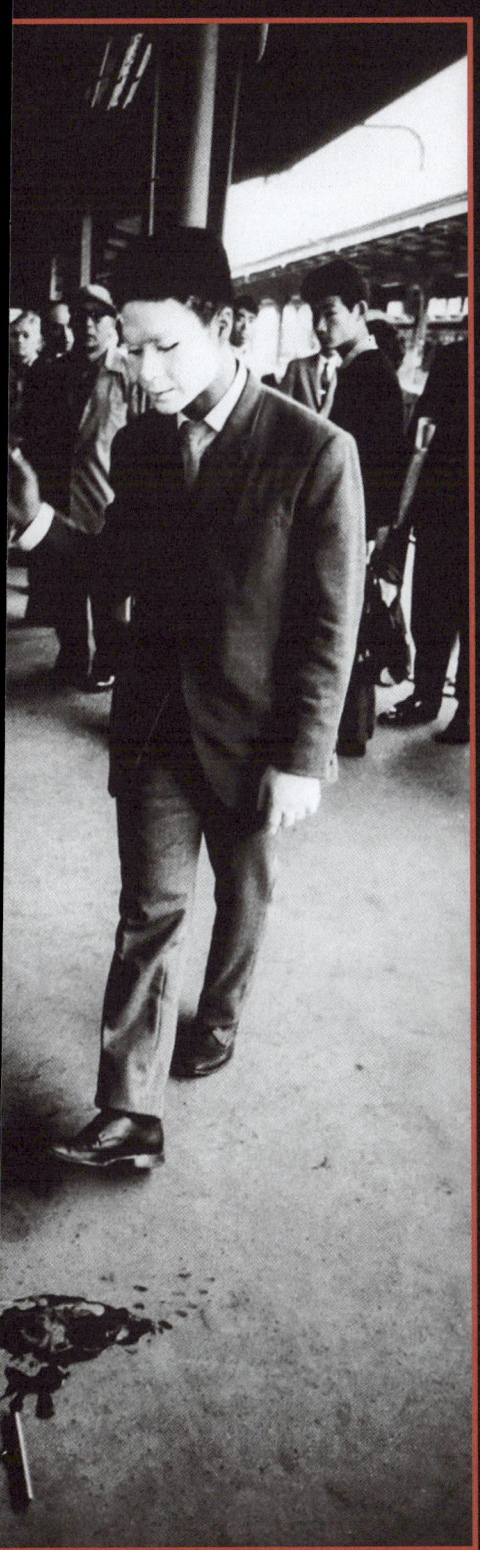

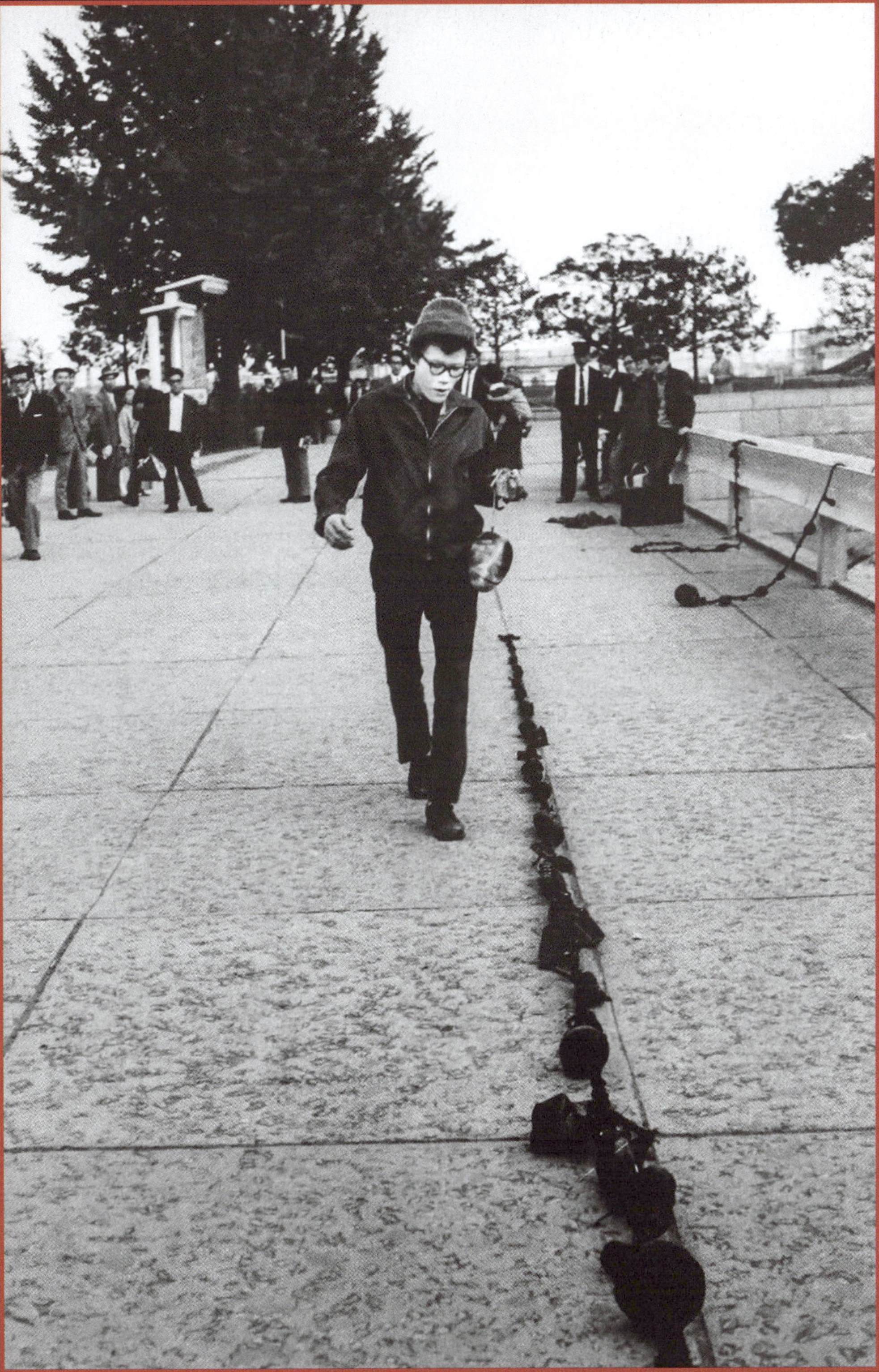

ハイレッド・センター

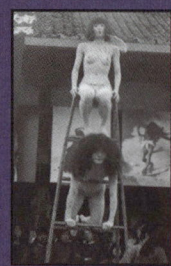

HANAGA MITSUTOSHI
1933–1999

羽永光利

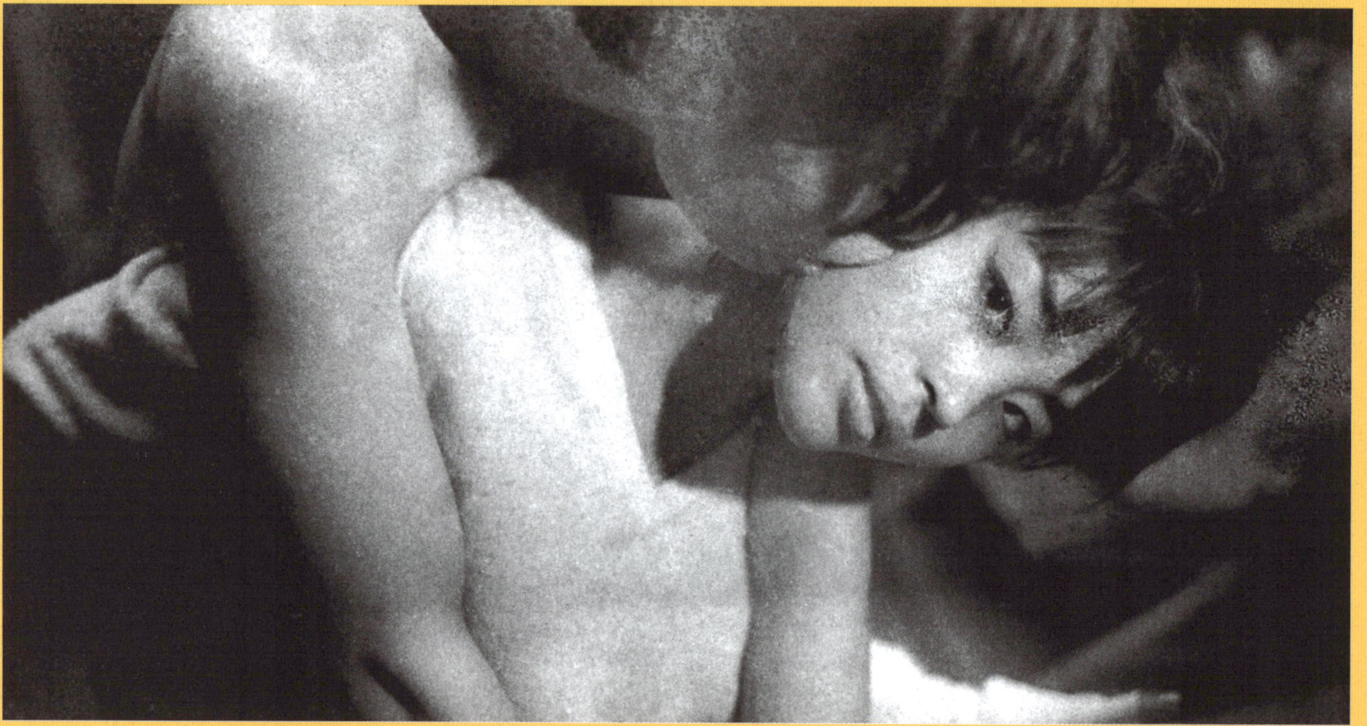

Hanaga Mitsutoshi, *Young People*, 1962, gelatin silver print.

Opposite (above left): **Hanaga Mitsutoshi**, *Kuni Chiya Dance Research Institute's Six Select Butoh Flowers at Honmokutei in Ueno, Tokyo, April 26, 1969*, gelatin silver print.

Opposite (above right): Photograph from **Hanaga Mitsutoshi**, *The Butoh* (1983).

Opposite (below): **Hanaga Mitsutoshi**, *Dream Tantric School, Revenge of Tantra: A Demonstration of Tantric Rituals at La Maison Franco-Japonaise in Ochanomizu, Tokyo, September 26, 1980*, gelatin silver print.

I was born in July 1970 as the eldest son of Hanaga Mitsutoshi. That year, he was extremely busy. In March, Expo '70 opened in Osaka. Around the same time, the Japan Red Army hijacked the Yodo plane. In June, there was the anti-ANPO struggle that attempted to stop the automatic extension of the Japan–US security treaty. Nationwide, cities suffered photochemical smog, a byproduct of Japan's high economic growth. In November, novelist Mishima Yukio killed himself by *seppuku*. Indeed, 1970 was a year full of newsworthy events.

HANAGA TARO, 'INTRODUCTION', *MITSUTOSHI HANAGA 1000* (2012)

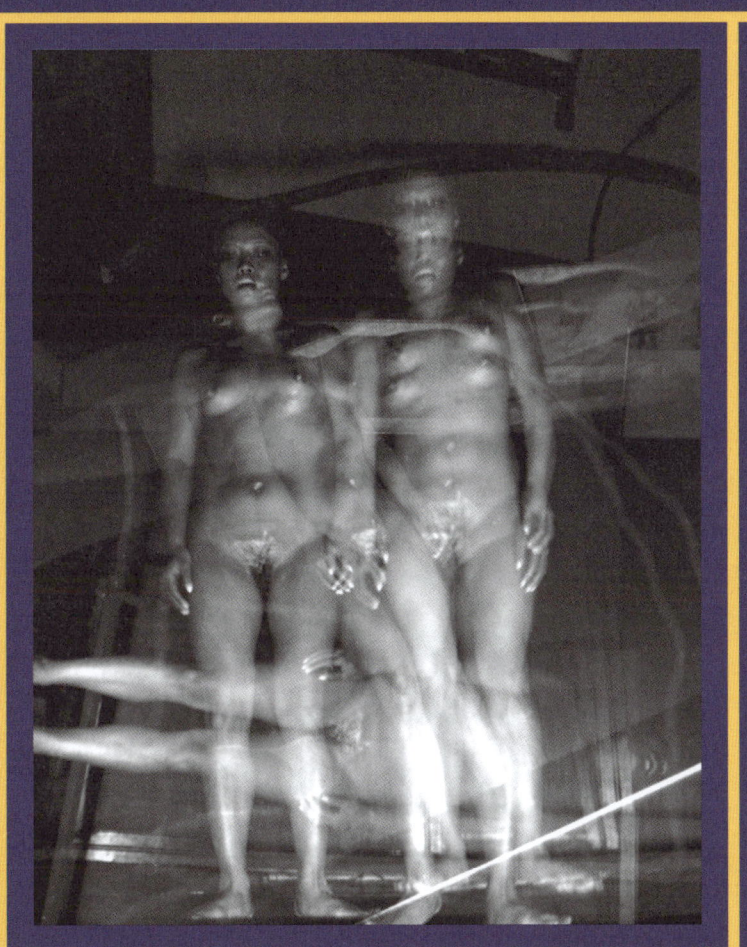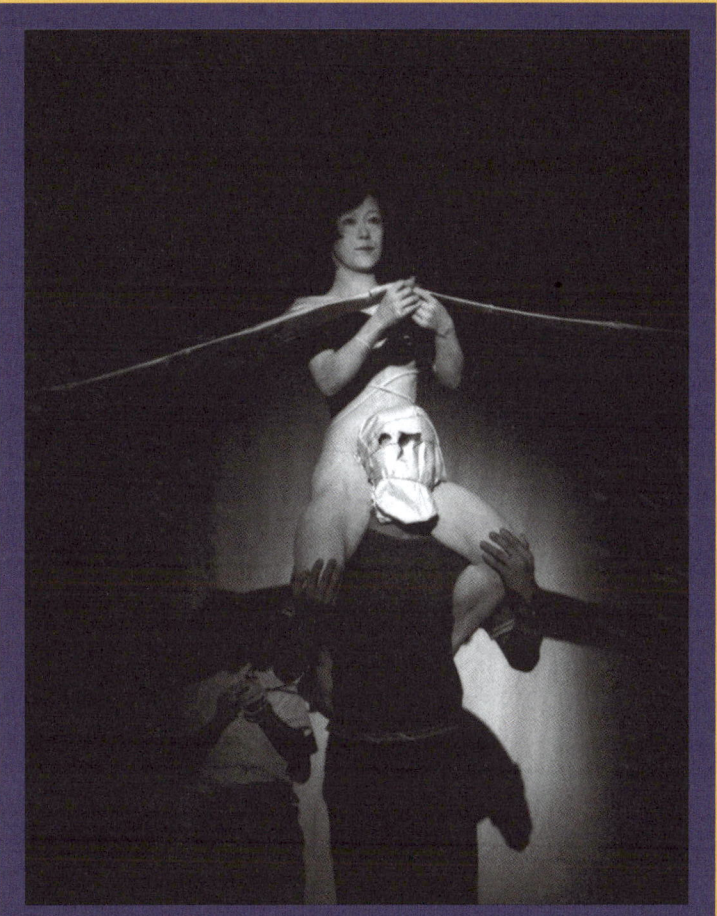

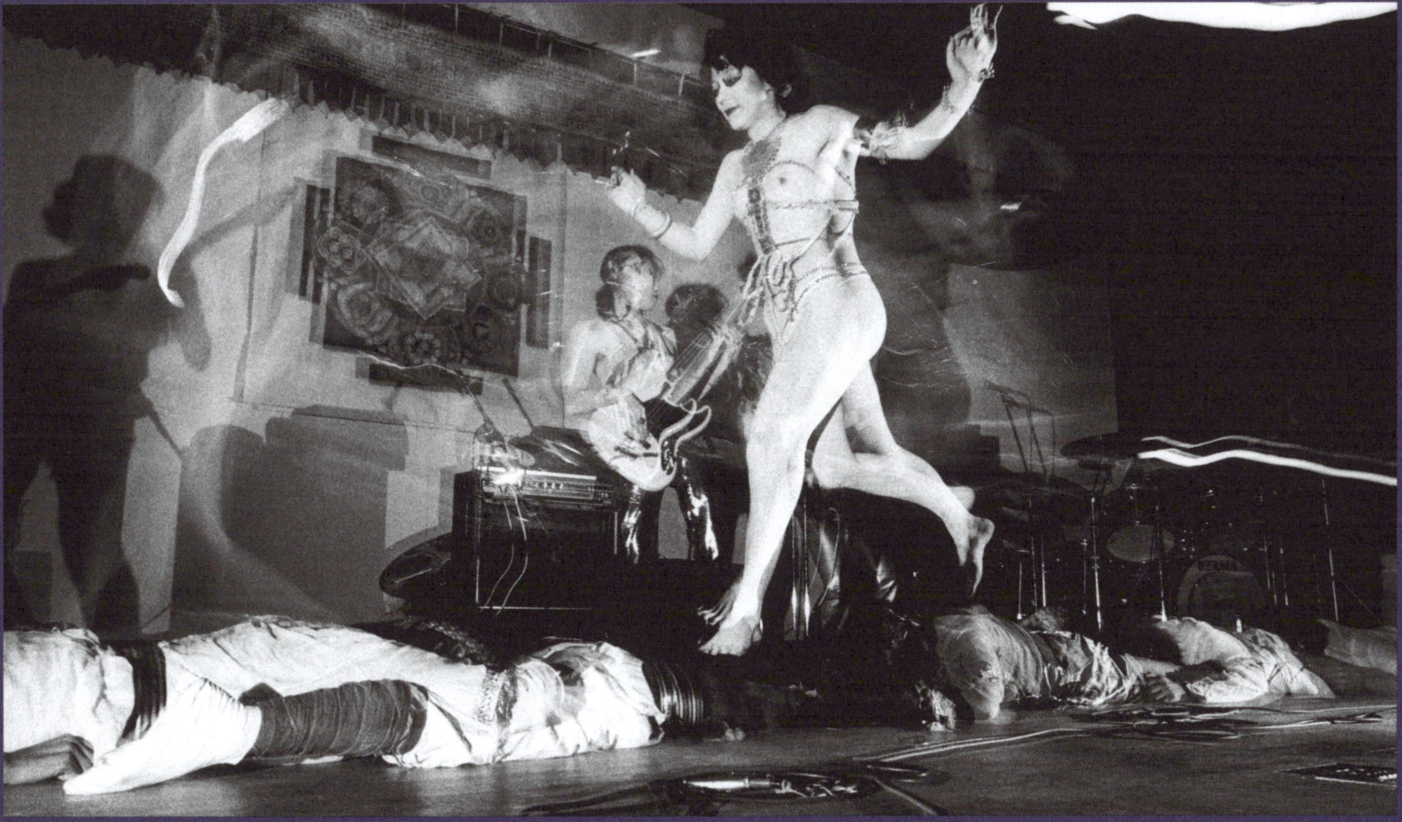

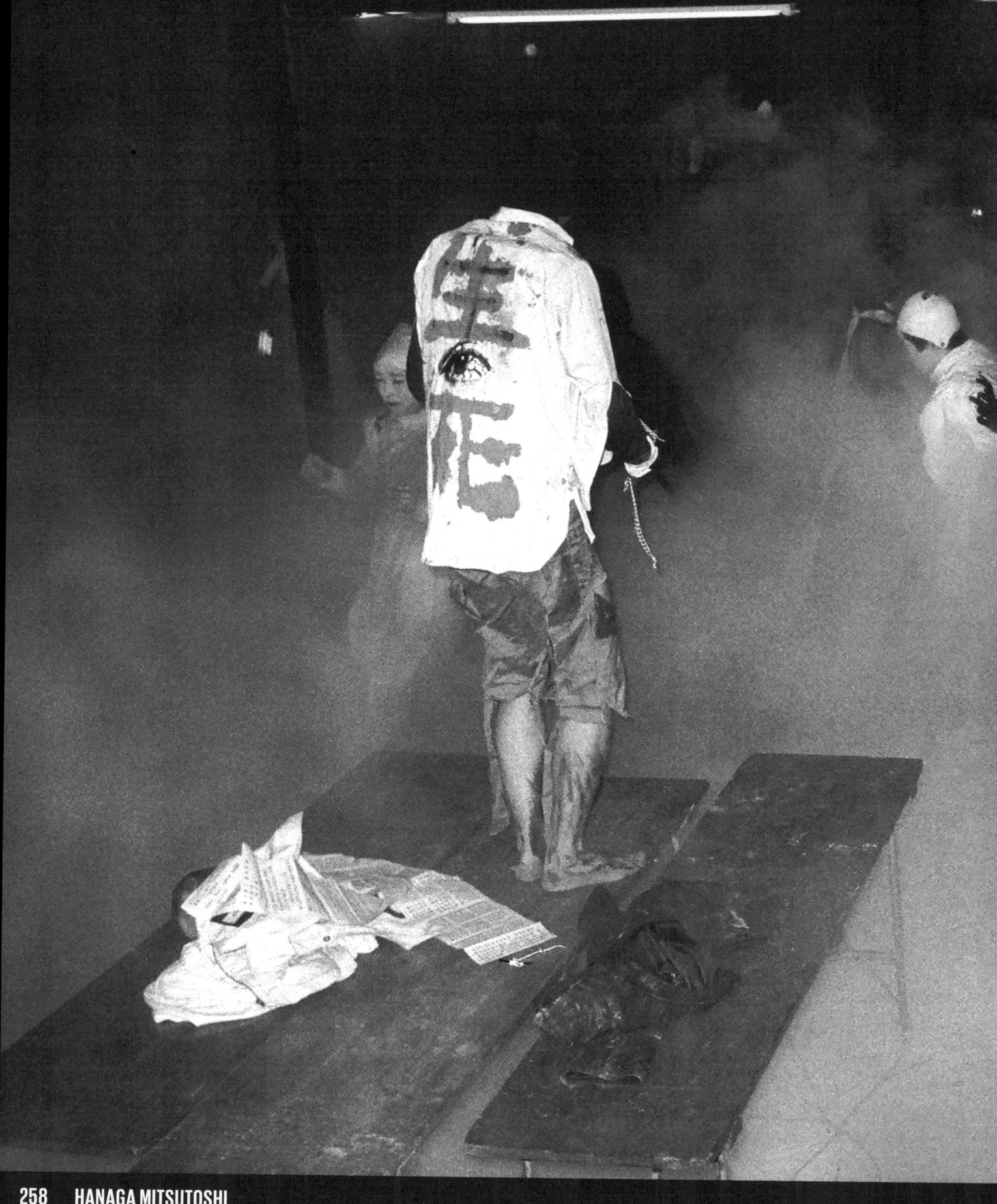

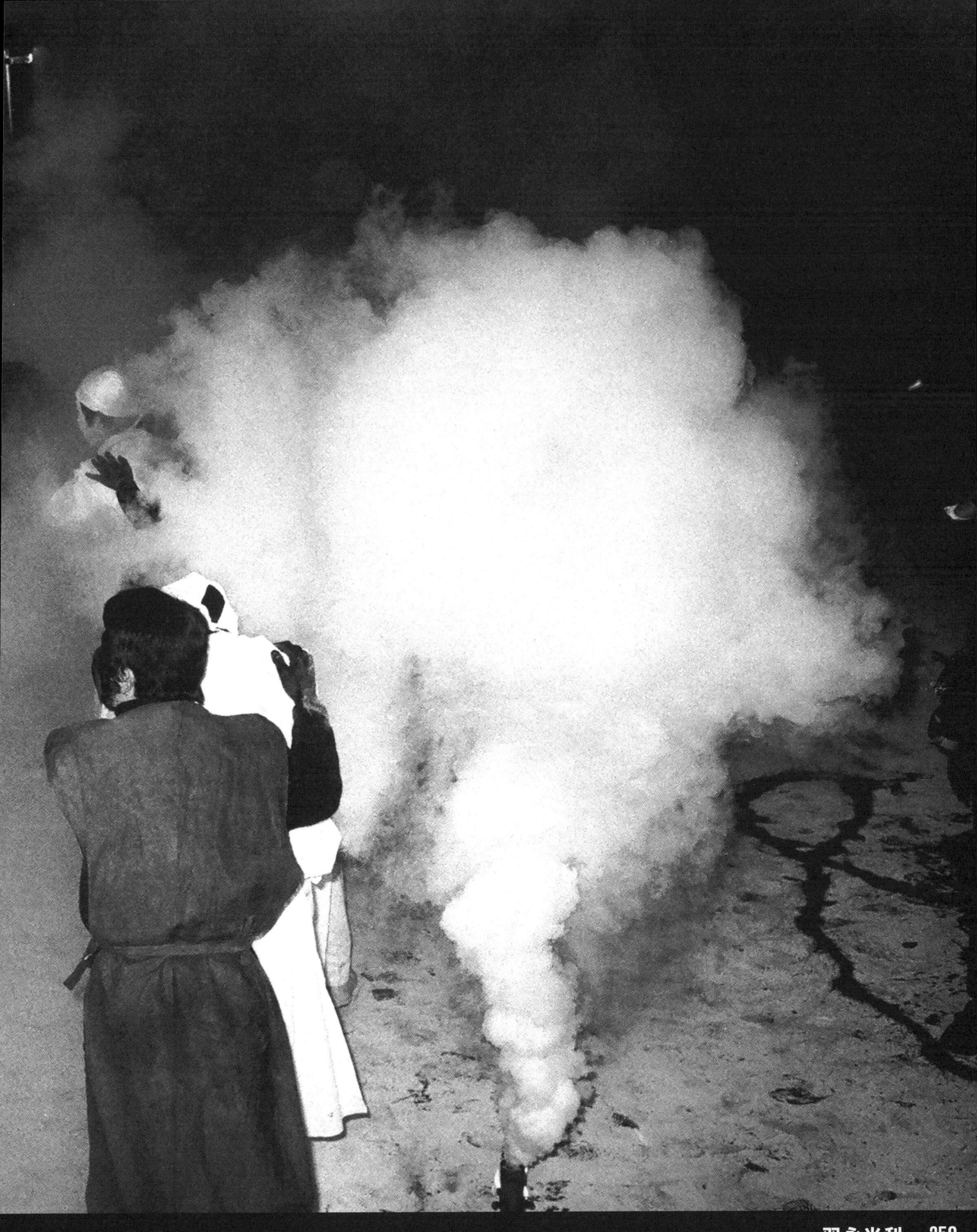

羽永光利 259

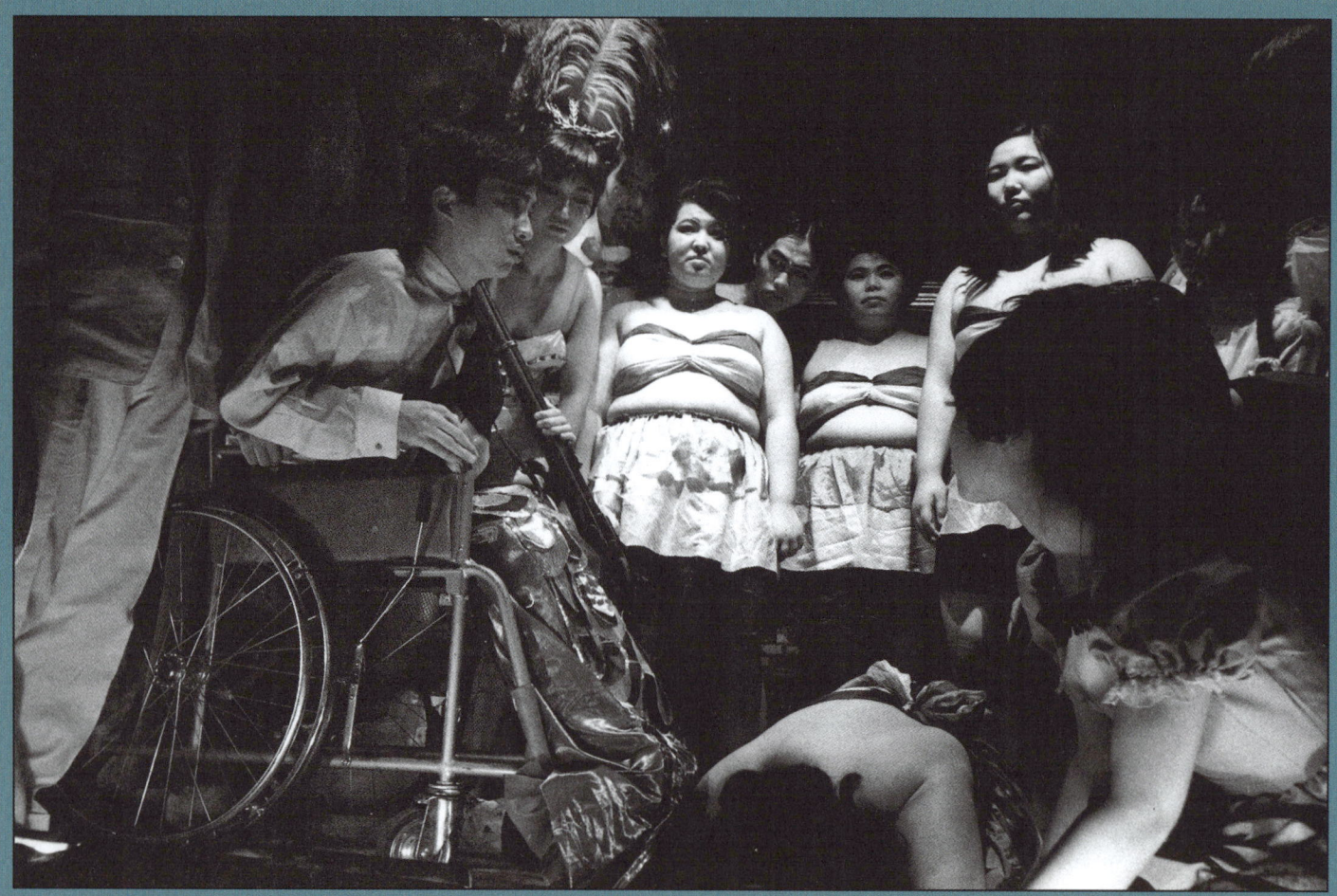

pp. 258–59: **Hanaga Mitsutoshi**, *All Kyushu 1st Outdoor Art Show – Gazing at One World at parking lot in front of Yahata Citizens Hall in Kitakyushu, February 25, 1969*, gelatin silver print.

Above: **Hanaga Mitsutoshi**, *Tenjō Sajiki, Crime of Ōyama Debuko at Suehirotei in Shinjuku, Tokyo, June 27, 1967*, gelatin silver print.

Opposite: **Hanaga Mitsutoshi**, *Hi Red Center's Great Panorama Exhibition at Naiqua Gallery in Tokyo, May 12, 1964*, gelatin silver print.

Overleaf: **Hanaga Mitsutoshi**, *Kobayashi Saga and Ashikawa Yoko in Hijikata Tatsumi Bangi Daitokan*, 1970, gelatin silver print.

Born in 1933, my father was part of the so-called 'war-experienced generation.' In the early 1950s, when Japan recovered from the wreckage of WWII, he succumbed to tuberculosis, with one lung removed.

Subsequently, he fell on a mountain and underwent surgery to remove a patella from his right knee, which crippled his right leg. In his early twenties, he thus became physically handicapped.

During a recession following the Korean War, the kinds of work the handicapped could find were limited – repairing shoes, repairing watches, lining men's suits – which were all menial works in the 'shadows.'

Since he could not get a good position through public job placement offices, he chose to be a freelance photographer, taking advantage of his eyes and hands as good as those of the non-handicapped.

His disadvantages led to his anti-authority spirit, prompting him to persistently direct his camera to the shadows of society.

He became particularly interested in the 'underground' world that society tended to view with prejudice – which encompassed the student movement, the environmental problems, avant-garde art, underground theater, and butoh. He was sympathetic to legitimate expressions that were condemned as 'anti-establishment.'

HANAGA TARO, 'INTRODUCTION', *MITSUTOSHI HANAGA 1000* (2012)

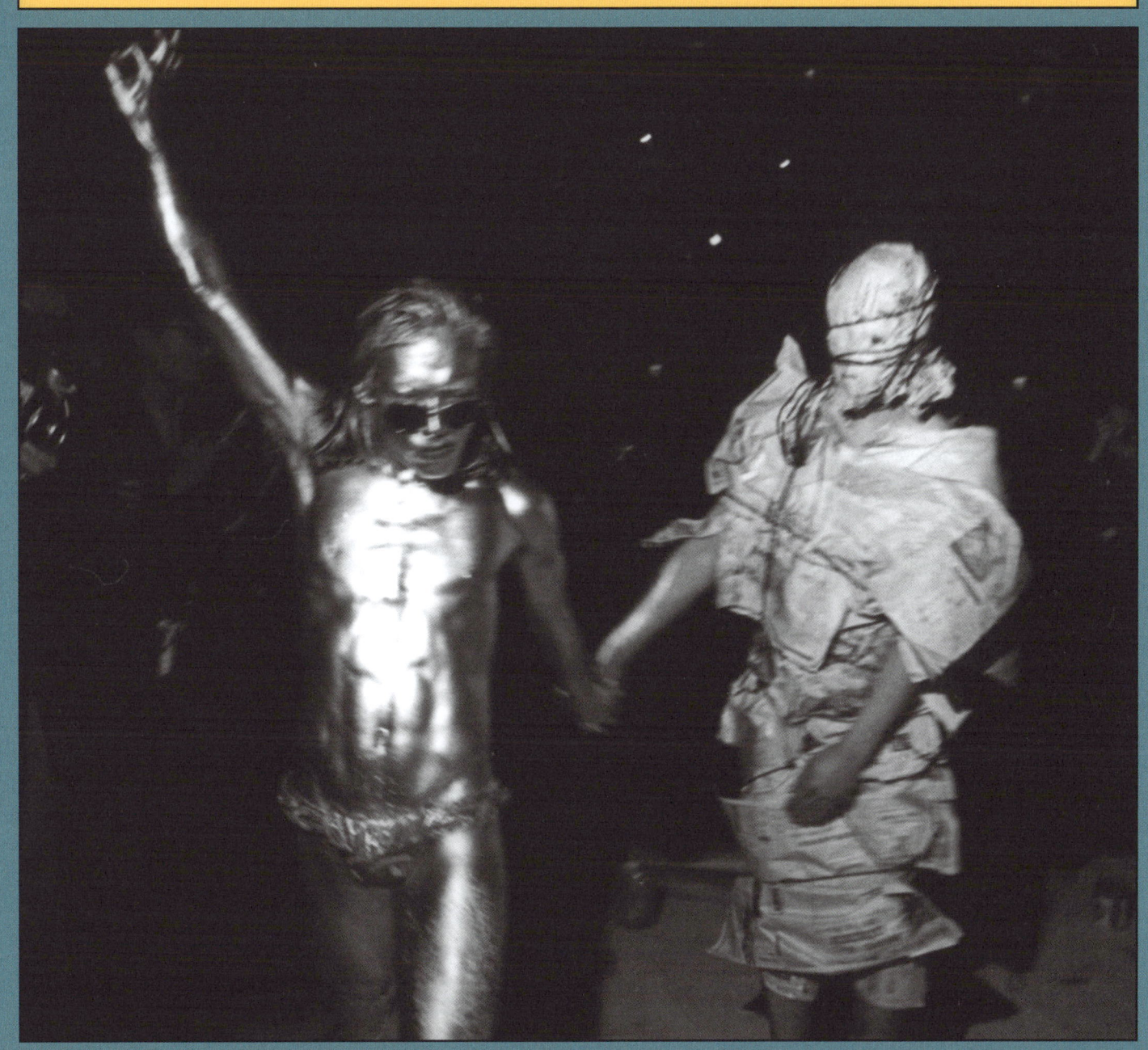

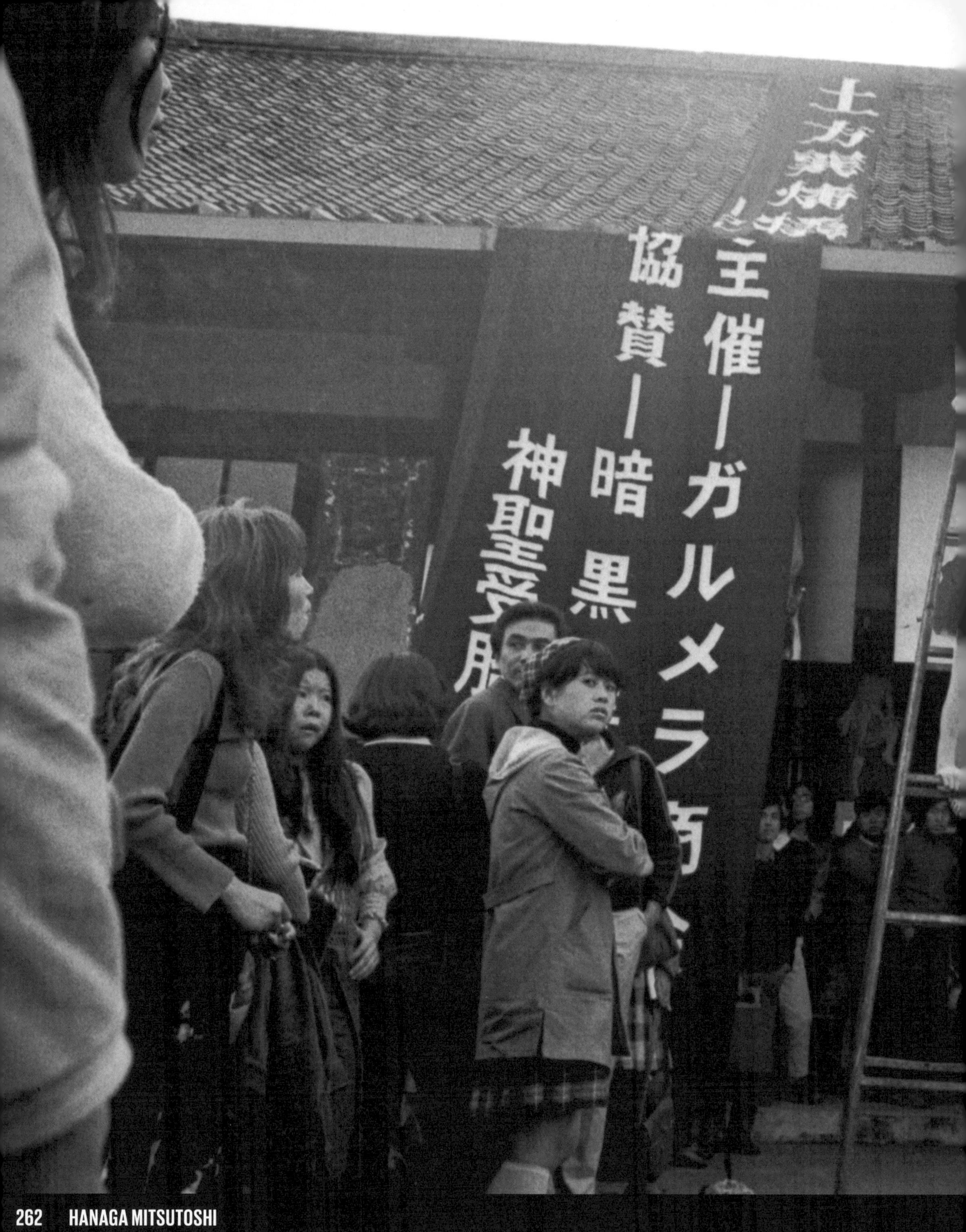

主催――ガルメラ商
協賛――暗黒
神聖受胎

土方巽好

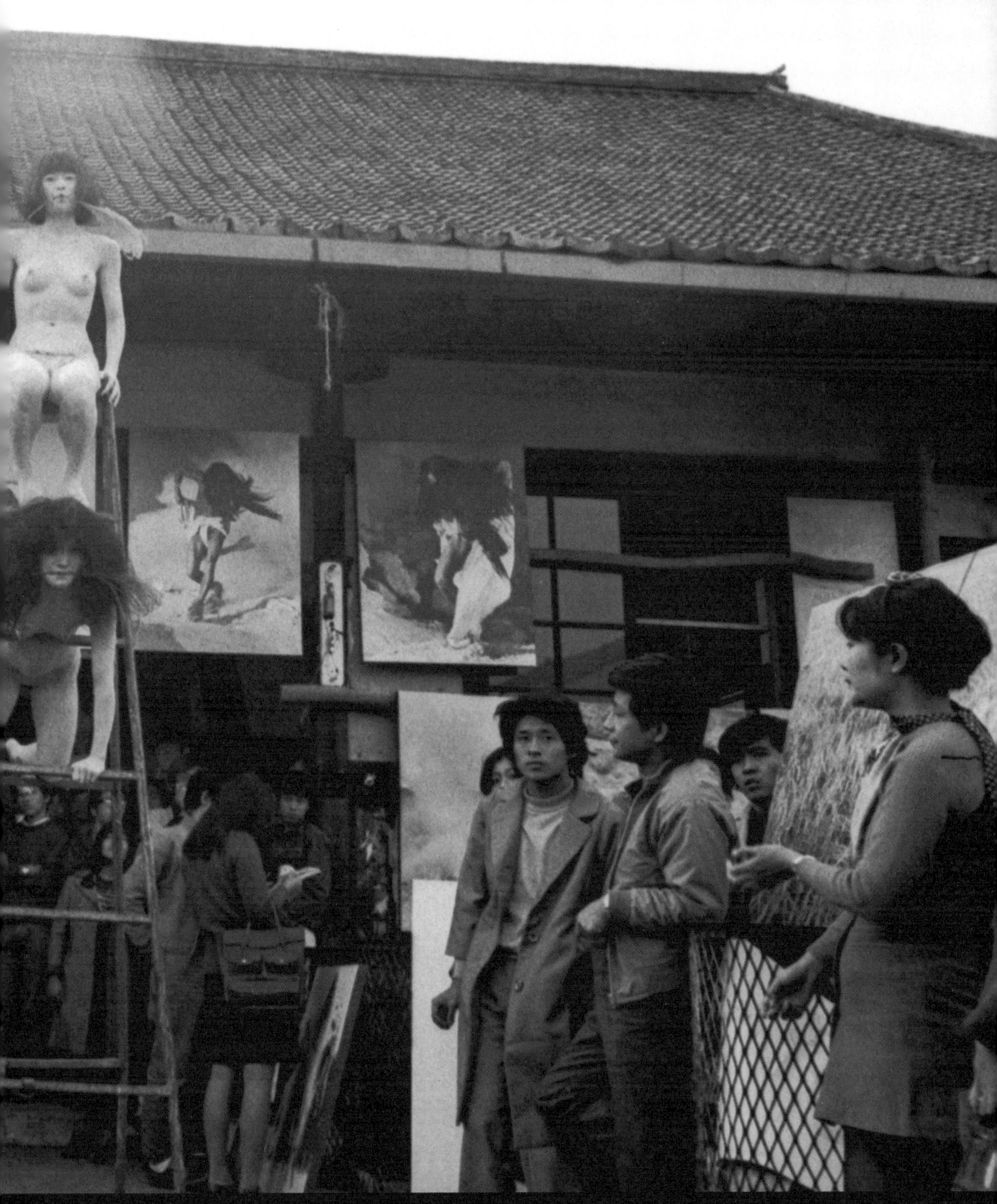

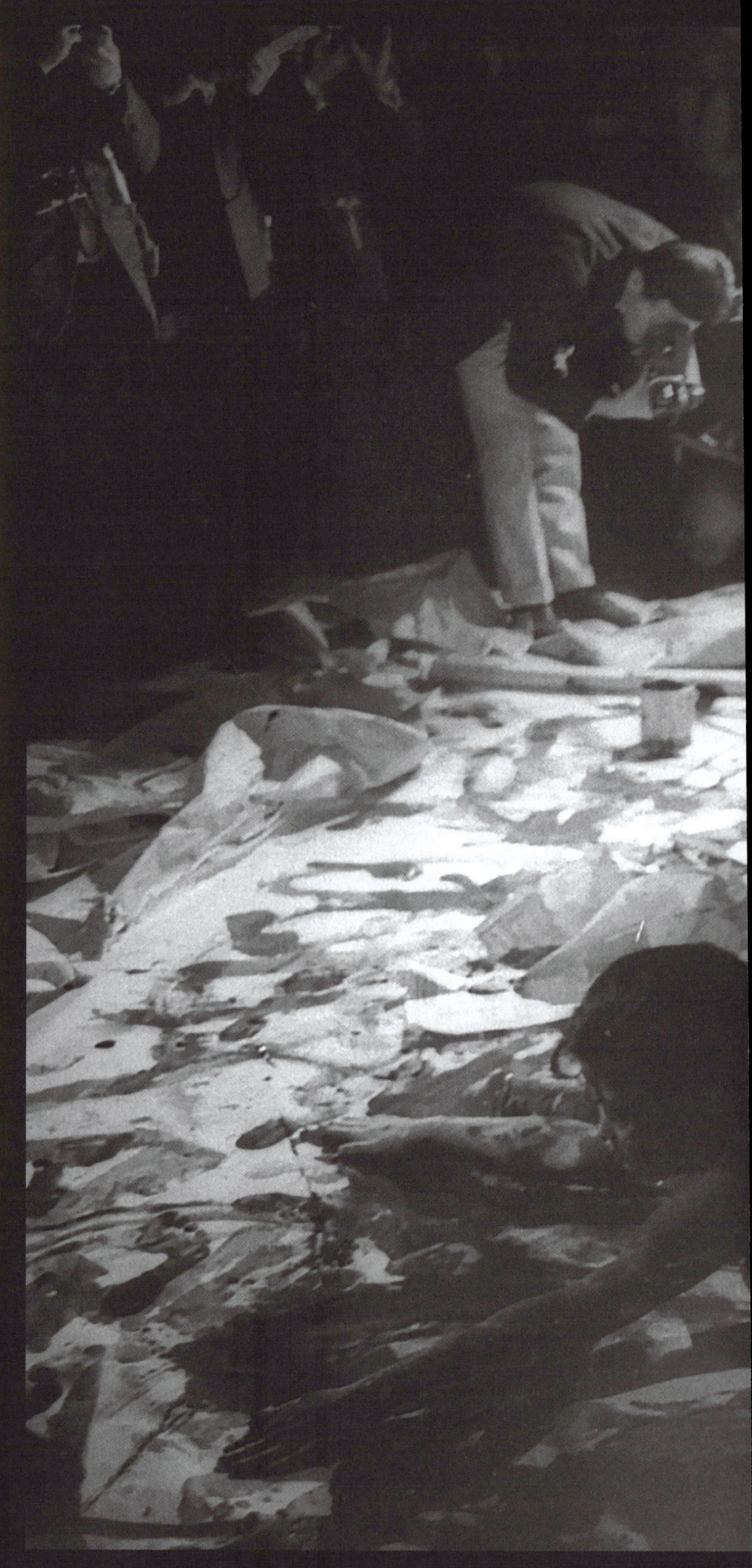

HANAGA MITSUTOSHI'S SYMPATHY WAS DIRECTED NOT SO MUCH TOWARD THE INDIVIDUAL WORKS PER SE AS TO THE ARTISTS' IDEAS AND THOUGHTS THAT UNDERSCORED THEIR WORKS.

HE PHOTOGRAPHED NOT ONLY COMPLETE WORKS BUT ALSO CREATIVE PROCESSES, NOT ONLY THE STAGE PRESENTATION OF DANCE AND THEATER BUT ALSO THE PRACTICES AND BEHIND THE STAGE, NOT ONLY THE NATION'S ECONOMIC GROWTH BUT ALSO ITS ENVIRONMENTAL ILLS.

HANAGA TARO, 'INTRODUCTION', *MITSUTOSHI HANAGA 1000* (2012)

Hanaga Mitsutoshi, *'Swinger Party' at Shinjuku Milan in Tokyo*, 1967, gelatin silver print.

Overleaf: **Hanaga Mitsutoshi**, *Yamamoto Keigo Fire and Smoke Event series at Echizen Coast*, date unknown, gelatin silver print.

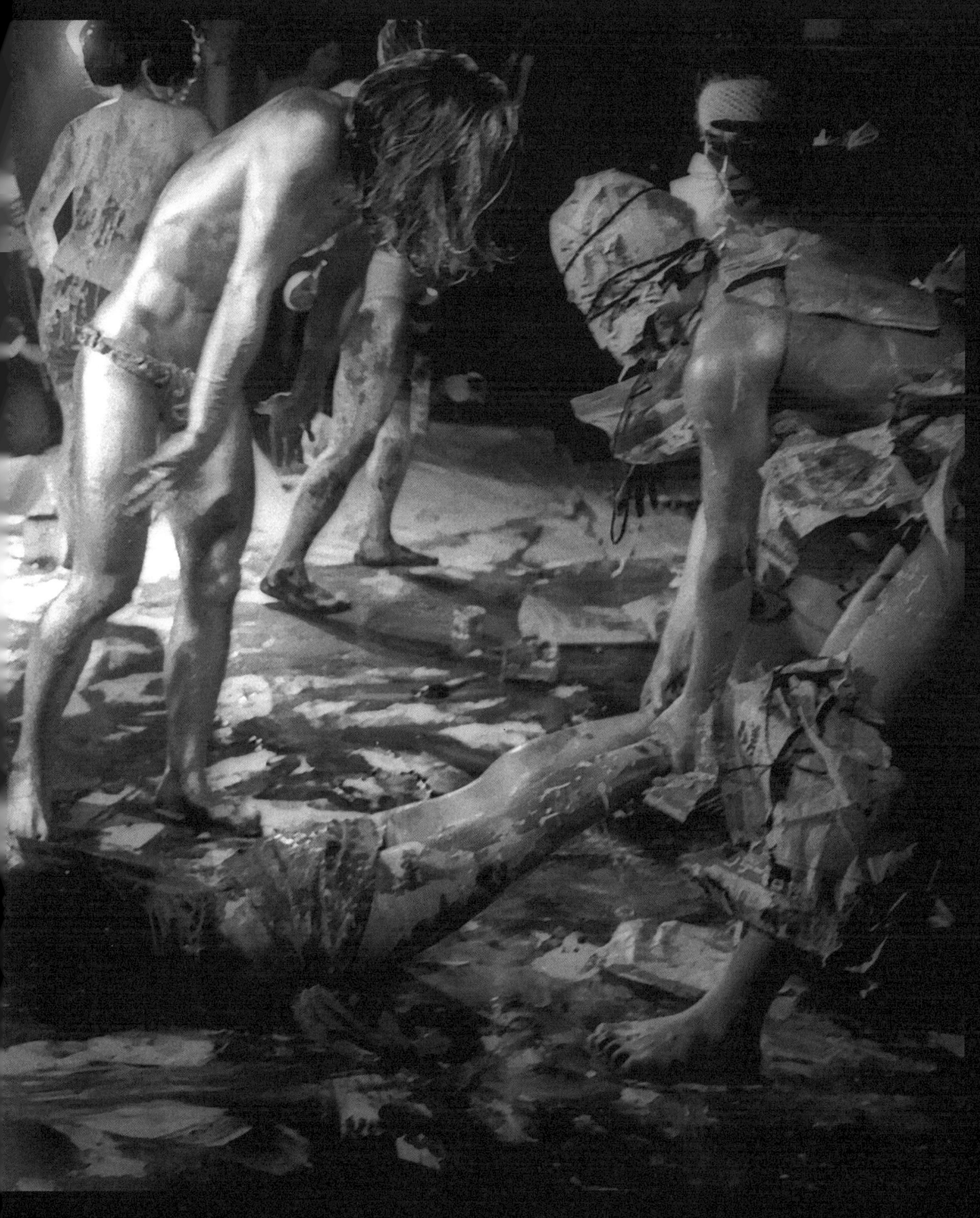

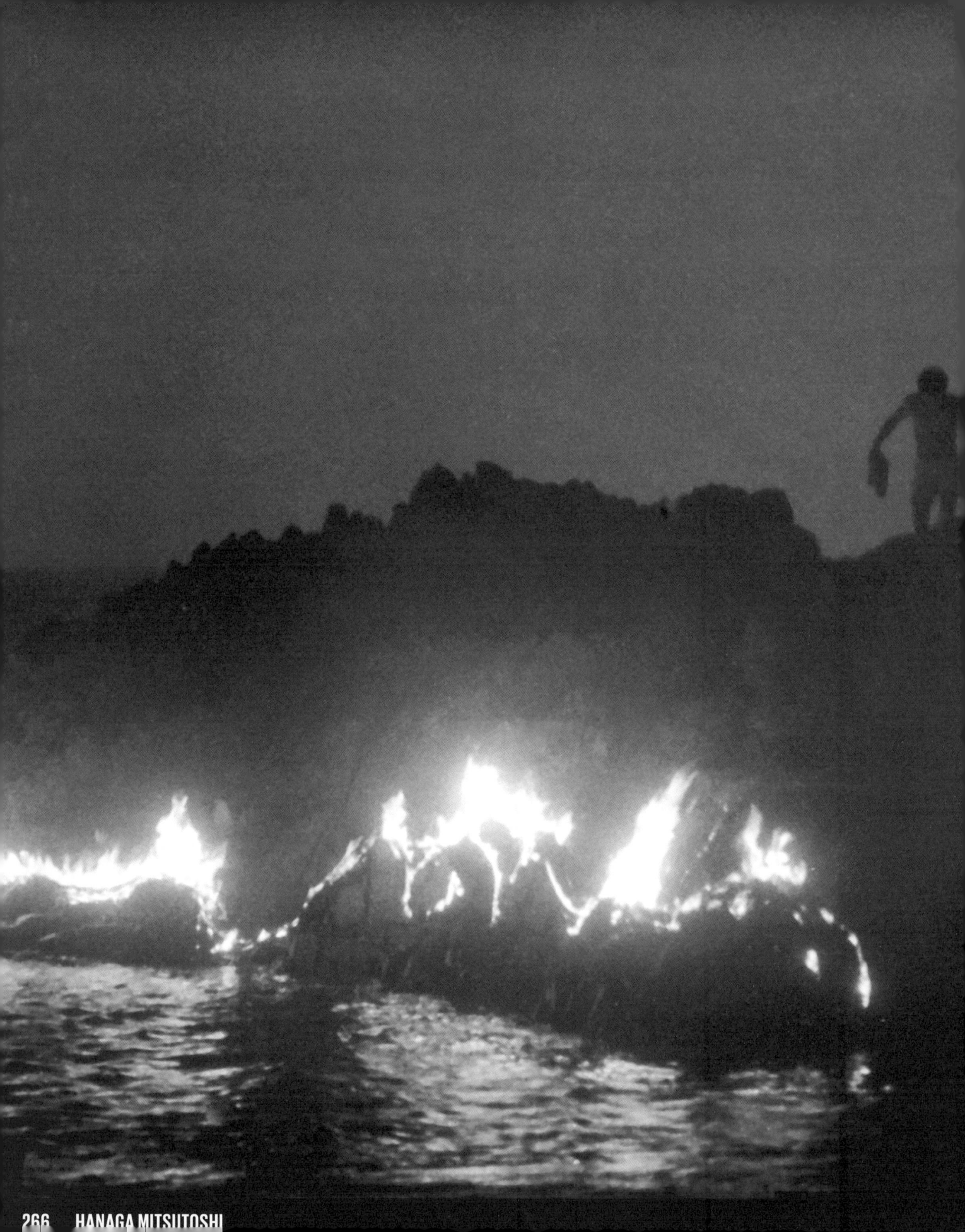

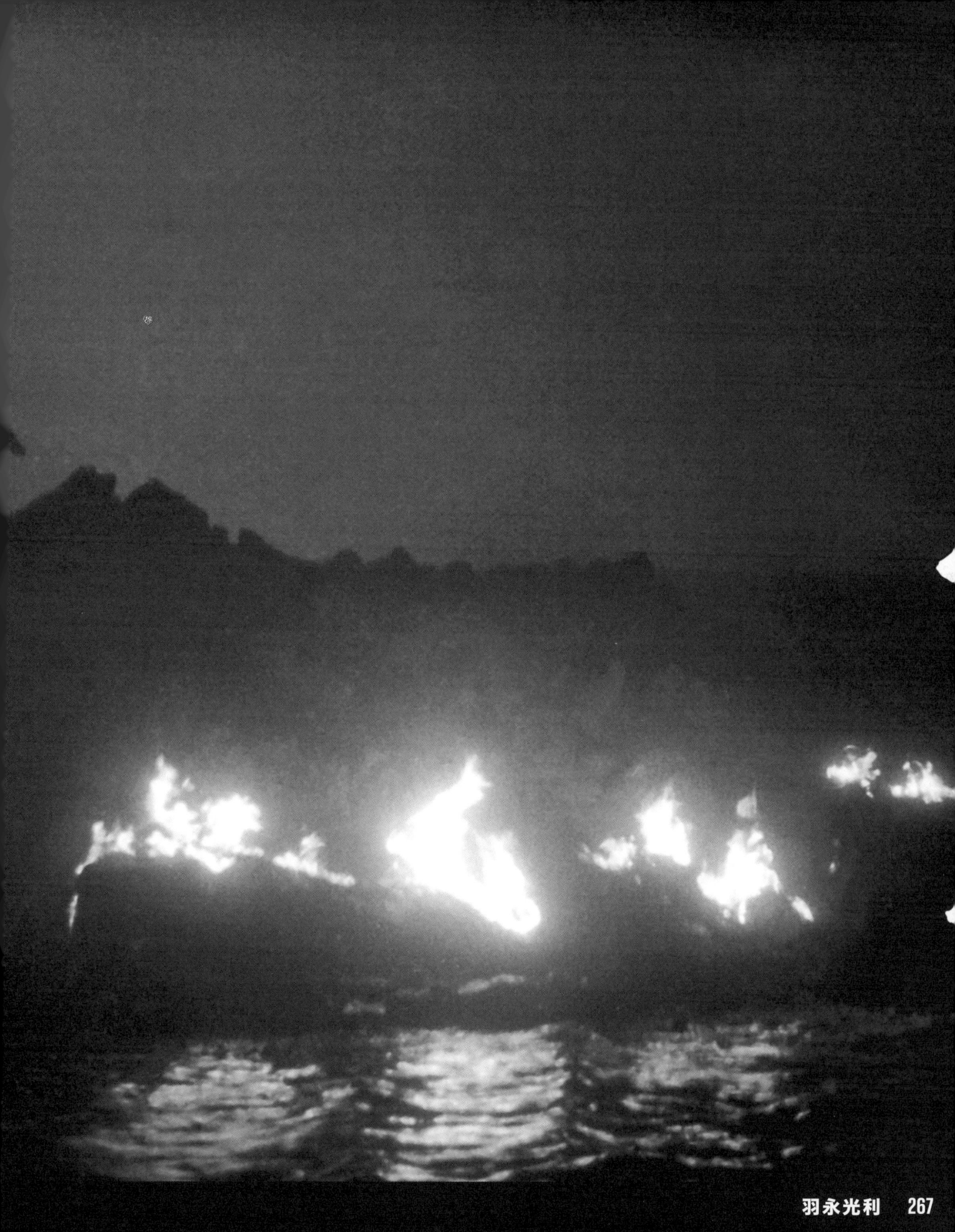

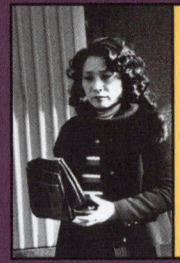

ISHIUCHI MIYAKO
1947–

石内都

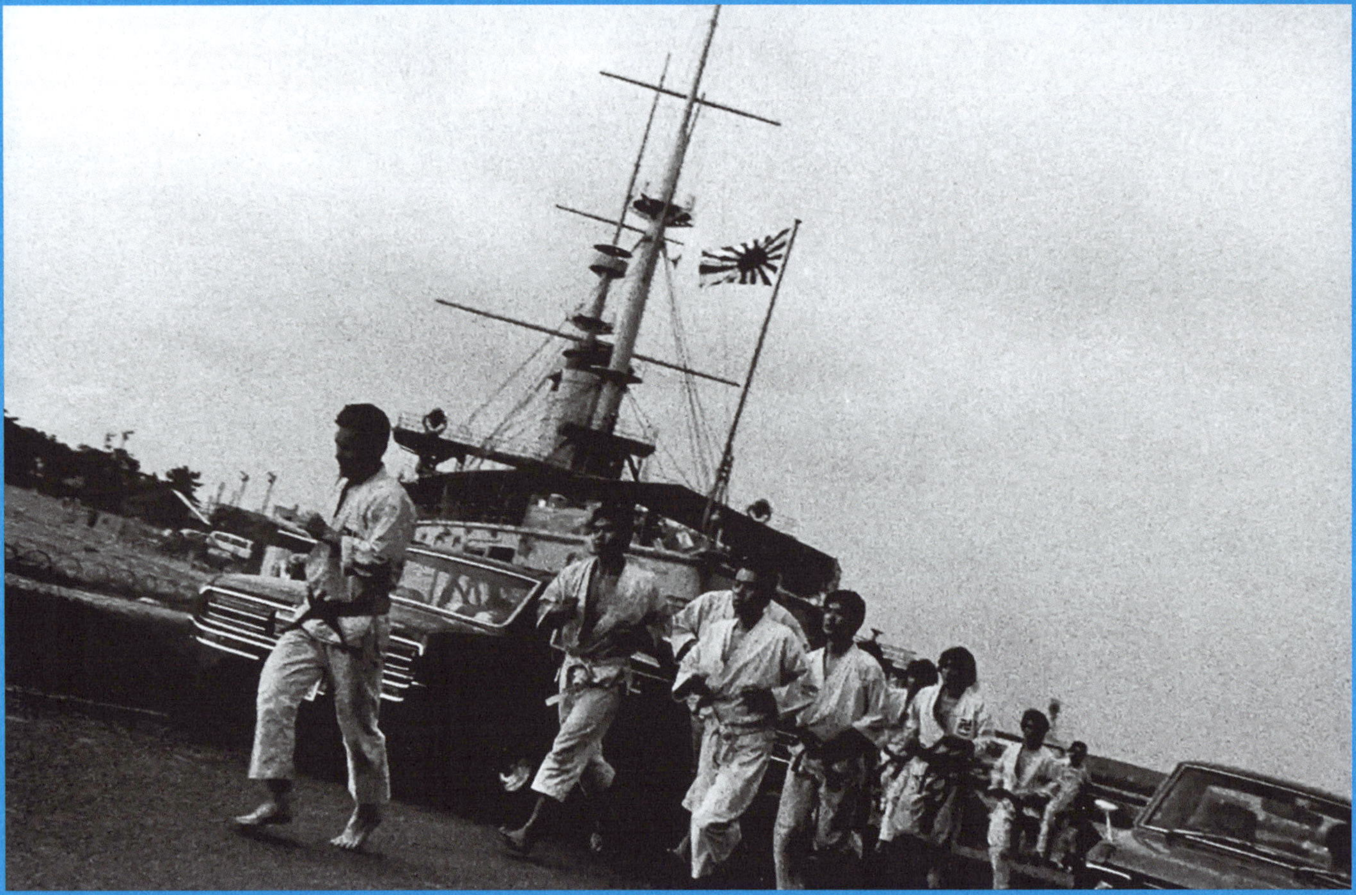

Ishiuchi Miyako, *Yokosuka Story #6*, 1977, gelatin silver print.

Opposite (above): **Ishiuchi Miyako**, *Yokosuka Story #73*, 1977, gelatin silver print.

Opposite (below): **Ishiuchi Miyako**, *Untitled, Yokosuka*, 1981, gelatin silver print.

Overleaf: Photograph from **Ishiuchi Miyako**, *Yokosuka Again, 1980–1990* (1998).

'When I first saw the Occupied territories, it felt very strange and I wondered what on earth it was. In front of my eyes was the national border, which was strange to me, but their culture and music were also very appealing. So there was a part of me that admired American culture, and another part that felt guilty about it. They were complex feelings. I decided to use photography as a way to avenge those pent-up resentments.'

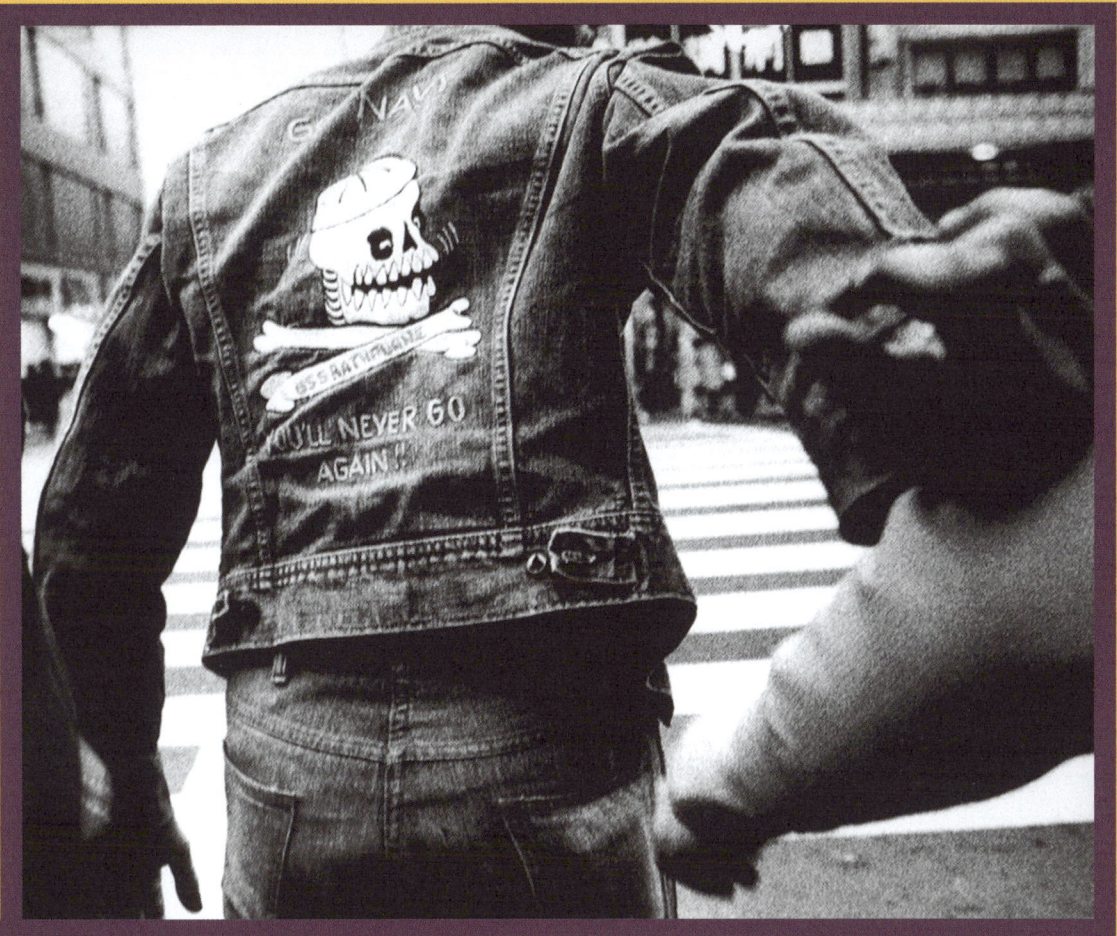

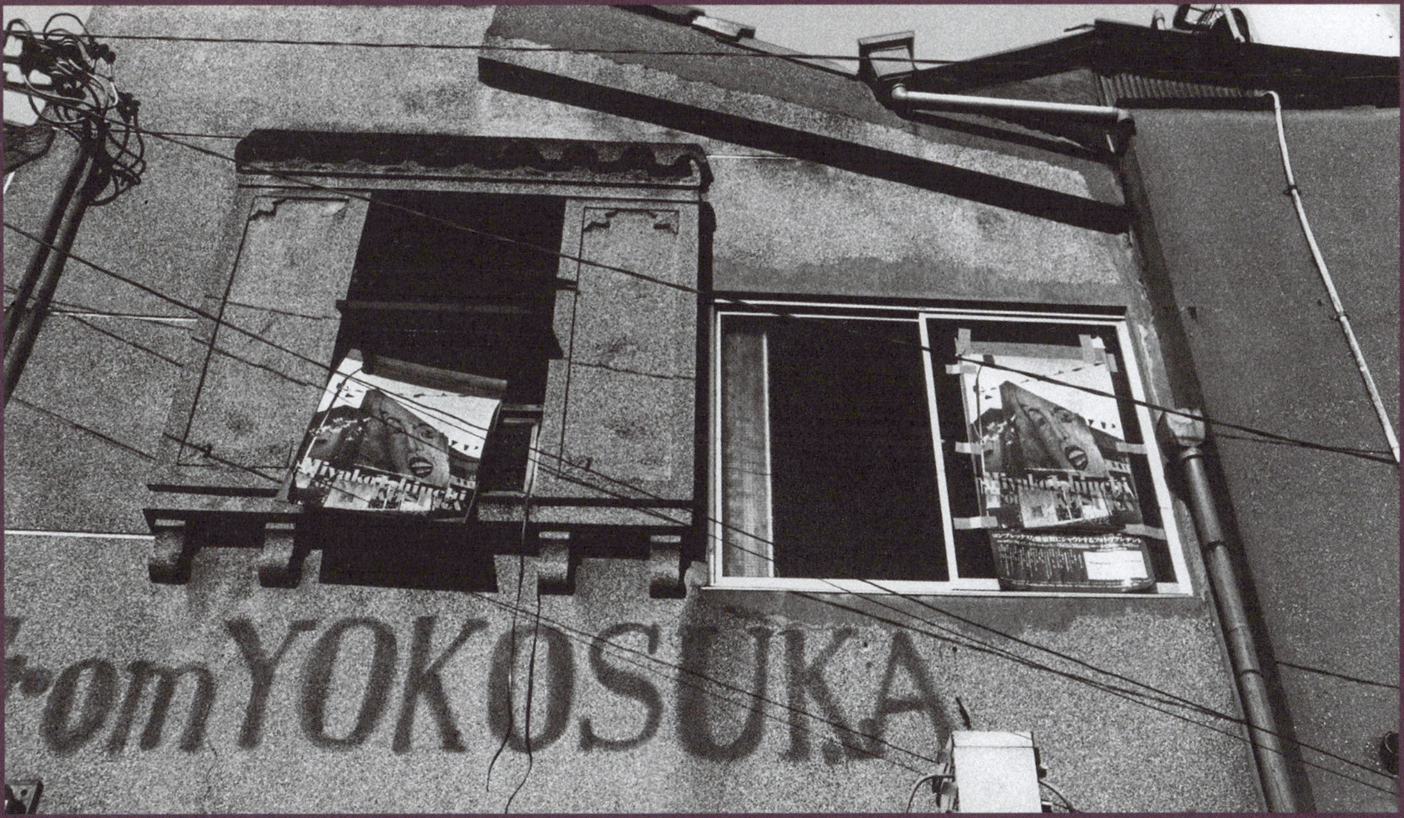

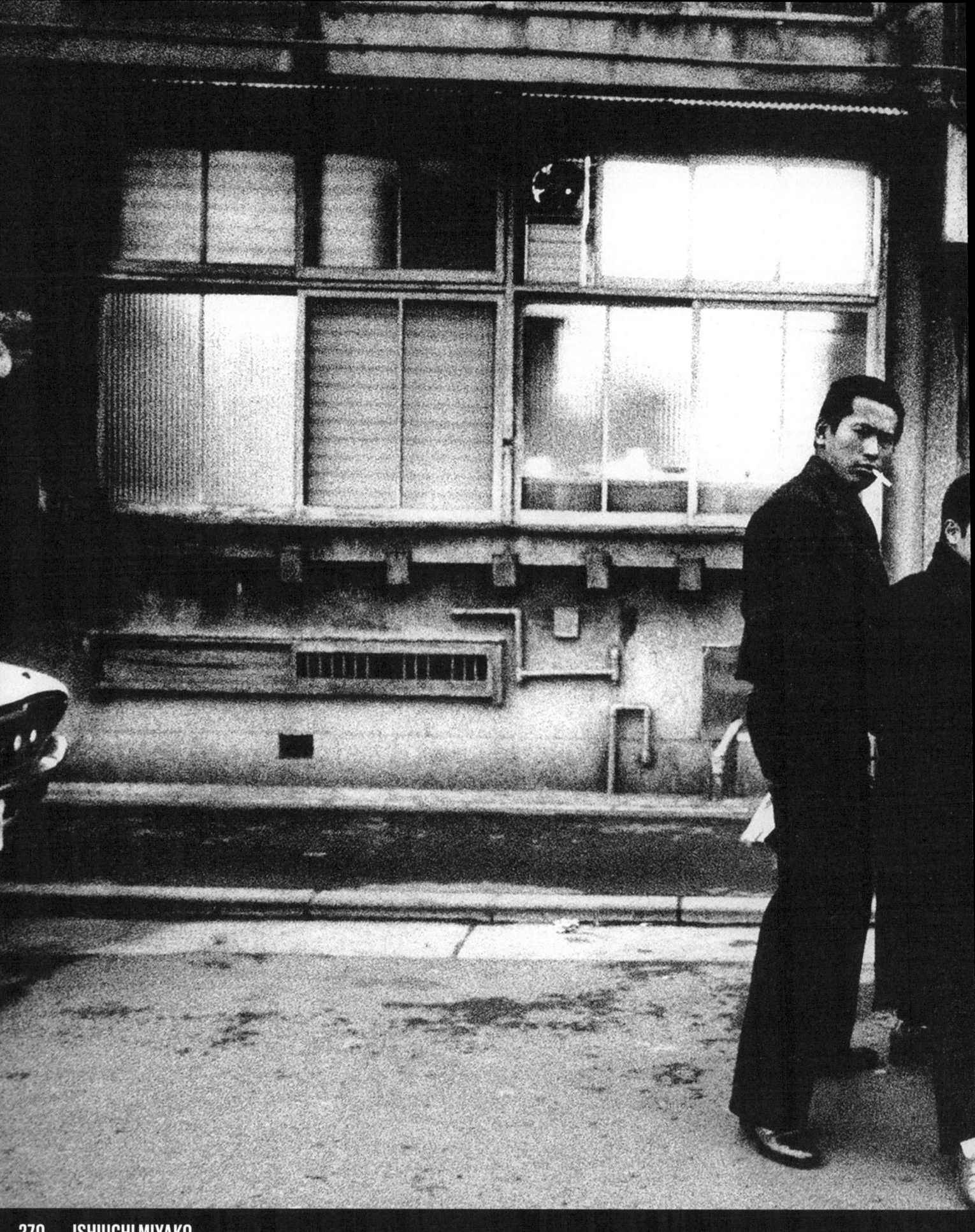

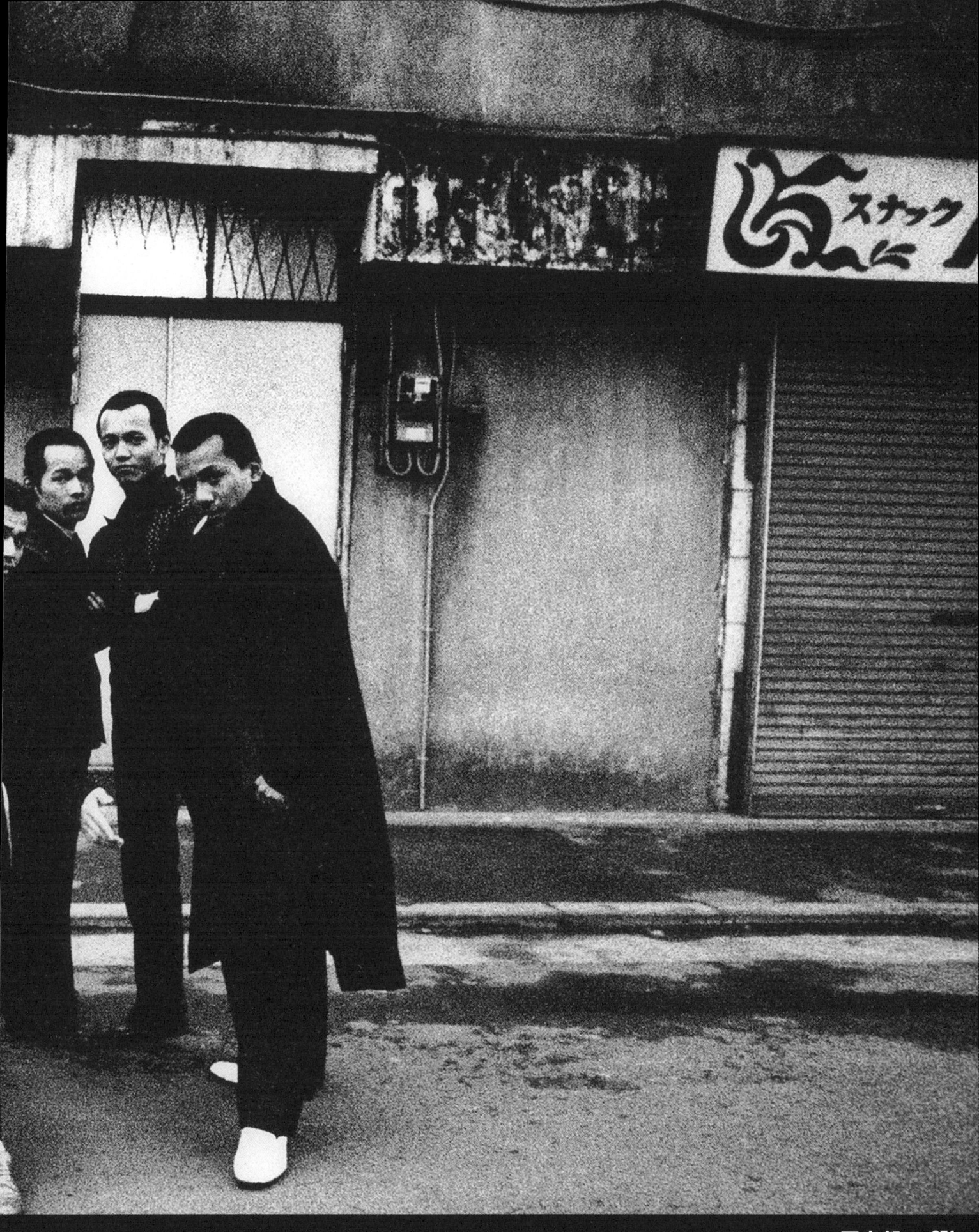

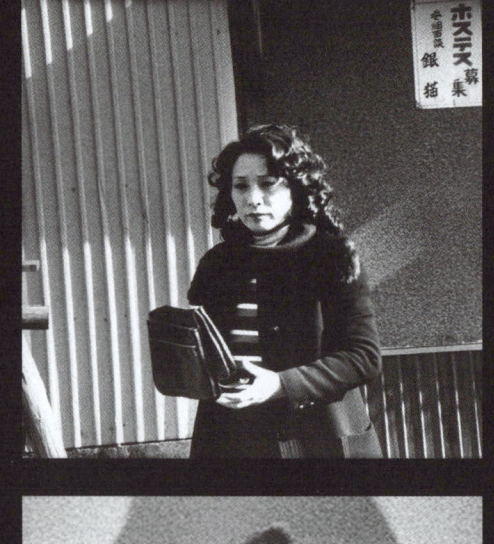

Despite growing up in Yokosuka between the ages of nine and sixteen, Ishiuchi Miyako does not recognize this place as her hometown. Ishiuchi would return in 1976, more than a decade after she thought that she had left the city behind for good, following the onset of her interest in photography. This journey developed into her acclaimed debut body of work, *Yokosuka Story* (1977).

Ishiuchi has described Yokosuka as a haunted place, charged with memories from her adolescence. After the American Occupation of Japan ended in 1952, the city continued to host one of the largest overseas US naval bases, and the foreign military presence made a lasting impression on Ishiuchi. Between the move away from her childhood home and the culture shock she experienced in this new city, the tense atmosphere that characterized Ishiuchi's early encounters with Yokosuka is conveyed in her pictures as an adult through a subjectivity which blends personal and political acuity.

LUCY FLEMING-BROWN

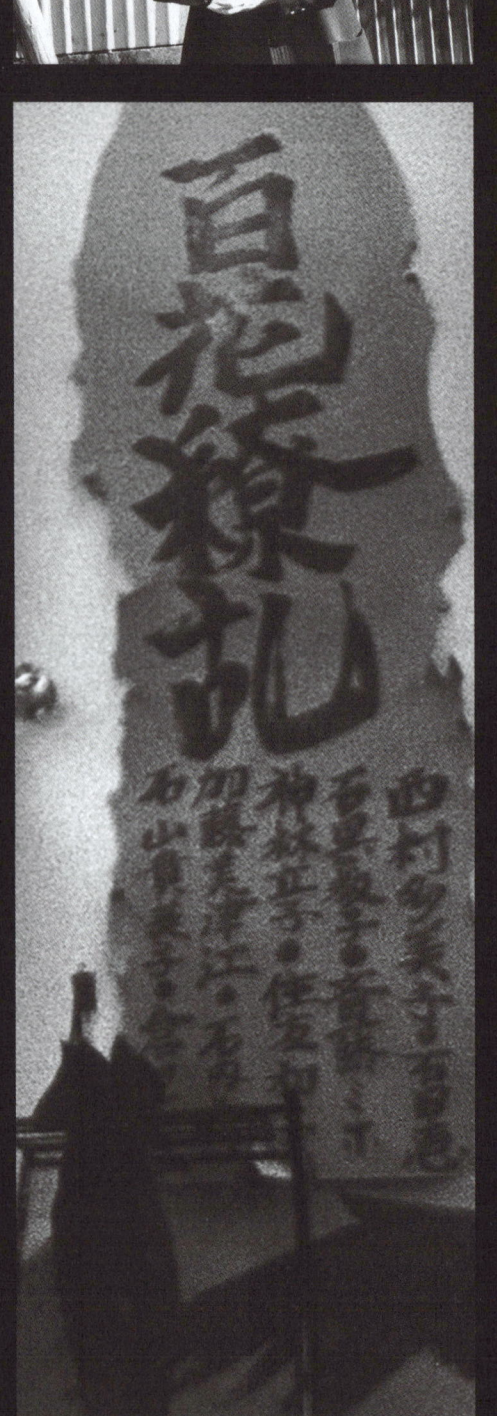

'I USE PHOTOGRAPHY TO EXPRESS MYSELF. IN *YOKOSUKA*, *APARTMENT* AND *ENDLESS NIGHT*, I WAS TAKING DOCUMENTARY-LIKE PHOTOS, BUT I INSISTED TO EVERYONE UNTIL MY FACE TURNED BLUE THAT THIS WAS NOT A DOCUMENTARY. THE BASIS OF PHOTOGRAPHY IS TO RECORD, BUT I WANTED TO PUSH BACK AGAINST IT.

PHOTOGRAPHY IS NOT ABOUT JUST DOCUMENTING, IT IS MAKING, SO I WAS SAYING FROM EARLY ON THAT THIS IS SOMETHING I CREATED. THE YOKOSUKA I SEE IS VERY GRAINY AND HAS PARTICLES. THE PARTICLES ARE ON THE FILM, AND WHEN WE ENLARGE THE 35MM FILM YOU CAN SEE ALL THE GRAINS. IT REALLY IS BEAUTIFUL.

I ALSO LEARNED THE HARD WAY FROM THE BASE THAT I AM A WOMAN. WHY? THERE WAS A STREET THAT WOMEN COULD NOT WALK ON; IF YOU WENT THERE, YOU GOT RAPED. I BECAME FASCINATED WITH THESE SEEDY PLACES THAT MOST PEOPLE WOULD IGNORE, THE PLACES PEOPLE WOULD AVOID, PLACES THAT WERE ONCE SUNNY AND NOW IN THE SHADOWS. IT FELT REALLY GREAT TO PHOTOGRAPH THESE THINGS.'

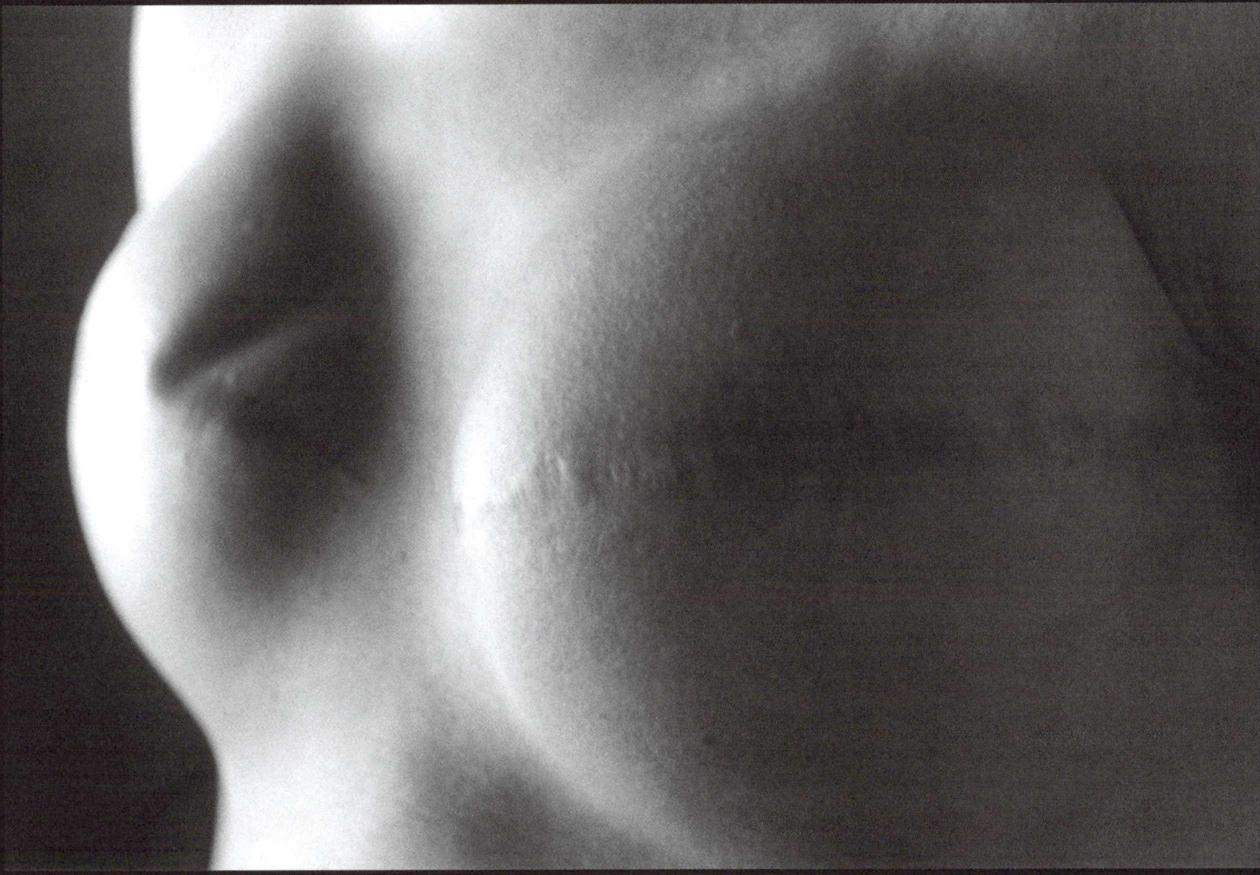

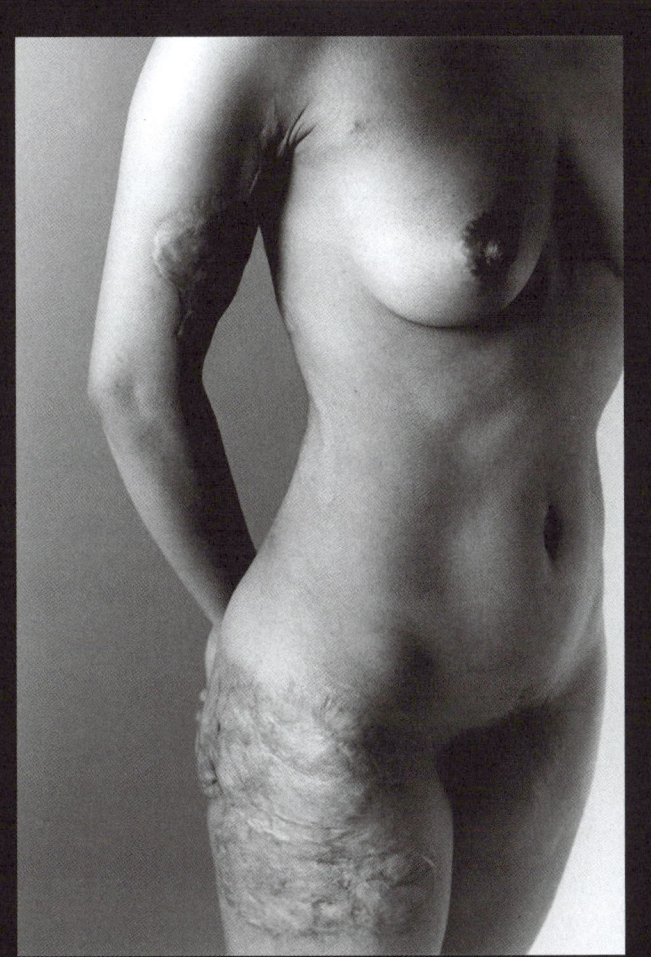
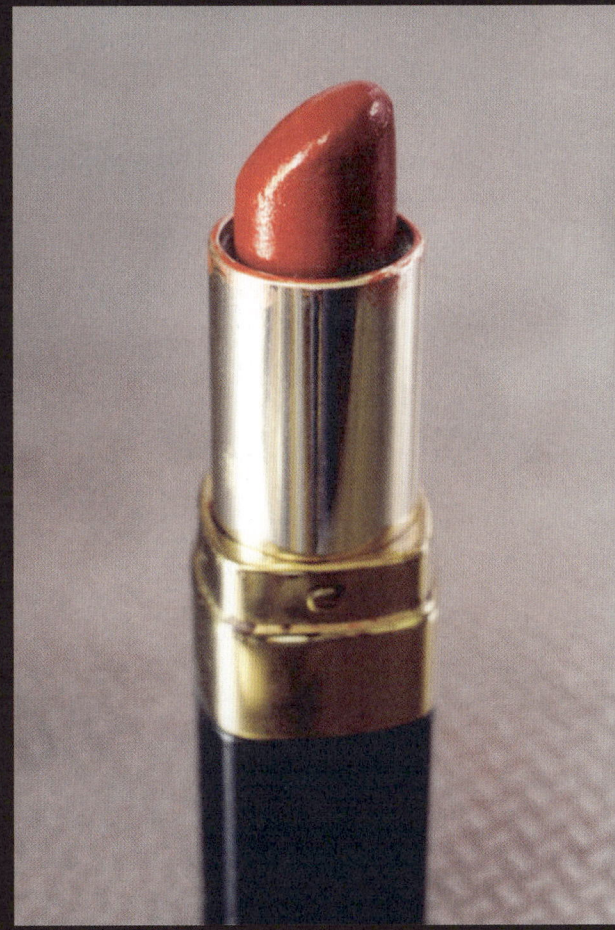

石内都

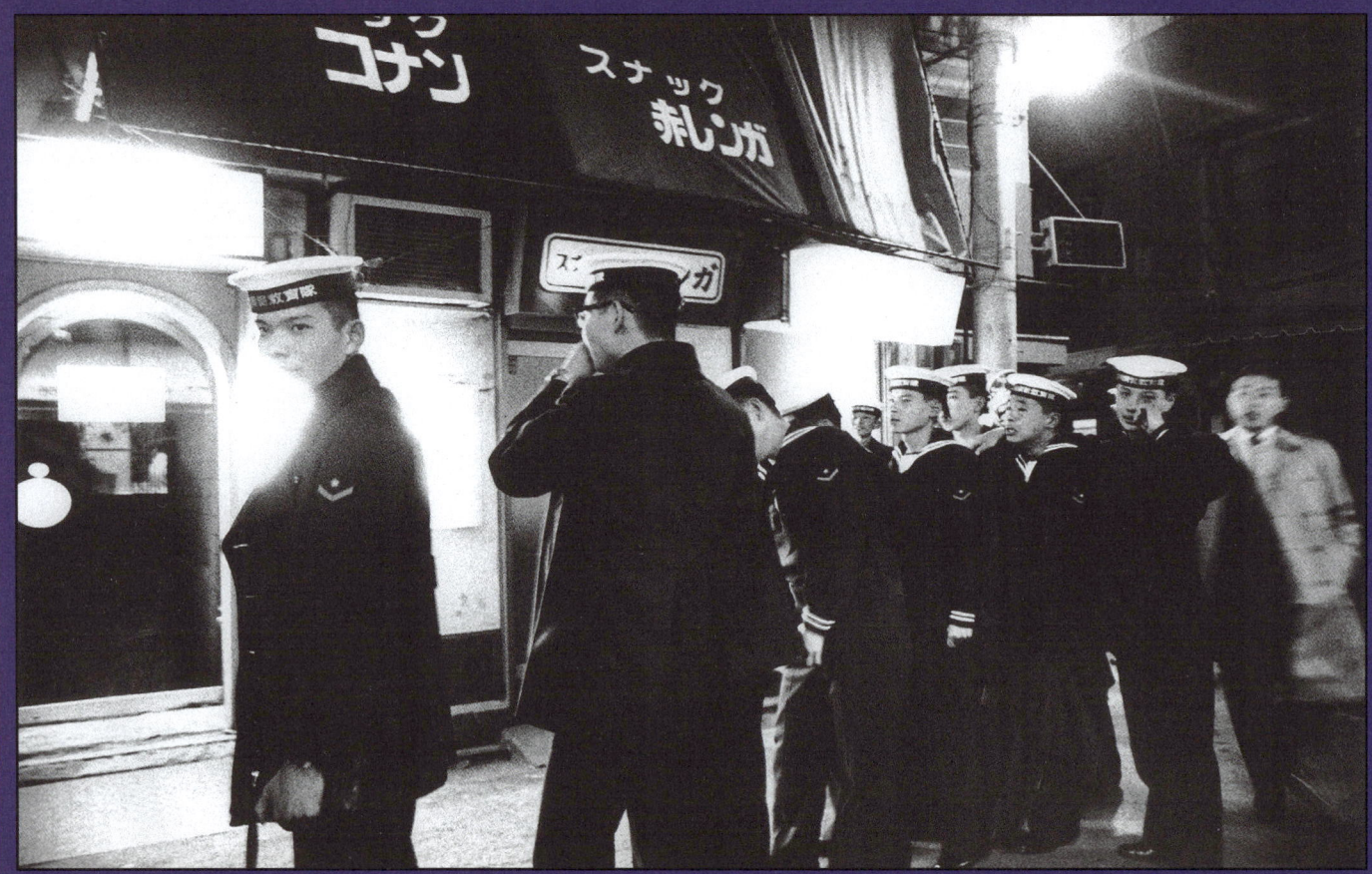

p. 272 (above): **Ishiuchi Miyako**, *Yokosuka Story #121*, 1977, gelatin silver print.

p. 272 (below): **Ishiuchi Miyako**, 'Hyakka Ryōran', March 1976.

p. 273: Photographs from **Ishiuchi Miyako**, *Yokosuka Again, 1980–1990* (1998).

Above: Photograph from **Ishiuchi Miyako**, *Yokosuka Again, 1980–1990* (1998).

Opposite: **Ishiuchi Miyako**, *Yokosuka Story #98*, 1977, gelatin silver print.

Overleaf: **Ishiuchi Miyako**, 'Hyakka Ryōran' flyer, March 1976.

pp. 278–79: **Ishiuchi Miyako**, *Yokosuka Story #30*, 1976–77, gelatin silver print.

'FROM THE VERY BEGINNING, I HAVE ALWAYS BEEN SELFISH – COMPLETELY SELF-CENTRED, YOU COULD SAY. I DON'T LET MYSELF BE SWAYED BY THOSE AROUND ME. ONCE I DECIDE SOMETHING, THAT'S IT. I DON'T REALLY LISTEN TO WHAT OTHERS SAY. THAT INCLUDES MY PARENTS – I NEVER LISTENED TO THEM EITHER. I'VE JUST LIVED MY LIFE DOING WHATEVER I WANTED.

BUT THE REASON I WAS ABLE TO BE SO WILFUL IS THAT, IN SOME WAY, I CARRIED A CERTAIN KIND OF VALUE. IT WASN'T JUST RECKLESS SELFISHNESS. WHILE I MAY BE SELF-CENTRED WHEN IT COMES TO MY OWN WAY OF THINKING, I HAVE ALWAYS UPHELD A SENSE OF INTEGRITY TOWARDS SOCIETY, THE WORLD AND OTHER PEOPLE. BUT WHEN IT COMES TO MY PERSONAL PERSPECTIVE, THAT IS SOMETHING THAT BELONGS TO ME ALONE, AND I REFUSE TO COMPROMISE ON THAT.'

'I CREATED THIS IMAGE OF A TOUGH WOMAN. BACK THEN, THERE WAS NO WORK FOR FEMALE PHOTOGRAPHERS. PHOTOGRAPHY WAS THOUGHT OF AS A MAN'S JOB. A WOMAN TAKING UP A HANDICRAFT AND EARNING HER LIVING, IT WAS NOT THE TIME FOR THAT.

YOU CAN'T DO PHOTOGRAPHY WITHOUT YOUR OWN POINT OF VIEW AND VALUES. EVERYONE IS DIFFERENT, WHETHER IT IS ARAKI, MORIYAMA OR TŌMATSU, EVERY PHOTOGRAPHER IS DIFFERENT. THEIR WORKS ARE NOT SIMILAR AT ALL. I WANTED TO MAKE SOMETHING COMPLETELY DIFFERENT, IN MY OWN WAY, SO I COULD BE ON THE SAME LEVEL.'

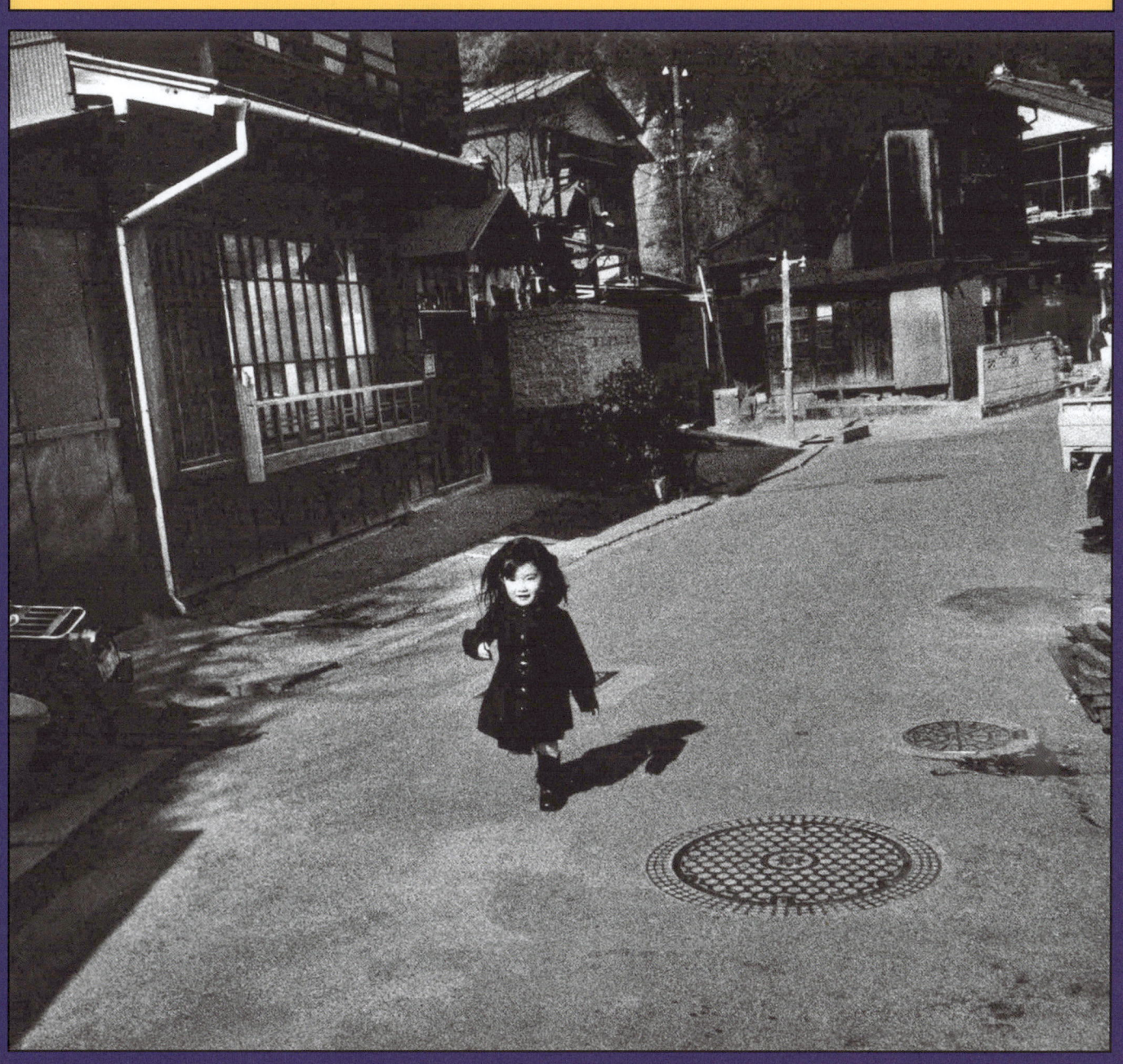

'WE EXHIBITED "HYAKKA RYŌRAN" DUE TO THE WOMEN'S LIBERATION MOVEMENT. I PLANNED IT WITH ANOTHER WOMAN, AND WE GATHERED TEN PHOTOGRAPHERS. EACH ARTIST WAS A YOUNG FEMALE, AND WHEN THINKING ABOUT THE THEME, WE SAID, "LET'S MAKE IT ABOUT MEN."

WHY? BECAUSE WE ARE ALWAYS THE ONES BEING LOOKED AT. SO LET US BE THE LOOKERS. THERE ARE SO MANY FEMALE NUDES AND MEN ARE NEVER IN THE SHOT. SO WOMEN ON THE OTHER SIDE OF THE LENS MUST SHOOT MEN. NO ONE LOOKS CLOSELY AT THE MALE BODY AND THERE AREN'T MANY PHOTOS. THERE ARE THESE MACHO NUDES, HISTORICALLY, BUT THERE ARE NO NUDES OF NORMAL MEN.'

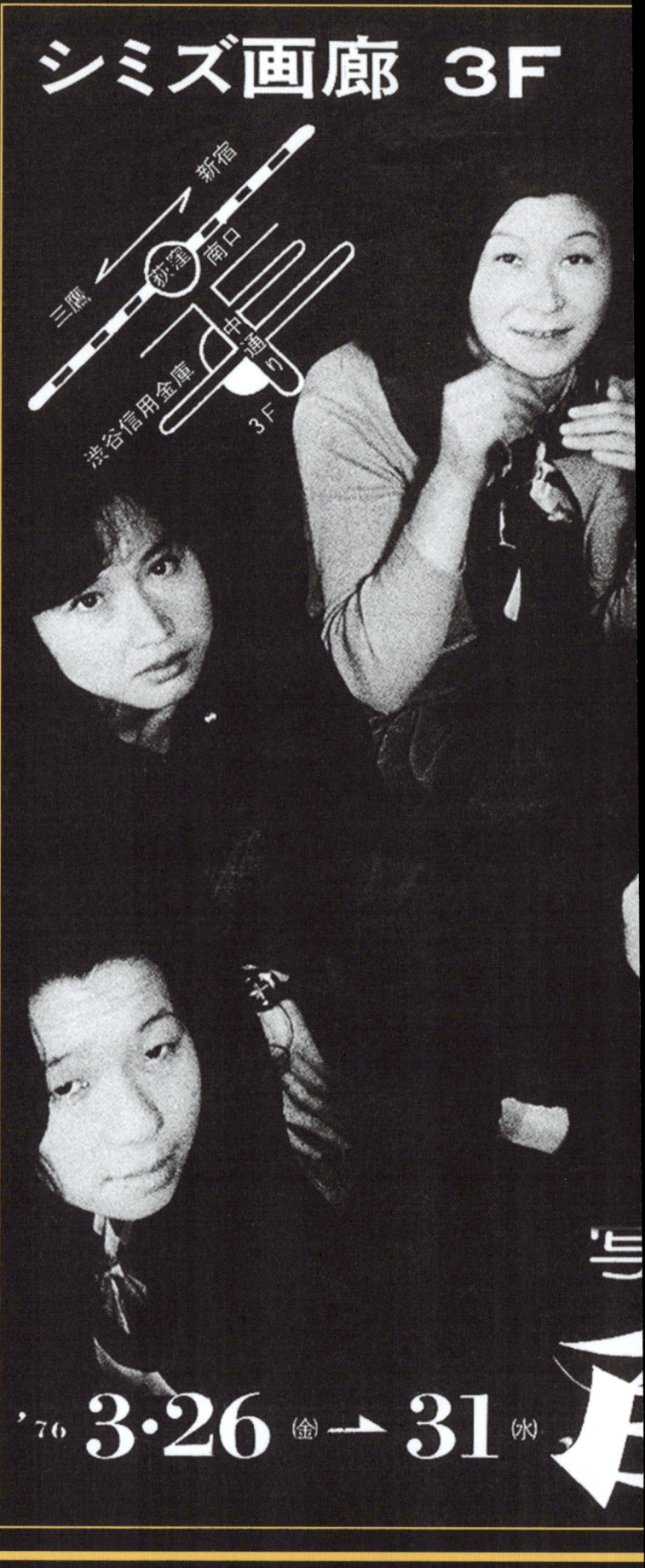

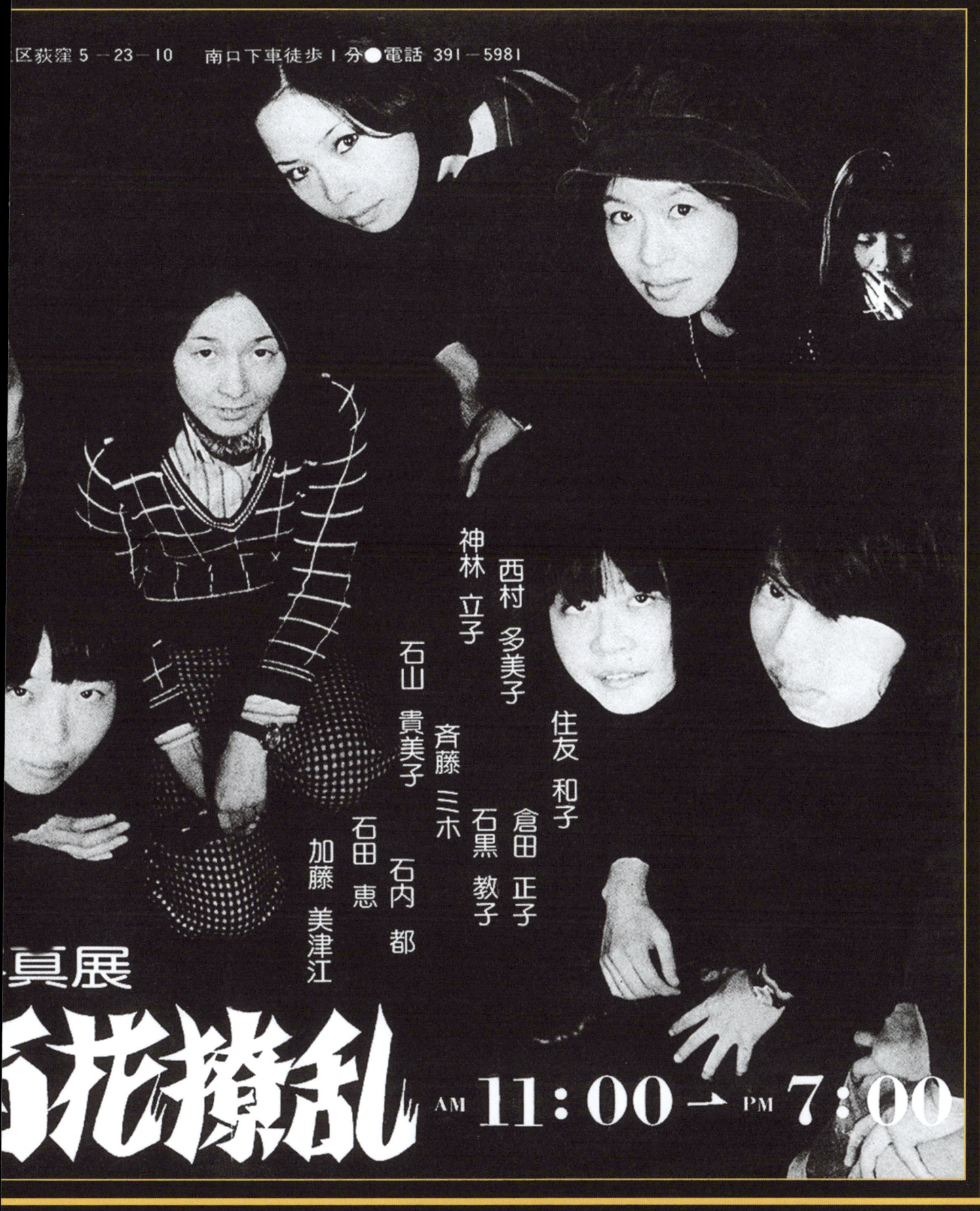

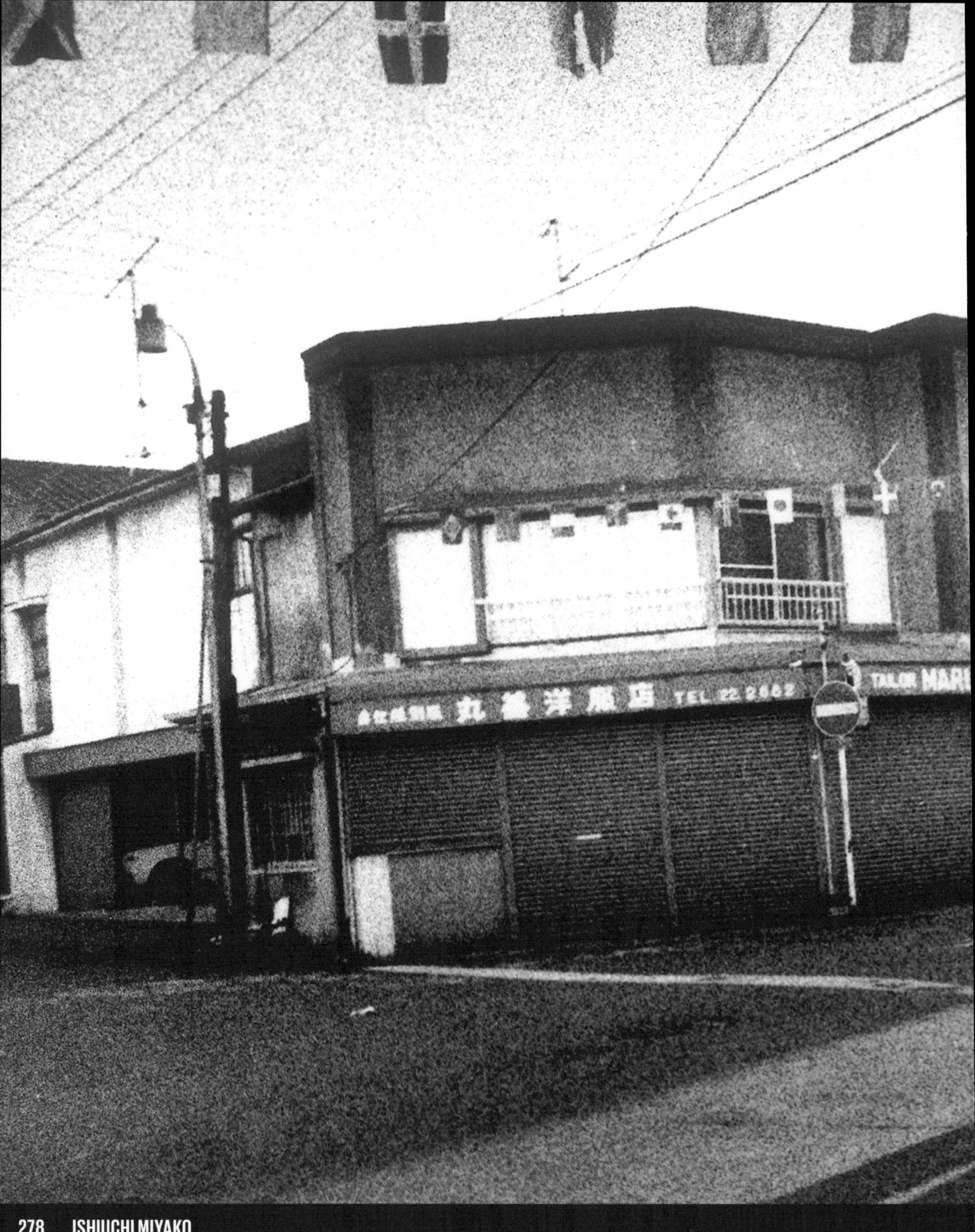

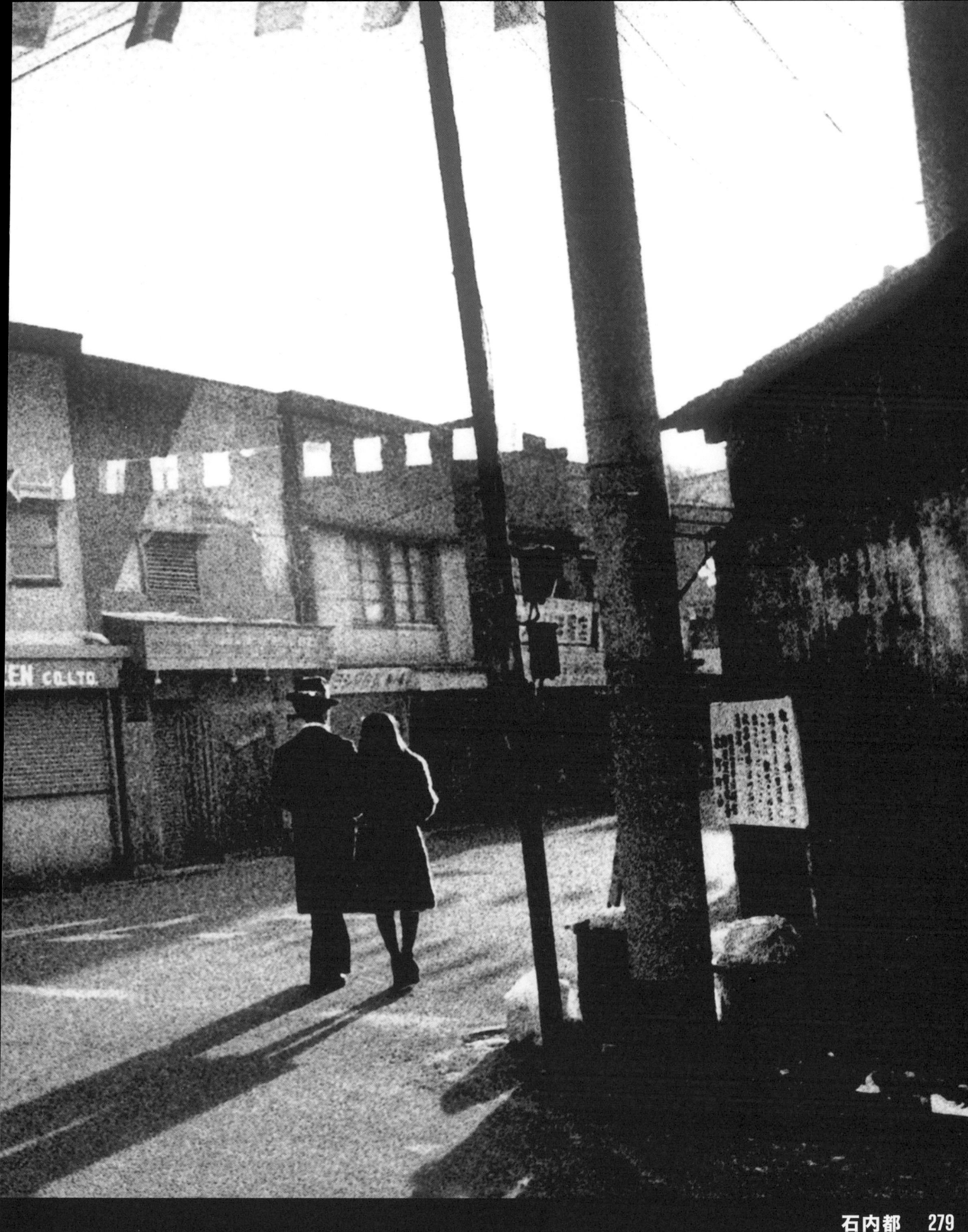

SAEKI TOSHIO
1945–2019

佐伯俊男

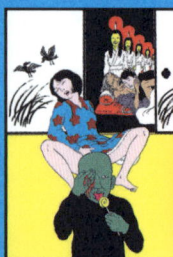

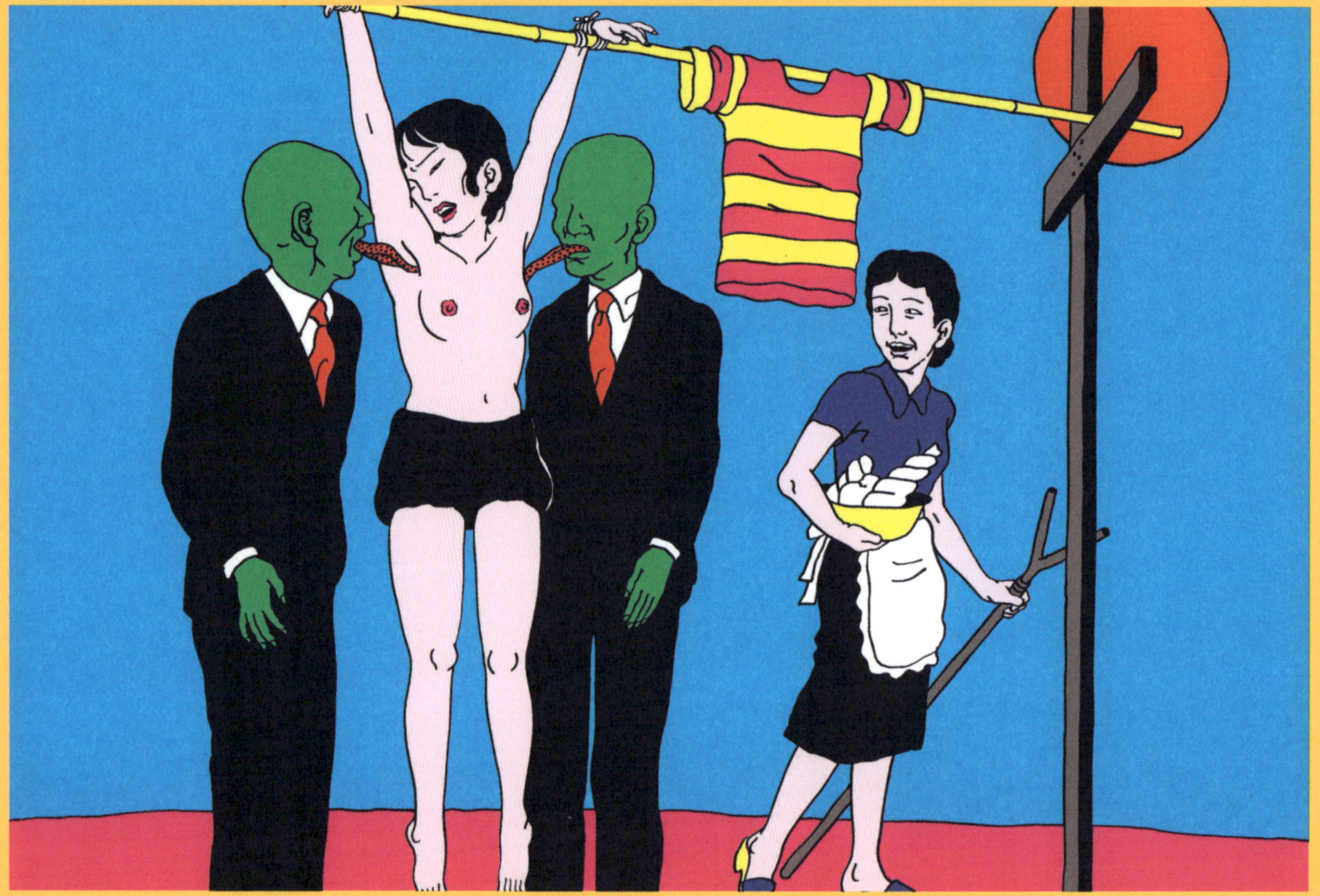

Image from **Saeki Toshio**, *Fièvres nocturnes* (2022).

Opposite (above, left and right): Images from **Saeki Toshio**, *Rêve écarlate* (2016).

Opposite (below): Image from **Saeki Toshio**, *Fièvres nocturnes* (2022).

Overleaf: **Satoshi Saikusa**, *Saeki Toshio*, date and materials unknown.

'The possession of Ero is the fate of human beings. On the other side of Ero, a hint of death can be seen through. When I make my drawings, I have no hesitation or doubts to haul into this theme.'

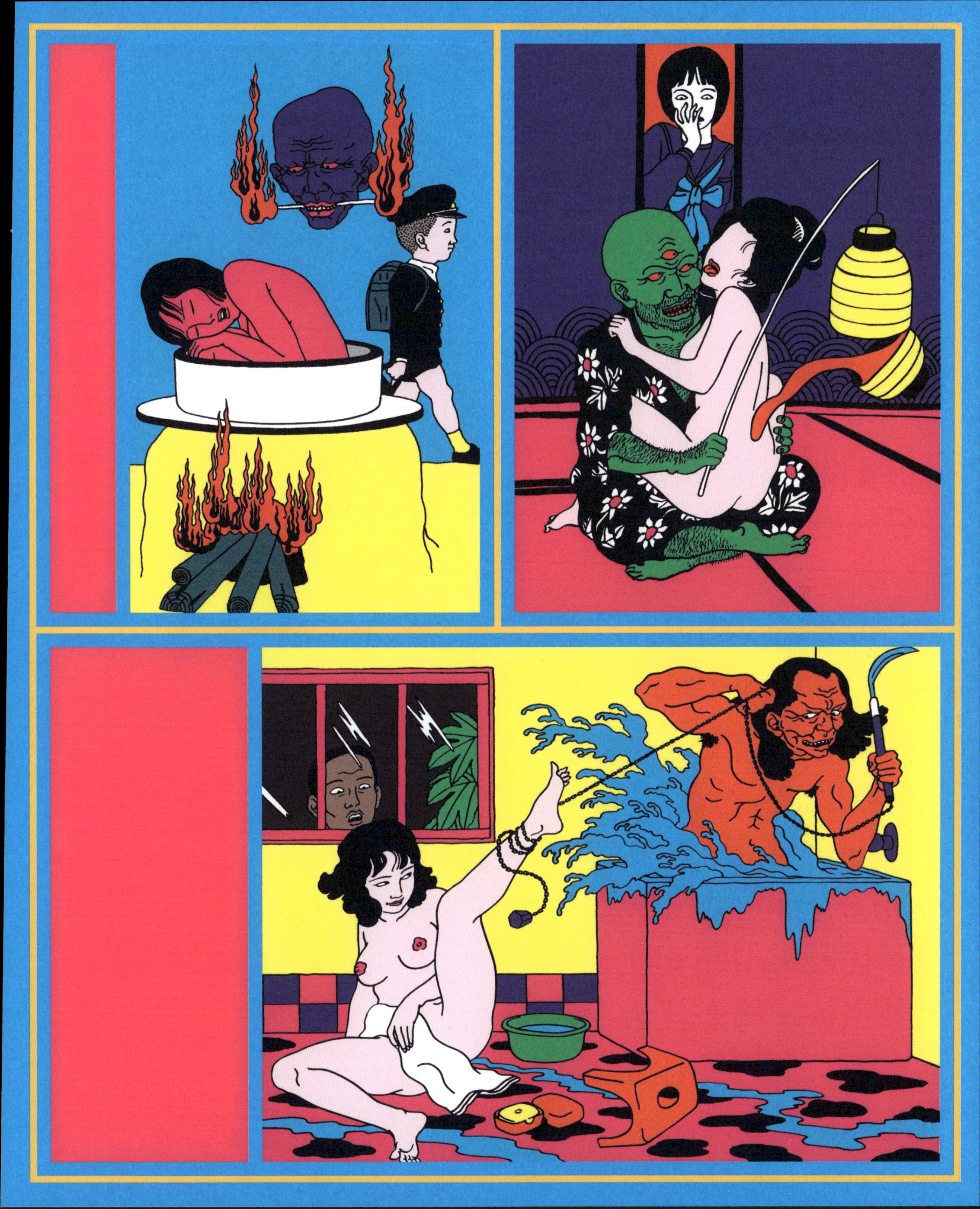

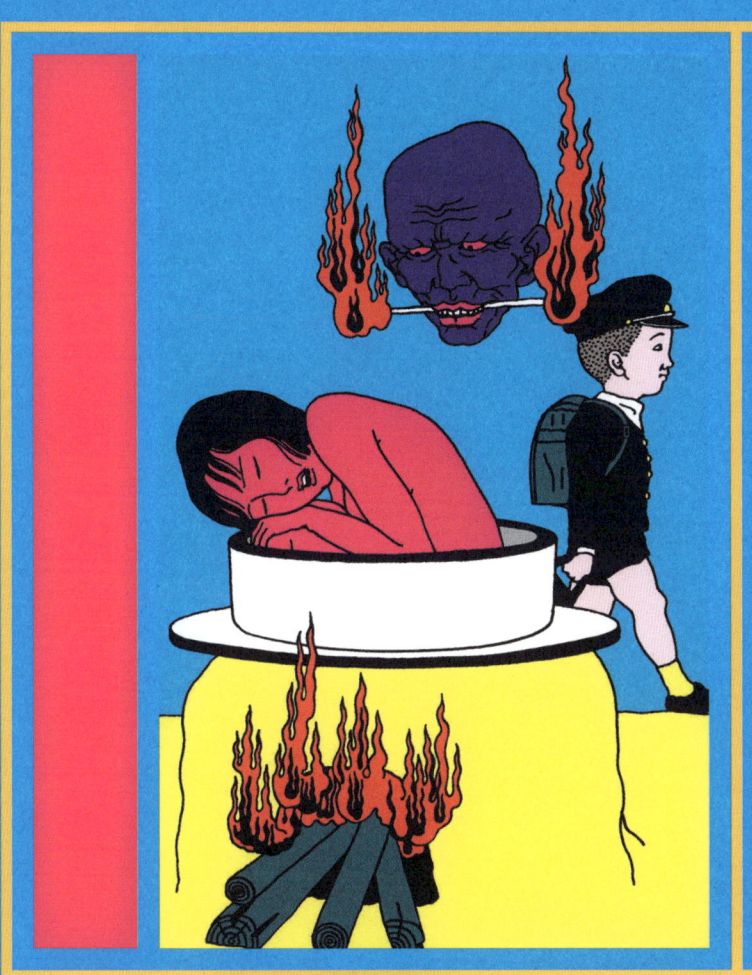
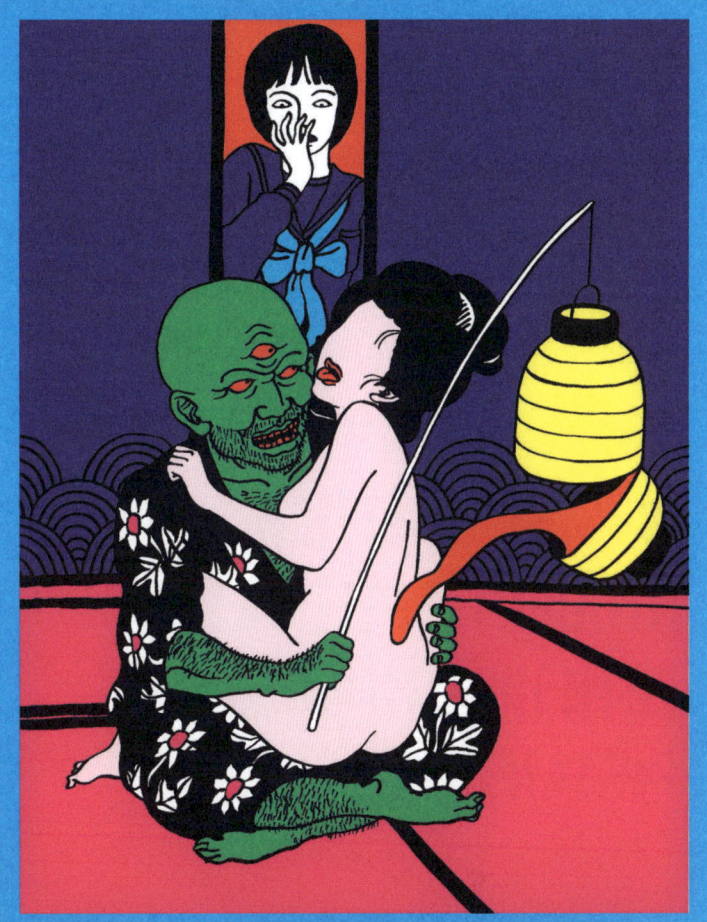

佐伯俊男

I WAS SAEKI TOSHIO'S PARTNER FROM 2007 UNTIL HIS DEATH IN 2019. I DISCOVERED SAEKI'S ARTWORK IN 1997, WHEN I WAS STILL A HIGH SCHOOL STUDENT. I FELL IN LOVE WITH HIS ARTWORK INSTANTLY.

SAEKI'S ARTWORK IS RATHER HAUNTING, THOUGH IT'S ALSO FULL OF HUMOUR AND VERY FUN. COMBINING DARK THEMES AND HUMOUR IS A BIG FEATURE OF HIS ART. HE APPROACHED ART IN A FUN, JOYFUL AND LIGHT WAY.

SAEKI YUKA

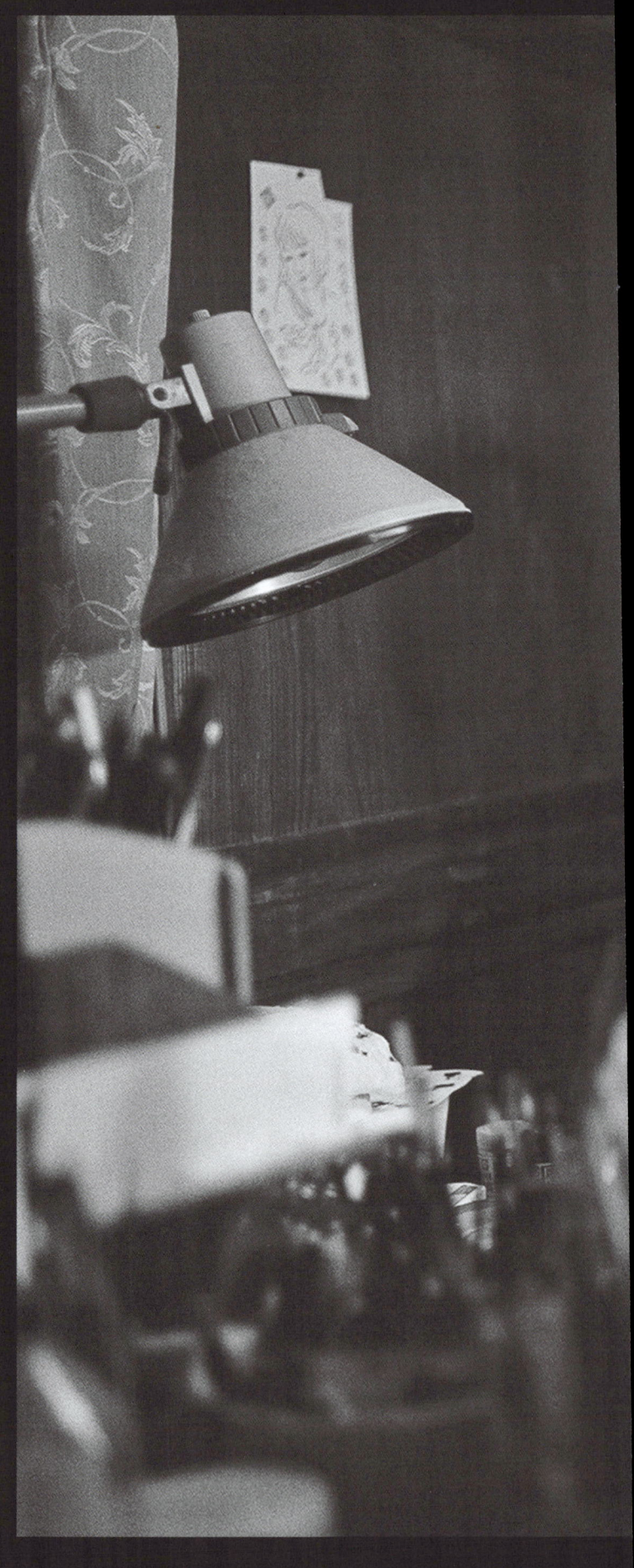

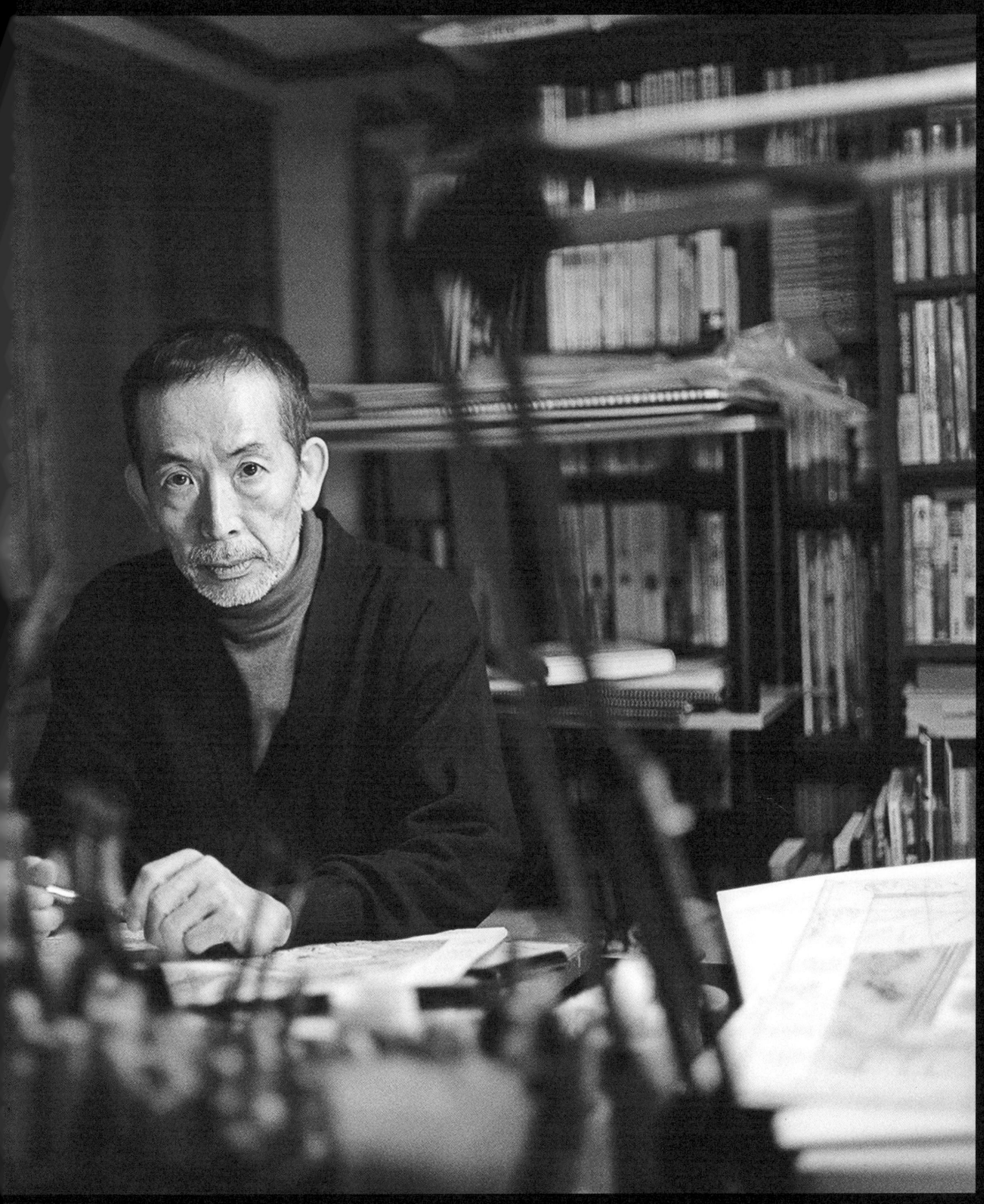

佐伯俊男

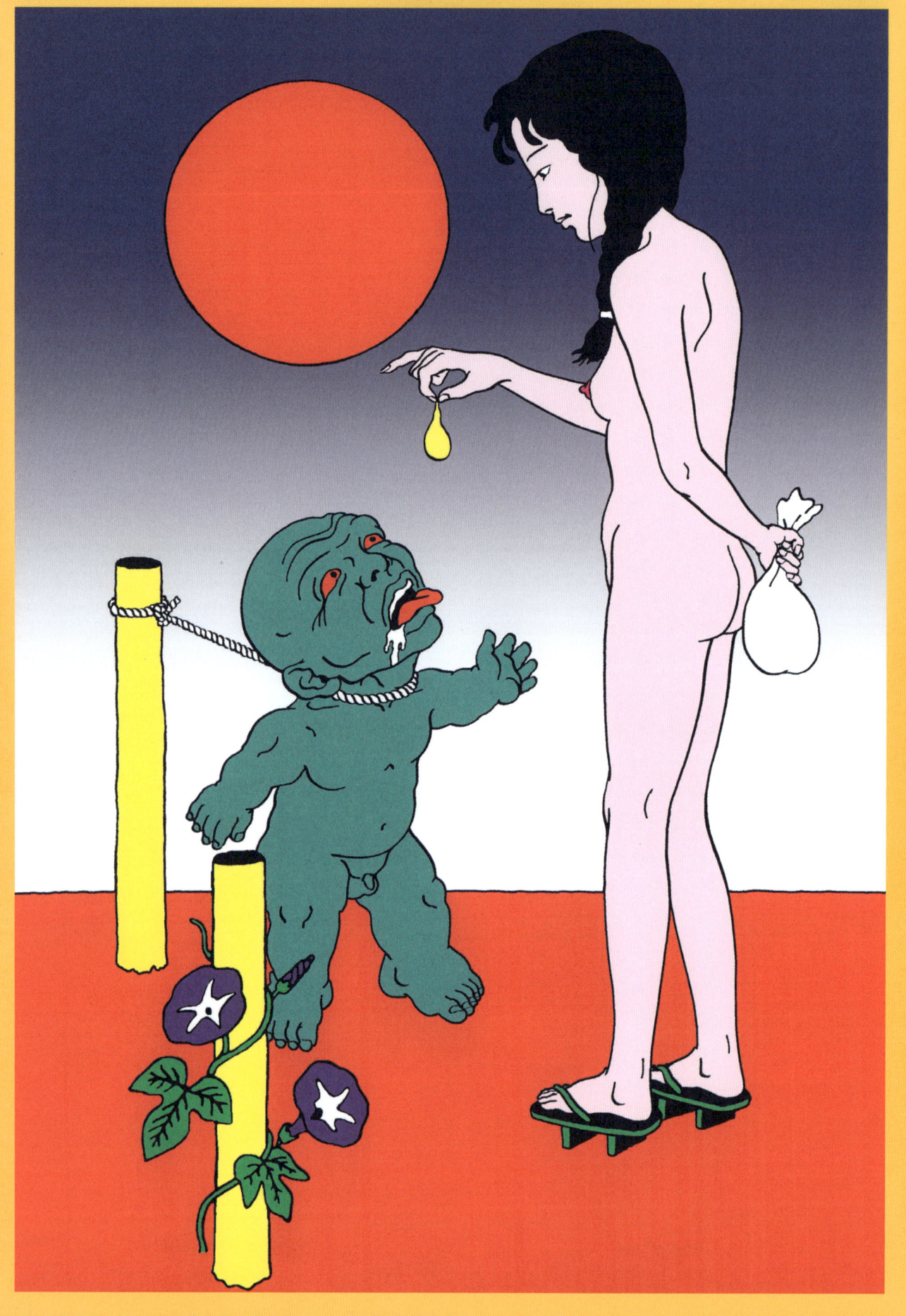

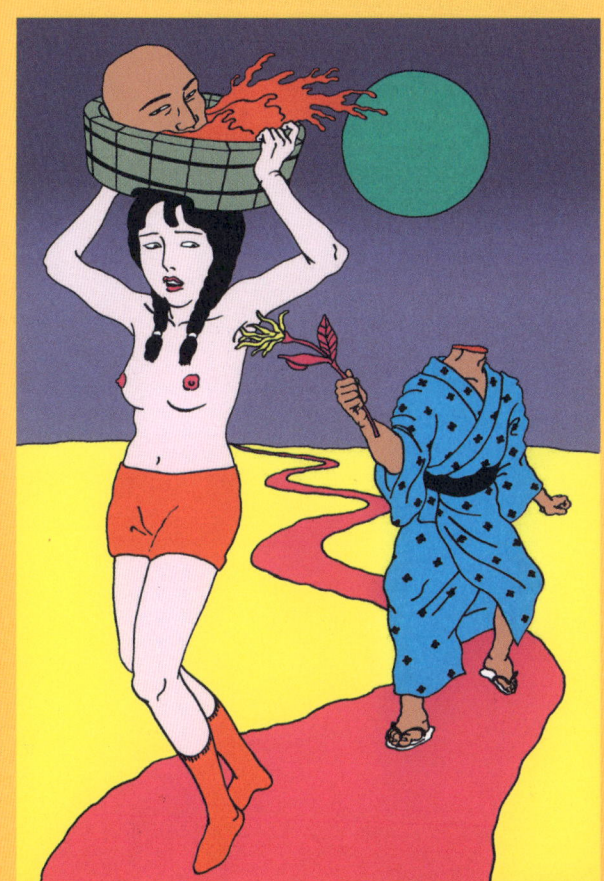

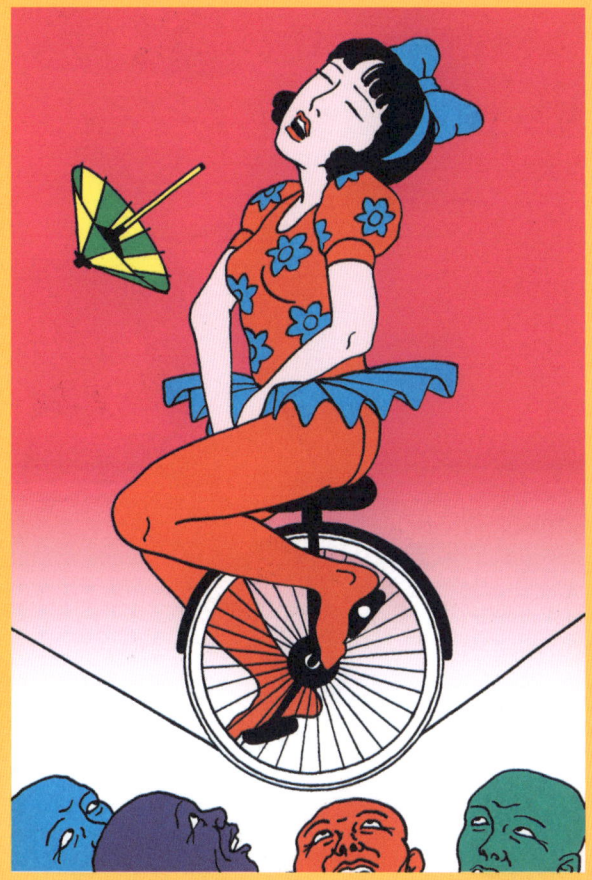

'The year 1970 was an unforgettable turning point in my professional career. In the spring of the previous year, I moved from Osaka to Tokyo, hoping to work in the publishing industry. In a beat-up apartment with cheap rent, I spent many oppressive tough days searching for various images. When summer was almost over, a certain style of drawing appeared that surprised even myself. I knew that was what I had been searching for, and my confidence drove me to create fifty drawings at once.

With these works in hand, I started to visit publishers, but none of them showed interest to publish them at first, and reality seemed grim. But as the times moved on into the '70s, things started to change all of a sudden. My efforts to create prints of the fifty works and to resend them to the publishers bore fruit, and the popular men's magazine *Heibon Punch* published a special feature of my works in their photogravure section.

That year, while the Japan Osaka World Exposition 1970 celebrated the country's high economic growth, it also marked the beginning of a memorable and dramatic new era, with such major events as the Yodogo hijacking incident by the Red Army faction of the Japan Communist League and the suicide by mutilation of Mishima Yukio which both shook the world. The hippie culture from the 1960s, which had been born in the wake of the Vietnam war, also progressively permeated various fields, revolutionizing the customs and behaviours of young people in particular.'

夢でない夢

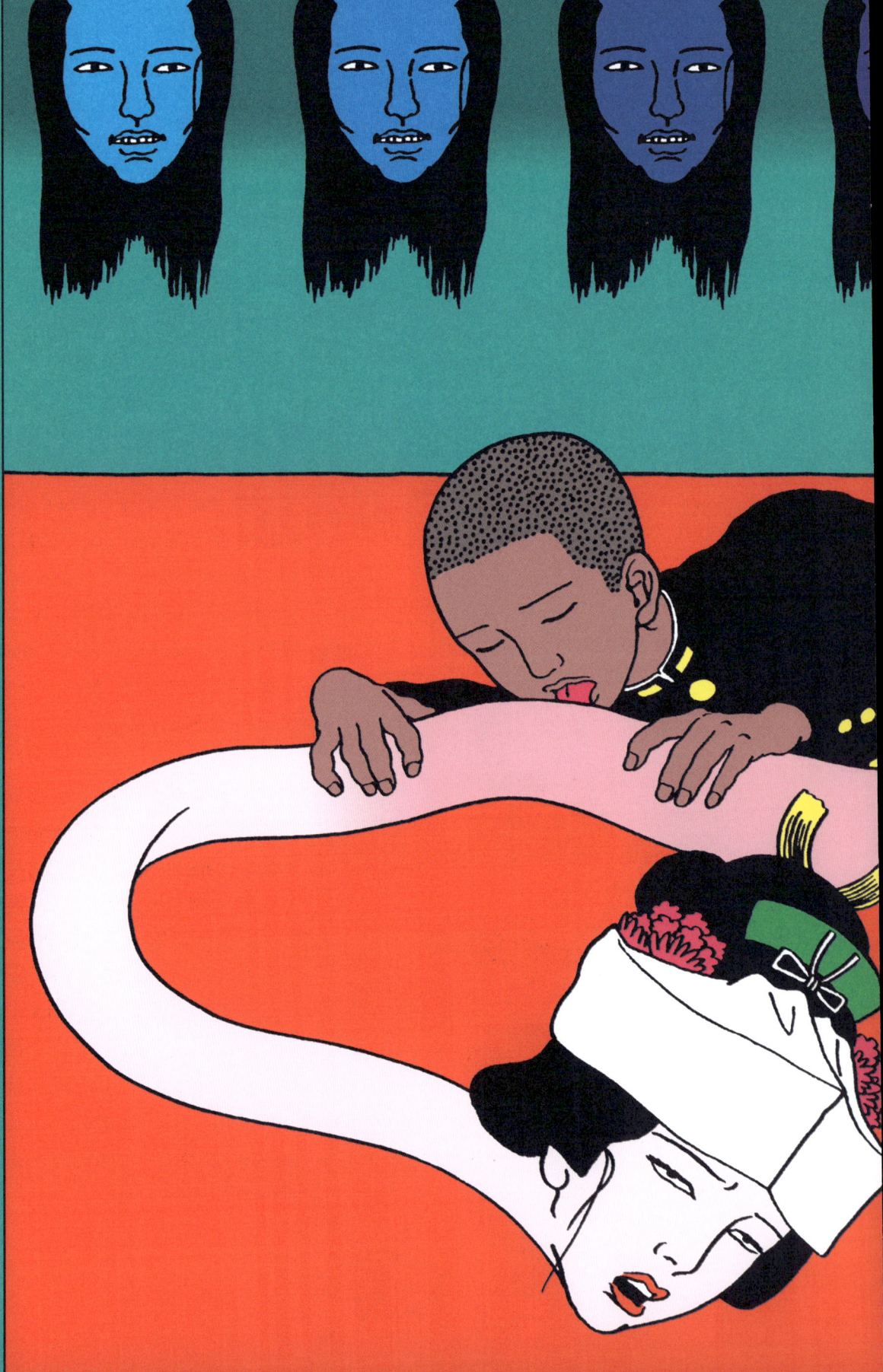

pp. 284–85: Images from **Saeki Toshio**, *Fièvres nocturnes* (2022).

Right: Image from **Saeki Toshio**, *Fièvres nocturnes* (2022).

pp. 288–89: Images from **Saeki Toshio**, *Rêve écarlate* (2016).

p. 290 (above, left and right): Image from **Saeki Toshio**, *Fièvres nocturnes* (2022).

p. 290 (below): Image from **Saeki Toshio**, *Rêve écarlate* (2016).

p. 291: Images from **Saeki Toshio**, *Rêve écarlate* (2016).

pp. 292–93: Image from **Saeki Toshio**, *Rêve écarlate* (2016).

A DREAM THAT IS NOT A DREAM

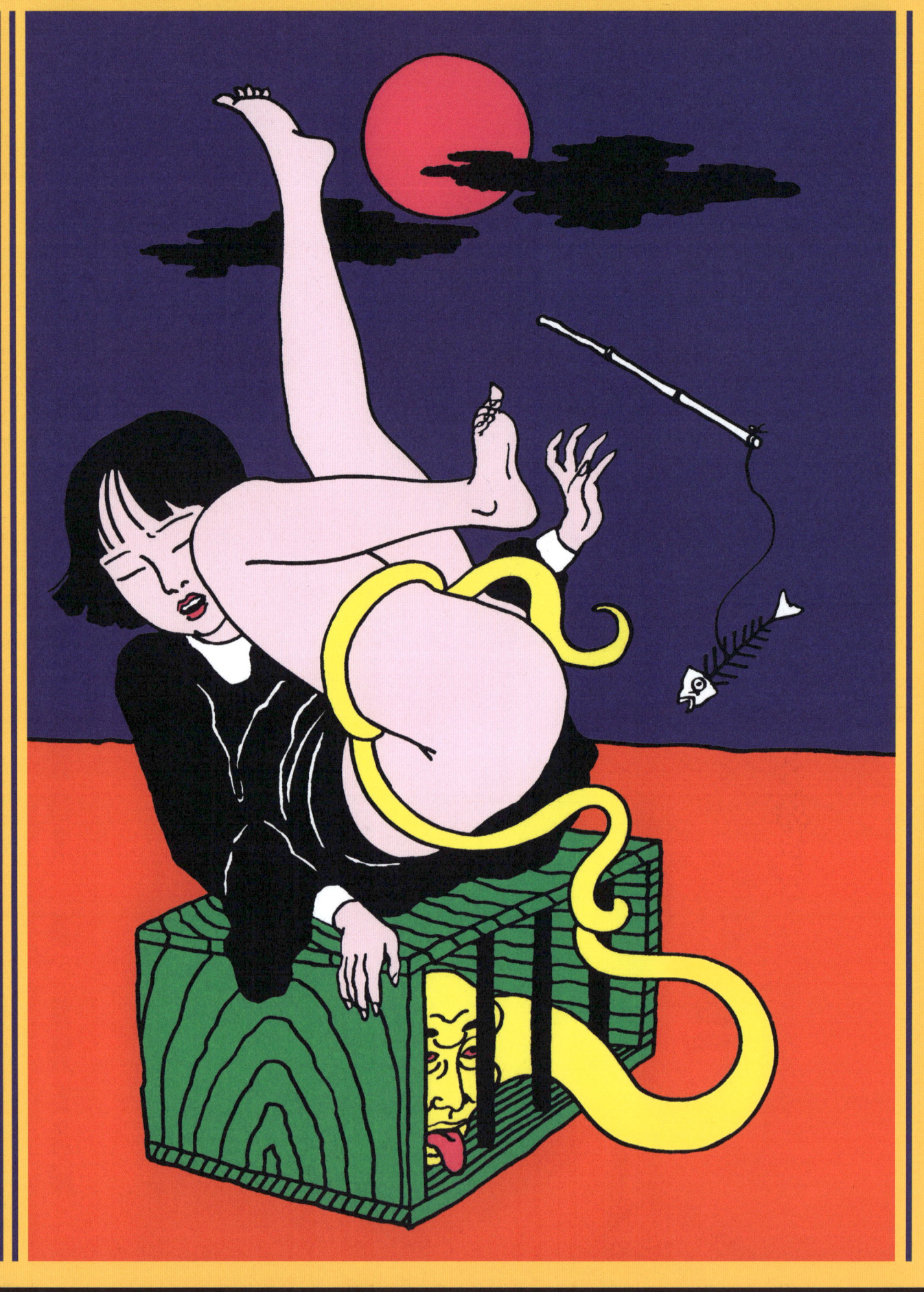

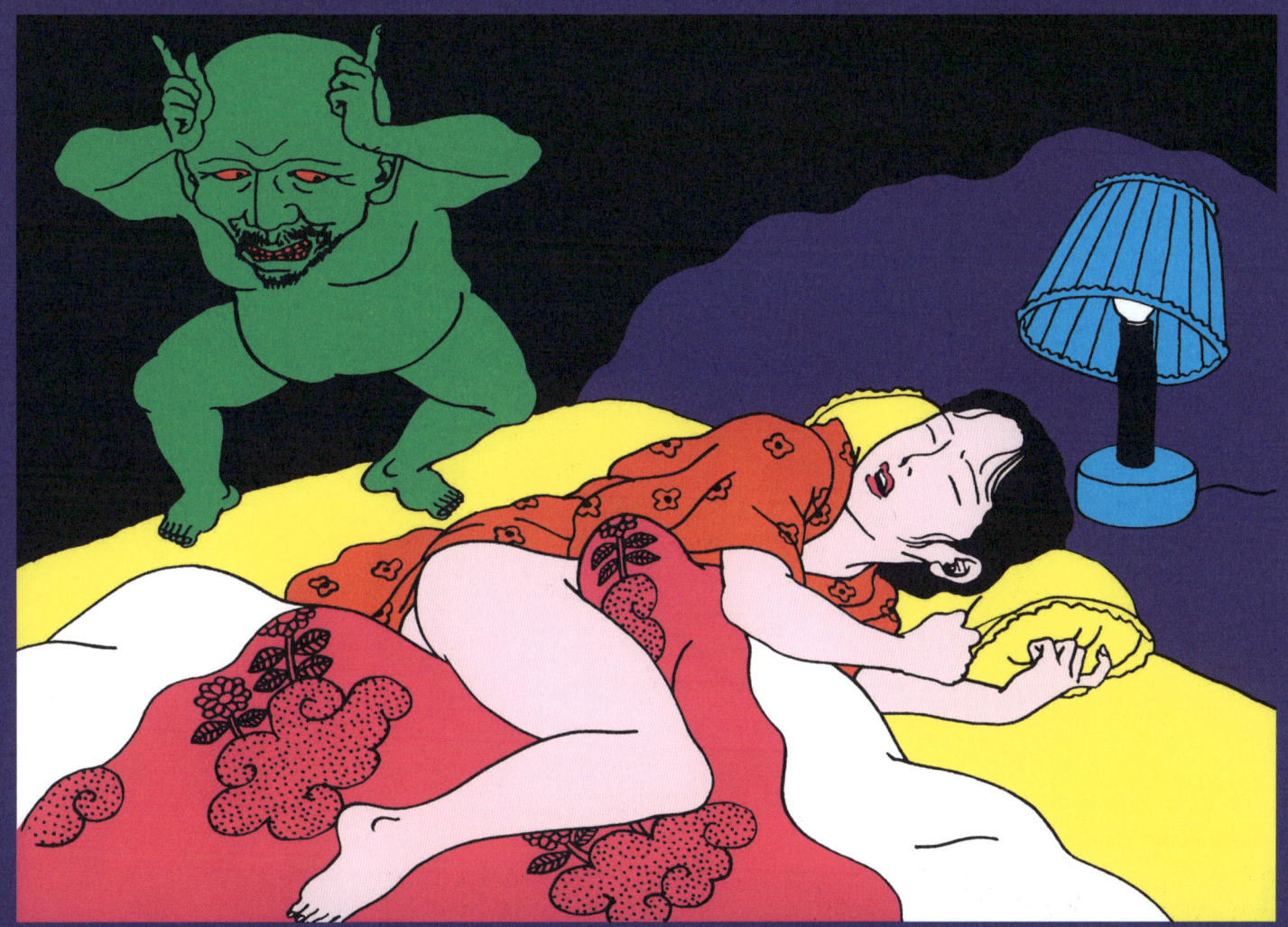

SAEKI'S ART GIVES OFF HAUNTING ENERGY. IT'S INSPIRED BY MYTHOLOGY AND FOLKLORE, BUT IT LOOKS VERY POP TOO.

Dreams and the unconscious were significant elements in Saeki's artwork. He often used the term 'dream' in the titles of his artworks and books. If you're Japanese, you'll notice a lot of famous ghosts, vengeful spirits and monsters culturally familiar to the Japanese. In addition to that, his own original fun, erotic and comical ghosts and monsters often appear.

To analyse spirituality from the perspective of the unconscious or dreams, Saeki thought how interesting it was to create something without understanding the reason why he drew it. Getting inspiration from unconscious ideas of unknown provenance was fascinating for him.

SAEKI YUKA

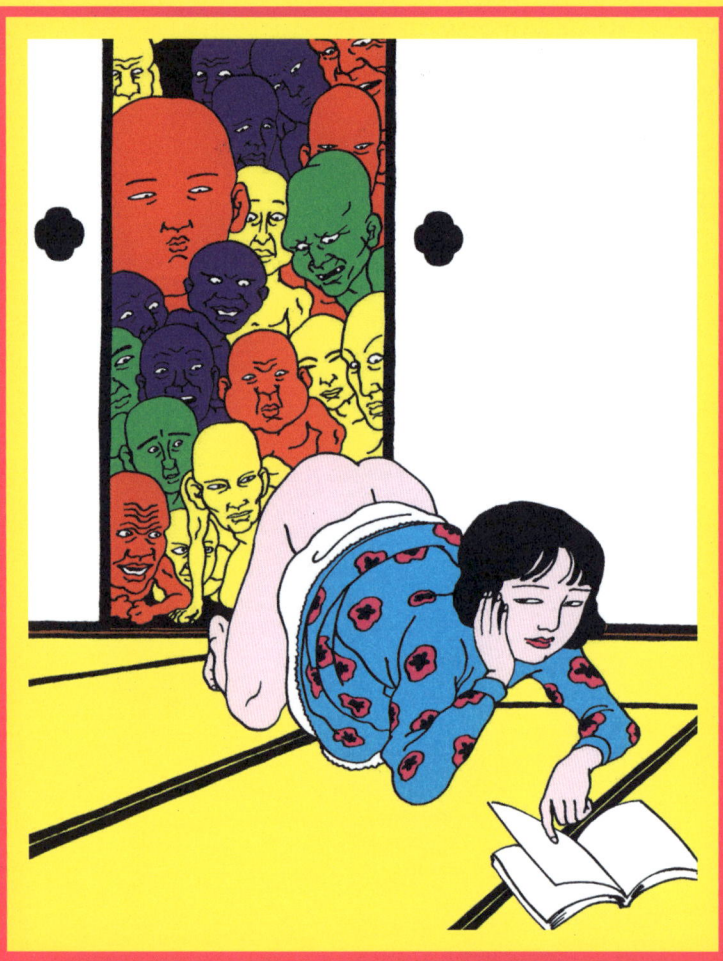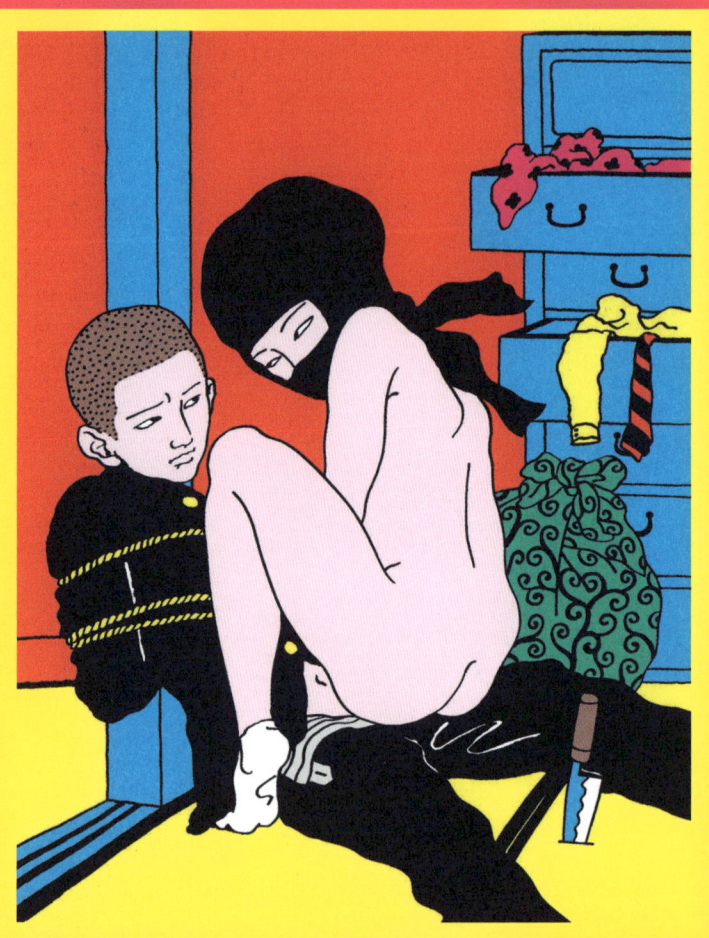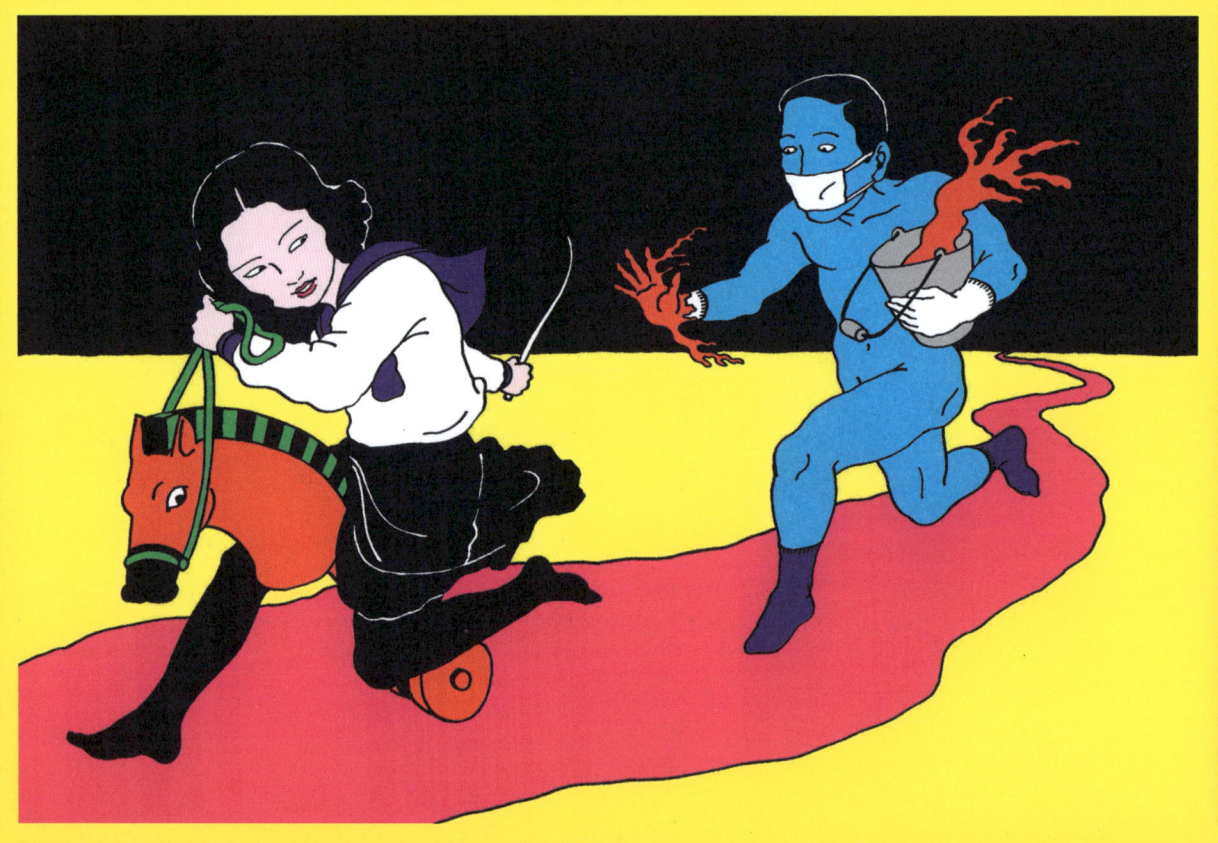

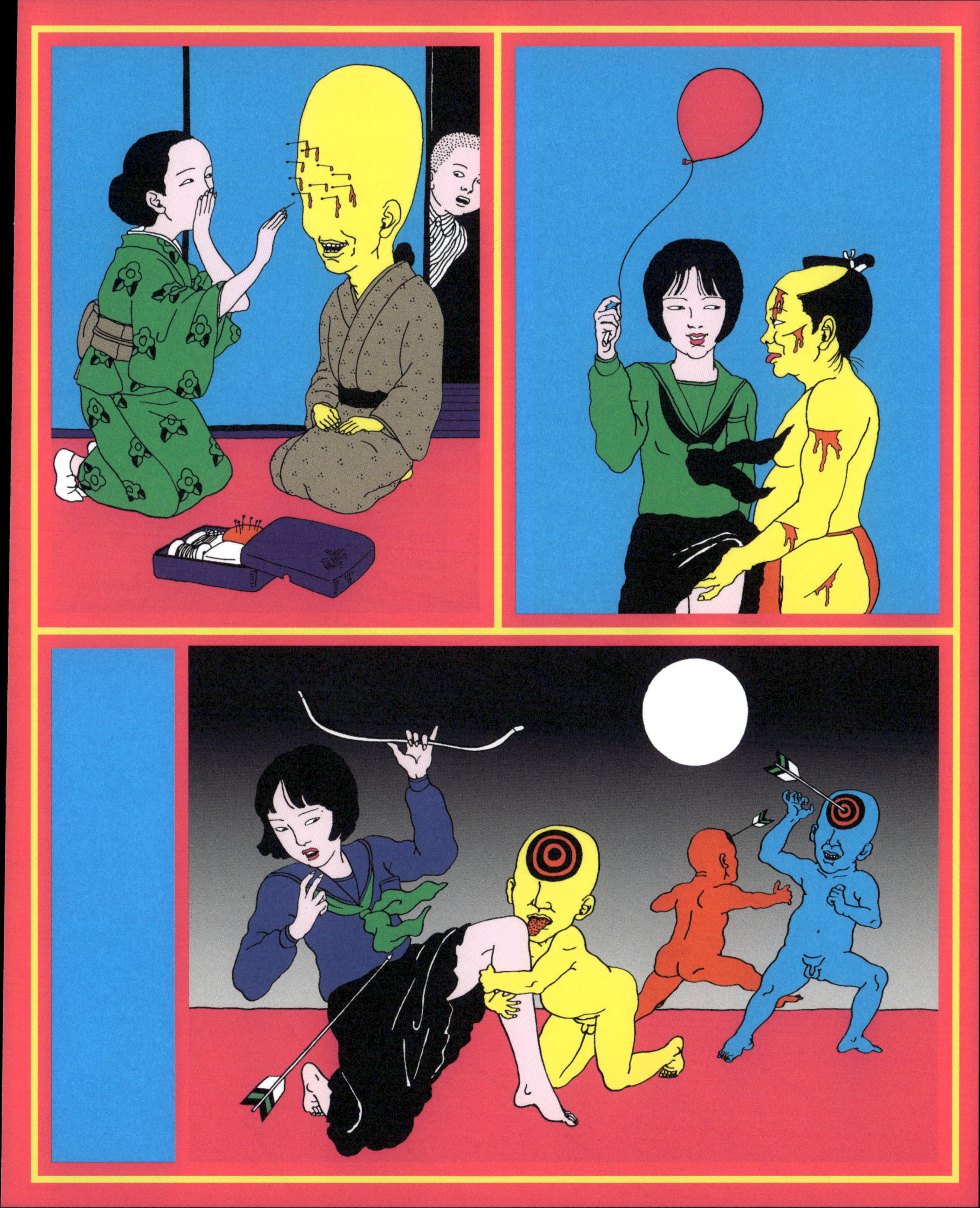

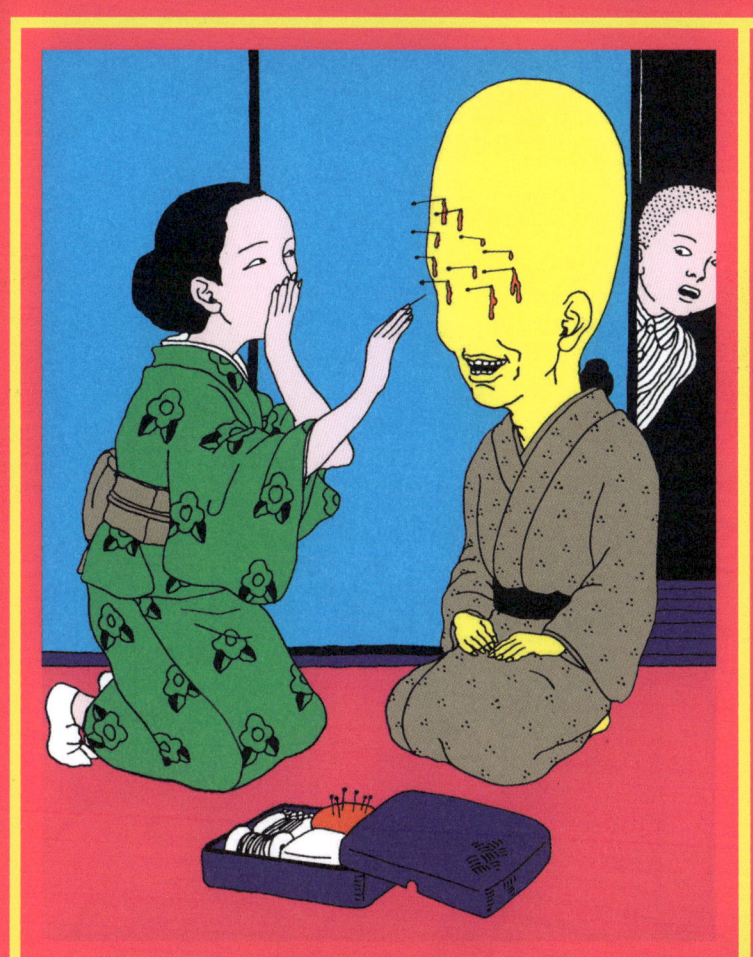
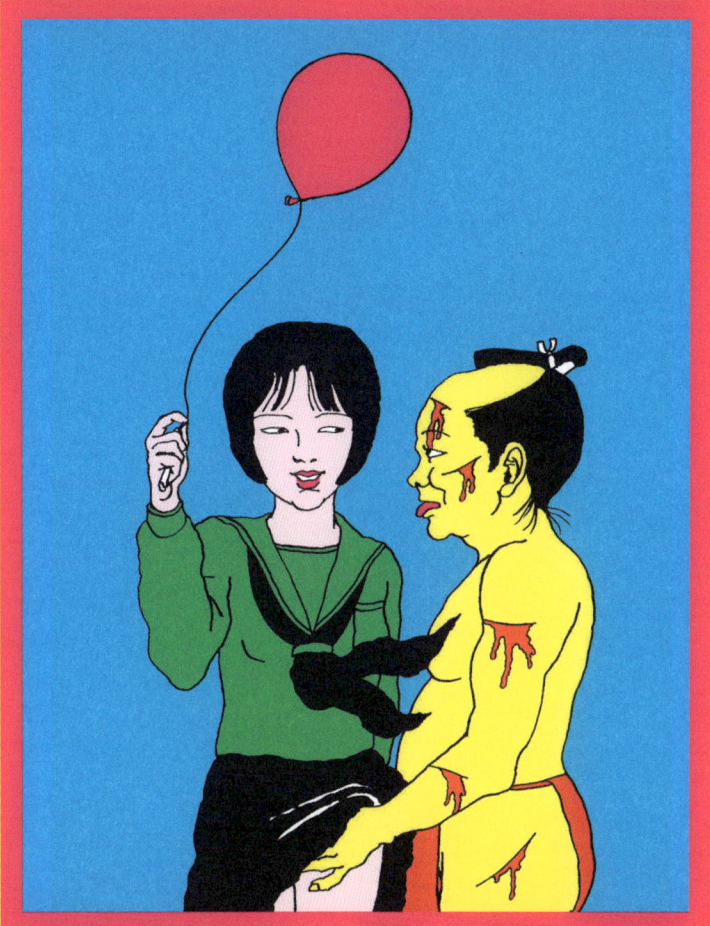

佐伯俊男

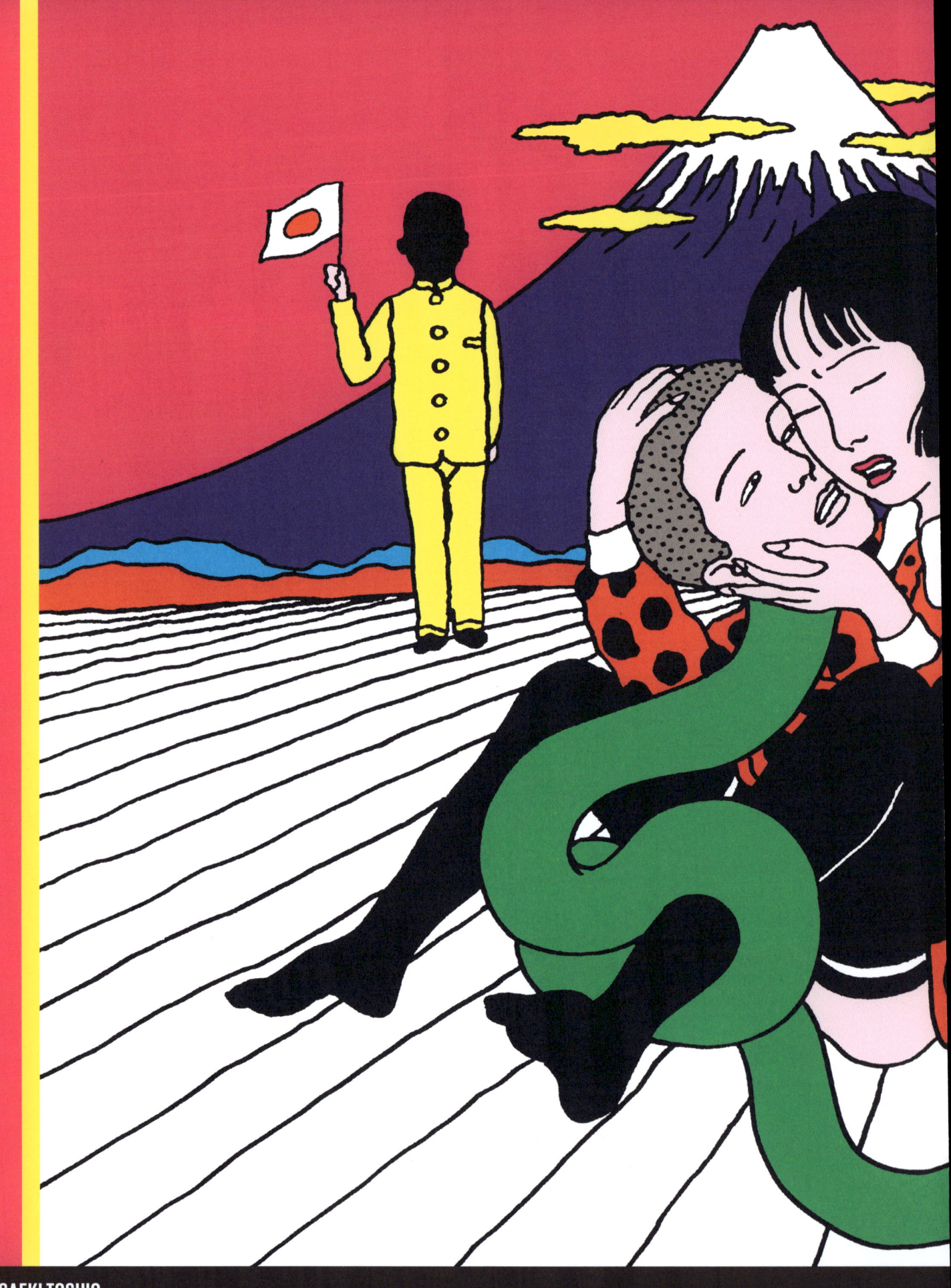

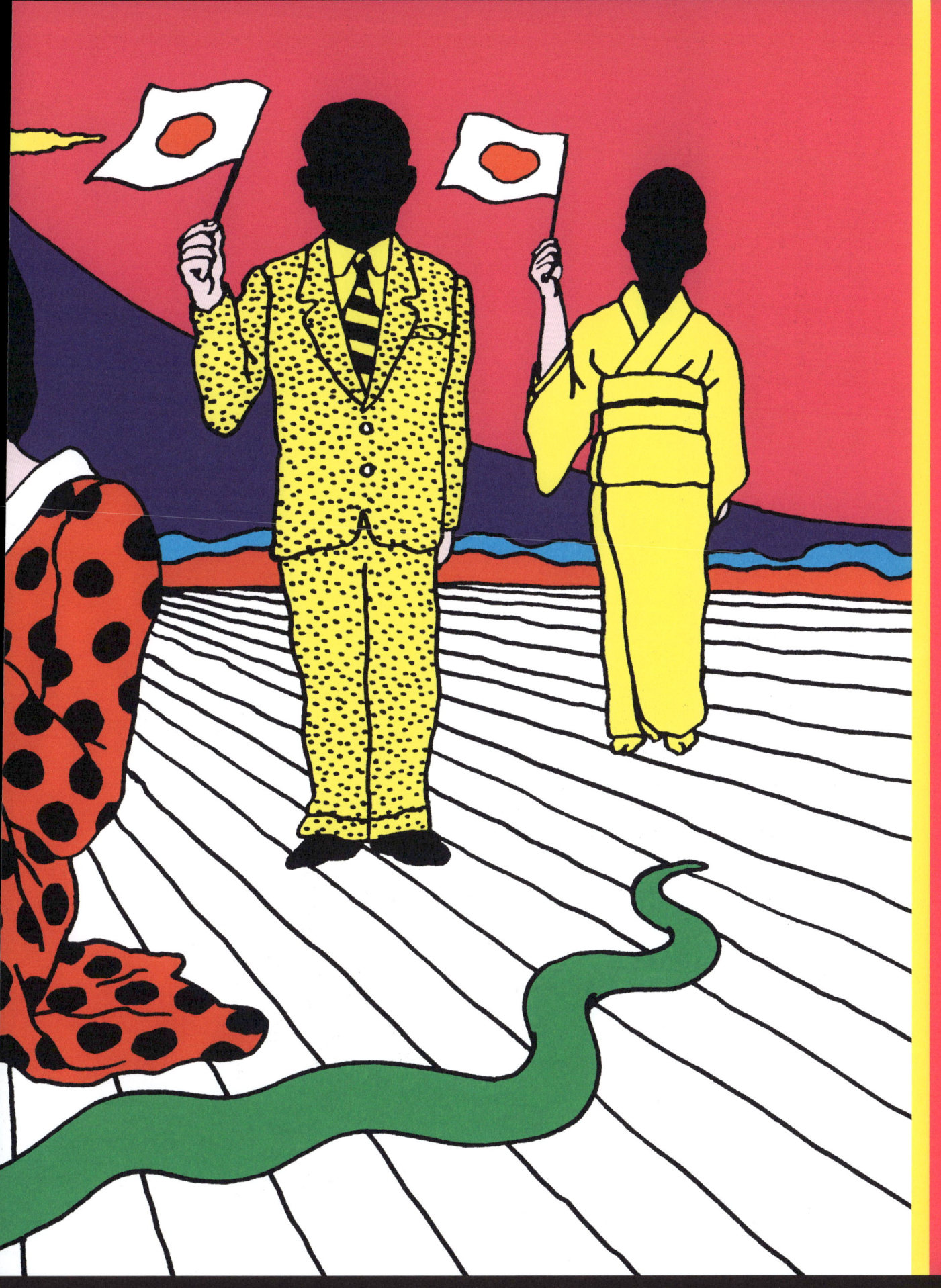

佐伯俊男

ERO GURO NANSENSU

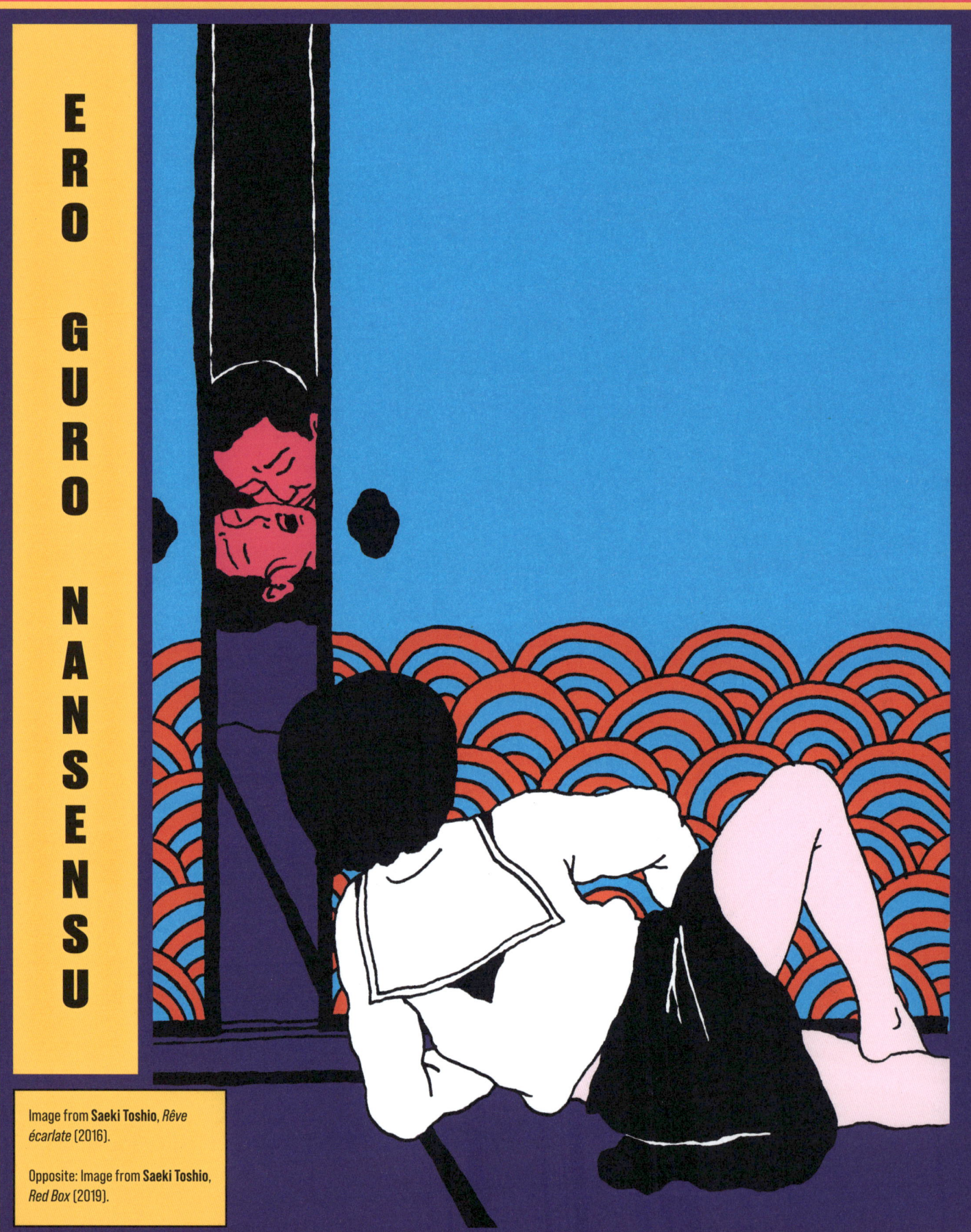

Image from **Saeki Toshio**, *Rêve écarlate* (2016).

Opposite: Image from **Saeki Toshio**, *Red Box* (2019).

Saeki drew a lot of women masturbating, which left an impression on me. I felt like his art could see through my mind when I fantasize or think of naughty things.

I think he did a realistic portrayal of women. He may have had a tendency to draw women more beautiful and men more ugly, but he also depicted women imagining vulgar things or becoming demons and biting someone.

Those are regardless of gender and there is a lot of free imagination in it.

SAEKI DID MANY DRAWINGS OF A PERSON PEEPING AT SOMEONE WHILE ALSO BEING WATCHED FROM BEHIND BY ANOTHER STRANGER. AUDIENCES ARE ALSO WATCHING THAT SITUATION FROM OUTSIDE. A MULTI-LAYERED STYLE OF WATCHING.

SAEKI YUKA

エログロ

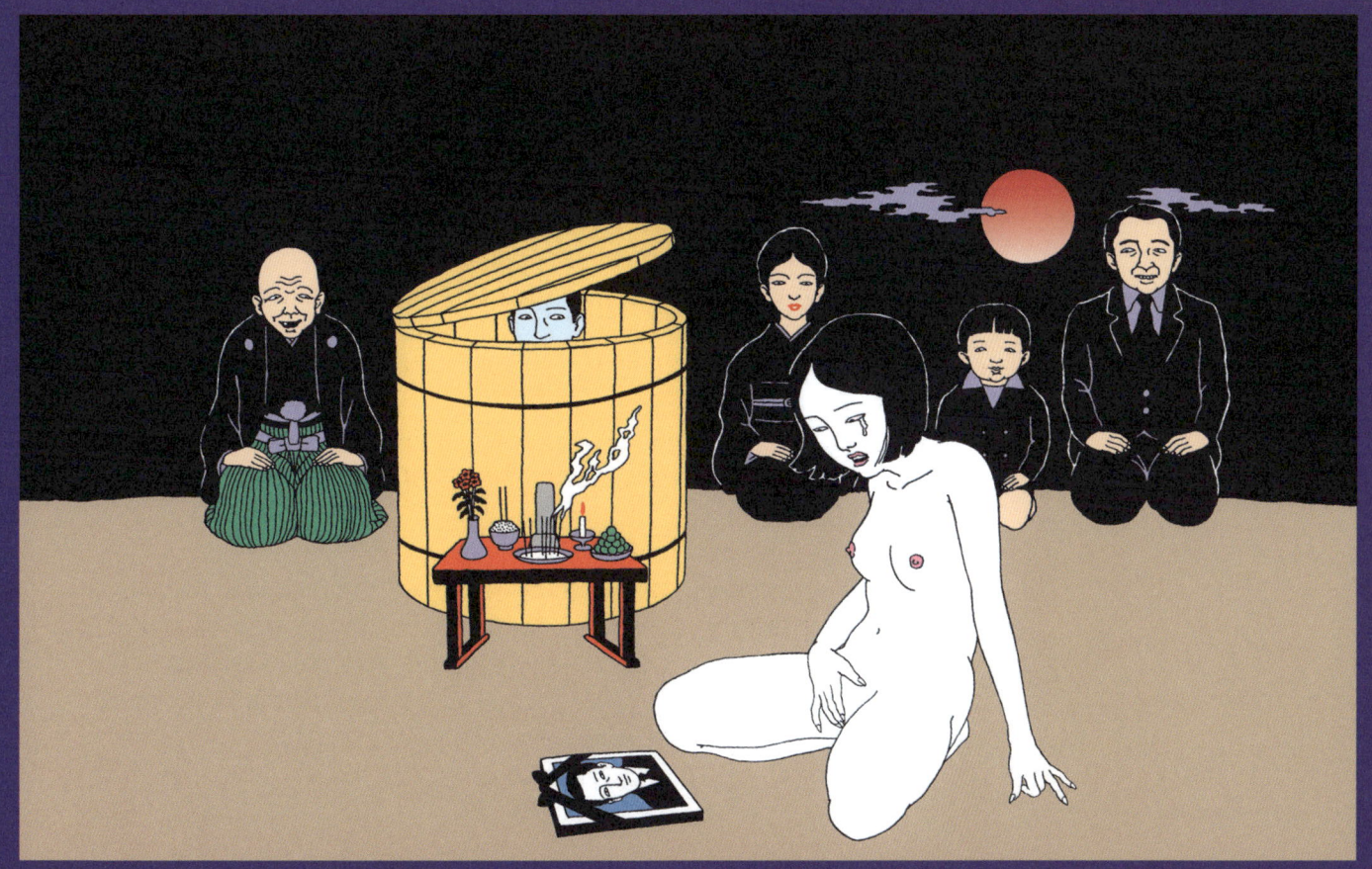

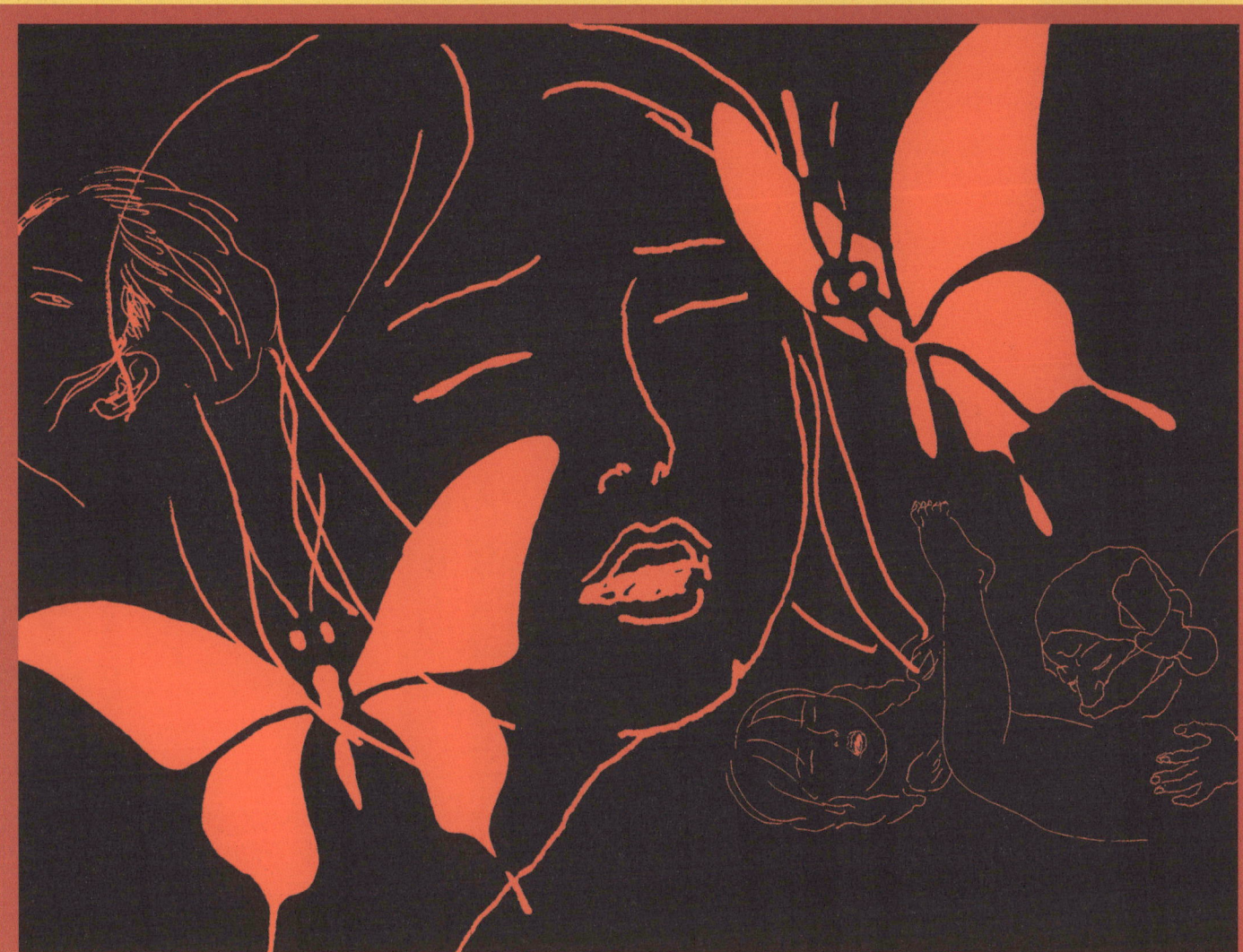

Image from **Saeki Toshio**, *Red Box* (2019).

Opposite (above left): Image from **Saeki Toshio**, *Red Box* (2019).

Opposite (right): **Photographer unknown**, *Saeki Toshio*, 1970, gelatin silver print.

Overleaf: Image from **Saeki Toshio**, *Red Box* (2019).

Growing up during the chaotic post-war era, there was hope for a better future after the war ended. The war was still going on when Saeki was born. He was born in February 1945, and the war ended in August. I believe being born at this time, which was a chaotic period for Japan, had a huge effect on Saeki's life.

Eroticism was an extremely significant theme for Saeki's artwork. Eroticism allowed him to see the real part of the world and the human mind.

Saeki Toshio wanted his works to allow viewers to realize each of their individual senses, their true feelings and their sensibility. If it scares you, you might not be able to enjoy it. There's no pressure. But if his art intrigues you . . . I want you to conceive why you were drawn to his art, or how it makes you feel.

SAEKI YUKA

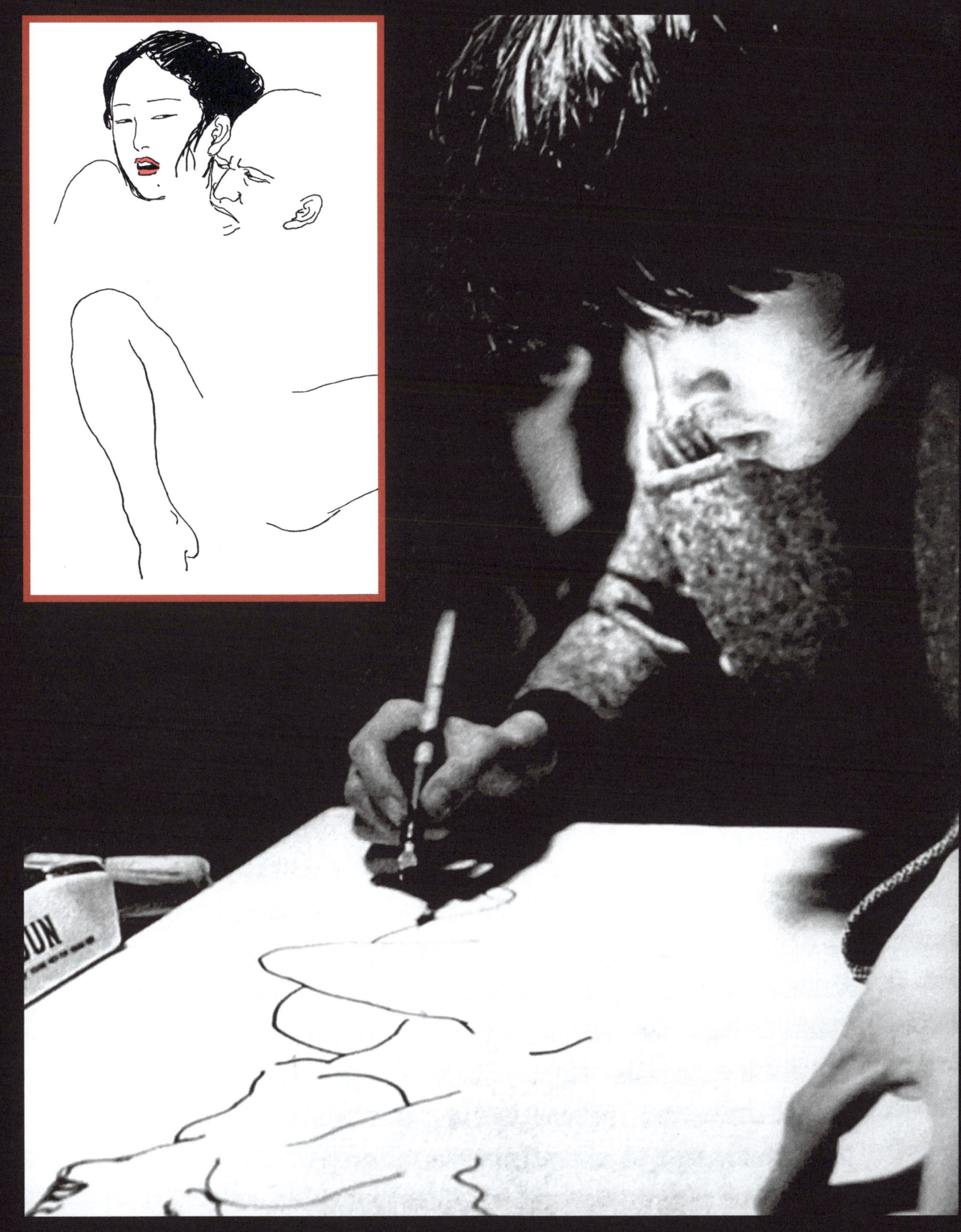

佐伯俊男　297

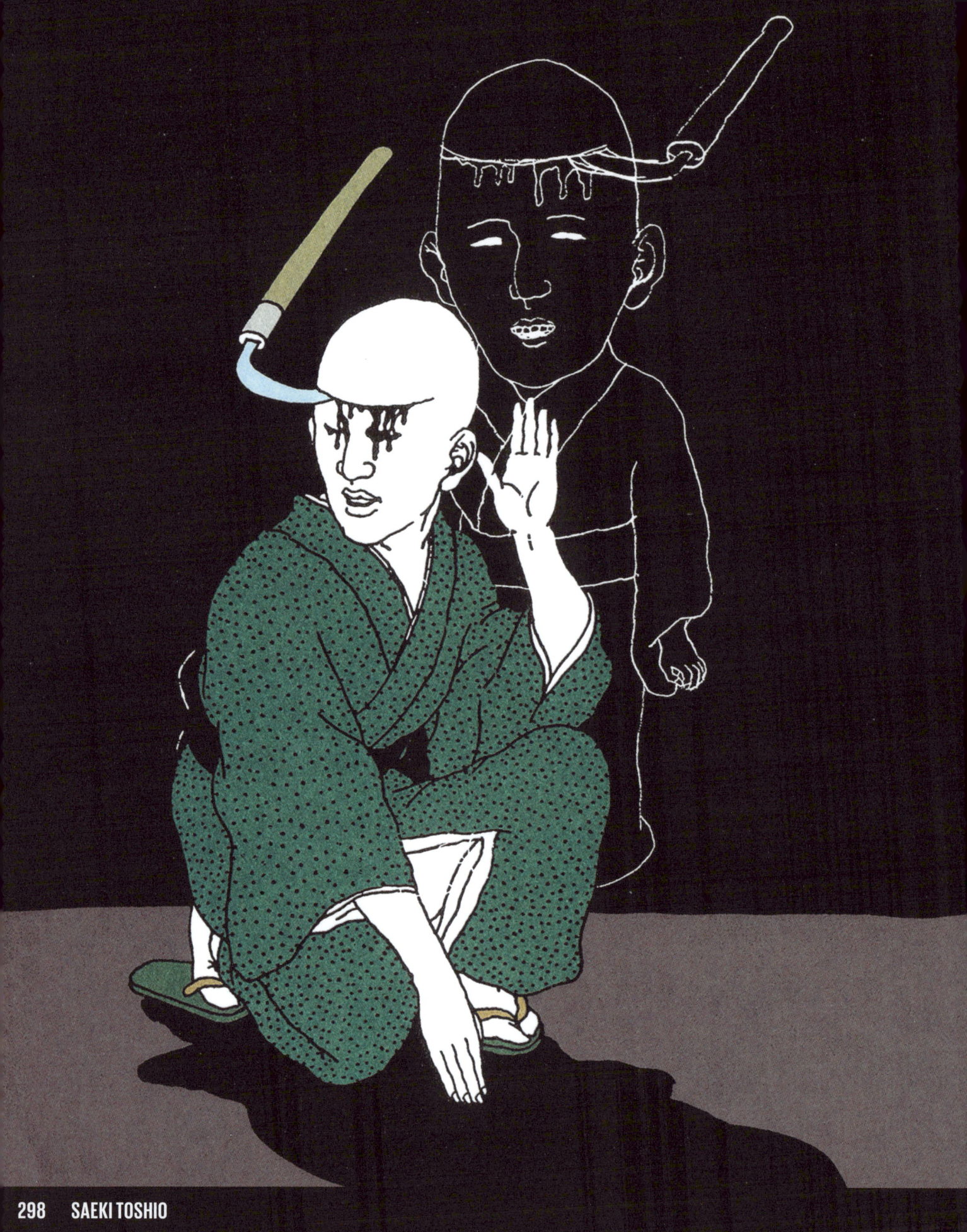

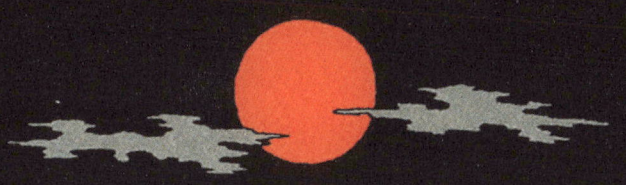

'It was not long after the beginning of the seventies that I received a call from Terayama Shūji. It was a request for an interview because he had been asked to write an article about me to be published in Chuo Koron's literary magazine *Umi* (Sea). Terayama had already written an interesting essay for my first book of drawings.

Terayama appeared in the coffee shop of the Tenjō Sajiki theater troupe wearing a black turtleneck and a brown jacket. His friendly atmosphere, as if he had known me for a long time, made me forget the nervousness of our first meeting. The interview began, and the topic of the conversation turned to our childhood sexual experiences.

When I was in the first grade of elementary school, my classmate Uemura-kun showed me an ukiyo-e shunga in the back corner of the classroom. I think they were prints made on Japanese paper. The scene in the extremely colorful picture was so outrageous and erotic that I was struck with dizzying surprise and bewilderment. In that a man and a woman were engaged in a somewhat embarrassing kind of "play," it was somewhat similar to the "playing doctor" I had already experienced with a girl earlier, but there was no way I could understand the grotesque joining of the bottom half of their bodies. I had to convince myself that this must have been the work of a demented adult who had skillfully created a picture of a disgusting imagination that could not exist in this world.

"What position were they in?" With a mischievous smile, Terayama held out a pencil and a small piece of paper. I thought he just wanted a simple sketch to grasp the image, so I made him a very simple drawing of a seated posture as seen from above, but instead of just leaving it on the table, he carefully tucked the piece of paper into the pocket inside his jacket. Later, when I saw the interview, the memo-like drawing was the first thing that jumped out from the page.'

'During this period, I often engaged in thoughts about "eternity." And I tried to reflect those thoughts in my works secretly. "I wonder why you draw one way roads."

Terayama's observation, as if he could see right through me, shook me inside, but I tried not to show it. I replied in a roundabout way, not mentioning the concept of "eternity," saying, "I don't know why but I end up drawing them a one way road that goes on forever."

In the text, Terayama says that "the idea of reincarnation is a metaphor for a one way road," and concludes that "the straight road is an anti-modern self-injection, a will to return to the darkness of the unconscious realm."'

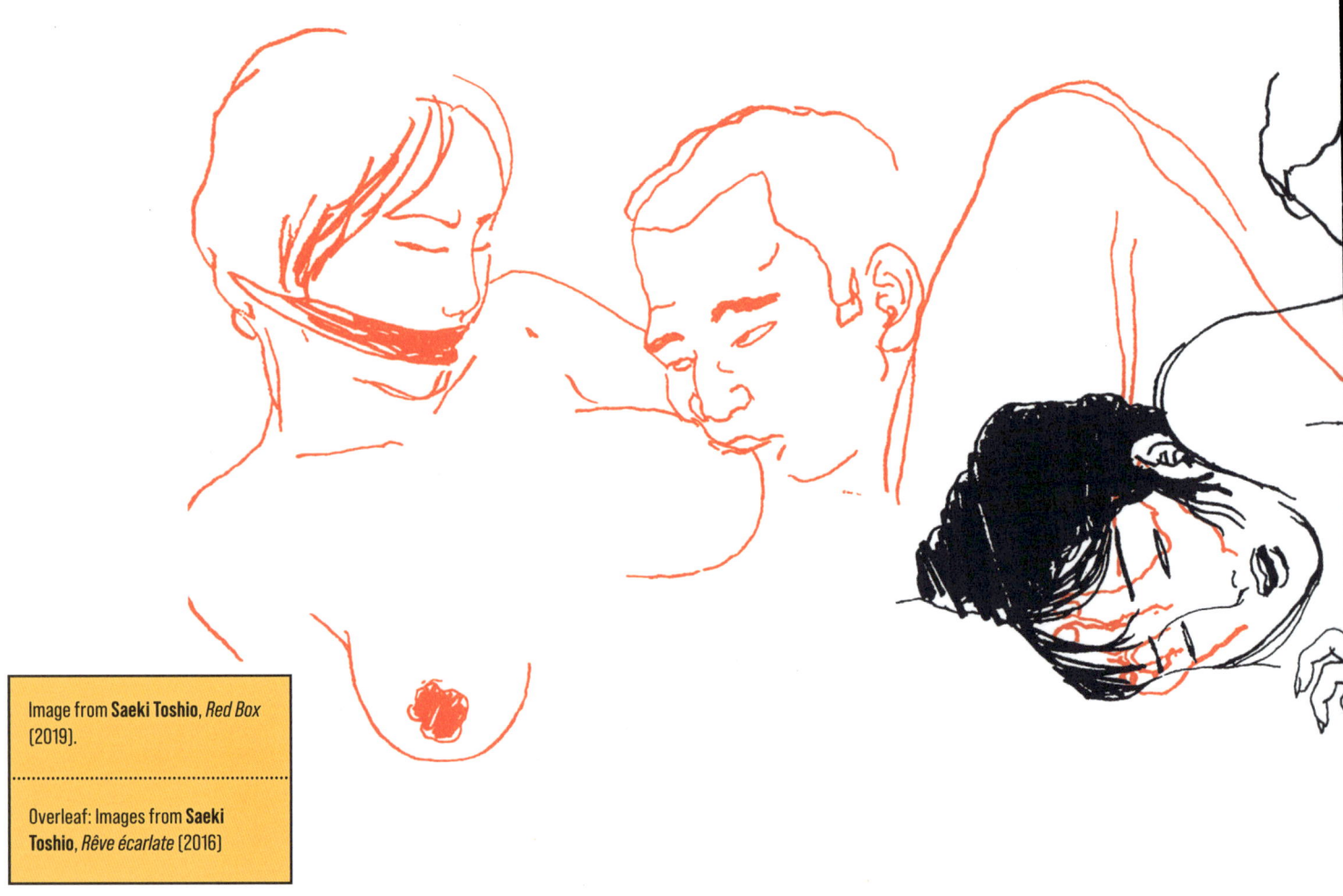

Image from **Saeki Toshio**, *Red Box* (2019).

Overleaf: Images from **Saeki Toshio**, *Rêve écarlate* (2016).

> One big distinction from other artists is that his painting style is very flat, using lines and surfaces thoroughly. I think that is very Japanese. Saeki's art comes alive once it is printed on paper or in a magazine. He took a very simple method for his art materials, he only used Kent paper and ink. In his early years, he used many vivid colours, such as the three primary colours, yellow, blue and red. In his later years, the colours changed to milder and more complex colours. It's because the printing technology itself had been improved so he was able to specify more colour variation.
>
> SAEKI YUKA

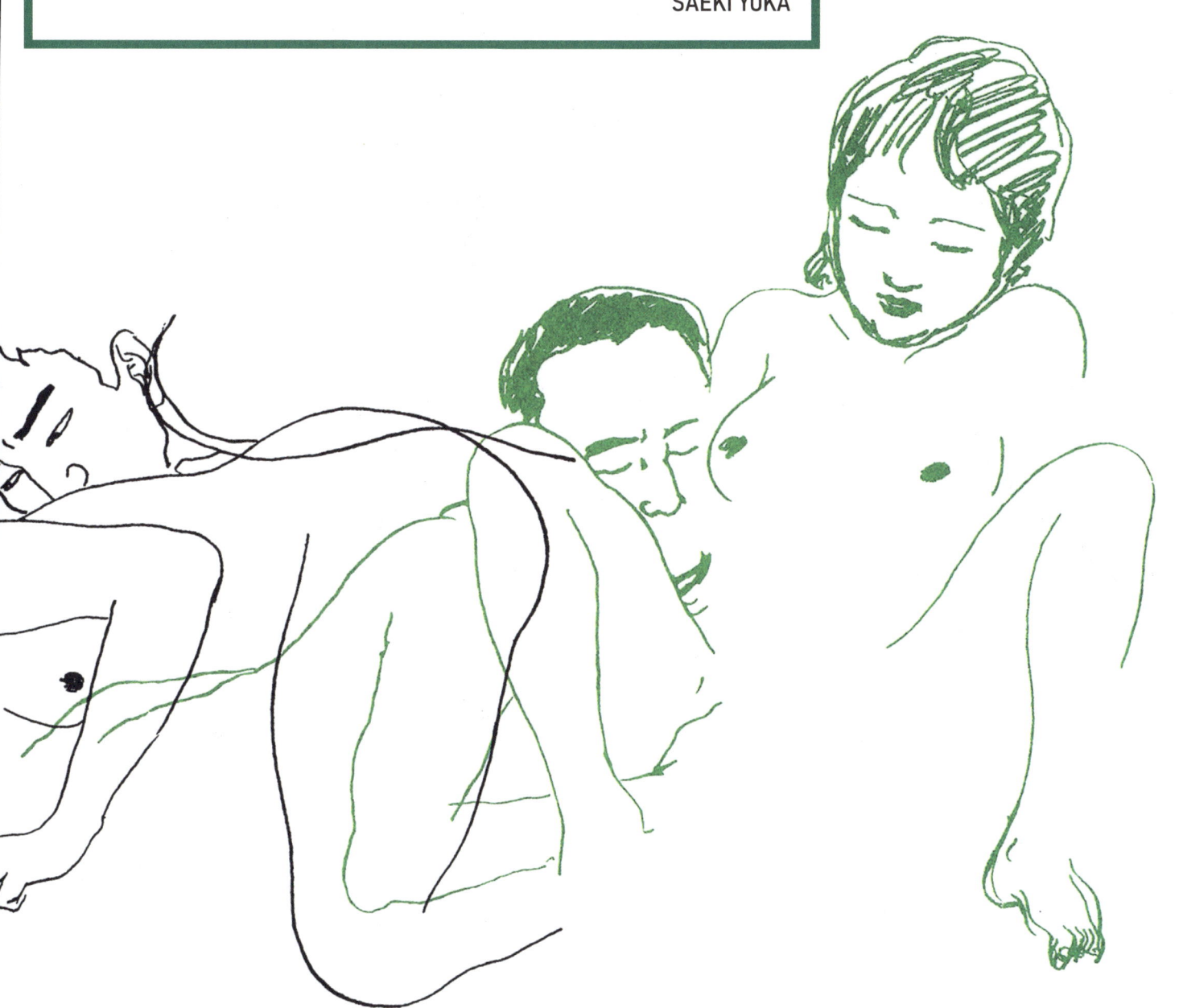

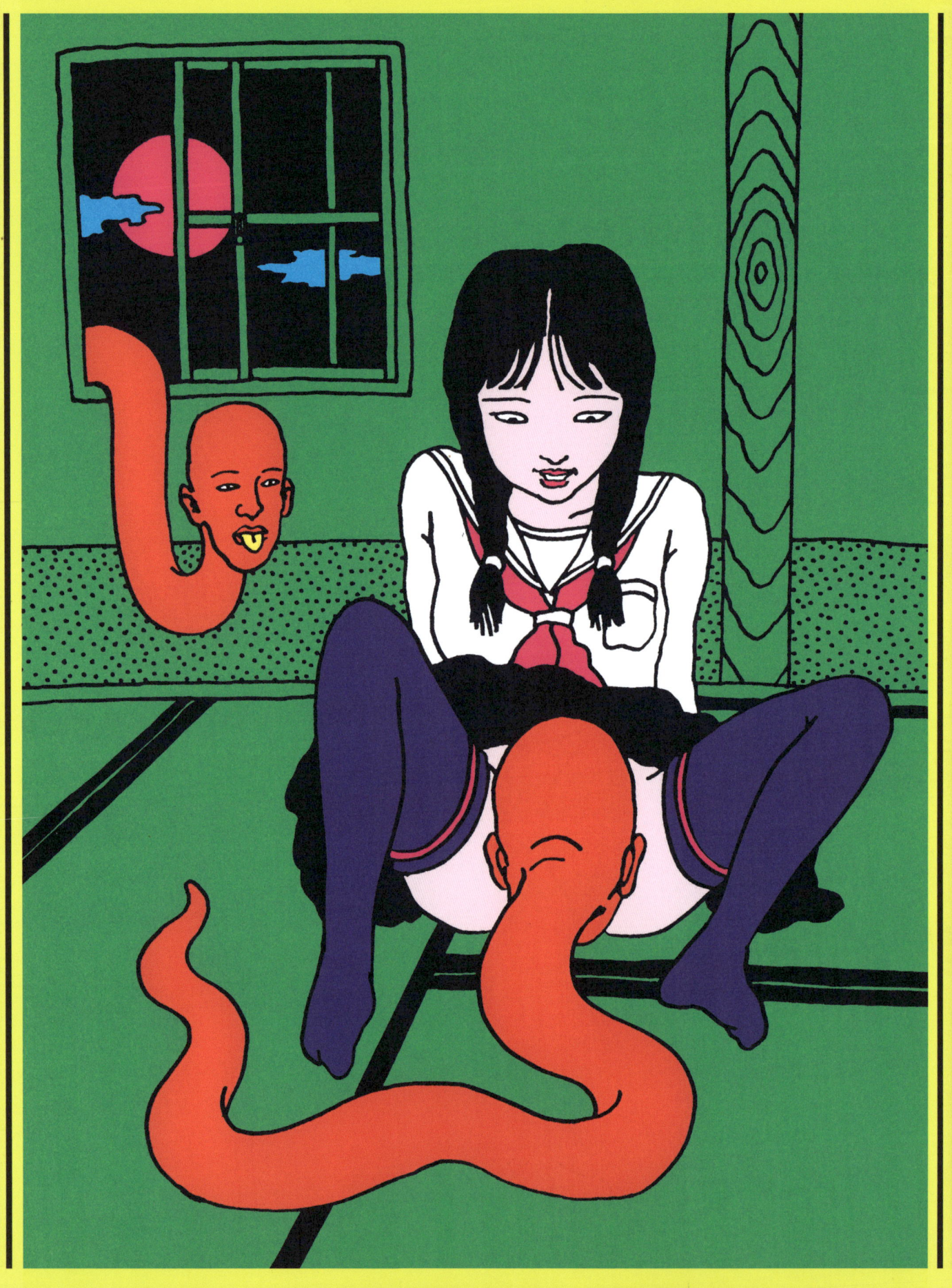

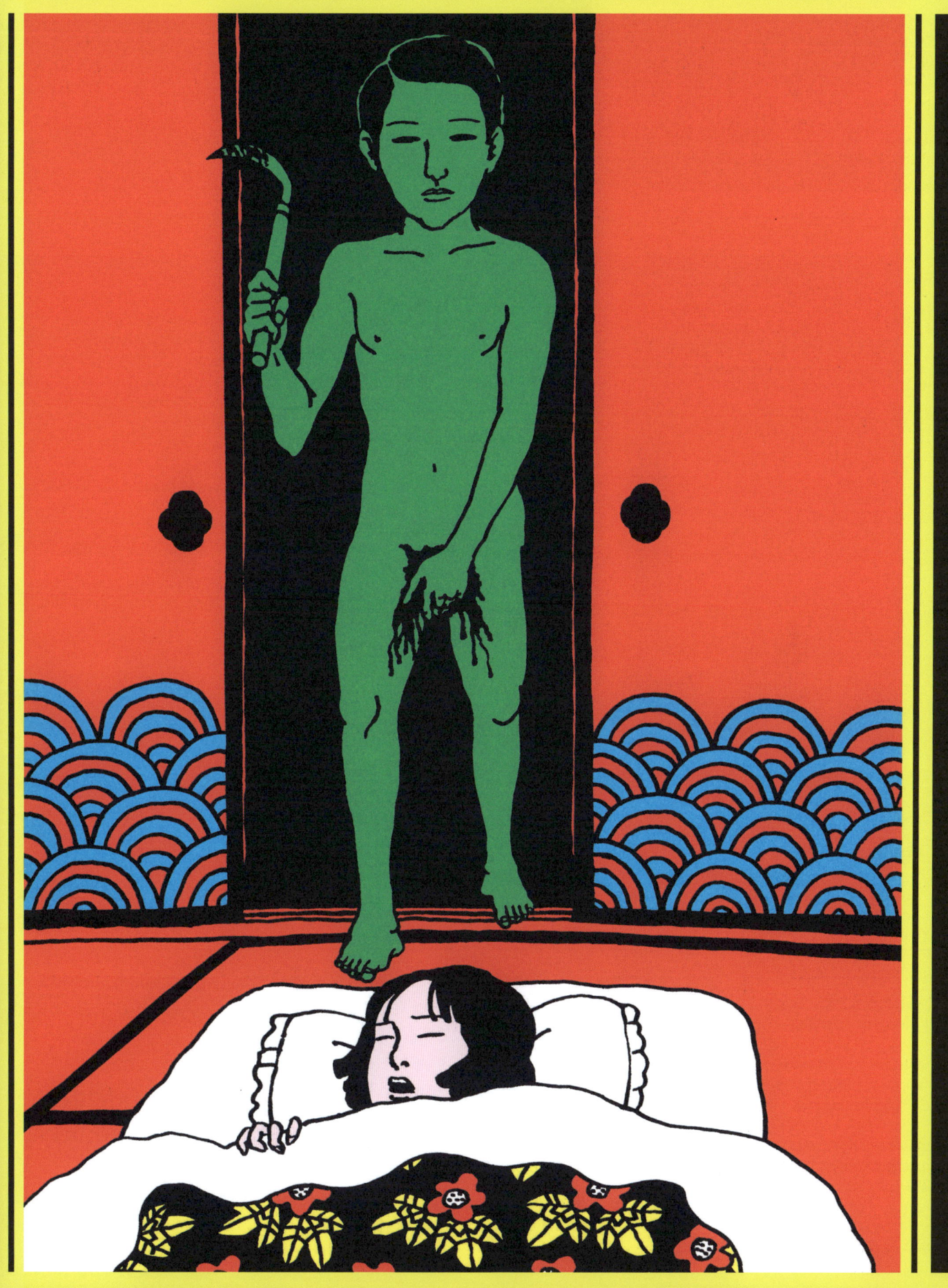

YOKOSUKA NORIAKI

1937–2003

横須賀功光

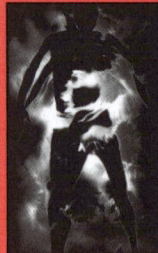

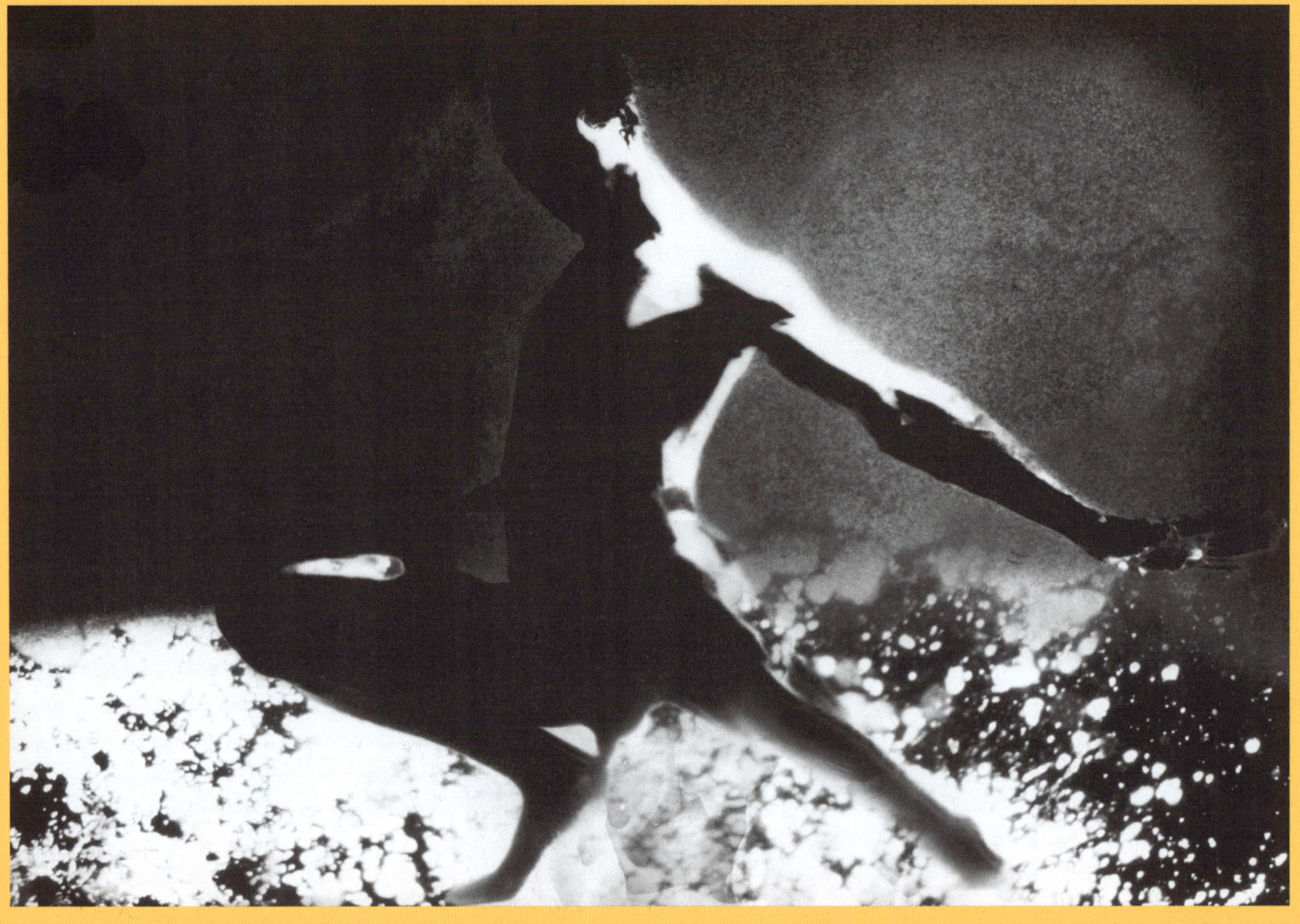

Yokosuka Noriaki, *Optical Isomers #10*, 1994, gelatin silver print.

Opposite (above left): **Yokosuka Noriaki,** *The Light Silver Incident #21*, 1989, gelatin silver print.

Opposite (above right): **Yokosuka Noriaki,** *Optical Isomers #18*, 1994, gelatin silver print.

Opposite (below): **Yokosuka Noriaki,** *The Photon & Ogre* (2005).

Noriaki Yokosuka used to call himself 'an animal shepherd', referring to the animal that watches over the herd and warns it of danger. He sought to be the first to detect signs from above that were wells of creation. He revealed the thrill, the pain and the hurt of those driven to create, the inescapable feelings of one's chosen work.

YANO YURIKO

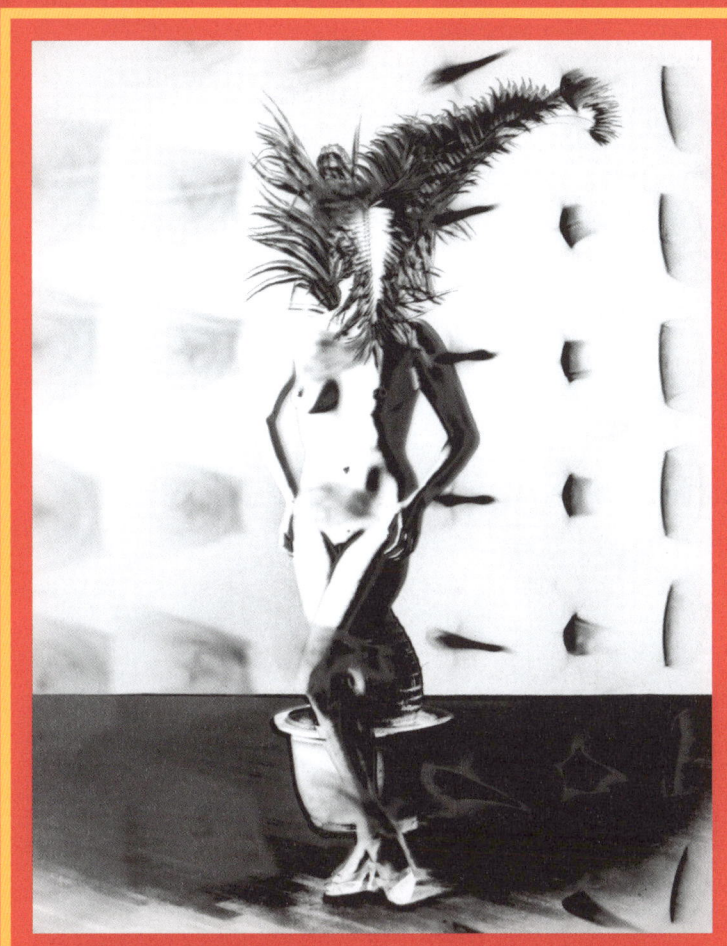
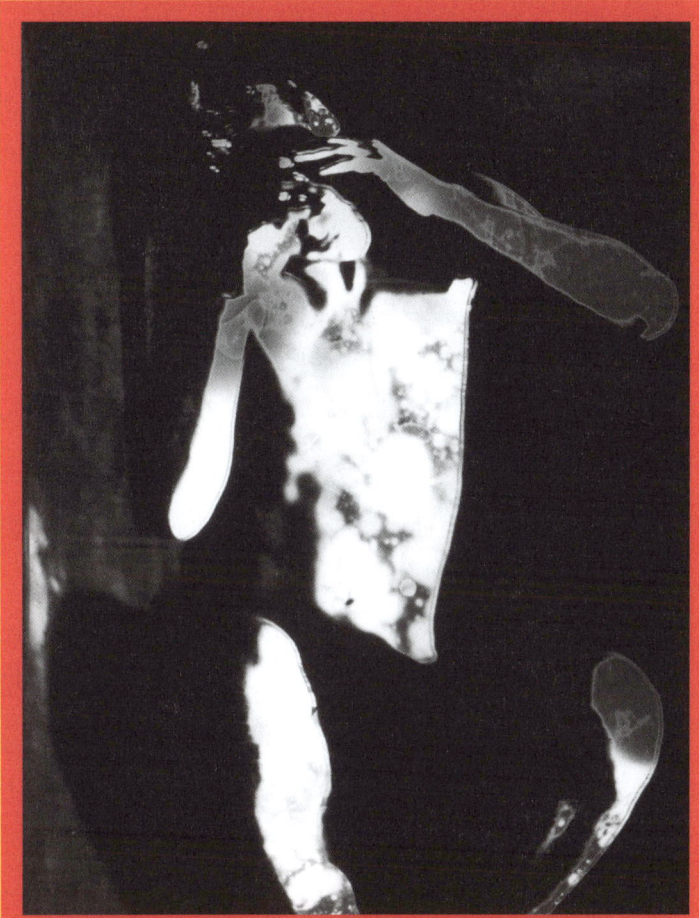

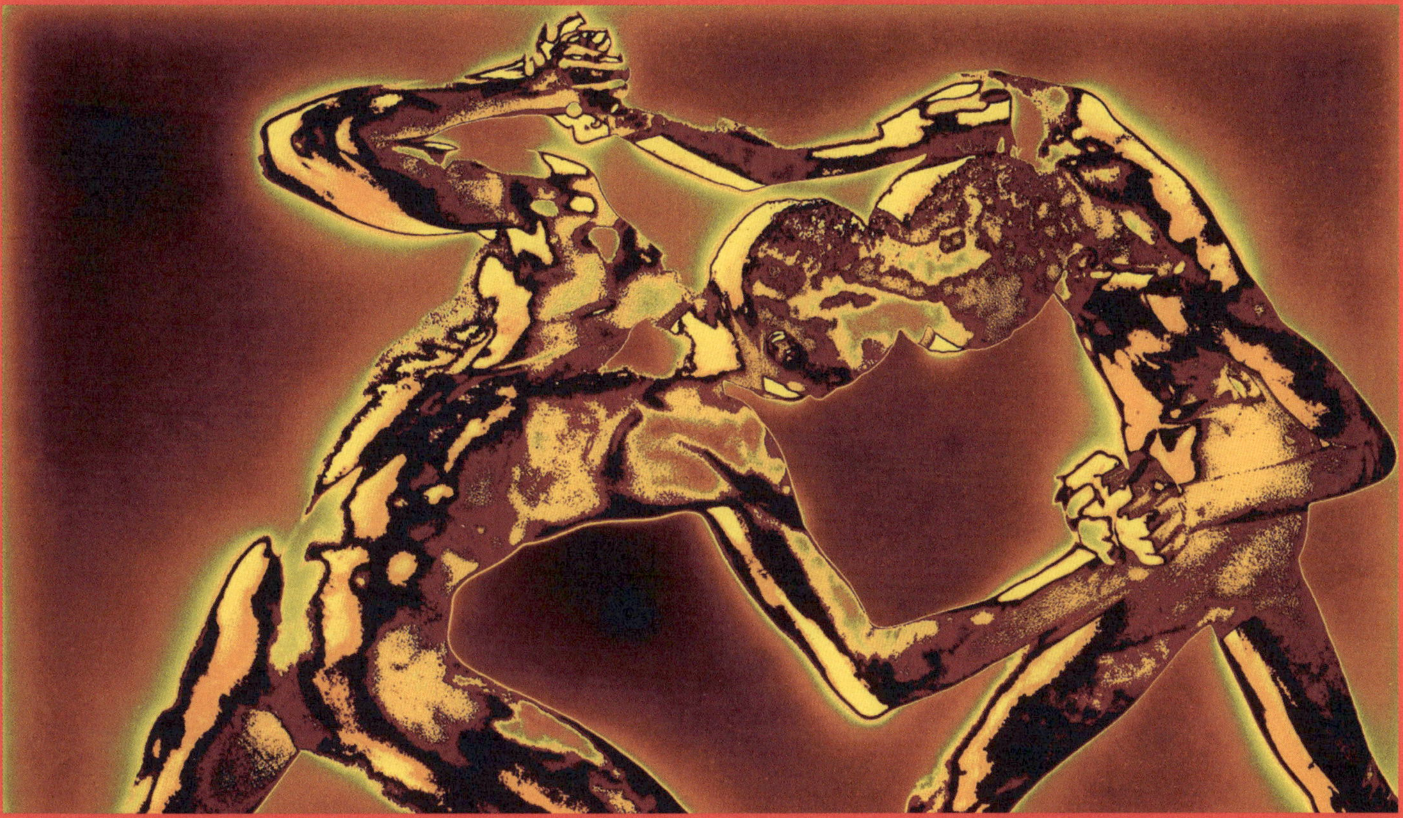

横須賀功光

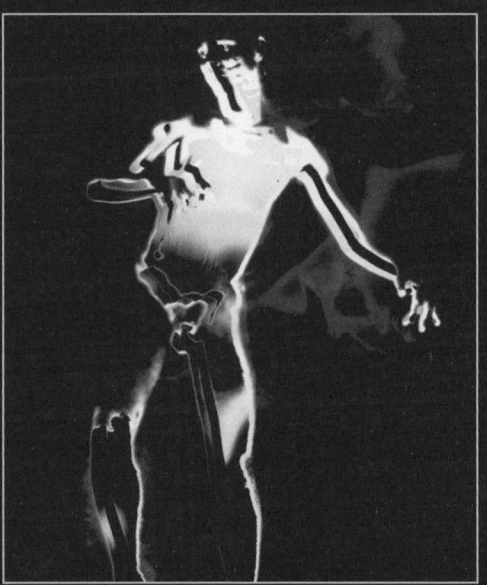

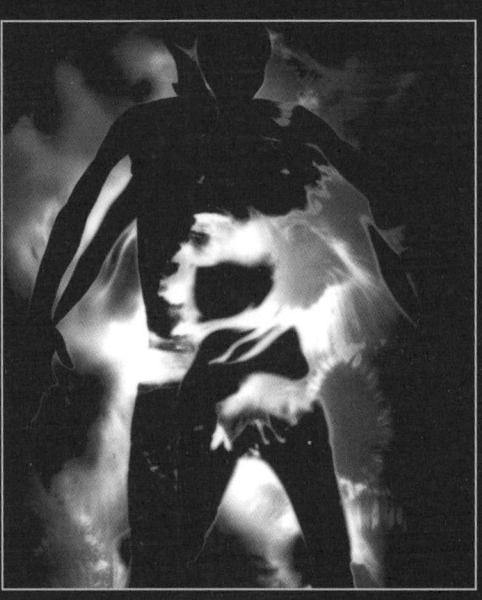

Above: **Yokosuka Noriaki**, *Optical Isomers #20*, 1994, gelatin silver print.

Below: **Yokosuka Noriaki**, *Optical Isomers*, 1994, gelatin silver print.

Opposite: **Yokosuka Noriaki**, *Cage 01*, 1969, gelatin silver print.

Overleaf: Photograph from **Yokosuka Noriaki**, *The Photon & Ogre* (2005).

pp. 310–11: **Yokosuka Noriaki**, *Castle*, 1964, gelatin silver print.

'The human mind's capacity for imagination is boundless.
It has the power to redefine the essence of matter,
expanding possibilities across dimensions.
Imagination fuels our obsession with space,
and our desire to explore the universe.

My imagination lets me peer into the unknown,
and discover the phenomena that transpire
between me and my subject.
What I capture is not what my eyes
see in that moment.
It is the truth unseen,
hidden in the play of light and shadow.
It is bigger than anything my
imagination could construct.

There is no art as intimately entwined with
light and shadow as photography.
A photograph is a visualization of that
intricate interplay, capturing what I refer
to as the 'invisible incidents of
elementary particles'.
I playfully term these incidents
"A Case of Light and Silver".

I once had a strange dream.
I was a cyborg,
riding a Mobius strip in an eternal loop.
yearning to reclaim my
diminished heart and body,
on a perpetual search for
that elemental human instinct.'

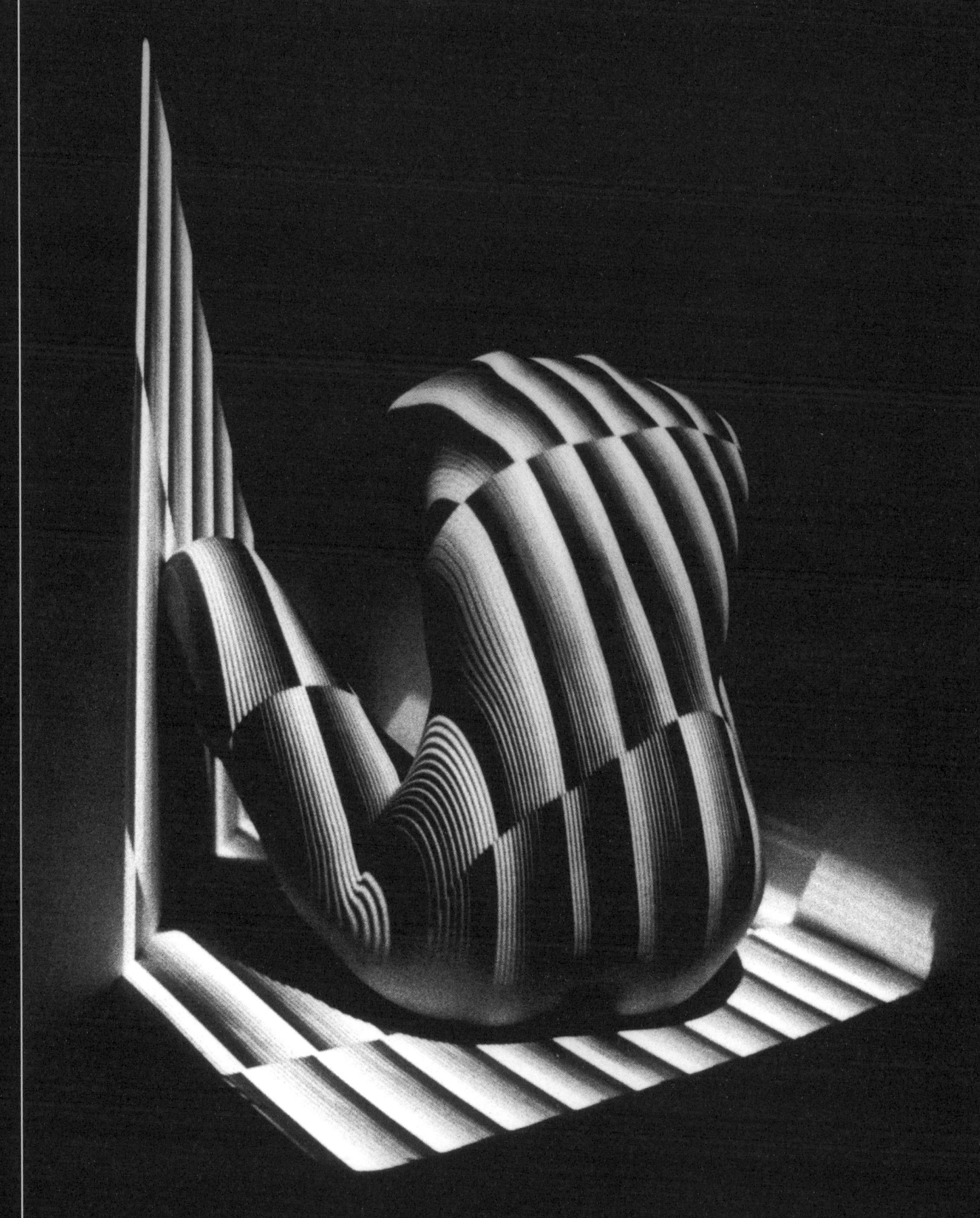

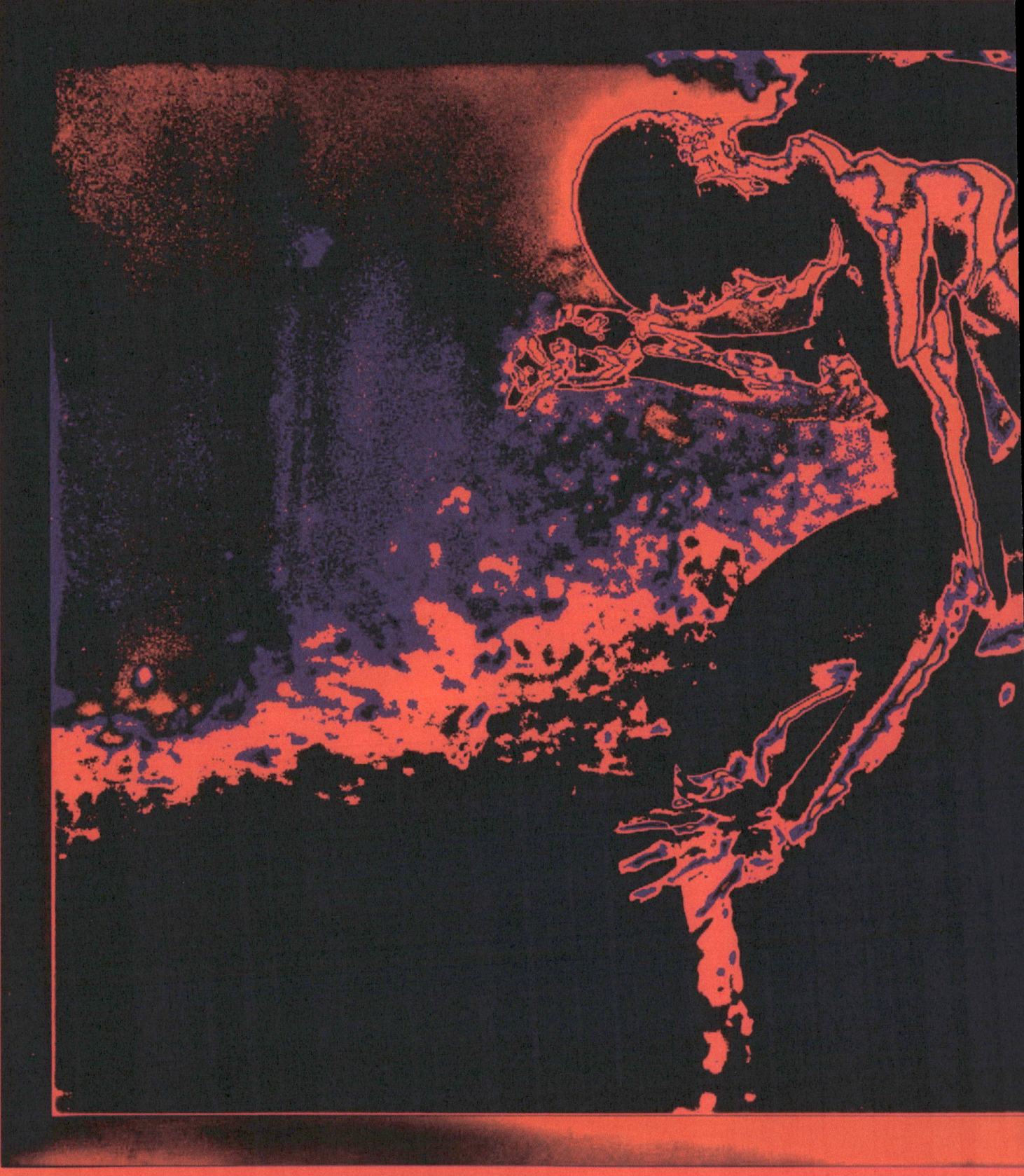

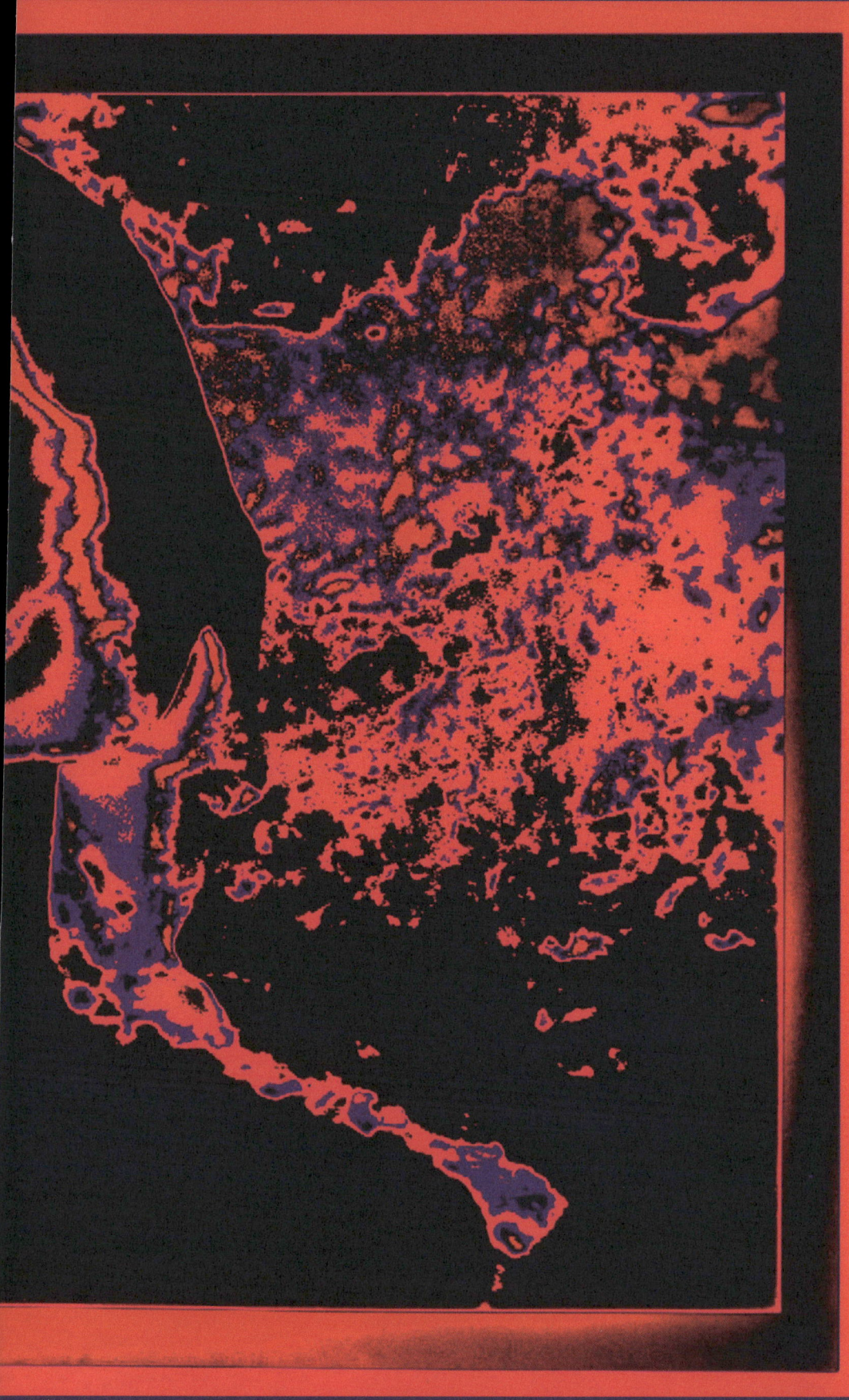

> Beauty that eliminates everything; emotional heat, humanity, love and idyllic incidents.
>
> SAITŌ MAKOTO

> He rarely talked about light or angles.
>
> He spoke of the 'scent,' 'gaze' or 'sorrow' of the woman beyond the camera.
>
> His penetrating eyes saw what normal people did not. He could go beneath the surface and uncover that hidden essence.
>
> KIMURA SOICHI

> His photos were created from an unparalleled aesthetic and undeterred spirit.
>
> ISSEY MIYAKE

> Noriaki wanted to be a silver halide, perhaps even a photo.
>
> ARAKI NOBUYOSHI

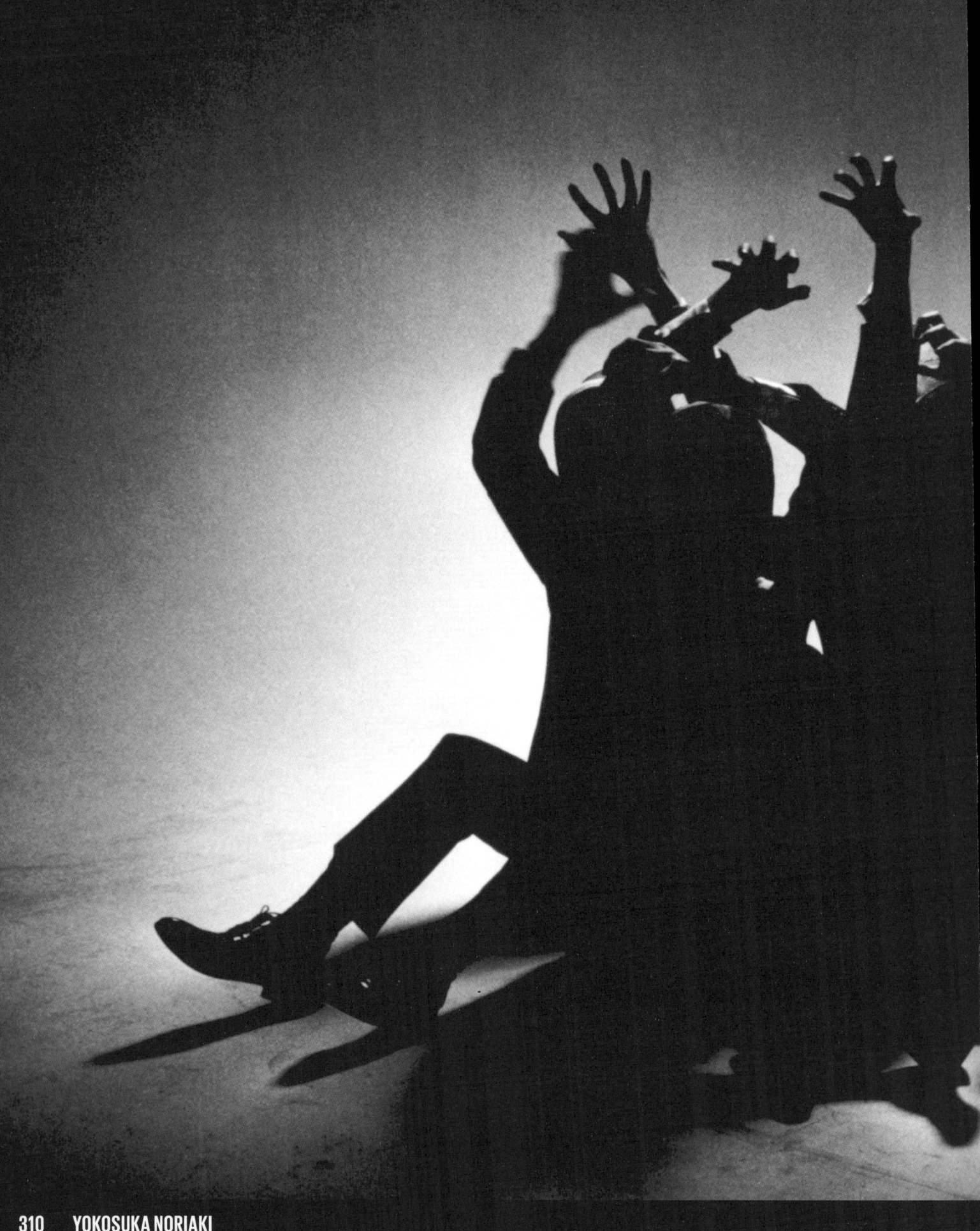

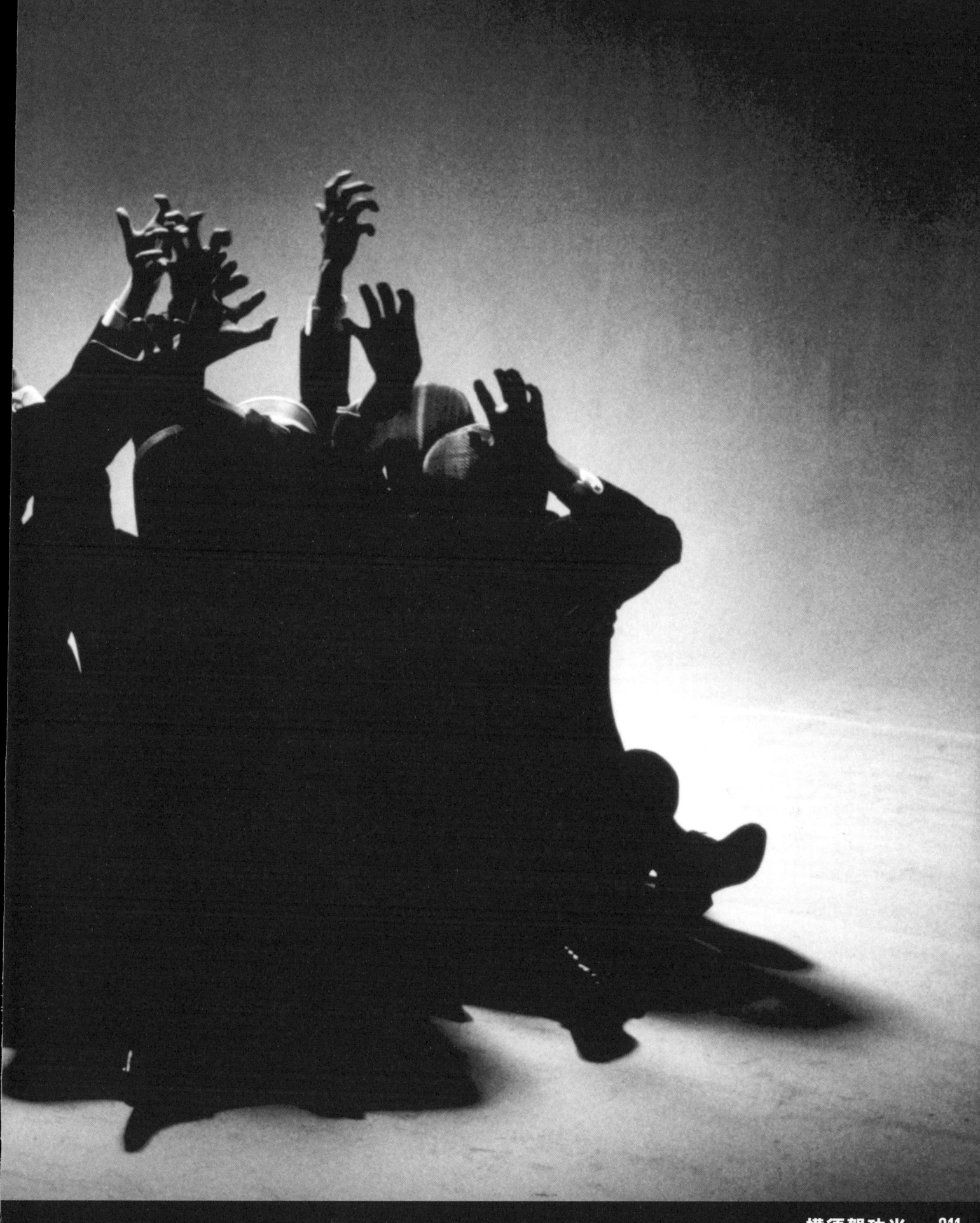

ARTISTS

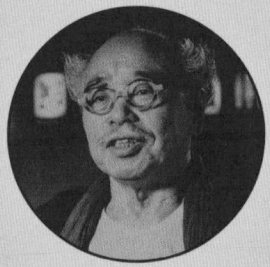

ARAKI NOBUYOSHI
Photographer
1940–

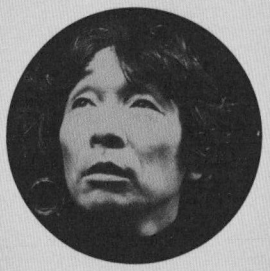

AWAZU KIYOSHI
Graphic Designer
1929–2009

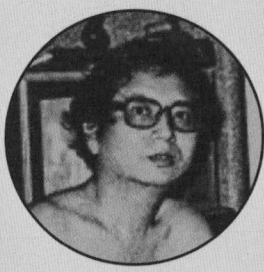

HANAGA MITSUTOSHI
Photographer
1933–1999

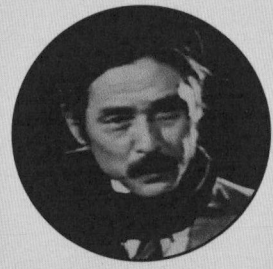

HIJIKATA TATSUMI
Butoh Founder
1928–1986

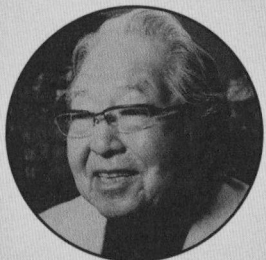

HOSOE EIKŌ
Photographer
1933–2024

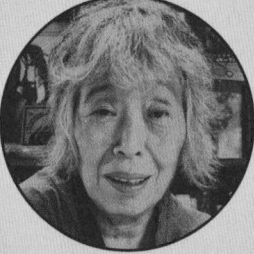

ISHIUCHI MIYAKO
Photographer
1947–

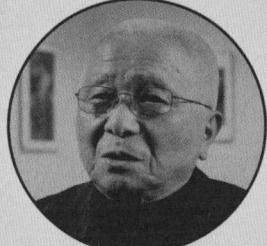

KAWADA KIKUJI
Photographer
1933–

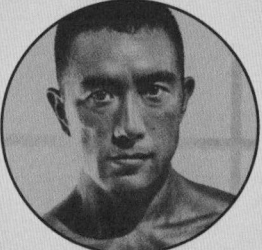

MISHIMA YUKIO
Writer
1925–1970

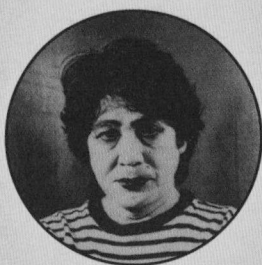

MORIYAMA DAIDO
Photographer
1938–

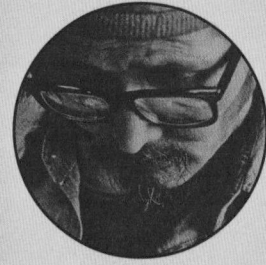

NAKAHIRA TAKUMA
Photographer
1938–2015

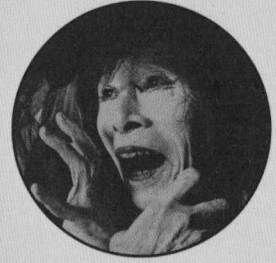

OHNO KAZUO
Butoh Dancer
1906–2010

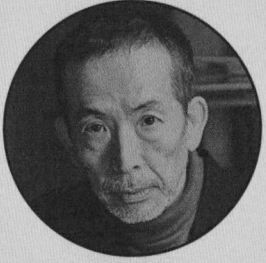

SAEKI TOSHIO
Illustrator
1945–2019

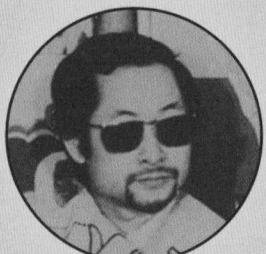

TANAAMI KEIICHI
Artist
1936–2024

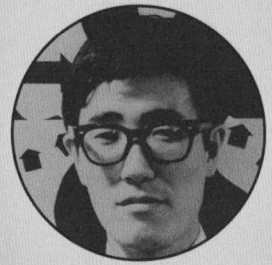

TANABE SANTARO
Performance Artist
1939–2017

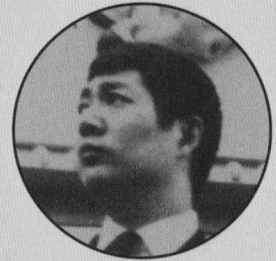

TERAYAMA SHŪJI
Poet and Dramatist
1935–1983

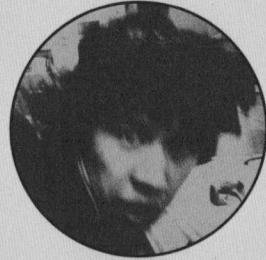

YOKOO TADANORI
Artist
1936–

CONTRIBUTORS

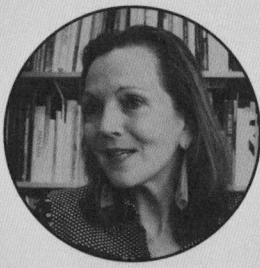

ALEXANDRA MUNROE
Curator-Scholar
Guggenheim Museum

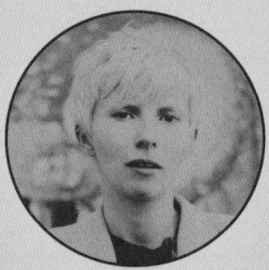

AMÉLIE RAVALEC
Filmmaker-Artist
Circle Time Studio

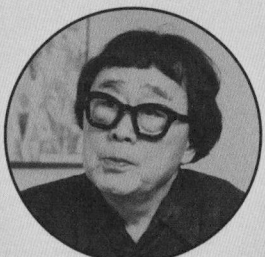

ENOMOTO RYŌICHI
Art Director
Tenjō Sajiki

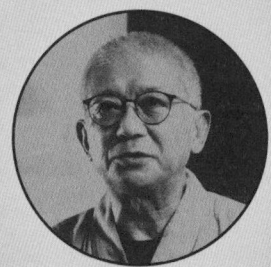

KANEKO RYŪICHI
Historian of Photography
Tokyo Museum of Photography

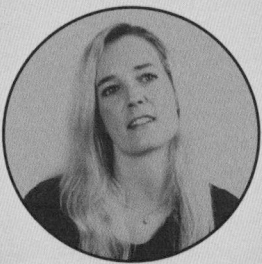

LENA FRITSCH
Curator-Scholar
Ashmolean Museum

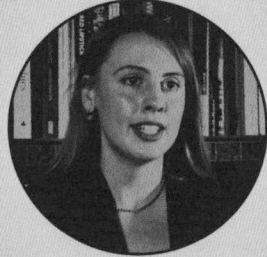

LUCY FLEMING-BROWN
Scholar
Daiwa Scholar

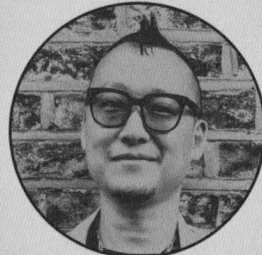

MAASERHIT HONDA
Filmmaker
WhatsOpp Inc

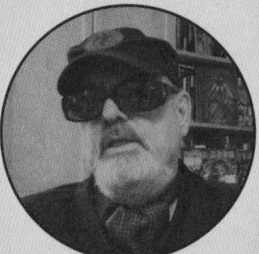

MASTER K
Rope Master
Kinbaku Scholar

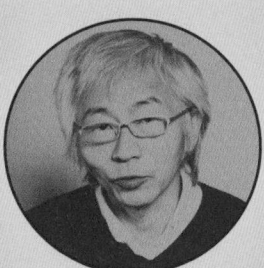

MIZOHATA TOSHIO
Archivist
Dance Archive Network

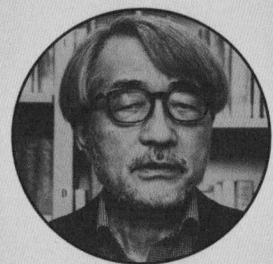

MORISHITA TAKASHI
Archivist
Hijikata Tatsumi Archive

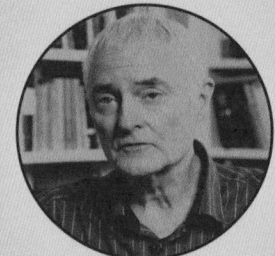

PETER TASKER
Author-Scholar
Terayama Shūji

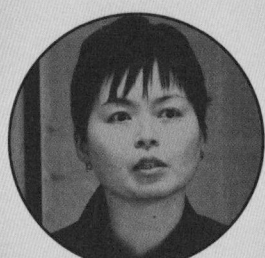

SAEKI YUKA
Archivist
Saeki Toshio Archive

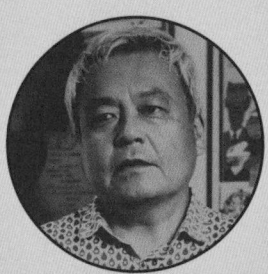

SASAME HIROYUKI
Archivist
Poster Hari's Company

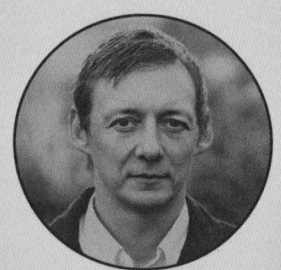

STEVE RIDGELY
Writer-Scholar
UW-Madison

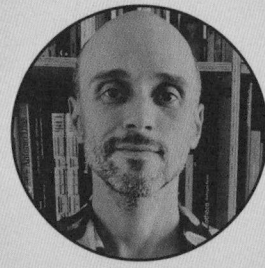

THYAGO NOGUEIRA
Curator-Scholar
Instituto Moreira Salles

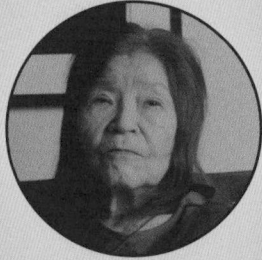

WATANABE HITOMI
Photographer
1942-

ACKNOWLEDGMENTS

My sincere thanks to the artists whose work appears in this book: Araki Nobuyoshi, Hosoe Eikō, Ishiuchi Miyako, Kawada Kikuji, Moriyama Daido, Tanaami Keiichi, Watanabe Hitomi and Yokoo Tadanori; as well as the many contributors whose insights helped shape this project: Alexandra Munroe, Enomoto Ryoichi, Kaneko Ryūichi, Lena Fritsch, Lucy Fleming-Brown, Master K, Mizohata Toshio, Morishita Takashi, Peter Tasker, Saeki Yuka, Sasame Hiroyuki, Steve Ridgely and Thyago Nogueira.

I'm very grateful to everyone who granted access to archives and images, or helped make connections along the way: Aoyama Meguro, Awazu Ken, Christian Russo, Daido Moriyama Photo Foundation, Dance Archive Network, Eikoh Hosoe Photographic Art Institute, Erin O'Toole, Galerie Da-End, Galerie Écho 119, Goto Saori, Hanaga Taro, Hana Miriam Tanabe, Hosoe Kenji, Ian Buruma, Iimura Akiko, Ishimoto Kae, Itaya Yuki, Ivan Vartanian, Jörg Colberg, Kamemura Yoshihiro, Kamiyama Teijirō, Keio University Art Center and Butoh Laboratory, Kevin Carr, Master K, Michael Rogge, Mitsutoshi Hanaga Project Committee, Moriyama Sohey, Murai Eri, Murai Takefumi, Musashino Art University Museum and Library, Nakahira Gen, Nanzuka, Nitesha, Noelle Colin, Odate Natsuko, Ogawa Takayuki, Ohira Akiko, Osiris, Ōtsuji Tetsuo, PGI, Poster Hari's Gallery, Preparatory Office for Takahiko Iimura Archiving, Sasame Hiroyuki, Sawada Yoko, SFMOMA, Takahashi Sayaka, Taki Kentarō, Terayama World Co., The Third Gallery Aya, Tokunaga Akemi, Yokoo's Circus Co. and Yokosuka Anri. Additional thanks to my translators Genta Komatsu, Julia Smith, Mari Matsutoya, Serina Kurahashi and Sona Ryang.

I am deeply grateful to Thames & Hudson for entrusting me with this book, especially to my wonderful editors Marc Valli and Phoebe Colley; Tristan de Lancey for his design guidance and cover design; Brett Weekes, who took my design to the finish line; Julie Bosser for her expert colour repro; and Yasmin Garcha and Domniki Papadimitriou for picture research support.

I could not have made this book and its accompanying film without the unwavering support of my co-producer, Maaserhit Honda. My heartfelt thanks to all the artists, estates and institutions who entrusted me with their work, it has been an honour. This project was five years in the making, and I'm deeply thankful to my partner and family for their constant support throughout the journey.

IMAGE CREDITS

B = Bottom; C = Centre; L = Left; R = Right; T = Top

2-3 © Terayama Shūji. Courtesy of Sasame Hiroyuki, Terayama World Co. 4-5 © Hosoe Eikō. Courtesy of Eikoh Hosoe Photographic Art Institute 6-7 © Hanaga Mitsutoshi. Courtesy of Mitsutoshi Hanaga Project Committee 8 © Yokosuka Noriaki. Courtesy of Yokosuka Anri 9 © Daido Moriyama Photo Foundation. Courtesy of Daido Moriyama Photo Foundation 10 © Yokoo Tadanori. Courtesy of Yokoo's Circus Co. 12-13 © Ōtsuji Tetsuo. Courtesy of Musashino Art University Museum and Library, Tokyo 14 © Terayama Shūji. Courtesy of Sasame Hiroyuki, Terayama World Co. 18 © Daido Moriyama Photo Foundation 19 © Hanaga Mitsutoshi. Courtesy of Mitsutoshi Hanaga Project Committee 20-21 © Michael Rogge. Courtesy of Michael Rogge 22 © All University Joint Struggle Committee of Nihon University 23 © Unknown 24-25, 28-29 © Unknown. Courtesy of Kiemow 26 © All University Joint Struggle Committee of Nihon University 30-35 © Watanabe Hitomi. Courtesy of Galerie Écho 119 36-55 © Tanaami Keiichi. Courtesy of Nanzuka 56-63 © Kawada Kikuji. Courtesy of PGI 64-69 © Hosoe Eikō. Courtesy of Eikoh Hosoe Photographic Art Institute 70-71 © Shinoyama Kishin 72-76 © Hosoe Eikō. Courtesy of Eikoh Hosoe Photographic Art Institute 78-79 © Yokoo Tadanori. Courtesy of Yokoo's Circus Co. 80-81 © Hosoe Eikō. Courtesy of Eikoh Hosoe Photographic Art Institute 82-85 © Shinoyama Kishin 86-105 © Yokoo Tadanori. Courtesy of Yokoo's Circus Co. 106-7 L-R © Nakatani Tadao. Courtesy of Keio University Art Center and Butoh Laboratory, Japan 107 B © Mitsutoshi Hanaga. Courtesy of Mitsutoshi Hanaga Project Committee 108 © Torii Ryōzen. Courtesy of Keio University Art Center and Butoh Laboratory, Japan 109 T Nakatani Tadao. Courtesy of Keio University Art Center and Butoh Laboratory, Japan 109 C © Mitsutoshi Hanaga. Courtesy of Mitsutoshi Hanaga Project Committee 109 B © Torii Ryōzen. Courtesy of Keio University Art Center and Butoh Laboratory, Japan 110 © Nakatani Tadao. Courtesy of Keio University Art Center and Butoh Laboratory, Japan 111 © Mitsutoshi Hanaga. Courtesy of Mitsutoshi Hanaga Project Committee 112 © Iimura Takahiko. Courtesy of Akiko Iimura, Preparatory Office for Takahiko Iimura Archiving 113 © Ouchida Keiya and Tatsumi Hijikata. Courtesy of Keio University Art Center and Butoh Laboratory, Japan 114 © Ōtsuji Tetsuo. Courtesy of Musashino Art University Museum and Library, Tokyo 115 © Nakatani Tadao. Courtesy of Keio University Art Center and Butoh Laboratory, Japan 116-17 © Hosoe Eikō. Courtesy of Eikoh Hosoe Photographic Art Institute and Kenji Hosoe 119 © Nakatani Tadao. Courtesy of Keio University Art Center and Butoh Laboratory, Japan 120-26 © Hosoe Eikō. Courtesy of Eikoh Hosoe Photographic Art Institute 127 © Ikegami Naoya. Courtesy of Ikegami Naoya 128-29 © Dance Archive Network. Courtesy of NPO Dance Archive Network and Mizohata Toshio 131 © Hosoe Eikō. Courtesy of Eikoh Hosoe Photographic Art Institute 132-33 © Ikegami Naoya. Courtesy of Ikegami Naoya 134-35 © Teijiro Kamiyama. Courtesy of NPO Dance Archive Network 136-47 © Awazu Yaeko. Photo by Kioku Keizo. Courtesy of 21st Century Museum of Contemporary Art, Kanazawa 148-73 © Terayama Shūji. Courtesy of Sasame Hiroyuki, Terayama World Co. 174-89 © Nobuyoshi Araki Foundation 190 © Fuji Aiko 191 © Unknown. Kitan Club 192 © Unknown. From "Hojojutsu: The Warrior's Art of the Rope". Courtesy of Christian Russo 193 T-B © Itō Seiu. Courtesy of Master K 194-95 © Fusoku Soshi. Courtesy of Master K 196, 198-99 © Unknown. Kitan Club 197 B © Daido Moriyama Photo Foundation

200–19 © Daido Moriyama Photo Foundation 220–21 © Estate of Taki Koji 222–23 © Nakahira Gen. Courtesy of Osiris 224 © Daido Moriyama Photo Foundation 226–33 © Nakahira Gen. Courtesy of Osiris 234–35 B © Hanaga Mitsutoshi. Courtesy of Mitsutoshi Hanaga Project Committee 235 T, L, R © Santaro Tanabe's Estate. Courtesy of Hana Miriam Tanabe 236–41 © Hanaga Mitsutoshi. Courtesy of Mitsutoshi Hanaga Project Committee 242–43 © Santaro Tanabe's Estate. Courtesy of Hana Miriam Tanabe 244–45 © Hanaga Mitsutoshi. Courtesy of Mitsutoshi Hanaga Project Committee 246–55 © Murai Tokuji. Courtesy of Murai Eri 246–67 © Hanaga Mitsutoshi. Courtesy of Mitsutoshi Hanaga Project Committee 268–79 © Ishiuchi Miyako. Courtesy of The Third Gallery Aya 280–81 © Saeki Toshio. Courtesy of Toshio Saeki Estate 282–83 © Satoshi Saikusa. Courtesy of Galerie Da-End 284–303 © Saeki Toshio. Courtesy of Toshio Saeki Estate 304–11 © Yokosuka Noriaki. Courtesy of Yokosuka Anri

TEXT CREDITS

Artist and contributor texts in this book were derived from interviews with the author, with the exception of texts by Lucy Fleming-Brown, Thyago Nogueira and Steve Ridgely; and sources listed below.

56–63 'Interview – Kikuji Kawada on the Atomic Bomb Dome and Postwar Japan', 2016 © Courtesy of the San Francisco Museum of Modern Art 68, 74, 78, 118, 122 'Interview – Eikoh Hosoe: Does photography reflect truth?', 2018 © Courtesy of the San Francisco Museum of Modern Art 70, 74, 76, 80 Mishima Yukio, 'Preface for Eikoh Hosoe' (*Afterimage*, November 1972) © Courtesy of Afterimage/Ordeal by Roses 148–52, 171 'Tenjō Sajiki Video Anthology' © Courtesy of Sasame Hiroyuki, Terayama World Co. 152 *Terayama Shūji, Japanese Dream*, trans. Peter Tasker (Minato: Zen Foto Gallery, 2013) © Courtesy of Peter Tasker 158, 174 Ian Buruma, *A Tokyo Romance* (London, 2018) © Courtesy of Ian Buruma 178–89 'Interview with Nobuyoshi Araki in Japan', 2016 © Courtesy of the San Francisco Museum of Modern Art 200–17 'Interview with Daido Moriyama', 2016 © Courtesy of the San Francisco Museum of Modern Art 226 Nakahira Takuma, 'Why an Illustrated Botanical Dictionary?', trans. Franz K. Prichard (Tokyo, 1973) © Courtesy of Osiris 243 Quoted in Nick Kapur, *Japan at the Crossroads: Conflict and Compromise after Anpo* (Cambridge, MA: 2018) 256–67 Hanaga Taro, 'Introduction', *Mitsutoshi Hanaga 1000* (Tokyo, 2012) © Courtesy of the Mitsutoshi Hanaga Project Committee 280, 285, 299–300 Saeki Toshio, 'Afterword', *Toshio Saeki 70* (Tokyo, 2016) © Courtesy of Toshio Saeki Estate 306–9 Video of Yokosuka Noriaki's work *SAYOKO YAMAGUCHI*, produced in 2023 © Yokosuka Noriaki. Courtesy of Yokosuka Anri

INDEX

Page references in *italics* indicate illustrations

Fuji Aiko *190*
Akasegawa Genpei *19, 235,* 238, 243, 246, 250
American occupation 22, 200, 204, 268, 272
angura (underground) scene 93, 96
ankoku butoh see butoh
Anpo Treaty, opposition to 20–29, 256
anti-art 234
Aquirax Uno 93
Araki Nobuyoshi 11, 16, 170, 174–89, *178, 189,* 220, 275, 309
   Bondage 175
   Geisha Girl with Watermelon 174
   Journal intime 188
   Kakyoku 175
   Past Tense – Future 176–77, *179*
   Personal Sentimentalism in Photography 183
   Pseudo-Reportage 182, *182*
   Sachin and his Brother Mabo 180–81
   Sentimental Journey 184, *184, 185*
   Winter Journey 184, *185, 186–87*
Asahi Camera magazine 216
Ashikawa Yoko *262–63*
avant-garde *(zen'ei bijutsu),* defined 18
Awazu Kiyoshi 17, 136–47, 168
   posters *136–37, 139, 142–43, 145*
   Scrapbook 138, 140–41, 146–47
   Tenjō Sajiki, prints for *137,* 138, *144*

Buruma, Ian 158, 174
butoh 16, 106–13, 126, *257, 264–65*
   see also Hijikata Tatsumi

Dalí, Salvador 153, 170
death 16, 52, 78, 82, 98, 184, 280
Demokrato collective 66

Enomoto Ryōichi 27, 168
eroticism 16, 43, 118, 170, 188, 196, 280, 296
Expo '70, Osaka 103, 256, 285

Fleming-Brown, Lucy 20, 36, 64, 66, 78, 93, 122, 130, 136, 138, 154, 182, 184, 188, 204, 208, 214, 230–31, 234, 238, 246, 272
Fritsch, Lena 60, 130, 183, 210
fūkei (landscape) 230
Fusoku Soshi magazine *194–95*
Fuwa Mansaku *6–7*

Hanaga Mitsutoshi 256–67
   butoh dancers *107, 109, 111, 257, 262–65*
   Neo-Dada Organizers *234, 236–37*
   performance artists *19, 235, 238–41, 244–45, 266–67*
   underground theatre scene *6–7, 258–59, 260*
   Young People 256
Hanaga Taro 256, 260–61, 264
Heibon Punch magazine 285

Hi-Red Center 15, 238, 246–55, *261*
Hijikata Tatsumi 11, 64, 66, 106, 109, 114–25, 130
   Asbestos Studio *107, 110*
   Bangi Daitokan 262–63
   Cine-Dance (with Iimura Takahiko) *112*
   Forbidden Colours (Kinjiki) 106, *114,* 122
   Gibasan, from *Twenty-Seven Nights for Four Seasons* 109, *115*
   Rebellion/Revolt of the Body 108, *115, 119*
   A Story of Smallpox (with Ouchida Keiya) *113*
   Yokoo Tadanori, collaboration with *94, 95,* 96
Hiroshima, Atomic Dome 60, 63
Hosoe Eikō 11, 15, 64–69, 74, 78, 96, 118, 130
   Butterfly Dream 66, *126, 131*
   Kamaitachi 64, *116–17, 120–21,* 122, *123–25*
   Man and Woman 64, *65,* 66–67
   Ordeal by Roses (*Barakei*) *4–5,* 64, *65,* 69, *71, 72–73, 75–77, 80–81*

Ichiyanagi Toshi 11
Iimura Takahiko, *Cine-Dance 112*
Ikegami Naoya *127, 132, 133*
Ishiuchi Miyako 27, 60, 268–79
   'Hyakka Ryōran' *272,* 276, *276–77*
   Yokosuka Again 1980–1990 270–71, 273–74

Yokosuka Story 268–69, 272, 272, 275, 278–79
Issey Miyake 309
Itō Seiu 193

Japan Red Army 256, 285
Jazz Film Laboratory 66

Kamiyama Teijirō *134–35*
Kaneko Ryūichi 27, 60, 208, 224
Kara Jūrō 11, 96
Kawada Kikuji, *The Map* 16, 56–63, *56–63*, 204
Kerouac, Jack 204
Kimura Soichi 309
Kinbaku 190–99
Kitan Club magazine *191*, 196, *196–97*, *198–99*
Kobayashi Saga *262–63*
Kuni Chiya 257
Kurosawa Akira 11
Kusakabe Kimbei 193

Life of Asakura, The, painting 192

martial arts 193
Master K 190, 193
Metabolism (architecture) 138
Minami Yusuke 103
Mishima Yukio 11, 15, 66, 70–85, 96, 256, 285
   The Death of a Man (with Shinoyama Kishin) 70–71, 82–85
   Ordeal by Roses (with Hosoe Eikō) *4–5*, 64, *65*, 69, *71, 72–73, 75–77, 80–81*
   Yokoo Tadanori, collaboration with 78, *78–79*, 100, *100*

Mitsutaka Ishii 107
Mizohata Toshio 109, 118, 126, 130
Morishita Takashi 27, 109, 110, 118
Moriyama Daido 11, 66, 200–19, 224, 275
   Accident 216, *216–19*
   Boku 212
   Color 206–7
   Dog and Mesh Tights 201, 213
   Entertainer on Stage, Shimizu 202–3
   Farewell Photography 205, 217
   Japan: A Photo Theater 208, *208*, 209, *210–11*
   Kariudo, Hunter 209, *214–15*
   Lips 213
   Mayfly 197
   Northern Series 201
   for *Provoke* 224
   RECORD No. 36 201
   Self-Portrait 9, 18
   Soldiers, Hamamatsu 200
   Whore, Yokosuka 212
Munroe, Alexandra 18, 74, 82, 106, 109, 110, 114, 242, 250
Murai Tokuji, *Yamanote Line Incident* 246–55

Nagisa Ōshima 11, 96
Nakahira Takuma 224, 226–33, *231, 232–33*
   Circulation: Date, Place, Events 222–23, 228–29
   For a Language to Come 226, 230
   Provoke 225, 227, 230
Nakajima Natsu *6–7*

Nakanishi Natsuyuki, *Yamanote Line Incident* 246, *246–55*, 250
Nakatani Tadao *106–7*, 110, 115, 119
Neo-Dada Organizers 15, 234–45
Nihon University, student protests 22, *24–25*, 26, *28–29*, *30–35*
Nogueria, Thyago 217
NON magazine 23
Nureki Chimuo 190

Ohno Kazuo 66, 126–35
   Admiring La Argentina 127, 133
   The Dead Sea 127, 132, 133
   My Mother 133, 134–35
   The Old Man and the Sea 128–29
Ohno Yoshito 114
Okada Takahiko 224
Ōtsuji Kiyoji *12–13*, 114
Ouchida Keiya, *A Story of Smallpox* (with Hijikata) 113

Pop art 36, 93
Provoke 15, *22*, 220, 220–25, *221, 227*, 230
psychedelic art 99

Ravalec, Amélie 15–17
Ridgely, Steve 164
Rogge, Michael *20, 21*
Ryūkansai 122

Saeki Toshio 16, 280–303, *282–83*, 297
   Fièvres nocturnes 280, *284–87, 290*
   Red Box 295–97, 298–301

Rêve écarlate 281, 288–89, 290–94, 302–3
Saeki Yuka 282, 289, 295, 296, 301
Saikusa Satoshi, *Saeki Toshio* 282–83
Saitō Makoto 309
Sasame Hiroyuki 96, 168, 170
Shimooka Renjō *192*
Shinohara Ushio 36, *238–41,* 244–45
Shinoyama Kishin, *The Death of a Man* (with Mishima Yukio) 70–71, 82–85
Sugiura Kōhei 63, 66
Surrealism 96, 153, 170

Taiheiki 192
Takamatsu Jirō 238, 246, 250
Takanashi Yutaka 224
Takemitsu Tōru 11
Taki Kōji *220–21,* 224, 225
Tamano Koichi *109*
Tanaami Keiichi 36–55, 242
  Big Bargain 36
  Clock Work Marilyn 42, 43, 48–49
  Collage Book 44–45, 52–53
  Dream Diary 37, 52
  Ephemerality and Eternity 39
  Jakuchu: Birds and Flowers 50–51
  The Last Supper 54–55
  Mother and Child 38
  No More War 40–41
  A Pancake for Breakfast_6 42
  Study of the Virgin in School Uniform 47
  Why 46

Tanabe Santaro 235, 239, *242,* 243
Tasker, Peter 27, 153, 168, 170
Tenjō Sajiki theatre troupe 15, 47, 96, *137,* 138, *144,* 153, 158, 168, 170, *260,* 299
Terayama Shūji 11, 96, 148–73, 208, 299, 300
  Butterfly 153, 164
  The Cage 152, 164
  Emperor Tomato Ketchup 156, 164
  The Labyrinth Tale 156, 164
  No Kamen Gaho 149
  Photothéque imaginaire de Shuji Terayama 2–3, 14, 15, 17, 149, *158–63, 165, 168–73*
  The Shuji Terayama Theatre Museum: 1935–2008 148, *150–51, 154–55*
  A Tale of Smallpox 167
  The Trial 164, *166*
  A Young Person's Guide to Cinema 164, *165*
  see also Tenjō Sajiki theatre troupe
Tokugawa Bakuhu Keijizufu 192
Tokyo University 26, 34
Tōmatsu Shōmei 22, 66, 204, 275
Torii Ryōzen *108, 109*

ukiyo-e woodblock prints 93, 299
Umi (Sea) magazine 299
underground scene 93, 96
US–Japan Security Treaty *see* Anpo Treaty

VIVO collective 66

war, experience of 16, 38, 66, 89, 130
Warhol, Andy 47, 204
Watanabe Hitomi, *Tōdai Zenkyōtō 30–33,* 30–35, *35*
WORKSHOP photography school 66

Yamamoto Keigo *266–67*
Yano Yuriko 304
Yokoo Tadanori 11, 15, 17, 66, 86–105, 153, 204
  The Complete Tadanori Yokoo Book 102
  Hijikata Tatsumi, collaboration with *94, 95,* 96
  Mishima Yukio, collaboration with 78, *78–79,* 100, *100*
  paintings *86, 87, 91, 98, 104–5*
  posters *10, 86, 87, 88–90, 92–94, 96–98, 99, 101*
  Seni-kan (Expo 70, Osaka) *103*
  Tenjō Sajiki, collaboration with 96
  Torture 100
Yokosuka Noriaki 304–11
  Cage 307
  Castle 310–11
  The Light Silver Incident 305
  Optical Isomers 304, 305, 306
  The Photon & Ogre 8, 305, 308–9

Zengakuren 34, 224
Zenkyōtō *see* Nihon University; Tokyo University

Amélie Ravalec is a Parisian film director, producer and colourist. She directed her first documentary, *Paris/Berlin: 20 Years of Underground Techno* (2012), at the age of sixteen, winning the Festival Pick Award at Sydney Fringe Festival. She has gone on to direct multiple films on underground arts, including two documentaries on the Japanese avant-garde (2025 and 2026), the first of which, *Japanese Avant-Garde Pioneers*, this book is based on. Her films have been shown at cinemas, festivals, museums and cultural institutions across fifty countries, and acquired by TV networks including ARTE, Sky Arts UK and ORF Austria.

First published in the United Kingdom in 2025 by Thames & Hudson Ltd, 6–24 Britannia Street, London WC1X 9JD

First published in the United States of America in 2025 by Thames & Hudson Inc., 500 Fifth Avenue, New York, New York 10110

Japan Art Revolution: The Japanese Avant-Garde, from Angura to Provoke © 2025 Amélie Ravalec

All Rights Reserved. No part of this publication may be reproduced or transmitted in any form or by any means, electronic or mechanical, including photocopy, recording or any other information storage and retrieval system, without prior permission in writing from the publisher.

EU Authorized Representative: Interart S.A.R.L.
19 rue Charles Auray, 93500 Pantin, Paris, France
productsafety@thameshudson.co.uk
interart.fr

A CIP catalogue record for this book is available from the British Library

Library of Congress Control Number 2025936752

ISBN 978-0-500-02910-7
01

Printed and bound in Italy by L.E.G.O. S.p.A.

Be the first to know about our new releases, exclusive content and author events by visiting
thamesandhudson.com
thamesandhudsonusa.com
thamesandhudson.com.au